Sephardim in the Americas
STUDIES IN CULTURE AND HISTORY

Edited by
Martin A. Cohen
and
Abraham J. Peck

Published in Cooperation with
The American Jewish Archives
by
The University of Alabama Press
Tuscaloosa and London

> Judaic Studies Series
>
> Leon J. Weinberger, General Editor

> For my father and to the memory of my mother, both of whom experienced the darkness of the Shoah and the light of liberation with Sephardim from the Greek community of Saloniki
>
> AJP
>
> To the grandeur of the Sephardic experience
>
> MAC

Copyright © 1993 American Jewish Archives
All rights reserved
Manufactured in the United States of America

Library of Congress Cataloging-in-Publication Data

Sephardim in the Americas : studies in culture and history / edited by Martin A. Cohen and Abraham J. Peck.

p. cm. — (Judaic studies series)
Published in cooperation with the American Jewish Archives. Includes bibliographical references and index.
ISBN 0-8173-0707-9
   1. Sephardim—America—History. 2. Jews—America—History.
3. America—Ethnic relations. I. Cohen, Martin A. II. Peck, Abraham J.
III. American Jewish Archives. IV. Series: Judaic studies series (Unnumbered)
   E29.J5S46   1993
   970'.004924046—dc20   93-20083

British Library Cataloguing-in-Publication Data available

0-8173-1176-9 (pbk: alk. paper)

CONTENTS

Introduction: Sephardim in the Americas

Part I
Families and Futures: The Early Sephardic Phenomenon

The Sephardic Phenomenon: A Reappraisal   1
  Martin A. Cohen

Stones of Memory: Revelations From a Cemetery in Curaçao   81
  Rochelle Weinstein

Portuguese Sephardim in the Americas   141
  Malcolm H. Stern

The Fidanques: Symbols of the Continuity of the Sephardic Tradition in America   179
  Emma Fidanque Levy

Part II
The Sephardic Experience in Latin America

"Those of the Hebrew Nation..." The Sephardic Experience in Colonial Latin America   209
  Allan Metz

Sephardim in Latin America after Independence   235
  Victor C. Mirelman

Part III
Hidden Roots: Sephardic Culture in North America

The Sephardim in North America in the Twentieth Century   267
  Joseph M. Papo

Language of the Sephardim In Anglo-America   309
  Denah Lida

The Sacred and Secular Musical Traditions of the Sephardic Jews in the United States Israel J. Katz	331
Judeo-Spanish Traditional Poetry in the United States Samuel G. Armistead	357
Tradition and History: Sephardic Contributions to American Literature Diane Matza	379
The Secret Jews of the Southwest Frances Hernández	411
Notes on the Contributors	455
Index	457

Introduction:
Sephardim in the Americas

In a revealing passage, written in an article on self-perception among American Sephardim, Diane Matza describes a tenuous relationship to her Sephardic heritage:[1]

> I am a third-generation Sephardic Jew, Monastirli on my mother's side and Yanioti on my father's. I speak no Judeo-Spanish and no Greek. I can faithfully duplicate only a few traditions of the Yanioti Passover, such as the style of the *Dayenu* chant; others are but shadowy memories. Like many third-generation ethnics, food provides my closest attachment to my heritage... Between me and authentic cultural practice, then, lies an unbridgeable gulf.

At first glance, this is not a statement out of the American Jewish mainstream. With a different geographic background it might have been written by almost any third-generation American Jew whose roots lay in Poland or Germany.

But it was written by a Sephardic Jewish woman who cannot just pick up a volume and grasp the essence of the American immigrant world of her fathers and mothers because so little exists about that world.

Indeed, at a time when most twentieth-century immigrant Jews to America asked "what does it take to become an American?," the Sephardic Jews — the so-called "Eastern" or "Levantine" Sephardim — from Turkey, Greece, Bulgaria, or Syria were forced to ask "what does it take to become a Jew in the eyes of an East European Jewish immigrant?" Or perhaps that same immigrant was forced to ask "what does it take to be accepted by an already established 'Spanish-Portuguese' or Western Sephardic community?"

The year 1992 and the observance of the Columbus quincentenary marked a special moment in the history of the American Jewish experience.

While mainstream America celebrated the five hundredth anniversary of Columbus' discovery of the New World, both groups of American Sephardim recalled with sadness Jews expelled from Castile and Aragon in 1492, and through them other Jews and descendants of Jews, before and after, who felt compelled to leave the Peninsula because of their Jewish identity.

For centuries the image of their beloved Iberia gripped the imagination of the Sephardim wherever they lived and however their ethnic composition changed through the absorption of local peoples.

In their language, music, religious custom, whether they had settled in the lands of North Africa and the Ottoman Empire or in the cities of Western Europe, in their mysticism and poetry, religious philosophy, ballads and romantic songs, all Sephardim belonged to Jewish Spanish high culture, a culture which much of the Sephardic world held dear for several centuries of its exile. We must ask: how was it that while other peoples who after their arrival in alien cultures disappeared with no trace, the Sephardim held on to their Castilian Spanish identity, an identity that Paloma Dias-Mas has characterized as "Spaniards without a homeland."[2]

To a degree, this identity was a strategy for survival. What else could bind a Moroccan Jew with a Turkish one, a descendent of a Marrano family in Amsterdam with a Sephardi in Bordeaux or Venice? It was this collective fantasy about a brilliant past and a beloved homeland.

Such a strategy was even more successful than the Sephardim could have imagined. Research in American Jewish history has shown that the first significant Jewish immigrants to America and to the Western Hemisphere were Jews from the West Indies and Europe who traced their ancestry to the Jewish communities in Spain and Portugal.

The Spanish-Portuguese Sephardim dominated the religious, social and economic life of American Jewry and the Jewry of the Western Hemisphere during the colonial and early federal periods, despite the growing numerical superiority of the Ashkenazim, already evident in the third decade of the eighteenth century. By the early 1830s, however, the Sephardim were overwhelmed numerically by a flood of Jewish immigrants from German-speaking Central Europe. These German Jews soon developed much of the institutional framework that would serve as the foundation for a future American Jewish community.

Introduction

The first American Sephardim soon became part of American Jewish myth. They were viewed as the "Grandees" of American Jewish society. They constituted an aristocratic, acculturated group that has now all but vanished as a factor in the American Jewish community of the twentieth century. Yet the Sephardic community continued to carry a certain mystique that led Ashkenazim to join and even take over Sephardic congregations and to claim Sephardic origins. To that degree, the Sephardic *minhag* or style of worship was the "American" Jewish style until well into the nineteenth century.

But if the "Spanish-Portuguese" Sephardim held a respected and even aloof position in the pantheon of American Jewish immigrant groups, the several thousand Eastern Sephardim who came to American shores in the first two decades of the twentieth century did not.

The new Sephardim numbered somewhere between thirty and fifty thousand and despite numerous languages and origins they also looked back to an Iberian past with a sense of longing and of pain.

Jóse Estrugo was a Sephardic Jew from the Balkans who visited Spain in the first part of the twentieth century, nearly five centuries after the Expulsion:[3]

> From my infancy Spain filled my imagination like a fairy tale...In October 1922 I first arrived in Spain...I was rejoining an ancient country from which my ancestors had been expelled so cruelly!...For the first time in my life I felt truly at home, like a native. Here I was not, I could not be an intruder!...For the first time I felt completely at home, much more so than in the Jewish quarter where I was born! I am not ashamed to confess that I bent down, in an outburst of indescribable emotion, and kissed the ground on which I was standing.

An equally strong identification of these Sephardim with the lands of their exile and their Jewish identity impelled the editors of the Sephardic newspaper *El Avenir* to write that "we are not a 'Spanish people scattered throughout the world.' We are Jews and as such we should not allow ourselves to be acquired by any nation, since we esteem all peoples equally without differentiating race and religion." And, the newspaper concluded, "we are Ottoman subjects and we should work for the general interest of the country that shelters us and grants us so many favors."[4]

Turkey, however, the "sick man of Europe" and the dying architect of Ottoman rule could not, by the beginning of the twentieth century, grant many more favors to its loyal Sephardic subjects. Those who left the lands in which their families had lived for centuries to come to America came for many of the same economic reasons that pushed the East European Jews to leave Poland, Romania, and Russia.

Instead of Warsaw and Grodno or Zhitomir and Pinsk, these Jewish immigrants identified themselves as Monastirli, Castorli, Rhodesli, Yanioti or Salonikli. They spoke Judeo-Spanish or Greek and Arabic. Their religious practices, their songs and poetry were all their own.

Because most of them were not educated they could not explain to the native Jewish community, neither to the East Europeans nor to the established Sephardim, that they, too, were the spiritual descendants of Don Isaac Abravanel, Judah Halevi, Maimonides and Joseph Caro.

Imagine the pain and the shame of having to live two separate lives as one Sephardic immigrant businessman was forced to do in order to make a living among his east European Ashkenazic clientele. He changed his name to Cohen in his store and learned Yiddish. At home, among the Sephardim of Brooklyn he retained his family name, Kassorla.

Imagine, too, the pain when the immigrants from Rhodes, Turkey or Bulgaria walked the streets of the lower East Side of New York—where many of them settled—and came upon small Ashkenazic congregations who called themselves Anshei Sefarad (Men of Spain) and whose members would not even accord them recognition as fellow Jews.

In the pages of this volume, the reader will find scholarly essays by some of the most outstanding interpreters of the Sephardic experience in the Americas. These dozen essays, multidisciplinary in nature, examine the historical and cultural history of the Sephardic experience from pre-expulsion Spain to the phenomenon of the contemporary "hidden" *conversos* of the American Southwest. They document especially the Sephardic presence in the Western Hemisphere and North America.

This volume could not have been possible without the generous support of the Maurice Amado Foundation of Los Angeles, a superb representative of an American Sephardic community which has found a highly successful and secure place within American and

American Jewish life. We are also grateful to Dr. Tamar Frank, the program consultant of the Maurice Amado Foundation, for her help and encouragement.

Our thanks also go to Malcolm M. Macdonald, the director of the University of Alabama Press, and to Nicole Mitchell and Professor Leon Weinberger, also of the Press, for their belief in the importance of the volume.

We must also thank Tom Bell and Jan Flesch of Cobb Inc., and Rick McGowan of Rosenthal Printing for their technological magic in the printing process.

Finally, a sincere thank-you must go to Robert Milch. Bob has been the finest copy-editor and indexer working in the field for a very long time. His brilliance is once more reflected in the pages of this book.

Martin A. Cohen
Abraham J. Peck

Notes

1. Diane Matza, "Self-Perception Among American Sephardim," *Melton Journal* Autumn, 1992, p. 11.

2. Paloma Diaz-Mas. *Sephardim: The Jews from Spain*. Chicago and London: University of Chicago Press, 1992. p. 169.

3. Quoted in Paloma Diaz-Mas, *Sephardim*, p. 171.

4. Quoted in Diaz-Mas, *Sephardim*, p. 173.

5. Diane Matza, "Self-Perception Among American Sephardim," p. 11.

Part I
Families and Futures:
The Early Sephardic Phenomenon

The Sephardic Phenomenon: A Reappraisal

Martin A. Cohen

Preface

The story of the Sephardic Jews in the Americas is part of a saga that began in the Iberian Peninsula under the Roman Empire, if not earlier, and eventually intertwined with the experience of all Europe, Asia, Africa, North America and South America. The Sephardic Jews were instrumental in the transmission of ancient culture, the creation of medieval Iberian civilization, and the development of modern Europe, and from it the modern world. The role of the Sephardic Jews in the New World is understandable only through their prior history, and this history is best understood by following the unfolding of the Sephardic phenomenon from earliest times.

Introduction

The year 1992 marks the quincentenary of the Edict of Expulsion of the Jews from Spain. The edict was issued in the city of Granada on March 31, 1492 by King Fernando of Aragon and Queen Isabel of Castile, the Catholic Monarchs, as they were dubbed by Pope Sixtus IV. It ordered all Jews to leave the territories belonging to the royal couple within four months, precisely by the end of July. According to tradition and perhaps historical reality, the deadline was eventually extended from July 31 until August 2. In the Jewish religious calendar this date corresponded to the ninth day of the month of Ab, the anniversary of the destruction of the Jerusalem Temple by the Romans in the year 70 C.E.

In reality, the Jews were not expelled from any political entity known as Spain. The Catalans in particular liked to call Ferdinand the king of Spain, but the name Hispania remained a geographical designation, and the Portuguese at no time took kindly to its political adoption at the expense of their exclusion. The name Spain for non-

Portuguese Iberia is hardly appropriate before 1512, when King Fernando added cys-Pyrenean Navarre to the dyarchy of Castile and Aragon. The edict of Ferdinand and Isabella consequently referred only to Castile, Aragon and their possessions. The independent Iberian kingdoms of Navarre and Portugal actually opened their doors to at least some Jewish refugees.

The number of Jews in Castile and Aragon at the time of the Edict could hardly have exceeded 100,000. Of these a minority of no more than 15,000 lived in Aragon, and the rest in Castile. At the time the Jewish population of Portugal could hardly have exceeded 30,000 and that of Navarre half that number. The numbers of Jews in Castile and Aragon had been greatly diminished in the previous century. The massacres of 1391 claimed anywhere from 15,000 to 20,000 Jewish lives, while conversions beginning at that time and continuing throughout the fifteenth century claimed several times that number. The number of Jews who left the Peninsula in the wake of the Edict may have exceeded 50,000, although it is possible that only a minority left. The remaining Jews converted to Christianity, as did many who returned in the years immediately following their departure. Of those leaving a considerable number went to Portugal, where they were almost all converted by force or fiat in 1497.

Nevertheless, the Expulsion of 1492 remains one of the watersheds of Jewish history. This is because of its impact upon the psyches of the affected Jews and their descendants, and the resonance of this experience ever since in the Jewish community at large.

The issuance of the decree of Expulsion was the centerpiece of the three major Iberian events in that fateful year. On January 2 the Catholic Monarchs had conquered the Kingdom of Granada, the last independent Muslim polity in the Peninsula. And at dawn on August 3, presumably on the heels of the last refugees, Christopher Columbus, a Christian of possible Iberian Jewish descent and a crew that included Christians of unquestionable Jewish descent, set sail for the Catholic Monarchs on their first and most momentous voyage. Together the three events bespeak a policy of unification and expansion that was to catapult the nation of Spain, once formed, into the vanguard of the modern world.

The Sephardic Phenomenon

With rare exceptions, the refugees, like their ancestors, were natives of the Peninsula. Jews had been present in Iberia as far back as the days of imperial Rome. According to legend, they had come even earlier, during the Babylonian exile in the sixth century B.C.E. and even King Solomon's reign 400 years before. By 1492 the Jews, like the rest of the Iberian population, comprised a racially mixed but distinctively Iberian community. Their small numbers in Roman days had continuously swelled with people of indigenous stock and periodically with immigrants from Africa and Asia.

Their expulsion, therefore, weighed heavily upon these Jews. And although they left their beloved land behind, they long continued to live in it psychologically, clinging to its language, customs poetry, and melodies. In 1906, a Spanish senator, Angel Pulido y Fernández, coming across the descendants of these Jews while he was traveling in the Middle East, was so impressed by the retention of their Iberian identity, that he called them *españoles sin patria*, Spaniards without a country.

To the exiles the Hebrew term *Sepharadi* was now applied. The word *Sepharadi* and its generic plural, *Sepharadim*, are simultaneously nouns and adjectives, meaning "Iberian," or, in the later political sense, "Spanish." As such they were previously applied to all Iberians, non-Jews and Jews alike. Popular usage has typically contracted the words to *Sephardi* and *Sephardim* respectively and created the English adjective "Sephardic." These words are parallels to the terms "Ashkenazi," "Ashkenazim," and "Ashkenazic," referring to German and Eastern European Jews.

The word "Sephardi" derives from the noun *Sepharad*, a biblical place-name which by the eighth century was commonly used by Jews to designate the Iberian Peninsula. The name *Sepharad* appears only once in the Hebrew Bible, in the twentieth verse of the Book of Obadiah. There, we read: "And this host of the children of Israel in captivity shall possess Phoenician territories as far as Zarephath, while the exiles of the Jerusalem community who are in Sepharad shall take over the towns of the south."

It is not possible to determine the identity of Zarephath and Sepharad in Obadiah. They appear to be cities: Zarephath in southern Phoenicia and Sepharad in Asia Minor. But in the early centuries of the present era Zarephath and Sepharad came to be identified with two principal Jewish settlements in Western Europe: Zarephath with the French regions, the Roman Gallia, and Sepharad with Iberia, the Roman Hispania. By the eighth century the identification of Sepharad with Hispania, though apparently still not universal, appears to have been sufficiently common. By that time also the term *Ashkenaz*, in Genesis 10:3, Jeremiah 51:27, and I Chronicles 1:6, originally referring to a land bordering on the Euphrates and Armenia, had come to signify the Germanic areas.

From these original immigrants and their descendants the term *Sepharadi* was gradually extended to denote three other groups: expatriate Iberian Christians who declared themselves Jews; the Jews of the Iberian Peninsula prior to the Expulsion; and Iberian Christians under Spanish or Portuguese rule who were presumed to be secret Jews. From this the appellation "Sephardi" may be further extended to all Iberians of real or presumed Jewish descent who lived and died as non-Jews both in Sepharad and elsewhere. The justification for such extension lies in the fact that in large measure the fate of these people and therefore their options in life were linked to the reality or in some cases the presumption of their Jewish ancestry.

In modern times the term has been further broadened to include Jews of non-Iberian ethnic background who have become part of Sephardic communities, and further, in modern Israel, to many non-Iberians who identify as Sephardim on cultural grounds.

The Expulsion connects the two broad phases of the Sephardic phenomenon, the first transpiring in the Iberian Peninsula and the second in what has felicitiously been called the Sephardic Diaspora. The two phases overlap chronologically. The Sephardic Diaspora may be said to have begun in the wake of the Iberian persecutions of Jews in 1391, a full century before the Expulsion, while the Iberian phase continues long after the Expulsion in the experiences of its Jews who converted to Christianity and the descendants of these converts. The Iberian phase fashioned the distinctiveness of the Sephardic community. The Sephardic Diaspora carried this distinctiveness through much of Europe, Africa, Asia, and the Americas. In both Peninsula and Diaspora the Sephardim reflected the world of Europe, medieval and early modern: its products, of which they were creators; its pathology, of which they were victims; and its promise, of which they were paladins.

Until the beginning of the eighteenth century the Sephardim were more numerous than the Ashkenazim. Historical circumstances have since catapulted Ashkenazic Jewry to numerical superiority in the Jewish world. Today, of the nearly 15 million Jews in the world, no more than 10 percent by the ethnic definition can be called Sephardim.

The quincentenary of the fateful decree provides an appropriate juncture for the reassessment of the Sephardic phenomenon. In the past century and a half, dating back to Elias Hayyim Lindo's still useful *History of the Jews of Spain and Portugal* (London, 1849) and the studies on Spain by José Amador de los Rios, culminating in his *Historia social, política y religiosa de los judíos de España y Portugal* (3 vols., Madrid, 1875–1876), scholarship on the manifold facets of this complex phenomenon has incrementally proliferated. The sheer extraction and publication of archival material can aptly be described as breathtaking. No less importantly, the same period has witnessed the development of sophisticated social scientific techniques for the analysis and reconstruction of the world to which the raw data attest. Cecil Roth, one of the twentieth century's most eminent investigators of the Sephardic phenomenon in all its complexity, often counseled the younger scholars at his side to create new comprehensive visions of the Sephardim. In the process he explicitly urged them to undertake a trenchant critique of all older reconstructions, including that of his own epochal *The History of the Marranos* (Philadelphia, 1931), which he had completed when he was only thirty years old. Indeed, although the discovery of more data, particularly from archival research, in all areas of the Sephardic phenomenon, continues to be as necessary as it is welcome, the need for new reconstructions of their totality occupies an even more pressing priority.

All reconstructions depend upon the interpretation of the available data, and interpretation in turn is a function of the matrix of assumptions with which any phenomenon is approached.

When approached with an assumptive system that ensures a maximum possible detachment from the data and the assistance of current social scientific techniques for coherent and consistent reconstructions, the many facets of the Sephardic phenomenon weave a distinctive pattern. Such an approach helps to puncture three categories of pervasive misconceptions found among historians of Sephardic Jewry.

The first is a racial myth. The myth makes of Iberian Jews, and, indeed, all Jews, a race of Eastern Mediterranean origin. This myth depicts Jews as inherently different and readily distinguishable from all other Iberians. It therefore treats Jews as outsiders whose activities are at best tangential to authentic Iberian experience.

Implicit in this myth is the notion that Jews possess certain traits. Among these are a penchant for commerce and finance, an aversion to soldiering, an obsession for religion, a clannishness and even xenophobia.

Derivative from the myth is the implicit notion of a demonic power possessed by Jews. As a result of this power, Jews, the paucity of their numbers notwithstanding, can control powerful institutions and even entire kingdoms.

Connected to the myth is the conception of a "Jewish problem" nettling every government and requiring special attention. This egregious misconception even leads one author, in connection with the policy of King Egica toward Jews, to speak of it as an effort toward a "final solution."

Accompanying this myth all too often has been what may charitably be called a distanced understanding of Judaism on the part of writers who appear to have had inadequate personal contact with its textual past or its social realities past or present.

The second myth is a religious one. It is the myth of the strength and unity of Roman Christianity in Iberia. The reality was quite different. Roman Christianity in Iberia, as frequently elsewhere, was continually beset by internal conflicts, alternative forms of Christianity, and rooted pagan cults. Its strength, like that of all other forms of Christianity, derived from the towns; the more populous countryside could not be effectively converted prior to the feudal age. In Navarre, fiercely independent, this process was not completed until the twelfth century. If, as appears to be the case, the Roman Church had become the strongest institution in Iberian life by the fourth century, its strength was relative; by conservative estimates, its adherents could at no time prior to the Muslim conquest have exceeded 15 percent of the total

Iberian population. These realities are essential for an understanding of the diverse relationships between Jews and Christians in Iberia.

The third category of misconceptions relates to general methodology. It includes:

(1) the tacit acceptance of documents without analysis of their biases. This results in the objectivization of such biases;

(2) the explanation of historical events by assumed insight into the psychology of the leaders involved. Such explanation is usually ad hoc and little more than a projection of the biases of the writer;

(3) the injection of filiopietism and ethnocentricity, in their various forms, into historical reconstructions, with the resultant distortions of apologetics and polemics:

(4) the confusion of authority and power. This results in the depiction of authority figures, popes and kings included, as

operating independently, capriciously, and even without accountability in their respective institutional settings;

(5) the equation of the promulgation of legislation with its enforcement. This results in the societal reconstructions based upon the false assumption that the behavior patterns demanded by constitutions and decrees constitute societal reality;

(6) the supposition that societal groups, including institutions, are structurally uniform and ideologically monolithic at a given time and even through time. This results in reductive presentations of sociopolitical and socioideological diversity as well as an inattention to variations, however subtle, resulting from differences in sociohistorical context;

(7) the assumption that societal structure is best understood as composed of broadly defined classes, which struggle with one another as solid blocs for primarily or exclusively economic ends. This results in a failure to discern the complexity of all societal spectra, where establishment and nonestablishment elements cut across the Marxist lines of class, and where ideological and political motivations are no less and often more important than the economic;

(8) the conviction that only documentary evidence is fundamental to successful reconstructions of historical situations. This results in a failure to recognize that, even where abundant, documentary evidence alone can never fully describe a historical situation. Documen-

tary evidence regularly presents the position of victors and their successor establishments, and other positions only rarely, and then usually only in proportion to their strength. Wherever possible, the presentors have selected, packaged and promulgated the evidence in the documents through the biases of their assumptive systems. As a result, any effort at the comprehension of historical situations must rely on the restoration of the missing links of societal activity through a typological reconstruction consistent with the available documentary evidence and the evidence of the broader societal context. To be sure, such methodology is not without its own intrinsic biases, but these are theoretically neutral toward the presentor and equally available to public scrutiny and correction.

The removal of these impediments and the application of contemporary social scientific methodology pave the way for a more comprehensive analysis of the Sephardic phenomenon. From such analysis the Sephardic phenomenon emerges as the distillate of the progressive interaction betweeen individuals and groups we can retrospectively label as Sephardic with the total environments of which they formed an integral part. In this light every culture in which the Sephardim were active participants becomes indispensable for an understanding of the totality of Sephardic experience. So too every phase of this experience becomes indispensable to an understanding of its unfolding.

The Sephardic phenomenon is divisible into seven major phases: (1) its foundation, from its beginnings until the Muslim conquest in 711–715; (2) its formation, in Muslim Iberia until the Almoravid conquest around 1150; (3) its "Occidentation," in Christian Iberia until around 1360; (4) its bifurcation, in Christian Iberia until 1497; (5) its rationalization, in Christian Iberia and its colonies; (6) its consolidation, in the Eastern Sephardic Diaspora and (7) its universalization, in the Western Sephardic Diaspora.

In every one of these phases, in varying forms, four constants appear: an impressive variety of Sephardic economic and political activity in the community at large; a high degree of Sephardic integration into the broader community; the numerical growth of Sephardic Jewry through the absorption of non-Jews; and, in addition to devoutly religious components in the Sephardic community, the presence of considerable numbers characterized by tepidity toward their traditional faith.

The Foundation of the Sephardic Phenomenon

The Sephardic phenomenon was first contoured by the geography of the Iberian Peninsula. As the westernmost point of Mediterranean Europe, Iberia was long believed to be the *finis terrae*, the end of the earth. As such it provided a natural goal for Rome's dreams of western expansion. Roman subjects settled in Iberia, as they did in Gaul and Germania, as early as the third century B.C.E. Among the early Roman settlers were Jews, who, like others, were particularly attracted to Iberia's southern lands and Mediterranean littorals.

The presence of these Iberian Jews is marked by tombstones. Yet aside from these slabs they left little trace during the heyday of imperial Rome. The original Jewish settlers may have included Roman prisoners as well as voluntary immigrants. The emigration of the latter from places where Jewish communities were almost certainly larger makes it reasonable to assume that for at least some the maintenance of the Jewish way of life in the fullest was subordinated to other motivations.

By the middle of the first century, however, the Jews had apparently attained sufficient importance to induce Paul of Tarsus, who had been preaching his message to Jews in many other parts of the Greco-Roman world, to consider a visit to the Iberian Peninsula.

No literary sources dealing with Jews appear in the Iberian Peninsula before the fourth century and none from Jewish hands before the ninth. Yet, individually and in their totality, the surviving documents testify to the numerical growth of the Jewish population, the integration of the Jews into the general society, and the importance of the Jewish community to both establishments and anti-establishments in the political process.

The earliest sources, all in Latin and of Catholic derivation, consist of conciliar canons, royal decrees, polemical tracts and historical works like Isidore of Seville's *History of the Goths*. A few of these documents derive from the Roman period, which may be said to have continued until the Visigothic assumption of a tenuous hold over the

Peninsula during the fifth century. In general, the documents exude an anti-Jewish hostility which derives from the earliest Christian literature and is enshrined in the Roman Catholic legislation that culminated in the Theodosian Code of 438.

This spirit is evident in the canons of the Council of Elvira, a pan-Iberian conclave of prelates that met sometime during the first decade of the fourth century, when the Roman Catholic Church was well on its way to becoming the official religion of the Roman Empire. Four canons of the council seek to curtail contact between the faithful and the Jews: they forbid Christians to marry Jews (nos. 16 and 78), have their fields or crops blessed by Jews (49) and eat at the same table with Jews. (50).

Though scant, all evidence reveals the importance of Jews in Iberian society. Jews were active in agriculture and viticulture, in crafts, trades, commerce and the professions. They mingled freely with non-Jews and married them, doubtless with the prior conversion of their partners to Judaism. They appear to have proselytized with more than a modicum of success. Above all, Jews held public office, received high titles, bore arms and served as trusted garrisons. A valuable glimpse into Jewish life in the early fifth century is preserved in a letter purportedly written by Bishop Severus of the Balearic island of Minorca. The letter recounts the miraculous conversion of Minorca's entire Jewish community through some of the recently discovered relics of the martyred St. Stephen. It depicts the Jews as acculturated and integrated into Minorcan society, with Greek names and titles, wealth and status, high honors and important offices. Some scholars claim that this document was a forgery retrojected to the early fifth century by a later writer for his own polemical battles. Even if so, its obiter dicta on the Jews, one of the fulcra of its claims to authenticity, are credible for the earlier period and additionally reflective of the later.

The spirit that pervaded the Council of Elvira is evident in the pronouncements of the Roman Catholic Visigoths, beginning with King Reccared (586–601) from the time of his conversion in or shortly before 589 and continuing with some of his successors, notably Sisebut (612–621), Sisenand (631–639), Receswinth (649–672), Erwig (680–687) and Egica (687–702). Their decrees and those of the church councils heaped restrictions upon the Iberian Jews. For all their variations, these fall primarily into seven categories: (1) the manumission of slaves owned by Jews; (2) the exclusion of Jews from public office and witness against Christians; (3) the prohibition of marital or concubinary unions between Jews and non-Jews, and the compulsory baptism of the issue of such unions; (4) the diminution of Jewish rights in court, travel and worship; (5) the forced conversion of the Jews, explicitly or implicitly with the alternative of exile; (6) the imposition of penalties against Jews and Christians for aiding the religious recidivism of Jewish converts; and (7) on the basis of the actual or putative religious recidivism of some converts, the generic attribution of recidivist inclinations to the converts as a group and the resultant preemptive imposition of disabilities upon them. Among the more ignominious disabilities was the *placitum,* or compulsory profession of religious fidelity, first imposed in Toledo by King Chintila (636–640) in December 638 upon converts from Judaism to Christianity. In this statement, the former Jews solemnly renounced their erstwhile beliefs and practices, promised to surrender their Jewish books, and swore to stone any backsliders among them.

Far from supporting an unrelieved Jewish adversity beginning with Reccared's conversion, the reiteration of this legislation betrays the difficulty of its enforcement. Contributing to the difficulty was the apathy or opposition to anti-Jewish legislation by several Visigothic monarchs after Reccared, notably Swintila (621–631) and Chindaswinth (641–649), and possibly also Liuva II (601–603), Witteric (603–610), and Gundemar (610–612). Such opposition cannot be responsibly dismissed by the occasionally proferred contention that these monarchs were "Arianizers." Besides, as the anti-Jewish legislation itself attests, Roman Catholic laity and clergy, including bishops, often supported the Jews, encouraged the return of exiled Jews, and even assisted Jewish converts to Christianity in their reversion to Judaism. Enemies charged these Roman Catholics with selling out to Jewish money. But this allegation, with its irresponsible imputation of corruption to large segments of the church, not to speak of its reductive appraisal of Jews, is nothing more than the excrescence of partisan hostility. Hardly surprisingly, it finds support in neither direct nor circumstantial evidence. It does, however, effectively divert attention from the deeper causes of the rift within the Iberian church and, indeed, all of Iberian society.

The rift exemplified the perennial and ubiquitious conflict between the advocates and the resisters of change, between an Old Guard zealous to preserve its power and prerogatives and a New Guard seeking to harness them to new power sources within its reach. In Iberia, in its simplest terms, the Old Guard supported strong regional autonomy, ecclesiastical and lay, while the New Guard promoted strongly centralized lay and ecclesiastical control. In this struggle, clergy, nobility, and laity were ranged on both sides of the issue, and on each side along a spectrum of visible and typological diversity, within which the principal political issues of the time and all auxiliary issues can be understood. In all phases of the struggle religious ideology was regularly put to the service of political agendas.

Aside from obvious political gain, the centralizers could not have overlooked the military and economic advantages of unification, especially as the Visigoths absorbed other independent enclaves and even finally, under Swinthia (622–631), the Byzantine foothold in the southeastern part of the Peninsula. The apparently incremental growth of Roman Catholicism, particularly among the native Iberian population, provided the paradigm for unification. The goal of unification is discernible in the unsuccessful efforts of King Leovigild (568–586), an Arian, to join Roman Catholics and Arians in a unified Christianity, under the control of the Arianism, or, as the Arian bishops called it, "our Catholic faith." It is seen as well in the revolt of Leovigild's son, Heremenegild, a Roman Catholic with both Arian and Roman Catholic support. Though unable to effect it politically, the Visigoths achieved unification legally by eventually extending Visigothic law over the entire Iberian polity. This took place under King Recenswinth (649–672), who completed the monumental revision of Visigothic law begun by his father Chindaswinth (642–653), with whom he had shared the crown for four years. Prior to Receswinth Iberia's two principal communities, the Visigothic ruling minority and the Roman subject majority, each lived under separate laws. The Visigoths iived under King Euric's (466–484) formulation of Visigothic law. The Romans were guided by a digest of the Theodosian Code arranged by the Visigothic King Alaric II (484–507) and known as the Alaric's *Breviary* (*Breviarium Alaricianum*).

The continued turmoil in Visigothic Iberia suggests that its Old Guard blocked the implementation of Receswinth's code as well as all other efforts at centralization. It suggests as well that the opposing attitudes of Iberian leadership toward the Jews were a function of this struggle. In this struggle the support of Jews and converts from Judaism by the Old Guard nobility, clerics, and laity implies that the Jews, far from being a thorn in an otherwise united society, were in effect a plum of surpassing importance in an internecine struggle for political power. On the other hand, the opposition to the Jews corresponds to the determination of the centralizers to separate them from the Old Guard.

The effort at separation consisted in prying Jews from their traditional identity and principal occupations. Conversion to Christianity made Jews religiously and, at least in theory, politically equal to the Old Guard. It therefore, in most of their activities, reduced the indispensability of their reliance on Old Guard protection. Besides, since the power derived from their activities was generally far less than that of the Old Guard, the converts who chose to break with the Old Guard tended to fall into the camp of the New Guard. The removal of recalcitrant Jews from their principal occupations, agriculture and viticulture, sought to undermine the benefits to the Old Guard of Jewish productivity in these areas. It was, of course, accomplished through the prohibition against Jewish ownership of Christian slaves. The prohibition carried a transparent tender of freedom for slaves converting to Roman Catholicism and an equivalently transparent admission of the existence of more than a few who were not Roman Catholics. Jews who converted kept their slaves, but, like other converts, could bolt from their dependence upon the Old Guard.

A political perspective thus fully explains why the centralizers preferred the Jews' conversion over their exile and their exile over their maintenance of the status quo. It also explains why the Roman Catholic clergy, nobility, and laity of the Old Guard, in order to retain the status quo, favored Jews and helped converts return to Judaism.

It is difficult to ascertain how many Jews converted under the pressures of the Catholic Visigoth monarchs, how many fled the country not to return, how many converts remained Jewish secretly, and how many returned to Judaism when they had an opportunity.

The internecine political struggles in the Peninsula and the apparent entrenchment of the Old Guard under Erwig and Egica explain as well the dynamics behind the invitation to the Muslims to enter the Peninsula. Clearly the New Guard invited the Muslims as allies, and Jews allied with the New Guard could not have been unhappy at their arrival. But the myth of collective Jewish responsibility for the Muslim invasion of an implicitly united Christian Peninsula must be categorically rejected.

The Formation of the Sephardic Phenomenon

Under Muslim rule the Jews of Sepharad became the premier Jewish community of Europe. In the process they evolved many of the traits that thereafter generally characterized all Sephardic communities.

The Muslims, under a captain named Tarik, invaded Iberia in 711 near the promontory thereafter known as the Rock of Tarik (Gibral-Tarik; Eng.: Gibraltar). By 715 they had occupied Iberia's south-central and northeastern areas and, except for some Pyrenean pockets, tributized the rest. The Muslims called the Peninsula al-Andalus, an enigmatic name sometimes derived from the hypothetical "Vandalicia," land of the "Vandals," after the Germanic tribes that had preceded the Visigoths into the Peninsula. Crossing the Pyrenees, the Muslims pushed northward until 732, when they were finally defeated between Tours and Poitiers by Eudes of Aquitaine and Charlemagne's grandfather, Charles, who earned the sobriquet Martel ("Hammer") for his prowess.

The occupation of Iberia, followed in the ninth century by the subjugation of Sardinia and Corsica and the gradual conquest of Sicily, climaxed the conversion of the Mediterranean into a Muslim lake. The Muslim world then inaugurated a period of spectacular achievement while Western Europe, landlocked, entered the provincialism of the feudal age.

The history of Muslim Iberia or al-Andalus is divisible into seven segments: (1) the chaos: 715–756, characterized by continuous internecine struggle, largely between Berber and Arab tribes; (2) the emirate: 756–929, promoted by coalitions successful in the gradual, if spasmodic, advance of peace, order, and productivity; (3) the caliphate: 929–1031, proclaimed by the erstwhile emir Abd-ar-Rahman III (912–961), which propelled al-Andalus to its greatest political centralization and inaugurated its cultural Golden Age; (4) the taifas, "party states," or city-state emirates: 1031–1086, often in struggle with one another but collectively reaping the harvest of the Golden Age; (5) the Almoravid province (1086–1147), appended to the Almoravids' West African headquarters and marking the onset of Al-Andalus' cultural decline; (6) the Almohad caliphate (1148–1238), which suffered extensive territorial losses to the Christians and witnessed the end of al-Andalus' cultural hegemony; and (7) the principality of Nasrid Granada (1232 or 1237–1492), a homogeneous and culturally productive remnant which capitulated to the Christians in 1492.

In al-Andalus the Muslims developed a unique society with a considerable degree of political, economic and social rationalization. Its population, possibly exceeding 7 million, was highly urbanized, and its cities, often built on Roman sites, were the largest and cleanest in Europe. Foremost among them was Cordova, home to 100,000 people by the caliphal period, and the capital of Emir/Caliph Abd-ar-Rahman III (912–961) until he built his majestic palace city of Madinat az-Zahra ("the Golden City") three miles away. The Muslims' wealth derived from their exploitation of al-Andalus' limited (and not, as often stated, generally abundant) resources with advanced scientific techniques. The Muslims introduced new crops and innovative irrigation. They stimulated mining, manufactures, and commerce. They built a fleet that plied the Mediterranean and connected with the Middle Eastern trade routes to India. It carried the raw materials and finished products of al-Andalus, including its vaunted silk cloth, and brought back the riches of these lands, not least among them the gold of the Sudan. Many of the Arabic terms related to these activities are retained in the vocabulary of Christian Iberia.

The economy of al-Andalus generated increasing wealth through much of the caliphate. This wealth in turn gave rise to increasingly self-indulgent courtiers and intellectuals. The courtiers, the caliph and his successors foremost among them, turned to the patronage of culture. The intellectuals, schooled de rigeur in Koran and Tradition (*hadith*), and as well in the scientific pursuits of the time, not the least medicine, increasingly invested their leisure in cultural creativity. In their growing worldliness both groups began to reassess the traditional world-view of their heritage, thus inaugurating in Europe what has been called, if somewhat infelicitously, the confrontation between reason and revelation.

As is always the case, this confrontation was resolved in one of three ways: the rejection of reason, the rejection of revelation, or a synthesis of the two. The rejection of reason was politically secure and could be publicly trumpeted, given the fact that society and government were grounded in Islam's revealed texts and sacred traditions. The rejection of revelation was politically most dangerous, since it courted punishment for treason, and therefore compelled all but its doctrinaire proponents to remain intellectually closeted. The intermediate solution of synthesis strove for the compatibilization of reason with revelation in such a way as to support the societal structure while permitting a rational understanding of its underlying ideology. Articulated by and on behalf of people uneasy with the traditional coordinates of revelation, this solution generated the creative philosophical syntheses of al-Andalus.

The artistic renaissance is justly called the Golden Age of al-Andalus. Its beginnings may at least symbolically be dated with the arrival of Ziryab the singer from Baghdad during the emirate of Abd-er-Rahman II (822–852) and its climax in the melodious poetry and sophisticated philosophy of the caliphate and taifas. The poetic florescence was pedestaled on scientific studies of the Arabic language. Grammar, philology, and lexicography uncovered Arabic's natural rhythms and directed its linguistic creativity. The philosophical counterpart couched the inherited tradition in the forms of ancient Greek philosophy, especially Neoplatonism and Aristotelianism. It culminated in the works of the Aristotelian Averroes (1126–1198).

In al-Andalus a new Jewish community came into being. The community was composed of three strata: the Jews of Visigothic Iberia, those overrun by the Muslim advance, and those subsequently returning from exile; immigration from elsewhere in the Muslim world, particularly as al-Andalus prospered and other Muslim lands declined;

and, in all likelihood, the continued adoption of Judaism by non-Jews, comparable to the massive non-Muslim adoption of Islam, particularly in the tenth and eleventh centuries. Concentrated in the newer cities, especially in the south, the Jewish community of al-Andalus, with a population by the end of the caliphate of 150,000 and possibly more, was by far the largest in Europe.

As elsewhere under Islam, the Jew of al-Andalus was a *dhimmi*, or "protected person." As dhimmis, Jews were regarded to be inferior to the Muslims and subjected to heavier taxes. Yet Jews lived with far greater physical and emotional comfort in al-Andalus than in any other country, Muslim or Christian, of the time. In al-Andalus they engaged in the widest range of occupations and professions. They were landowners and farmers, artisans and craftsmen, local and international merchants, physicians and scholars. They served the community at large as administrators, diplomats, and even soldiers, beginning with their garrisoning of captured cities in the early days of the conquest. In many of these activities Jews had regular contact with Muslims professionally and, especially in the higher echelons of society, intellectually and socially as well.

In their communities, or *aljamas*, as they were called, the Jews of al-Andalus, as elsewhere, lived quasi-autonomously under talmudic law. The heads of their communities were typically Jewish courtiers approved if not appointed by the Muslim leadership. In the early caliphate, when Abd-er-Rahman III strove to centralize his domains, he selected his body physician, Hasdai (sometimes called Hisdai) ibn Shaprut as prince (*nasi* in Hebrew) of the entire Jewish community of al-Andalus. Hasdai was also one of the caliph's principal diplomats, distinguishing himself not only with Muslims, but with the Christians of imperial Germany, the Byzantine Empire, and the Iberian state of Asturias-León. In the case of Asturias-León, he added his medical knowledge to his diplomatic skills when he provided a remedy for the obesity of its monarch, Sancho the Fat (956–966). As nasi of the Jewish community, Hasdai went to the rescue of beleaguered Jews in foreign lands and established contact with the Jewish kingdom of the Chazars in Russia.

The advent of the party states provided Jewish administrators with more abundant opportunities for preferment, and even titles which were not attainable during the caliphate. In one of these states, the emirate of Granada, a Jew named Samuel (Ismail) ibn Nagdela (993–1055 or 1056), rose meteorically to become commander of the army and even vizier. He headed the Jewish community of Granada with the title of *naggid*, or "leader." He composed works on halakhah and Hebrew poetry of distinction, including poems from the battlefield. Like Hasdai and other Jews in the service of the court, Samuel spoke and wrote Arabic, and like many another Jew he was versed in the Koran. But he also wrote on the Koran, composed poetry in Arabic, began a biblical lexicon in Arabic, and translated from Arabic sources into Hebrew.

In the light of these realities it is only natural that the impress of its Muslim surroundings should have broadly pervaded the Jewish life of al-Andalus. Revealing this influence were the dress, institutions, and architecture of the Jews and even the chants and prayer mats of their synagogues. The influence was evident as well in the fact that the Jews' language of daily discourse was Arabic, which for internal use they apparently generally wrote in Hebrew characters. The Muslim parallel is also reflected formally in the Jews' focus on their own heritage: in their emphasis on scriptural commentaries, legal compilations, grammatical and related studies, religious and secular poetry, and philosophical syntheses between reason and revelation.

The Muslim influence is apparent as well in the mechanisms of Jewish governance. Until the caliphate the Jewish courts and academies of al-Andalus were subordinated to the Jewish legal establishment in Baghdad and the presiding scholar, known as the gaon ("excellency") of its academy of Sura. When the caliphate estabished its independence from Baghdad, the Jewish community of al-Andalus acted correspondingly. Although it continued cordial contact and not infrequent support of the geonic institutions, it proceeded to create an independent legal structure.

The architect of the transition was Hasdai ibn Shaprut. Toward the goals of autonomization and centralization, Hasdai stimulated legal studies. He purchased talmudic manuscripts abroad, thereby significantly increasing the copies available in al-Andalus, and revamped the Jewish legal establishment by importing an Italian scholar, unencumbered by the Jewish factionalism of al-Andalus and beholden to no one but the nasi, to preside over the leading talmudic academy at Cordova. The scholar, Moses ben Enoch, is one of the principals in the famous Legend of the Four Captives, which seeks to repair the rupture of legal continuity between the geonic center and its Diaspora offshoots, both in al-Andalus and elsewhere. The legend presents the founders of the major secessionist academies as emissaries of the geonic academies who were captured by a Muslim pirate and cast off onto the shores of the lands where their leadership was soon established.

Although the fragmentation of the caliphate into party states decentralized the legal systems of both Muslims and Jews, the principle of unity appears to have been retained. This was achieved through the influence of the major centers of the succeeding emirates and the occasional moves toward the organization and codification of halakhah, or talmudic law, and the corpus of its pertinent applications. The process of halakhic organization produced distinguished legal compilations, beginning with the long-influential *Sefer ha-Halakhot* of Isaac of Fez (Alfasi; 1013–1103) in Lucena and culminating nearly two centuries later, outside of the Peninsula, with the *Mishneh Torah* of the Cordovan Moses ben Maimon (Maimonides; 1135–1205), whose father had studied at Lucena under Alfasi's successor.

The Muslim influence carried over as well into the Jewish culture of al-Andalus. Following their Muslim counterparts, courtier Jews like Hasdai, Samuel ibn Nagrela, and their colleagues created and sustained al-Andalus' Jewish Golden Age. Beginning with the grammarian poets Menahem ibn Saruk and Dunash ibn Labrat in Hasdai's time, the study of grammar led to the classic articulation of the triliteral Hebrew root by Judah ben David Hayyuj (ca. 945–ca. 1000) and the grammatical masterpieces of Jonah ibn Janah (first half of 11th cent.). Out of these sciences came a rich Hebrew poetry, secular and religious, that paralleled its Arabic counterpart in variety and beauty. The creativity of world-class poets like Solomon ibn Gabirol (ca. 1020–ca. 1057), Moses ibn Ezra (1055–1135 or later), and Jehuda Ha-Levi (ca. 1070–ca. 1141) ranks with the finest in any language.

The great poets were also engaged actively in medicine and other scientific disciplines. They were often also involved in creative religious scholarship in halakhah and biblical commentary, as well as linguistic studies and philosophy.

The Muslim milieu is also strikingly evident in the philosophical synthesis of Jewish al-Andalus. Indeed, the oldest extant synthesis in al-Andalus is the *Keter Malkhut* ("Royal Crown"), a long Hebrew poem by Solomon ibn Gabirol, in which the coordinates of Jewish theology are Neoplatonically framed. The *Keter Malkhut* is the only major Jewish synthesis of al-Andalus to have been composed in Hebrew. The others, including the Neoplatonic *Hovot ha-Levavot* ("Duties of the Heart") by Bahya ibn Pakuda (second half of 11th cent.), the Neoplatonic and Aristotelian *Cuzari* by Jehuda Ha-Levi, the Aristotelian *Emunah Ramah* ("Exalted Faith") by Abraham ibn Daud (ca. 1110–1180), whose historical work the *Seder* (or *Sefer*) *Ha-Kabbalah* ("Book of Tradition") carries the Legend of the Four Captives, and the Aristotelian *Moreh Nevukhim* ("Guide of the Perplexed") by Moses Maimonides, were written with Hebrew characters in Arabic prose.

Though differing in form, approach, and purpose, the common effort of all these works to articulate the Jewish revelational system through the framework of another system ineluctably results in procrusteanization. Even a cursory reading of the Jewish philosophy of al-Andalus reveals alterations in the philosophical priorities of the thought of the inherited Jewish tradition and the details of their articulation. Thus, in different degrees, all these works effect changes in the inherited understanding of God, creation, providence, election, revelation, Torah, mitzvah, sin, atonement, reward and punishment, immortality, resurrection, and Messiah. Not surprisingly, this parallels the syntheses of the Muslim philosophers.

To be sure, such philosophical lucubrations were intended primarily for a small circle of intellectually conflicted believers. Aside from these and other intellectuals, including those positionally opposed to their efforts, there was no reading public, as some contemporary scholars occasionally imagine. However, this small circle constituted an influential group, who doubtless by nonverbal example as much as by articulated ideas modeled patterns of thought and behavior for the lower echelons of Jewish society. Although opposition could not have failed to mount from the beginning, the aggregate following of this synthetic thought, Muslim as well as Jewish, could not, for a variety of reasons, have been negligible. To the extent to which the synthesizers enjoyed establishment support, their philosophical positions, even if not majoritarian, must be called societally tonal.

Perhaps the classic literary example of the acculturation of the Jews of al-Andalus is to be found in Gabirol's other philosophical work, of which there remain only fragments in Hebrew and a Latin translation, titled *Fons Vitae* ("Fountain of Life"). The original of this work, occasionally presumed to be in Hebrew, could just as easily have been in Arabic. Grounded in Neoplatonism like the *Keter Malkhut*, the *Fons Vitae* differs in its avoidance of all biblical, talmudic, or other religious terminology or allusions. Though forgotten among Jews in al-Andalus as Aristotelianism became their philosophical fashion, the *Fons Vitae* enjoyed a popularity among Christian scholastics, who believed that its author, his name now corrupted to Avicebron or Avicebrol, was a Muslim or even a Christian!

The Jewish Golden Age in al-Andalus reached its apogee in Moses ben Maimon, known as Maimonides or by the acronym Rambam. Maimonides lived in al-Andalus for little more than the first thirteen of his seventy years. He and his family left Cordova in the wake of the Almohad arrival and wandered through Christian Iberia, Muslim North Africa, and the Middle East before settling in Egypt. But Maimonides carried the culture of al-Andalus and spent the rest of his life in its energetic expression. The comprehensiveness of his activity is evidenced in his work as as a physician (he served Saladin's powerful vizier, al-Fadil, in this capacity), as leader of the Jewish community, and as a prodigious writer in Arabic on medicine, and in Arabic and Hebrew on a variety of dimensions of Jewish law and philosophy.

All these writings are models of precise organization and unambiguous clarity. So are at least the first two of his three monumental works: the *Luminary* (1168), his commentary to the Mishnah, in Arabic, known as the *Maor* in Hebrew; and the *Repetition of the Torah*, 1180, his code of Jewish law in Hebrew, known as the *Mishneh Torah* and also the *Yad ha-Hazakah* ("Strong Hand"). But his third and culminating work, *The Guide of the Perplexed* (1190), his synthesis of Jewish revelation and Aristotelian philosophy, in Arabic, known as the *Moreh Nevukhim* in Hebrew, appears to have a double meaning, one apparent from a superficial reading, and the other, as Maimonides himself tells us, attainable by individuals grounded in philosophy through the careful juxtaposition of critical elements seemingly scattered in various chapters.

That the synthesis of reason and revelation in the *Moreh Nevukhim* is thoroughly Aristotelian is beyond any cavil. Aristotle's influence pervades Maimonides' treatment of all Judaism's theological coordinates. But what appears to be uncertain is Maimonides' real position on Aristotle's belief in the eternity of matter, with its obviously implicit denial of creation out of nothing and its challenge to corollary concepts. Maimonides was fully aware of the centrality of eternity of matter to Aristotle's thought. Yet, though he unequivocally accepted Aristotle's other fundamental propositions, he appears to hedge on the full acceptance of the eternity of matter into his synthesis.

Indeed, Maimonides' possible attraction to the eternity of matter was not lost on the commentators supportive of the *Guide* in the three centuries following its publication, for example, those of Shem Tob ibn Falaquera (ca. 1225–1295), Joseph ben Abba Mari Ibn Kaspi (1279–1340), and Moses ben Joshua ben Mar David of Narbonne (d. 1362), also known as Narboni. Kaspi went so far as to claim that, appearances notwithstanding, Maimonides had not refuted the doctrine of the eternity of the world. Nor was it lost on the commentaries that challenged the position of the *Guide*, among them most prominently that of Shem Tov ibn Shem Tov (ca. 1390–ca. 1441).

But whatever their views, the commentaries implicitly attest to the impact of Maimonidean thought and the cogency of its articulation for a environment that foreshadowed Jewish society in the modern world.

The "Occidentation" of the Sephardic Phenomenon

The distinctive characteristics of Sephardic life in al-Andalus were transferred to a Christian environment with the unfolding of Christian Iberia. This unfolding is known as the Reconquista, or the Christian reconquest of the Peninsula.

In retrospect, the Reconquista may be said to have begun in 722, when a Visigothic nobleman named Pelayo successfully skirmished with the Muslims near the village of Covadonga. It did not end until the annexation of the emirate of Granada by the Catholic Monarchs seven centuries and seven decades later. Legend romantically depicts the Reconquista as an irrepressible and heroic crusade against the infidel. Yet, in reality, it consisted of desultory campaigns, fueled by material prospects, in which Christians and Muslims often fought side by side. At one time the emir of Zaragoza was aided by the greatest Christian hero of the Reconquista, Rodrigo Díaz del Vivar, who has been immortalized by his Castilian-Arabic sobriquet, El Cid.

Chronologically the Reconquista falls into three major phases. The initial expansion culminated in a rout of the Almohads at Navas de Tolosa in 1212. It produced a Christian Iberia that stretched from below the Tagus River on the Atlantic to some fifty miles south of Barcelona on the Mediterranean. The intermediate period comprised four electrifying decades, through the middle of the thirteenth century. During this time Christian forces occupied the heartland of southern Iberia, leaving al-Andalus with the kingdom of Granada and a small pocket on the southern coast. In the final phase, the pocket was absorbed in the fourteenth century and Granada in 1492.

The Reconquista carved out various Christian kingdoms: Asturias in the west; six counties in the east: Aragon, Sobarbe, Ribagorza, Urgel, Pallars, and Barcelona; and between them the fiercly independent kingdom of Navarre. Eventually from Asturias there emerged Portugal and León-Castile; the six counties fused into Catalonia and Aragon, which in the twelfth century were brought together under a single crown, though with separate administrations; and Castile, once an outpost, had definitively absorbed León under King Fernando III "the Saint" of Castile (1217–1252) and León (1230–1252).

Around a Visigothic residue the Christian population of Reconquista Iberia grew through the absorption of mozarabs, mudejar converts, and, by no means least, adventurers from across the Pyrenees. Known as the Franks in Christian Iberia, these adventurers informed the Reconquista with the biblical faith and crusading militancy of feudal Christianity.

The Reconquista generated a social order based on military achievement. It comprised two strata: warrior-leaders, developing into an aristocracy, and their raggedy followers. With the advance of the Reconquista the warrior-aristocracy diverged toward two extremes: the older and more comfortable, and the newer and more ambitious. To the constellations of warrior-leaders around these extremes the terms "Old Guard" and "New Guard" may be respectively applied.

At this point a further word about the terms "Old Guard" and "New Guard" is in order. Like so many others, these useful terms are arbitrary labels. They refer to the opposing segments a sociopolitical spectrum and cover a wide variety of positions on either side, each with its own agenda and lesser alignments. These constellations, like their constituent components, become activated in direct proportion to their need for political or military confrontation, at which point they bank their differences and federate against the common foe. It is important to bear in mind that although the conservative and liberal perspectives on the sociopolitical spectrum labeled Old Guard and New Guard remain unchanged, the historical context and ideological content of these positions are always undergoing modification, as is obviously the case with the identity of their personnel. It thus can happen that today's New Guard position becomes the position of tomorrow's Old Guard. In addition, both constellations, and their individual components, strive to co-opt prospectively useful noncentrist elements of their opposition, even at the expense of some internal strife and even the restructuring of their own groups.

In Iberia, the distinctions between Old Guard and New Guard were expectedly more defined in its more settled areas and more fluid at the frontiers.

Jews in Reconquista Iberia are documented from the beginning of the ninth century. Their presence therefore may be presumed to be earlier. The Jewish population in Reconquista Iberia derived from four principal sources: established communities overrun by Christians, refugees from al-Andalus, immigrants from across the Pyrenees, and, not least, converts into Judaism. By the heyday of the Reconquista, Jewish communities of 50 to 100 families were to be found throughout the Peninsula. Such communities were sparser in the west and north of Iberia and more abundant in the south, center, and east. Large concentrations, of 200 or more families, included Valencia, Barcelona, Zaragoza, Huesca, and Toledo. Toledo's Jewish community' the largest, may have reached 350 families, though not the thousands of people reported by legend.

As they did in al-Andalus, Jews in Reconquista Iberia enjoyed quasi-autonomous political status under talmudic law. But in Reconquista Iberia, with its multiple polities, the Jewish communities were not centralized. Typically, every major city had independent jurisdiction, and, customarily, some degree of control, often loosely structured, over its neighboring settlements. It is of note that although Aragon was progressively centralized, its Jewish communities, despite various efforts, at no time achieved a central organization.

As in other lands, Jewish social and political structures in Reconquista Iberia revealed the influence of their environment. The Jewish community comprised two strata: the populace at large and the aristocracy. The Jewish aristocracy, however, derived not from military prowess, but from knowledge and and skills which were put to the service of their Christian overlords. Politically the Jewish communities were headed by a royal favorite who appointed the chief rabbi or chief judge, or served in this capacity himself.

The Jews of Reconquista Iberia were heirs to the world-view that had pervaded al-Andalus. Sophisticated, elitist, rationalistic, and decidedly acculturative in its articulations, this world-view fostered strong currents of religious tepidity and skepticism that variously affected nearly all of Jewish society. Throughout Reconquista Iberia almost to the eve of the Expulsion from Aragon and Castile, Jewish moralists fulminated against these currents and often indicted them for the ethical and moral corruption in their midst.

The influences of this world-view informed the rich Jewish literature of Reconquista Iberia. Though often fused with the literature of the Jewish Golden Age in al-Andalus or relegated to secondary status, this creativity, in the absence of its predecessor, would have sufficed to locate Iberian Jewry among the most innovative in history. This Silver Age of Iberian Jewry continued the forms of grammar, poetry, and philosophy developed in al-Andalus, but not without significant modifications. In language, Hebrew became the standard idiom, its rabbinic and medieval components blending with the biblical idiom dominant in the Golden Age. In poetry the conventions of al-Andalus were modified by greater topicality, specificity, and even preciosity, and the Hebraization of new genres, like the *maqama*, the Arabic dramatic dialogue in poetry and prose. And in philosophy the rational structures of Neoplatonism and Aristotelianism were harnessed to the defense of the Judaism of tradition.

The traditionalists in Jewish society attributed its erosions of faith and moral laxity to the blandishments of Aristotelian thought. To the followers of its teachings they frequently gave the appellation Averroists. They employed this term pejoratively, and often in lieu of the term "Maimonidean" (or "Maimunist"), referring to a follower of Maimonides, who rather than Averroes, represented the culminating link between Aristotle and Judaism. The opposition to the Maimonideans by the traditionalists, or anti-Maimonideans, formed the basis of a prolonged and at times incandescent struggle. Begun before the death of Maimonides, it continued for three centuries in Castile, Aragon and Provence, until it was stilled by the decree of the Expulsion.

The internal struggles beweeen Maimunists and anti-Maimonideans in Iberia had been preceded by an international struggle following the appearance of Maimonides' *Mishneh Torah*. There the center of opposition was Baghdad, the seat of the gaonate, whose followers correctly understood the *Mishneh Torah* as a frontal attack on the gaonate's claim to leadership of the Jewish world. In Europe also the Maimonidean controversy was ignited by the *Mishneh Torah* because of its challenge to the Jewish establishment, and, with the publication of the *Guide for the Perplexed*, for its underlying philosophy as well. But it was the Aristotelianism of the *Guide* that became the battle line in Europe. The struggle had two peak moments. The first came in 1233 or 1234, when, by order of the Dominicans and possibly at the instigation of the anti-Maimonideans, the writings of Maimonides were burned in the public square of Paris. The second occurred in 1305, when the sage of Barcelona, Solomon ibn Adret, issued a ban against the study of the sciences, except for medicine, and metaphysics by any Jew below the age of twenty-five. Besides their philosophical substance, the struggles all had decidedly political dimensions. What was at stake was nothing short of the control of the direction of the regional and even universal Jewish world.

Not unconnected to the anti-Maimonidean position was the bloom of intellectual mysticism in Reconquista Iberia. In Aragon-Catalonia this occurred in the second quarter of the thirteenth century in the city of Gerona. A circle of mystics, formed around the legendary Isaac the Blind, wrote sophisticated mystical works, like those steeped in Neoplatonism scripted by Isaac's disciple Azriel. In Castile a parallel movement culminated in the 1280s with the completion of the *Zohar* ("[The Book of] Splendor"). The cardinal work of Jewish mysticism, the *Zohar* is a collection of a number of tracts, which, with the exception of two, penned shortly thereafter, were the work of Moses ben Shem Tob (ca. 1240–1305) of León. The intellectuals connected to these works often reflected the ascetic tendencies of traditional Judaism, which, along with popular mysticism, were particularly in evidence in times of sociopolitical stress. But the works themselves were of the highest philosophical caliber. They were clearly intended for the cultured few in their struggle to shore up support for their position and countervail that of their opponents. In their address of social and moral issues, including their criticism of religious and moral laxity, these works are therefore reflective of the realities of their society and are not to be studied, as they sometimes are, independently of this context.

The gradual assumption of political ascendancy by the anti-Maimonideans in Reconquista Iberia reflected the dominance of the traditional, God-irrupting view of the world nurtured by feudal Christianity and enshrined in the epics, poetry and drama of medieval Christian Iberia. This world-view survived the challenges of Christian scholasticism. Yet at the same time scholasticism's Hellenic heritage struck receptive chords among Iberia's growing Christian elite, whose sophistication, worldliness, skepticism, and religious apathy gave them much in common with their counterparts among the Jews.

Jews in Reconquista Iberia continued the manifold activities of their involvement in al-Andalus. They helped to repopulate numerous conquered areas. In Cordova, Seville, Valencia, Majorca, and elsewhere they were given land and houses. They cultivated fields and vines, crafts and trades, local and international commerce. They served militarily in a variety of capacities, especially the defense of captured towns. They excelled in medicine, astronomy, and eventually cartography. Their scholars studied science, law, and language. Their legists were often consulted by royal jurists on the laws of the land. A most illustrious consultant was the Catalonian Isaac bar

Sheshet Perfet (1326–1408), known acronymically as the Ribash. Along with Muslims and Christians, Castilian Jews were among the Translators of Toledo, rendering Greek and Arabic scientific classics into Latin for Alfonso X (1252–1284), the Wise.

Above all, they Jews were prominent in administration and diplomacy. They were charged with the organization of royal finances and the collection of taxes. Their familiarity with both Christian and Muslim culture made them invaluable for diplomacy. They were often sent on sensitive political missions, as in the case of Don Meir ibn Shoshan for Ferdinand III of Castile and León. Jews served as ambassadors, court physicians, astrologers, secretaries, and interpreters. The alfaquim, or court physician, was often simultaneously the principal royal counselor. In Portugal, he held a seat on the royal council. Throughout Reconquista Iberia such Jews formed a courtier class. As such they often wielded enormous power not only in the Jewish community but in the polity at large.

Unlike other lands of the Christian feudal world, the Jews of Reconquista Iberia enjoyed considerable professional, social, and cultural contact with their non-Jewish neighbors. Jewish thinkers, even mystics like Azriel, were in contact with Christian scholasticism. And, among the earliest Iberian vernacular poetry are verses from a number of Hispano-Jewish poets, among them Jehuda Ha-Levi (ca. 1070–after 1141), whom the distinguished Spanish polygraph, Marcelino Menéndez y Pelayo, calls the first Castilian poet. The contact between Jews and Christians was greatest among the aristocracy, but it was far from absent among the ordinary people. The greater social openness of Reconquista Iberia is evident from the patterns of Jewish residence. The Jews of Reconquista Iberia did not live in restricted communities. Some cities had predominantly Jewish quarters which facilitated the accessibility of communal institutions, but elsewhere, particularly in smaller towns, Jews were to be found in many neighborhoods.

More importantly, Jews and Christians, primarily from the secularized strata, were drawn to one another by their increasingly convergent outlooks on life. And their greater propinquity, geographical, occupational, cultural, and religious, facilitated the transfer of religious commitment from one group to the other. Although few names survive of converts to Christianity, and these usually belong to important personalities, especially scholars like Solomon ha-Levi of Burgos, who became Paul of Burgos, and eventually bishop of that city, it is likely that the converts were not limited to the Jewish aristocracy. Nor is it unlikely, reciprocally, that there was no movement on the politically more perilous road of conversion from Christianity to Judaism.

Leading princes throughout Reconquista Iberia thrived on Jewish service. Though zealous Christians, they issued Jews charters of privilege that were at least tacitly and often explicitly supported by the church. These charters, generally typical of those issued to Jews throughout the feudal world, placed the Jews under the protection of their benefactors. They assured fair treatment for Jews in litigation with Christians and frequently gave them the right to inflict capital punishment.

Jews were especially useful as well because they were powerless and therefore dependent upon the goodwill of their patrons. At the same time, the service they rendered to establishments made Jews an impediment to non-establishment leaders. These therefore spared no opportunity to arouse the populace against them. For this purpose they summoned the farrago of anti-Jewish canards that had accumulated during the Middle Ages. Most vicious were the charges of host desecration, well poisoning, and ritual murder. These myths were continually exploited to siphon popular discontent onto the Jews. Such exploitation was always possible because of the perennial and ubiquitous existence of popular discontent. It proved successful and enduring in direct proportion to the spread and continuity of such discontent, particularly during times of drought, disease, wars, and inflation. Establishments, ecclesiastical no less than lay, vigorously defended Jews against such charges, out of justice in all likelihood and self-interest certainly. But when their own security was threatened, these establishments frequently took over the leadership in the scapegoating of the Jews in order to derail their adversaries' momentum.

As the Reconquista unfolded, the clamor against Jews became more persistent. Reflective of the intensification of sociopolitical stress, this clamor also formed the background for the creation of a new political horizon in Iberia and a radically new direction in the history of its Jews.

The Bifurcation of the Sephardic Phenomenon

By the the fourth quarter of the thirteenth century, Navarre, Portugal and Aragon-Catalonia had completed their respective territorial expansions, leaving the culmination of the Reconquista to Castile. These events were to prove profoundly significant for the fate of Iberian Jews. They were to prove no less significant for the history of all Iberia, and, beyond, the trajectory of Western European civilization.

The kingdom of Navarre was active in the Reconquista only until the middle of the eleventh century. Its participation ended in the reign of Sancho III "the Greater" (1004–1035), when Navarre essentially reached its final boundaries, no less at the expense of nearby Christian lands in León, Ribagorza, Sobarbe and Aragon than the disintegrating Muslim caliphate. At the time Navarre was Iberia's principal Christian state. But its primacy did not survive the reign of Sancho's eldest son and successor, García (1035–1054), as it was quickly overshadowed by its neighbors, Aragon and Castile.

The remaining Christian polities in Iberia completed their major roles in the Reconquista around the same time. Portugal, having achieved its most spectacular gains under Sancho II (1223–1246), rounded out its boundaries under his brother, Afonso III (1246–1279). Aragon-Catalonia completed its section of the Reconquista under Jaume I (1213–1276), and Castile its principal phase under Fernando III. In all three the process occasioned dramatic transformations in the interrelationsips of their respective Old and New Guards.

Until the conclusion of the Reconquista, New Guards could anticipate their aggrandizement through the further pursuit of the Reconquista, especially since the farther south its penetration, the richer the Muslim territories became. The impending termination of the Reconquista exhausted such prospects. It therefore put the New Guards in each advancing realm on a collision course with their Old Guards. Unable to generate additional power through the desiccating Reconquista, the New Guards faced two alternatives: to wrest power forcibly from the Old Guard or to generate new and potentially decisive sources of power. The implementation of the first alternative was the more difficult, because of the sensitivity of the entrenched Old Guard to any disquieting move. The second, initially not as confrontational, but at no time without its own attendant risks, comprised the centralization of the polity with the help of noncentrist elements of the Old Guard, and its expansion through territorial conquest. Centralization entailed the rationalization of the prerogatives of each polity ultimately under a single regime, while territorial expansion offered the prospect of incalculable wealth through the exploitation of conquered territories. The New Guard quite naturally preferred the second alternative.

If the Old Guards of the various Iberian Christian polities perceived a threat to their dominance in this process, they could not have failed to realize its potential for the enrichment of their states, and the maintenance of their competitiveness against one another and equivalently ambitious politics outside the Peninsula. Considerations such as these inevitably led to struggles within the Old Guard, all the while that it was maintaining a fragile unity against the common New Guard adversary. Basically two distinct positions emerged within the constellation of the Old Guard: one favoring the status quo and an unrelenting campaign against the New Guard; and the other recognizing the decisive power potentially derivable from New Guard activities and therefore interested in the fashioning of a new political scenario. This scenario would include the promotion of sociopolitical rationalization and territorial conquest by the state in accordance with the New Guard agenda. But at the same time it would create mechanisms to ensure that the power deriving from these activities was diverted toward the Old Guard, or, more precisely, a coalition within it. This coalition would therefore do everything within its power to control the New Guard. It would supervise its enterprise, reward its achievement, and incorporate some of its people into its midst as it deemed desirable or necessary. But at the same time it would not hesitate to block any New Guard thrusts toward dominance with every means at its disposal. The Old Guard coalitions which promoted this scenario of controlled modernization were the first of their kind in Western Europe. On them the label "Modern Old Guard" may be affixed.

The emergence of the Modern Old Guard was neither swift nor easy in any polity. In all it came about only after continuous and often violent struggles. These struggles were fought not only between the Old Guard and New Guard constellations, but among elements within each, depending upon their perceptions of threat or opportunity. A Modern Old Guard at no time achieved dominance in Navarre. In the other polities the constellational advantage shifted continually. A Modern Old Guard finally established itself in Aragon-Catalonia in the mid-fourteenth century, in Portugal in the early fifteenth, and in Castile in the mid-fifteenth. Thereafter these Modern Old Guards managed, often, however, only with great difficulty, to retain their establishment status against continuous and often relentless New Guard opposition until the end of the eighteenth century in Portugal and the nineteenth century in Spain.

The struggles of the Modern Old Guard were of varying intensity, depending on the polity. In Aragon-Catalonia the emergence of the Modern Old Guard is traceable to the reign of Jaume I (1213–1276); its consolidation to the attainment, by the broader constellation of the Old Guard, of the "General Privilege" under Pere the Great (1276–1285); and its primacy to the political understanding after the military defeat of a more conservative coalition of the Old Guard in 1348 by Pere the Punctilious (1336–1387). By the middle of the thirteenth century, the rationalization of Aragon-Catalonia sociopolitically and its expansion militarily and economically were well under way, led by Catalonia, its more advanced component. For a variety of reasons, including war, famine, and financial collapse, Aragon-Catalonia declined rapidly and irremediably by the end of the fourteenth century.

Though bitter and often bloody, the struggles between the constellations were least devastating in Portgual. This was because Portugal had been the least feudalized of the three large Iberian polities. It had been pointed toward centralization with the separation of its first ruler, Afonso Henriques (ruled 1128–1185), from the hegemony of Castile. Signposts indicating the emergence of its Modern Old Guard are evident in the systematization of Portuguese law under Afonso II (1211–1223), the sociopolitical rationalization under Diniz the Farmer (1279–1325), and Pedro the Justicer (1357–1367), and the massive restructuring of power alignments under João I (1384–1433), by which time a Modern Old Guard had clearly risen to dominance. The Modern Old Guard successfully met new challenges at the end of the fifteenth century and reestablished its dominance on a firmer basis by the middle of the sixteenth.

Castile was the last of the surviving Iberian states to emerge. Though destined to outstrip its neighbors in territory, population, and power, its modernization was later and slower than the others' and the struggle between its Old and New Guards was longer and more bitter. By the culmination of its Reconquista, Castile had generated an overwhelmingly feudalized Old Guard and a rapidly growing New Guard eager to assume control of the kingdom. The emergence of a Modern New Guard is discernible in the sociopolitical rationalization under Alfonso X the Wise (1252–1284) and Alfonso XI (1312–1350) after his thirteen-year minority, but its empowerment was long obstructed by the right wing of the Old Guard. With the growing power of the New Guard, and the unrest brought on by the epidemics and economic disasters of the first half of the fourteenth century, the struggle between the Old Guard and the New Guard kept the specter of civil war continually over Castile through the third quarter of the fifteenth century.

The first major confrontation came late in the reign of Pedro I (1350–1369) when, under Pedro, the New Guard came to the fore and the Old Guard constellation aligned itself behind Pedro's halfbrother, Count Enrique of Trastámara, whose platform included the strong anti-Jewish components traditional for Iberia's anti-establishment positions. Aragon and France entered the fray on Enrique's side, while Edward, England's "Black Prince," came to Pedro's aid. The Black Prince actually turned the tide of battle in Pedro's favor in 1367, but when he suddenly withdrew, the Old Guard forces moved in for the coup de grace. The war culminated spectacularly with Enrique's capture and murder of his royal half-brother.

The war was devastating. It sapped Castile's resources and decimated the aristocracy on both sides of the conflict. It also left unresolved the underlying problems of Castilian society, including the unremitting pressure for its modernization.

When the count of Trastámara mounted the throne as Enrique II (1369–1379), he replenished the old Guard with military officers and family members. He also mitigated his former anti-establishment position toward the Jews. If by these actions he sought to develop a Modern Old Guard, he was frustrated by the conservative Old Guard. The policies it promoted under the Trastámaras permitted it to accumulate nearly half the land of Castile. This kept the Modern Old Guard relatively weak and played into the hands of the New Guard, leading to the recurrent threat of New Guard dominance and civil war.

But neither Enrique nor his son, Juan I (1379–1390), could quell the turbulence of their realm. Powerless against the economic crises of Western Europe which reverberated most emphatically in the Aragonese crash of 1381, and the disaffection of the populace throughout Castile, the Castilian leadership, Old Guard and New, stood again on the brink of civil war and mutual destruction. If civil strife did not abate for many decades, full-scale civil war was for the nonce averted. In the process the Modern Old Guard grew in strength.

In the struggles between the Old Guard and the New and the emergence of the Modern Old Guards, the Jews in the various polities played a seminal role. For all the differences that existed in detail, Jews in all these areas had one critical element in common: in all they were traditionally engaged in New Guard activities but were predominantly under the protection of the Old Guards. The Old Guard sought to keep them as Jews precisely as the Old Guard in Valencia sought to preserve the Muslims in their religious identity. If for no other reason this was because their conversion to Christianity would tend to add to the numbers of the New Guard and therefore threaten their power. But Modern Old Guards, in line with their efforts at rationalization and consolidation of their control, pursued a different policy once they had become dominant in the Old Guard and begun to subordinate the New Guard. This policy promoted the conversion of the Jews, the admittance of a small number into the Old Guard, and the relegation of the rest to the controlled New Guard.

As in the case of the Catholic monarchs among the Visigoths, the conversionist policies of the Modern New Guard corresponded as least as much to a secular political agenda as it did to religious zeal.

In Navarre, which had been centralized since Sancho el Mayor, the Modern Old Guard is discernible in the concerted efforts at international commerce, albeit on a small scale, during the reign of Juana I

(1274–1305). The Jews of Navarre played an important role in these activities. Yet Navarre remained basically a feudal country with dominant power vested in a feudalized Old Guard.

In Portugal, the Jews were also few. Prior to the last decade of the fifteenth century, their numbers could not have exceeded 30,000. With the comparatively smooth transition to the primacy of the Modern Old Guard, the Jews continued to work under the protection of the various segments of the Old Guard constellation. They were molested only by the fringes of the sociopolitical spectrum, and most notably in the difficult, plague-ridden reign of Afonso IV (1325–1357), who was constrained to pass disabling legislation against Jews in the face of New Guard pressure and popular unrest.

In Aragon, where the number of Jews probably approached 100,000 in the thirteenth century, the Modern Old Guard clearly pursued a conversionist policy toward them. The implementation of this policy may have begun early in the second quarter of the century, when the Dominicans became the chief missionaries for the church in Provence and Aragon. Evidence of the zeal of the Dominicans is attested by the Disputation of Barcelona in July of 1263. Convoked under the aegis of King Jaume and the Aragonese anti-Pope Benedict XIII and paid out of their budgets, the disputation ostensibly set out to resolve the shopworn questions of the Messiah's identity, nature, and arrival. But the real agenda was to support the pope and the secular centralizers and, in the process, to induce conversions of Jews. The disputation relied on the Dominicans' study of rabbinic literature in support of Christian doctrine. This study led a dozen years later to the completion of the *Pugio Fidei* ("Dagger of Faith") by Raymund Martí, one of the participants in the Disputation of Barcelona. This massive Latin work was clearly intended to provide Christian missionaries with material for their conversionist activities. Aided by royal enactments, like that of Pedro III in 1279, requiring Jews to hear conversionist sermons, these activities continued steadily and successfully through the fourteenth and fifteenth centuries.

In Castile the Modern Old Guard also adopted the conversionist policy. But, because of Castile's later development and more difficult ascendancy, this policy was implemented more slowly than in Aragon. Despite scant information on its origins, the policy is inferable from

Christian polemicists like the former Jew, Abner of Burgos, whose activity in the second quarter of the fourteenth century leaves little doubt about their conversionist intentions. Conversion may well have also been the motive behind the call for the expulsion of the Jews by Gonzalo Martínez de Oviedo, the majordomo of Alfonso XI (1312–1350). Opposed by other leading Christians, the expulsion did not take place. But not a few Jews converted to Christianity at that time and subsequently, especially during and after the Castilian civil war.

Further indicative of a conversionist policy was the anti-Jewish preaching of Ferrán Martínez beginning in 1378. Martínez was the archdeacon of Ecija, judicial representative of the archbishop of Seville, and confessor to Queen Leonor. Hardly fortuitously, his preaching was concentrated in Seville, Castile's wealthiest Jewish community and a major New Guard center. Martínez's connection with the establishment is evidenced by his undiminished vitriol despite repeated orders to desist obtained by the frightened Sevillian Jewish aljama and its supporters from the pope and even the king. This suggests that the papal bulls were rendered ineffective; that the royal documents were mere formalities and that Martínez, as he himself intimated, enjoyed the support of Castile's highest echelons. Martínez continued undisturbed in his activity for seventeen years. He was finally arrested in 1395 by order of King Enrique III "the Sickly" (1390–1406) in response to circumstances unclear to the chroniclers of the time. But even then his punishment appears to have been little more than a slap on the wrist.

In addition to conversions, Martínez's preaching could not have failed to contribute to the violence against the Jews of Castile which began in March of 1391 and by the summer had spread throughout Castile, Aragon, and the Balearic Isles. These events occurred at a time of heightened unrest in both Castile and Aragon. Castile was reeling from its defeat at the hands of the Portuguese at Aljubarrota in 1385, a depleted treasury, a disoriented populace, and incandescent tensions between the Old Guard and the New Guard, with the New Guard making progress and another devastating civil war on the horizon. Aragon, in the meantime, was not faring much better, as it strove to overcome the ravages of a decade of economic turbulence, revolts in its Mediterranean possessions in 1391, and mounting problems of dynastic succession.

In many places, beginning with Seville, the massacres were stopped by royal orders. These were issued only after enough destruction had taken place to suggest that total destruction was not an impossibility. As in the case of the pogroms against the Jews in Russia 490 years later, there is every likelihood that the eruptions of 1391, which at first glance appeared spontaneous, had been contoured by the establishment and executed with the collusion of important nonestablishment power sources in both Castile and Aragon.

The extent of the losses in life or property during these assaults cannot be accurately determined. Nor can the number of refugees they created. But there can be no question about the magnitude of the numbers or the resultant disorientation of the Jewish communities throughout Iberia. In view of the considerable acculturation and religious ambivalence within the Jewish community, it is not surprising that the violence generated massive conversions to Christianity from all echelons of Jewish society. The number of conversions in all probability exceeded the combined total of Jewish casualties and refugees. Many Jewish communities were decimated, and some, including Barcelona, were closed for lack of Jews.

The sudden governmental termination of the violence and the approved, if not sponsored, conversions in both Castile and Aragon lead ineluctably to the conclusion that in neither country did the leadership wish to destroy all its Jews. Indeed, the massacres of 1391 served a dual purpose: to defuse the impending civil war through the calculated diversion by societal leadership of popular anger and fanaticism onto the Jews, and, at the same time, to make conversion, now as an escape hatch, all the more palatable. Unconverted Jews in Aragon and Castile, though diminished numerically and circumstantially terrorized, retained their communities, self-government, prerogatives, and protection.

Significantly, despite anti-Jewish traditions in both Navarre and Portugal, and the existence of elements ready to turn them into political action, both countries remained comparatively quiet during this period.

That conversion was the official policy of Castile and Aragon is evident from the intensification of conversionist efforts after the massacres. Conversionist preaching was particularly evident in Aragon in the first two decades of the fifteenth century under the fiery Dominican, Vincent Ferrer (1350–1419). Connected to the highest echelons of state and church, and in a position at least twice to call for Pope Benedict's abdication, Ferrer spent the last two decades of his life as an itinerant apostolic preacher in Iberia, France, Lombardy, Switzerland, and the Low Countries. Within this activity, he devoted considerable efforts to the missionization of the Jews.

Ferrer's were also turbulent times, marked by an uneasy political stalemate between the death of King Martí (1395–1410) without issue and the enthronement of the Castilian regent, Fernando de Trastámara, as his successor. An outsider, Fernando was tied to no Aragonese power source aside from the Modern Old Guard establishment. Yet the successes of Fernando I (1412–1416) and the prosperity under Alfonso V (1416–1458) were insufficient to resolve Aragon's deeper sociopolitical problems. This was evidenced by the Catalan revolt under Juan II (1458–1479). Encompassing all of Peninsular Aragon and the Balearic Isles, the revolt was a complex web of civil strife, urban and rural, with intricate shifts of Old and New Guard elements. By the end of the century Aragon, drained and debilitated, was no match for its more populous neighbor, Castile.

Stemming from Ferrer's activity was the Disputation of Tortosa. Convoked by Benedict XIII in 1413 and continuing to November of 1414, the disputation's official agenda comprised a discussion of the Messiah's nature and the Talmud's alleged hostility to Christianity. But here, too, the real agenda of the disputation appeared to be the stimulation of conversions and thereby the enhancement of both Benedict's papacy and the secular establishment.

Appreciable numbers of Jews converted during the disputation and in its wake. By 1415 the Jewish community of Aragon was only a pathetic shadow of its former self. In his philosophical chef d'oeuvre, the *Ikkarim*, completed that year, Joseph Albo reflects the defensiveness of the Jewish community in the wake of the disputation by classifying the belief in the Messiah not as a root but as a derivative principle in Judaism.

The Sephardic Phenomenon

The conversions cohered with the official Christian program for the missionization of the Jews and the acceptance of all converts as neonates, fully cleansed of all their past shortcomings. This explains why, on conversion, the erstwhile Jews, now known as *conversos* or New Christians, a term which eventually acquired a distinctive connotation, found unimpeded opportunity in all areas, including marriage to Old Christian aristocracy and high office in both secular callings and the hierarchy of the church. Politically, the massive conversions strengthened the ranks of the New Guards and stimulated the empowerment of Modern Old Guards.

Indeed, conversion appears to have underlain the clamor for the expulsion of the Jews by both New Guard and Modern Old Guard and for the major expulsions edicted in the closing decades of the fifteenth century: the expulsion from Andalusia in 1483 and from all Castile and Aragon in 1492.

By the time of the Edict of Expulsion, the Modern Old Guard had clambered to the top of a precarious power ladder in Castile. This came about through four temporally overlapping steps: the integration into the New Guard of the majority of the converts beginning in 1391; the struggles of the New Guard, thus strengthened, with the dominantly feudal Old Guard throughout the nearly six decades between 1391 and 1449; generated by this clash, the realignments within the Old Guard that favored the growth of its modern component; and, beginning in 1449, late in the reign of Juan II (1406–1454), when the New Guard was enjoying a brief period of dominance, the implementation of a new policy under the aegis of the Modern Old Guard.

In that year a decree issued in Toledo and known as the *Sentencia-Estatuto* ordered all conversos, by which it intended not only the converts of 1391 and those of subsequent years but all their descendants as well, to be removed from any public offices they might hold and to be henceforth ineligible to occupy them.

The rationale given was that none of these people could be trusted as Christians and that all were actual or potential practitioners of Judaism. The expression of Judaism by Christians through deed or word was, of course, as it always had been, heresy. The *Sentencia-Estatuto* explained the New Christians' proclivity for Judaism by the assertion that as descendants of Jews they could not be *cristianos lin-*

dos, complete or perfect Christians. Through this assertion, the *Sentencia-Estatuto* gave an impetus to the promulgation of the doctrine of *limpieza de sangre,* "blood cleanness," or perhaps more precisely, "blood purity." *Limpieza de sangre* was taken to be the mark of a true Christian. It was regarded as absent from the Christian descendants of Muslims, and especially, judging from its more common application and emphasis, the Christian descendants of Jews.

The doctrine of *limpieza de sangre* injected a bifurcated definition of Jewish identity into the Iberian Peninsula. Henceforth there were two definitions of the Jew: the traditional definition denoting the open adherents of the Jewish faith who lived under Jewish law, and the new definition, covering the converts from Judaism and their descendants, who, though baptized or presumed to be, and though officially Christian, were suspected, by virtue of their Jewish ancestry, of being irremediably bound to their ancestral faith.

For the apprehension and punishment of the heretics among the New Christians, a call was immediately issued for the creation of an Inquisition. Permission for the establishment of such an Inquisition, with unusually broad powers, was given by Pope Nicholas V in 1451. But nothing was done for its implementation. However, advocacy for an Inquisition continued strong, and in 1478, papal permission was granted again, and the Inquisition was established two years later.

The inquisitorial pursuit of the New Christians' heresies was not a tangential eddy in the stream of Iberian history. On the contrary, it represented a critical part, if not the centerpiece, of the policy by which eventually all the Modern Old Guards of Iberia, despite continuing opposition, managed to retain control of their respective regimes for centuries.

The struggles between the Old Guard, the New Guard, and the growing Modern Old Guard continued during the tumultuous reign of Enrique IV (1454–1474), when again Castile found itself on the brink of civil war. Once again the impasse was solved by compromise: the marriage of Princess Isabel of Castile, not originally in line for the throne, to Fernando of Aragon and the cession of effective power to the Modern Old Guard. Under the Catholic Monarchs, as they came to be called, Castile and Aragon retained their distinctiveness and autonomy, and their leadership, in both cases Modern Old

Guard, with the help of the subordinated New Guard, again sought peace, stability, and the development of their dyarchy in line with the New Guard agenda. In the process their Catholic subjects of Jewish descent were to play a prominent role.

The Rationalization of the Sephardic Phenomenon

Under its two identities, internal and imposed, Sephardic Jewry was swept into the vortex of political, economic, social, and ideological rationalization throughout its dispersion in the Western world.

Through this process of rationalization, the Catholic Monarchs catapulted Castile-Aragon and its successor state of Spain into the forefront of the modern world. To be sure, their polity was not the first in Europe to embark on modernization. By the usual definitions of the term there were precursors, as early as twelfth-century Flanders, thirteenth-century Italy, perhaps thirteenth-century Aragon-Catalonia, and certainly early-fifteenth-century Portugal. But Spain enjoyed a superiority over the other states in population, material, and intellectual resources, and not least, a sense of manifest destiny toward "the glorious age in which heaven promises one flock and only one shepherd," in the words of the sixteenth-century poet Hernando de Acuña, the age when there will be "one king, one empire, and one sword."

The Catholic Monarchs also, though in this case unintentionally, catapulted Sephardic Jewry into the modern world through expulsion, conversions, *Limpieza de sangre,* and Inquisition.

The impulse to rationalization explains the efforts by the Catholic Monarchs and their predecessors to unite their polities religiously through the conversion of their Jews, whose contributions they did not wish to lose through expulsion. So, too, their reliance on *limpieza de sangre* to mark the potential for heresy and on the Inquisition to extirpate its actualization fully coincide with their agenda for unification.

Traditionally, *limpieza de sangre* and Inquisition have been regarded as primarily, if not exclusively, religious institutions created to confront the New Christians' irrepressible tendency to judaize. Indeed, appearing to testify to pervasive clandestine Judaism are thousands of inquisitorial dossiers of New Christians often generations and centuries removed from ancestral conversion, and hundreds of inquisitorial martyrs for Judaism. Appearing to testify to the irrepressibility are not only its continuity but its powerful reemergence years and even decades after its apparent extirpation in places like Peru, Mexico, and most dramatically, Majorca and its residual continuity among contemporary Christians in various parts of the Iberian world.

Jews have often lionized the New Christians arrested by the Inquisition as paladins of faith, and have exalted the opprobrious term *marrano,* meaning "pig," popularly hurled against the New Christians, particularly of Spain, into a badge of Jewish religious fidelity. They have even composed stirring fictional reconstructions of secret Judaism, like the one in the Hebrew trilogy *Shelomo Molkho* (1928–29) by the novelist A. A. Kabak. So, too, Christian defenders of the Inquisition have regarded the institution primarily as an instrument designed to protect the purity of the faith against various infractions and heresies, not least the heresy of New Christian judaizing.

Jews and Christians with views focusing on the Inquisition's religious role have tended to treat its activity, however important they may have regarded it, as tangential to the general history of the Iberian empires.

However, a closer look at the vast records of the Inquisition and the related records of imperial Spain and Portugal during the Inquisition's lengthy duration suggests that while rationalization was clearly a critical goal, and *limpieza* and Inquisition were clearly directed toward this goal, their function was quite different from its traditional portrayal.

Pointing to this conclusion are at least thirty-six major anomalies which challenge the traditional view. These challenges may be arranged in seven categories, as follows:

Category A. If Jewish blood carried an indelible stain and compulsion to Judaism,

1. Why was there such eagerness to convert Jews at all times and places, and especially in the Iberian Peninsula in the late fourteenth century and throughout the fifteenth?

2. And why did nearly six decades elapse between the mass conversions of 1391 and the promulgation of the *Sentencia-Estatuto*?

3. And why, certainly for at least the first three of these nearly six decades, were there almost no notices of judaizing practice or com-

The Sephardic Phenomenon 43

plaints about the political and ecclesiastical promotion of people with impure blood?

4. And why, throughout the Iberian Peninsula, did many Old Christians, especially aristocrats, marry New Christians, with the result that by the end of the fifteenth century few noble families in Castile and Aragon retained *limpieza de sangre*?

5. And why was the principle of *limpieza de sangre* conventionally disregarded for descendants of Jews who converted prior to 1391, thus sparing as Old Christians, incidentally, the entire Spanish monarchy descended from King Fernando II of Aragon, who issued the Decree of Expulsion and whose Jewish ancestry came through his mother, Juana Enríquez?

6. And why, for conversions after 1391, was the principle of *limpieza de sangre* only selectively applied to the nobility and on occasion even formally nullified through royal certification of Old Christian status, some of the most dramatic nullifications coming from King Manuel of Portugal in the wake of the conversions of Jews to Christianity in 1497?

7. And why did the organizations adopting *limpieza de sangre* constitute only a relatively small number, thus leaving many segments of Iberian society exposed to New Christian infiltration?

8. And why did the authorities not seriously prosecute the industry of false genealogies which further muddled the lines between Old Christians and New Christians?

9. And why did so many New Christians live exemplary Christian lives, among them nuns, monks, priests, bishops, and cardinals?

10. And why, in the case of New Christian religious deviation, was this deviation so often expressed not through Judaism, but through marginal Catholicism, heterodox Catholicism, Protestantism, Deism, and skepticism?

11. And why did the vast majority of New Christians in the Iberian empires leave no record whatsoever about their religious activities, thereby suggesting, in view of the presumably strict inquisitorial vigilance, that there is no responsible basis for regarding this group as in any way divergent from official Catholic practice and belief?

12. And why, instead of punishing the New Christians for engaging in religious practices that were hematicly induced, did the

authorities not follow the often-proffered advice to expel all New Christians from their domains instead of favoring their retention and even at times prohibiting their emigration?

13. And why are there examples of individuals certified, known, or believed to be Old Christians who were prosecuted for judaizing?

Category B. If inherent in Jewish blood there resided an impulse to passionate and even sacrificial devotion to Judaism, then

14. Why, prior to 1492, and particularly in the last two centuries, do the Jewish communities of Iberia appear to have been riddled with considerable apathy and secularization?

15. And why, in reaction to the massacres of 1391 and the conversionist preaching before and after that date, did such a large number of Jews chose conversion over the available alternative of martyrdom, which, incidentally, many New Christian judaizers preferred?

16. And why, after leaving in 1492, did many Jews return to the Iberian Peninsula and embrace Catholicism?

17. And why, when the opportunities did exist for emigration from Spain and Portugal, did the majority of New Christians opt to remain in the Peninsula?

18. And why, among those who did leave, did so many migrate to lands within the Spanish and Portuguese orbit and therefore subject themselves anew to *limpieza de sangre* and the Inquisition?

19. And why, among those who did not migrate to Spanish and Portuguese colonies, did so many go to other Catholic lands, where, even though there was no Inquisition, they could not openly practice Judaism?

20. And why, in lands like Italy, where they had the option of living openly as Jews, did so many New Christians hesitate to do so?

Category C. If the New Christians' devotion to Judaism secretly preserved the Jewish faith, then

21. Why, even in the early days of the Inquisition, did their secret Judaism manifest a dramatic and, in many instances, almost total discontinuity from the traditional Judaism of Iberian Jews?

22. And why did the contacts between New Christians and authentic Jews in Iberia prior to 1497, and thereafter in various parts of the world, including Iberia, leave only desultory reflections of authentic Judaism in crypto-Jewish liturgy and practice?

23. And why, above all, does an astonishing correlation appear between the details of the New Christians' crypto-Judaism on the one hand, and, on the other, aside from the influence of the Vulgate, the eclectic catalogue of presumed Jewish practices and beliefs found in the Edicts of Grace that were promulgated with the advent of an Inquisition to a new seat and the Edicts of Faith issued periodically thereafter for reinforcement?

Category D. If the New Christians were the enemy, then

24. Why did *limpieza de sangre* encounter powerful opposition from the moment of its promulgation, from sources as high as the king and the pope, who pointed to its contradiction of canon law?

25. And why, from that moment on, did it elicit a spate of condemnatory tracts seeking the abolition of the principle of *limpieza de sangre*, or at least its modification?

26. And why did this opposition elicit spirited defenses of *limpieza de sangre*, culminating in the early 1670s in the *Centinela contra judíos* ("Sentinel Against Jews") by the Franciscan friar Francisco de Torrejoncillo, which contained a hefty catalogue of canards against Jews, with whom New Christians were fully identified?

27. And why, when New Christians were attacked by mobs, especially in 1449, 1467, and 1472, were they successfully defended by strong forces whose numbers had to have been larger than the number of New Christians unless the New Christians' numbers were already unusually high?

28. And why, similarly, did the introduction of the Inquisition in all four Iberian kingdoms encounter powerful opposition that often spilled into violence?

Category E. If the Inquisition was concerned with the extirpation of heresy, then

29. Why did it accept damaging evidence that was flimsy, uncorroborated, or patently concocted?

30. And why did it operate with an a priori assumption of guilt which blocked defendants from knowing their accusers and their inquisitorially approved lawyers from presenting an objective defense?

31. And why did it create an environment that induced false denunciations out of vengeance by enemies or fears of torture or death by prisoners under duress?

Category F. If the judaizing of the New Christians, vigilantly pursued by the Inquisition, was widespread, then

32. Why, in view of the ever-growing number of New Christians, which increased with the progeny of every marriage between New Christians and Old, was the number of New Christians prosecuted for judaizing by all the Inquisitions, though cumulatively large, surprisingly small in percentage, even in the periods of the Inquisitions' intensest activity?

32a. And why, between the first auto-da-fé in Seville in 1481 and the abolition of the last Inquisition in 1834, could the total number of individuals indicted for judaizing by all the Spanish and Portuguese Inquisitions, by conservative estimates, not have exceeded 5 percent of the total number of available New Christians, this term defined inclusively as all individuals with any Iberian Jewish descent beginning with the conversions of 1391?

32b. And why, for the same period, and by the same inclusive definition and conservative estimates, could the total number of individuals burned at the stake for judaizing not have exceeded 1 percent, from which there would have to be subtracted a significant number of convicts: those safely ensconced in lands beyond the jurisdiction of the Inquisition, who paid their supreme penalty in effigy; and the dead, both those whose bones were within reach of the Inquisition and could be incinerated in retroactive punishment and those whose remains were beyond the Inquisition's reach and were, like the absent living, punished in effigy?

33. And why were the majority of those convicted for Judaism reconciled to the church, and, except for a minuscule percentage, never heard from again, unless these former heretics, whose activities were presumably closely scrutinized for recidivism, gave no further evidence of deviation from strict Catholic orthodoxy?

34. And why, if the New Christians' compulsion toward Judaism was genetic and irrepressible, were there in many places feverish peaks of inquisitorial activity followed by decades of relative inactivity, of which the Balearic Islands furnish the classical example, or even

total inactivity, as in the case of Spain after 1530, when records of judaizing all but disappear until after the influx of Portuguese New Christians with the union of Spain and Portugal in 1580?

35. And why, if the New Christians were, by virtue of their lack of *limpieza*, unfit for political office, beginning with the very promulgation of the *Sentencia-Estatuto*, were New Christians appointed to the universities, church hierarchies, and some of the highest offices of state, even by monarchs and popes?

Category G. Above all, if there was a focused dedication to the identification and extirpation of Judaism, then

36. Why do the records appear repeatedly to suggest the utilization of alleged judaizing in cases of transparently political significance, against individuals regarded as dangerous to the establishment, as is dramatically exemplified by the indictment, at the beginning of the nineteenth century, of Father Miguel Hidalgo y Castilla, one of the two principal martyrs in the Mexican war for independence, who, in addition to Judaism, was accused of Lutheranism, Calvinism, atheism, and materialism, and not least, liberalism and sedition?

The anomalies can all be resolved. Their resolution must begin with the fundamental recognition that, although overlaid with religious language, the doctrine of *limpieza de sangre* is a societal myth. Like all other societal myths, the myth of *limpieza de sangre* is generic, simplistic, reductive, and affective. In a society where Christianity functioned as the fundamental unifier and anti-establishments trumpeted Judaism as the Enemy before the popular consciousness, *limpieza de sangre* declared that all New Christians were Jews; that as such they were irremediably different from the Old and true Christians, hostile to them, unassimilable into their society and, in a society where demons and spirits roamed the human imagination, even demoniacally dangerous because of their Christian camouflage. The New Christians were, indeed, the Enemy of the people. *Limpieza de sangre* is therefore, purely and simply, in the full sense of the term, a racist myth.

Like all other such myths, *limpieza de sangre* was created for societal control. The Inquisition was the instrument for this control. To be sure, the Inquisition possessed a religious function, both historically and canonically, and the inquisitorial establishments pursued their duties with religious perspective, texts, and customs. But, and this is the critical element, in both the Spanish and Portuguese empires, the Inquisition was subordinated from its start to a nonreligious political agenda.

Defenses of *limpieza de sangre* regularly equated the New Christians with unconverted Jews. The culmination of this equation in Torrejoncillo marks a straight-line development from the first major literary defense of *limpieza*. This was the *Fortalitium Fidei*, completed in 1459 by another Franciscan monk, Alfonso de Spina. In this work, dedicated in part if not primarily to the dissemination of the *limpieza* myth and intended as a vademecum for preachers, Spina issued the first call for an Inquisition against the judaizing heresy.

The myth's underlying agenda readily unfurls. The percentage of judaizers indicted in the 350 years of what may justifiably be called worldwide inquisitorial activity may have been small, and the percentage executed far smaller, but the terror that accompanied the Inquisition's selectivity was pervasive. It was reinforced by the continuous fear of denunciation, the spectacles of the *autos-da-fé* and the display in churches of the signs of family obloquy. All of this leaves little doubt that the goal of the Spanish and Portuguese authorities ultimately pulling the strings of their respective Inquisitions was not the destruction of the entire New Christian community, but its intimidation and subordination. On the other hand, the rejection of expulsion as an obvious solution to their New Christian problem, coupled with the often draconian measures for the retention of the New Christians, leave little doubt of the considerable importance of the New Christians as a group to Spanish and Portuguese society. The myth of *limpieza de sangre* was clearly utilized to control the entire New Christian community by selectively prosecuting some and keeping the rest insecurely dangling in unrelieved vulnerability.

But the control of the New Christian community meant as well the subordination of the entire New Guard through the myth of *limpieza de sangre* and the institution of the Inquisition, since the New Guard had become so interlaced with New Christians as to be functionally coterminous with them. Formally inaugurated with the *Sentencia-Estatuto* less than sixty years after the beginnings of the massive conversions of Iberian Jews to Christianity, this policy appears to have been conceived at least in principle long before that time, and possibly as early as the beginning of the Trastámara dynasty. Because of the large New Christian presence in the New Guard, and because, contrary to the myth, the New Christians had, aside from their societal roles, become increasingly indistinguishable from all other Christians, it was possible for the Old Guard to identify all New Guard elements as hematicly impure, or to imply that any conspicuous group within the New Guard, like its large-scale merchants, was composed entirely of "Jews." It could in the process, without regard to genealogical truth, create "Jews" by race at will. By focusing on such New Guard groups, it was derivatively possible to declare all New Christians to be wealthy, powerful, and exploitative of all Old Christians. In reality, through the Inquisition, fear was sown throughout the New Guard, from its courtiers to its writers, from its scientists to its artisans, among everyone indeed whose position of wealth, creativity, or political preference was at any given moment perceived as a threat to the power of the Old Guard establishment. This fear was enhanced by the realization that the Inquisition could at any time choose to strike or not to strike based largely on its own internal agenda, a factor that best explains the apparent waves of recurrent judaizing in various parts of the Iberian world. At the same time the unclean blood of Old Guard aristocrats was conveniently overlooked, except if aberrantly they proved to be religiously maverick or politically incorrect.

Also on the basis of political incorrectness the Inquisition at different times pursued New Guard individuals who could not be identified as judaizers, but were Erasmians, Protestants, mystics, Jansenists, Freemasons, devotees of the Enlightenment, and others at odds with official Catholic thinking. That the Inquisition's perception in such cases was colored by political realities is dramatically evident in the eighteenth century, when it stigmatized as heretical and "Jansenist" a variety of expressions that were perceived as challenges to Ultramontanism, the doctrine of papal supremacy. It is evident as well in the prosecution of distinguished Catholics like Talavera and Carranza, whose prosecution was motivated primarily by political considerations. The inquisitorial tactics in such cases were summed up by the eminent sixteenth-century religious and belletristic writer Fray Luis de León, when from his inquisitorial cell he declared: "Here envy and falsehood have kept me imprisoned" (*Aquí la envidia y la mentira me tenían encerrado*).

The Inquisitions of Spain and Portugal were modeled after the Papal Inquisition that had been established in the second quarter of the thirteenth century to extirpate the Cathari, or Albigensians, as they soon came to be called. This heresy and later ones that attracted this Inquisition, like the heresies of the Franciscan Spirituals and the Waldensians, were reflections of dissatisfaction with the church which had deep social, political, and economic roots, as well as ideological. Heresy, of course, was nothing new to the church. Heresy is always someone else's view on a subject, and it becomes institutionalized into the Enemy whenever there is an Orthodoxy. Prior to the thirteenth century, however, the correction of heresy through *inquisitio*, or inquiry, into matters of faith, was the responsibility of the local bishop in accordance with the procedures of canon law. The Papal Inquisition, placed largely in the hands of the newly formed Dominican order, was freed from canon law and followed new procedures which, with some modification, became the norm for the Iberian Inquisitions.

The arrival of an Inquisition was preceded in all places by an Edict of Grace, urging all who had committed or abetted heresy to confess their wrongdoing within a specified period of time. The Edict of Grace was subsequently periodically reinforced by the Edict of Faith, which specified all the punishable heresies and other wrongdoings. The Inquisition gathered its evidence and, wherever possible, made its arrests in secret. It assumed its prisoners to be guilty unless proven innocent, but hobbled their defense by withholding the identity of their accusers and appointing defense counsels whose main purpose was to secure their confessions. It subjected its prisoners to torture to extract confessions and information, though it could not have failed to be aware that the information thus elicited was frequently false and given primarily to satisfy the torturers and end the infliction of pain. Voluntary confessors and repentant prisoners were reconciled to the church with a variety of penalties, while the unrepentant and the second offenders were sentenced to death at the stake, with the possibility of being garroted rather than burned alive if they repented prior to execution. Technically the Inquisition, as a religious institution, did not inflict the supreme penalty. Instead, it delivered, or, in its language, "relaxed," the condemned to the secular authorities for appropriate action. The secular authorities at no time misunderstood the implications of such delivery. To have done so would have invited the Inquisition's scrutiny of their activities.

The Papal and the Iberian Inquisitions were religiously grounded and, like all other institutions, were politically directed. There were, however, major differences between them in two areas: ultimate control and primary targets. For the Papal Inquisition ultimate control rested in Rome; for the Iberian Inquisitions it rested with the state. For the Papal Inquisition the original primary targets, the Cathari and their positional successors, were, with rare exceptions, connected by physical proximity; in the Iberian Inquisition their counterparts, the New Christians, were connected by putative genealogy.

To the question in the Iberian Inquisitions of *cui bono*, who benefited from their formulation and imposition of political correctness, the answer could not be clearer. It was the Old Guard, under the leadership of the Modern Old Guard, which, in order to preserve its power against the encroachments of the New Guard, created the myth of *limpieza* as the primary ideology of political correctness and the Inquisition as its general instrument of control.

The recognition of this role for the Inquisition explains the nature and extent of the opposition to it from the very beginning of its Iberian existence. Within this opposition it explains as well the presence of a large number of clergy who publicly and eloquently advocated the limitation or elimination of the Inquisition, often at the price of personal subjection to its mercy.

In detail the implementation of this process differed from place to place and period to period. Yet its fundamental trajectory and discernible purpose with respect to the New Guard was in every place the same. This can be appreciated by a division of the Inquisition's tonal activity into five chronolgically ordered periods:

period 1: 1481–1492, in which the New Guard's political ascendancy in Castile and Aragon is braked;

period 2: 1492–1580, in which the New Guard in Spain is effectively subordinated, and the process of its control in Portugal is begun;

period 3: 1580–1640, in which the ascendancy of the Spanish New Guard, reinvigorated with the invited arrival of Portuguese New Christians, is blocked;

period 4: 1640–1765, in which the struggles between Old Guard and New Guard in Portugal and Spain lead to greater swings of tolerance and persecution of New Christians before sputtering out of existence, and in which increased attention is given to liberals, Freemasons, and others regarded as politically incorrect (and often called Jews);

period 5: 1765–1834, in which the the Old Guard control, as hitherto known in Spain and Portugal, dissolves with the de jure abolition of the distinctions created by the *limpieza de sangre* myth, and there emerge new sociopolitcal spectra of Old and New Guard constellations.

From all of this it follows that the myth of *limpieza de sangre* notwithstanding, it was not blood but sociopolitical position which principally determined one's New Christian or Old Christian status. And it was Old Guard policy, through the leadership of its modern wing, which determined whether to make an issue of New Christian status or not. Therefore while many New Christians were caught up in the nets of the myth, often for generations, others, in New Guard no less than Old Guard activities, were long or forever unscathed.

Contrary to the oft-articulated belief, the Inquisition could not have invented crypto-Judaism or crypto-Jews. What it could and did do was to inflate a phenomenon whose existence had a basis in fact sufficient to impart credibility to the inflationary process. The massive conversions in Aragon, Castile, Navarre, and especially in Portugal could not have been followed quickly by the complete absorption of the conversos into orthodox Catholicism. Sociopsychologically, the conversos could not have failed to show a spectrum of deviation, including full retention of Jewish identity, even though such instances appear to have been increasingly scattered. At the same time, the myth of *limpieza de sangre* and its implementation by the Inquisition often turned the imputation of an inescapable Jewish identity into a self-fulfilling prophecy for many people whose commitment to Jewish identity had been slim or nonexistent and who had been striving for full assimilation into the general society. Similarly, for purposes of group trust and solidarity, the myth often turned these people, who had increasingly few recollections of authentic Judaism, to the practice of a Judaism enriched by the Vulgate, the Edicts of Grace, and the Catholic religious environment. In this sense the Inquisition did, of course, create Jews by religion and in appreciable numbers.

Also noteworthy is the fact that, however unorthodox the Judaism of the New Christian judaizers might have been, the devotion in the name of Judaism with which it was practiced was often, if not regularly, exemplary. The records permit no doubt of the sincerity of Jewish identification on the part of many New Christians, the eagerness of many to learn as much as possible about Judaism, to teach others about it and, if need be, to die a martyr's death.

The divergence of the judaizers' faith from authentic Judaism is best dramatized by the disillusionment of Gabriel (Uriel) Da Costa (1585–1640) on his arrival in Amsterdam. There he had hoped to live openly as a Jew with a faith derived primarily from the Vulgate and the New Christian environment of Portugal. But there the faith he carried with him clashed with the authentic Judaism he found in the Amsterdam Jewish community, and this ultimately led to his excommunication, humiliation, and suicide.

The recognition of the operative role of *limpieza de sangre* and Inquisition reveals a critical dimension of crypto-Judaism. Because crypto-Judaism, sincere and fervent though it often was, was, especially in the course of time, essentially a sociopsychological response to a political agenda, its primary stimulus is attributable not to ancestral continuity but rather only to situational reality. All other elements being equal, Old Christians in the New Guard were therefore more likely be regarded as New Christians and to be judaizers than New Christians in the Old Guard.

Given this context, it becomes meaningless to speak of Iberian Christians who openly and formally embraced Judaism in the Diaspora as "returning" to Judaism. It also suggests the possibility that at least some of these people left Iberian lands without any crypto-Jewish attachment, became Jews for situational reasons in the Diaspora, and then claimed a history of secret Judaism in order to enhance their status within the Jewish community.

Related to the myth of *limpieza de sangre* is the Iberian and especially the Spanish concept of honor. Medieval in its origins and Old

Christian in its associations, this concept exalted the warrior, depreciated commerce in particular and New Guard activity in general, and reinforced a pride in racial purity. It even spawned what may be called an anti-work ethic. All of this intended to keep the New Guard as identified by the Old Guard separated from the rest of the populace, and therefore isolated, exposed, and subordinated.

The sociopolitical reconstruction best explains the potent opposition to the concept of *limpieza de sangre* and the institutions of the Inquisitions and its claim that in their absence all judaizing would cease. This is, of course, what happened with the end of the Inquisition in Spain, and, three quarters of a century earlier, the destruction ordered by the marquis of Pombal of all Portuguese registers of New Christian families. Left throughout the Iberian world were Christian individuals with traditions of ancestral crypto-Jewish practice and isolated pockets of Christians still called Jews but fully Catholic in their identity and practice.

With its racist doctrine, the Modern Old Guard created the first modern totalitarian states. A direct line of development links inquisitorial Spain and Portugal to the totalitarianisms of the modern world, with their demands for political correctness, their efforts at thought control, their unscrupulous treatment of opposition through rigged trials, their terrorization of multitudes by the persecution of selected individuals and the heaping of obloquy upon their families, their utilization of the myth of the Enemy, which, all too often, has been the Jew, and, above all, their creation of an external definition of the Jew which has led to a variety of understandings of self-identity on the part of those who have been so defined.

Within the, Iberian world, the known and putative New Christians of the New Guard contributed spectacularly to its development and modernization. Their names abound in the records of commerce, industry, diplomacy, the sciences, the humanities and the arts, and not least, the literature of both Portugal and Spain.

The Consolidation of the Sephardic Phenomenon

Within the diverse environments of their refuge, the Spanish and Portuguese exiles contoured their Iberian heritage into the modern and now classical structures of the Sephardic ethos.

There were actually three groups of exiles: one in 1492, one before, and one after. The first, after the events of 1391, comprised mostly Jews and apparently some conversos. Both groups could have remained in the Peninsula, the Jews as Jews and the conversos as Christians, but both, except possibly for some conversos, sought a Jewish life under happier skies. The emigrants of 1492 were mostly Jews, who could not have remained in the Peninsula except through conversion to Christianity. Added to these should be the smaller numbers of Jews who left Portugal in the wake of its expulsion order in 1496. The third emigration comprised Iberian New Christians, primarily Portuguese. It began after 1497, crescendoed after the Lisbon massacres of New Christians in 1506, and continued for decades.

In the first emigration the refugees in search of a Jewish life faced limited options. The Christian lands of Western Europe were closed to them, except for underdeveloped Portugal and several Italian states which offered limited immigration. A number of Muslim countries were also open: Morocco, where the refugees' lot was precarious; Egypt, where it was generally favorable; and Algeria, where it was most favorable.

The emigrants of 1492 had more sanguine options. Some Italian states were more receptive, as was the now imperial Portugal; while in the Muslim world, where Algeria was less hospitable and Morocco somewhat more, a warm welcome awaited the Jews in the rapidly expanding Ottoman Empire.

The third group of emigrants enjoyed the broadest options because they were Christians when they left the Peninsula. They could go to the Muslim world, where they had to become Jews; or the Italian Peninsula, where in most places they could choose Judaism or continue in Christianity; or the Christian lands of Europe closed to Jews, like England, France, Germany, the Low Countries, where they had to live, at least ostensibly, as Christians; or the colonies and other territories of

Portugal or Spain, where they not only had to live, at least ostensibly, as Christians, but also continously in fear of inquisitorial molestation.

Sephardim from all three emigrations settled in the Muslim world, and from the second and third especially in the Ottoman Empire. According to a seventeenth-century Jewish source (Immanuel Aboab), Sultan Bayazid II (1481–1512) chided King Ferdinand for allowing such valuable subjects to slip out of his grasp.

In the Ottoman Empire the Sephardim came across four groups of Jews, each jealous of its own identity and generally unfriendly to the others. Two had been there as far back as memory could trail. They were the Greek-speaking Romaniotes, or Gregos, of the former Byzantine Empire and the Arabic-speaking Jews of the former Muslim caliphates, themselves divided into "Easterners" and "Westerners." The other two were more recent arrivals: the Karaites, who had appeared in the Byzantine Empire in the eleventh century; and non-Sephardic Europeans from the Italian Peninsula and Sicily, the Franco-German regions, Central Europe, and Provence, who had come largely in the fifteenth century because of unrest in their native lands.

In all Muslim areas the resident Jewish populations were threatened by the the newcomers' skills and culture. In Morocco and elsewhere, friction between the *megorashim*, as the refugees were called, and the natives, or *toshavim*, diminished, though hardly to the point of disappearance, with the assimilation of the Sephardim and their irrepressible rise to community dominance.

Exacerbating the friction, especially in the Ottoman Empire, was the animosity among the Sephardim themselves, particularly between the earlier Jews and the subsequent New Christians. Though advanced over the native groups, the Jews proved no match for the New Christians' practical knowledge and cosmopolitan sophistication. Besides, the immigrants of 1492, with few exceptions, arrived in poverty, while the New Christians often brought considerable wealth.

The relative underdevelopment of the Muslim lands facilitated the entree of the Sephardim into a broad spectrum of service, and, not infrequently, their rise to prominence.

In the Ottoman Empire their activities fall into four broad areas: commerce, from local shopkeeping to international trade and banking, in which they were aided by the Iberian trade routes and their own worldwide mercantile contacts; manufacture of innumerable items, among them textiles, leather, wine, jewelry, and munitions; medicine, in which they produced scholars as well as practitioners, and even court physicians like Joseph Hamon, under Bayazid II and Selim I (1512–1520), his son Moses, under Selim I and Suleiman I (1520–1566), "the Magnificent," and Daniel de Fonseca under Ahmed III (ruled 1703–1730); and administration, ranging from the collection of tolls and supervision of finances to international diplomacy, in which court physicians, preeminently Daniel de Fonseca, were known to excel. Among the distinguished Sephardic diplomats at the Ottoman Court were Joseph Nasi (ca. 1524–1579), from a distinguished Portuguese banking family, who served under Suleiman I and Selim II (1566–1574), and, during Selim's reign, was named duke of Naxos and its neighboring islands; and Solomon ibn Yaish (1520–1603), who served under Murad III (1574–1595) and Muhammad III (1595–1603) and was named duke of Mytilene in 1585.

These activities produced considerable wealth and prominent families like the Catani, Kadoorie, and Sassoon, but the percentage of wealthy Jews was small. Most Jews hovered near the subsistence level, many comfortably above in prosperous times and at least as many precariously below during economic adversity.

The zenith of the Ottoman Empire and its Jewish community coincided with Suleiman the Magnificent (1520–1566). But by the last two decades of his reign the empire had spun into an irreversible decline. Beginning, at least symbolically, in 1571, with its naval defeat at Lepanto, the empire was wracked for two centuries by corruption, disorder, brigandage, revolts, secessions, impoverishment, ignorance, despair, disease, and, all too often, depopulation. The Jewish communities, never strangers to these calamities, suffered additionally from Muslim scapegoating and persecution in areas of Christian conquest. Significant amelioration did not come until the reforms of Abd al-Majid I (1839–1862) especially the Rose Law of 1839, reissued in 1856, which opened the way to legal equality for non-Muslims.

Until this time, the Ottoman Jewish community lived in functional sociocultural isolation and sociopolitical fragmentation. Like other subject communities, the Jewish community was officially regarded as a corporate entity: a *ta'ife*, or *cema'at*, or, in retrojection from broader nineteenth-century usage, a *millet*. But its unity was a gossamer. The millet was in reality composed of politically autonomous religious congregations, of which there were some thirty in Salonika alone. These congregations were socially, intellectually, and culturally self-contained, since their link with the ambient society was, with some exceptions, like their access to Muslim courts, almost exclusively economic and professional. This is evidenced, inter alia, by the absence of conversions into the community and the rarity of conversions out.

The congregations were controlled by wealthy oligarchies. These served the sultans by ensuring the peace of their communities and the timely submission of their taxes. They adamantly opposed all efforts at democratization despite the advocacy of such measures by sages like Isaac Adarbi (1510?–1584?), and they zealously protected their parochial interests within the community umbrellas that had been created for mutual benefit. Each congregation possessed its own administrative structure, headed by a rabbi. The rabbi, not ordained because there had been no ordination among the Sephardim, was, among other occasional titles, called *hakham* (sage), *marbits Torah* (disseminator of Torah) or *dayyan* (judge).

Largely obstructed from significant exposure to the contemporary world, the Sephardim in the Ottoman Empire were compelled to look inwardly to their own traditions for their ineluctably difficult adjustment to exile and immigration.

The adjustment to exile was emotionally traumatic for the Sephardim. They had been deeply attached to their Iberian horizons, and when they left, they held on to as much as they could. The land was behind them, but they carried its atmosphere with them pyschologically, culturally, and linguistically, and they were thereafter indelibly shaped by its influence. In their departure they searched vainly, as their literature attests, for earthly or heavenly explanations of their plight. They had been loyal subjects of their rulers. The Jews among them had been unswervingly faithful to their God, while those who had became Christian, whatever their religious proclivities, were under the shelter of canon law against generic suspicion or ancestral aberrance. Disoriented, the Sephardim were gripped by perplexity and guilt.

The Sephardic Phenomenon

Insofar as is reconstructible, the reactions of the Sephardim to their calamity were manifold: they ran the gamut from uncompromising faith to inconsolable despair. In between were a plethora of speculations, popular even more than scholarly, on the purpose of God and the meaning of life. Not infrequently these speculations contained elements of questionable authenticity within the flexible parameters of Jewish thought.

A unifying thread in this fragmentation was the increased focus on the messianic advent. Many people could make sense of what was happening only in eschatological terms. They came to believe that their calamities, logically incomprehensible, could only presage what the Jewish tradition calls the pangs or footsteps of the Messiah. Some were certain that if they but exercised more patience, the messianic proximity would become ever clearer.

Reinforcing the messianic beliefs were the events unfolding before their very eyes. The Muslim soldiers of the Ottoman colossus had pushed dauntlessly into Christian Europe, approaching the gates of Vienna in 1529. Two years earlier the holy city of Rome, the very heart of Christianity, had been sacked and Pope Clement VII had been taken prisoner by the troops of none other than the Holy Roman emperor himself. Besides, with Luther's bolt, Christianity had begun to splinter. What else could these miracles signify save that the old order was, like night, being dispelled by the dawn of the new day?

This atmosphere illuminates the attraction of the mysterious David Reubeni in the 1520s. Many European Sephardim, both New Christians and Jews, considered him a messianic precursor, and in some cases, perhaps, the Messiah himself. It also explains the enthusiasm stirred by the messianic pretender Solomon Molkho (ca. 1500–1532), the former Portuguese New Christian known as Diogo Pires, who had been inspired by Reubeni.

Events like these galvanized apocalypticism, notably in Italy, North Africa, and the Ottoman Empire. From sages like Isaac Abravanel (1437–1508) to humble folk, predictions of the redemption for various years, especially 1503, 1512, 1540, and 1541, reverberated throughout the Mediterranean basin. These events also turned many ordinary people, apocalyptics as well as non-apocalyptics, to traditional Kabbalah, popular mysticism and superstitious practice.

Simultaneously, many sages, including the most renowned, combined their talmudic learning with blends of kabbalistic study, mystical speculation, apocalyptic expectation, and ascetic exercise, often with thaumaturgic dimensions. At least some were open to a divine voice, called a *maggid*, which instructed the listener to record its revelations. The origin of the maggidic appearances has been linked to Joseph Taitazak (1487/88?–before 1545), a renowned talmudist as well as kabbalist, whose inspiration could not have failed to play a role in the founding of Safed's kabbalistic circle by his students. Even better known is the maggid, personifying the Mishnah, who appeared to Taitazak's famous pupil Joseph Caro (1488–1575). It is of interest that Solomon Molkho studied Kabbalah under Taitazak for a while in Salonika, where the master spent his final years.

The adjustment to immigration was by no means easier. Though encompassed within the same millet, the individual communities of Ottoman Jewry governed themselves by a bewilderment of laws and customs. The Karaites diverged from the rabbinic Jews in tradition and even calendar. But the rest, although entirely rabbinic, were only in a generic sense more united. Sharp differences in tradition and practice separated not only the constellations of Greek-speaking, Arabic-speaking, European non-Sephardic, and Sephardic Jews, but also the individual congregations within each constellation. This situation was particularly apparent among the Sephardim, where fierce loyalties to the traditions and practices of Iberian regions and cities, without the curb of centralization, precipitated bitter internecine disputes.

As a result, the manifold concerns of adjustment among the Sephardim, as within the community at large, were addressed with an unbridled luxuriance of rabbinical responses, and these often in sharp conflict with one another. The concerns included the perennial and ubiquitous problems of personal, interpersonal, family, business, and community involvement. But they comprised as well the special conditions of Ottoman life, including the relations between Jews and Ottoman Muslims, and, even more, the differences between and within the Jewish communities. Additionally and most critically for all Sephardim, particularly those with a New Christian past, were the questions relating to their own or their family's Jewish roots, their entitlement to community privileges, and, in some cases, even the validity of their contractual arrangements.

The responses of the Ottoman rabbis, the Sephardim most prominent among them, constitute the richest and most varied corpus of responsa literature in all of Jewish history. Their repertory would be even greater if many responsa, known through references in the extant literature, had not been lost. Responsa were scripted by almost every hakham. The most renowned, Rabbi Samuel di Medina (Rashdam; 1506–1589), also a disciple of Taitazak, left over a thousand responsa, some to questions from Christian Europe. His responsa on the New Christians reflect an openness to their plight and a desire to facilitate their full incorporation into the Jewish community. Still largely unanalyzed for historical purposes, the responsa of the Ottoman Jews provide an indispensable source for the appreciation of their daily activities and transcendent ideals.

The consolidation of the Sephardic phenomenon resulted from the confrontation between the Iberian and Ottoman contexts of life. In al-Andalus, even in the *taifas*, and certainly within Christian Iberia, the Sephardim had generated regional, if not pan-Iberian unities. And throughout their Iberian experience, whether as politically autonomous Jews or politically integrated Christians, they had regularly interacted with the majority community in social and intellectual openness.

Many Sephardic sages of the Ottoman Empire reflect this openness in their cosmopolitanism, acculturation, and intellectual syntheses. The polymath Rabbi Moses Almosnino (ca. 1515–ca. 1580), wrote on Al-Ghazali and Aristotle's *Nicomachean Ethics*. Gedaliah ben Tam Ibn Yahia (16th cent.), a physician and Maecenas of learning, translated the *Dialoghi d'amore* of Leone Ebreo (Judah Abravanel) from Italian into Spanish. Joseph Taitazak composed a commentary on Ecclesiastes (*Porat Yosef*) following Thomas Aquinas, whom he calls "the Sage." The breadth of cultural experience, including, besides philosophy, such varied disciplines as history, science, and rhetoric, sparkles delightfully in many of the religious compositions of the Sephardic elite.

Such sages, where immune to centrifugal politics, naturally inclined toward community solidarity. In scholarship they were characteristically collectors, organizers, and consolidators. This is engagingly evident even in their commentaries to biblical and rabbinic texts. Notable in the latter category is the commentary *Kesef Mishneh* by Joseph Caro (1488–1575) to Maimonides' *Mishneh Torah*. Emblematic of this process was the projection by Rabbi Solomon ben Jacob Almoli (before 1483–1542) of an entire encyclopedia of Jewish knowledge.

Outstanding personalities of this stamp, always, to be sure, with substantial support, stimulated efforts at reining in the fragmentation of Ottoman Jewish life. In the process they unleashed a creative tension, which persisted through much of the period of decline, between the existentially centrifugal and historically centripetal elements in Sephardic Jewry.

There were seven principal avenues toward this consolidation. They were different from one another in substance, intensity, and duration. Six were initiated by Sephardim. The seventh debouched from historical forces beyond their control.

The first aimed for the political unification of Jewish life. It sought to accomplish this religiously and in conformity with the prescriptions of Maimonides, through the restoration of ordination and the Great Court, the Bet-Din Hagadol, later called the Sanhedrin, of proto-rabbinic and early rabbinic Judaism. The initiative for this move was taken in Safed by the Castilian Jacob Berab (ca. 1474–1541). In 1538, Berab convoked an assembly of twenty-five sages, who collectively ordained him, and in the process ignited an expectable controversy with the Jerusalem hakham, Levi ibn Habib. Before long Berab was expelled from Safed by the Ottoman Turks, but not until he had ordained four disciples, among them Joseph Caro. While these eventually ordained others, Berab's effort left no residue except perhaps a continued longing for Jewish political unity.

Reflective of the longing for political unity were the later efforts to retroject the title or function of chief rabbi (*hakham bashi*) upon the revered sages Moses Capsali (1420–1496 or 1497) and Elijah Mizrahi (ca. 1450–1526).

The second avenue involved the systematization of the Kabbalah, whose study was recommended as a propellant of the messianic coming. There was much activity in this regard in Morocco, and an important center in Salonica, but pride of place belongs to Safed. In the century between the birth of Moses Cordovero (1522–1570), its first towering figure, and the death of Hayyim Vital (1542–1620), its culminating genius, Safed was the unrivaled navel of the Jewish mystical world. Symbolic of its centrality is the fact that the major commentaries to the *Zohar* in this period were all products of Safed, with the exception of the one written in Fez. Cordovero, and his disciples after him, strove to weave the inherited strands of Kabbalah into an organic and philosophically laced unity. The Ashkenazi Isaac Luria (known acronymically as the Ari, 1534–1572), raised by his Sephardic mother and her family after his father's premature death, was Cordovero's pupil for a while. His theoretical Kabbalah, with its focus on the cosmic signficance of all human actions for the *tikkun*, or redemptive completion of the world, carried a powerful messianic thrust. Since Luria preferred to communicate his system orally, it is known largely through four independent traditions, most notably that of Vital. Though philosophically inferior to Cordovero's, Luria's Kabbalah resonated greater intelligibility, implementability, and above all, messianic urgency to a broader constituency.

Within a generation after Vital's death the Lurianic Kabbalah had informed the doctrines of the Sephardi Shabbetai Zevi (1626–1676), whose messianism attracted Jews not only in Muslim Asia and Africa, but throughout Europe, some of them, as in Amsterdam, among the lay and religious leadership of the community. It also attracted Christian millenarians and men of practical affairs. Contributing to the impact of Shabbetai Zevi was the general disorientation in Jewish life consequent upon the disintegration of the Ottoman Empire, and in Europe, the destruction of Jewish communities during the Chmielnicki massacres of 1648 and the Russian-Swedish War of 1655.

The initial successes of Shabbetai Zevi and the support of eminent sages and power brokers in many parts of the Jewish world and in some of the Christian do not suggest a leader psychologically aberrant and followers all bovinely credulous. On the contrary, they point to two confluent realities: on the one hand, the sweeping intolerability of life in a messianically charged environment, and on the other, the inevitable political and economic vultures ready to capitalize on the instability of the Ottoman realm.

The failure of Shabbetai Zevi and the typical post-messianic trajectories of his movement further testify to the rootedness of the preconditions for its response.

The third avenue was the determination in all congregations, often in concert, to transmit the sacred tradition of Judaism through educational institutions on all levels, from elementary schools to advanced academies where scholarly symposia often paved the way for halakhic decisions. Academies (yeshibot) of this kind, often endowed by individuals like the grande-dame Doña Gracia Mendes Nasi, transmitted the traditions of Judaism through the methods of instruction brought over from the Iberian schools.

The fourth comprises the efforts to channel Jewish faith and practice through the structures of traditional thought and law. The distinguished name in the category of thought is Jacob ibn Habib (1445?–1515/1516), whose *Ein Yaakov* ("The Fountain of Jacob"), a compilation of Babylonian talmudic lore (aggadah) and a sampling from the Jerusalem Talmud, was intended as a guide to traditional faith and religious values. Ibn Habib was also a talmudist and commentator on the *Arba'ah Turim* ("Four Rows"), the innovatively organized masterpiece of Jewish legal compilation by the Iberian Jacob ben Asher (1270?–1340).

The decisive work in the category of law was left for Joseph Caro. He undertook to provide authoritative rulings on all points of Jewish law, and to construct them systematically upon a solid scholarly foundation, beginning with the Talmud and proceeding through the often labyrinthine trajectory of their subsequent applications. His work, the *Bet Yosef* ("House of Joseph"), the fruit of twenty laborious years, is framed as a commentary to the *Arba'ah Turim*. Caro's decision to do so proved to be of momentous significance in the history of Jewish law. It gave the organization of the *Turim*, which was becoming the cynosure of jurisprudence in the Ashkenazic no less than the Sephardic world, a de facto canonicity which made it the model for all subsequent Jewish legal compilations.

Caro's digest of his work, the *Shulhan Arukh* ("Prepared Table"), intended as a functional code buttressed by the scholarship of the *Bet Yosef*, achieved renown throughout the Sephardic world. With adjustments that were soon called the *Mappah* ("Tablecloth") after the description by its author, Rabbi Moses Isserles (1525–1572), it became standard in the Ashkenazic world as well.

Reinforcing Caro's work was the massive *Kenesset ha-Gedolah* ("Great Assembly") by the hakham Hayyim Benveniste (1603–1673). Writing in the heat of the Sabbatian movement, which he opposed, Benveniste set out to strengthen the chain of halakhic tradition by elucidating the halakhic works, including responsa, since Joseph Caro and some earlier ones which he had not mentioned.

The fifth avenue was the tenacious preservation of fifteenth-century Castilian as the primary Sephardic language. Known by the Sephardim as Espanyol or Judezmo, and popularly if imprecisely as Ladino, its use as a primary language was concentrated in the Eastern Mediterranean, inasmuch as Western European Sephardim spoke current Spanish and Portuguese. Unaffected by the changes in later Castilian, Judezmo reveals certain peculiarities of syntax, grammar, and language attributable to Iberian regionalism, natural development, and the impact of Hebrew or the languages of the new Sephardic environments. The varieties of Judezmo have been subsumed into two groups: Western (Bosnia, Macedonia, Romania, Salonika, and Serbia) and Eastern (Constantinople, and Smyrna).

In this language of daily discourse the Sephardim preserved their Iberian heritage of popular stories, proverbs, and especially *romansas* (known as *romances* in the Peninsula). The romansas are ballads whose music and words were on the lips of the Sephardim long after many had been forgotten in Iberia. These have been transmitted generally unaltered except for the removal in most cases of Christological allusions. The Sephardim also composed original works like Almosnino's ethical work, *Regimiento de la Vida* ("Direction of Life," 1564), which also touches on theology, education, astronomy, and even dreams.

The Sephardim also prepared translations of their religious classics from Bahya ibn Pakuda's *Duties of the Heart* to Joseph Caro's *Shulhan Arukh*, and above all, the Bible. The Psalms (1540) and the Pentateuch (1547) appeared in Constantinople and the Prophets in Salonika (1572), two centuries before Abraham Assa's translation of the entire Bible (Constantinople, 1739–1745). But the culmination of their achievement in Judezmo was the *Me'am Lo'ez* ("From a People of a

Strange Tongue"), a title taken from Psalm 114:1. An encyclopedic masterpiece conceived, named, and begun by Rabbi Jacob Culi (ca. 1685–1732) in 1730, and continued by others through the nineteenth century, the *Me'am Lo'ez* is a treasurehouse of traditional Jewish lore and law. Written as a commentary to the Holy Scriptures and the *Ethics of the Fathers*, and combining selected elements of the tradition with the explanations of the authors, it was intended as a source of Jewish learning during the time of the Ottoman decline. It became the most popular of all productions in Judezmo, and in many ways the most influential.

The sixth was the printing press. From its establishment in Constantinople by Sephardic immigrants in 1504, 224 years before the appearance of its Turkish counterpart, the Jewish press in the Ottoman Empire reinforced the unity and continuity of the Sephardic heritage. In Egypt, Safed, Syria, Salonika and Izmir, as well as Constantinople, despite interruptions and often tortuous histories, the Jewish presses, notable among them the Jabez press in sixteenth-century Salonica, combined for a cornucopia of publications. These included, besides books in Judezmo, translations of Iberian classics, the sacred classics of the Jewish tradition, and contemporary works of Hebrew law and lore. In the early decades of the sixteenth century, their publications ensured the preservation of many works scripted in the Iberian Peninsula and carried in manuscript into exile.

The seventh avenue was the trajectory of the decline itself, especially the disorientation in the Jewish community in the wake of Shabbetai Zevi. This debacle accelerated the acceptance of the *Shulhan Arukh* as the de facto authority of Jewish law. It converted the *Me'am Lo'ez* into a major vehicle of Jewish education. It compelled increased cooperation and centralization within the beleaguered Jewish community. And in the process it completed the establishment of the Sephardim as the dominant element of the Jewish community and Judezmo as its primary language. All of this, in turn, facilitated the sultan's imposition of centralization in the reforms of the nineteenth century.

With these events the consolidation of the Sephardic heritage was essentially completed. Although this heritage was strongly preserved in many circles, the nineteenth century witnessed its gradual recession from centrality in Sephardic life through increased acculturation and secularization. This is evident in the dominantly secularized Judezmo press, the advent of the French-oriented Alliance Israélite Universelle, the inclusion of the Turkish language and Ottoman culture in the curricula of Jewish schools, and the eagerness of many Jews for participation in the general community. Jews, among them Chief Rabbi Hayim Bejarano, were active in the Young Turkish Committee of Union and Progress that led the coup d'etat of 1908 and in the ensuing nationalism of the Turkish Republic. The Jews as a community also responded alacritously to the constitution of the Republic of Turkey in 1925, with its creation of a secular state and guarantee of equal rights for all its citizens. They renounced their community rights, reemphasized the centrality of the Turkish language, and adopted Turkish names.

A tragic end to this process came with the Nazis' decimation of the Sephardic Jews in the lands of what was once the Ottoman Empire that fell under their control. Some 50,000 Jews perished from Salonika alone.

More than three quarters of a century before the Holocaust, a stream of migrations of Sephardim from the Muslim world, predominantly from the Ottoman Empire to Central and Western Europe and the Americas, had modestly begun. The migrations reached their peak between 1908 and the Immigration Act of 1924 in the United States, which all but closed its borders to Jewish immigrants from many lands. By that time, however, the United States had received some 70,000 Sephardic immigrants and perhaps more, by far the largest number of any country. Of this number nearly 50 percent remained in the Greater New York area, while the others formed substantial communities in various cities, including Atlanta, Chicago, Cincinnati, Los Angeles, Portland, and Rochester. In all of these the Sephardim and their descendants have contributed immeasurably to Jewish life and the life of the general American community.

Since World War II many Sephardim in Muslim lands have emigrated, frequently in a new exodus from persecution, to the State of Israel. There the Sephardim today constitute the majority of the population. With the aid of other nonestablishment groups that are attracted to Sephardic culture, they bid fair to preserve and further develop the heritage of the Sephardic consolidation.

The Universalization of the Sephardic Phenomenon

The Western Sephardic Diaspora differed significantly from its Eastern counterpart. On the one hand, the activity of the Western Sephardim, Christians as well as Jews by our definition, was not concentrated in a single area: it circumscribed the entire planet, radiating its influence through much of Asia, the Americas, and Europe. On the other, although all the Western Sephardim had been Catholics, at least titularly, in the Iberian Peninsula, they were at no time in their Diaspora concentrated in one religious group. Many affirmed Judaism, some on their departure from the Peninsula, but even by the most inclusive reconstruction, they could not in their totality have constituted more than a small fraction of the Sephardic emigrants and their descendants. Other Sephardim became Protestant, and others still, when opportunities arose, drifted away from all religious identification. In their Diaspora many Sephardim shifted between one faith and another before making a faith commitment and even thereafter. But, by any count, the vast majority of the emigrating Sephardim remained Catholic, as have the vast majority of their descendants. To be sure, changes of faith among later generations of the Western Sephardim have not been infrequent. Occasionally the changes have been from Catholicism or Protestantism to Judaism, but more often they have involved the exchange of Judaism for the dominant Christianity of the environment. Conforming to this pattern, for example, were the conversions of large numbers of North African Jews to Catholicism after immigrating to Spain with freedom of religion during the nineteenth century.

Within the numbers of these Sephardim must be included the numerous descendants of their marriages, if not unblessed liaisons, with the natives of the various continents of their sojourn.

The Sephardim emigrated for three reasons, in varying degrees of intensity: religious zeal, economic opportunity, and fear of persecution. Since autobiographical rationalizations for depature tend to be self-serving, the reasons have to be estimated on the basis of broader contextual coordinates. By any reconstruction, the aggregate number of New Guard individuals who emigrated constituted only a small percentage of their total number in Iberia. The vast majority, neither zealous nor lured nor frightened sufficiently, remained in the Peninsula.

In choosing their spheres of refuge, the Sephardim had to weigh risk and reward in three areas: economic opportunity, social acceptance, and physical security. The best mix of these elements was to be found in the far-flung colonies of Portugal and Spain. Although these territories were in one form or another subject to the Inquisition, their distance from the Iberian power struggles, their linkage to the crown and therefore the Modern Old Guard, and, not least, their critical dependance upon the emigrants' activity, seemed to carry the promise of inquisitorial restraint. At the same time, the colonies beckoned with visions of untapped riches and replications of the familiar society of the Iberian Peninsula.

Not surprisingly, by the middle of the sixteenth century, perhaps as many as 50,000 Iberians had emigrated to the colonies. The number classifiable as New Guard was considerably smaller and probably no more than a third of the total. The emigrants included some nobles connectible to the Old Guard and peasants, similarly definable, who became soldiers in the colonies. Once in the colonies, these often turned to New Guard pursuits. Outside of the Spanish and Portuguese orbits, where only the New Guard was needed, and where different politics controlled their immigration, the total Spanish and Portuguese immigration was considerably lower.

In Italy and the Low Countries they were also subject to Inquisitions. But here, as elsewhere in the non-Iberian world, the Sephardim faced additional problems. Being outsiders in these countries, they were for this reason socially and politically marginal. They were especially vulnerable as Iberians whenever their hosts found themselves in strained relations or open warfare with Portugal or Spain.

All Western Sephardim were linked to one another not by religion but by their New Guard status, with its characteristic range of skills, including their broad general culture and linguistic versatility, and its conditioning toward risk orientation, marginality, and alienation. The implications of their New Guard status render otiose the attempt to connect all Western Sephardim to Jewish descent, assuming that such connection were possible in the face of the widespread blurring of bloodlines in the Peninsula and outside through official and unofficial certification.

In no case can the reception of the Sephardim in any polity be fruitfully attributed to altruism or whimsy on the part of any ruler. In every case the motivation is explainable on the basis of the polity's political and economic needs. All of the admitting establishments were composed of Modern Old Guards or New Guards. All were in stiff competition with one another in their progress toward rationalization and modernization against internal as well as external obstacles. The New Guard qualities of the Western Sephardim were therefore understandably useful and eagerly sought by these establishments.

Each of these polities differed in the circumstances of its history. Only a detailed analysis of the particulars of each history will convincingly support an appreciation of the similarity of their contours, and therefore, for all the differences involved, the fundamental similarity of the role of the Western Sephardim throughout the lands of their Diaspora.

After 1492, all five regions of eventual Sephardic settlement were bustling with modernization. Portugal and Spain were speeding toward their imperial zeniths. Spurred by Vasco da Gama and Afonso de Albuquerque, Portugal would soon secure a trade route to India, 10,000 miles from Lisbon, with critical bases at Ormuz (1509), Malacca (1511), and Goa (1510), which was chosen as the nub of the Portuguese Orient. Spain, led by Castilians, was opening the Western Hemisphere and scanning the Pacific Ocean as far as the Philippines. The quiltwork of Italian city-states, the duchies of Ferrara, Savoy, and Modena, the republics of Florence, Genoa, and Venice, the marquisates of Saluzzo and Montferrat, the kingdom of Naples and Sicily, and the Papal States, though incapable of rivaling the Iberian powers and often in conflict with one another, nevertheless promoted every potential augmentation of their wealth and peninsular power. France and England were embarked on different routes toward the goal of modernization. New Guards in both militantly pursued power, often through vehicles of religious dissent. England underwent more rapid transformation with the establishment of a national church, the creation of a largely New Guard government under

Cromwell, and a Modern Old Guard polity after the Glorious Revolution. In the meantime France's Modern Old Guard, led by such stalwarts as Cardinals Richelieu and Mazarin, was bolstering its "Old Regime" against revolts from left and right, even to the point of revoking the Edict of Nantes (1685), which less than a century before (1598) had given its Huguenot Protestants freedom of worship and civil rights. The Low Countries, in Hapsburg hands since 1477, were soon to pass to Emperor Charles V, who was also Charles I of Spain (ruled 1516–1556), and to be exploited as a mercantilist bastion by Charles's son and successor in Spain, Philip II (1556–1598). Seething with resentment against Spain, the Catholics and Protestants of the Low Countries would agree in 1576 to join against the Spanish "blackbeards." This alliance foundered, but the predominantly Protestant Northern Provinces, with powerful New Guard leadership, were to secede in 1581 to form the Dutch republic.

Throughout their Western as in their Eastern Diaspora, the Sephardim, with differences of detail specific to each locale, continued the complex economic, political, and social roles they had played in the Peninsula. They served New Guards and Modern Old Guards. These invited the Sephardim and, within the parameters of their own security, protected them against their natural enemies of the antiestablishment and their competitors from within the local New Guards. As elsewhere, the enemies of the Sephardim resorted to the equation of all the Sephardim with Jews and summoned against them the medieval anti-Jewish canards of the kind that had received defacto canonization by Alfonso de Spina. In all cases the effectiveness of the opposition to the Sephardim was inversely proportional to the stability of the polity as a whole. In instances of heightened instability, the establishments often felt compelled to pass legislation and take action against the Sephardim, although the legislation passed was often not thoroughly implemented and the action taken was just as often milder than anticipated.

This matrix makes it possible to structure the often bewildering vicissitudes of the Sephardic experience in the various polities. Thus, for example, in Italy it can account for the rejection of Iberian Jews in 1492 by cities like Genoa and their admission by others like Rome, where, incidentally, Jewish merchants were among the opposition;

the expulsion of New Christians from Milan in 1540 and Venice in 1497 and 1550, on the one hand, and, on the other, their guarantee of freedom from persecution by Ferrara (February 12, 1550) and the famous Leghorn charter, known as *La Livornina* (July 10, 1593), which specifically extended a welcome to Jews, even if they had lived elsewhere as Christians. In France, it accounts, on the one hand, for the favorable response of Iberian New Christians to the charter of Louis XI (1474), which extended privileges to foreigners, except the English, and even more to the authorization of freedom of residence to New Christians by Henry II (1550); and, on the other, the many attacks against New Christians by merchants in Bordeaux, Bayonne, and the French Caribbean, and charges of host desecration at St. Jean de Luz (1622) or of collusion with the Spanish enemy, as at La Ligne (1596) and St. Esprit (1630).

In England, it explains the quiet admission of Iberian refugees, initially in very small numbers, under Henry VII (1485–1509), Henry VIII (1509–1547), and Elizabeth I (1558–1603), as well as Cromwell's interest in the the Jews' formal readmission. It explains as well the persistent opposition to the Sephardim from many quarters (including Spain, when it could pressure Henry VII), leading to the dissolution of their early communities and the obstruction of their formal readmission. It also accounts for the sensational charges against prominent Sephardim, most notably that Rodrigo López, physician to Queen Elizabeth I, had conspired to murder his royal patient.

In the Dutch Republic it explains not only the fundamental openness of the country's borders to the Portuguese, but numerous special considerations, as, for example, the grant to Jews, on July 12, 1657, of the status of subjects of the states of Holland, Zeeland, and West Friesland. It explains as well the currents of opposition by the Remonstrants and other, but far from all, elements in the Dutch church, leading to efforts at disabling legislation. In this connection, it can account, in New Netherlands, for the efforts by the governor, Peter Stuyvesant, on September 22, 1654, to dissolve the inchoate Jewish community there and prohibit future Jewish immigration, and at the same time, the obstruction of these efforts by the Dutch West India Company, for reasons that transcended the significant number of Jews who were "main participants" in that company.

In the Iberian colonies, it will explain, on the one hand, the rise to prominence of many New Christians and, on the other, the persistent efforts to obstruct the emigration of New Christians to these territories and the crescendos of inquisitorial activity evident, for example, in the so-called Great Conspiracy in Peru, culminating in 1639, and its counterpart in New Spain a decade thereafter.

In all of these areas, despite occasionally successful restrictions, the Sephardim engaged in the full gamut of New Guard activities.

Contrary to the myth reiterated by their enemies, the Sephardim of the Western Diaspora, for the most part, were neither rich nor famous. The majority were ordinary folk, eking out a subsistence as artisans, craftsmen, or petty merchants. Poverty was not always a stranger to them, and was often painfully visible, as among the Sephardic Jews of Amsterdam after the French subjugation of the Netherlands in 1794. Although these Sephardim did not make history by the drama of their individual lives, they provided the indispensable support for their communities' achievers.

The achievers constituted only a small minority of the total Western Sephardic population. But their aggregate contribution can only be characterized as extraordinary.

The tonal activity of this minority was international commerce. The varied skills of the Sephardim in this area, and their connections in the Eastern and Western Diasporas, with fellow Sephardim, Catholics and Jews, and most often family members similarly engaged, could not have failed to promote their favorable reception and spectacular successes. From the Far East they brought herbs, including pepper, and tea, silk, diamonds, and pearls. From the West Indies they carried cocoa and cotton, wood and sugar, tobacco, silver, and gold.

Western Sephardim were involved in a host of related economic activities: shipbuilding and privateering; the mining of gold and silver; the development of plantations for cocoa, tobacco, and sugar; the stimulation of industries to move raw materials toward finished products; and the advancement of banking techniques and insurance.

But no less impressive was the breadth of Western Sephardic activity and achievement in the broadly defined areas of political administration, the hard sciences, the humanities, and the arts. The names and achievements of distinguished Sephardim in these areas, many within the Iberian empires, would fill many pages. In administration the Western Sephardic Diaspora has produced prime ministers, ambassadors, judges of the highest national courts, high-ranking military officers, including generals and admirals, and innumerable government officials in other high-level positions. In the sciences Western Sephardim have been prominent in medicine, some even serving as royal physicians in Iberia, England, Sweden, and Russia; in medical research, some becoming renowned authors in a variety of fields; and in disciplines like physics, chemistry, minerology, and even conchology, and critical related fields, like mathematics. In the humanities, Sephardim have achieved renown in areas like history, anthropology, sociology, economics, philosophy, and biblical criticism. In the arts, their names are to be found among the leading figures of music, painting, and literature in almost every country of their sojourn. Indeed, in many of these disciplines Sephardim have been in the forefront of developments in numbers far beyond their percentage of their country's population.

In many cases it is impossible to determine whether the Jewish identity of Western Sephardim was accepted prior to their emigration or subsequently. The difficulty derives from their tendency to retroject the origins of Jewish identity as far back as possible. Connected to this tendency was the adoption by many Sephardic Jews of traditional Hebrew names like Cohen or Levi. But whatever their origins, the self-identification of the Sephardim as Jews, clandestine or open, was always an amalgam of commitment and circumstance.

We have examined these circumstances in the Iberian empires. Throughout the Iberian world, a formal Jewish identity was denied to all its inhabitants throughout the inquisitorial period, even though, for reasons that can best be fathomed politically on the basis of the Old Guard–New Guard struggle, nonresident Jews in areas like commerce and diplomacy were tolerated, as was commercial contact between resident Iberian New Christians and their Jewish relatives abroad. Outside of Iberia's orbits the circumstances varied more greatly and therefore produced different results.

In Italy, many places permitted Jews and even New Christians to live openly as Jews without molestation. There were New Christians who became Jews, but many clearly did not. The widespread religious ambivalence of New Christians in early-sixteenth-century Italy motivated Samuel Usque to write his Portuguese classic, *Consolation for the Tribulations of Israel* (1552), in whose prologue he attests: "I have seen members of our [Portuguese] nation, recently pursued and routed from the realms of Portugal, vacillating in their faith."

In France New Christians all lived as Catholics until the beginning of the eighteenth century, although culturally in distinctively Portuguese communities. Not uninfluenced by this isolation, some, notably in Bordeaux, seem to have slackened their Catholic practice for several decades prior to their official recognition as Jews. Ironically, the imposition of conformity among Frenchmen through the revocation of the Edict of Nantes (1698) may have facilitated the emergence of the New Christians as Jews. These actions disrupted the largely New Guard Huguenot communities and created a vacuum for Sephardim, who because of their social distinctiveness were less threatening to France's Old Guard and Modern Old Guard. It is of interest that the imposition of conformity strengthened the opponents of the Sephardim in France's distant possessions, like Martinique, where a non-Sephardic, non-Huguenot New Guard was eager to seize the opportunities the Sephardim had helped create. The continued social marginality of the French Sephardim is dramatically evidenced by the questions posed by Napoleon to the Assembly of Notables (1806) and the Great Sanhedrin (1807).

In the Low Countries Judaism appeared slowly among the Sephardim in the Dutch republic. An appreciable settlement of Portuguese merchants began in the early 1590s, but open Judaism did not appear until 1603. The account of the Yom Kippur service in 1596, interrupted by the Dutch authorities, is a legendized retrojection of what appears to have been an illegal Christmas mass.

The public emergence of Judaism was at least partially conditioned by the Dutch hostility toward Spain, to which Portugal was united until 1540, and an equivalent animus to Catholicism.

In England any Iberian Jews who may have arrived in 1492 and 1496 either disappeared or were absorbed as Christians into the English population. The Iberian Christians who followed found increased opportunity for becoming Jewish with Henry VIII's break with Rome, the Commonwealth (1649–1660), and the Glorious Revolution (1688).

When the Western Sephardim left Catholicism for Judaism, they were as a group religiously more zealous than knowledgeable. They were ignorant of the traditions, language, and customs of authentic Judaism. The first center of their integration into Judaism was Italy, where authentic Jewish communities, Iberian included, had long existed, and where the so-called "Marrano Press" at Ferrara, during four years (1552–1555), published translations into Spanish of the liturgy and the Bible (the renowned Ferrara Bible [1553]), Usque's *Consolation for the Tribulations of Israel*, in Portuguese, and two other works, one in Portuguese and the other in Spanish, whose connection to the New Christians appears clear but whose exact purpose remains enigmatic.

The liturgy and Bible profoundly influenced the second center, Amsterdam. Under Spanish-speaking teachers from Italy and the Muslim world, the Amsterdam Sephardim confirmed their link to the Iberian heritage of learning, custom, and liturgy (the *Minhag Sepharad*), and have preserved this heritage with nuances derived from the context of the Western world.

Within a few decades, Amsterdam became the spiritual cynosure of Western Sephardic Judaism. Its community was rich with traditional Jewish study, and its Talmud Torah, founded in 1615, was renowned for the range of its teaching and its rabbinic and belletristic alumni. Amsterdam was astir with an intellectual ferment that amalgamated the Iberian heritage, the Jewish faith, and the contemporary context. It made significant contributions to Jewish scholarship and many fields of general learning, and, not least, the literature of the Spanish Golden Age. And, with its Jewish printers, beginning with Manasseh ben Israel (1627), the Amsterdam community supplied books throughout the Sephardic world. Simultaneously testifying to the sophistication of this community, the novelty of Judaism for many erstwhile Sephardic Catholics, and the wavering marginality of others are the numerous apologetical and polemical works composed in Amsterdam and its offspring communities by distinguished thinkers, among them Immanuel Aboab (ca. 1555–1628), Saul Levi Morteira (ca. 1596–1660), Isaac (Fernando) Cardozo (1604–1681), Isaac

(Baltasar) Orobio de Castro (1620–1687), and David Nieto (1654–1728).

Directly, or indirectly through its offspring, Amsterdam became the mother city for the Sephardic congregations in England, Germany, France, and the New World.

Amsterdam Sephardim provided the religious foundation for the first openly Jewish community in the Western Hemisphere. This community arose in the city of Recife and its suburb of Mauricia within the independent Dutch enclave carved into Portuguese Brazil in 1630. During the twenty-four years of the existence of this enclave, many Portuguese New Christians, or perhaps, more correctly, New Guards, openly adopted Judaism. They were soon joined by Sephardim from various places in Africa and Europe, especially Holland.

On recapturing the enclave in 1654, the Portuguese gave its Jews and Protestants three months to leave. Some former Portuguese Christians, despite the dangers of the Inquisition, appear to have remained in possessions under Iberian control, including Peru and the Río de la Plata region. Large numbers of Jews returned to the places of their origin, especially Holland. Others sailed northward, developing Sephardic communities in the Caribbean, in the Guianas, English Barbados, Dutch Curaçao, and elsewhere. A group of twenty-three, arriving in New Amsterdam early in September 1654, where two Jews had preceded them, founded the first American Jewish community, and the first American synagogue, which they appropriately named Shearith Israel, the "Remnant of Israel."

The Brazilian Jewish community generated a rich panoply of Jewish institutions on the Amsterdam model, including an educational system that offered advanced talmudic study. It was enriched by the arrival in 1641 of Hakham Isaac Aboab da Fonseca (1605–1693), the first rabbi in the Western Hemisphere, and with him Hakham Moses Raphael de Aguilar (d. 1679). Other American Sephardic communities continued to be guided by the Amsterdam model, and some, like Barbados, Jamaica, and Curaçao, achieved an appreciable level of Jewish life in the century after their arrival. The Jamaican community produced two distinguished authors: Daniel Israel López Laguna, a Portuguese, who while in Jamaica wrote his famous *Espejo fiel de vidas* "Faithful Mirror of Lives," (London, 1720), with reflections of his inquisitorial incarceration, and Rabbi Joshua Hezekiah de Cordova, author of *Reason and Faith* (Jamaica, 1788), which was to become the first English book on Judaism reprinted in North America (Philadelphia, 1791).

In the North American colonies Shearith Israel became the model for other American colonial Sephardic congregations, in Newport, Philadelphia, Savannah, and Charleston. Long after the year 1720, by which time the Sephardim in the colonies had become a minority of the Jewish population, it continued to set the tone for all of American Jewish religious life, modeling a dedicated involvement in the general life of the American community with a passionate devotion to the Iberian traditions of Judaism. Its concern for internal Jewish unity was never better expressed than by its distinguished hakham, Henry Pereira Mendes (1852–1937, rabbi 1877–1923), who came to Shearith Israel on the recommendation of his brother, Rabbi Frederick de Sola Mendes (1850–1927), at the time rabbi of the neighboring Congregation Shaarey Tefila in New York.

From their first settlement the Sephardim in North America, as elsewhere, became increasingly integrated economically, socially, and politically into the community. In the colonies and the nations of the United States of America and Canada, they have contributed significantly not only to material life but to every phase of scientific, scholarly, and artistic endeavor. In these countries dedicated to New Guard progress, they have been the quintessential New Guard. In the twentieth century, the Eastern Sephardic immigrants to America have joined in these achievements.

But throughout the New World, as in the Old, the Sephardim have suffered the erosions that inevitably accompany acculturation. Deep knowledge of Judaism, even where available in abundance, has not characterized large numbers of Sephardic Jews in the Western Hemisphere, any more than it has the Ashkenazic. Apathy, marginality, and defection, often through marriage, have numerically eroded many communities. The strength, dedication, organization, and inspiration within the surviving remnants remain, as in the past, the strongest guarantee for Sephardic survival.

Note

The foregoing is a précis of a multi-volume work in progress. Spatial limitations in this volume and the complexity of the subject matter have made necessary the omission of numerous facets of the Sephardic experience. They have also required the postponement of notes and other scholarly apparatus until the publication of the larger work.

Stones of Memory: Revelations from a Cemetery in Curaçao

Rochelle Weinstein

The Sculptured Tombstones of Ouderkerk and Curaçao in Historical Context

In a garden like setting at the Ouderkerk Portuguese Jewish cemetery in the Netherlands lies the marble monument to Mosseh de Mordechay Senior, who died on July 2, 1730. The white slab was prepared in his lifetime, according to the terse Portuguese epitaph. It is covered with reliefs of elaborately garbed men and women posing and gesturing within an ornate framework of arches and tall pilasters. The composition resembles a Baroque building facade. The names, carved in Hebrew Bible phrases beneath each image, match the first names of all the members of Mosseh's family: his parents and grandparents as well as his ten siblings, their spouses and offspring (Figures 1–3).

Mosseh's father, Mordechay de Judah Senior, was born in Amsterdam to Portuguese New Christian refugees from religious persecution. Mordechay and his brother Jacob de Judah spent their young manhood in Recife, Pernambuco, in service to John Maurice, governor general of Dutch Brazil, until its recapture by the Portuguese in 1654. Mosseh, born around 1676, was ninth in a family of eleven siblings: Judah, Jacob, Ester, David, Isaac, Abraham, Rachel, Benjamin, Mosseh, Ribca, and Selomoh. Mosseh's eldest brother Judah and cousin Judah de Jacob Senior Henriques (married to Mosseh's sister Ester) belonged to the group of Jewish magnates in the Hague circle of Stadholder William III, later King William III of England. Mosseh's mother Sarah Lopes, aunt Ester Lopes (married to his uncle Jacob de Judah), aunt Ribca Lopes Henriques (married to Dr. Daniel Semach Aboab), and uncle David Lopes Henriques were allied, through

Figure 1: *Left side: Tombstone of Mosseh de Mordechay Senior, July 2, 1730, Ouderkerk. Right side: Tombstone of Abraham and Isaac Rephael Senior, sons of Benjamin Senior, September 16 and 24, 1727, Ouderkerk* Photo R. Weinstein

Figure 2: *Detail of the top portion of the tombstone of Mosseh de Mordechay Senior*
Photo R. Weinstein

David's wife Abigail Isidro, to the powerful Hamburg merchant family Isidro, alias Baruch. They had obtained economic leverage unavailable to Dutch Sephardim by serving Portugal after it regained independence from Spain in 1640. Mosseh's sister Ribca married Isaac, community circumcisor (mohel), and son of Dr. Daniel Semach Aboab. Mosseh's aunt Ribca Senior and sister Rachel married, respectively, Abraham and his son Jacob Fundam, traders based in Recife, Barbados, London, and Curaçao. Brother Abraham Senior married Batseba Aboab Cardoso, of the family based in Amsterdam and Curaçao. Brother Benjamin was business partner and universal heir of bachelor Mosseh. Unmarried Curaçao brother Jacob, as Captain Philippe Henriques, commanded brigantines through the trade lanes of the Spanish Main as factor for the States General of the United Netherlands, the king of England, and the Royal African Company of Portugal. We have been able to confirm these and other family ties and obligations with archival sources. Especially useful are the 1680 will of Mordechay Senior, the 1686 will of his widow Sarah Lopes, the 1728 will of Mosseh Senior (copied and grouped with other Senior instruments in the Amsterdam Municipal Archives collection Da Costa 946), and the 1733 will of David Senior (stored at the Hague National Archives as Old Archives of Curaçao, no. 1.05.12, portfolio 821). Also very useful is the Portuguese Jewish community archive of the *Dotar*, the ("Holy Company for Dowry of Orphans and Young Girls"), stored at the Amsterdam Archives as PA 334:1141–1145 (1615–1787). The numbered membership places in the society were usually passed down from father to eldest son, and the members were named with full patronymics as well as aliases.

Half a world away, in the Jewish cemetery on the Dutch island of Curaçao, lie four more stones for members of the Senior family, ornamented with biblical personages in compositions echoing Mosseh's. They form part of a group of about forty slabs with similar figural reliefs and epitaphic date range in a cemetery of around 2,500 stones, the oldest dated 1660/69. Like all monuments on Curaçao, which is poor in building stone, they had been prepared in the home country and shipped to the island. Like Mosseh's they were prepared in life, for the families of his brothers, David, Jacob, Isaac and Selomoh, who sought their fortunes and made their homes in the New World. Recognized since 1657 by the States General as Dutch nationals, and permitted freedom to trade and settle in all Portuguese colonies according to the 1661 treaty, Jews were protected from foreign persecution at home and abroad. Doubly represented, at Ouderkerk and at Curaçao, are symbolic tombstone portraits of brother Selomoh's wife Ester, brother David, David's son Ishac Haim Senior, and Ishac Haim's wife Rachel (Figures 12, 16, 14, 15).

Figure 12: *Tombstone of Esther, wife of Selomoh Senior, December 4, 1714, Curaçao*
Collection of the American Jewish Archives

Figure 16: *Tombstone of David Senior, September 14, 1749, Curaçao*
Collection of American Jewish Archives

Figure 14: *Tombstone of Ishac Haim Senior, April 17, 1726, Curaçao*
Collection of the American Jewish Archives

Figure 15: *Tombstone of Rachel, wife of Ishac Haim Senior, July 14, 1746, Curaçao*
Collection of the American Jewish Archives

Furthest back in time of Mosseh's family namesakes in stone is that of grandfather Judah Senior, Amsterdam freighter of Brazilian sugar, and scion of the family Henriques Pimentel, alias Abeniacar. In Constantinople Judah's father Mordechai and uncle Alvaro Pimentel, alias Rabbi Jacob Abeniacar, were Jewish community leaders as well as diplomats in the sultan's service. They were closely connected to the Venice Jewish community, home base of Judah's brother Afonso Henriques, alias David Senior. As a New Christian merchant in the French court of Henri IV, Judah's uncle Manuel Pimentel, alias Isaac Abeniacar, won fame as the king's favorite gambling partner. He stayed at court as late as 1608, increasing the monarch's treasury through his notorious skill at cards and dice. With Manuel in France was brother Garcia Pimentel, alias Mordechay Abeniacar, as a Portuguese merchant, operating in Lisbon, North Africa and the Levant and also, as of 1594, in Amsterdam. Young Judah Senior visited the French court and traveled with and for uncle Manuel to Florence, Livorno, Venice and Dubrovnik. He survived occasional robberies and even murder attempts while receiving valuable tutoring in international trade and diplomacy. The brothers Pimentel/Abeniacar moved to Venice and then to Amsterdam. Garcia/Mordechay was the first Jew buried in the first Jewish cemetery in the Netherlands: Groet near Alkmaar, purchased in 1602 and inaugurated with his burial in 1607. Groet predated Ouderkerk but went into disuse after the new site's official 1616 opening. By 1626 the remains of seventy-four Groet burials had been transferred to Ouderkerk, in actual use since 1614 and the oldest European Jewish cemetery still in use. Manuel/Isaac, instrumental in the purchase of Ouderkerk, was the first adult buried there, in 1614.

Commemorated symbolically at Ouderkerk but buried at Curaçao is Mosseh's brother Jacob, who carried grandfather Judah's alias, Philippe Henriques. He disclosed his Jewish name as well as his alias when he was arrested in 1699 by the Inquisition at Cartagena while on a trading mission for William III of England, former stadholder of the Netherlands. Next to Mosseh's stone, bearing the relief of Abraham sacrificing Isaac, is the 1727 stone for two "anjos" (boys under thirteen years of age), Isaac and Abraham Raphael. The children had previously been identified as members of the family Senior Teixeia. But in view of new Senior Henriques family information and the absence of the name Teixeira in the epitaph, it is equally possible that Mosseh, a bachelor, was deliberately placed in eternal spiritual guardianship over two infant nephews. They were sons, according to the epitaph, of Senior, Mosseh's brother and, according to his 1728 testament, his universal heir.

The figures on the monuments of Mosseh and his Curaçao brothers represent Jewish heroes and heroines of religious history, copied in stone from contemporary prints. Such images served as popular models of thought and behavior in the national imagination of the Dutch Republic, a highly visual culture. For the Protestant Dutch, who had attained independence from Catholic Spain in 1609, Hebrew Bible protagonists represented nobility and courage. They were historical embodiments of human virtue to imitate, not churchly idols to bow down to. For Mosseh, art collector and booklover, and for those who visited the Jewish cemetery, these images served as a gallery of symbolic family portraits. Mosseh's stone is the most complex in a group of forty or more slabs, among the 27,000 in Ouderkerk's oldest part (pre-1800), carved with figured biblical reliefs during a century beginning with a monument dated 1667.

Mosseh's ancestors were New Christians who had fled Portugal for Venice and the Netherlands in the 1590s, under numerous aliases. For them to take biblical names was a way of asserting and reaffirming ancestral ties they had almost lost. For them especially, re-entry into Judaism, with all the accompanying precepts and rituals, including circumcision, was a pledge of body and soul to renewed faith. This identity became the heritage of their progeny. Inscribed on the tombstone, the names and images served to remind those who inherited the names of their forebears and of their religious and social responsibilities.

The atypical Baroque Jewish monuments with figured reliefs are found only in regions governed by the Dutch or near the free city of Hamburg, whose official religion was Lutheran. These competing sometimes allied, sovereignties permitted Sephardic settlement at about the same time. They welcomed affluent refuges from Portugal and Spain. Comparable figured reliefs are found on two upright slabs, dated 1713 and 1717, at the Dutch Ashkenazi cemetery of Muiderberg, inaugurated in 1648. A 1746 stone with figured relief is at the Hague Scheveningsweg Jewish cemetery ground purchased in 1694. Reliefs on Sephardic monuments epitaphically dated 1648–1737 are found on approximately forty horizontal slabs and prisms among the 2,500 at the Jewish cemetery of Altona-Königstrasse, now part of greater Hamburg. They share the burial site with approximately 6,000 Ashkenazi upright slabs, the two main groupings separated by a pathway. The first Sephardic burial in Hamburg/Altona cemetery took place in 1611, the year of purchase; the first Ashkenazi burial took place in 1616. It was closed in 1869 when the Jewish section at Hamburg's Ohlsdorf cemetery was opened. Founded in 1620 as a short-lived Danish competitor to Hamburg, the port city of Gluckstadt preserves a small Jewish cemetery of approximately fifty slabs, for Ashkenazim and Sephardim who worked or settled there during the ensuing century. Among them are two Sephardic figured slabs dated 1694 and 1716.

In their exuberance and visual appeal these monuments are unlike any other markers associated with traditional Jewish or Protestant monumental ritual. Most members of the Dutch Jewish community,

Ashkenazim and Sephardim alike, had simple native bluestone slab grave monuments. They were similar to those of their Dutch Protestant countrymen except for the epitaphic language. For Ashkenazim, the script was Hebrew on a vertical slab; for Sephardim it was Portuguese and Hebrew, with occasional Latin, on a horizontal slab, more rarely on a rectangular or triangular prism. The latter structure represents the more usual type of tent tomb (*ohel*) favored by Ashkenazim to commemorate rabbis and other community leaders. The prototype, which had arrived in Europe with the Romans, evolved as a tabletomb monument in all religious denominations.

Like the Jews, the majority of Dutch Protestants and the smaller Catholic populace placed their modest monuments outdoors; by their tradition in the churchyard. In contrast, Protestant gentry, including the newly evolved aristocratic merchant class, as well as those with titles of nobility, commissioned slabs for placement in churches as either floor stones or wall epitaphs.

Among patrician Protestants and many Dutch and also Hamburg Sephardim, ancestral crests crowned the more elegant, sometimes marble, architectonic Baroque slabs. Such Sephardim also commissioned marble prism-form table tombs as seen in Jacob van Ruisdael's two seventeenth-century paintings of the Portuguese cemetery at Ouderkerk. Prominent in both paintings is the tomb prepared in 1614 for Dr. Elijah Montalto by his patron, Queen Marie de Medici of France. Many stylish Protestant and Sephardic slabs and table tombs were embellished with Renaissance reworkings of classical mortality motifs, such as winged hourglasses, scallops and other seashells, skull and bones, genii, smoking torches, urns, plus wreaths of laurel and symbolic flowers and fruits.

Many tombstones of the seventeenth to nineteenth centuries at the Prague and Czernowitz Ashkenazi cemeteries have vivid reliefs as a play on the name, profession, or tribal descent of the deceased. These emblems of trade or brotherhood recall similar seventeenth- and eighteenth-century reliefs in the Netherlands. Members of some Dutch craft guilds commissioned for their tombstones figured narrative or allegorical reliefs showing particular occupations. Special sailors' cemetery markers included ship reliefs. The motif might first have appeared as the facade stone of a home or a place of business, or as the distinguishing element on the medallion issued with entry date to each dues-paying member of a guild. At the burial of a guild brother, all members were expected to attend or to send their medallions as tokens of attendance.

We know that Uri Phoebus Halevy, who became a member of the Amsterdam book publishers' guild in 1664, owned such a medallion with the image of a winged Mercury, armed with book and staff. The guild had opened its doors to Jews as proofreaders and printers after its 1661 separation from the St. Luke's artists' guild. The St. Luke's guild, like most craft guilds, refused Jews admittance.

This restriction severely hampered Amsterdam publishers. They wished to maintain their justly deserved reputation throughout Europe for the most accurate editions of the Bible and its translations. In 1661 Joseph Athias (1635–1700), was the first Jew admitted to the guild. In 1661 and again in 1667 Athias published a translation and commentary on the Bible by Dutch Reform theologian and Hebrew scholar Johannes Leusden. For its beauty and accuracy the later edition, subsidized in part by Jeronimo Nunes da Costa alias Moses Curiel, earned the gold medallion and chain of the States General. Rabbinical approbations for it, in Hebrew and Latin, dated Nisan 5, 5427, came from Aaron Sarfati, Moses Raphael d'Aguilar, and Isaac Aboab da Fonseca. Shortly after Athias, David de Castro Tartas gained admittance and, in 1664, an administrative post. In this milieu Dutch Jews had easy access to prints for ornamenting their books or for collecting as art objects with diverse applications.

Rarest of all among the sepulchral adornments which added dignity to the burial service in early modern Europe are examples of the brass armorial which covered the casket of the deceased. In shape and size they resemble Torah breastplates. We know that just such a shield with armorials in the style of a casket plate, was commissioned in Amsterdam in 1656. The assignment to brassfounder (*geelgieter*) Gillis Wijbrandts came from Johan Lopes Chilon and Ruleff Lobatto. We know that in 1657 the parnassim of Amsterdam sent the Jewish community of Barbados two Torah scrolls and their ornaments. They charged Abraham Chillon and Abraham Mesiah with delivery of the first scroll set. In Amsterdam also at that time was Abraham Cohen Lobatto and son Isaac alias Rehuel.

The most ambitious Dutch Protestant monuments were prepared in marble for national leaders such as stadholders and admirals. In these, the recumbent effigy was surrounded by free-standing allegorical figures and richly populated narrative and emblematic wall reliefs, all placed as close as possible to the main altar in the chief church of their birth city. The complexity of the chapel-sized monuments for Dutch national heroes contrasted with the austerity of the interiors in which they were placed. During the iconoclastic 1590s, Northern Netherlands churches had been divested of all Catholic imagery as prelude to the "alteration" when Reform Dutch Protestantism replaced Catholicism as the new official religion of the United Provinces. In the early decades of the new Dutch Republic, major commissions went to emigre or migrant sculptors from the South Netherlands, still under Spanish Catholic rule. These were sometimes the only artisans deemed able to produce monuments with the degree of skill and evocative power to match the importance of the deceased. Formally, the Dutch marble sepulchral tours de force echoed the design of Baroque Catholic monuments in churches throughout Europe. But the Dutch made a careful distinction between painted and sculptured imagery in houses of worship to which one bends the knee in idolatrous worship, and those images of heroism and history, both religious and classical, from which one takes a moral lesson in how to live a better life. Prefaces to readers, in editions of profusely illustrated Bibles, spelled out the distinction.

One such Dutch Protestant Bible history, first published in Amsterdam in 1704 and illustrated by Romeyn de Hooghe (1645–1708), chief print maker, pamphleteer, and commissioner of mines for William III, contained in its list of subscribers the names of Sephardim Joseph Barsely, Abraham van Aaron da Fonseca, and Benjamin Signora. The last-named was possibly Mosseh Senior's brother. Two of de Hooghe's etchings served as models for reliefs on Curaçao stones: one for that of Haham Eliau Lopes, d. 1713; the other for that of Jahacob Alvares Correa, d. 1714. Lopes, the community's second chief rabbi, had followed Josia Pardo in service beginning in 1692; Alvares Correa, a community parnas and leader, was one of the richest settlers on the island.

During the century 1650–1750, when the most elaborate Sephardic monuments were designed, the most ambitious Dutch Protestant sepulchral monuments were commissioned for heads of state and military heroes. Recognizing the unique historical situation of the Dutch Jews and of certain Sephardic families in particular, plus conditions of religious and artistic monumental style in the Dutch Netherlands, we are better prepared to comprehend the nature of the Sephardic monuments typified by those of the Senior family and others like them at Ouderkerk and Curaçao. The monuments express not only an attitude toward the Jewish religion but a sense of being at home, at last, in a specific moment and place, in a long history.

Some members of the Dutch Sephardic community, with great political influence in the home country, left dignified, architectonically elegant, monuments. They are simple by comparison with the narrative fullness of the Senior stones and others like them. But wills and other documentation from these families indicate a life equally rich in personal possessions, such as portraiture, jewelry, and handsomely furnished homes in town and country. Mid-eighteenth-century family papers contain payment receipts for tombstone cutting from craftsmen whose names are associated with church sculpture, and stucco and marble ornament for mansions and town halls. Pieter Pantel's name appears; François Absiel's name appears repeatedly. In 1704 Johannes Ebbelaer prepared two marble wall plaques for the Circuits House (Rodeamentushuis) at Ouderkerk.

The question of these Jewish monuments' suitability does not hinge on their degree of extravagance, however much virtue may be attached to simplicity. A self-conscious show of austerity might also be interpreted as a form of vanity. Stones, ornate or simple, are traditionally agents of memory for Jews. Their chief function is to serve as a sign, to activate in the beholder the memory and spirit of the departed, and thereby keep the loved one forever alive in the heart of the living; by means of memory metaphorically "bound up in the garland of everlasting life."

The sculptured Curaçao and Ouderkerk tombstones of the Senior family can be traced to images printed in Bibles originating or available in Amsterdam. Archives from Curaçao, Amsterdam, and the Hague have helped to identify the specific family members symbolically portrayed. The century and a half during which this dynasty evolved was unlike any other in Jewish or general European history. The stones and the archives help us to reconstruct a time and a place which nurtured the growth of certain aspects of human freedom and understanding and the expansion of scientific and economic methods which are enduring legacies to our world.

Description and Analysis of the Senior Monuments of Ouderkerk and Curaçao

Although the Senior stones under discussion have been reproduced previously, they have never been analyzed as a group of related monuments. David Henriques de Castro was responsible for the initial restoration of many of the handsomest stones and for recording the epitaphs or epitaphic dates, and for mapping the location of approximately 27,000 monuments in the oldest (pre-1800) part of Ouderkerk cemetery. His 1883 Dutch publication about the stones of Ouderkerk (*Keur van Grafsteenen*) reproduced, among others, the Senior stone when it was first unearthed. Because of the cemetery's marshy terrain, most of the stones had sunk below the ground surface in the course of the almost three centuries the site had been in use. The epitaphs were gradually lost to posterity, but this situation had the advantage of protecting the subtle sculpture on many stones. De Castro set the stones he reproduced on brick platforms to prevent their re-sinking. The contrast between his original black-and-white photos and the color slides I took in the 1970s and 1980s shows the erosion that occurred over the last century. Some figured stones which de Castro had not supported with bricks were brought to light and photographed in black-and-white in raking light, for maximum epitaphic clarity, in the 1970s and 1980s. This was part of an up-to-date conservation program under the direction of the Hague Monumental Restoration division: the Portuguese-Israelitisch Begraafplaats Wergroep. The recently unearthed stones retain the delicacy of carving which so moved de Castro; after photographic records were made some of the stones were reburied to maintain their surface integrity.

Isaac Emmanuel's richly documented publications on the Jews of the Netherlands Antilles featured photos of the visually outstanding stones of Curaçao but with no discussion of their relationship to the imagery and forms of related stones at Ouderkerk. Curaçao's Jewish cemetery was originally surrounded by West India Company plantations less than a day's journey from Willemstad, the capital city built on the two arms (Punda and Otrabanda) of Schottegat harbor on St. Anna Bay. As the island's economy shifted to oil production, fumes from the Shell refineries built on these plantations, especially after the 1940s, began to erode the surfaces of many of the tombstones in varying degree. There have been attempts at restoration. Maquettes of some of the handsomest figured stones have been installed in the courtyard of the Jewish Historical Museum, site of the recently restored ritual bath (mikveh). The courtyard adjoins the present site (the fourth structure, inaugurated in 1730) of synagogue Mikve Israel–Emanuel. It is the oldest Jewish congregation in continuous operation in the New World, founded in 1674 on a plantation near the cemetery site whose earliest stones date from that decade. Of the four chandeliers hanging in the present synagogue, two date from the 1703 third building. One of the later ones was donated by Mordechay de Isaac and Ester de Marchena. Carilho Marchena is the surname of Ester, wife of Selomoh Senior; of Sarah, wife of Selomoh's brother David Senior; and of Rachel, wife of Ishac Haim Senior, David's son. Set next to Ishac Haim's tombstone is the equally ornate figured stone with epitaphs for Isaac de Marchena, with Ester and young son Mordachay. Despite erosion of the reliefs on the Curaçao stones, we have been able to match many of them with prints from illustrated Bibles. By retrieving details of form in this way we can perhaps recover some of the initial impact of the stones and see what the families saw in them.

Mosseh Senior's Stone at Ouderkerk

The organization of Mosseh's stone at Ouderkerk, the most complex of the monuments of the Senior family, also governs the general composition of four of the Senior stones at Curaçao. The impression is that of a four-story Baroque building facade, probably similar to one in which Mosseh lived in Amsterdam or which he used as a warehouse or office for his family business. The attic or top course, set on a parapet, is divided into three parts by a central window-like niche. It rests on a pair of colossal order pilasters which frame the second and third stories. The pilasters rest atop the fourth story, which resembles a stage with a carved curtain drawn up to reveal a central dramatic episode flanked by two narrators standing on platforms. The left platform is inscribed with a pair of entwined letters M, probably the Senior company monogram "Mosseh de Mordechay," which Mosseh called his "cypher" in his will. The right platform is embellished with a relief of a three-masted ship in full sail, probably one of the seagoing galliots referred to in documents written by Mosseh's Curaçao brothers David and Jacob.

Inside the top niche a half-figure representing Moses holds the tablets of the law, which are inscribed with the Hebrew initial words of the Ten Commandments. On a projecting ornamental keystone above Moses' head is a small relief of a figure kneeling on a mountaintop; at its base stands a crowd of witnesses, from its summit a cloud billows up and out. Inscribed in Hebrew in the niche arching over Moses' head is the phrase "Moses received the Law from Sinai," from the Babylonian Talmud, Tractate Avot, chapter 1, which follows the Sabbath prayers in the Siddur.

On the parapet below Moses is inscribed part of Exodus 19:19: the moment "Moses spoke," after the sounding of the horn, and before God answered him by a voice. The scene in the keystone comes from Exodus 19:20: "And the Lord came down upon Mount Sinai, on the top of the mount; and the Lord called Moses up to the top of the mount; and Moses went up." The specific nature of the Hebrew inscriptions and the passages represented in stone reveal Mosseh's attention to the details of his symbolic portrait. Outside the niche, on the viewer's right, a full-length figure in a long robe, representing Abraham, kneels bare-headed at the entrance to his tent, grazing up at the moon and star-studded heavens. Beneath him, on the parapet, are inscribed words from Genesis 15:5, when God told him to "look toward heaven" to count the stars, so numerous would be Abraham's progeny. To the left of the niche sits a crowned, bearded David on an elegantly carved throne; he plays a harp embellished with a genie head; his backdrop a richly embroidered curtain. Beneath him, on the parapet, are the Hebrew words which preface Psalms 38 and 70, referring to David as God's "chief musician," who brings God's promise to our "remembrance."

In the center of the high second story, framed by the pilasters, is the Portuguese epitaph flanked on the right and left respectively by reliefs from the lives of Solomon and Jacob. The epitaph reads: "Sepultura/qua Preparou em/sua vida Mosseh/de Mord:y Senior/F:o em 17 Tamus/A:o 5490/S:A:G:D:G." The abbreviations stand for *Sua Alma Goze da Gloria*, the Portuguese Jewish equivalent of the Hebrew acronym for "let his/her soul be bound up in the garland of life."

In the Solomon relief the young crowned king, enthroned under a canopy, scepter in his right hand, feet resting on a pillow, wears a classical warrior's breastplate over his robe. On each of the six steps of the throne rest a pair of lions, traditionally representing the twelve tribes of Israel. The six lions on the far right are partially hidden by the pilaster. At the foot of the steps, near a collection of precious vessels, kneels the Queen of Sheba, on sacks of gifts. She is accompanied by three maids-in-waiting, one of whom shelters her with an umbrella. The Hebrew inscribed beneath, from I Kings 10:13, identifies the scene of Solomon's generosity to the Queen: "King Solomon gave to the Queen . . . "

At the left of the epitaph rises a ladder of angels toward a sun framed by a gloriole. At the foot of the ladder Jacob sleeps near his vessels of food and water, walking staff firmly grasped in his right hand. The Hebrew beneath, from Genesis 28:12, translates as "And he dreamt, and behold, a ladder set up on the ground."

The third story resembles a triple-arcaded porch or balcony. The wide, lively center scene is skillfully carved so as to show receding surface levels in imitation of aerial perspective as our attention moves from close up into the distance. In the arches on either side are tableau-like figures set within slightly curved recesses. The tableau at right shows Rachel at the well with two of her flock. Below her are inscribed Hebrew words from Genesis 29:6: "Behold, Rachel comes with the sheep." In the left arcade the infant Isaac frolics at the knee of his mother Sarah; the Hebrew below, from Genesis 21:6, referring to how God made Sarah laugh, translates as "And Sarah said, God made (laughter) for me." It is a word-play on the noun for "joke" (*tz'khak*) and the proper noun "Isaac" (*Itzkhak*).

The wide center arcade is a marvel of atmospheric and linear perspective rendered in stone. At right an exotic caravan of camels and drivers progresses from the foreground up and back toward a turreted city near the horizon. The figures gradually get flatter and smaller as they recede. At the left, close up, is the encounter scene between Rebecca and the servant of Abraham, as indicated in the Hebrew below from Genesis 24:45: ". . . behold, Rebecca came forth with a pitcher on her shoulders and she went down to the spring." Rebecca is attired in a gown whose low-cut décolletage reflects contemporary royal portraits. The servant wears the boots, cape, and short jacket of a cavalier. The sculptor drew on a popular set of images first created in the 1590s but revised details for the 1730 commission. In the background left a dolphin rears its flukes to the arcade frame. In the original print the fountain was embellished with a statue of a sea god reclining on the beast, but this pagan image was removed to suit the sensibilities of the Jewish client. The cityscape in the distance is a reference to Genesis 24:18, wherein Abraham's servant Eleazar stands outside his home city, Nahor, in the evening, near a well, praying for the event which will fulfill his mission.

The bottom story of the composition is designed to resemble a stage divided into three sections; a carved curtain is shown drawn up to reveal the drama taking place. In this the relief reflects an aspect of stage practice of the mid-seventeenth century which followed principles established with the 1637 formation of the Amsterdam theatre. Rather than imitate lifelike behavior the actors assumed strictly regulated emblematic gestures and stance. To the degree that they were recognizable to an educated audience it was a kind of collaborative theatre. In the center section a symbolic tableau-vivant plays out in front of a spacious backdrop of architecture and landscape. Both side sections contain allegorical representations in traditional costume: shepherd at right, Roman warrior at left. They were stock figures found in many plays, an allusion to the classical, venerable and therefore solemn nature of the presentation.

The Hebrew inscription from Genesis 49:27 under the figure in the right section identifies him as the symbol of the tribe of Benjamin, the head eroded even in de Castro's time; at his feet the "wolf devouring its prey." Beneath Benjamin, in a cartouche, is a three-masted ship, a symbol of the seagoing galliots in which Moses Senior Henriques and Company plied their trade. The Hebrew under the left figure, from Genesis 49:9 describes him as the symbol of the tribe of Judah; "the lion's whelp" crouching beside him. In the cartouche below is the pair of entwined M's for "Mosseh de Mordechay": most likely Mosseh's company monogram. In real life Benjamin and Judah were Mosseh Senior's closest brothers. Metaphorically in his monument they form the supporting and enclosing components of his extended family structure. They form the symbolic base of the family together with Mosseh's father Mordechay, represented in the center section with Hebrew from Esther 8:15.

In the center panel, Mordechay's biblical namesake, Mordecai, in royal apparel, goes "out in the presence of the king" while the city of Shushan rejoices. The sculptor displays the same bravura handling of atmospheric and linear perspective evident in the Rebecca panel above. At the far right, on a five-stepped viewing stand draped with swags, sit King Ahasuerus and Queen Esther on an ornate double throne. The stand resembles a small Roman temple. On the spine of the roof stand two or three little figure resembling acroteria or guardian spirits. In this instance they are city people who have climbed up for a better view of the parade. On the long side of the temple, framed by two pillars, two larger figures lean out to watch the proceedings. Farther back, toward center, smaller and in flatter relief, a workman appears to be operating the winch of a gibbet or gallows or perhaps pushing someone up the ladder. To the left a woman, her head draped in a veil, leans out of a window of a building, pouring something from a basin in her hands. A figure cringes at the base of the building as if to avoid the direct impact of what is coming from the basin. In Amsterdam, by then the century-old global center of the Bible translating and publishing industry, the Dutch sculptor was probably familiar with the episode from Midrash Megillah 16a wherein Haman's daughter pours refuse on her father's head, mistaking it for Mordecai's.

In front of this animated backdrop Mordecai passes majestically along a high grassy road, riding a horse with a tasseled saddle and plumes in its mane. He is outfitted like a Renaissance condottiere, in classical breastplate, skirt, cape and boots, but crowned with an Eastern potentate's feathered turban. Trumpet-blowing young equerries accompany him on both sides. The legs of one or more can be seen behind the horse's legs. A bearded man his own age, more sedately attired in a many-buttoned jacket, leads the horse. It is possible that this is Haman, although he already appears in a less-dignified situation in the background. Alternatively it is Harbona, one of the chamberlains who reminded the king, at the moment Haman's villainy was exposed, that the vizier had prepared a gallows for Mordecai. Whereupon the monarch ordered Haman's execution on it. According to Midrash Esther Rabbah 7:9, the prophet Elijah appeared in Harbona's guise to urge Haman's punishment. This story of political intrigue, hidden identity, and the triumph of virtue through divine but masked intervention (the name of God never appears in the Book of Esther) has counterparts in the personal histories of the Senior family.

The Artistic Milieu of Amsterdam and the Hague

The curtain as an artistic device was popular in painting of the Dutch Golden Age, such as Jan Vermeer's *The Artist's Studio* of the mid-seventeenth century. The curtain alluded, among other things, to the amateur and professional dramatic and literary societies called rhetoric chambers, popular in both the South and North Netherlands in the sixteenth and early seventeenth centuries. In the years preceding and shortly following Dutch independence the chambers performed pageants with political messages. They were often drawn from biblical episodes, designed to encourage the populace in the fight against Spanish tyranny. A favored subject was the story of Esther. Plays based on the Book of Esther were among the most frequently written and performed in the nation. Designs for the dramas must have abounded in Amsterdam, offering countless opportunities for artistic invention within the boundaries of the written scriptural directives. The chief playwrights of the day, such as Pieter Hooft, Gerbrand Bredero and poet-Laureate Joost van Vondel, contributed to these productions. In the United Provinces in 1637 the rhetoric companies evolved into the Dutch national theatre with these and other writers among its founding fathers.

The Muiderberg literary circle, a loose association of some of the most famous writers, included Hooft, Casper van Baerle, Anna Maria Schurman, Roemer Visscher, his daughters Anna Roemer and Maria called Tesselschade, Jacob Cats and Constantijn Huygens the elder (1596–1687), secretary to Stadholders Frederick Henry, William II, and William III, later King William III of England. Van Baerle corresponded with Manasseh ben Israel, and wrote poetry in praise of the rabbi, including an encomium to his *Creatione Mundi*. Jacob Cats was an investor in overseas enterprises of Amsterdam Sephardim. The Antwerp art dealer Gaspar Duarte, his son Diego (who later settled in the Hague as Jacob), and Gaspar's daughter Francesca "De Fraansche Naghtegael" attended musical soirees at Muiderberg. Francesca's nickname was a play on words of the title of Cats' famous poetry collection *De Zeeuwsche Naghtegael*. Huygens the elder, and his son Constantijn the younger, who followed him as secretary to the princes of Orange, was regularly in touch, officially and socially, with Sephardic magnates such as the Suassos, the Lopes de Liz, Machados, Pereiras and the members of the Senior Henriques family established at the Hague. Huygens wrote a eulogy for Gaspar Duarte, who died in 1654; it is the subscript to an engraved portrait of the collector by Lucas Vorsterman, the printmaker on whom Rubens relied for engraved records of all his paintings.

Mosseh Senior, his brothers Benjamin and Jacob, and his Hague-based uncle Jacob de Jeuda Senior Henriques were in touch with the literary and artistic currents of the day. Certainly they were familiar with the concept of the rhetoric chamber from two examples in the Amsterdam Sephardic community: Los Floridos (fl. 1685) and Los Sitibondos (fl. 1676–77), formed by Isaac Nunes Belmonte, alias Manuel Baron Belmonte.

The Art Collections of Mordechay and Mosseh Senior

From Mosseh's testament we know that he had a library and an art collection ("Syn Bibliotheecq, en Curiosityten") which he willed to be equally divided among those of his brothers' sons bearing the name of his father, i.e., the name Mordechay. We have begun to trace that collection to see what was in it that might have served as models for the remarkable tombstone designs in his family. We have constructed a genealogy of the Senior/Henriques family, using archives of the Portuguese Jews housed at the Hague and the Amsterdam Municipal Archives, plus records of engagement and burial. Amsterdam has recorded its inhabitants' baptisms, engagements, and burials since the late sixteenth century, to form one of the fullest extant demographic files in Europe, if not the world. Using these we have come to a tentative conclusion about the fate of the library and art collection.

We know of six siblings' sons named Mordechay as well as a son and a grandson of Mosseh's uncle Jacob. Two named Mordechay Senior, with the respective patronymics Jacob and Judah, died in Curaçao in 1756 and 1757. Sons to brothers Selomoh and David of Curaçao died, respectively, in 1711 and 1750. Of sons to sisters Rachel Fundam and Ribca Semach Aboab, Rachel's son died in Curaçao in 1763; Ribca's son died before 1781. A son of Benjamin, Mosseh's universal heir and executor, died in 1766. Benjamin de Mordechay Senior himself died November 23, 1750. Of Benjamin's sons who were circumcised by his brother-in-law Isaac Semach Aboab we have records for Jacob in 1712, Judah in 1718, David in 1719, although none, apparently, for son Mordechay (1707–1766). We know that a Jeuda de Benjamin Senior died April 21, 1782.

We suggest that whatever had been owned separately by the sons named Mordechay eventually reverted to a single universal collector in the family, most likely the son of Mosseh's universal heir. This guess is supported by evidence of an auction in Amsterdam, between November 4 and 9, 1782, of the collection of books, dramatic scripts, musical instruments, paintings, drawings, and prints belonging to the late Juda van Benjamin Senior. The different spellings here of Judah/Jeuda/Juda reflect the diversity in archival spelling. They also signal the caution to be exercised when attempting to stabilize the identity of the owner of the 1782 collection and locate him within the Senior genealogy. On the basis of the richness of the collection, it is likely that Mosseh and his brothers owned or had ready access to all the illustrated publications which served as print sources for the reliefs on his tombstone and those of his family in Curaçao. We plan to analyze the auction catalogue of that art collection in depth in the future.

Of all the brothers, Judah, Mosseh, and Benjamin stayed closest to the arts. The Seniors contributed to the Amsterdam, Curaçao, and Hague synagogues and participated in special prayer honors. But it was Benjamin Senior, living in Amsterdam ("morador a Amsterdam" in David da Fonseca's manuscript report of the planning and inauguration), who gave to the new 1726 Hague Honendel synagogue a cover for the "Teba and Sepher" of green velvet bordered with gold and silver, on June 23, 1726. In February 1725, the sons of widow Ester Senior Henriques (Mosseh's sister, married to his cousin Judah de Jacob [d. 1716]) had donated ornamental cedarwood paneling in her name. The synagogue's construction, in the style of state architect Daniel Marot, was supervised by his student, François Dusart. A portrait bust of Antonio alias Isaac Israel Baron Lopes Suasso I (1614–1685), has been ascribed to Rombout Verhulst (1625–1696), who with a François Dieussart (1600–1661) portrayed many of Europe's nobility. Suasso financed William III's ambitions, both military and political, which finally put him on the English throne. At the Hague, seat of government and center of high society and fashion, a Judah Senior supported new directions in opera and theatre, as did members of the De Liz, Pereira, and Arredondo families.

It was to Judah that Mordechay, in his 1680 will, bequeathed five family portraits: two of Mordechay's parents, and three of his grandparents, one of the latter perhaps a double portrait. These were probably miniatures, following the fashion of the time. They have yet to be located and identified. They would have portrayed Judah/Philippe (1589–1656) and his cousin Ester (b. 1600), whom he married in 1617, daughter of Judah's uncle Garcia/Mordechay. The grandparents would have been Violante Pimentel and Mordechay (Henriques?) of Constantinople; and Garcia Pimentel/Isaac Abeniacar and wife Leonore Gutieres, alias Sarah Lindes. Prudentia Pimentel, alias Abigail Abeniacar, Ester's sister, depended first on Judah and then on his son Mordechay. During a 1621–1623 dispute between the heirs of Manuel Pimentel/Isaac Abeniacar over his 250,000-guilder legacy, Judah was proxy for Abigail and her husband Simao Vaz Silva, alias Jacob da Silva. The couple was then living in Gluckstadt, where Jacob was trying without success to start industries for the processing of soap, oil, and sugar. They returned to the

Netherlands, where Jacob died in 1626. When Abigail died intestate in 1661, her *Dotar* no. 263, of which she was prime possessor, was ceded to Mordohai Abenjacar with Mordechay Senior as one of the witnesses.

In Mosseh's 1728 will he bequeathed his gold snuffbox, engraved with his cypher, to Ester de Jacob Fundam, daughter of Ribca, Mosseh's aunt and wife of Mosseh's brother Judah. To brother Benjamin's wife Rachel, daughter of their uncle Jacob de Judah Henriques, Mosseh bequeathed a gold ring with an emerald and a sack of fine solid gold instruments ("een goud sack kookertje daarin Vyff massive gouwe instrumenten"). To his nineteen-year-old nephew Abraham de Isaac Semach Aboab, son of sister Ribca and mohel Isaac, Mosseh bequeathed a ring with a green emerald and two diamonds. Emerald was the generic term for Brazilian topaz. We know that at the 1712 liquidation of the assets of jeweler Abraham da Fonseca the bookkeeper was an Abraham Semach Aboab (possibly a relative) who owned a group of Hebrew manuscripts, with catalogue, of the works of Haham Saul Levy Morteira. Many of Morteira's works are lavishly decorated with biblical illustrations drawn from printed Bibles by community artists. On such was Judah Machabeu, who returned from Brazil to Amsterdam and among other artistic pursuits from 1650–1661 was forging permits for Dutch trade in the Spanish East Indies. The 1650 Spanish Dutch commercial treaty had freed Dutch ships in Spanish ports from boarding and inspection as long as their certificates, signed by Dutch admiralty college officials, affirmed that no French or Portuguese cargo was aboard.

The Prototypes for the Tombstones of Mosseh and His Family: Isaac Aboab's "Parafrasis" and His Portrait

The title page on which Mosseh's stone is based also governs the composition of the Curaçao stones of his brother David, David's son Ishac Haim, and Ishac Haim's wife Rachel. No doubt the book which it—and its frontispiece—adorned was in Mosseh's collection. (Figure 4: frontispiece; 5: title page; 14: Isaac Haim's stone 15: Rachel's stone; 16: David's stone).

The title-page plate, prepared by etcher Johan van den Aveele, was used by the Amsterdam publisher Jacob Haim ben Moses Raphael de

Stones of Memory

Figure 4: *Mezzotint portrait of Rabbi Isaac Aboab da Fonseca by Aernout Naghtegael, 1686*
Collection of the American Jewish Archives

Cordova e Brazil for the 1681 commentary on the Five Books of Moses written in Castilian by Isaac Aboab da Fonseca (ca. 1605–1693). At the time Aboab was chief rabbi (haham) of the Amsterdam synagogue Talmud Torah, the congregation formed from the 1639 union of Bet Jacob, Bet Israel, and Neve Shalom. The title of the work reads:

Parafrasis Comentado Sobre el pentateuco por el illustrissimo s'(eñor) Ishak aboab H(aham) del K(ahal) K(ados) de amsterdam estampado en caza de Iaacob de Cordova 5441. It translates as: "Commentary paraphrasing the Pentateuch by the illustrious Chief Rabbi of the sacred congregation of Amsterdam printed at the shop of Jacob de Cordova 1681." The etcher's signature at lower left and right reads: "Ioh. vander Avele (in)ventit et fecit"; translated as: "Johan van den Aveele designed and made." Below these are the Hebrew words for "year" and "truth," the latter a chronogram word-play on the date.

In Aveele's etching two fluted pillars enclose the title and continue up past a parapet to terminate as a niche. The pillars rest on a platform with two projecting side sections. On the platform stand two bearded, robed representations of patriarch Isaac: at right he sows, at left he carries the harvest. Below, in the recess between the projections Isaac stands and supervises workers who dig and resurface a well. The Hebrew on the projecting edges comes from Genesis 26:12 referring to Isaac's sowing and harvesting with God's blessing. On the recessed edge the phrase from Genesis 26:18 refers to Isaac's restoration of the wells dug by his father Abraham which the Philistines had stopped up after his death; wells which Isaac called again by the names which Abraham had given them. This is a remarkably apt and dramatic allegorical description, in words and images, of Aboab's mission in Recife, where he served as rabbi from 1642 to 1649. During that period he guided the New Christian Portuguese settlers back to the ancestral faith and supervised the rites and rituals whereby they assumed new identities and new Hebrew names.

Mosseh's father, Mordechay Senior, and his uncle, Jacob Senior, spent their young manhood in Brazil. Mordechay Senior and Jaacob Senior signed the Minute Book (dated 1648–1653) of Congregations Zur Israel of Recife and Magen Abraham of Mauricia, Brazil. Egon and Frieda Wolff made a detailed examination of signatures and paraphs of the names, among others, of Jacob and Mordechay Senior. Paraphs are signature flourishes which are as personal as fingerprints and also at times help guard against forgery. They firmly matched the Minute Book signature of Mordechay Senior with that among those added to the complimentary letter written to Sabbatai Zevi in 1666 by the members of the Amsterdam charitable society Yeshuot Mashiho

("Nobility of the Anointed"). The letter was never sent, as it coincided with delivery of the news of the apostasy of the false messiah. The letter was reproduced in J. S. da Silva Rosa's 1925 history of the Amsterdam Portuguese Jews; in Moses Gans's sumptuous 1971 atlas of Netherlands Jewry, *Memorboek*; and most recently in the 1980 Jerusalem catalogue of the loan exhibition of a selection of manuscripts in the Amsterdam Ets Haim Library.

We have matched the signature of Mordechay Senior (1620–1680) on the letter with the one he used in 1674, signing in as Mordechaj de Jeudah Senior, member no. 396 of the *Dotar*. Mordechaj's *Dotar* paraph, especially the "*j*" descender, is identical with that of 1666, except that in 1674, he added the patronymic "de Jeuda." In 1682, Jacob de Judah Senyor signed into the *Dotar* as no. 409. In public and private papers Jacob de Judah Senior and his offspring regularly used the double surname Senior Henriques. We assume this was Mordechay's brother Jacob (1631–1705) and the uncle of Mosseh and his siblings. On the basis of surname consistency, signature paraphs, and *Dotar*, we have been able to develop a fairly reliable genealogy of the Senior–Senior Henriques family.

The upper-class membership of Yeshuot Mashiho was pious rather than given to diligent Torah study. In their 1666 letter they cite another, sent from Amsterdam's yeshiva Torah Or ("Law is Light"), which praised Haham Isaac Aboab as their revered spiritual leader and example. Mordechay's signature on the 1666 letter suggests the love and esteem he must have felt for the haham. It dated from his days as one of Aboab's congregants in the New World Jerusalem of Dutch, lately Portuguese, Brazil. In Mordechay's family the image of the haham was potent enough to incorporate as a symbolic name portrait on a tombstone. It appears in a niche, in a design based on the Aveele titlepage, at the top of the 1726 Curaçao monument for Mordechay's grandson, David's son Ishac Haim Senior. We have determined that the prototype for the image on Ishac Haim's stone is a 1686 mezzotint of Haham Isaac Aboab da Fonseca. We believe that it was an author portrait, placed as a frontispiece facing the Aveele title page to his 1681 *Parafrasis*. The late Moses Heiman Gans kindly provided the photo of the *Parafrasis* title page, from the volume in his collection, which we here reproduce.

In the Aveele title page, the top register, with parapet and niche, shows images, right to left, of Abraham, Moses and David. It governs the design of the stones for Mosseh and three of his Curaçao kin. Abraham kneels near his tent looking up at the stars and a flood of rays, a landscape in the distance. In the niche Moses holds the tablets of the law inscribed in Hebrew with initial phrases from the Ten Commandments. At left sits a crowned David on an ornate throne playing a harp capped with a genie head, in front of a richly embroidered curtain. Beneath Abraham, on the parapet, are inscribed the first words of Genesis 15:5, referring to God's pact with the patriarch, as in the tombstone relief. Beneath David, as in the relief, is the Hebrew preface to Psalms 38 and 70, alluding to God's faithful servant. Surrounding Moses, on niche and parapet, are Hebrew phrases from Deuteronomy 4:44, 33:4, and Psalms 19:8, referring to his mission as law-giver. This Hebrew differs from that inscribed in the relief, from Genesis 19:19 and the Talmud. It shows that Mosseh made sure that the cutter of the stone followed his inscriptional choices, not what came with the image. The image of Abraham, moreover, differs slightly from what appears in the relief. The actual sculptural model came from the printed source used for most of the reliefs below the top register.

Aveele (b. mid-17th cent., Netherlands, d. 1727, Stockholm) was a lay preacher who later emigrated to Sweden in the service of King Charles XI. He had studied with Romeyn de Hooghe (1645–1708), William III's chief printmaker, two of whose etchings for the 1704 Bible history served as models for Curaçao tombstones. Like his teacher, Aveele produced topographical views and plans of buildings and gardens which were much in vogue in the Netherlands in the late seventeenth century. The Dutch, who had spent so much energy rescuing their land, first from Spanish tyranny and then, with dikes, from the encroachment of the North Sea, took great pride in their landscapes, both urban and rural. In the early 1690s Aveele produced a series of large-scale and detailed images of "Het Schoone Perk van Sorgevliet" (Beautiful Sorgvliet Park), a Hague suburban villa on the route to Scheveningen, owned since 1675 by Lord William Bentinck, who became King William III's closest confidant. Its gardens and sculpture impressed the circle of the princes of Orange. It became a model for other suburban gardens, including those of Hague-based

Sephardim with country retreats along the Vecht and Amstel rivers. Nearby was the Portuguese Jewish cemetery for Jews from the Hague area which opened around 1698, the time they began to gain financial and social access to the refined precincts of the capital city. In 1691 the Sephardic artist Bartolomeus Brandon, who with brother Jan Hendrick entered the Hague artists' "Confreri Pictura" at this time, painted a watercolor frontispiece for just such an album of sculpture-garden views. He was paid for it in 1692 from the account of William Bentinck, privy purse for King William III.

Accounts show that well-to-do Sephardim took pride in sculpture gardens, as artist, owners or visitors. It would seem then that the Dutch Jewish cemetery, known as the House of Life (Bet Haim) was perceived as an extension of the concept of garden: a Garden of Eden.

Because of Jacob de Cordova's connection to the flourishing Amsterdam book publishers' guild he was able to acquire Aveele's etched titlepage. Jacob had apprenticed to both Joseph Athias and David de Castro Tartas and had also worked for Uri Halevy. His father, Moses de Isaac Cordova, a proofreader from Constantinople, arrived in Amsterdam in 1641/42. Jacob's son Isaac Hisquiahu de Cordova Kuzin was inscribed in the publishers' guild after his arrival from Brazil at the end of the seventeenth century. In 1688 Isaac printed the Spanish sermons of Jehosua de Silva, d. 1679, a disciple of Amsterdam rabbis Aboab and Saul Levy Morteira, who served as haham in the London Sephardic synagogue. By 1721 Isaac de Cordova had returned from Hamburg to Amsterdam and was working for Ashkenazim as well as Sephardim.

The "Theatrum Biblicum" and Antwerp Print Ateliers

The remainder of the print prototypes we have matched to Mosseh de Mordechay's stone come from an album of engraved Bible illustrations, which, in its different editions, had as many as 470 images. These were drawn from the Hebrew Bible, the New Testament, and , as a separate section, the Acts of the Apostles. The album is entitled *Theatrum biblicum, hoc est Historiae Sacrae Veteris et Novis Testamenti tabulis aeneis expressae*, issued in Amsterdam by Claes Jansz Visscher in a number of editions beginning in 1614. The 1674 edition we consulted, folio size, with two prints per sheet, comes from the Robert L. Stuart Collection,

Rare Books and Manuscripts Division, The New York Public Library; Astor, Lenox and Tilden Foundation. We gratefully acknowledge the Library's permission to reproduce six engravings from the work.

Many of the *Theatrum* prints were first published together in oblong quarto format under the title *Thesaurus Sacrarum*, by Gerard de Iode, 1585, Antwerp. In the two-volume set in the Spencer collection of the New York Public Library, the 1585 engravings are handcolored, with superscripts in ink by a previous owner. The *Theatrum*, while later in date, is more complete, as it contains images that seem to be missing from certain identical engraved series in the *Thesaurus*. The albums belonged to that class of illustrated religious and classical history found in all homes of the educated European bourgeoisie after the advent of movable type. The most typical was the illustrated Bible, especially popular in Northern Europe, embellished profusely with woodcuts, engravings or etchings by master craftsmen working for the presses of Lyons, Strassburg, Paris, Wittenberg, Frankfurt on Main, Antwerp and Amsterdam. With exotic renderings of ancient locals and costumes, sometimes based on actual report, these miniature print galleries became affordable luxury items of anthropological and spiritual edification. In the top course of Mosseh's stone, the kneeling Abraham is actually derived from the front center figure in an Ascension scene in the *Theatrum*, inscribed "Luke 24:51," in a series designed by Martin de Vos and engraved by Anthony Wierix.

The *Theatrum* engraving of the sleeping Jacob, missing in the *Thesaurus* group, comes from a de Vos design in a four-plate series, here inscribed "Genesis 28:20" (Figure 6). Parts of the engraving were used in the same sense, parts reversed and protracted to fill the elongated space to the left of the epitaph on Mosseh's monument. The image represents, among other persons, Mosseh's brother Jacob, alias Philippe Henriques, whose tombstone at Curaçao is dated November 15, 1718. A similar elongation transforms the *Theatrum* engraving of Selomon and Sheba at the right of the Epitaph (Figure 7). Inscribed "I Kings 10," it is part of a multi-print cycle, probably engraved by Jan Sadeler after a design by de Vos. The stone cutter added the six-stepped throne to fill up the space. The image of the king refers to Mosseh's brother Selomoh, who died in Curaçao November 28, 1758, widower of Ester de Marchena y Carilho, whose 1714 tombstone is part of our discussion.

Figure 6: *Jacob asleep near the ladder of angels, engraving,* Theatrum Biblicum, *Claes Jansz Visscher, 1674, Amsterdam*
Robert L. Stuart Collection, Rare Books and Manuscripts Division, The New York Public Library, Astor, Lenox and Tilden Foundations

Figure 7: *Solomon and Sheba, engraving* , Theatrum Biblicum, *Claes Jansz Visscher, 1674, Amsterdam*
Robert L. Stuart Collection, Rare Books and Manuscripts Division, The New York Public Library, Astor, Lenox and Tilden Foundations

The relief with Rebecca and the servant in the center of the third register of the stone has as prototype a de Vos engraving from the *Theatrum* inscribed "Genesis 24" (Figure 8). The naked river god adorning the fountain is absent; the dolphin flukes fill its space; the remaining entourage around the fountain has been omitted for clarity and dramatic effect. In the bottom register, the figures right and left showing the tribe-brothers Benjamin and Judah, inscribed, respectively "Genesis 49:27" (Figure 9), and "Genesis 49:9" (Figure 10), come from a twelve-plate *Theatrum* set called "The Sons of Jacob," designed by Crispin van den Broeck, engraved by Jan Sadeler. They are further inscribed with Latin distiches by Dutch poet-laureate Joost van Vondel praising them as heroes of religious history worth emulating by the Dutch. In the Mordechay scene a match exists between the porch couple and a detail in the *Theatrum* set of Acts of the Apostles, inscribed "Acts 25:23." It was reproduced in our unpublished 1979 doctoral dissertation, "Sepulchral Monuments of the Jews of Amsterdam in the 17th and 18th Centuries." It shows Paul standing before Agrippa and Berenice (both nominally Hebrew according to New Testament scripture) on their stepped throne, surrounded by an audience. This episode was engraved by Acts publisher Philip Galle after the design of Johan Stradanus.

Figure 8: *Rebecca and Eliezer, engraving,* Theatrum Biblicum, *Claes Jansz Visscher, 1674, Amsterdam*   Robert L. Stuart Collection, Rare Books and Manuscripts Division, The New York Public Library, Astor, Lenox and Tilden Foundations

Figure 9: *Benjamin, engraving,* Theatrum Biblicum, *Claes Jansz Visscher, 1674, Amsterdam*
Robert L. Stuart Collection, Rare Books and Manuscripts Division, The New York Public Library, Astor, Lenox and Tilden Foundations

Felix ante alios fratres ego dicor Iuda;   Non mihi verba pater inuidiosa dedit.
Sed me victorem dixit, fortéq; Leonem.   Hostes qui superes urbus ecce suos.

Figure 10: *Judah, engraving,* Theatrum Biblicum, *Claes Jansz Visscher, 1674, Amsterdam*
Robert L. Stuart Collection, Rare Books and Manuscripts Division, The New York Public Library, Astor, Lenox and Tilden Foundations

Alongside Mosseh's stone at Ouderkerk is that for the "anjos" Abraham and Isaac Raphael, sons of Benjamin Senior, with epitaphic dates of Tisri 3 and 11, 5488/September 16 and 24, 1727. In a more naive sculptural handling Abraham, in long buttoned jacket, boots, and beret, wields a scimitar over Isaac, who kneels in a loincloth on the altar of stacked wood. An angel emerges from clouds at left to stay Abraham's hand. Incense rises from an urn at right, and the ram stands with its horns tangled in the brambles at left. The eighteenth-century Portuguese Jewish community records show that the grave site next to that of Mosseh was reserved for an Isaac Senior. The much later maps by de Castro identify the two graves by the names in the epitaphs. The probable prototype for the boys' stone was the *Theatrum* engraving inscribed "Genesis 22" from a cycle designed by Martin de Vos (Figure 11).

Figure 11: *Abraham's Binding of Isaac, engraving,* Theatrum Biblicum, *Claes Jansz Visscher, 1674, Amsterdam*
Robert L. Stuart Collection, Rare Books and Manuscripts Division, The New York Public Library, Astor, Lenox and Tilden Foundations

The Senior Stones of Curaçao

On Curaçao is the stone for David Senior's son Ishac Haim Senior, dated Nisan 16, 5486/April 17, 1726 (Figure 14). In the central niche at the top is a relief of a bearded man in a skullcap holding a book; he is seated against a background of table, curtain and bookshelves. At bottom is a relief of a deathbed scene. We have discovered that the prototype for the niche relief is a mezzotint portrait of Haham Isaac Aboab, aged eighty-one in 5446/1686, by the artist Aernout Naghtegael (1658/59–after 1719) (Figure 4). It may have been planned as the author-portrait frontispiece for the *Parafrasis* of Aboab (d. II Adar 27, 5453/April 4, 1692) (Figure 5). The mezzotint was probably done from life, in a Dutch tradition of rendering important personages. Another Aboab portrait, posthumous, by the proselyte Abraham bar Jahacob, has much less artistry. Unlike Ashkenazim generally, the acculturated Sephardim were pleased to commission images of still-living hahamim. We have the undated image of Jacob Sasportas, by P. van Gunst and the three portraits of Manasseh ben Israel by Rembrandt, Jan Lievens, and Sephardic artist Salomo Italia. The 1629 engraving of Joseph del Medigo by Willem Duyster after Willem Delff, was a frontispiece to his *Sefer Elim*, Aboab's portrait must have been very popular, as it circulated in two editions, the second of 5449/1689 with the haham's age changed to eighty-four and the substitution of Spanish for the Hebrew inscription on the parapet. Most importantly, it must have commanded sufficient name-recognition power to be appropriate as a model for a symbolic memorial portrait on Isaac Haim's stone. Identical in print and relief are details such as the clerical gown with square-tabbed plain collar, the cloak encircling the shoulders. The symbolic portrait of Isaac Haim, framed by the niche, is a variation on the niche portrait of Mosseh.

The figure of Abraham half-kneeling at right of the niche borrows directly from the Aveele title page, as shown by details of drapery and the position of the legs. However, Abraham in the relief appears to wear a skullcap, which sets him apart from the bareheaded versions in Aveele and in Mosseh's relief. Mosseh chose his image of Abraham not from Aveele but from a detail in the *Theatrum's* "Luke 24:51." The figure of David comes directly from Aveele. His crowned

Figure 5: *Johan van den Aveele's etched title page for Isaac Aboab's* Parafrasis, *printed by Jacob de Cordova, 1681, Amsterdam* Collection of Moses H. Gans

head rests straight on his shoulders as he gazes to the left. In Mosseh's relief his head tilts downward, eyes closed, dreaming to the sacred melody. The crowned parapet in the Aboab mezzotint is replaced in Isaac Haim's stone with a fringed curtain bearing the Portuguese epitaph. On the frame of Ishac Haim's niche and on a horizontal band beneath the curtain are biblical Hebrew phrases.

Because the inscriptions were never published by Emmanuel, who first published the photo of the stone, we have here transcribed and translated the Portuguese and the Hebrew. The Portuguese reads: SEPULTURA/Do Incurtado Virtuozo/e muy Capas Varao Ishac/Haim Senior qui nascer de/Sua Ydade Passou desta/amihor Vida o Segunda dia/de Pessah Sendo 16 de Nissan/do Anno 5486 Avendo/Padezido Infenittos/Martirios na Enfermidad/(Hebrew acronym). Translated as: "Tomb/of the Departed Virtuous and Very Able Gentleman Ishac/Haim Senior who, born of/His Age Passed from This/to a Better Life on the Second Day/of Pessah being 16 Nissan/of the Year 5486, Having Suffered Infinite Martyrdoms of Illness/(Hebrew acronym for Let His Soul be Bound Up in the Garland of Life)." The Hebrew around the niche, reading right to left, translates as: "Look now to heaven" (Genesis 15:5); "a crown of glory shall she deliver to you" (Proverbs 4:9); "to David for remembrance" (Psalms 38:50 and 70:50). The Hebrew below the curtain translates as: "Mine eyes are ever toward the Lord; for He shall pluck my feet out of the net" (Psalms 25:15). It is conceivable that the stone was designed and the motifs were chosen by David Senior. The eloquent epitaph confirms the feelings of a grieving father predeceased by his son. In his 1733 will David repeatedly refers to Ishac Haim as the son whom God has taken.

The tombstone for Isaac Haim's wife Rachel is dated Tamuz 26, 5506/July 14, 1746 (Figure 15). The top register resembles the format of the stones of Mosseh and Ishac Haim. But the side figures of Abraham and David differ in details. Abraham, at right, lacks a tent, but has the moon and stars. His outstretched arms and upturned head complete a spiral dance-like movement rising from his sandaled feet. The body turns partly to the front as though to engage the viewer in the emotion. The David figure is crowned but now in warrior costume. No longer enthroned, he appears to be seated on a rocky ledge. He plays the harp as though taking a break from maneuvers in the wilderness. The banderole between the figures is inscribed in Hebrew "the pillar of Rachel's grave" from Genesis 35:20. The arched niche beneath is inscribed "Sepultura" (grave). Rachel is symbolically portrayed as a shepherdess, partially undraped in a classical chemise and sandals. A hair ribbon flutters in back of her. Staff in her right hand, she guards three sheep. With Isaac she had three sons: David, Abraham and Mordechay. Mordechay, like her husband, predeceased her and died young in 1737. According to Emmanuel, Rachel was the daughter of Abraham de Marchena and Sarah Carilho. She was related to Sarah, wife of David Senior.

David Senior's stone is dated Tishri 1, 5510/September 13, 1749 (Figure 16). The top register resembles the format of the stones of Mosseh, Isaac and Rachel but the figures at the side in the niche are entirely different. In the niche is a winged hourglass; above it is a scallop with a cloud billowing to the left. Both niche elements are post-Renaissance reworkings of classical motifs. The hourglass represents mortality as time's flight; the scallop represents eternal life and was the vessel upon which the goddess of love reached earth's shores from her ocean birthplace. The arching banderole is inscribed in Hebrew "and David's days grew near to death," from I Kings 2:1. At right a young crowned king in flowing cape, short gown and boots sits on a pedestal playing a harp, his face turned to the right. On the left side of the niche is the confrontation between David and Goliath. The young hero looks almost childlike with his softly curled hair, shepherd's jacket and boots, and the huge sling hanging from his right shoulder. He is dwarfed by the helmeted warrior in boots, billowing skirt and chest armor resembling chain mail. Goliath carries a lance in his right hand; the hilt of a sword emerges from behind his left hip, in a sheath slung from his right shoulder.

Born in 1664, David was the longest-lived of all the Senior brothers. Third eldest of Mordechay's sons after Judah and Jacob, he outlived his Curaçao brothers, except for Selomoh. Brother Isaac had died in an epidemic on June 25, 1693, shortly after arriving on the island. Brother Jacob had died in 1718, apparently unmarried. David's son Ishac Haim, with whom he had gone into business, had died in 1727. In the Hague, cousin Judah Senior Henriques (d. 1716) and brother-in-law Abraham Fundam (d. 1717) had left thousands of guilders in unresolved accounts partly connected with Curaçao enterprises. Much of David's 1733 will was concerned with explaining to his surviving sons, Jacob, Abraham, and Mordechay Haim, how to pay off the debts of the company of David Senior and Sons. Some of the accounts were registered in the name of Philippe Henriques, others in the name of Isaac Senior. As Mosseh noted in his 1728 Amsterdam will, David's affairs were hamstrung by legal entanglements (*bodemaryen*). Like his father Mordechay before him, David told his sons to pay off strangers first, so as to keep an honorable name; then pay off relatives. Above all, don't sell property unless forced to by natural catastrophe or war. And in that case let the city houses go but keep the plantations, especially Bloempot (Flowerpot), so beloved by David's late wife Sarah Hana, who died in 1730. In 1715 David owned a warehouse near the waterfront in the name of Philipe Henriquez (Senior). He lived on the same street as the synagogue, in a townhouse about five doors away. His son Ishac Haim had donated the *tebah* for the 1703 synagogue. The Marchena Carilho in-laws had contributed one of the chandeliers to the 1730 synagogue building. In the first decades of the eighteenth century, when he was truly prosperous, David had purchased from the government the plantations Suikertuin and Habaai.

The source of the David imagery is a series of ten engravings from the life of David designed by Martin van Heemskerch and published by Hieronymous Cock, 1555–1559, Antwerp. The image of David with harp comes from the scene where David tries to cool Saul's wrath with music and turns aside to avoid the king's javelin (Figure 18). The engraving is inscribed "I Kings 18," aimed, as it was, for a Christian audience. The episode comes from the Hebrew book of I Samuel 18:10. The scene between David and Goliath comes from the engraving inscribed "I Kings 17" (Figure 17). In reality the episode comes from I Samuel 17:49. The engravings are from the Print Collection of the Miriam and Ira D. Wallach Division of Art, Prints and Photographs of the New York Public Library, Astor, Lenox and Tilden Foundations. We gratefully acknowledge the Library's permission to reproduce them. The main elements from each print are boldly translated into relief on the stone. The relief at left of the niche suppresses the figures, tents and landscape of the Goliath print. A simpler armor

Figure 18: *David before Saul, engraving after Martin van Heemskerch, in "The History of David"*, Hieronymous Cock, 1555-59, Antwerp
Print Collection, Miriam and Ira D. Wallach Division of Art, Prints and Photographs, The New York Public Library, Astor, Lenox and Tilden Foundations

Figure 17: *David and Goliath, engraving after Martin van Heemskerch, in "The History of David"*, Hieronymous Cock, 1555-59, Antwerp
Print Collection, Miriam and Ira D. Wallach Division of Art, Prints and Photographs, The New York Public Library, Astor, Lenox and Tilden Foundations

style replaces the Mannerist intricacies. The lance is now in the right hand. But the hilt of the sword still emerges menacingly at the hip. The relief of David as a shepherd omits his lance but retains the sling, boots, and the flutter of his garment. And it carries all the bravado of the original: the young hero still strides boldly out; still thrusts his left arm forward in challenge to the giant. The relief on the right side of the niche selects only the image of David with harp from the Saul print. In the engraving, David stands as he turns away from the king's anger. The relief retains the twist of his body and grasp of the harp. But it transfers the serpent head from Goliath's sword hilt to the harp. And the addition of a crown and a simple throne has transformed the now-seated youth into a confident young king.

The tombstone for Ester (de Marchena y Carilho) Senior is dated Kislev 27, 5475/December 4, 1714 (Figure 12). Ester was the wife of Selomoh, who died November 28, 1758. David does not mention brother Selomoh in his will. Selomoh's sorrows included, besides the early death of his wife, the death of his son Mordechay in 1711. Selomoh took his son's place in the Amsterdam *Dotar* as no. 493, which Mordechay had inaugurated and held for only about half a year. In 1740 the *Dotar* went to Mordechay's son David. Selomoh, who outlived David by nine years, appeared in lists of shipowners in 1738, 1740, 1746, 1748. After 1748 the name Senior in independent capacity appears to have vanished from Curaçao's maritime records.

Illustrated Bibles from Lyons

The relief on the stone for Ester comes from Esther 8:3–4, wherein the young queen reveals her Jewish identity to the king and begs him to set aside Haman's decree of destruction to her people: ". . . and Esther fell down at his feet and wept, begging him to set aside Haman's cruelty. . . . then the king held out the golden scepter toward Esther. So Esther arose."

The relief is almost a line-for-line copy of a woodcut by Pierre Eskrich (also called Pierre du Vase), which appeared first in 1562, and again in 1581 in the *Biblia Sacra* published in Lyons by, respectively, Phillipe and Guilleaume Roville (Figure 13). It is one of two illustrated Lyons Bibles which served as print sources furthest removed in

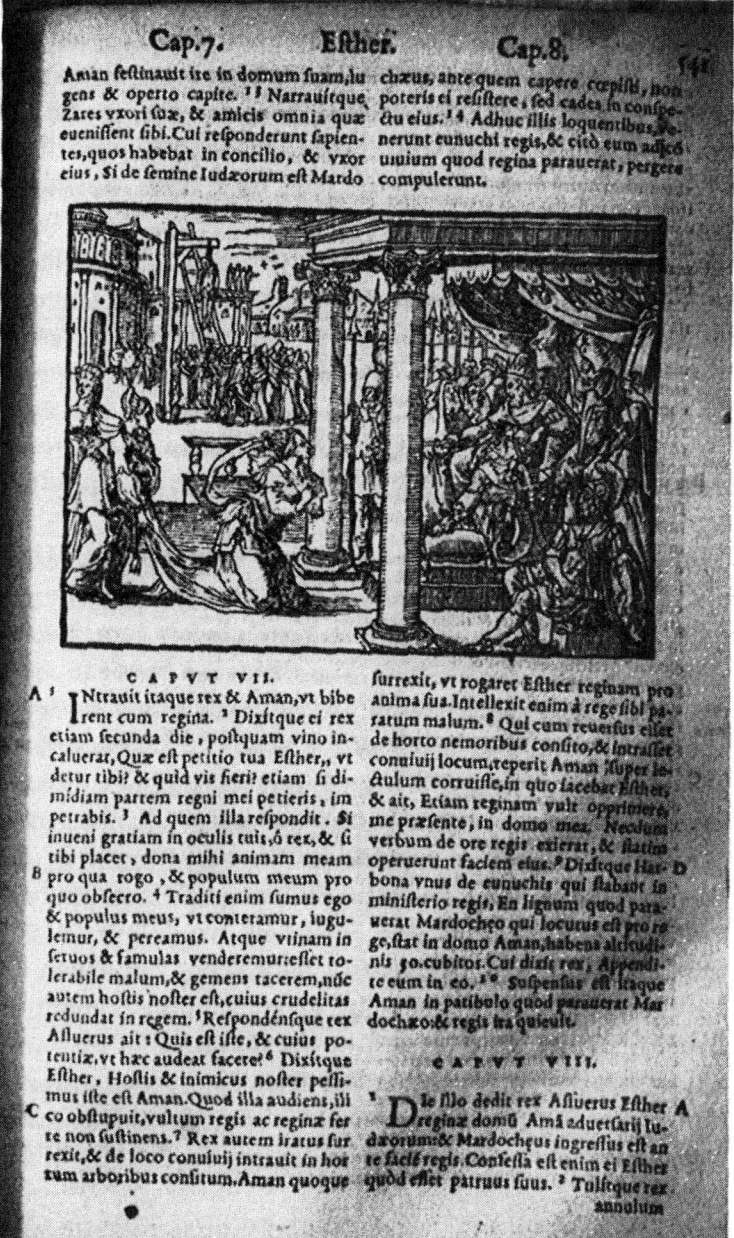

Figure 13: *Esther before Ahasuerus*, woodcut by Pierre Eskrich, Biblia Sacra, Guillaume Roville, 1581, Lyon
Rare Books and Manuscripts Division, The New York Public Library, Astor, Lenox and Tilden Foundations

time from the seventeenth- and eighteenth-century tombstone reliefs we have studied. The delicate French woodcuts were copied for two centuries in Bibles all over Europe. The images emerged in applications ranging from embroidery, to furniture carving, to stucco wall decoration. A similar Esther scene ornaments the title page of a book of biblical poetry by the Sephardic poet Juan, alias Mosseh, Pinto Delgado, who died in Amsterdam on December 23, 1653. His *Poema de la Reyna Ester*, dedicated to Cardinal Richelieu, was published by David du Petit Val, 1627, Rouen. The Rouen image was copied from a woodcut by Bernard Salomon for *La Sainte Bible*, first issued by Jean de Tournes, 1553, Lyons. We consulted the 1581 copy of the Roville *Biblia Sacra* in the Rare Books and Manuscript Division; The New York Public Library; Astor, Lenox and Tilden Foundations. We gratefully acknowledge the Library's permission to reproduce the woodcut.

In both relief and print King Ahasuerus sits back languidly on a canopied throne, his feet on a pillow. With his right hand he stretches out his scepter toward Esther, who kneels before him. Two maids attend her; one holds up her train. She clasps her hands in supplication. Surrounding the king within his columned porch are his attendant soldiers and advisers. Four of the hooded advisers and two of the soldiers, one standing with a spear and one sitting at lower right with sword and shield, appear in identical poses in print and relief. In the upper left the relief reproduces the round tower with high doorway and the building behind with high gable seen in the print. The relief omits everything else, including the gallows. Instead it substitutes, behind the building, two tall towers. The oblong frame of the woodcut becomes, in the relief, an arched proscenium to frame the dramatic scene. Plays based on the Book of Esther had long enjoyed popularity in the Dutch Republic. The 1714 Curaçao relief for Ester Senior found its complement in the Mordechay relief sixteen years later on the tombstone of her brother in law Mosseh at Ouderkerk.

Emmanuel published the relief detail of Ester's tombstone but he never transcribed or translated the Portuguese epitaph below it or the Hebrew inscribed in the frame around it. We take the opportunity to do so here. The Portuguese is on a fringed curtain below the framed relief. On either side hang clusters of fruit and flowers, a *vanitas* device alluding to mortality. Three winged genie heads, also mortality symbols, nestle amidst two more swags of vegetation at the top. The Portuguese reads: SEPULTURA/Da yncurtada dona/Ester muller que foy/De Selomoh Senyor/Faleceo em 27 de Kisleu/Do anno 5475/S(ua) A(lma) G(oze) d(a) G(loria). It translates as: "Grave of the departed lady/Ester who was wife to/Selomoh Senyor/who died on Kislev 27/Of the year 5475 (Let her soul drink of glory)." Leaf fronds as mortality devices fill the two top corners around the relief. On the arch is a conflation of passages from Esther 2:15 and Jacob's dream episode in Genesis 28:11: ". . . found grace . . . and lay down to sleep and dreamed." Below is a conflation of a phrase from Esther 2:8 and a paraphrase from 8:5: ". . . and Esther was brought to the king's house . . . and nullified the decree."

The Amsterdam-Hague-London-Hamburg Orbit

Romeyn de Hooghe's 1704 etchings served as models for two Curaçao stones. His student Aveele produced a title page dated 1681 which influenced the design of five more, there and at Ouderkerk. De Hooghe had earlier completed a cycle of etchings for the Sephardic publisher David de Castro Tartas. They graced a collection of sermons and addresses by community scholars celebrating the 1675 inauguration of the new Portuguese synagogue of Amsterdam. Besides various views of the new Sephardic building, he depicted the new 1671 structure housing the Hoogduits, or German Jewish, congregation across the way on Houtgracht plaza (site of the present Amsterdam Jewish Museum on Jacob Meijerplein), rituals of the Portuguese Jews, and Amsterdam townhouses of three prominent Sephardim. The homes were those of: David de Pinto, Breestreet, later called Jodenbreestraat (restored and now a public library); Manuel Baron Belmonte, alias Isaac Nunes Belmonte, on Herengracht (Gentlemen's Avenue, now no. 586); and Jeronimo Nunes d'Acosta, alias Moses Curiel, on what is now Nieuwe Herengracht 49 (restored as the site of the present municipal waterworks administration). Da Costa/Curiel was, with Belmonte, the Jewish community representative to the Hague government. He was also consul in the Netherlands for the king of Portugal with power of attorney for the deputies of the Portuguese Brazilian Company.

The Nieuwe Herengracht was an extension of the original avenue in the section newly laid out southeast of the central city. Da Costa/Curiel lived on the same street as Judah de Jacob Senior, who also lived in the Hague. Judah owned two houses facing what had been the Academy Tuin, Botanical Gardens for growing herbs and other medicinals used by the medical profession. To enter the Gardens one had to present a token, for which one paid annual dues after passing a license exam; it was similar to the medallion of the craft guilds. It is likely that the Semach Aboab relatives were members. In 1711 Judah Senior Henriques of the Hague gave his Amsterdam-based brother, Moses de Jacob Senior Henriques, proxy to mortgage the properties as pro forma security on his promise to deliver rye he owed the City of Amsterdam and its private investors. He also mortgaged his two houses on the southeastern side of Nieuwe Amstelstraat, a street parallel to and northwest of Nieuwe Herengracht. Cousin Mosseh de Mordechay Senior lived nearby in the house of Benjamin Senior, on Weesperstraat off Nieuwe Keisersgracht. Weesperstraat is a cross-street between Nieuwe Keisersgracht on the southeast and Nieuwe Herengracht on the northwest.

Judah Senior Henriques (d. 1716) was the son of Mordechay Senior's brother Jacob de Jeuda Senior Henriques. On November 19, 1695, a Jeuda Senior Henriques signed a certificate of noninheritable rights of citizenship (*poorterscedul*). It was likely he who participated in a 1698 contract to deliver forage for the company Machado and Pereira, provisioners (*Providoors*) in King William III's service. In 1730 Judah's heirs were still liable to the state for outstanding debts. Judah (de Mordechay) Senior and sister Ester, widow of Judah Senior Henriques, were co-executors of his will. In 1718–1719 they had to sign numerous papers on behalf of the late Judah, who was described as an Amsterdam merchant with considerable business negotiations and who had left many accounts open at his death. In order "to avoid shame and difficulties to families" some agreements required the signatures of Judah Senior Henriques' two London-based sons Jacob and Judah (*sic*). Included in these agreements was Mosseh's sister Rachel, then in London to attend to the affairs of her late husband Abraham de Jacob Fundam, partner of the late Judah. Jacob Fundam had been a comrade from the days he, the brothers Mordechay and Jacob de Jeuda Senior, and their father Judah Senior/Philippe Henriques managed Brazilian sugar. Fundam's children intermarried with Seniors first in Amsterdam and then in Curaçao, completing the cycle of return to the New World.

In 1704 the company of Moses Senior Henriques and Company, together with brothers and brothers-in-law at home and abroad, imported cocoa, cotton, pepper, sapon wood, snuff tobacco and Varinas tobacco. We know this from records of the Amsterdam Chamber of the West India Company, the 1728 will of Mosseh, and the 1733 will of David. Mosseh stored diverse merchandise in a warehouse on Swanenburgerstraat, and tobacco in a shed on the Breestraat under the aegis of Semach and Lopes. Mosseh's uncle, David Lopes Henriques, was brother to: (1) Mosseh's mother Sarah, who had married Mordechay Senior in 1658; (2) Ester, who married Mosseh's uncle Jacob de Judah Senior the same date; and (3) Ribca Lopes Henriques, who in 1668 married Dr. Daniel Semach Aboab.

David Lopes Henriques' wife Abigail was the daughter of Isaac Rodigues Isidro, alias Isaac Baruch. Isaac was the nephew and business associate of the wealthy Hamburg-based Manuel Isidro, alias Manuel Dirksen, alias Jacob Baruch, who handled Portuguese Moroccan trade after the 1640 restoration at a time when this enterprise was closed to the Dutch. Manuel (d. 1666) and son Jacob the younger spent time in Madrid and Cadiz. From the latter city in 1668 Jacob sold their Hamburg house on Walstrasse to cousin Isaac. For a Sephardic Jew to own property in the city of Hamburg at that time betokened a great deal of wealth. As a young man Isaac tended to stretch the rules by which the Hamburg Jewish community operated; his uncle interceded for him regarding fines and demerits. In 1666 he got a sharp reprimand from the governing board for upsetting his family by traveling to Lubeck for two weeks in the company of non-Jews. In 1670 Isaac was recorded as a new settler in Gluckstadt. In 1674, when Isaac's daughter signed the marriage bans with David Lopes Henriques, David's mother Rachel attended. Abigail was identified as from Seville, and it was her grandmother who attended her.

In the 1674 Amsterdam tax assessment on the 200th penny, David Lopes Henriques was recorded as living in the city with his mother and two brothers, not named. No mention was made of his three sisters who had already married. The 1668 Amsterdam marriage bans for sister Ribca and Dr. Semach Aboab note her living on Batavierstraat. This was about half an hour's walk south to the synagogue area, Vlooienburg, where David's mother lived, and the Nieuwe Herengracht. Daniel Levy de Barrios' 1683 saga of the Portuguese Jewish community of Amsterdam, "Triumpho del govierno popular," notes that members of the charitable society Aby Yetomim that year included Jacob de Juda Senior and deceased legatees Jacob Lopes Henriques and Raquel Lopes Henriques. Jacob Lopes Henriques may have been David's father although David entered the *Dotar* on his own in 1675, as no. 367, right after Mordechay Senior's 396. In 1716 David's son Jacob inherited his place in the *Dotar*.

One of David's brothers may have been Selomo de Jacob Lopes Henriques, who in 1678 married Sara de Moses Gabay Henriques. She was the sister of Ester, who married Daniel de la Penha, later president of the Rotterdam Portuguese congregation. The figured de la Penha tombstones of Ester (d. 1697) and Daniel (d. 1717) are as beautiful as those of Mosseh Senior and his family. Widower Selomo remarried in 1689 to Rebecca Henriques Faro, branches of whose family settled in Curaçao and Hamburg. A Moses Lopes Henriques based in Curaçao may have been David's other brother.

The Curaçao Connection:
Jacob Senior and the Inquisition at Cartagena

Manuel Belmonte, with David and Jacob Senior among others in lesser capacities, was a silent partner in the Koeymans 1685–1689 Curaçao assiento. Earlier and afterward he managed the fortunes of the Dutch state especially in its maritime negotiations with Spain. Apart from trade agreements he secured Dutch aid to Spain, the erstwhile oppressor, now an ally against the common enemy, France. Belmonte was considered so important in these matters that, as count palatine and resident of the king of Spain in the Netherlands, he was given a place of honor in the 1677 funeral cortege for battle hero Admiral Michiel de Ruyter. He had successfully lobbied to obtain a dukedom for de Ruyter from the Spanish crown. Unfortunately it was posthumous, as the admiral had died on April 29, 1676, in the battle of Syracuse, the month the title was conferred. Belmonte was placed not with the official leaders of the Sephardic Jewish community, or even with other consuls, such as those of Spain and Genoa, but farther ahead, with the commissioner of the crown of Denmark and the immediate de Ruyter family members. The royal pomp and circumstance of the procession in Amsterdam's Dam Square, with horses, equerries, trumpets, banners, an honor guard, and scores of diplomats, scholars and community leaders, was commemorated in a contemporary print of the event by Daniel Stopendael, the same artist who made engravings of Amsterdam country homes along the river Vecht, including those of prominent Sephardim.

The stones are our visual, metaphorical connection to a group of people whose skills and motivations, conditioned in part by their religion and national origin, brought them into the center of history at a critical moment. These monuments were not aberrations and not marginal to Judaism at the time and the place in which they were commissioned. They were very fitting monuments; in the world system of that time the families who commissioned them might have been invented had they not already existed. Their financial, linguistic and diplomatic skills, and their family and business networks in an evolving global economy, made them welcome in the developing maritime capitals of Venice, Constantinople, London, Hamburg and Amsterdam. Political and religious despotism, which forced them to leave their earliest European homeland, Roman Catholic Spain and Portugal, confirmed their adherence to Judaism. It also gave them an advantage as agents of countries competing with Spanish imperial ambitions. Their widespread business and kinship associations nurtured Dutch fortunes as long as Spain remained an economic threat and before England assumed maritime dominance in the mid-eighteenth century.

By examining situations selected from 150 years of Senior history, and by placing them within a known general historical framework, we can begin to form a collective biography of a family. This is a theoretical construct, subject to later refinements and revisions. Documents presently available have permitted us to see exactly how particular family members responded to events. They offer glimpses of how they perceived themselves and what they did. When we review personal wills, deeds and reports, and read beyond the formulas of seventeenth- and eighteenth-century officialese, we are able to hear the particular voices and temperaments of various members of the family. We get to know who and what they cherished, desired, feared, honored, dismissed or held in contempt. This documented self-awareness and the sense of the moment and meaning of an act carries over into their choice of Jewish gravestones. The monuments should be compared to those of other public figures in Dutch history who took the greatest risks due to their historical situation and achieved the greatest measures of success and glory.

The greatest risk-taker in the family Senior was Jacob Senior, alias Philippe Henriques. He was the Curaçao factor for the Portuguese Royal African Company and commander of a fleet of brigantines and galliots that plied Spanish trade routes. Relatively poor in arable land, Curaçao had the best harbor in the Western Hemisphere. In 1675 Curaçao was recognized by as a free port and hub by all participants in the Spanish/Portuguese slave assiento in the New World. The assiento had become an instrument of international diplomacy. It had begun as a joint asset during Spain's annexation of Portugal, 1580–1640. Afterward, as their bankruptcy increased, the two countries competed in assigning the assiento to the highest bidder at international peace conferences. To obtain this exclusionary trade agreement was equivalent to signing a treaty of alliance. The contract went from the Genoese in 1660 to the Dutch in 1661. At first the Dutch were guaranteurs for the Genoese, but by the 1670s the Dutch West India Company took over active management. The West India Company subcontracted to Denmark, Sweden, Brandenburg and England. The French won it as part of a settlement with Spain in 1696 but lacking the necessary finances, ceded it to the English in 1713. The English South Sea Company managed it until its suspension and cancellation, 1739–1748, during Anglo-Spanish hostilities. By that time foreign penetration into the Spanish Empire, encouraged by the assiento, had weakened the contract's effect as Spain's bargaining chip.

Loopholes permitted unofficial (or silent) participation in one or another country's assiento. The Amsterdam Chamber of the West India Company nominally controlled the Dutch assiento, with a factor and associates in the home country serving as a form of checks and balances to a factor and associates on the island. In reality the factors received direct orders from the States General, effectively from the stadholder, bypassing West India Company supervision although they were required to make reports to it. Curaçao was also the depot for transport of manufactured goods or home country items to colonists: merchandise, or "cargacoims," as described in David Senior's will. These were traded for New World goods and reached Europe on the return voyage, with stops in both directions at all ports sharing in the contract. Certificates of control signed by the cooperating countries' admiralty boards attested to the legality of the ship's lading. This was to assure that no contraband was aboard which might be illegally delivered to ports of countries with which the partner countries were at war. This was a typical measure in the first half of the seventeenth century when Spain embargoed all Portuguese ports. In practice there was much contraband trade. It flourished by means of forged certificates and collusion with business partners operating under aliases in countries outwardly hostile to each other. New Christian agents in Portugal especially benefitted from their associations with Sephardic relatives in the Netherlands and Hamburg.

On May 22, 1699, Jacob set sail in command of a fleet of ships ferrying merchandise and slaves from Curaçao to his long-time patron Don Gaspar de Andrade, factor general of the Portuguese assiento based in Cartagena. It was also the seat of the Holy Tribunal of the Inquisiton in the Spanish dependencies. In spring 1697 the city and environs had been sacked by the French. After this attack the tribunal went into a decline from which it never recovered . The seat also became a base from which French religionists, including Franciscan Capuchins, sent out missions. Discovery of embarrassing misdemeanors among ranking members of the Spanish civic and religious personnel caused rapid turnovers and shifts in leadership, coupled with xenophobia and paranoia. On June 7 Jacob learned that Governor Don Diego de los Rios y Quizada and his entourage had been relieved of their posts and replaced by Don Juan Dias Pimiento and staff.

Jacob reached port on June 10, hoping to recover heavy debts from the king of Spain incurred to his company by the former governor. Spanish royal officials arrived to transfer the cargo of slaves and merchandise to Portuguese vessels and bring them to land. Jacob himself remained in the harbor awaiting permission to land from the lord inquisitor. Friends showed up, surprised at the delay. Midday, June 15, a canoe of twelve soldiers and some civilians approached his ship. Several soldiers, armed, sprang aboard asking for Captain Philippo Henriques. Jacob, incognito, told them they were on the brigantine of Philippo Henriques, that the captain was in town but would return soon, and asked what they wanted. They insisted on delivering the message personally to Henriques and returned to their canoe. Shortly afterward Jacob, in captain's uniform, announced himself as Henriques and asked what they wanted. A man of sixty or seventy appeared who told him he was under arrest and was to be brought by armed guard to the prison of the Holy Inquisition. They ignored his protests that he was a Netherlands citizen not subject to the Inquisition. Jacob/Philippo then instructed his crew to relay this news to Governor Bastiaan Bernagie of Curaçao and to his friends there, and he was led away.

In Jacob's August 21, 1700, report to the West India Company, requested by Curaçao Governor Nicolaas van Beck, he described his seventy-three day ordeal of imprisonment. We have consulted the copy of the report stored at the Hague Royal Library as Hamelberg Collection no. 120-B-10:XVI-E. For the first two months he was kept ignorant of the nature of his crimes while he suffered from a fever and from daily audiences with the inquisitor, Don Juan de la Isaca Alvarado. To his interrogator he pointed out that he was a Jew, born in the Netherlands, who served his country, the States General of the United Netherlands. Additionally, in the last war with France he had served as a captain under the command of the former stadholder, now king of Great Britain. As he gave daily depositions, which a secretary copied down for him to sign, he repeatedly asked to be told the nature of his crimes and to be confronted by his accusers so that he might respond and acquit himself. He also pointed out that in the days of Governor Don Martin de Gomez de Cavallo y La Cerna, he had been received cordially by the former inquisitor, Don Gomez de Figueroa. To all this Alvarado would repeat that he'd find out everything soon enough, after which Jacob would be marched back to his cell and locked in for the night. Jacob was put in the care of an Augustin padre, Fray Lucas de St. Joseph, who tried to convert him so as to save his soul and mitigate the eventual judgment. He failed in his efforts but visited almost daily with Latin scriptural texts, which Jacob could not read, to discuss the nature of salvation and faith. Concerned about the illness, he obtained a doctor known to Jacob, although not much could be done to ease him. Despite the padre's repeated assurances that things would turn out well, Jacob continued to languish from fever and anxiety. Among other things he worried about the fate of his commanderless crew and fleet, and his financial obligations.

Not until August 13 was Jacob confronted by his accuser, the former secretary and acting *fiscael* of the Inquisition, Captain General Don Miguel de Icharri y Daois. He was the man who had originally captured him. In the trial deposition Jacob/Philippo was accused of: (1) trafficking in the West Indies in a trade where no Jews were allowed on order of the king of Spain; (2) doing this knowing the rules against it; (3) publicly slaughtering and koshering animals; (4) forcing the crew and passengers to eat meat he or a servant had slaughtered; (5) trying to convert his crew and passengers to Judaism by leading them in Hebrew prayers. His responses to the five accusations give some idea of his attitude toward the whole business. He pointed out that: (1) for eleven or twelve years he had been navigating these waters on behalf of the Portuguese sovereign; (2) he never knew the assiento was restricted to Roman Catholics; (3) he would never slaughter animals even if permitted because he would have it done by someone who knew the koshering laws; (4) as commander of a vessel which was like a home to him he would not dishonor anyone aboard with the indignity of making them eat or behave in any other manner by force; (5) it would be difficult for the crew and passengers to be converted if they couldn't understand Hebrew prayers. Moreover, he noted, it was not likely that he was recognized as a Jew because he did not engage in any outward display of the religion in which he was brought up. And in any case he would not merit the trust he had enjoyed from colleagues all these years if he had engaged in the appalling behavior of which he was accused. To the five accusations the *fiscael* added new ones at the last minute, provided by unnamed witnesses, about Jacob's attempts to convert others to Judaism and he asked what he had to answer. Jacob retorted that the whole business was a "bagatelle" not worth dignifying with a reply and that all further questions should be referred to his attorney. The real purpose of the investigation and threats was to discover who his Curaçao investor friends were, who was in his debt and how much was owed him. In fact the king of Spain was his greatest debtor, for 5,000 pesos spent on arms and ammunition. But Jacob had learned soon after his arrival that the present governor was not liable for the debts incurred during a previous administration and that he would have to settle matters directly with the former governor.

His judge was the inquisitor who had interrogated him all summer. His lawyer was the Spanish padre who had daily looked after him. On August 27 the record of the trial and judgment were presented to him in duplicate copies which he had to sign. After he received the judgment, a fine of fifty pieces of eight, he was warned to desist from sailing in the area again or risk a fine of 2,000 pieces of eight and imprisonment in a dungeon for two years. Upon his release Jacob was met with a carriage and taken to the cloister of San Diego to recover. All his papers and personal belongings which were with him in his cell were brought to the cloister. There he was greeted by confidants whom he had known and done business with in the past. Especially upset by news of his experience was Governor Pimiento, who promised to do all in his power to help him, putting his house and domains at his service. On August 28 Jacob received from the inquisitional secretary all of his identification papers. He also received, for signature, a bill for the fine plus a separate bill for 335 pieces of eight and 8 reales, the cost of food and shelter during his imprisonment. Thirteen pieces of eight and 8 reales were deducted from the bill, being the money Jacob had on him when he was arrested. At the end of his report to the West India Company Jacob wrote that he thanked God he was free of the Inquisition and was chiefly concerned that he could carry out the contract that had been delegated to him by Governor Bernagie and his investor friends in Curaçao. He continued sailing the Spanish Main for Portugal, England and his own country, the Netherlands, until 1711. Outraged at the shabby treatment he had received at the hands of the Inquisition he took the opportunity in 1704 of smuggling to Curaçao a Capuchin friar, Victor de Dôle. The Frenchman was a member of the Franciscan opposition to the Spanish in the competition for Roman Catholic souls. Jacob died November 15, 1718, and was buried with his people in the Jewish cemetery on Curaçao.

Curaçao may have shaped the Senior family's destiny more than any other geographical and economic sphere in which they moved. It was the Dutch stronghold in the New World after the loss of Brazil and New Netherlands. As a colony chartered under the auspices of the Amsterdam chamber of the West India Company, Curaçao was permitted, even encouraged, to evolve in response to local conditions with greater independence than any other Dutch possession. The West India Company had reorganized in 1674 with a director general normally administering Curaçao (and New Netherlands until the English conquest) in the name of the central government at the Hague. The director/governor transmitted procedures designed by the company's board of Ten Gentlemen (*Heeren X*) in direct conferral with the stadholder's executive office. The States General at the Hague gave advice and consent. But West India Company directors, who rotated duties every four years, were more like monitors and reporters of local conditions than strong enforcers of conduct. It was hard to impose a system of economic, political and social conformity and obedience such as had operated so successfully in the territories of the East India Company. The New World was filled with too many competing political entities. The colonists in each national territory were not necessarily bound by ties of loyalty to their home country. The New World was rich in opportunity but also in danger. Piracy on the high seas and attacks on colonies became the way one nation might take revenge for the loss of a battle or negotiating point in Europe. The original West India Company, chartered soon after Curaçao was captured from Spain in 1634, had a poor economic and defense strategy for the island. This ended in its bankruptcy and loss of faith in it by the settlers. The new 1674 West India Company delegated economic and political power to the island council. The Seniors were leading participants in Curaçao self-government. They were members of the ruling class, like the patricians in the home country. Moreover, because of their strategic geographical placement they were in a unique and unparalled position to help shape Dutch fortunes both politically and economically throughout the world during the century of the Republic's greatest growth.

Because of his diplomatic and linguistic skills and the fact that he had an economic investment there, David Senior was sent to Coro in 1722 as a personal representative of Curaçao's governor, Jan Noach Du Fay. His mission was to claim reparations for a galliot stranded off the coast of Venezuela while fleeing pirates. He succeeded. It was also David who lobbied in 1726 in the town council against a special surtax to be levied on goods from Spain received by residents, which meant Sephardic merchants. Money for extra fortifications and for a hospital was being raised, in the wake of recent French piracy. Certain anti-Semitic members of the government resented the fact that citizens so connected with the recent Spanish enemy should benefit from civic protection. They claimed that the Jews were responsible for Curaçao's vulnerability. In these and in public and private forums David was an outspoken and fervent defender of his faith. It explains why the Hebrew epitaph to David Senior, by David Franco Mendes, includes the phrase: "and the governor heeded his counsel."

The members of the Senior family effectively, sometimes dramatically, found appropriate outlets for their skills in a dynamic, evolving early modern European world. Their contributions to Jewish life are documented in every city in which they lived during the century and a half of their greatest energy. The high point of their collective visibility and success coincides with that of the Netherlands in the seventeenth and eighteenth centuries. Nowhere else at that time could Jews participate in the world and believe in the future with the zest and confidence that should be considered a human birthright.

In this way Mosseh in Amsterdam and his brothers in the Hague and Curaçao affirmed permanent ties to Judaism. Their stones of memory still speak to us today. They recall for us, after more than three centuries, a dynasty spanning the European continent past the Mediterranean, and reaching across the Atlantic to the new worlds in the Americas.

End Note

Data for this discussion were in part derived from published and unpublished material cited in footnotes and bibliography in my 1979 New York University doctoral dissertation, "Sepulchral Monuments of the Jews of Amsterdam in the 17th and 18th Centuries," now being revised for publication. Further data, including the Senior genealogy, were obtained from the following agencies and persons: Released time and funding: from a 1982 National Endowment for the Humanities Post-Doctoral Summer Grant; a 1982 fellowship from the Memorial Foundation for Jewish Culture; a 1983–1984 City University of New York Faculty Research Award; a 1985–1986 City University of New York Sabbatical and Scholar Incentive Award. Gracious guidance in examining and securing copies of data at Amsterdam's Municipal Archives came from Hans Ernst, S. A. C. Dudok van Heel, and Odette Vlessing. At Amsterdam University's Rosenthaliana Library expert assistance came from Chief Librarian Dr. A. K. Offenberg and Dr. F. J. Hoogewoud. At Amsterdam's Jewish Museum help and hospitality came from the curator, Dr. Rabbi Edward van Voolen. Coaching in translations came from Wim Heijnen of Amsterdam, who is completing a study of the Sephardic Palache family. At Ouderkerk cemetery, beginning in 1971, help came from late Secretary Emeritus of the Portuguese Jewish Community L. A. Vega, and in summer 1988 from Rabbi and Mrs. H. Rodrigues Pereira. In Hamburg Professor Dr. Peter Freimark, Director of the Institute for the History of German Jewry, provided extraordinary personal and professional support and encouragement, as did Dr. Ina Lorenz and Günter Marwedel. Hamburg Municipal Archivest Jurgen Sielemann provided guidance in examining and securing copies of data. At the New York Public Library Dr. Roberta Waddel exemplified the fine help given by the Special Collections staff. At the Hebrew Union College–Jewish Institute of Religion, Chief Librarian Dr. Philip Miller and staff provided the same, plus guidance in Hebrew arcana. Dr. Herman Prins Salomon, Professor of Romance Languages at the State University of New York, Albany, shared his inventory of Sephardic arcana and imagery. Mary Joyce A. Hardey of the Royal Netherlands Embassy, Washington, D.C., made, for comparison purposes, recent photos of many of the sculptured tombstones of Curaçao.

Portuguese Sephardim in the Americas
Malcolm H. Stern

Recife

The year was 1654. For twenty-four years the Dutch had held the bulge of Brazil that extends into the Atlantic Ocean, the province of Pernambuco, with Recife as its capital. Jews from Holland arrived in ever-growing numbers to join New Christians from Portuguese Brazil who had converted to their ancestral faith. Eventually two congregations were formed, Zur Israel in the island city of Recife, and Magen Abraham on the mainland at Mauricia. By 1641 they had imported from Amsterdam Rabbi Isaac Aboab da Fonseca and the haham (scholar) Moses Rafael de Aguilar, and public Jewish worship was held for the first time in the New World. Synagogues were built as the community grew and flourished.

In 1645, however, the Portuguese began a guerilla campaign that ultimately spelled the end of Dutch dominion. Four years later, the colony was besieged. For five years the Dutch held out despite starvation and lack of ships and supplies from the homeland. By 1654, when the Dutch surrendered to the Portuguese, the Jewish population, which had peaked at about 1,450 in 1645, had diminished to about 600.

The Portuguese commander, Barreto, agreed to give Dutch citizens the right to emigrate within three months. Despite a paucity of available ships, every professing Jew left. The majority seem to have gone to Amsterdam, whence some of them returned to the New World. Others had already been trading in the Guianas and the Caribbean and found their way to new homes in these areas.[1]

Caribbean Jewry

The Spanish settlements in Mexico and Peru had attracted many Portuguese New Christians, no small number of whom were accused by the Inquisition of judaizing. Of the islands discovered by Columbus, only the larger ones were under Spanish rule in 1654: Cuba, Hispaniola (later subdivided as Santo Domingo and Haiti), Puerto Rico, Jamaica, Trinidad, and Tobago. The Spanish rulers sought gold or other mineral wealth and abandoned the smaller islands to be fought over by Holland, England, France, and Denmark, which made them bases from which to prey on Spanish shipping carrying the wealth of mainland America.

Sephardic communities soon came to be established in many parts of the Caribbean. Since refugees leave few records, it is difficult to document the arrival of the first Jews in any locality. The existence of laws forbidding Jews to live in a place cannot be taken as evidence that there were none there, for Jewish survival has always required ignoring or bending man-made laws, and living as a Jew meant taking risks. Thus, although Jews were prohibited from settling in England before 1655 and in most of France after 1390, secret Jewish communities existed in both countries; in the same manner, refugees from Dutch Brazil undoubtedly found homes in the island provinces before their presence was officially countenanced. While individual Jews can be found on almost every island of the Caribbean prior to the abandonment of slavery in the mid-nineteenth century, here we shall describe only those areas where congregations were organized and synagogues built.[2]

Surinam

The legend of El Dorado, a city of gold purported to be in the hinterland of the Guianas, led to futile explorations by Sir Walter Raleigh and other sixteenth-century adventurers. The discovery of well-watered, tropical coastland brought settlers and inevitable fighting among the English, French, and Dutch that eventuated in the formation of three Guianas, one belonging to each nation.

Surinam, originally British, but Dutch after 1667, may have had Sephardic settlers by 1639. The Amsterdam Jewish archives contains a *ketubah* (marriage certificate) from Surinam dated 1643. A shipload of secret Jews from England came with Lord Willoughby in 1652. Eager for colonists, he had assured them freedom of worship and endenization (the right to settle and trade). By 1665 they had built a synagogue in Paramaribo, the capital.

Farther north in Cayenne, in 1662, a colony of Dutch Jews was organized by Abraham Cohen, as financier, and David Cohen Nassy, as manager. Nassy was typical of the Portuguese New Christian seeking to flee the Inquisition. Born in Portugal about 1612 with the name Christovão de Tavora, he escaped to Holland and adopted the name Joseph Nuñes da Fonseca. To conceal his trail, or perhaps to protect relatives still in Portugal, he became David Cohen Nassy.

Nassy was the founder of a prolific and important family in the Dutch colony. His sons, Samuel and Joseph Cohen Nassy, became military leaders in the Guianas and played a major role in the founding of Surinam's second congregation in 1605, in the hinterland upriver from Paramaribo at what came to be known as the Joden Savanne. Again, a synagogue was built, the ruins of which, along with a cemetery, can still be seen in the jungle.

The census taken in 1694 shows the Dutch colony of Paramaribo as having ninety-two Sephardic families and a dozen Ashkenazic ones. The following century brought such growth that the Ashkenazim opened Congregation Neve Shalom in 1734. The community's prosperity brought a rise in anti-Semitism despite the fact that Jewish militia units had helped to defend the colony against slave uprisings. The abolition of the slave trade in 1819 and the formal emancipation of slaves in 1863 made plantations unprofitable and so decimated Jewish trade that the Paramaribo congregations all but disappeared.[3]

Barbados

Barbados is one island for which there is documentary evidence of the arrival of refugees from Brazil. In the minutes of the Barbados Council for November 8, 1654 can be found: "Ordered that the consideration of the jews and foreigners brought from Barzele to the Island be presented at the next sitting of the Governor and Assembly."

In January 1655, months before England sanctioned their presence, it was enacted that the Jews of Barbados, provided that they "behav[ed] themselves civily and conformably to the Government of this Island . . . shall enjoy the privileges of Laws and Statutes of the Commonwealth of England and of this Island, relating to foreigners and strangers."

In April of 1655 Oliver Cromwell issued a pass to Dr. Abraham de Mercado and his son David to go to Barbados "to exercise his profession." Both had been residents of Recife, returned to Amsterdam, then lived for a time on the island. The doctor returned to Amsterdam a second time and died there in March 1669. David died in Barbados in 1685 and was buried in its Jewish cemetery.

By the end of the seventeenth century the Jewish population of Barbados had grown to 250, sizable for an island that measured only 14 by 21 miles. Its Jewish community was organized by another refugee from Recife who later returned to Amsterdam, known as Luis Dias, alias Joseph Jesurun Mendes.

Born in Portugal in 1616 as Ludovico Luis Gutteres, Mendes settled in Bridgetown with his wife and six children. By the early 1660s, he had prevailed on his fellow Jews to found Congregation Nidhe Israel ("The Scattered of Israel"), purchase ground, and erect a synagogue. Following the traditional pattern of English churchyards, their cemetery, subsequently enlarged, surrounds the synagogue on two sides.

The large number of Jewish merchants in Bridgetown, the capital of Barbados, is indicated by the fact that Swan Street, its main business thoroughfare, was dubbed "Jew Street." As the Jewish community grew, so did its property. A house was erected for a rabbi. Other buildings surrounding a smaller graveyard for suicides and intermarrieds were purchased for various functions. And in due course a second congregation, Semach David ("Sprout of David"), was founded in Speightstown.

The Speightstown synagogue was destroyed in 1739 during an anti-Semitic riot occasioned by a non-Jewish imposter's claim that he had been falsely accused of theft during a Jewish wedding. The

Bridgetown synagogue was almost totally destroyed in an 1831 hurricane, but was handsomely rebuilt and rededicated two years later.

Unfortunately, economic depression resulting from the earthquake and the emancipation of slaves led to the emigration of many of the island's Jews. In 1869, the remaining members of the community, by deed of trust, vested the ownership of the Bridgetown congregation's property in the Spanish and Portuguese Synagogue of London.

By the beginning of the twentieth century the synagogue was still open for worship solely because of the dedication of a lay member, Edward S. Daniels. Upon his death, only the two elderly Baeza brothers remained. One of them secured power-of-attorney from the London congregation and sold the synagogue to a local lawyer, who offered to a make it into a law library for public use. The government, however, did not accept this proposal.

On his death in 1934, another attorney acquired both the synagogue and the cemetery. He converted the former to rental office space and began erecting garages over the graves. Many of the synagogue's fittings were sold. The eight handsome wrought-iron chandeliers were purchased by Henry S. Du Pont for his museum at Winterthur, Delaware (where two of them may be seen on an upper porch).

At this point a history-minded solicitor, Eustace M. Shilstone, who had visited the synagogue as a boy with members of the Daniels family, endeavored to buy the properties, but the owner rebuffed him. On the latter's death two years later, Shilstone prevailed on the island government to put the cemetery in perpetual trust for the use of the new community of Jews then arriving from Europe. He also created a Barbados Museum in a former prison and included several items from the synagogue in its collection, among them a pew, a clock, a brass Hanukah menorah, and an alms box. He then proceeded to teach himself Hebrew, Spanish, and Portuguese, had the cemetery cleared of tropical growth, and copied the 472 surviving epitaphs.

Fortunately these were published, for after Shilstone's death, the self-appointed leader of the new Jewish community conceived the unfeasible notion of digging up the tombstones and plastering them into the walls, with the resultant ruin of hundreds of the stones. In 1984, the government threatened to tear down the dilapidated synagogue to replace it with a building for the supreme court. A native Jew, Paul Altman, persuaded the government that the synagogue restored would prove a tourist attraction. With a group of Jewish winter visitors he began an effort to restore the synagogue, enlisting the support of the American Jewish Congress. Although much still needs to be done to achieve the building's original beauty, a service was held in it on December 18, 1987.[4]

Martinique

A few of Recife's refugees found their way to Martinique, where they were joined by Portuguese Jews from southwestern France. Encouraged by Colbert, King Louis XIV's minister, the community grew and by 1676 was able to build a synagogue in the capital town of St. Pierre. That same year Benjamin da Costa Andrade went to Amsterdam to acquire both a bride and a Torah scroll, which he brought back to the island. A 1680 census lists eighty Jews; a subsequent one, three years later, lists ninety-six. But in 1685, the Jesuits, who controlled trade in the French colonies, took advantage of Colbert's loss of power to persuade the king to introduce the Code Noire (Black Code), banishing all Jews from the French colonies. The majority of them left for Curaçao. Any surviving traces of this short-lived community disappeared when St. Pierre was wiped out in the eruption of Mount Pelée in 1902.[5]

Curaçao

From a Jewish standpoint, Curaçao is the most important island in the Caribbean. It has maintained a functioning Jewish community for nearly three and a half centuries. From its historic Mikve Israel synagogue went founders of other Jewish communities. Rabbis, cantors, and financial aid were supplied to struggling North American congregations. By 1745, Curaçao's Jewry numbered 1,500, more than the entire Jewish population of contemporary North America.

A Dutch fleet captured Curaçao from the Spanish in 1634. On board as interpreter was a Portuguese New Christian, Samuel Cohen, who had lived in Brazil in the 1620s and was fluent in Dutch, Spanish, and Portuguese, as well as in Indian dialects. Cohen searched the island unsuccessfully for gold and returned to Amsterdam, leaving behind at least one other known New Christian, Juan or Julio de Araujo, who moved on to Mexico.

In 1651 the Dutch West India Company contracted with João de Yllan, a former New Christian who had been active in the Brazil trade, to bring fifty Jewish settlers to the island, but he succeeded in enticing only twelve. Discouraged by the island's barren soil, they all left. Eight years later, Isaac da Costa in Amsterdam enlisted seventy fellow-refugees from Brazil to establish Curaçao's first permanent Jewish settlement. Some of their descendants are still there as members of the synagogue.

Although de Yllan's group undoubtedly met for worship, Mikve Israel can be documented only from 1659. It was probably then that land was purchased for a cemetery, although no records survive prior to 1668. Enlarged many times, the cemetery came to be known for its sepulchral art. As individual Jews prospered they demonstrated their status by ordering tombstones carved in Holland with scenes illustrative of the biblical figures who were their namesakes. Unfortunately, a twentieth-century oil refinery's fumes have obliterated much of this art, but it survives in photographs and in a few examples preserved in the synagogue's recently established museum.

Imitating Amsterdam's congregation, the *adjunta* (trustees) of Mikve Israel enacted *hascamot* (regulations) to govern the lives of Curaçao's Jews for the next two centuries. Infractions were often punished by excommunication. By 1674 the congregation was able to bring over its first rabbi, Haham Josiau Pardo, a scion of Amsterdam rabbis. Nine years later he departed for the growing congregation in Port Royal, Jamaica, where he perished in the earthquake of 1692.

The slave trade helped Curaçao to prosper, and her Jewish community grew rapidly, enlarged with every ship by immigrants both from the French colonies and from Holland. Until its first synagogue building was erected in 1703, the congregation worshipped in rented quarters. Within a generation the community had outgrown the edifice, so funds were raised for the present handsome building, dedicated in 1732, the oldest surviving synagogue in the Western Hemisphere. Two chandeliers remain from the earlier structure; and as a memorial to the clandestine worship of their Portuguese forebears, the congregants covered the floor with sand to muffle footsteps. Until 1880 some of the sand came from Palestine to symbolize the congregation's close ties with Eretz Israel.

The factionalism so endemic in Jewish life was exacerbated in an insular community like Curaçao, at times necessitating the intervention of the local government or of the public authorities in Holland. A few months after the synagogue's dedication in 1732, Jews living across the inlet that bisects the capital city of Willemstadt organized Congregation Neve Shalom ("Dwelling of Peace"), which became the focal point of rebellion against Mikve Israel. By 1746 Neve Shalom had its own synagogue, but it was abandoned in 1817 when the majority of the members moved to other parts of the city.

In 1863 another split occurred, more between members of the same families than ideological. This arose when an El Porvenir Society, ostensibly created to further reforms in worship, published an editorial vilifying individual members of Mikve Israel, including the incumbent rabbi, Aron Mendes Chumaceiro (1810–1882). This precipitated the birth of Dutch Reform Congregation Emanu-el, named for its New York counterpart. By 1867 its members had erected a handsome temple not far from Mikve Israel.

Nearly a century later, this congregation engaged Rabbi Simeon Maslin, the first graduate of the Hebrew Union College–Jewish Institute of Religion to serve on the island. He found the remaining 750 Jews spilt into three congregations, an Ashkenazic Orthodox one, Shaare Tsedek, having been formed by newcomers from Eastern Europe. Rabbi Maslin bridged the groups by organizing a chapter of B'nai B'rith for cultural activities. He subsequently persuaded the leaders of Mikve Israel and Emanu-el to reunite under the banner of Reconstructionism. Emanu-el's building has become a community center.

The merger was made easier by Mikve Israel's unhappiness with the stringent orthodoxy of its incumbent rabbi, Isaac S. Emmanuel, who came to the synagogue from Salonika, Greece, in 1936 and resigned three years later. World War II kept him in Curaçao, where he worked as a government librarian. After the war, supported by a generous grant from Joshua ("Jossy") M. L. Maduro, a member of one of the island's oldest families, Emmanuel recorded the entire cemetery and researched his two-volume history of the Jewish community.[6]

Jamaica

Jamaica remained a Spanish possession from its discovery by Columbus until the British captured it in 1655. Thereafter it became the largest Caribbean island open to Jewish settlement until the Spanish-American War in 1898 liberated Cuba and Puerto Rico. Individuals of Marrano origin settled in Jamaica throughout the Spanish period. When the English conquered the island, they noted that about half the white population were "Portugals." One of them, Captain Campoe Sabbatha, guided the invading British fleet into Kingston Bay to capture the capital, St. Jago de la Vega, which they renamed Spanish Town. The Spanish surrender was negotiated by Acosta, a New Christian who succeeded in having all the Spanish residents banished except the "Portugals."

Port Royal, at the mouth of Kingston Bay, was the first spot in Jamaica to attract Jewish settlers, who were granted rights by Cromwell, later confirmed by King Charles II of England. Jews immigrated from all parts of the Caribbean as well as from England. By the late 1660s a cemetery had been secured across the bay at Hunt's Bay, where the oldest surviving grave dates to 1672. An attempt to restore the cemetery in 1938 has long since given way to squatters and tropical growth.

Kahal Kadosh Neve Tsedek ("The Holy Congregation, the Abode of Righteousness") was the name taken by Port Royal's Jews for their congregation and for the synagogue they erected in 1676. The name was probably chosen to counteract Port Royal's evil reputation as a haven for pirates and other criminals. Preying on the Spanish galleons carrying the riches of Mexico and Peru to Europe proved a very lucrative trade for some of the town's inhabitants, but Port Royal's prosperity was seriously diminished by a destructive earthquake in 1692. The synagogue was rebuilt, but the town was destroyed again by a fire in 1815.

Meanwhile, many of Port Royal's Jews left after the earthquake and settled in Spanish Town. The Sephardim soon founded a new congregation there, Neveh Shalom ("Abode of Peace"), and were able to erect a synagogue by 1704. The Ashkenazim separated themselves into Congregation Mikveh Israel and built their own synagogue two years later.

With Port Royal in ruins because of the earthquake, Kingston became Jamaica's economic center. As a result, Spanish Town's Jewish population began to decline, and by 1844 the two congregations had to merge. In the aftermath of another earthquake in 1907, the surviving Sephardic synagogue was permanently closed and its furnishings moved to Kingston, by then the island's capital. Vestiges of this once-thriving community may still be seen in the synagogue building and in the remnants of four Jewish cemeteries in Spanish Town.

Kingston's Sephardic community created Congregation Shaar Hashamayim ("Gate of Heaven"), but it was 1744 before they could build a synagogue and eventually a community house, both destroyed by a fire in 1882. Meanwhile the "English and German Jews," as the Ashkenazim styled themselves, formed Congregation Shaangare Yosher ("Gates of Righteousness") in 1797, and built a synagogue. Their first hazzan (cantor) was Myer Lyon ("Leoni"), best known for his adaptation of the Slavic folk-melody to the Hebrew hymn *Yigdal*.

Growing faster than the Sephardim, the Ashkenazim built a larger synagogue in 1837, only to have it destroyed in the 1882 fire. This led to the creation of an Amalgamated Synagogue, but diehards of both groups attempted to keep separate congregations functioning. The 1907 earthquake compelled them to strive for a merger, not totally achieved until 1921, ten years after the present synagogue was built. The hurricane of 1989 caused the small surviving community to attempt another reconstruction of the synagogue. Two Sephardic cemeteries, the older opened in 1716, and an Ashkenazic one begun in 1798, are visible in Kingston.

At the beginning of the eighteenth century, eighty Jewish families were recorded in Jamaica. The Assembly found them so convenient a source of taxation that they were repeatedly forced to appeal to the crown for relief, which finally came in a 1737 edict of King George II.

Thereafter, imitating the local Christian leadership, the Jewish community made certain to present a handsome gift to the island's governor annually. This earned Jews honorific posts in the militia. By 1831, Jews could hold office, a right not granted in England until 1858. So many Jews won elective posts that in 1849 the Jamaican Assembly adjourned for Yom Kippur.

The growth of the sugar industry enlarged the Jewish immigration and a number of Jews became plantation owners. More than a dozen scattered Jewish cemeteries attest to the location of Jews in many towns. Montego Bay's Congregation Beth Yangakob ("House of Jacob") erected a synagogue in 1844, but by the end of the century there were too few Jews to keep it open. A 1912 cyclone destroyed the building. The abolition of slavery in the British dominions lowered the economy and scattered the Jews. Intermarriage also had an effect on the dwindling population.

In 1942, the discovery of bauxite, the source of aluminum, on the plantation of Sir Alfred d'Costa, created a new mining industry. Two world wars brought new Jewish immigrants to the island, many of them from the Ladino-speaking lands of the eastern Mediterranean, and the leadership of today's Sephardic community is largely of Ladino origin.[7]

Nevis

The existence of a seventeenth-century synagogue on the island of Nevis was comparatively unknown until this author learned of it serendipitously. In 1957, he served as a chaplain on a cruise ship sponsored by the Virginia State Chamber of Commerce, which was endeavoring to promote the 350th anniversary of the settlement at Jamestown. The cruise's itinerary included the places visited by Captain John Smith's expedition en route from England via the Caribbean to Virginia in 1607. Among these was Nevis.

The author already knew the tale, substantiated in his son's biography of him, that Alexander Hamilton, born out of wedlock on Nevis, had been denied admission to the Anglican school there and thus had been educated at the island's synagogue. When our cruise ship arrived in the harbor of Charlestown, we asked to be shown the location of the synagogue. A black native designated a vine-covered ruin as "the Jews' school." This was connected by a path known as "Jews' Walk" to an overgrown field in which goats were feeding, labeled by our guide as "Jews' Burying Ground." There the author and his wife discovered sixteen flat tombstones in Portuguese, Hebrew, and Elizabethan English, which they copied and subsequently published.

The article caught the attention of a Philadelphia attorney, Robert D. Abrahams, and his late wife, Florence. They visited the island and purchased a ruined plantation that they converted to a vacation home in which they installed their collection of Admiral Nelson memorabilia. Over the years they collected donations from visitors to their Nelson museum for the purpose of having a wall and gates erected for the cemetery. On February 25, 1971, a ceremony of rededication was held.

Jews were in Nevis as early as 1671, when the British separated the administration of their Caribbean islands into Leeward and Windward. The presence of mineral springs made Nevis a popular health resort and the population grew. A muster roll from 1678 lists five Jewish heads of families. A decade later the community had enlarged sufficiently to erect the synagogue. The outbreak of a tropical disease, followed in 1707 by French raids, may have taken a toll of Jews, but in 1723 the Anglican minister reported to England that one-fourth of the island's white population was Jewish, with the Jews catering well to the plantation owners but resented by the Christian merchants. The tombstones, dating from 1679 to 1730, show the brief span of the active community.[8]

St. Eustatia and St. Martin

Starting in 1660, Jews from Curaçao began to settle on the Dutch island of St. Eustatia. Although driven out by the French in 1709, they soon returned because of the island's rich soil and because the harbor of Oranjestad offered convenient trading with neighboring British, French, Danish, and Spanish islands. A census of 1722 showed twenty-one Jews. These acquired the cemetery, still visible.

By 1737 the community had founded Congregation Honen Dalim ("Kindness to the Poor") and was ready to build its synagogue, which was dedicated two years later. When French raids resumed, the Jews fled to Curaçao, taking along the synagogue appurtenances. By 1744 they were back. A hurricane in 1772 leveled the synagogue, but it was rebuilt in three months with financial help from individuals in New York and Curaçao.

The Jewish population of St. Eustatia reached its zenith during the American Revolution, when the island became a major supply base for the patriots. This brought an attack in February 1781 by British Admiral Rodney, who confiscated all Jewish property and exiled all able-bodied Jewish males without their families. Because some of his victims were Jews loyal to Britain and some of the confiscated merchandise belonged to British shippers, he was denounced in Parliament by Edmund Burke, who defended the Jews.

The families of many of the exiles joined their menfolk on St. Croix and St. Thomas, and St. Eustatia never regained its Jewish population. The synagogue and cemetery fell into disrepair as the Jews disappeared. The last epitaph dates from 1843. Attempts to have the synagogue restored have so far been unsuccessful.

The small island of St. Martin/St. Maarten was divided between the Dutch and the French by the simple expedient of having two sailors, one of each nationality, walk around the island in opposite directions; where they started and met again became the boundary line. The Dutch settlement attracted occasional Jewish traders from Curaçao, but it was Rodney's raid on nearby St. Eustatia that enlarged the population to the point of building a synagogue. This community was short-lived, however, and a Dutch traveler in 1828 noted that the synagogue, probably devastated by a hurricane, was a rubble-heap.[9]

St. Croix and St. Thomas

St. Thomas was colonized by Denmark in 1672. Because it is the closest to Europe of all the Caribbean islands, it was a strategic lair for privateers preying on Europe-bound vessels. In 1684, Gabriel Milan, a Jewish soldier-of-fortune, was appointed governor of St. Thomas by the Danish government, but after two years of misrule and apparently criminal behavior, he was brought back to Copenhagen, tried, and hanged.

In 1733, the French sold St. Croix to Denmark. When the official documents reached St. Thomas a year later, the governor sent Emmanuel Vass, a Jewish resident, to Martinique to complete the negotiations with the French colonial governor. There is evidence of a synagogue at Christianstad on St. Croix by 1760, but the Jewish community had disappeared before the end of the nineteenth century. An overgrown cemetery had eleven decipherable epitaphs, dating between 1779 and 1867.

The majority of the refugees from Rodney's raid on St. Eustatia settled in St. Thomas and soon thereafter purchased a cemetery no longer extant. Its epitaphs, predominantly Sephardic, were recorded between 1792 and 1802. By 1796 Congregation B'racha V'shalom ("Blessing and Peace") had been organized and had erected a synagogue. The community was enlarged when a number of Sephardim moved there during the British occupation of Curaçao between 1807 and 1816. The community also acquired members from Jamaica and from the United States.

A new cemetery was purchased in 1837, by which time there were 400 Jews on the island, almost half its white population. The original synagogue and several of its successors were destroyed by fire, until the present brick and stone structure was erected in 1833. In the hubris of dedicating their new synagogue, the congregation renamed itself B'racha V'shalom Ugemiluth Chassadim ("Blessing and Peace and Loving Deeds").

Steam navigation ended the era of sailing ships, destroying the island's economy and diminishing its Jewish population, which included the family of native-born artist Camille (born Jacob) Pissaro. An 1867 hurricane heightened the economic disaster, while an outbreak of cholera, brought on a ship from India in 1895, sent many of the women and children to join relatives in Panama, and few returned.

In 1917, at a ceremonial marking the United States purchase of the Virgin Islands from Denmark, the synagogue provided the island's only clergyman for the occasion. Rev. Moses David Sasso, as a pious youth, had sat at the feet of his predecessor, Rev. David Cardoze. When the latter, at age ninety, had a stroke on the pulpit and was being carried out of the synagogue, he pointed to Sasso and said,

"You must carry on." Sasso kept the synagogue functioning from 1914 to 1965 despite a paucity of Jewish families.

Another Sephardi, Morris Fidanque de Castro, was appointed governor of the Virgin Islands by President Truman, after having served as acting governor in the 1930s. Among his successors was Ralph Paiewonsky, son of Romanian immigrants. Following World War II, tourism rebuilt the island's economy, and many North Americans, including author Herman Wouk, enlarged the congregation's membership. The synagogue joined the Reform movement, and since Rabbi Sasso's retirement it has been served by a series of graduates of the Hebrew Union College.[10]

Haiti

In 1697 Spain ceded the western third of the island Columbus had named Hispaniola to the French. They restored its Indian name, Haiti. Under Spanish rule Marranos were to be found on the northern coast at Isabella. Despite France's Black Code, prohibiting Jewish settlement, there are indications of Jews doing business with almost every port on the island during the seventeenth and eighteenth centuries. The Gardis and Mendes families of Bordeaux maintained trade depots after the 1750s. A tax list, dated January 16, 1765, shows twenty-nine Jewish heads of families in Cap-Haïtien plus eight others as either plantation owners or in widely scattered areas. Cap-Haïtien undoubtedly had a congregation and a cemetery, but the black uprising of 1790 slaughtered or scattered Haiti's white population. The majority of the surviving Jews migrated to other islands or to the North American mainland.[11]

British North America

All the communities described so far were totally dominated by Sephardim through much of their history, although almost all of them had an admixture of Ashkenazic settlers. North America was different in this respect: the colonial communities were tonally Sephardic, but the rapid accretion of Ashkenazim soon outnumbered the "Spanish-Portuguese," and, as we shall demonstrate, often challenged Sephardi domination. Until well into the nineteenth century, however, the Sephardic minhag (rite) was the American way of Jewish worship in the congregations we shall describe.

New Amsterdam/New York

As is well known, the first Jewish settlement in what became the United States was in Dutch New Amsterdam. The generally accepted history is that in late August or early September of 1654, a French ship, called variously the *St. Catherine* or *St. Charles*, captained by Jacques de la Motthe, arrived in the harbor of New Amsterdam with a number of Dutch refugees, including twenty-three Jewish men, women, and children, presumably from Recife. The surviving documentary references have given rise to a number of theories regarding the route and circumstances that brought these pioneers to Peter Stuyvesant's small village.

At least two Jews met the boat: Solomon Pieters or Petersen, who appears briefly in the Dutch records as advocate for the Jews in their first dealings with Stuyvesant; and Jacob Barsimson, an Ashkenazi trader who had just arrived in the colony. Captain de la Motthe sued his Jewish passengers for the promised fare, and when they were unable to meet his demands, two heads of family were imprisoned as hostages until funds to pay the debt could be obtained from relatives in Amsterdam.

Stuyvesant, who objected to any settlers who were not members of the Dutch Reformed Church, attempted to evict the Jews, but Jewish stockholders in Amsterdam prevailed on the Dutch West India Company to order the narrow-minded governor to let them remain. Possibly at the instigation of the Amsterdam Jewish community, six heads of Sephardic families, led by Abraham de Lucena, went to New Amsterdam as settlers in March 1655 to investigate its business potential. They brought a Torah scroll with them, an indication that a private synagogue was created.

Stuyvesant, determined to drive the Jewish settlers out of New Amsterdam, made efforts to restrict their trade, prohibited their owning property, and taxed them to pay for the town watch. When Barsimson and Asser Levy, the community butcher, both Ashkenazim, protested that they had "burgher" (i.e., citizenship) rights from Amsterdam and should be allowed to take their turn as guards on the town wall, Amsterdam ruled in their favor. In 1655, the Jews applied for a plot of land for a cemetery, but the governor denied the request, pointing out that no one had yet died. The following year the death of one of the Jews compelled him to designate "a little hook of land" beyond the town wall. This site has long since disappeared.

Stuyvesant's recalcitrance and the extreme cold of New Amsterdam's winters led the Sephardic Jews to depart for Amsterdam, London, or the Caribbean, where relatives were better established. By 1663, the Torah scroll had been returned to Amsterdam. In 1664 a large British fleet forced Stuyvesant to surrender without firing a shot, and all residents who remained in what was now New York were required to sign an oath of allegiance to the English crown.

The one Jewish name on the list was Asser Levy's. He seems to have maintained the only Jewish presence of record in British New York until he was joined in 1680 by relatives from Amsterdam. Levy's death on February 1, 1681/82 and burial in the old cemetery unquestionably led Sephardi Joseph Bueno de Mesquita to purchase a separate burying ground for his own family and for a growing group of Sephardim in the community.

The earliest mention of Jewish worship dates to 1682, but public worship was proscribed until a decade later. A map from 1695 shows a rented synagogue location on Beaver Street; five years later the synagogue had moved to a house owned by John Harpendinck, shoemaker, on Mill Street. By 1728, probably inspired by the erection of a number of churches, the Jewish community purchased a plot adjacent to the Harpendinck house and built America's first synagogue.

The papers of Nathan Simson, a former president of the congregation who moved back to England in 1722, show that in his day the Ashkenazim already outnumbered the Sephardim. The new synagogue, completed in 1730, set the tone for colonial American Jewry by continuing to use the Sephardic form of worship already in place since the arrival of its first lay reader, Saul Brown (né Pardo). Why? Because the community was too small to underwrite the building fund and relied heavily on donations from the wealthier Sephardic communities.

The incumbent hazzan, Moses Lopez da Fonseca, was the son of Curaçao's rabbi. That community sent the most generous contribution to New York with the stipulation that even though New York was full of "Tedeschi" (Portuguese for "Germans"), the gift was predicated on New York's using the Sephardic ritual. Although Nathan Simson had referred to the congregation as Shearith Jacob ("Remnant of Jacob"), its official title became Shearith Israel.

Another factor may have favored the maintenance of Sephardic custom: In the small town that New York was, Jews lived among non-Jews, and the latter found Jews and Jewish worship of some interest. Sephardic worship, led by a hazzan, must have been considered more dignified for non-Jewish observers than the unstructured babel that was Ashkenazic worship.

The congregation, recognizing that the Ashkenazim were more versed in halakhah (Jewish law), engaged them for such synagogue functions as shochet and bodek (kosher butcher and inspector), and mohel (circumciser). However, for the conduct of worship the New York congregation sought Sephardim who could chant in the Sephardic mode. They were greatly assisted by the appearance in 1761 of an English translation of the Sephardic prayerbook for the eve of the holidays, followed five years later by a more complete prayerbook for the year, both presumably the work of Isaac Pinto, an educated layman.

Shearith Israel was often hard-pressed to find a qualified hazzan. Those it did obtain did not stay long. How the members must have welcomed in 1768 a native son reared in the congregation, Gershom Mendes Seixas! He served for forty-eight years, interrupted by the Revolutionary War. In August 1776, when it was apparent that George Washington was losing the Battle of Brooklyn Heights, Seixas gathered the synagogue's scrolls and appurtenances in a wagon and joined other patriot congregants and his relatives from Newport, Rhode Island, in Connecticut.

The British remained in control of New York until the surrender in 1783. Those members of the community who had no other place to go kept the synagogue open, joined by an occasional Tory hazzan and by

Jewish Hessian soldiers who opted to remain in New York when their contracts with the British army ended. The majority of New York's Jews were either shopkeepers or international traders.

Following the Revolution, the scattered leaders of Shearith Israel returned. By this time, the congregation's leaders were almost all Ashkenazic, but they were so accustomed to the Sephardic ritual that it has remained the minhag. Shearith Israel's strict control of Jewish religious life in New York was all-pervasive. Every Jew who arrived in the community was required to affiliate and to contribute as his means permitted. The congregation was also the sole social-service agency, dispensing charity and caring for the aged, the sick, and the transient.

Following the Napoleonic Wars in Europe, there was a revival of immigration of Ashkenazic Jews. The newcomers asked permission to hold their own separate services under the aegis of Shearith Israel, but when their request was denied, they broke away and in 1825 organized B'nai Jeshurun, New York's first Ashkenazic-rite congregation. By mid-century, Shearith Israel's preeminence in New York's Jewish communal affairs was gradually yielding to the far larger German immigrant community.[12]

Newport

Roger Williams's reaction to intolerant Puritan Massachusetts was to create a colony in Rhode Island open to all faiths. This may have attracted Jews as early as 1656 or 1658, but the first documented evidence of settlement is the deed for the purchase of a cemetery in 1678. Mordecai Campanall and Moses Pacheco of Barbados had visited Newport a year earlier and been favorably impressed. After returning home to collect their families and some fellow-Jews eager to escape the sugar taxes, they established New England's first Jewish community.

Lacking British endenization (the right to trade), the Jewish settlers, as aliens, were subject to arrest and trial for violating the Navigation Act. Their goods were impounded and they were brought to trial. The jury, apparently grateful for the economic benefits they had brought to the town, acquitted them. However, frightened by this experience, and for other reasons as yet undiscovered, most of them left for more-established Jewish areas. No tombstones of this era survive in the cemetery.

Although we get glimpses of occasional Jewish traders, it was not until the 1740s that Newport's Jewish population began to grow with the town's development as an important whaling and shipping port. The French and Indian War enhanced the town's importance as a supply base for British troops moving on Canada. In 1759, the Jews, already formed into Congregation Yeshuat Israel ("Salvation of Israel"), engaged a Christian architect, Peter Harrison, to erect a handsome building, completed in 1763, and now the oldest surviving synagogue in North America. Once again, the city had to rely on gifts from other Jewish congregations, including New York's Shearith Israel. Here, too, the population included as many Ashkenazim as Sephardim, but the ritual was Sephardic, and the hazzan, Isaac Touro, was a Sephardi.

Newport's Jews prospered with the community. Aaron Lopez, import-export merchant and shipowner, sent his vessels around South America to the whaling grounds. He and other Jews were involved in the triangular slave trade. With his cousin Jacob Rivera, he joined Christian merchants in 1761 to form the United Company of Spermaceti Candlers, controlling the price and manufacture of luxury whale-oil candles.

Newport's Sephardim and Ashkenazim met socially to form a card-playing club, the first Jewish social club of record. Its existence is known only from surviving bylaws that prohibited conversation on synagogue matters on penalty of bottles of good wine.

The Inquisition in Portugal, which the Lopezes and Riveras had fled, reverberated in Newport with the arrival of Aaron Lopez's half-brother Michael, age fifty-six, and his three sons, Duarte, twenty-eight, José, twenty-four, and João, seventeen. In keeping with the well-established custom of New Christian converts to Judaism, the four men were circumcised in suburban Tiverton, Rhode Island, and given the biblical names of Abraham, Moses, Samuel, and Jacob, respectively. The mohel (ritual circumciser) was Abraham I. Abrahams of New York, who had previously serviced members of the Lopez family.

Newport lacked a mohel until 1772, when Moses Seixas, a prominent resident, learned the ritual by correspondence with Abrahams. The correspondence and the silver surgical implements made for Seixas by New York's outstanding silversmith, Myer Myers, are preserved at the American Jewish Historical Society.

Thanks to the copious diaries of Rev. Ezra Stiles, later president of Yale University, we know much about the colonial Jews of Newport. In 1760 Stiles reported the town as having fifteen Jewish families, totaling fifty-eight souls. By 1774, according to a census, they numbered 121.

The outbreak of the Revolution sent Newport's leading Sephardic families elsewhere. The Lopezes and Riveras moved first to Providence, then north into Massachusetts. The Seixas clan went to Stratford, Connecticut, where, as mentioned above, they were joined by Rev. Gershom from New York.

Newport remained under British control until 1779, when the French helped the patriots to capture it. Those merchants who had remained under the British, largely Ashkenazim, were accused of Toryism and fled. Hazzan Touro, a Tory sympathizer, moved to New York and then to the Caribbean, where he died suddenly, leaving his young wife and three children to find their way to the home of her brother, Moses Michael Hays, in Boston.

One of the hazzan's sons, Abraham Touro, died unmarried in 1822, leaving a bequest to preserve the Newport synagogue and cemetery. His better-known brother, Judah, whom we shall meet in New Orleans, amassed a fortune. Dying unmarried in 1854, he left a bequest to pay the "minister" of the Newport synagogue. As a consequence, the synagogue, the cemetery, and the connecting street all acquired the Touro name.

After the Revolution a few of Newport's merchants returned, but the town's importance as a port was finished. Moses Lopez, "the last Jew," left for New York in 1822. The synagogue was closed, its key turned over to the New York congregation, the cemetery vested in the Newport City Council.

During the nineteenth century, Newport became a summer resort and the synagogue was occasionally opened for worship. By the 1880s area Jews sought permission from Shearith Israel to hold holy day services in the sanctuary. Permission was granted with the proviso that they engage a Sephardic hazzan. After several years of this, the area Jews sued to sever the hold of Shearith Israel, but the court upheld the requirement that the Touro Synagogue follow the Sephardic rite. The disgruntled Ashkenazim held their own services elsewhere until more recent generations capitulated and returned to the Touro Synagogue and a Sephardic service.[13]

Savannah

In the 1720s, the Portuguese Inquisition renewed its rigor, causing new flights of refugees, a number of whom descended on the London Jewish community, taxing the Sephardic synagogue's resources. Meanwhile, around 1730, several members of Parliament began efforts to create a buffer colony between the Carolinas and Spanish Florida, intending it as a new home for many of the inmates languishing in London's prisons as debtors.

When the trustees of the new colony issued a call for commissioners to raise funds for the venture, they were delighted to accept an offer from the leaders of London's Spanish and Portuguese Synagogue in Bevis Marks. The latter, hoping to relieve the congregation of its numerous refugees, applied for permission to send colonists at no cost to the trustees. After some debate the trustees concluded that Jewish settlers might be a detriment and denied permission, with a request that the synagogue's leaders give up their commissions.

Ignoring this, the synagogue proceeded to charter a vessel, the *William & Sarah*, under Captain Hanton, and put forty-three passengers aboard. Outbound for Georgia the ship sustained some injury while in the Thames River. Repairs having been made, she again set sail and, after a storm-tossed voyage, arrived in the five-month-old colony at Savannah on July 11, 1733. Nine of the passengers were Ashkenazic; the other thirty-two, Sephardic. One child had died at sea.

Leading the group was Dr. Samuel Nuñez (1668–?), born in Portugal as Diogo Nuñez Ribeiro, a former physician to the Portuguese king. He had become an active judaizer in Lisbon and was proscribed by the Inquisition, but had escaped with his family to London. There he and his wife were remarried in 1726 as Jews. Seven years later, with his mother, two sons, a daughter, and a manservant, he arrived in Savannah. His wife brought other family members on a later ship.

The first arrivals found the Savannah community suffering from an outbreak of dysentery that had already killed twenty people. The London trustees wrote to James Oglethorpe, the founder of the colony, objecting to Jewish settlers, and ordered him to "use your best endeavors that the said Jews may be allowed no kind of settlement." This crossed a letter from Oglethorpe to the trustees reporting the arrival of the forty Jews with a physician who had stopped the plague.

The trustees responded with an expression of gratitude to the physician and the hope that Oglethorpe would pay him off but not grant him land. However, Oglethorpe had already sought legal advice from Charleston, since Georgia was governed by the liberal constitution of the Carolinas. Charleston must have ruled that any adult males who came at their own expense were entitled by the trustees' plan to a town plot of five acres for house and garden, and a farm of forty-five acres outside the town. Oglethorpe assigned property to each Jewish family and even allocated a plot for a Jewish cemetery on the town common. Although the graves can no longer be found, a monument now marks the site.

Every ship brought new Jewish arrivals, and the first shipload "brought with them a Sefertora with two Cloaks and a Circumcision box which was given by Mr. Lindo a merchant in London for the use of the congregation they intended to establish." But it was July of 1735 before Congregation Mickve Israel was created.

Quarrels between Sephardim and Ashkenazim contributed to the delay. What precipitated worship was undoubtedly proselytizing by Christians. According to a letter of Oglethorpe's, one Jew had been converted. Nuñez's sons, Moses and Daniel, born Catholic, were reported by the Anglican minister as occasionally attending his service, although not as Christians. He and other Christians noted differences between the more assimilated Sephardim and the rigidly orthodox Ashkenazim, especially in matters of kashrut.

The notion that viticulture might flourish in Georgia was a fondly held dream of the London trustees, so they willingly made a loan to Abraham de Lyon, Nuñez's son-in-law, who had experience with wine-growing in Portugal and secured vines and vignerons from that country to carry out his ambitious plans. Unfortunately for him, the Georgia soil proved unconducive.

Even before he came to that conclusion, however, Oglethorpe had made some unsuccessful raids against the Spanish in nearby Florida. When it was rumored that the Spaniards, in reprisal, might overrun Georgia, the Sephardim, all of whom had been born in Iberia, fled the colony in fear of the Inquisition, leaving only the Ashkenazic Minis and Sheftall families.

Moses and Daniel Nuñez returned to Savannah in 1750, the former working as a trader and interpreter with the Indians, and later as port inspector. Both were leaders of Savannah's Masonic lodge. Their nephew, Isaac de Lyon, returned from Charleston in the 1760s.

Meanwhile, the colony was suffering from the trustees' idealistic insistence on no slaves or liquor, and the consequent economic failure compelled the trustees to relinquish the colony to the crown in 1752. With more Jews arriving, the community petitioned to enlarge the cemetery. The Georgia Assembly, responding to the objections of neighborhood residents, denied the request, whereupon Mordecai Sheftall deeded a piece of his suburban property to the Jewish community for the erection of a synagogue with an adjacent cemetery. However, only the cemetery came into being; the remainder of the property was sold, and the proceeds were used by later generations for the erection of the synagogue's community house.

By 1774 Congregation Mickve Israel had been reestablished in the home of Mordecai Sheftall, but its development was totally interrupted by the Revolution, which again scattered Georgia's Jews. It was July of 1786 before the communal record kept by the Sheftalls could report the permanent establishment of Mickve Israel, soon chartered by the new Georgia General Assembly. By this time only two of the leaders of the predominantly Ashkenazic community were Sephardim: David Nunes Cardozo, gabay (treasurer), and Emanuel de la Motta, hazzan (lay reader).

Economic difficulties, intensified by a major fire in 1796, forced the congregation to use a rented facility. When this was sold by its owner, the congregation was compelled to build a synagogue. It was dedicated in 1820 with a noteworthy address by attorney Jacob de la Motta, the last Sephardi of influence in the community until the arrival as "rabbi" in 1877 of Jamaican-born Isaac Pereira Mendes (1854–1905). Mendes came in time to dedicate the congregation's present synagogue building, but Mickve Israel was already veering toward Reform and gradually moved from the Sephardic liturgy, although Sephardic terminology (e.g., *adjunta* "board"; *tebah* "altar," etc.) remained in use at least in the temple's minutes.[14]

Charleston

A friendly rivalry has existed between Savannah and Charleston as to which is the older Jewish community. As we have indicated, Savannah can date its origins as an organized Jewish settlement to 1733, its congregation to 1735. However, periodic losses of population led to lapses and revivals. Charleston can date its first Jew of record to 1695, when the governor used an unnamed Jew as interpreter to a delegation of Spanish-speaking Indians. Two years later, four Jewish names, one undecipherable, were appended to a petition. The others were Abraham Avila and Jacob Mendes, Sephardim; and Simon Valentine, an Ashkenazi and a nephew of New York's Asser Levy.

Avila and Valentine lived out their lives in Charleston, but few Jews joined them. It was not until 1849 that ten heads of family, led by Joseph Tobias, were available to form a minyan, the quorum needed for the congregation they named Beth Elohim ("House of God"). Of the founding families, six were Sephardic, four Ashkenazic, including Mordecai and Levi Sheftall, both of whom were temporary residents from Savannah.

The Sephardic majority, evidently determined to dominate decision-making, accorded their best-informed layman, Moses Cohen, the honorific titles *Hacham v'Abh Beth Din* ("chief rabbi and chief of the ecclesiastical court"). Isaac da Costa, a leading merchant, functioned as hazzan. It was he who purchased ground for a cemetery in 1762. Two years later he deeded it to the congregation, but named as trustees the leaders and membership of Sephardic congregations in London, "King's Town, Jamaica," and "Bridgetown, Barbados." In the deed a dash separates these from the three North American congregations, also named with their mixture of Ashkenazic and Sephardic leaders.

Charleston's Jewish growth was interrupted by the Revolution. In 1780, the British captured the city, and Da Costa joined other Jewish patriots in Philadelphia. In his absence, the congregation's leadership was assumed by Ashkenazim. When peace was declared in 1783, Da Costa returned to Charleston. He died within a few months, and his remains were interred in a separate cemetery at Hampstead, subsequently described in the local press as belonging to "the Portuguese Congregation of this City, called `Beth Elohim Unveh Shallom.'"

A split had developed, but the two groups seem to have reunited sometime between 1791, when the Ashkenazim determined to abandon their rented facility and build their first synagogue building, and 1794, when it was dedicated. The agreement seems to have included abandoning the separate Sephardic cemetery, but this led to further friction and compromise, for Sephardic burials continued there until 1847.

By 1800 Charleston had the largest Jewish population of any city in the United States, numbering about 600. The congregation maintained strict control over the actions of individual members. Rev. Moses Cohen and his successors as hazzan were all Sephardim, with the exception of Abraham Alexander, and the Sephardic ritual prevailed.

Some restlessness must have existed, though, for in 1820 the congregation issued a new and very stringent constitution. The hazzan of the moment was another Ashkenazi, Rev. Hartwig Cohen, a native of Wartha, Poland. He was dismissed in 1823, and his place was taken by Selomoh Cohen Peixotto, a native of Curaçao, where he had served as ribi (teacher) and shochet (kosher butcher). He had left during the British occupation of the Dutch island between 1807 and 1816 to become hazzan in St. Thomas, and had come to Charleston in 1818.

Peixotto's election may very well have been a precipitating factor in the formation a year later of the Reformed Society of Israelites. One of their complaints was that the Spanish and Portuguese prayers and hymns comprising Beth Elohim's liturgy were meaningless to the membership. However, when Reform leader Isaac Harby prepared a prayerbook for the insurgents, it was the Sephardic prayerbook that he translated.

The two groups eventually reunited, but when a new synagogue, built by David Lopez, a Sephardi member, replaced the old one, which had burned down in 1838, the agitation for an organ and other reforms led to another breakoff.

The new Orthodox congregation, Shearith Israel, led at first by Jacob de la Motta, formerly of Savannah, still followed the Sephardic minhag. It prospered while Beth Elohim struggled. As late as 1854, Beth Elohim's Reform proclivities undoubtedly eliminated it from a benefaction in the will of New Orleans philanthropist Judah Touro. Following the example of Rebecca Gratz of Philadelphia, Miss Sally Lopez instituted a Sunday school in 1838 which she directed for four years, obtaining weekly lessons copied for her by Rebecca Gratz.

The depredations of the Civil War and the economic depression it engendered in the South led to a reunion of the two congregations in 1866. They agreed to use the "Portuguese minhag" with a shortened version of the Orthodox service. Rev. Joseph H. Chumaceiro, son of Curaçao's hazzan, was elected in 1868 and served for six years. By 1875, the congregation had acquired a growing influx of German immigrants who were assuming leadership. The liturgy was modified and the board agreed to accept the prayerbook of its incumbent hazzan, David Levy.[15]

Philadelphia

As an inland port, Philadelphia was slow to attract a Jewish community. As early as 1735, Nathan Levy, son of an Ashkenazic leader of New York's Shearith Israel, had moved to Philadelphia, to be joined shortly thereafter by his brother Isaac and their nephew David Franks. In 1738, the death of Nathan's child motivated him to purchase a suburban plot for a cemetery. Two years later, he acquired a larger plot, presumably for a family burial ground, but it eventually became the property of the emerging Jewish community and may still be seen on Spruce Street, near Ninth.

Worship may have been held by the 1740s, but no formal congregation was organized. By 1761, Philadelphia's Jews had obtained a Torah scroll on permanent loan from New York, but their worship—like the membership—was undoubtedly Ashkenazic. Ten years later they opened a synagogue in rented facilities and named their congregation Mikveh Israel. With the exception of Curaçao-born Solomon Marache, all the leaders were Ashkenazim.

The Revolutionary War brought Philadelphia under British occupation from November 1777 to June 1778. With its restoration to American control and the return of the Continental Congress, Jews from all the coastal communities converged on the federal capital, swelling its Jewish population to nearly 1,000 souls. In 1780, Gershom Mendes Seixas was ordered by the leaders of his New York congregation, now domiciled in Philadelphia, to bring the synagogue appurtenances and serve as hazzan to this growing community.

The rented synagogue soon proved far too small. After considerable difficulties, funds were raised to purchase ground and erect a synagogue, designed in the Sephardic manner. It was dedicated in time for the High Holy Days of 1782, but less than a year later the war ended and the majority of the Jews returned to the communities from which they had fled. This left the Philadelphians with a heavy mortgage. To add to their problems, the New Yorkers demanded the return of their "minister," proposing their latest wartime incumbent, Rev. Jacob Raphael Cohen, as a replacement for Seixas. The trade was effected.

The Philadelphia congregation grew slowly. By 1795, new Ashkenazic immigrants had created their own minyan out of which they formed, in 1800, "the Hebrew German Society" Rodeph Shalom, America's oldest Ashkenazic congregation. It too was slow to grow despite the continuing arrival of immigrants from northern Europe. Rodeph Shalom's use of varied rented quarters continued until 1847, when it acquired a church as its first synagogue building. This led the early German immigrants, as they prospered, to join the more established Mikveh Israel.

Following the death of Jacob Raphael Cohen in 1811, his son served as "acting Reader" until the congregation secured from Charleston Rev. Emanuel Nunes Carvalho, who died within a year of his arrival. After a hiatus of eight years, Mikveh Israel elected the hazzan of Barbados, Rev. Abraham Israel Keys, who dedicated a new synagogue for the expanding community. Following his death, the congregation elected as hazzan the man who was to make Philadelphia the center of American Judaism for most of the century, Isaac Leeser (1805–1868).

Like other Ashkenazim who came to head "Sephardic" congregations, Leeser had studied and worshipped under a Sephardic hazzan. His *Occident and American Jewish Advocate*, published mostly as a monthly from 1843 to a year after his death, was literally the only Jewish medium for half of its history. Beginning as a voice of moderation, but gradually becoming an opponent to Reform, it provoked a number of other papers espousing other viewpoints, helped to create institutions, and disseminated both news of world Jewry and knowledge of Judaism.

In 1850 Mikveh Israel and Leeser parted company, and a number of members joined him in forming a second Sephardic-rite congregation, Beth El Emeth, which survived him and two Sephardi successors before dying out in the 1890s. In the interim Mikveh Israel brought to its pulpit Sabato Morais, a native of Leghorn, Italy, and a recognized scholar and communal leader. He became the instigator for the creation of New York's Jewish Theological Seminary.

Mikveh Israel has retained its Sephardic traditions, although its membership has been overwhelmingly Ashkenazic for most of its history. After years in North Philadelphia in a deteriorating neighborhood, the congregation, as its observance of the American Bicentennial in 1976, joined what has become the National Museum of American Jewish History to erect a synagogue and museum facility in the area redeveloped as Independence National Historic Park.[16]

Montreal

Permanent Jewish settlement in Canada began with the British defeat of the French in 1759. Within nine years enough Jews had arrived in Montreal, some from New York, to form a congregation which they named after New York's Shearith Israel. They adopted the Sephardic rite, even though the entire founding group was Ashkenazic, the majority of them either merchants or fur traders. Canada's ongoing ties with England, especially during and after the Revolution, led Shearith Israel to look to London's Sephardim for guidance in its bylaws and use of terminology. By 1777 the congregation had built a small synagogue on property belonging to a member, David David. When he died in 1825, the property reverted to his estate, and whatever worship was conducted took place in private homes, led by lay members or, on special occasions, by a hazzan summoned from New York.

Even without a building, in 1837 the congregation passed a resolution to continue the use of "Portuguese Service of Prayers and Ceremonies from now on." This would seem to indicate an Ashkenazic counter-effort, which came to fruition in 1846 when members broke away to establish Montreal's first Ashkenazic congregation.

Meanwhile, the "Portuguese" congregation had completed a new synagogue in 1838 and engaged Rev. David Piza from London as hazzan. He was followed by Rev. Abraham de Sola (1825–1882), who, at the request of London's Sephardic rabbi, published a new edition of Sephardic prayerbooks in 1878. On his death, he was succeeded by his son, Rev. (Aaron David) Meldola de Sola (1853–1918), Canada's first native-born minister.

Demography caused the congregation to erect a new synagogue on Stanley Street in 1890. The building fund received a gift from the congregation's New York namesake with the proviso that the Montrealers continue the Orthodox Sephardic rite. At this point, imitating both London and New York, the congregation changed its corporate name from "Portuguese" to "Spanish and Portuguese." This may well have been precipitated by preparations for the 1892 celebration of Columbus' discoveries.

The years after the hazzan's death in 1917 brought two short-term successors, but the congregation went into a serious decline in membership. The westward movement of the city's Jews urged a new synagogue, but it was not until after World War II that this proved feasible. With the completion of its present sanctuary in 1960, the congregation has taken on new growth, largely through the arrival of Sephardim from the former Ottoman Empire.[17]

Richmond

Although occasional Jewish traders visited Virginia as early as the 1650s, the colony's plantation economy retarded the development of cities. Richmond, at the head of navigation of the James River, attracted its first Jewish settlers in 1769. The earliest surviving record of a congregation is its mention in correspondence of the New York and Philadelphia congregations regarding a congratulatory letter to George Washington after his April 1790 inaugural.

An 1856 list of twenty-eight founders mentions only one Sephardic name, but since almost all the founders came from the more established communities, the Sephardic minhag was unquestionably the rite of Richmond's Congregation Beth Shalome ("House of Peace"). The town's first Jewish resident, Isaiah Isaacs, contributed a lot for a communal cemetery whose site has been preserved, although most of the graves have long been covered over.

By 1818 Beth Shalome had purchased land for a synagogue, dedicated five years later. Isaac H. Judah functioned as hazzan. He was succeeded by Isaac B. Seixas, a nephew of New York's Gershom Mendes Seixas, and then by the latter's scholarly son-in-law, Israel Baer Kursheedt.

The 1830s saw an influx of immigrants from the Rhineland and Bavaria who joined Beth Shalome, but by 1839 they had broken away to form German-rite Beth Ahabah ("House of Love"). With the passing of generations the social distinctions between the descendants of Beth Shalome and the rising Beth Ahabah gradually diminished. In 1877, Rev. Isaac Pereira Mendes departed for the Savannah pulpit, and a move was begun to merge the two congregations. Beth Shalome maintained its independence with a lay reader even after its building was sold to the Orthodox Sir Moses Montefiore Congregation, but in November of 1898 the surviving twelve members accepted an invitation to join Beth Ahabah, and Beth Shalome went out of existence.[18]

New Orleans

The last community in North America to form a "Portuguese" congregation was New Orleans. Banned by the French Black Code until 1803, when Louisiana became part of the United States, Jews were slow to settle in New Orleans. Few of the early arrivals were family men, and intermarriage was rife. Thus it was 1828 before a congregation was formed. This seems to have been entirely instigated by the efforts of a Sephardi temporary resident from Philadelphia, Jacob da

Silva Solis, who apparently conducted services and wrote the constitution and bylaws before returning to his home city.

The name of the new congregation was Shanarai-Chasset, a spelling that reflects the Sephardic pronunciation of Shaarai Chesed ("Gates of Mercy"), but aside from Solis, only one other founder, "Souza, Sr." was Sephardic. Following Solis's departure, the president, Manis Jacobs, became officiant. He wrote to Solis, "I do not know much about the portuguaise [sic] minhag."

The constitution of Shanarai-Chasset specified that the "prayers offered shall be after the custom of the Portuguese Israelites." The officers were to be two parnassim ("senior wardens") and three gabaim ("junior wardens"); at least one of each had to be married. Because of the high rate of intermarriage, no child was to be excluded from the school, and no spouse excluded from burial unless he or she had formally converted to another faith.

The congregation purchased a cemetery plot in the somewhat remote suburb of Lafayette. By 1829 it had also purchased a lot for a synagogue, but none of the wealthy Jews of New Orleans would either join the congregation or contribute to the building fund. The majority of them were fully secularized and had abandoned the Orthodoxy they had left behind in Europe.

Judah Touro, son of Newport's hazzan, was probably the wealthiest Jew in New Orleans. He made a token contribution to the congregation when it organized, but was deaf to further Jewish appeals until about 1847. Until then his philanthropies were totally to Christian enterprises.

The arrival in New Orleans of Gershom Kursheedt had a remarkable effect. Kursheedt was an ardent Jew, a disciple of Isaac Leeser, grandson of Gershom Mendes Seixas, and son of the learned Israel Baer Kursheedt. He convinced Touro to become a pre-publication subscriber to Leeser's *Occident*. Kursheedt found the congregation being led by an actor, A. J. "Roley" Marks, whose antics were an embarrassment to observant Jews.

Meanwhile, the Jewish population of New Orleans was growing. The end of slavery in the Caribbean saw Jews from the islands arriving almost daily in Louisiana, among them many Sephardim. Kursheedt determined to start a new "Portuguese" congregation. In 1845, appealing to the American-born as well as to the West Indians, he organized Congregation Nefutzoth Yehudah ("Dispersed of Judah"), a name that he hoped would flatter Judah Touro into affiliation.

Although Touro refused to join, Kursheedt prevailed on him, possibly through Touro's best friend and lawyer, Rezin Shepherd, to remodel as a synagogue the building being abandoned by Shepherd's Episcopal church. Three years later, when the remodeling was completed, Leeser came to dedicate the building and Touro was so impressed that he became a regular attender, built a schoolhouse next to the synagogue with an apartment for Kursheedt, and even became a strict Sabbath observer.

Rev. Moses N. Nathan was imported from St. Thomas as hazzan. However, the congregants had come to rely on Kursheedt and Touro, so Nefutzoth Yehudah did not prosper. Shanarai-Chasset had become the "German" congregation.

Following Touro's death in 1854, Nefutzoth Yehudah sold its synagogue and surrounding property for a large sum and erected a synagogue closer to the members' homes. Reform came to New Orleans after the Civil War, and Temple Sinai was established in 1870. The two older congregations merged in 1881 to become Touro Synagogue, a Reform congregation in the manner of Charleston and Savannah, with Sephardic traditions.[19]

Sephardic Customs and Influences

In addition to the terminology used in these founding synagogues, which has often persisted to the present, the use of "ng" to transliterate the Hebrew letter *ayin* is a Sephardism.

The Sephardim differed from the Ashkenazim in naming traditions. Until well into the nineteenth century, they followed a strict protocol in which the firstborn children were named for the paternal grandparents, the next children for the maternal grandparents. The Ashkenazim preserve a pious superstition of not naming a child after a living person.

As late as 1858, uncle-niece marriages were not unusual among the "Portuguese Jews," and first-cousin marriages were common, especially in the Caribbean. These practices undoubtedly reflected the tradition of the Hapsburg rulers of Spain.

The dignity of the Sephardic service, led by a hazzan, made it the early American way of worship. Sermons in the vernacular were first introduced by Isaac Leeser in 1830 over great objections from his Philadelphia congregation. The hazzan's English title of "reader" or "minister" and his role as preacher and pastor were modeled on the dominant Protestant mode. All these patterns became standard for the American synagogue by the time of the German immigration of the 1840s, whose ordained rabbis were forced to accept the established customs, but differentiated themselves from the hazzan by being dubbed "Reverend Doctor."

The majority of the Sephardic congregations kept careful vital records—births, marriages, and deaths. Even though some of these have been destroyed through fires or natural disasters, enough records have survived to make it possible for us to recapture the names of most of the Sephardim in the communities we have mentioned.

Those Sephardim who left Portugal for the freedom of Holland, England, and America were far more comfortable with Christian neighbors than their ghettoized Ashkenazic counterparts. As a consequence, while strongly observing the protocols established by their synagogues, the Sephardim were often lax in keeping kashrut and other ritual observances at home.

A mystique of elitism developed around the Sephardim that led Ashkenazim to join their congregations, and many a latter-day Jew laid claim to Sephardic origins. The East European masses that came to America after 1880 evidently shared this feeling, for a number of the small ghetto synagogues they organized labeled themselves Anshei Sfarad ("Men of Spain").[20]

Sources for Lists of Sephardic Jews in Each Community

(Bibliographic details on works cited will be found in the notes.)

BRAZIL: Wiznitzer, *Jews in Colonial Brazil*, pp. 137 f.; amended in I. S. Emmanuel, "Seventeenth-Century Brazilian Jewry: A Critical Review," *American Jewish Archives* 14 (April 1962): 32 ff.

CARIBBEAN JEWRY: Many specifics are in the collections of Zvi Loker, former Israeli ambassador to Haiti, now residing at 32 Palmach Street, Jerusalem; Mordechai Arbell, former Israeli ambassador in Colombia and Central America, now at 50 Pinkas Street, Tel Aviv; and in the genealogical notebooks of the late Florence K. Abrahams, in the library of the Historical Society of Pennsylvania, 1300 Locust Street, Philadelphia, PA 19107, that include data from V. L. Oliver's periodical, *Caribbeana* (London, 1910–1919).

SURINAM: Rev. P. A. Hilfman, "Notes on the History of the Jews in Surinam," *Publications of the American Jewish Historical Society* 18, pp. 179 ff.; Portuguese Congregation, records of births, marriages, and deaths (microfilm, in AJA).

BARBADOS: "A census of the Island of Barbados, West Indies, with the names and ages of all the White Inhabitants of the Island . . . Taken in . . . 1715" (typescript in AJA); and in works cited in n. 4.

MARTINIQUE: Censuses of 1680 and 1683; Cahen, "Les Juifs de Martinique," *Revue des études juives* 31, pp. 102, 114 f.

CURAÇAO: Separate records of male and female births, indicating some death dates (photostats in AJA); marriages in Emmanuel, *Netherland Antilles*, Appendix 17, pp. 841–1007; deaths in Emmanuel, *Precious Stones*.

JAMAICA: Andrade, *Jews of Jamaica*; H. P. Silverman, "The Hunt's Bay Jewish Cemetery, Kingston, Jamaica, British West Indies," *Publications of the American Jewish Historical Society* 37, pp. 327 ff.; "List of [Jewish] Wills [in the West Indies Institute, Kingston]," typescript compiled by Mrs. Dorrit Wilson of Jamaica (copy in AJA); "Deaths in K.K. Shaar Hashamayim, Kingston, Jamaica" [1825–26], compiled by Rev. M. H. Nathan (photostat in AJA).

NEVIS: Sources cited in n. 8.

ST. EUSTATIA: Emmanuel, *Netherlands Antilles*, pp. 104 ff.

ST. CROIX: Epitaphs copied by Rabbi Bernard Heller and Florence K. Abrahams (in AJA).

ST. THOMAS: Births, 1796–1847, compiled by Enid M. Baa (microfilm in AJA); marriages, 1841–1869 (photostats in AJA); burials, 1792–1802 (ibid.); "298 Epitaphs from the Jewish Cemetry [sic] in St. Thomas, W.I., with an Index, compiled from Records in the Archives of the Jewish Community in Copenhagen," by Jul. Margolinsky, Librarian (typescript, Copenhagen, 1957) (copy in AJA).

HAITI: Source cited in n. 11.

BRITISH NORTH AMERICA: M. H. Stern, *First American Jewish Families: 600 Genealogies, 1654–1988* (Baltimore, 1991); Alan Corré and M. H. Stern, "The Record Book of the Reverend Jacob R. Cohen," *Publications of the American Jewish Historical Society* 59 (September 1969): 23 ff.

NEW AMSTERDAM/NEW YORK: Shearith Israel vital records (microfilm in AJA); Pool, *Portraits*; Leo Hershkowitz, *Wills of Early New York Jews (1704–1799)* (New York, 1967).

NEWPORT, R.I.: Epitaphs in *Publications of the American Jewish Historical Society* 27, pp. 191 ff.

SAVANNAH: Sources cited in n. 14.

CHARLESTON: B. A. Elzas, *Jewish Marriage Notices from the Newspaper Press of Charleston, S.C. (1775–1906)* (New York, 1917); idem, *The Old Jewish Cemeteries at Charleston, S.C.: A Transcript of Their Tombstones, 1762–1903* (Charleston, 1903); Stern, "South Carolina Jewish Marriage Settlements," *National Genealogical Society Quarterly* 66 (June 1978): 105 ff.

PHILADELPHIA: Sources cited above for BRITISH NORTH AMERICA; "Record of the Spruce Street Cemetery presented to Congregation Mikve Israel, with notes by Leopold D. Goodman" (1912) (manuscript, photostat in AJA).

Note: Vital records for MONTREAL, RICHMOND, and NEW ORLEANS have not been found, but almost all names recorded in these Sephardic congregations seem to have been Ashkenazic.

Notes

1. Arnold Wiznitzer, *Jews in Colonial Brazil* (New York, 1960); idem, *The Records of the Earliest Jewish Community in the New World* (New York, 1954).

2. J. R. Marcus, *The Colonial American Jew* (Detroit, 1970), vol. 1, chap. 2.

3. S. R. Cohen, trans., *Historical Essay on the Colony of Surinam, 1788* (Cincinnati, 1974); Robert Cohen, "Surinam," *Encyclopaedia Judaica* (1972), 15:529 f.; also frequent references in *Publications of the American Jewish Historical Society* (cited in Cohen article).

4. Bernard Postal and Malcolm H. Stern, *American Airlines Guides to Jewish History in the Caribbean* (New York, n.d.), pp. 16 f.; E. M. Shilstone, *Jewish Monumental Inscriptions in Barbados* (New York and London, n.d.), pp. xiv–xxvii; W. S. Samuel, "Review of the Jewish Colonists in

Barbados in the Year 1680," *Transactions of the Jewish Historical Society of England* 13 (1936): 1–111; 14 (1940): 44 ff.; Samuel Oppenheim, "The Jews in Barbados in 1739: An Attack upon Their Synagogue. Their Long Oath," *Publications of the American Jewish Historical Society* 22 (1914): 197 f.; B. W. Korn, "Barbadian Jewish Wills, 1676–1740," in *A Bicentennial Festschrift for Jacob Rader Marcus* (New York, 1976), pp. 303 ff.; conversations with the late E. M. Shilstone; correspondence of the author with Paul Altman, 1984 f.

5. Postal and Stern, *American Airlines Guide*, pp. 76 f.; Abraham Cahen, "Les Juifs de la Martinique au XVIIe Siècle," *Revue des études juives* 31 (Paris, 1895): 93–121; L. M. Friedman, *Jewish Pioneers and Patriots* (Philadelphia, 1942), chap.7; I. S. Emanuel, "New Light on Early American Jewry," *American Jewish Archives* 7 (January 1955): 22.

6 Postal and Stern, *American Airlines Guide*, pp. 31 f.; I. S. Emmanuel and S. A. Emmanuel, *History of the Jews of the Netherlands Antilles*, 2 vols. (Cincinnati and Curaçao, 1970); I. S. Emmanuel, *Precious Stones of the Jews of Curaçao: Curaçaon Jewry, 1656–1956* (New York, 1957).

7. Postal and Stern, *American Airlines Guide*, pp. 43 f.; J. A. P. M. Andrade, *A Record of the Jews in Jamaica from the English Conquest to the Present Time* (Kingston, 1941) (typescript name index, compiled by Paul F. White, 1963–64, available in American Jewish Archives); Henry Phillips Silverman, *The Tercentenary of the Official Founding of the Jewish Community of Jamaica, B.W.I.; A Panorama of Jamaican Jewry, 5415–5715/1655–1955* (Kingston, 1955).

8. Postal and Stern, *American Airlines Guide*, pp. 82 f.; Stern, "Some Notes on the Jews of Nevis," *American Jewish Archives* 10 (October 1958): 151 ff.; idem, "A Successful Caribbean Restoration: The Nevis Story," *American Jewish Historical Quarterly* 61 (September 1971): 19–32; J. C. Hamilton, *The Life of Alexander Hamilton* (New York, 1834–40).

9. Postal and Stern, *American Airlines Guide*, pp. 85 f.; Emmanuel and Emmanuel, *Jews of the Netherlands Antilles*, pp. 518 f., 1048 f.; John Hartog, "The Honen Daliem Congregation of St. Eustatius," *American Jewish Archives* 19 (April 1967): 60 ff.; T. C. Hansard, ed., *The Parliamentary History of England from the Earliest Period to the Year 1803* (London, 1814) XXII, 218 ff.

10. Postal and Stern, *American Airlines Guide*, pp. 64 f.; Hartog, "Honen Daliem Congregation," p. 65, n. 13; Isidore Paiewonsky, *Jewish Historical Development in the Virgin Islands, 1665–1959* (St. Thomas, 1959); S. T. Relkin and M. R. Abrams, eds., *A Short History of the Hebrew Congregation of St. Thomas* (St. Thomas, ca. 1983).

11. Postal and Stern, *American Airlines Guide*, p. 79.; Abraham Cahen, "Les Juifs dans les colonies françaises au XVIIIe Siècle," *Revue des études juives* 4–5 (1882).

12. Egon Wolff and Frieda Wolff, "The Twenty-Three Jewish Settlers of New Amsterdam," *Studia Rosenthalia*, August 1981, pp. 169–177, challenges the accepted story that appears in Wiznitzer, "The Exodus from Brazil and Arrival in New Amsterdam of the Jewish Pilgrim Fathers," *Publications of the American Jewish Historical Society* 44 (1954): 80 f.; David de Sola Pool and Tamar de Sola Pool, *An Old Faith in the New World* (New York, 1955); D. de Sola Pool, *Portraits Etched in Stone* (New York, 1953); H. B. Grinstein, *The Rise of the Jewish Community of New York, 1654–1860* (Philadelphia, 1945); "The Earliest Extant Minute Books of the Spanish and Portuguese Congregation Shearith Israel in New York, 1728–1786," *Publications of the American Jewish Historical Society* 21; "The Lyons Collection," *Publications of the American Jewish Historical Society* 27.

13. Morris A. Gutstein, *To Bigotry No Sanction* (New York, 1958); Abram Vossen Goodman, *American Overture: Jewish Rights in Colonial Times* (Philadelphia, 1947), pp. 32–68; Jacob R. Marcus, *Early American Jewry*, vol. 1 (Philadelphia, 1951), pp. 116–157; Lee M. Friedman, "America's First Jewish Club," *Jewish Pioneers and Patriots* (Philadelphia, 1942), pp. 197–206; *Rhode Island Jewish Historical Notes* (Providence, 1954 to date), passim.

14. Saul J. Rubin, *Third to None; the Saga of Savannah Jewry, 1733–1983* (Savannah, 1983); M. H. Stern, "New Light on the Jewish Settlement of Savannah," *American Jewish Historical Quarterly* 52 (March 1963): 169–199; idem, "The Sheftall Diaries: Vital Records of Savannah Jewry (1733–1808)," *American Jewish Historical Quarterly* 54 (March 1965): 243–277; B. H. Levy, *Savannah's Old Jewish Community Cemeteries* (Macon, Ga., ca. 1983); Jacob R. Marcus, *Early American Jewry*, vol. 2 (Philadelphia, 1953), pp. 277–373.

15. B. A. Elzas, *The Jews of South Carolina from the Earliest Times to the Present Day* (Philadelphia, 1905); Charles Reznikoff with Uriah Z. Engelman, *The Jews of Charleston: A History of an American Jewish Community* (Philadelphia, 1950); William A. Rosenthall, *The Story of K.K. Beth Elohim of Charleston, South Carolina* (Charleston, 1981); Solomon Breibart, "Two Jewish Congregations in Charleston, S.C. Before 1791: A New Conclusion," *American Jewish History* 69 (March 1980): 360–363; Marcus, *Early American Jewry*, 2:226–257; Elzas, *The Reformed Society of Israelites of Charleston, S.C.* (New York, 1916); *The Isaac Harby Prayerbook* (facsimile reproduction of manuscript) (Charleston, 1974).

16. H. S. Morais, *The Jews of Philadelphia: Their History from the Earliest Settlements to the Present Time* (Philadelphia, 1894); Edwin Wolf II and Maxwell Whiteman, *The History of the Jews of Philadelphia from Colonial Times to the Age of Jackson* (Philadelphia, 1957); Marcus, *Early American Jewry*, 2:3–164; Murray Friedman, ed., *Jewish Life in Philadelphia, 1830–1940* (Philadelphia, 1983).

17. Esther L. Blaustein, Rachel A. Esar, and Evelyn Miller, "Spanish and Portuguese Synagogue (Shearith Israel), Montreal, 1768–1968," *Miscellanies of the Jewish Historical Society of England* 8 (1971): 111–142; Marcus, *Early American Jewry*, 2:198–285; Benjamin G. Sack, *History of the Jews in Canada* (Montreal, 1965).

18. H. T. Ezekiel and Gaston Lichtenstein, *The History of the Jews of Richmond from 1769 to 1917* (Richmond, 1917); Myron Berman, *Richmond's Jewry, 1769–1976: Shabbat in Shockoe* (Charlottesville, Va., 1979).

19. Bertram W. Korn, *The Early Jews of New Orleans* (Waltham, Mass., 1969); Jacob R. Marcus, *United States Jewry, 1776–1985*, vol. 1 (Detroit, 1989), passim.

20. The author has been compiling unpublished Sephardic genealogy for many years, and these conclusions derive largely from his research. Naming protocol is outlined in Herbert C. Dobrinsky, *A Treasury of Sephardic Laws and Customs* (Hoboken, N.J., 1986), p. 3; congregations named "Anshei Sfard" appear in lists of Jewish institutions in *American Jewish Yearbook*, 1907–1908, 1919–1920, and in Kehillah of New York City, *The Jewish Communal Register of New York City, 1917–1918* (New York, ca. 1918).

The Fidanques:
Symbols of the Continuity of the
Sephardic Tradition in America*

Emma Fidanque Levy

Loyalty to family, faith in God, and pride in the Jewish community were the values of the family which surrounded me during my childhood. Long before I learned about the Fidancs of Saragossa (ca. 1279) or the Duarte-Rodríguez-Fidanques of Hamburg (ca. 1612),[2] I had a strong sense of connection with the past and with family history.

The family detective's work depends on identification by name. In truth, we place and understand ourselves best when we know not only the origins of our name but also the symbolism the name carries. The earliest records, dating from the thirteenth century in Saragossa, name us Fedanc. In seventeenth-century Hamburg, we appear as Fidanque, having at some point lost the appellation Duarte-Rodríguez that preceded it. It has not been possible to document the family's journey from Saragossa to Hamburg, nor to discover how the ancient name was transmuted to a new spelling. It is known, however, from testimony taken by the Spanish Inquisition that "they [the Fidanques] are baptized Christians and in said city of Hamburg had themselves circumcised and . . . continued in the synagogues of Hamburg to use the tallit and tefillin and to say the prayers of the *Shema* and *Amidah* and to perform the other ceremonies which the Jews are accustomed to perform."

*This article is dedicated to "Uncle Bill," Elias Alvin Fidanque (b. 1905).[1] For well over fifty years he has searched and researched the history of our family and created our first family tree. His correspondence with scholars all over the world is voluminous, his reading prolific. In fact, his efforts made it possible to write the story that follows.

I accepted the invitation to undertake this assignment with pride, and in the spirit of "successor" to our beloved uncle.

Another interesting fact concerning the family's religion during the years of persecution on the Iberian Peninsula was discovered by Herman P. Solomon in a document from the Lisbon Inquisition. It is the confession of one Gaspar Bocarro, who says that around 1631 he resided in Hamburg and "knew [David] Duarte-Rodríguez-Fidanque, born in this city, merchant, 60 years old, lives in Hamburg as a member of the Protestant congregation, having abandoned the Mosaic denomination which he was previously professing."[3] In spite of David's change of heart, the sons and cousins who came after him present a more faithful story.

Through the centuries of forced conversion, expulsion, intermarriage, and even acceptance by the dominant societies in many different cultures, the descendants of our earliest known ancestor, Azmel Fidanc of medieval Aragon, time and again found their way back to the synagogue, tenaciously bound to God and the traditions of Jewish life.

The name Fedanc, or Fedanch, appears to be an old Catalan-Aragonese derivative of the Latin *fidens*, denoting "a man of faith." For over six hundred years, despite numerous changes, the family's name has retained its root meaning. Through the generations, the members of the family have lived up to the spirit the name embodies, apparently sensing its meaning even though they lacked scholarly knowledge of its etymology.

* * *

Our large family circle was headed by my great-grandparents, Emma Fidanque (1850–1935) and Joseph Fidanque (1844–1933), whose memories of their parents took us as far back as the early nineteenth century. The stage was set for us to feel part of history.

As small children we learned about faraway places reached only by ocean voyages as we welcomed cousins of many degrees of kinship arriving from France, Germany, England, Cuba, Colombia, Venezuela, St. Thomas, Curaçao, and Jamaica. It seemed as if everyone in the communities of what Bill Fidanque calls "La Nacion"[4] was related in some way. Our children's world was enriched and our horizons broadened by the seamless and seemingly endless connections with people all over the world.

The outstanding characteristics of our family have been faith in God, devotion to the synagogue, and a strong sense of duty and per-

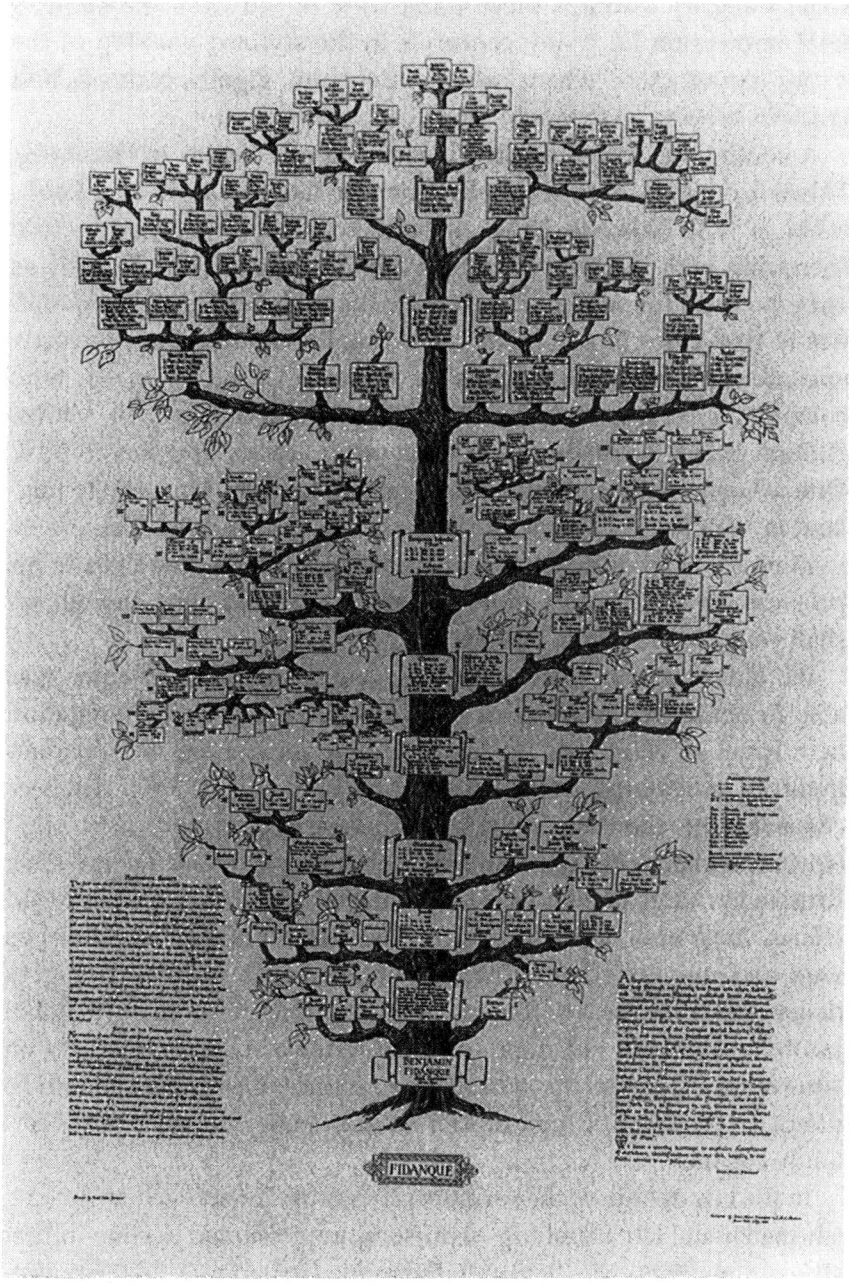

The Fidanque Family Tree. The original was collated by Elias Alvin "Bill" Fidanque and J. N. L. Maduro. (Courtesy of Emma Fidanque Levy)

sonal integrity. Perhaps these traits were honed from the family's total immersion for many centuries in the stylized worship of the *esnoga* (synagogue),[5] where habits of decorum, dignity, courtesy, and gracious bearing were taught, practiced, and revered.

A continuous record of the Fidanque family begins in Hamburg. This information came originally from the late David de Sola Poole, rabbi of K.K. Shearith Israel in New York City, who had a close friendship with the local branch of the Fidanque family. As early as 1923, he used his worldwide connections with Sephardic communities to find clues to our history. Our family archives include correspondence with such figures as Alfonso Cassuto (1928), who compiled a list of every Fidanque tomb in the cemetery in Altona, Haham Rabbi Solomon Gaon in London (1953), and Reverend I. Duque (1953) of Bevis Marks Synagogue in London. On a trip to England in 1938 Rabbi Poole wrote home to say, "By the way, I have been hunting for Fidanques, but with little success." In another note on his progress, he was slightly more optimistic: "If I live long enough we shall yet have the family history."

Bill Fidanque continued the search, and finally H. P. Solomon was able to obtain the minutes of the Portuguese Jewish Congregation Beth Israel, of Hamburg. We learn of three generations of Fidanques involved in congregational activities as *parnassim de hebra* (trustees charged with the care of the poor and sick), *gabbay de terra santa* (trustee in charge of Holy Land charities), and *parnas de Talmud Torah* (trustee in charge of education). The entries indicate honors bestowed (*Hatan Torah* and *Hatan Bereshit* on the festival of Simhat Torah) as well as fines levied for unruly behavior and public apologies demanded from the *teba* (the officiant's reading desk). In 1686, Rabbi Jacob de Abraham Fidanque (d. 1702) wrote a supercommentary on Abravenel's *Commentary on the Earlier Prophets*. We cannot claim to be direct descendants of the Rif, Ribi Ya'acob Fidanque, but we are certainly cousins.

In the last decade of the seventeenth century, many well-to-do Jewish merchants left Hamburg because of an economic decline in that city. Among them was Benjamin Fidanque (1635–1704), who emigrated to Amsterdam in 1694 with his three sons. Picking up stakes and establishing oneself elsewhere occurs quite often in our family, and, I suspect, in many Sephardic families which found it easier to leave and look for opportunities in the general Western European culture rather than wait to be pursued.

In his foreword to *Beth Haim van Ouderkirk van de Amstel* ("Images of a Portuguese Jewish Cemetery in Holland") by the Queen's Commissioner for the Province of North Holland,[6] Mr. F. J. Kranenburg wrote:

> [Here] we see before us the striking encounter between a Holland in the process of liberating itself and striving ahead and the exiled Sephardim; an encounter which led to a unique, mutual, spiritual impregnation of both peoples. The Dutch . . . thirsted for spiritual elevation and culture. The . . . Sephardim . . . brought erudition, artistic sense and skill, and the colorful Mediterranean art of living. . . . In the midst of other Amsterdamers, there grew and flourished in the Portuguese Jewish community a group of merchants certainly, but also theologians, jurists, philosophers, physicians, and printers for whom the ideas of Amsterdam had already been common spiritual property for many generations.

Fidanques lived in Amsterdam and are recorded there until late in the nineteenth century when the male line ended with the death of David of Isaac (1857–1881).[7] Our own direct forebear, Josseph Fidanque (ca. 1682–1748), left in 1698, bound for a real adventure. He was off to join his cousins who had settled in Curaçao, which had been seized from Spain by the Dutch republic. The island was rich in natural resources and was, of course, an excellent base in the Caribbean. By 1643, when Peter Stuyvesant was governor, the slave trade was flourishing and the Dutch West India Company needed more colonists to stabilize and build up the island. A proclamation was issued inviting groups from Holland to settle. The Amsterdam parnassim, who were loyal Hollanders, encouraged members of the Jewish community to answer the call and even financed their journeys. And so it was that in 1651 the first small group of Jewish settlers arrived in Curaçao under a contract made with Joao de Yllan.

When the Dutch were forced to abandon their attempt to take Brazil from Spain, in 1659, six hundred Jews retreated with them. We quote from Cecil Roth's *History of the Marranos*:

> The reconquest of Brazil by the Portuguese and the consequent break-up of the local communities of Marranos returned to Judaism under Dutch protection

was an episode of the highest importance in Jewish history, a majority of the older American communities owing their origins to the minor dispersion that catastrophe brought about.[8]

When the Dutch government offered inducements to attract settlers to Curaçao. Isaac da Costa, one of the first Jewish settlers in Brazil, convinced several Amsterdam Jewish families to emigrate, "More than 70 souls, adults as well as children of our nation."[9] They took with them a *Sefer Torah* lent by the parnassim of the Portuguese community.

The privileges granted to the da Costa group were far superior to those in earlier contracts. The local government committed itself to support the group's disciplinary measures against its members, granted the Jewish settlers the right to buy slaves directly and to build houses, and, most important, gave specific guarantees of religious freedom. However, the settlers were not granted citizenship.

Although the earlier settlers of 1651 had given their small community the name K(ahal) K(adosh) Mikve Israel ("Hope of Israel"), it is in fact the members of the da Costa group of 1659 who are considered the founders of Curaçao's Jewish community—families such as Cardozo, Aboab, Jesurun, DeLeon, Marchena, and de Castro. They wrote their own *hascamoth* (regulations) based on those of the Amsterdam community. Following are some of the interesting regulations they imposed:

- Arguing or holding forth on the street in the synagogue district is prohibited.
- It is absolutely forbidden to found another synagogue.
- It is forbidden to open another's mail.
- Members having a dispute among themselves shall be obliged to submit to arbitration by the Mahamed.
- Anyone writing verses, sonnets, or satires injurious to another shall pay 24 florins to the community.

And, to remind the congregation of their obligations,

- The *hascamoth* shall be read [in the synagogue] every six months.

They also chose a *haham* (lit. "sage"; title given to the rabbi of a Sephardic congregation). The *hascamoth* embraced almost every phase of behavior and minhag (custom). There had been a house of worship in the walled city of Willemstad since 1671. Now a proper synagogue was built. A country synagogue was built for the convenience of the plantation owners who lived outside of the city. In addition, the community imported teachers, a cantor, and ritual slaughterers.[10]

By the time Josseph Fidanque arrived, the Jewish community was well established. The management of the community was entrusted to the Mahamad, a committee of three elected by the parnassim.

From all accounts Josseph was an aggressive businessman and entrepreneur who made and lost several fortunes. He is listed as a "merchant and licensed broker," a profession that would remain a family mainstay through the generations. Applying a verse in Genesis to Josseph, one of his contemporaries wrote of him, "His hand is on everyone, and the hand of everyone is on him"—similar, perhaps, to having a finger in every pie. He owned the sailing ship *Koningen Esther* and had interests in several others. From an agreement he made with one of his creditors after a substantial loss, we know that he owned slaves. His erratic career never daunted him, and he was proud enough to have ordered a special tombstone from Amsterdam many years before his death. (It can be seen today in the cemetery in Curaçao.) When the day arrived, his affairs were in good order and his widow, Sara Jesurun Henriquez Fidanque (d. 1768), was able to carry out his generous bequest to provide dowries for five orphan girls.[11]

Josseph was very active in the affairs of the Jewish community. He served as treasurer and as parnas of Talmud Torah. He gave a Torah scroll to the synagogue with the condition that memorial prayers be said for him and his brother Jacob (d. ca. 1739). In an old manuscript found and translated by J. (Jossy) L. Maduro (1891–1964),[12] reference is made to the donation by Jahacob (Jacob Fidanque), a brother of Josseph who resided in Amsterdam, of a Torah scroll to Mikve Israel in Curaçao for two *escavoth* (memorial prayers), one for himself and one for his wife. It is not clear whether these different stories concern the same scroll; what is clear is that the ties between the Amsterdam family and the Curaçao branch were close and remained that way for generations.

Josseph's will indicates that he was survived by eight children, one of whom was Yacob (1717–1791). During Yacob's life, several Jewish communities were established in the American colonies.[13] When the British took over New Amsterdam in 1664, renaming it New York, the Jews there, who had arrived from Brazil in 1660 and had been permitted, under Dutch rule, to have their own cemetery but not the right to build a synagogue, were now given permission by the British to do so. In 1730, Shearith Israel ("The Remnant of Israel") built its first synagogue with financial help from the Curaçao community. So it was also in Newport, where the Curaçaoans also responded generously to the request from a settlement of Jewish families who named themselves K.K. Yeshu'ath Israel. In 1740 a third congregation in the colonies with ties to Curaçao was established in Charleston, South Carolina, K.K. Beth Elohim. The families were mainly immigrants from Curaçao and Jamaica. The liturgy they used was in Hebrew, but the selection for synagogue honors was conducted in Spanish.

In 1733(?) forty Jews of Spanish-Portuguese ancestry arrived in Savannah, Georgia. They had fled Portugal by way of London. The Sheftall diaries tell of constant movement between the families of Savannah and Curaçao, Jamaica and St. Croix.[14] The first Jewish congregation founded in Philadelphia appealed in 1782 to their "brethren" in the West Indies for assistance in building a synagogue.

The social and familial records of the colonial congregations and those of the islands reveal many close connections. Sons and daughters were betrothed to cousins, marriages were arranged, and in this manner the purity of the Sephardic families was maintained. Business ties were also strong. Among the first Marranos in Portugal, the phrase *E dos nossos* ("He is one of us") was like a pledge of mutual trust. Centuries later this trust bound together the early Jewish settlers in the New World.

A picture of Yacob Fidanque (1717–1791) emerges from the pages of the appendices compiled by Isaac and Suzanne Emmanuel in volume 2 of their monumental *History of the Jews of the Netherlands Antilles*. Yacob was a licensed broker in Curaçao, as was his father.

During the seventeenth and eighteenth centuries, Sephardic Jewish brokers (called "Portuguese"), with their worldwide family connections, were in a most favorable position to advise their clients on the best investments in goods or money or on the risks involved. They had the reputation of having a fine sense of business, diplomacy, and experience in international trade. In many cases a foreign government was the client. The broker was also a merchant's agent, a judge of merchandise, an appraiser of ships, a real-estate agent, and, always, a financial adviser. In Curaçao at that time, Jewish brokers outnumbered others by four or five to one. Although Yacob's son was the last Fidanque broker in Curaçao, his descendants through the years remained interested in international trade, representing businesses on many continents.

Yacob's name also appears on the list of slaveowners drawn up by the Emmanuels for the year 1764. Slaves were not permitted to work on the Sabbath or the holy days. Yacob's wife, Bathsheba Jesurun Henriquez (1727–1772), inherited a large estate from her parents. Yacob's financial standing declined after her death, and he was no longer able to maintain his son-in-law and daughter, Sara, as he had agreed to, and as was the custom in those days. Yacob served as parnas and as treasurer of the congregation. He signed the *hascamoth* of 1671 after a bitter conflict within the congregation. Yacob and Bathsheba were evidently pillars of the congregation; her tombstone, with a Portuguese inscription, praises her for "heroic deeds and virtuous works. . . . I hope she will rejoice in life eternal, reserved by God for those who fear Him."[15] We know of four children who survived: Sara, Hannah, Abraham Haim, and Mordechay, the fourth generation in this line of Fidanques.

Mordechay Fidanque (1760–1826) lived during the years of revolution in the New World and in France. This upheaval did not bypass the small and hospitable island the Fidanques called home. In fact, the Jews of Curaçao were very much involved—sometimes by choice and at other times by the force of events. When French revolutionary forces conquered Holland in 1795, the French government sent an agent to govern Curaçao. The islanders resented this interference, however, and resisted the French takeover attempt. In 1796 they formed a National Guard for defense, and the merchants, who were mostly Jews, were taxed repeatedly for local government loans. The local forces successfully repulsed the first French naval attack, and during the second attack, one month later, English ships appeared to help turn back the French. The English then seized the island for themselves. After an occupation of some two years, it was returned to the Dutch by the Treaty of Amiens (1802), only to be attacked again by the English. The National Guard bravely defended their territory but could not repel a second surprise attack in 1807. The second English occupation lasted nine years and ended only through local government action. Since the Jews were the most successful merchants, they not only made the largest contributions but also suffered the largest losses from the interruption of trade.

During the American Revolution, Curaçao and St. Eustatius, also under Dutch control, were centers for the shipment of arms and provisions to the revolutionaries. Many Jewish Curaçaoan shipowners participated in this potentially very profitable enterprise. However, the risk was quite great, for ship and cargo could be lost if intercepted by English warships, and life as well, since the owners often accompanied their cargoes. Trade of this type came to an end with the English seizure of St. Eustatius in 1780.

During these years, the conflict among nations was echoed by ever-present conflicts between families in the synagogue, new regulations adopted by the parnassim, and constant appeals to the Amsterdam parnassim for rulings.[16]

The conflicts, for the most part, revolved around the question of the power of the local parnassim and their interpretation of the *hascamoth*. For example: Could a young couple who had premarital relations be refused a proper marriage ceremony? Could the parnassim banish or excommunicate a member of the community (or refuse him synagogue honors or a Jewish burial) for so-called unruly behavior or disturbing the peace? On one hand the governor, who represented the Dutch West India Company, could be asked to settle the dispute; or the parnassim of Amsterdam, which represented a higher religious authority, could hear the appeal. In some cases, the disputes reached the court of the States General of Holland. By 1783, the orders and decisions of the parnassim were so continually challenged that qualified men did not want to be elected to these positions. Because of this problem, the *hascamoth* were amended to allow for the fining of anyone who refused to serve, defied the parnassim, did not attend the general meeting, or was insubordinate in any way. Very strong measures taken in an age of revolution!

At first glance it may seem strange that Mordechay's name appears only in the marriage records of Mikve Israel. The answer might be that Abraham Haim was the *bekhor*, the firstborn son, who, in the Jewish tradition, often received special privileges. However, in this case he earned his privileged position as well. Abraham Haim was the last Fidanque to be listed as a broker in Curaçao. In addition, he was president of the congregation, a cantor, and a teacher—all told, a most important and accomplished person in the community.

Our Mordechay married Rebecca Henriquez Fereyra (ca. 1777–1845). They had two daughters and two sons. The eldest son was Jacob, born in 1801 in Curaçao (d. 1885). He is the subject of our next portrait.

Jacob emigrated to St. Thomas as a young man. His motives for leaving Curaçao, the island that had been home to four generations of Fidanques, were, we assume, due to two very different causes—economics and uncomfortable Jewish communal conflicts. In the early years of the nineteenth century Curaçao suffered consecutive disasters: a devastating drought, a severe hurricane, three yellow fever epidemics, and a smallpox epidemic. Though certainly secondary to the human suffering caused by these events, their confluence had a devastating effect on the island's economy.

Between 1807 and 1816, controlled at the time by the English, Curaçao's port was completely paralyzed. When war broke out in 1812, it fell victim to the conflict between America and England and was bypassed by shippers in favor of St. Thomas, a free and open port. The Sephardic Jews of the United States also suffered from the war because of the loss of the reciprocal overseas market in the Caribbean.

Moreover, the Curaçao Jewish community was divided by a conflict surrounding Hazzan Joshua Piza (1772–1850), who had been sent from Amsterdam, with recommendations from the Dutch parnassim, to serve Mikve Israel. The trouble started when Piza was reprimanded for disobeying the regulations. The Amsterdam parnassim wrote to him warning that he was not to make innovations when reading the Torah. The next complaint was that he mispronounced the word *haguefen* when blessing the wine. He said *hagafen*, as was the custom in Amsterdam. It appears that the parnassim resented his "independence," which, according to family lore, was really stubbornness.

There is no doubt that Piza was another victim of the authoritarianism of the parnassim. The conflict pitted the parnassim against the "separatists" for six long years. Many families were divided by quarrels between supporters of the two sides. We know that there were Fidanques in both camps. As for Joshua Piza, who had been accused of being "hoarse, deaf and unpleasant," the community asked the government to mediate. Prevailed upon to resign, he received a monetary settlement and left to become hazzan in St. Thomas.[17] (There is an interesting aside to this story which shows how events shape local idioms. In Papiamento, the Creole dialect of Curaçao, the phrase *Bo ta parnas* [lit. "you are like a parnas"] came to mean, "you are stubborn and unbending.")[18]

After these events many Jewish families decided to leave Curaçao for other areas of the Caribbean where they had connections. Some went to Jamaica, Cartagena, Caracas, or Santo Domingo. Like many others, however, Jacob Fidanque headed for St. Thomas.

Founded in 1665 as a Danish Lutheran colony, St. Thomas became a free port in 1764. The first settlers included immigrants from many nations and a large number of slaves. In time the Danish language gave way to Dutch, Negro Dutch Creole, and, after the second English invasion, English became the language of trade. In the first half of the nineteenth century, "the golden age of the Danish islands, St. Thomas became the commercial emporium of the Antilles and one of the great ports of the world."[19]

Denmark proclaimed religious tolerance for Jews and Catholics as early as 1685. The first Jewish birth recorded was in 1794. At that time many Jews had fled to St. Thomas from St. Eustatius after it was sacked by the British. Congregation B'racha v' Shalom, which still exists today, was formed in 1796.

Jacob moved to the bustling town of Charlotte Amalie in 1825. By that time the Jewish population of St. Thomas was made up largely of Curaçaoans. He established his own business, selling "dry-goods and earthenware," and in 1830 married Rebecca Mendes-Monsanto (1810–1863), whose parents had lived in Curaçao for generations. Jacob and Rebecca, who was fifteen years his junior, had eight children; only four survived.

St. Thomas records show that the largest number of births to Jewish parents occurred in 1831, the year of Morris's birth (d. 1915). (Two of the sons of Jacob and Rebecca, Morris, the eldest, and Joseph, were great-grandfathers of mine.) In that year the congregation's third wooden synagogue was burned to the ground in a devastating fire. Two years later, a beautiful new sanctuary built of stone and brick was dedicated and consecrated with appropriate ceremony. This lovely building, designed by a French architect, with mahogany benches, lamps with Baccarat crystal hurricane shades, ancient scrolls, and original furniture, was restored by the congregation in 1973.[20]

In 1851 the congregation had grown to number almost four hundred. Ten years before, an anonymous English author wrote the following about the Jews of St. Thomas: "The flock of Israel's fold is thick and fares well at this place."[21] The Danish government proclaimed emancipation for all "Colored" in 1848 and free compulsory education for every child. This was twenty years before President Lincoln's Emancipation Proclamation. While the Danish government issued liberal decrees and Jewish communities in the United States were beginning to free themselves from what Max I. Dimont describes as "blind observances of ceremonial law,"[22] the Jews of St. Thomas prospered and multiplied and continued to observe the Sephardic rituals of their ancestors. They did so without the controlling and all-encompassing rules of the Curaçao parnassim, which remained the root of the constant quarrels at Mikve Israel.

Jacob Fidanque became one of the leading merchants in Charlotte Amalie. He served as honorary reader of the congregation for ten years. His son Joseph wrote of him, "It can be said that he never lost a friend or made an enemy."[23] He and Rebecca, his accomplished and beautiful wife, owned a home on Crystal Gade, known even today as Synagogue Hill. There, at the top of the hill, where legend has it that the most important people lived, they raised their family in a community admired and respected by its Christian neighbors. On Jacob's seventieth anniversary he received a testimonial scroll from the congregation. The scroll states in part: "The number of signatures attached will evince in some measure, the estimation in which you are held by us."

Our family's oldest mementos are the portraits of Jacob and Rebecca that hang in the home of Vito (Vivian Joshua) Fidanque (b. 1896) of New York City, who also is the custodian of four *Parassah* volumes (books containing the weekly Torah readings) and a Rosh Hashanah prayerbook published in 1770. The books are inscribed with the name

J. Monsanto, which was used by Jacob. The prayerbook includes a prayer in Portuguese for "the State of Holland and West Vrieland . . .

> *St. Thomas, 1st January 1885.*
>
> M_____
>
> *Dear Sir,*
>
> *I beg to inform you that I have this day established a Commercial House in the city of Panama, U. S. C., and admitted my sons* **J. M.** *and* **B. D. Fidanque** *as partners thereof, under the style of*
>
> ## M. Fidanque & Sons.
>
> *Soliciting for the new firm a continuance of the confidence which my establishment in this Island has enjoyed for the past twenty-nine years, and requesting your attention to the respective signatures at foot,*
>
> *I remain,*
> *Dear Sir,*
> *Your Obdt. Servt.,*
>
> *M. Fidanque.*
>
> *M. Fidanque will sign* M. Fidanque & Sons
>
> *J. M. Fidanque* " "
>
> *B. D. Fidanque* " "

A letter informing the recipient of the establishment of a Fidanque business presence in Panama. (Courtesy of Emma Fidanque Levy) and high and serene Prince William, Prince of Orange and Nassau . . . and the venerable Burgomeisters and Magistrates of the city of Amsterdam."

In 1856 Morris, then twenty-five years old, established the second Fidanque firm in St. Thomas, the first being that of his father, Jacob, which still flourished at the time, importing "dry-goods and earthenware." Morris called his firm M. Fidanque and Brothers, importers and exporters. That same year he married Rachel Delvalle (1837–1882), the daughter of Benjamin Shalom Delvalle (1811–1896), who had served as hazzan and parnas in the Curaçao congregation. He too emigrated to St. Thomas to avoid the constant communal quarrels.

Benjamin Shalom served as honorary hazzan in St. Thomas for several years. Family legend has it that he died on Yom Kippur at the very hour of the *Minha* service at which he had always officiated. Morris and Rachel had ten children, eight of whom survived.

In 1867 a devastating hurricane and earthquake struck St. Thomas. In the years that followed, as steam replaced sail, other islands became the main service ports for ships plying the Caribbean, and the economy of St. Thomas declined rapidly. By 1884 Morris decided to send his two eldest sons to establish a branch of his business in Panama. This coincided with the plans of French financiers who, having gained a concession from Colombia, were attempting to build a canal across the isthmus.

Several Sephardic Jewish families from St. Thomas, and some others from Jamaica and Curaçao, had already settled in Panama. Evidence shows that a burial society (Kol Shearith Israel) had been formed and a Jewish cemetery consecrated.[24] Joseph, the seventh child of Jacob and Rebecca Fidanque, married Emma Levy Maduro in 1867. Emma's father, Samuel Levy Maduro (1780–1867), another hazzan who was dismissed from his position in Curaçao, had taken the position in St. Thomas.

When Jacob retired, Joseph took over the business, naming it J. Fidanque & Co. It was not long before he too decided that future success depended on a move to Panama. And so we find, in the last quarter of the nineteenth century, Joseph and his two nephews in separate firms in Colón, the Atlantic port of the isthmus of Panama. And in 1887, Rebecca (1868–1947), the only child of Joseph and Emma

Fidanque, married her cousin Benjamin Delvalle (1863–1937), son of Morris and Rachel.

Panama has always held a unique position in world commerce. A narrow neck of land situated between the two great American continents, it serves as the shortest land distance between the Caribbean and the Pacific Ocean. In the fifteenth century, when Columbus was searching for a route to India, he explored the Caribbean coast of Panama to find a way across. In the days of the Conquistadors, as treasure from Peru, Chile, and Mexico was transported to ships bound for Spain, the cities on both coasts of Panama prospered. "Gold and silver bars were piled up like firewood in the Royal Treasury Building."[25]

When the nationalist-revolutionary movement started in South America, Panama was part of Spanish Nueva Granada, which included present-day Colombia, Venezuela, and Ecuador. In 1821 Panama declared its independence from Spain and became part of La Gran Colombia. During the next eighty-two years, colorful and sometimes fanciful schemes and plans for routes across the isthmus figured importantly as it became the transshipment point for gold and for people. In 1885 the Panama Railroad, built by the United States, was opened—a somewhat more secure and efficient way to cross the isthmus.

Then followed the failed attempts by the French to build a canal across the neck. The United States government stepped in to negotiate a treaty with Colombia which would have permitted the conclusion of the project. By 1903 it was apparent that no treaty would be negotiated, propelling Panama to declare her independence from Colombia and sign the Hay–Bunau-Varilla Treaty, which gave the United States the right to construct a canal. My grandfather Benjamin Delvalle Fidanque (1863–1937) at that time represented Belgium as consul. Belgium was one of the first countries to recognize Panama as an independent nation. The next ten years of canal construction brought great advantages to the country and in particular to the port cities, as sewers were built, streets paved, and yellow fever eradicated. The canal was opened in 1913.

As the country prospered, so did the Jewish community. The story of Congregation Kol Shearith Israel is the story of the families who have nurtured it for the last 114 years. The Fidanques, Maduros, Cardozes, de Castros, and many others who left St. Thomas to settle in Panama were looking for a better life in a new homeland—similar to their ancestors who had left the Iberian Peninsula, then western Europe, for the Caribbean. In St. Thomas they had practiced their Judaism in an atmosphere of openness and confidence, no longer dependent on the *hascamoth* of Curaçao, no longer under the dominion of the parnassim of Amsterdam. The winds of change and of self-determination were in the air.

Among the emigrants were readers and elders of the St. Thomas congregation and offspring of the Curaçao hazzanim. Bill Fidanque posits the theory that the majority of the members of Kol Shearith Israel in 1976 were descendants of the four Curaçao–St. Thomas hazzanim: Joshua Piza, Samuel Levy Maduro, Benjamin Shalom Delvalle, and David Cardoze, Jr. (1824–1914).

In every generation Fidanque men and women have been among the most eminent and supportive members of the congregation, not only with their financial resources but, more important, through their leadership. The commemoration of one hundred years of Jewish life in Panama held in 1976 testifies to the devotion of this small and loyal offshoot of the people Israel. They had moved from one country to another, indeed, crossing the ocean between continents, for over four hundred years, yet they always found the voice (or way) "to sing Adonai's song in a strange land."

During its first fifty years, the original Kol Shearith Israel Benevolent and Burial Society became an organized religious community with "a clearly defined congregational dignity, pride and self-reliance that are its distinguishing characteristics."[26] Functioning without the formal structure of the Curaçaoan model, the members held and conducted worship services, performed life-cycle events, assisted members in need, contributed to appeals from the larger community, helped travelers, answered appeals from Palestine for support of Jewish institutions, and also prepared their sons to become Bar Mitzvah. Readers will recall that the tradition of help for Israel goes back to Hamburg in the seventeenth century where a *gabbay de terra santa* was in charge of "Holy Land charities."

In 1918 the congregation rented a large second-story hall in a building in downtown Panama City. The expense was shared by the

YMHA, which had set up a Panama branch to serve Jewish military personnel stationed in the Canal Zone.

Soon thereafter a special meeting was called to consider changing the Sephardi traditional rite to a more modern form of worship. The proponents of change stated that since most of the members did not understand Hebrew, sections of the service should be conducted in English. The decision was made to retain the Hebrew reading of the Torah and the traditional Curaçaoan chants and hymns, but that as much as possible should be read from the Reform *Union Prayer Book*.

Before the time when mixed seating was approved in the 1930s, I remember as a small child sitting with my father in the men's section looking across the aisle to my mother as she sang in the separate women's choir.

During the second fifty years our first rabbi, ordained by the Hebrew Union College in Cincinnati, arrived to serve the congregation.[27] In the fall of 1932, Bill Fidanque, president of the congregation, had proposed that Rabbi Norman Feldheym (1906–1985) be invited to serve for a three-month trial period. Happily for the group, Norman Feldheym accepted the modest offer of $350 plus his steamship fare! In a letter setting forth the terms, Bill Fidanque wrote,

> . . . we use the Union Prayer Book exclusively except for *Yom Kippur* when we also read from the Orthodox ritual and we like our minister to wear a cap and gown and to call up certain members to the Law each Saturday. Also there are a few other picturesque Spanish and Portuguese forms and chants we still adhere to.

Norman Feldheym more than lived up to his recommendation by the president of the Hebrew Union College as "a wonderful human being." He was a man of great abilities, unusually resourceful, sincere, a sound thinker, and a fine preacher. He remained in Panama for five years.

During that time, a sanctuary and community hall was built and dedicated. The formation of a sisterhood followed, an important step which allowed the women of the congregation to participate more fully in every phase of congregational life. Because of the persistence of the first president of sisterhood, women of the congregation gained the right to vote on congregational matters.

It was also during these years that the Kol Shearith Benevolent and Burial Society officially took its name as Congregation Kol Shearith Israel. Jewish community organizations were formed, and two more groups established synagogues.[28] The Albert Einstein Hebrew Day School was started as a joint venture.

Today the fourth generation of Fidanques and related families continue to enjoy the esteemed respect of the dominant Catholic community in Panama, a framework beautifully built and nurtured by their great-grandparents in the early days before and since the republic was formed.

Our grandparents, Benjamin Delvalle and Rebecca, were the proud parents of nine sons and one daughter, all of them born in Panama, with the exception of their second son, Joseph (1890–1970), who was born in St. Thomas during a visit there by his parents. One son, Stanley, died at the age of thirteen. The Fidanque firm in 1906 included Morris, Joseph (who had joined his agencies to those of his brother), and Morris's two sons, Benjamin Delvalle and Jacob. They represented several European shipping companies. They also imported needed goods and exported timber, tortoise shell, and fruit.

As the country enjoyed economic and cultural progress, the firm prospered. Family letters indicate that the older generation did quite a bit of traveling—Paris and Hamburg and "watering spas" in Europe seemed to be favorite destinations. However, skepticism about the effectiveness of the "cures" was expressed, as in the following letter:

> I have often thought of Ben Delv's anticipated trip to Europe to reduce flesh and this is a mistaken idea as it is not sustained after return inasmuch as the old habit of indulgence will be continued and no privations of any sort be maintained after those heavy sacrifices of money.[29]

Jacob (1858–1942) moved to New York City with his wife and opened a new branch of the business. He acted as the purchasing and forwarding agent for the Panama office. As the eldest son, Jacob was given advantages that his brothers and sisters never enjoyed. At the age of sixteen, he was sent from St. Thomas to attend school in Brussels and later at Dr. Kayserling's Academy in Hanover. From correspondence we learn that he and Rufus Daniel Isaacs were "good friends & pals" at Dr. Kayserling's. (Rufus Daniel Isaacs was later to be a prominent British politician, viceroy of India, and first marquess of Reading.)

"Uncle," as we called him, was considered the arbiter of good taste in the family. He wrote rather florid poetry for special family occasions and loved opera. He took upon himself the position of patriarch of the family, trying, with success at times, to control the personal relations and business activities of Delvalle's large family. He and his wife, Rebecca Sasso (ca. 1865–1919), had no children of their own, but they acted as surrogate parents to Delvalle's older sons as each was sent to New York to complete his education. It was to him also that his father opened his heart in old age. We quote from a poignant letter written by Morris a few years before his death:

> I cannot grow satisfied to live and end my days in this hot country [Panama] and its strange surroundings. . . . solely my religious belief & trust in All Merciful Heavenly Father supports me. . . . If only I would have my former affiliates for more companionship & enjoy the devotion of my heart in God's Temple!

We believe he meant Mikve Israel in Curaçao, where he had lived for some years before moving to Panama.

In 1913 Benjamin Delvalle and Rebecca moved to New York with their three younger children. In New York, the Fidanques joined K.K. Shearith Israel and were warmly welcomed. Although they were not related to the early New York families, there were enough strong Sephardic ties to make them completely acceptable. My grandmother, Rebecca, also joined Congregation Shaaray Tefila, a Reform congregation, where she preferred to pray.

Within seven years Delvalle was elected a trustee of Shearith Israel. He served as *segan* (vice-president) for twelve years and as president for a few months of that time. We quote here a part of the resolution adopted by the trustees at his death:

> Resolved that the Board of Trustees expresses & records the profound grief at the demise of Benjamin Fidanque. . . . Esteemed and respected . . . he was the exemplar of the finest type of American Hebrew. A faithful son of Israel passionately loyal to the religious traditions of this ancient synagogue, he stood unmoved amid the swirling passion for change, defending the ideals of his Faith and culture of his generations. Resolved: that the name of our late Vice-Presi-

dent be entered upon the Roll of *Perpetual Hashcaboth* [memorial prayers], that the Banca [seat of honor] which he occupied in the Synagogue be turned to the wall and draped in Mourning for a period of thirty days according to custom.[30]

In the community building of Shearith Israel there is a Benjamin D. Fidanque social room. The room was dedicated in his memory by my grandmother.

Before attempting to write about their sons (my father and my uncles) and their families, it seems appropriate to copy some lines of a printed letter written by Uncle (Jacob Fidanque) to his nephews, whom he addresses as "My Beloved Sons."

> The closing hours of nineteen-hundred-and-twenty-three recall the epochal year of eighteen-hundred-and-eighty-three, forty years ago: When jointly with your devoted father we laid the cornerstone of a co-partnership.... *Undaunted and unassisted we persevered—never ceasing to maintain in its integrity the name we inherited from our Sires, which was magical wherever and whenever we had to invoke it for assistance in our perilous climb* [emphasis added].... I ask you to pledge yourselves to maintain the house we have reared—by clinging together at any cost: and sacrifice and disregard differences which may and will arise at times. I ask you to pledge yourselves again, to pass on the blazing torch one to the other of solidarity, unification and responsibility.

Uncle's romantic exhortation had the desired effect for many years, but in time it proved to be unrealistic. Eight different temperaments would never fit into one mold. In actual fact, their different personalities were an asset in making it possible for each brother to find a place in the business.

As eldest brother, Morris (1888–1966) was expected to be a model. It was a role which he took very seriously and one at which he excelled. He married Inez Brandon (b. 1892) in 1911. Inez's father, David Henry Brandon (1855–1903), an American by birth, was, in fact, descended from one of the Sephardic groups from Jamaica. He and his brother were in business in Panama with their uncle. Inez's mother, Judith Maduro (1862–1940), was a granddaughter of two of our hazzanim from St. Thomas.

David Brandon is a hero to the people of Panama. He was an educated man of action who lived by the highest Jewish moral values. During the years he lived in Panama, his impact on the city was quite strong. He was a successful businessman and a great humanitarian, respected and loved by everyone who knew him. After a terrible fire almost destroyed the city, he accepted the challenge to modernize the fire department and, in effect, created a new corps of firefighters. He was named its commander-in-chief and, sadly, died within the year while supervising the work of providing catchment basins for proper waterpower. It is said that the church bells tolled the day he died. His obituary stated: ". . . from the day he first arrived on these shores he served its people . . . he practiced goodness with the sincerity of a Rabbi."[31] The Republic of Panama issued a stamp with his portrait in 1937. His memory is honored as well by a bronze plaque in the central fire station, Plaza de los Bomberos, in Panama City.

Inez recalls her childhood in Panama during those days, the death of her father, and her mother's return to New York with twelve children. Returning to Panama as the nineteen-year-old bride of Morris, Inez found a city with streets still unpaved and very few of the modern conveniences of New York in 1911.

Morris enjoyed a superior and unblemished reputation among his business associates. He was offered a position in a company which the firm represented, but rejected it without hesitation because he had never contemplated working in anything other than the family business. He served the congregation as reader, as treasurer for many years, and as president. In suburban New York after his retirement, he became a trustee of the Central Synagogue in Nassau County. Assigned to write to members with problems or in need on behalf of the trustees, his notes became such an integral part of the synagogue's communication that they were called "Fidanques." Today, some twenty-five years later, the congregants still use the term "Fidanque" to describe a message of concern.

Inez inherited from her father a love of culture and natural leadership traits. Appalled by the lack of reading material and music in Panama, she managed to have books sent to her and to have a piano placed in her home. She went beyond the confines of the Jewish community, participating in cultural activities with American women in the Canal Zone. She was the founder of the sisterhood, serving as its president for ten years. Through her efforts other women in the congregation were trained to assume leadership positions.

The Anniversary Volume contains an article which Inez wrote entitled, "I Remember Panama." The article closes with the following paragraph:

> When I remember Panama, I recall with gratification the part that Morris played in the building of the Synagogue and in the development of a strong and significant Jewish community. We lived in Panama for thirty-eight years in many sections of the city, but no matter where our home was situated, we were always part of one community, that of *Kol Shearith Israel*.

Morris made one of her fondest dreams come true when they moved to the United States, first to suburban New York and then to New York City, where she now lives—on the very same street where she was born ninety-eight years ago! Morris and Inez had five children: Benjamin Delvalle (b. 1912), also known as Val, Henry Brandon (b. 1914), Stanley (b. 1918) Emma (Emita), (b. 1920), and Ines (1923–1941), who died at eighteen.

When Delvalle and Rebecca moved to New York, the firm was left in the capable hands of Morris, Joe (Joseph), and Ben (Benjamin), (1893–1981). Joe had begun to work at age sixteen. His forte was salesmanship. In the firm, he managed the fire-insurance business and the steamship lines. Two years after Morris's marriage he married Sybil Maduro (1883–197?), a first cousin of Inez. The contrast between these two brothers was enormous, yet they worked together for thirty-eight years. Joe and Sybil had two sons, Jack (b. 1914) and Nelson (1917–1977). Joe remarried in 1937 to Lucille Wallenstein (b. ca. 1915) and had another son, Joe Jr. (b. 1940).

Ben joined the Panama firm at eighteen, having spent a year in Europe and another year in the New York office. In an interview recorded by his daughter Zelia (b. 1921) in 1974, he recalled working in the office at age ten, counting Colombian money into $1,000 bags. He also recalled the primitive facilities in his home when he was a child, as well as the cobblestone streets and the difficult time his parents had supporting such a large family. Ben's talent was in the accounting field. In 1917 he married Bertha Toledano (b. 1899), whose grandparents were also St. Thomas people. Ben and Bertha were "pillars of the congregation," a status she still holds. Ben served as congregational president three different times.

Bertha served the sisterhood in many different positions. Devoted as they were to the Jewish people and to humanitarian work, their special cause was the Albert Einstein Institute, the Jewish day school established under the aegis of the three congregations. Unlike Morris and Joe, when Ben retired he remained in Panama, using his desk in the office for his variety of interests. Ben and Bertha had three children, Benjamin Earle (b. 1918), Zelia, and Jacqueline (b. 1928).

These three brothers, their ten children, and their grandparents, Emma and Joseph, were a strong, close family unit. The family also included Cecil (1898–1985) and his wife, Gladys Toledano (1901–1973), who was Bertha's sister, and Bill and his wife, Elaine Maduro (1909–1987).

This history would not be complete without some words about Emma and Joseph, an extraordinary couple. In 1932 they celebrated their sixty-fifth wedding anniversary. The celebration was a Thanksgiving service. Rabbi Norman Feldheym addressed them as follows:

> The art of this blessed couple has been living, and the medium of expression has been life. . . . we are here to pay homage to your art woven out of the spirit, out of life. That art we find unparalleled, more, even unexcelled.

"Uncle Joe" and "Aunt Emma," as they were called by everyone, became the core, perhaps the heart, of the congregation and of their family. His optimistic view of life is demonstrated in this quotation from an autobiography he was asked to write: "On October 10, 1917, I consecrated the concrete Bungalow in Bella Vista as a home which I erected and presented to my wife on our Golden Wedding."

Cecil, the fourth partner in the Panama office, was not a leader, yet he added another dimension to the group. He did his work in a quiet way. He and Gladys had no children but lavished their affection on their nieces and nephews. His devotion to Judaism was characterized by his mitzvot.

Although Bill (Elias Alvin) spent most of his life in New York, he chose Panama when it came time for him to join the firm. Despite the fact that the differences between him and his older bothers were not perceived by them as assets, he successfully introduced innovative ideas and enlarged the scope of the partnership.

Bill was president of the congregation when the synagogue was built, and he was for many years the "search committee" charged with finding a rabbi. Even during the years he spent away, he maintained contact and remained very much at the center of Jewish activity in Panama. Today he has replaced his grandfather Joe as the person at the core of the congregation. Bill and his wife, Elaine, were so close in age to their nieces and nephews that they seemed more like a brother and sister to us. Their daughter, Lynda (b. 1936), is of course considered one of the *younger* cousins.

In New York, son Jack (Jacob) (1891–1948) succeeded his father and uncle as senior partner. His driving ambition was not in the tradition of most of his brothers. Perhaps he was more like our first Josseph rather than other family members who believed that hard work and a good name alone would inevitably lead to success. Jack was the treasurer of Shearith Israel in New York for twenty years. In addition he served as chair of many committees, as his interests included many Jewish causes other than the synagogue. He and his wife, Celina de Castro (1888–1984), had no children.

Six of the eight Fidanque brothers. Left to Right: Joe, Ben, Cecil, Morris, Jack, and Alvin. (1929). (Courtesy of Emma Fidanque Levy)

Fred (Frederick Reuben) (1901–1985) and Vito (Joshua Vivian) were the younger partners in New York. Vito, who succeeded Jack as treasurer of Shearith Israel, was the last family member who worked in the firm's New York office—an obligation he fulfilled for many years. He and his wife, Ruth Allen (1916–1964) had no children.

It seems impossible, but it is true that Rae (Rachel) (1907–1946), the last child and only daughter, was able to break the tradition of this conservative household by choosing as her husband George Himmelblau (1900–1976), an Ashkenazi Jew from an Eastern European background.

The years between World War I and World War II were very productive for the Fidanque brothers, joined in the last years by some of their sons. It was a time when the family was at the peak of its performance. It moved along with the times imaginatively, diversified its interests, and in spite of the depression of the 1930s was able to pass on a goodly heritage to the next generation (and, I can hear it being said, "With God's help!").

The years that followed brought additional changes. Some sons joined the firm, some chose different careers, some moved away, and the "seniors" began to retire. One hundred years after Morris Fidanque established his business in Panama, our cousin Joe Fidanque, Jr., now sole owner of the firm, celebrated the continuity.[32]

* * *

It remains for a family historian of another time to write with perspective about my generation. I know something about our achievements and our failures, of our love of Judaism—and our leaving it—of our loyalty to one another and our concern about the distances that divide us.

Our generation, once dispersed, chose their mates from a variety of backgrounds and cultures. Three of eleven cousins have married into Panama-related families. Four married Ashkenazi Jews, one married an Eastern Sephardic Jew, and three have intermarried. In spite of the fact that some family members have distanced themselves from the Jewish community, there is a core of commitment to Jewish life. Fidanques, their spouses, and their children continue to make an impact in the Jewish community and in the larger community where we have chosen to live.

As active participants in the Reform movement, we have been supporters of Reform synagogues from Panama to San Francisco to New York; from the suburbs of Pittsburgh to suburban New York. We can say with pride that we continue to be faithful to the synagogue in the tradition of our mothers and fathers.

In the process of writing this story, I discovered that certain family characteristics are repeated to this day. There have been leaders and followers, rebels and peacemakers, conservatives and liberals. My narrative has followed the paternal lineage of our particular branch of the Fidanque family tree.[33]

The Fidanques were a pure Sephardic family for six generations after our first Josseph left the European continent to come to the Western Hemisphere. At the present time, however, the three generations born in this century cannot be considered Sephardic. I believe that outcome was inevitable, indeed it was fostered by our parents. Jews cannot afford to be divided by place of origin any longer. Today, we and our children are scattered throughout the world; we are part of *K'lal Israel*, and we delight in melding our unique traditions with those of all other cultures found in the Diaspora and in Israel.

If the stories of our past generations have added richness to Jewish life, then our exploration goes beyond family pride and is a celebration. For the Fidanques, a Jewish family in the Western Hemisphere, I believe that the legacy of the past will continue to influence further generations. To paraphrase Leo Baeck, Jewish life is largely centered in the subconscious, in the memories and clues of past generations which are carefully handed down to each new generation, as land and more tangible reminders are among other ethnic groups. We are, after all, the people of the Book, and the stories of our forebears are our most precious legacy. The reminders of this legacy are contained in our family archives.

Notes

1. Bill is the youngest of the nine sons of Rebecca and Benjamin Delvalle Fidanque, and a direct descendant of Josseph Fidanque, who emigrated from Amsterdam to Curaçao in 1698.

2. H. P. Salomon, "The Fidanques: Hidalgos of Faith," *American Sephardi* 4, nos. 1–2 (Autumn 1970): 15–29. This article is the source for information on the Fidanque family in Spain, Hamburg, and Amsterdam.

3. I am grateful to Herman Salomon for this additional information.

4. Bill uses this appellation for the Caribbean Portuguese groups. In official Dutch documents they were always referred to as the "Portuguese Nation."

5. For this and other terms, see H. P. Salomon, "Sephardi Terminology," *American Sephardi* 3, nos. 1–2 (September 1969): 88, 103–105.

6. L. Alvares Vega, *Beth Haim van Ouderkirk* (Assen: Van Gorcum, 1979).

7. David of Isaac Fidanque served as administrator of the cemetery from 1857 to 1881. During that time he worked with David Henriquez de Castro on the restoration of the cemetery, which was established in 1614. Gravestones which had sunk under the ground were raised. Today many of these beautiful monuments can be seen in the meticulously cared for cemetery. A foundation jointly funded by the Portuguese Jewish community (Amsterdam), the state (Holland), the province, and the municipality (Ouder-Amstel) is in charge of this work.

8. Cecil Roth, *A History of the Marranos*, rev. ed. (Philadelphia: Jewish Publication Society, 1941), pp. 288–289.

9. Isaac S. Emmanuel and Suzanne A. Emmanuel, *History of the Jews of the Netherlands Antilles*, vol. 1 (Cincinnati: American Jewish Archives, 1970), p. 46.

10. Ibid., pp. 48–50.

11. Isaac S. Emmanuel, *Precious Stones of the Jews of Curaçao: Curaçaoan Jewry, 1656–1957* (New York: Bloch, 1957), biography 91, pp. 288–291.

12. Jossy M. L. Maduro (1891–1964) was a philanthropist, historian, and genealogist of the Jews of Curaçao.

13. E. Alvin Fidanque, "Early Sephardic Jewish Settlers in North America and the Caribbean," *Journal of Reform Judaism*, Fall 1978, pp. 77–82.

14. Ibid., p. 78; Sheftall Diaries, *Publication of the American Jewish Historical Society*, March 1965.

15. Emmanuel, *Precious Stones*, biography 127, p. 363. The monument reads: "Da Yncortada Honesta / Virtuosa aritativa / Matrona Dona Batseba / Hana Mulher de Yacob / Fidanque que de 45 Annos / Transportou Para Milhor / Vida Em 18 De Adar Seni / AO 5532 Que Comresponde / Em 23 De Marco A O 1772 Que / Por Suas Accoems Eroicas / Y, Obras Virtuosas Espero / QueEstara Viva Gozando / No Lugar Tem D S / Rezervado Para/Seus Tementes."

16. Emmanuel and Emmanuel, *History of the Jews of the Netherlands Antilles*, 1:283–303.

17. Ibid., p. 306.

18. Ibid., p. 482. "The dominant element [of the Papiamento dialect] is Portuguese due to the influence of the Portuguese Jews who spoke, preached, and wrote their epitaphs in that tongue ... it has in it also, Spanish, Dutch, French English, African and a little Hebrew. Thus: BO (corruption of Portuguese *VOS*) = YOU / *TA* (African) = ARE / *UN* (Spanish) = A / *PARNAS* (Hebrew) = PARNAS."

19. Jens Larsen, *Virgin Island Story* (Philadelphia: Muhlenberg Press), p. 144.

20. Stanley T. Relkin, ed., *Short History of the Hebrew Congregation of St. Thomas*, 1983.

21. Ibid., p. 27.

22. Max I. Dimont. *The Jews in America* (New York: Simon & Schuster, 1978), p. 96.

23. This and other quotations from members of the Fidanque family are taken from the collection of family documents of E. A. Fidanque which he has shared with me.

24. E. Alvin (Bill) Fidanque, Ralph De Lima Valencia, Eugene Sasso Maduro, Eleanor D. L. Perkins, and Joseph Melamed, *Kol Shearith Israel: A Hundred Years of Jewish Life in Panama, 1876— 1976* (Panama City, 1987), p. 73. We recommend this book, written in Spanish and English, for a complete account of this relatively small but important Jewish community. It was dedicated to

the memory of my father, Morris B. Fidanque, and was published during the presidency of my brother, Stanley Fidanque, B.

25. *Panama Canal Review* (Balboa Heights, C.Z.), November 1965, p. 59.

26. Fidanque et al., *Kol Shearith Israel*, historical material by E. A. Fidanque.

27. Rabbi Norman Feldheym, a graduate of the Hebrew Union College in Cincinnati, arrived in Panama in 1932. He was the first Reform rabbi to serve Congregation Kol Shearith Israel.

28. Congregation Shevet Ahim is an Orthodox Sephardic congregation founded by families from the Middle East after World War I. Congregation Beth El is a Conservative congregation founded by families from Western Europe after World War II.

29. See note 23 above.

30. Victor Tarry, retired executive secretary of Congregation Shearith Israel, made this information available to me.

31. *Kol Shearith Israel*.

32. Nadhji Arjona. *La Familia Fidanque: Cien Anos en Panama, 1885–1985* (Panama City: Impresora Panama, 1986).

33. For full details, see *The Fidanque Family Tree*, collated by E. A. Fidanque and J. M. L. Maduro, art work by Enid Eder Perkins (New York, 1951). A copy of the family tree is on display in the Beth Hatefusoth in Tel Aviv.

Part II
The Sephardic Experience in Latin America

"Those of the Hebrew Nation..." The Sephardic Experience in Colonial Latin America

Allan Metz

Introduction

The purpose of this paper is to provide a general history of a broad and complex subject—the Sephardic experience in colonial Latin America. This subject will be discussed as follows: first, with an historical overview; then geographically, according to areas with the largest Sephardic populations, such as Mexico, Peru, Brazil, and Cartagena, Colombia. The overview and geographic sections will touch upon such themes as religious observance and customs,[1] participation in colonial life, Christian perceptions (and misconceptions) of Jews and Judaism, and, related to these perceptions, the Inquisition.[2] Concerning terminology, Sephardic Jews in colonial Latin America are commonly referred to as New Christians, crypto-Jews, or conversos. Since these terms are similar in meaning, they will be used interchangeably for the sake of variety,[3] but the pejorative term "marranos" will not be used. The paper closes with a conclusion/summation. For readers interested in more detail than can be provided in a necessarily short treatment, the notes provide ample suggestions for further study.

Overview

Jews and conversos, involved in all events related to fifteenth-century Spain, were naturally linked to the transcendent act of the discovery of the New World.[4] Previously, such Jewish activity was essentially unknown, cloaked in a "veil of silence." In contrast, the argument has been made that the discovery was largely a Jewish enterprise. For example, many have contended that the discoverer of America,

Christopher Columbus, was Jewish. Supporters of this position (such as Salvador de Madariaga and José María Millás Vallicrosa) contend that Columbus may have been from a Catalan or Majorcan Jewish family. While not totally impossible, this theory lacks firm evidence.[5]

In contrast to the speculation regarding his origins, it is widely accepted that Columbus received assistance from individuals with probable or definite Jewish backgrounds, such as Father Diego de Deza and the marquis of Moya and, particularly, from the Aragonese ministers of King Ferdinand—Luis de Santángel and his cousin, treasurer Gabriel Sánchez. Santángel helped to negotiate the finances for Columbus's first voyage,[6] and the second voyage was partially financed by possessions confiscated from the Jews expelled from Spain.

The number of conversos who served as crew members on the first voyage is uncertain. This is understandable, since many wished to escape the Inquisition. Alice B. Gould identifies only one with certainty, Luis de Torres. However, others may have included Rodrigo Sánchez de Segovia, Alfonso de la Calle, Marco (the expedition's physician), and a certain Bernal who was jailed in 1490.[7] A more indirect influence of the Spanish Jews may be linked to the discovery: the knowledge contributed by important Jews such as astronomer and cosmographer Abraham Zacut and the Majorcan cartographers.

As noted previously, Aragonese conversos contributed to the financing of Columbus's first voyage. In addition, converso ministers in the latter years of Ferdinand's reign played a significant role in colonial administration. Not much concern, however, was given to the selection of officials and even less to the immigrants. With the adjustment in 1509 of the composición of Seville, imprisoned conversos were authorized to travel to the Indies and conduct commerce there.

The rules of emigration became more stringent with Charles V, who conceived of the idea of forming an "ideal society" in the Indies which would exclude those thought to be of detrimental influence. Besides the order of September 24, 1518 to the Casa de Contratación, the chamber of commerce established by Ferdinand and Isabella in Seville,[8] prohibiting the emigration to the New World of those jailed by the Inquisition,[9] newly converted Catholics (Moorish or Jewish) and their children could not emigrate without the monarch's consent. Later provisions reinforced and broadened these restrictions, which, however,

"*Those of the Hebrew Nation . . .*" 211

proved to have little effect in the long run.[10] (This was true for Portugal as well, since Portuguese conversos were able to take advantage of the vastness of Brazil's frontier, which was difficult to patrol.)

While there were no conversos among the famous conquistadors, several were involved in the conquest, probably including the chronicler Gonzalo Fernández de Oviedo and Pedrarias Dávila.[11] As governor of Castilla del Oro (Panama), Dávila left bitter memories, including the assassination of Vasco Núñez de Balboa, the discoverer of the Pacific Ocean. A possible descendant of Dávila's, Diego Peñalosa Briceño, was governor of New Mexico in the seventeenth century, was later jailed by the Mexican Inquisition, and eventually died in France.

The Carvajal family was a famous seventeenth-century New Christian family of the viceroyalty of New Spain. Luis de Carvajal y de la Cueva (1539–1591?) served as comptroller of the Cape Verde Islands and Spanish fleet admiral prior to going New Spain in 1568. He returned to Spain in 1578 and in 1579 was appointed governor of the New Kingdoms of León, later called Monterrey. The governor's wife, Guiomar, a secret Jewess, did not wish to go to New Spain. However, Carvajal's sister Francisca and her husband Francisco Rodriguez de Matos, both fervent judaizers, went to the viceroyalty with their nine children in 1580. The Inquisition arrested Carvajal in 1589, charging him with not having denounced his niece Isabel as a judaizer. Stripped of his authority and sentenced to a six-year exile, the ex-governor died in incarceration before he could leave the viceroyalty. Other members of the Carvajal family met a cruel death. The governor's nephew, Luis de Carvajal "El Mozo" ("the Younger," 1566–1596), his mother Francisca Núñez, and three of his sisters—Isabel, widow of the judaizer Gabriel de Herrera; Catalina, married to the adventurous merchant Antonio Díaz de Cáceres; and Leonor, married to the prosperous mine-owner Jorge de Almeida—were burned at the stake on December 8, 1596.[12]

As noted in the introduction, the Inquisition must be discussed in any treatment of the Latin American Sephardic experience. It was not established in the New World until relatively late, in relation to the Spanish and Portuguese Inquisitions—1570 for the Tribunal of Lima and 1571 for Mexico. In 1610, the northern portion of the Tribunal of

Lima (which previously had encompassed the whole South American continent) was constituted as Cartagena de Indias.

There were a substantial number of conversos (and others who had escaped from Spain) in the New World, since it was "the escape, the refuge of those in Spain who, for one reason or another, were not well-regarded." However, the converso population did not become a serious issue until a large number of Portuguese New Christians came to America. It may be speculated that the Catholic Church to some degree neglected "the problem of Crypto-Judaism" by focusing on other matters.

This is only a partial answer, however, because the inquisitorial records indicate that a vast majority of the victims of the trials were Portuguese (i.e., of "Portuguese origin"). Thus, it may be deduced that the Spanish conversos were more quickly assimilated. The latter were not "a cohesive group," did not share a common language, and, most importantly, were "authentic converts" who essentially wished to forget their backgrounds and emphasize their piety and religious foundations. In the New World, as in the Iberian Peninsula, "the distinction between both groups of conversos [i.e., Spanish and Portuguese] is essential."

The Inquisition in America did not display "the barbarous rigor" of that in Spain; and throughout America, over its 250-year existence, many fewer victims were sentenced to death. The sensational trials with the harshest sentences, selected for study by such scholars as Henry Charles Lea and José Toribio Medina,[13] may mislead the reader into thinking that the persecution was primarily due to the alleged Jewishness of the victims. However, this accounts for only a relatively small percentage of the total. The trials were dominated by charges of bigamy and witchcraft. Moreover, a large number of cases were against "clérigos solicitantes," since one of the goals of the Inquisition "was to correct the very lax behavior of the clergy." Since little confiscation of goods was involved in sentencing, the economic aspects of the Inquisition in the Americas were essentially inconsequential.[14]

Regarding Portuguese conversos, their arrival in the New World may be traced to the beginning of the discovery. However, not until 1580 did they begin to have an impact, due to the temporary union of Spain and Portugal, which allowed for legal authorization to travel and do business in the Indies and, more frequently, "clandestine immigration." This illegal immigration was facilitated by the entry of blacks and Portuguese ascendancy in Brazil. The black slave traffic was conducted by Portuguese businessmen, and the continual voyages of the slave ships provided frequent opportunities to violate the laws regarding the entrance of foreigners. (Despite the "personal union" achieved by Phillip II, the Portuguese were still viewed legally as foreigners in Castilla [Spain] and its American colonies.)

Portuguese ownership of Brazil provided another opportunity for foreigners to secretly enter the Spanish territories, for only a narrow coastal stretch of Brazil was settled. Between it and Peru lay the vast Amazonian jungle. To reach Lima or the Andean mining areas, a long journey was necessary—in the north, along the Venezuelan coast; to the south, via the Río de la Plata and the valley of Paraguay toward the region of Charcas (present-day Bolivia). The first route was the shortest and most frequently traveled.

Thus, the inquisitorial tribunal was established at Cartagena in 1610.[15] However, its principal victims were not crypto-Jews but persons accused of such "crimes" as witchcraft and sorcery. Because of the vigilance of the Cartagena tribunal, Portuguese conversos tended to select the southern route to the viceroyalty of Peru. This explains why, in light of its "low density" of white settlement, there was a substantial Judeo-Portuguese colony in the Río de la Plata region, which served as a "transition" zone, although many remained there.

On October 17, 1602, the king issued a royal decree to the Audiencia and to the bishop of Charcas, noting with concern the presence of Portuguese Jews from Río de la Plata in the province of Charcas.[16] This document reflects two basic reasons for the crown's mistrust of the Portuguese Jews: religion (i.e., suspect faith) and politics (i.e., trade with enemies). However, in this relatively neglected and ignored region of Spanish America, the Portuguese Jewish presence was valued for its economic contribution and its role in the defense of Buenos Aires. For these reasons, a threatened expulsion of Jews was not carried out in 1606.[17]

For similar reasons, a proposal for the establishment of an inquisitorial tribunal in Buenos Aires was rejected in 1619. Although Porto

Bello was the usual means of entry into Peru, the New Christians, in order to escape the Cartagena tribunal, chose the La Plata route.

Trials regarding faith/religion continued being referred to the Tribunal of Lima, with inherent delays due to the long distance. A little over one hundred procesos took place in what is now Argentina. Via the indirect route from La Plata, or directly from Cartagena or Porto Bello, so many conversos were entering Peru that the authorities became concerned, as did Spanish merchants who viewed them as serious competitors. Despite precautions, Portuguese Jews were persecuted by the Lima Inquisition. The Mexican Inquisition began its persecutions toward the end of the seventeenth century.

At the beginning of the eighteenth century, a papal exemption granted to the Portuguese conversos was made applicable to the New World. This order, issued on August 22, 1604, was circulated in Lisbon in 1605. The New Christians of Portugal were given a year to benefit from it; those in the New World, two years, due to difficulties in communication. During this period, those who sought pardon for their offenses were to be freed and their goods returned to them.

This order was not readily accepted by the Inquisition in the New World, so that in 1608 the order to release "those of the Hebrew nation of the Kingdom of Portugal" from jail and to return their confiscated goods had to be repeated.[18] This favorable ruling by Phillip III was initially continued by Phillip IV, resulting in an increase in the converso population. Although not very numerous, the conversos were concentrated in the cities and commercial areas. Their control of much of the commerce, and their tendency to do business mostly outside of existing legislation, eventually attracted the attention of the mother country. In addition to apprehensions due to these factors, there was a religious reason for the government's concern—i.e., to prevent those who "by religion and nature have such hatred" toward Spain from becoming "more powerful than the Castilians. The "psychosis of fear and jealousy" that this reflected led to incidents like the uprising in 1611 allegedly instigated by the Portuguese Jews of Huancavélica, Peru, the great mining area, whose output of mercury was necessary for the production of silver in Potosí.[19]

Nevertheless, this was, on balance, an age of tolerance which abruptly ended in 1635. The reasons are unclear; since the change corresponded with the beginning of the Thirty Years War, it may be speculated that Spain wished to take security precautions against potential enemies and, in the process, to confiscate goods. There is no doubt that due to the increasing numbers of those executed (usually, for the most trivial reasons), the Inquisition in the New World not only temporarily relieved its usual deficit, but sent considerable amounts of wealth to Spain. Those accused by the tribunals of the Inquisition lived in an atmosphere of worry and terror. The value of the goods confiscated in Peru during this period amounted to approximately 800,000 pesos, culminating in a famous auto-da-fé which took place on January 23, 1639.[20] And following this date, while some of the accused were released, the number of conversos held continued to be significant. The viceroy, Marquis de Mancera (calculating the figure to be 6,000), opted in 1646 for "total expulsion." The conversos managed to avoid this danger, but eventually, as a minority, slowly assimilated and disappeared as an "autonomous social group."

In Mexico, the connection between political events and persecution was more evident, because in New Spain, following a period of peace, repression of crypto-Jews was not unleashed until 1642. This date marked the discovery of a synagogue in the home of Captain Simón Vaez Sevilla, whose son was viewed by many as the Messiah. A man named Miguel Tinoco conducted the religious service and distributed the unleavened bread. A black slave, banging a drum, was sent to homes where the "faithful" lived in order to notify them of the religious services.

It is highly unlikely that such acts would go unnoticed by the Inquisition, which utilized a large spy network. The Mexican inquisitors may have been expecting word from Spain to act more vigorously, and this would have come as a result of what was known as the uprising of Portugal (so named since Jews were termed "Portuguese" in New Spain). Thus, it no longer was necessary to proceed with caution regarding a group who, in addition to being accused of religious heresy, also turned out to be threats to the state. A series of trials ended Mexican crypto-Judaism, at least outwardly. The year 1649 was a particularly difficult one regarding inquisitorial persecution.[21]

Following this date, "Judaism in Spanish America was limited to isolated cases." The crypto-Jews had assimilated sometime before, and the Portuguese Jews, who arrived in the Americas later, "also disappeared as a group by the second or third generation." There were few white women at the beginning of the colonization of the New World. The Portuguese did not wish to bring women there due to the dangerous conditions. Some Portuguese Jews married within their own nationality, others with women of color, and still others with Old Christians, which initiated the process of assimilation, a course which many, if not the majority, followed.

Documentation on the Inquisition tends to distort our perspective by emphasizing those who did not conform. In actuality, not all were willing to sacrifice their lives for reasons of faith. This was especially true of the Spanish conversos; to a lesser extent, it also held for the Portuguese conversos. A number of conversos became pious Christians or even joined the Catholic clergy. Many conversos were integrated into colonial Latin American society, choosing conversion over persecution.[22]

Geographical Survey

As indicated above, the major Sephardic population centers in Spanish colonial Latin America were in what are today Mexico, Peru, and Colombia (i.e., Cartagena).[23] Since the preceding overview emphasized Spanish America, it seems appropriate to begin the geographical survey with Brazil as well as to include other areas (such as Chile, Argentina, and Surinam) whose converso populations were not as large, but which nevertheless merit discussion.

Brazil

At least one person of Jewish origin, Gaspar da Gama (who was forcibly baptized by the Portuguese in 1497), accompanied admiral Pedro Álvares Cabral of Portugal to what is now Brazil in 1500.[24] In 1502, a group of conversos led by Fernando de Noronha received permission from King Manuel I to colonize and develop the new colonial possession. The consortium's main endeavor was the export of brazil wood to Portugal for dyeing textiles.

There is evidence to suggest that New Christians introduced sugar cane from Madeira to Brazil in the early 1500s. New Christian foremen and laborers likely were brought from Madeira and São Tomé around 1542, when the first sugar plantations and mills were built. In 1550, a New Christian, Diego Dias Fernandes, was the owner of one of the first five *engenhos* (sugar plantation and mill) in Brazil. Furthermore, by 1600, many of the 120 *engenhos* in Brazil were owned and run by New Christians.

While some of Brazil's New Christians were firm Catholics, most followed Jewish rituals and customs in secret and were actually crypto-Jews, known disparagingly as marranos by Catholics. Unlike Spanish America, the Inquisition was never officially established in Brazil. However, following 1580 (when Portugal united with Spain), the bishop of Bahia was given investigative authority from Portugal, and after 1591 officials of the Inquisition periodically visited Brazil. The first such group was in Bahia from 1591 to 1593 and then in Pernambuco until 1595; another commission was again in Bahia in 1618. "Denunciations" were the basis of the inquisitorial hearings, and the accused were arrested and brought to Portugal for trial.

Approximately 50,000 former Europeans lived in Brazil in 1624, many of whom were New Christians. They owned sugar mills and engaged in business, commerce, education, writing, and even religion as priests. Among other New Christian accomplishments, Bento Teixeira (also known as Bento Teixeira Pinto) wrote the "Prosopopéia," the first Brazilian poem, and Ambrósio Fernandes Brandão wrote *Diálogos das Grandezas do Brasil*, viewed as one of the best books about Brazil.[25]

By the end of the sixteenth century, Amsterdam had become a significant Jewish religious, cultural, and economic focal point. Holland, through the West India Company and supported by Dutch Jews who had fled the Inquisition, attempted to capture Bahia in May 1624, but was defeated in May 1625. The Dutch troops, including some Jews, were allowed to return to Europe. However, five conversos who had renewed the practice of Judaism while the Dutch were in control were accused of treason and hanged by the Portuguese.

The Dutch were more successful in capturing the ports of Olinda and Recife, located in Pernambuco. The Dutch government declared that the rights of everyone under its control in Brazil (including the Jews) were to be respected. Thus, once the Dutch established a hold on northeastern Brazil, many conversos in that area began to publicly practice their Judaism.

Jews fared well under Johan Maurits van Nassau, the governor-general of Brazil appointed in 1637. Many Jews were in the militia, and one of its four companies was entirely Jewish and did not have to serve on the Sabbath. However, the governor-general and Calvinist preachers attempted to convert both Jews and Catholics, although without success. A synagogue had been established in Recife by 1636 and a congregation was forming in Paraiba. The Jews of Recife made an inquiry to Rabbi Chayyim Shabbetai of Salonika regarding the appropriate time to say prayers for rain, thus making the New World's first contribution to the responsa literature.

By 1639, Dutch Brazil had a flourishing sugar industry. Jews owned six of the 166 sugar mills. Jews were also actively involved in the slave trade and commerce. These and other economic opportunities attracted more Jews to the area; in 1638, for example, Manoel Mendes de Castro brought 200 Jews to Dutch Brazil.

The Jewish community of Recife soon developed a communal structure. In response to a need for Hebrew teachers and cantors, the well-known Rabbi Isaac Aboab da Fonseca from the Amsterdam synagogue of Talmud Torah and the learned Moses Raphael d'Aguilar were asked to come to Recife in 1642 as spiritual leaders. By this time, two synagogues, Zur Israel in Recife and Magen Abraham in Maurícia, had already been established.[26] However, the fate of a certain Isaac de Castro was not as fortunate. He had arrived in Bahia (then under Portuguese control) from Amsterdam through Dutch Brazil, was seized for teaching Judaism to conversos, and then sent to Portugal, where he was executed in the auto-da-fé of December 15, 1647.

From 1645 to 1654, a civil war took place between the Dutch and the Portuguese, who wished to reassert their dominion over northeastern Brazil. The Portuguese prevailed, and many Jews were either killed or taken prisoner and condemned as traitors. It was during this struggle (in 1649) that Rabbi Isaac Aboab composed the first Hebrew poem in the New World, "Zekher Asiti le-Nifle'ot El" ("I Have Set a Memorial to God's Miracles").

At its height, the Jewish population in Dutch Brazil reached approximately half of the 1,500 European civilians living there in 1645. Despite the loss of Jewish life during the civil strife and the return of some Jews to Holland, around 650 Jews still remained in Recife and Maurícia.

The Jewish communal structure in Dutch Brazil was very organized, paralleling the communal structure in Holland. All Jews were subject to the community's rules, regulations, and taxes, and there were a school, yeshiva, cemetery, and general fund (*sedaca*, or "charity"). An executive committee (mahamad) maintained control over communal life (such as in settling disputes and law enforcement).[27]

New Christians were also to be found in other areas of Brazil which had not been controlled by the Dutch, including Bahia, Rio de Janeiro, São Paulo, and São Vicente. According to the protocol of January 26, 1654 (which ended the Dutch occupation), all Jews and Dutch had to leave Brazil within ninety days, selling off their possessions or taking what they could with them. Most of the Jews went to Holland, with some venturing to such Caribbean islands as Curaçao and Barbados, where they established the sugar industry. In early September 1654, twenty-three Jews left Brazil for New Amsterdam (later named New York, but then under Dutch rule), forming the foundation of the first Jewish community in what was to become the United States.

Following 1654, few conversos remained in Brazil. Approximately twenty-five were sent to Portugal for trial between 1650 and 1700. Persecutions and extraditions resumed in the 1700s. Hundreds of Brazilian New Christians were among the victims of the Lisbon autos-da-fé of 1709, 1711, and 1713. The economic ramifications of the persecution were great—the sugar industry temporarily ceased to function, and commerce between Brazil and Portugal was greatly hampered.

The most widely known Brazilian converso and martyr of the Inquisition was António José da Silva, an accomplished poet and playwright, also known as "o Judeu" (1705–1739).[28] Documentation regarding eighteen executed Brazilian conversos is located in the Archivo da Tôrre do Tombo in Lisbon.

On May 25, 1773, a royal decree issued in Portugal voided all laws in violation of the rights of New Christians. Since the decree pertained to all Portuguese territories, the conversos of Brazil, after this date, were safe from further inquisitorial persecution. Due primarily to the high degree of mixed marriages, Brazil's conversos became increasingly assimilated and gave up any retaining Jewish rituals and customs, thereby becoming practicing Catholics. Jewish immigration only resumed after 1822 with the attainment of Brazilian independence from Portugal.[29]

Chile

Conversos played a role in Chilean history from the very outset.[30] Rodrigo de Orgoños, one of the Spanish officers who accompanied Diego de Almagro (the discoverer of Chile in 1535), is believed to have been of New Christian ancestry. In 1540, Diego García de Cáceres of Plasencia, Spain, went to Chile with the conquistador Pedro de Valdivia and later attained a prominent post there. Forty years following his death, a pamphlet entitled *La Ovandina* claimed that Cáceres was of Jewish ancestry.[31] This work became a center of controversy, because it revealed the Jewish background of several famous families, and the Inquisition removed it from circulation. Cáceres's descendants included some famous figures of Chilean independence, such as General José Miguel Carrera and statesman Diego Portales.

When the Lima inquisitorial tribunal was set up in 1570, present-day Chile fell within its sphere. Although autos-da-fé were held in Lima, the converso population in this fairly remote corner of the Spanish Empire kept increasing. The height of inquisitorial activity in Chile occurred in 1627 in Concepción de Chile with the seizure of the prominent surgeon Francisco Maldonado de Silva, one of the most famous martyrs of the Inquisition, who was sent to Lima to be put on trial. After almost a dozen years in jail, he was "relaxed" in the January 23, 1639 auto-da-fé, the largest up to that point in the Americas.

Nonetheless, secret judaizing continued. Physician Rodrigo Henrique de Fonseca of Santiago and his wife were executed in Lima in

1644 on the charge of adhering to "the Law of Moses," and his brother-in-law, Luis de Riverso, chose suicide over burning at the stake. In the late 1600s, the inquisitorial tribunal learned of the existence of some twenty-eight New Christians in the area of Santiago, although apparently this report was not followed by any arrests. Other Chilean conversos received lesser punishments from the Inquisition, such as Francisco de Gudiel, born in Spain in 1518, who, according to his sentence, "was still awaiting the coming of the Messiah." (His daughter was wed to the son of another converso, Pedro de Omepezoa.) A converso soldier, Luis Noble, was charged in 1614 with the theft of a crucifix for the purpose of practicing "rites in the Law of Moses." In addition, the possessions of Captain León Gomez de Oliva were confiscated as partial punishment for observing Judaism in secret.

After the 1700s, there is no evidence of conversos or inquisitorial persecution of them, and Chile's independence in 1813 marked the end of inquisitional activities. As in other areas of Latin America, converso ancestry exists among a number of Chile's more well-established families.[32]

Colombia

The Jewish presence in Colombia may be traced to the coming of conversos with the Spanish conquistadors in the 1500s.[33] From the outset of the 1600s, due to the presence of the Cartagena inquisitorial tribunal, the secret practice of Judaism could prove fatal. In 1636, a number of New Christians in Cartagena were arrested, in part as an attempt to destroy the Complicidad Grande ("Great Conspiracy") in Lima,[34] and in 1638, the most famous of them, Juan Rodríguez Mesa, was sentenced to death in an auto-da-fé. In contemporary times, the existence of practices and traditions reminiscent of Judaism in the area of Antioquia led to speculation that a significant number of the region's inhabitants have converso backgrounds. However, subsequent research does not bear this out.[35]

Argentina

Following the temporary Spanish-Portuguese union of 1580, Portuguese of Jewish lineage started entering colonial Argentina.[36] Lightly settled, the region functioned as a staging area for contraband trade in which Andes silver was exchanged for African slaves, textiles from Europe, and other goods. The area was distant from Lima, the seat of the viceroyalty's government, and, beginning in 1572, of the Inquisition (although a Portuguese inquisitor was in Buenos Aires in 1618).

Coming directly to Buenos Aires, or arriving via São Paulo and Paraguay, the Portuguese immigrants located mainly in Buenos Aires, Córdoba, and Tucumán. Throughout the 1600s, "Jews," "Portuguese," and "merchants"—terms used interchangeably—were uniformly accused of "filling the land" and "monopolizing commerce." An expulsion decree of 1602 also associated "Portuguese" with "judaizers" or crypto-Jews.

The number of people referred to in these reports is unknown, as is their degree of Jewish observance, because the danger of being haled before the Inquisition, as well as the Spanish law prohibiting the entry of those who were not Old Christians, led them to keep their origins secret. Further complicating the question, Inquisition officials based their accusations of Jewish faith on such superficial factors as wearing clean linen, refusing to eat pork and to do labor on Sabbath, and not practicing Christian beliefs.

Among those persecuted in the famous auto-da-fé of January 23, 1639 in Lima was a surgeon from Tucumán, Francisco Maldonado de Silva, who tended toward mysticism and returned to his Jewish religious roots. Other prominent figures of Jewish-Portuguese background who were linked to Argentina were Francisco de Vitoria (d. 1592), a Tucumán bishop charged with judaizing and sent to Spain, and the Córdoba jurist Antonio de León Pinelo, a significant South American literary figure, who appealed against a fine levied on Portuguese living in the province of Buenos Aires by its governor.

However, one cannot assume that every Portuguese who resided in Buenos Aires was Jewish. (Around 1620, about 100 residents of Buenos Aires were Portuguese out a total population of 2,000.) There probably were fewer conversos in all of Argentina than in the mining area of Potosí in what is now Bolivia or in colonial Lima. Furthermore, "their Judaism, such as it was, failed to take root." In eighteenth-century Argentina, there are no reliable accounts of judaizing nor confirmation of whether any families had Jewish lineage.[37]

Mexico

Several New Christians accompanied Hernán Cortés in his conquest of Mexico in 1521.[38] From 1523 onward, only those who could prove Catholic lineage to the fourth generation, and thus be eligible for certification of *limpieza de sangre* (lit. "blood purity"), were allowed into Mexico. However, some Spanish and Portuguese conversos obtained certificates by illegal means. Immigrants from elsewhere in Europe, posing as Old Christians, continued arriving in Mexico throughout the colonial period. Veracruz and Campeche served as entry points for arrivals from Europe, and Acapulco for those from Brazil, Chile, and Peru. While the first auto-da-fé involving crypto-Jews occurred as early as 1528, relatively few conversos were arrested before the formal establishment of the Inquisition in Mexico City in 1571. Soon after this date, however, a trend of increased converso persecution became evident. By 1550 there were more Spanish conversos living in the capital than Spanish Catholics. From 1596 to 1659, crypto-Jews were involved in just about every auto-da-fé, and the period from 1642 to 1649 marked the highest incidence of inquisitorial activity, climaxed by the auto-da-fé of April 11, 1649, in which only thirteen survived from a total of 109.

Despite the persecution, crypto-Jews continued to settle in Mexico, where they thrived and were most responsible for the growth of commerce and trade. The persecution of New Christians may have stemmed from inquisitorial concern over an alleged Portuguese plot to seize Mexico as well as economic envy of converso merchants and the greed of Inquisition officials who were able to confiscate whole fortunes when the rightful owners were arrested.

Crypto-Jews were involved in all facets of Mexican colonial life and work. A number worked for the crown and even the church. For example, Ricardo Ossado, an Italian believed to be a Jew who fled

Mexico, compiled a reference work about Mayan herbs, remedies, and diseases known as *El libro del judío*.[39] While conversos were to be found throughout New Spain, most lived in Mexico City, Veracruz, and Guadalajara.

Regarding religious observance, inquisitorial documents indicate that communal prayers regularly took place in private homes. The manner of observance of the Mexican conversos largely resembled that of their fellow worshipers in the Iberian Peninsula and the rest of the world. The Mexican version, however, was characterized by an overemphasis on fasts and related acts of penitence, with consequent nonobservance of the norms of traditional Judaism. There is reason to believe that the Judaism practiced by the conversos in Mexico was more similar to the standards of normative Judaism than that observed by European conversos.

A number of Jews settled in Mexico with the notion that they would be able to practice their religion more openly there. While this was, in general, a misconception, the practice of circumcision was widespread and the dietary laws were also observed. The Mexican New Christians were able to communicate with Jewish communities in Europe and the Middle East, and on occasion raised funds for Eretz Israel—the collection called *farda*. Moreover, a few individuals regularly traveled from town to town to teach Jewish practices, although the degree of knowledge these teachers possessed is much exaggerated in the Inquisition's records.

By the mid-1600s, inquisitorial persecution of conversos had declined markedly. Eighteenth-century converso immigration to Mexico was in considerable decline as well, due to changing circumstances and growing tolerance in other nations. For several years the inquisitorial tribunal in Mexico City was directed to cease arresting Jews, and in the waning years of the colonial period those sought were generally well-known figures who held liberal views.

During the whole colonial period, about 1,500 individuals were convicted of judaizing and following the Laws of Moses and Jewish rituals. Fewer than 100 were burned at the stake, but about the same number perished in jail. The descendants of colonial conversos assimilated in the nineteenth century, and some Mexicans currently claim Jewish backgrounds.[40]

Peru

There were conversos in Peru from the very beginning of Spanish control, but it was not until after the Inquisition's formal establishment in the viceroyalty that judaizers attracted attention and efforts to identify them began.[41] The period from 1601 to at least 1625 marked a decline in the persecution of judaizers due to a general pardon and a substantial increase in the number of Portuguese New Christians (including many judaizers) who settled in the viceroyalty. The commercial activities of the conversos enabled them to accumulate considerable wealth, and their high social visibility was a definite factor in uncovering their secret religious practice.

In 1634, sixty-four people were accused of judaizing (just about all of them of Portuguese ancestry). Both Old and New Christians were much alarmed by this crackdown, as were their creditors, who worried that the Inquisition would confiscate the suspects' wealth. The persecution and flight of large numbers of New Christians came close to causing the financial ruin of the viceroyalty. The repression of this "Great Conspiracy" (referred to earlier) culminated in the great auto-da-fé of January 23, 1639, which included two of the most prominent judaizers in history: Manuel Bautista Pérez, Lima's richest merchant and the leader of the judaizers, and physician Francisco Maldonado de Silva.

Following this, Lima's inquisitorial tribunal considerably lessened its search for judaizers. Some cases were even dismissed, and very few accused persons were involved in an auto. There were even fewer cases in the eighteenth century, but three took place because of the commanding personalities of the accused—Teodoro Candioti, a Levantine Christian, noblewoman Ana de Castra, and nobleman Juan de Loyola y Haro.

A few Jews who cannot be termed New Christians occasionally were present in colonial South America, generally engaged in West Indian commerce. Currently, a number of Catholics in countries which once formed the viceroyalty of Peru acknowledge their New Christian and even judaizer backgrounds.[42]

Surinam

The small nation of Surinam, located in northeastern South America, holds the distinction of having the oldest Jewish community in the Americas.[43] Jews seem to have reached Surinam as early as 1639. A second group of Jews came from Great Britain in 1652, led by Lord Willoughby of Parham, who founded a permanent settlement.

The next group of Jews, led by Joseph Núñez de Fonseca (or, David Nassi), were mainly refugees of the Inquisition who had lived in Brazil until the Portuguese defeat of the Dutch in 1654 (as discussed earlier). Experienced in commerce and agriculture, they established many sugar plantations. In recognition of their important contribution to the colony, Surinam's Jews were granted religious freedom in 1665. This was reaffirmed by a 1667 decree which stipulated that they were to be viewed as British-born subjects.

When the Dutch took over Surinam in 1667, some Jews left. Those who stayed fared well, thanks to the abundance of slaves and plantations, and despite occasional attempts to restrict their religious freedom. In the first half of the eighteenth century, the Jewish community was doing well economically, but it experienced an economic decline toward the end of the century.

By 1836 Jews of Portuguese ancestry were outnumbered by more recent settlers of German origin. Meanwhile, in 1825, the special privileges granted the Jews earlier in Surinam's history became superfluous because of the rights to which they were entitled as subjects of the Dutch crown.[44]

Conclusion/Summation

On the quincentenary of the discovery of America, it is appropriate to note the Sephardic presence in the New World. While the supposed Jewish background of Christopher Columbus remains a questionable assertion, a number of his crew were New Christians. However, soon after Columbus's voyage to the New World, Spain and Portugal restricted access to it by New Christians and their immediate descendants. The prohibition continued but was periodically eased, particularly following Phillip III's general pardon of 1601. Despite the ban,

New Christians were able to enter the Americas rather consistently until at least the mid-1600s, sometimes with the complicity of Spanish officials who recognized the advantages of Jewish enterprise in the development of their colonial lands.

The Jewish history of colonial Latin America, it has been said, is essentially "that of . . . New Christians who were judaizers." The number of judaizers among the conversos who settled in America cannot be ascertained with any certainty, but not all New Christians secretly practiced Judaism, and for most, no doubt, the economic and social benefits which the New World was perceived to offer were the primary motivation for settling in America, and not the possibility of more openly observing their faith.

The effort to suppress judaizing in Spanish America began with "episcopal inquisitions" under the direction of secular or regular clergy (an auto-da-fé under such auspices took place in New Spain as early as 1528). Inquisition tribunals patterned on their Iberian counterparts were established in Lima, covering the viceroyalty of Peru, in 1570, and in Mexico City, for the viceroyalty of New Spain, in 1571. Later, in 1610, a third main center of inquisitorial activity was introduced in Cartagena for the viceroyalty of New Granada.

These tribunals conducted ongoing autos-da-fé until the close of the colonial epoch, but persecutions of judaizers occurred mainly before 1660. Inquisitorial activity was particularly acute in the 1580s and 1590s and again in the 1630s and 1640s in both New Spain and Peru. While the number of judaizers is difficult to determine, it was not much greater than the number of those actually arrested, and there is no evidence supporting the claim that judaizing was very widespread. In fact, a majority of the judaizers tried by the Inquisition had already come to terms with the church, or would in the future.

The judaizers had their unique religion. And while, as noted above, economic considerations were important, this did not mean that they were not ardently devoted to their secret faith, which they attempted, with some success, to spread to tepid New Christians. Some judaizers were martyred for their beliefs, which they regarded as authentic Judaism, but were really "a wild blend of biblical Judaism, post-biblical reminiscences," and Catholic influences.

Well represented in commercial, professional, and political activities, the New Christian presence greatly enhanced Latin America's development. While Jews were officially banned from entering the New World during the colonial period, and though the Americas did not represent the safest refuge for them, its territorial vastness, the small number of Europeans, and the relative laxity of the New World's inquisitors made it a much safer place than the Iberian Peninsula. Even in the most severe periods of repression, which occurred in both New Spain and Peru in the mid-seventeenth century, New Christians were more secure in the Americas than in Spain and Portugal.[45]

Notes

1. For more information on the important aspect of religious practice and observance, see Seymour B. Liebman, *New World Jewry, 1493–1825: Requiem for the Forgotten* (New York: Ktav Publishing House, 1982), pp. 100–130; Boleslao Lewin, Los criptojudíos: un fenomeno religioso y social, Ensayos (Buenos Aires: Editorial Mila, 1987), pp. 185–250; idem, *Creencias religiosas marranas en Hispanoamérica* (Córdoba: n.p., 1958). (The latter is an offprint from *Revista de la Universidad Nacional de Córdoba*; the focus is Mexico.)

2. For general treatments of the Inquisition in Latin America, see Boleslao Lewin, *Los judíos bajo la inquisición en Hispanoamérica* (Buenos Aires: Editorial Dedalo, 1960); idem, *Los criptojudios*; idem, *La inquisición en Hispanoamérica: judíos, protestantes y patriotas* (Buenos Aires: Editorial Proyeccíon, 1962), previously published in 1950 as *El Santo Oficio en América*; idem, *Que fue la inquisición*, Colección Esquemas históricos, vol. 15 (Buenos Aires: Plus Ultra, 1973); George Alexander Kohut, *Jewish Martyrs of the Inquisition in South America* (Baltimore: Friedenwald, 1895); Anita Novinsky, *A inquisióao*, Tudo e historia, no. 49 (São Paulo: Brasiliense, 1982); Jorge Randolph, *La inquisición en América* (Santiago: n.p., 1970); José Toribio Medina, *La primitiva inquisición americana, 1493–1569: estudio histórico*, 2 vols. (Santiago: Imprenta Elzeviriana, 1914); Domingo Faustino Sarmiento, *La inquisición en América*, Biblioteca Avante, vol. 4 (Tortosa: Monclus, 1917); Matilde Gini de Barnatan, "Los criptojudíos y la inquisición," *Todo es historia* 17, no. 216 (April 1985): 8–29.

3. Seymour B. Liebman essentially makes the same point regarding terminology in *New World Jewry*, pp. 213–215. For further discussion of these terms and related problems, see *Encyclopaedia Judaica* (1972), s.v. "Conversos," "Crypto-Jews," and "New Christians"; Harry Havilo, "Origen y desaparición del criptojudaísmo en América," *Sefardica* 1, no. 1 (1984): 67–74; Boleslao Lewin, "Resonancia del criptojudaísmo en Latinoamérica," ibid., pp. 27–33; Anita Novinsky, "Some Theoretical Considerations About the New Christian Problem," in *The Sephardi and Oriental Jewish Heritage*, ed. Issachar Ben-Ami (Jerusalem: Magnes Press, Misgav Yerushalayim, 1982), pp. 3–12; idem, "Cristianos nuevos: un problema historiográfico," *Sefardica* 1, no. 2 (1984): 51–68; and Ellis Rivkin, "How Jewish Were the New Christians?" in *Hispania Judaica: Studies on the History, Language, and Literature of the Jews in the Hispanic World*, ed. Joseph M. Sola-Sole, Samuel G. Armistead, and Joseph H. Silverman, vol. 1 (Barcelona: Puvill-Editor, 1982), pp. 105–115. For discussion of the term "marranos" and related problems, see Martin A. Cohen in *Encyclopaedia Judaica* (here-

after cited as *EJ*) (1972), s.v. "Marranos"; idem, "Toward a New Comprehension of the Marranos," in *Hispania Judaica*, ed. Sola-Sole, Armistead, and Silverman, vol. 1; Boleslao Lewin, *Los marranos, un intento de definición: contribución al estudio de los orígenes americanos y argentinos* (Buenos Aires: Colegio Libre de Estudios Superiores, 1946).

4. For other overviews/introductions to the subject, see Liebman, *New World Jewry*, 1982; idem, *Requiem por los olvidados: los judíos españoles en América, 1493–1825* (Madrid: Altalena, 1984); Alberto Liamgot, *Criptojudíos en Hispanoamérica*, Colección Hechos de la historia judía, no. 31 (Buenos Aires: Ejecutivo Sudamericano del Congreso Julío Mundial, 1970); Lewin, *Los criptojudíos*, 1987; Arturo Bab, *Los judíos en la América Latina de 1492–1930: ensayo histórico* (n.p., 1933?); Martin A. Cohen, ed., *The Jewish Experience in Latin America: Selected Studies from the Publications of the American Jewish Historical Society*, 2 vols. (Waltham, Mass.: American Jewish Historical Society; New York: Ktav, 1971), 1:xvlxx.

5. The following include discussions on Columbus's alleged Jewish background: Salvador de Madariaga, *Vida del muy magnífico señor don Cristobal Colón* (Buenos Aires: Editorial Sudamerica, 1940); José María Millás Vallicrosa, "Solución definitiva del problema de la patria de Colón," *Tesoro de los judíos sefardíes* 6 (1963): vii–xv; Michael Pollak, "The Ethnic Background of Columbus: Inferences from a Genoese-Jewish Source, 1553–1557," *Revista de historia de América* (Mexico) no. 80 (July–December 1975): 147–164; Alberto Liamgot, *Marginalidad y judaísmo en Cristobal Colón*, Colección Hechos de la historia judía 81 (Buenos Aires: Congreso Judío Latinoamericano, 1976); Charles Alperin, "Christopher Columbus–A Jew?,"*Midstream* 25, no. 3 (1979): 35–48; Sarah Leibovici, "Cet etrange Christophe Colomb," *Les nouveaux cahiers* (Paris) no. 10 (1977): 56–58; idem, *Christophe Colomb juif, defende et illustrations* (Paris: Maisonneuve and Larose, 1986); Francisco Cantera, "El origen judío de Colón y el monograma de su firma," *Atlántida: revista del pensamiento actual* (Madrid) 2, no. 9 (May 1964): 303–310.

6. For more detail regarding the contribution of the Aragonese conversos to the preparation for Columbus's voyages, see Manuel Serrano y Sanz, *Orígenes de la dominación española en América: estudios históricos*, Nueva biblioteca de autores españoles, 25 (Madrid: Bailly-Bailliere, 1918–). More specific information on the Santangel family may be found in Meyer Kayserling, *Christopher Columbus and the Participation of Jews in the Spanish and Portuguese Discoveries*, 4th ed. (1894; reprint ed., New York: Hermon Press, 1968).

7. Alice B. Gould, *Nueva lista documentada de los tripulantes de Colón en 1492* (Madrid: Real Academia de la Historia, 1984), originally published as a series of articles in the *Boletín de la Real Academia de la Historia*.

8. *Larousse gran diccionario*, 1st ed., s.v. "casa de contratación."

9. Henry Charles Lea, *The Inquisition in the Spanish Dependencies: Sicily, Naples, Sardinia, Milan, the Canaries, Mexico, Peru, New Granada* (New York: Macmillan, 1908), pp. 191–298.

10. For more information about these laws and, particularly, the means used to circumvent them, see Juan Friede, "Algunas observaciones sobre la emigración español a América," *Revista de Indias* 12, no. 49 (July–September 1952): 467–496.

11. See Pablo Alvarez Rubiano, *Pedrarias Dávila: contribución al estudio de la figuro del "Gran justador," gobernador de Castilla de Oro y Nicaragua* (Madrid: Consejo Superior de Investigaciones Científicas, Instituto Gonzalo Férnandez de Oviedo, 1944) (originally author's thesis, 1939) and idem, "Diego Arias Davila," *Estudios segovianos* 1 (1949): 367–372. This figure, also known as Pedro Arias de Avila, was the subject of another thesis: Michael Odell Lancaster, "Pedrarias Davila" (Ph.D. diss., University of Texas, 1965), as well as a play: Pedro de Gorostiza y Cepeda, *Pedrarias Davila: drama original en cinco actos, de los cuales el cuarto está dividido en dos cuadros* (Madrid: Impr. Nacional, 1838).

12. *EJ*, s.v. "Carvajal," by Martin A. Cohen. Further reading on the Carvajal family may be found in Alfonso Toro, *La familia Carvajal: estudio histórico sobre los jud´ios y la inquisición de la Nueva España en el siglo XVI, basado en documentos originales y en su mayor parte ineditos, que se conservan en el Archivo General de la Nación de la ciudad de México*, 2 vols. (Mexico City: Editorial Patria, 1944); Pablo Martínez del Rio, "Alumbrado" (Mexico City: Porrua Hermanos, 1937); *Procesos de Luis de Carvajal (el mozo)*, Publicaciones del Archivo General de la Nación 28 (Mexico: Talleres Gráficos de la Nación, 1935); Liebman, *The Enlightened: The Writings of Luis de Carvajal, el Mozo* (Coral Gables, Fla.: University of Miami Press, 1967); *Enciclopedia Judaica Castellana*, s.v. "Carvajal y de la Cueva, Luis de" and "Carvajal (El Mozo), Luis de"; Martin A. Cohen, "The Autobiography of Luis de Carvajal, the Younger," *American Jewish Historical Quarterly* 55 (1965–66): 277–318; idem, "A Brief Survey of Studies Relating to Luis de Carvajal, the Younger," *American Sephardi* 3 (1969): 89–90; idem, "The Letters and Last Will and Testament of Luis de Carvajal, the Younger," *American Jewish Historical Quarterly* 55 (1965–66): 451–520; idem, "The Religion of Luis Rodriguez Carvajal," *American Jewish Archives* 20 (1968): 33–62; and idem, *The Martyr: The Story of a Secret Jew and the Mexican Inquisition in the Sixteenth Century* (Philadelphia: Jewish Publication Society, 1973).

13. Regarding Toribio Medina's many works on the Inquisition in the Americas, see citations appearing under various countries below.

14. Lea, *Inquisition in the Spanish Dependencies*, pp. 191–298, and Maurice Birckel, "Recherches sur la trésoririe inquisitoriale de Lima," *Mélanges de la Casa de Velázquez*, 5:223–307.

15. For more detail on the Cartagena Inquisition, see José Toribio Medina, *La inquisición en Cartagena de Indias*, 2nd ed. (Bogota: C. Valencia, 1978), originally published as *Historia del tribunal del Santo oficia de la inquisición de Cartagena de las Indias* (Santiago de Chile: Imprenta Elzeviriana, 1899). The topic is partially treated in Manuel Tejado Fernandez, *Aspectos de la vila social en Cartagena durante el seiscíentos*, Publicaciones de la Escuela de Estudios Hispano-Americanos de Sevilla, no. 87, 1st ed. (Seville: Escuela de Estudios Hispano-Americanos, 1954).

16. The text of the decree will be found in Boleslao Lewin, *El judío en la época colonial: un aspecto de la historia rioplatense* (Buenos Aires: Colegio Libre de Estudios Superiores, 1939), pp. 52–53.

17. Ibid., pp. 78–85.

18. Birckel, "Recherches sur la trésoririe inquisitoriale," pp. 223–307.

19. For more information, see Fernando Montesinos, *Anales del Peru*, 2 vols. (Madrid: Imp. de Gabriel L. y del Horno, 1906).

20. This auto-da-fé is discussed in José Toribio Medina, *Historia del Tribunal del Santo Oficio de la inquisición de Lima, 1569–1820* (Santiago: Imprenta Gutenberg, 1887); 2nd ed. (Santiago de Chile: Fondo Histérico y Bibliogréfico J. T. Medina, 1956).

21. For more detail regarding this auto, see Matias de Bocanegra, *Jews and the Inquisition of Mexico: The Great Auto de Fé of 1649*, trans. and ed., with notes, bibliography, and introduction, by Seymour B. Liebman (Lawrence, Kans.: Coronado Press, 1974).

22. Antonio Domínguez Ortiz, *Los judeoconversos en España y América*, Colección Fundamentos, no. 11 (Madrid: Ediciones ISTMO, 1971), pp. 127–147 passim.

23. Other treatments of the subject on a geographical basis include Nissim Elnecave, *Los hijos de Ibero-Fraconia: breviario del mundo sefaradí desde los orígenes hasta nuestros días* (Buenos Aires: Editorial "La Luz," 1981); José Monin, *Los judíos en la América española, 1492–1810* (Buenos Aires: Biblioteca Yavne, 1939): Lewin, *Criptojudíos*, pp. 107–114.

24. A great deal has been written about the Jewish presence in colonial Brazil, including Arnold Wiznitzer, *Jews in Colonial Brazil* (New York: Columbia University Press, 1960); idem, *Os judeus no Brasíl colonial*, trans. Olivia Krahenbuhl (São Paulo: Pioneira, 1960): Anita Novinsky, *Inquisiçao: inventários de bens confiscados a cristaos novos: fontes para a história de Portugal e do Brasil*

(Lisbon: Impr. Nacional, Casa de Moeda: Livraria Camões, 1976–); idem, "Sistema de poder y represión religiosa: para una interpretación del fenómeno 'cristao novo' en el Brasil," *Sefardica* 1, no. 1 (March 1984): 17–24; idem, *Cristaos-novos na Bahia*, Estudos 9 (São Paulo: Editora Perspectiva, 1972); Evelyne Kenig, "Identitó des nouveaux-chrétiens portugais au Brésil au 16e siécle," in *The Sephardi and Oriental Jewish Heritage*, ed. Issachar Ben-Ami (Jerusalem: Magnes, Misgav Yerushalayim, 1982), pp. 73–83; *Breve história dos judeus no Brasil*, Biblioteca de cultura judaica, no. 10 (Rio de Janeiro: Edicoes Biblos, 1962); Rachel Ouziel, "Brésil–des marranes aux chrétiens: un effacement qui a dure trois siécles," *Nouveaux cahiers* no. 77 (1984): 50–57; José Gonçalves Salvador, *Cristaos-novos, jesuítas e inquisiçao: aspectos de sua atuaçao nas capitanias do 1530–1680*, Biblioteca Pioneira Editora (São Paulo: Livraria Pioneira Editora, 1969); idem, *Os cristaos-novos e o comércio no Atlântico meridional*, Biblioteca Pioneira de estudos brasileiros (São Paulo: Pioneira, 1978); idem, *Os cristaos-novos: povoamente e conquista de solo brasileiro, 1530–1680*, Biblioteca Pioneira de estudos brasileiros (São Paulo: Liveria Pioneira Editora, 1976); Elias Lipiner, *Os judaizantes nos capitanias de cima: estudos sobre os cristaos-novos do Brasil nos séculos xvi é xvii* (São Paulo: Editora Brasiliense, 1969); Isaac Izecksohn, *Os marranos brasileiros* (São Paulo: Impres, 1967); Solidonio Leite, *Os deus no Brasil* (Rio de Janeiro: J. Leite, 1923); Nachman Falbel, *Estudios sobre a comunidade judaica no Brasil* (São Paulo: Federaçao Israelita do Estado de São Paulo, 1984); Egon Wolff and Frieda Wolff, *Dicionario biográfico*, vol. 1, *Judaizantes e judeus no Brasil, 1500–1808* (Rio de Janeiro: E. and F. Wolff, 1986); Kurt Loewenstamm, *Vultos judaicos no Brasil: uma contribuçao a história do judeus no Brasil*, vol. 1, *Tempo colonial, 1500–1822*, trans. Kurt Hahn, Coleçao "Israel" (Rio de Janeiro, 1949), originally published as *Schicksal und Leistungen von Juden in Brasilien in Vergangenhei; un Gegenwart*; Nelson Omeqna, *Diabolizaçao dos judeus: martirio e presenca dos sefardins no Brasil colonial* (Rio de Janeiro: Distribuidora Record, 1969); N. M. de Braga Mella, *Os judeus no Brasil e nas Americas: (tentames)* (Rio de Janeiro: Lito-Tipo Guanabara, 1959); Afamio Peixoto, *Os judeus na historia do Brazil* (Rio de Janeiro: V. Zwerling, 1936); *Enciclopedia Judaica Castellana* (hereafter cited as *EJC*), s.v. "Brasil."

25. Bento Teixeira, *Prosopopéia*, 9th ed., Memoria literaria (São Paulo: Ediciones Melhoramentos, 1977); Ambrosio Fernandes Brandão, *Diálogos das grandezas do Brasil*, 2nd ed., Documentos para a historia do norieste, vol. 1 (Recife: Imprensa Universitaria, 1966).

26. For the records of these synagogues, see Arnold Wiznitzer, *The Records of the Earliest Jewish Community in the New World* (New York: American Jewish Historical Society, 1954).

27. Works focusing on Dutch Brazil include Arnold Wiznitzer, *Jewish Soldiers in Dutch Brazil, 1630–1654* (Philadelphia: Typ. M. Jacobs, 1956?); José Antônio Gonsalves de Mello, *Tempo dos flamengos: influéncia da ocupaçao holandesa na vida e na cultura do norte do Brazil*, 3rd ed., Estudos e pesquisas (Recife: Editora Massangana, 1987); Isaac Z. Raizman, *História dos israelitas no Brasíl desde o descobrimento até o fim do dominio hollandez* (São Paulo: Buch-Presse, 1937); Hermann Kellenberg, *A participaçao de companhia de judeus no conguisca holandesa de Pernambuco* (Paraiba: Universidade Federal da Paraiba, 1966); Charles Ralph Boxer, *The Dutch in Brazil, 1624–1654* (Oxford: Clarendon Press, 1957).

28. *EJ*, s.v. "Silva, António José da," by Godfrey Edmond Silverman.

29. *EJ*, s.v. "Brazil," by Arnold Wiznitzer.

30. For more detail regarding the Sephardic experience in colonial Chile, see Moshe Nes El, *Historia de la comunidad israelita sefaradí de Chile* (Santiago: Editorial Nascimento, 1984); Gunther Friedlander, *Los heroes olvidados* (Santiago: Editorial Nascimento, 1966); Gunther Böhm, *Nuevos antecedentes para una historia de los judíos en Chile colonial* (Santiago: Editorial Universitaria, 1963); idem, *Los judíos en Chile durante la colonia*, version aumentada (Santiago: Academia Chilena de la Historia, 1948); idem, *Historia de los judíos en Chile*, vol. 1: *Period colonial, judíos y judeoconversos en*

Chile colonial durante los siglos xvi y xvii, El Bachiller Francisco Maldonado de Silva, 1592–1639, Judaica iberoamericano, nos. 4–5 (Santiago: Editorial Andres Bello, 1984); José Toribio Medina, *Historia del Tribunal del Santo Oficio de la inquisición en Chile,* 2 vols. (Santiago: Impr. Ercilla, 1890); *EJC,* s.v. "Chile."

31. Pedro Mexía de Ovando, *La ovandina,* Colección de libros y documentos referentes a la historia de América, vol. 17 (Madrid: Suarez, 1915).

32. *EJ,* s.v. "Chile," by Gunther Böhm.

33. More information on the Jews of New Granada (which included Colombia) is found in Lucía García Proodian, *Los judíos en América: sus actividades en los Virreinatos de Nueva Castilla y Nueva Granada,* Publicaciones Ser. E., no. 2 (Madrid: Consejo Superior de Investigacioaes Científicas, Instituto "Aria Montano," 1966); Lewin, *Criptojudíos,* pp. 117–120; Tejado Fernández, *Aspectos de la vida social en Cartagena de Indias durante el seiscientos*; Itic Rotbaum, *De Sefarad al neosefardismo: contribución a la historia de Colombia,* 2 vols. (Bogotá: Editorial Kelly, 1967–71): José Toribio Medina, *Historia del tribunal del Santo oficia de la inquisición de Cartagena de las Indias* (Santiago: Imprenta Elzeviriana, 1899); idem, *La imprenta en Bogota y la inquisición en Cartagena de Indias* (Bogotá: Biblioteca Nacional de Colombia, 1952); *EJC,* s.v. "Colombia."

34. More detail on the Complicidad Grande may be found in Liebman, "The Great Conspiracy in Peru," *The Americas* 28, no. 2 (October 1971): 176–190.

35. *EJ,* s.v. "Colombia," by Moshe Nes El.

36. Additional reading on the Sephardim of Argentina may be found in Boleslao Lewin, *El judío en la época colonial: un aspecto de la historia rioplatense* (Buenos Aires: Colegio Libre de Estudios Superiores, 1939); idem, *Supresión de la inquisición y libertad de cultos en la Argentina,* Cuadernos, no. 3 (Buenos Aires: Universidad Nacional de La Plata, Instituto de Historia ie la Filosofía y del Pensamiento Argentino, 1957); idem, "Esbozo de la historia judía de la Argentina (desde el coloniaje hasta 1889)," *Indice: revista de ciencias sociales* 2, no. 5 (April 1969): 8–38; José Toribio Medina, *El tribunal del Santo oficio de la inquisición en las provincias del Plata,* Biblioteca enciclopedia argentino, no. 2 (Buenos Aires: Editorial "Huarpes," 1945); Ricardo Rojas, "Los judíos en la época colonial," *Vida Nuestra* 1, no. 2 (August 1917): 15–23 (a somewhat abridged version appears in Juan José Sebreli, ed., "Los judíos en los paises rioplatenses durante el coloniaje," *La cuestión judía en la Argentina,* Colección ensayos [Buenos Aires: Editorial Tiempo Contemporáneo, 1968]); *EJC,* s.v. "Argentina."

37. *EJ,* s.v. "Argentina," by Fred Bronner.

38. Further information on Mexico is contained in Eva Alexandra Uchmany, "De algunos cristianos nuevos en la conquista y colonización de la Nueva España," *Estudios de historia novohispana* 8 (1985): 265–318; Seymour Liebman, *The Jews in New Spain: Faith, Flame, and the Inquisition* (Miami: University of Miami Press, 1970) and in Spanish translation, *Los judíos en México y América Central: fé, llamas, inquisicion* (Mexico: Siglo XXI, 1971); idem, "From All Their Habitations, They Came with Cortes: Notes on Mexican Jewish History," *Judaism* 18 (Winter 1969): 91–102; Martin A. Cohen, "Some Misconceptions about the Crypto-Jews in Colonial Mexico," *American Jewish Historical Quarterly* 61 (June 1972): 277–293; idem, "Antonio Díaz de Caceres: Marrano Adventurer in Colonial Mexico," *American Jewish Historical Quarterly* 60 (1970-1971): 169–184; idem, "Don Gregorio Lopez: Friend of the Secret Jew," *Hebrew Union College Annual* 38 (1967): 259–284; Sara Bialostosky, "Situación social y jurídica de los judíos y sus descendientes en la Nueva España," *Revista de la Facultad de Derecho (Universidad Autónoma de México)* 26, nos. 101–102 (January–June 1976): 115–128; Jonathan Irvine Israel, *Race, Class, and Politics in Colonial Mexico, 1610–1670,* Oxford Historical Monographs (London: Oxford University Press, 1975); Alicia Gojman Goldberg, "Conservsos en la Nueva Espana, su idealismo y perseverancia," (thesis, Universidad

Nacional Autonoma, 1976); *EJC*, s.v. "Mexico."

39. Ricardo Osado (d. 1770), *Medicina doméstica: descripción de los nombres y virtudes de las llervas indígenas de Yucatan y las enfermedades a que se aplican* . . . (N.p.: n.p., 1939?).

40. *EJ*, s.v. "Mexico," by Nissim Itzhak.

41. Additional material on Peru includes Boleslao Lewin, *El Santo Oficio en América y el más grande proceso inquisitorial en el Perú* (Buenos Aires: Sociedad Hebraica Argentina, 1950); Ricardo Palma, *Anales de la inquisición de Lima: estudio histórico* (Lima: A. Alfaro, 1863); José Toribio Medina, *Historia del Tribunal del Santo Oficio de la inquisicion de Lima*, 2 vols. (Santiago: Imprenta Gutenberg, 1887); García de Proodian, *Judíos en América*; Elkan Nathan Adler, *The Inquisition in Peru* (Baltimore: Lord Baltimore Press, n.d.), reprinted from *Publications of the American Jewish Historical Society*, no. 12; Octavio Cavada Dancourt, *La inquisición en Lima: sintesis de su historia* (Lima: Libreria "El Inca," 1935); Hans Joachim Sell, *Briefe einer Judin aus Cuzco: eine do Kumentarische Erzahlung aus dem heutigen Peru* (Vienna: Herold, 1978): Juan José Vega, *Los conversos en los inicios del Peru moderno* (Lima: Editorial Todo el Peru, 1981); *EJC*, s.v. "Peru."

42. *EJ*, s.v. "Peru," by Martin A. Cohen.

43. For more information on Surinam, see Robert Cohen, ed., *The Jewish Nation in Surinam: Historical Essay* (Amsterdam: S. Emmering, 1982); *Essai historigue sur la colonie de Surinam, su fondation, ses révolutions, ses progrès, depuis son oriqine jusqu'à nos jours* . . . *avec l'histoire nation juive portuguise & allemande y étable, leurs privileges, immunites & franchises* . . . *le tout redigé sur des pieces authentichs y jointes & misen ordre, par les régens & répreesentas de ladite Nation Juive Portugaise* (Amsterdam: S. Emmering, 1968); Jacob R. Marcus and Stanley F. Chyet, eds., *Historical Essay on the Colony of Surinam*, trans. Simon Cohen, Publications of the American Jewish Archives, no. 8 (Cincinnati: American Jewish Archives, 1974); Rudolf Asveer Jacob van Lier, *Frontier Society: A Social Analysis of the History of Surinam*, trans. M. J. L. van Yperen, Koninklijk Instituut voor Taal-, Land- en Volkenkunde-Translation series, 14 (The Hague: M. Nijhoff, 1971); Jaap Meijer, *Pioneers of Pauroma: Contribution to the Earliest History of the Jewish Colonization of America* (Paramaribo: Typ. El Dororado, 1954); Frederik Oudschans Dentz, *Die Kolonisatie van de Portugeesch Joodsche natie in Suriname en de geschiedenis* (Amsterdam: S. Emmering, 1929); Sigmund Seeligmann, *David Nassy of Surinam and His "Lettre politico-theologico morale sur les Juifs"*, reprinted from *Publications of the American Jewish Historical Society* 22 (1914); Herbert Ivan Bloom, *A Study of Brazilian Jewish History, 1623–1654, Based Chiefly upon the Findings of the Late Samuel Oppenheim* (Baltimore, 1934), reprinted from *Publications of the American Jewish Historical Society* 33 (1934); *EJC*, s.v. "Surinam."

44. *EJ*, s.v. "Surinam," by Robert Cohen.

45. Martin A. Cohen, *Jewish Experience in Latin America*, 1:xxii–xxiv; idem, in *EJ*, s.v. "Latin America."

Sephardim in Latin America after Independence

Victor A. Mirelman

During the colonial period, Jewish life in the Spanish and Portuguese territories in America was manifested mainly in a clandestine way. Judaizers, usually as individuals but sometimes in groups, celebrated Jewish holy days with religious services of sorts and also observed some Jewish laws and customs. Most of these observances, however, became more and more diluted due to the lack of a formal Jewish community in close proximity that could be the source for accurate observance of the ritual laws and fix the proper dates for the celebration of festivals.

As result of the attainment of independence by the nations of Latin America, and the subsequent formal abolition of the Inquisition during the first quarter of the nineteenth century, Jews felt more free to wander into the various countries of the continent. Nonetheless, during most of the nineteenth century only a very small number of Jews opted to live there, and very limited organized Jewish life was attempted. The major waves of Jewish immigration to Latin America began in 1889 when a contingent of over 800 Jews from Russia moved to Argentina with the purpose of establishing an agricultural colony. However, among the first pioneering Jews who preceded the mass migration of the late nineteenth and early twentieth centuries we find a relatively strong Sephardic presence.

Curaçao

At the turn of the nineteenth century, the largest Jewish community in the Americas was on the Dutch island of Curaçao. These Jews were Sephardim, and they retained strong links with the Spanish-Portuguese community in Amsterdam, from where they or their ancestors had migrated. Most of them were merchants, actively involved in the island's trade with other parts of the world, including the Spanish territories in South and Central America. Since Curaçao is only 35 miles off the northern coast of Venezuela, it is understandable that considerable trade was transacted with the main ports of present-day Venezuela and Colombia.[1]

During the revolutionary period on the mainland, some of the Curaçao Sephardim, in line with the general policy of the British, who at that time had control of the island, favored the rebels and actively supported the uprising against Spain. Several of them established friendly personal relationships with Simon Bolivar and offered their help to him and his family. A few Curaçaoan Sephardim even enlisted in Bolivar's army.

Shortly after Bolivar's victory, Curaçao suffered a severe economic depression coupled with a dry spell from 1819 to 1825 which ruined the farmers and a smallpox epidemic in 1827 which claimed many victims. Significant numbers of people began looking for new horizons, and many opted to continue their trade and commerce in a different setting. Bolivar, now the ruler of Greater Colombia—as the short-lived union of Colombia and Venezuela was then identified—invited foreigners, including Jews, to settle in the new country. Greater Colombia ratified this policy on May 1, 1829 in a treaty with the Netherlands, granting full religious freedom to all immigrants.[2]

Coro

Small groups of Jews from Curaçao, sometimes only a handful of families, settled in the Venezuelan cities of Coro, Puerto Cabello, Cumaná, and Caracas. The most important Jewish presence was in Coro, a port on the Caribbean about 60 miles south of Curaçao, where Jews first arrived in 1824. Though there were Jews living in Coro almost uninterruptedly from 1824 to 1900, they always remained a small community numbering at the most 130–160 souls. All the Jews in Coro had come from Curaçao, and the traffic between these two points continued throughout the century.

Small as it was, the Jewish community of Coro made a substantial contribution to the town's economic and commercial development, mainly through the establishment of retail stores in which they sold goods imported from Europe, usually in Dutch vessels via Curaçao.

Jews were also involved in exporting goods such as hides and cacao from Venezuela to Curaçao and Europe. A few Sephardim from Coro participated with distinction in the political life of the state of Falcón and also at the national level.

The liberal spirit prevailing in Venezuela during the nineteenth century was what allowed for the early settlement of Jews in Coro. Most prospered, and many obtained Venezuelan citizenship, but nonetheless they were not spared from occasional outbreaks of anti-Semitism. In 1831 a band of hoodlums entered the house of David Valencia, where a few Jews were praying together, and injured some of them physically. They also attacked the homes and properties of other Jews in Coro. While the goal of the hoodlums was to "defend the Christian religion" and force the Jews to leave the country, these attacks did not have major consequences.

Similar incidents took place in February of 1855. This time the issue provoked a diplomatic impasse between Venezuela and Holland, which opted to protect the interests of its subjects, most of whom had left Coro because of the provocations. When the negotiations regarding reparations for the losses sustained by the Jewish merchants broke down, a Dutch fleet was sent to the port of La Guaira, threatening to attack unless restitution was paid. Through the efforts of the British consul in Caracas, the Dutch agreed to withdraw from the port. In later negotiations Venezuela agreed to pay a substantial indemnity to the Jews of Coro.[3]

With respect to the practice of religious rites other than Catholicism, the early Venezuelan legislation specifically singled out Dutch subjects as having all types of freedoms, "as long as they are observed in private homes." This was the major reason for having religious services in individual homes. In 1832 the Jews of Coro were allowed to establish a cemetery, and a total of 182 people were buried there during the period of the Jewish sojourn in Coro.

Interestingly, the tombstones in Coro do not include any Hebrew inscriptions, nor dates of birth and death according to the Hebrew calendar. This is a departure from the usage in Curaçao, where the tombstones contained not only names and dates in Hebrew, but also appropriate sentences or biblical verses in Hebrew. This is a tangible testimony to the rapid assimilation of the Coro Jews. While situated quite close to Curaçao, where Jewish life was enriched by the presence of rabbis, teachers, educational materials, and ritual objects provided by closer contacts with the "mother" community in Amsterdam, they were substantially removed from that aspect of Jewish life. Toward the end of the century the Jewish presence in Coro ceased to exist, leaving the cemetery as the only testimony to the life of that branch of Sephardic Jewry.[4]

The Caribbean "Diaspora"

The Jewry of Curaçao remained small in size throughout the nineteenth century, numbering between 783 and 1,265 souls, and many of them migrated to Spanish America immediately after the liberation from Spain and the abolition of the Inquisition. As early as the first third of the century we find vessels from Curaçao, laden with cargoes belonging to the island's Sephardic merchants, making frequent calls not only at the Venezuelan ports of La Guaira and Coro, but also in Colombia at Cartagena, Puerto Bello, Barranquilla, and Santa Marta, as well as ports in Mexico, Cuba, and Puerto Rico. A number of the island's Jewish merchants ended up settling in these port cities, establishing a Curaçaoan Sephardic "diaspora" whose constituent groups were dependent for Jewish nurturing on *their* "mother" community in Curaçao.[5]

In 1838, for example, a group of Caracas Sephardim petitioned the Mikveh Israel synagogue in Curaçao for help in acquiring a parcel of land for a Jewish cemetery. This petition was forwarded to the Sephardic community in Amsterdam with the addition of a note urging the Amsterdam synagogue officials to consider the request of the "Dutch subjects of the Hebraic religion" residing in Caracas. The petition was publicized through the Amsterdam community's publication in the hope that funds would be forthcoming from individual members.

This request, like later ones, did not accomplish much, but the reasons for the failure are not clear.[6] In other instances the Curaçao synagogue contributed directly to satellite groups in the South American mainland. Thus 100 florins were sent for a cemetery in Rio Hacha, and in 1868, when the Curaçaoan Jews sent 1,300 francs, through the

Alliance Israélite Universelle, for the relief of the Jews of Morocco and Tunis, they added 129 francs from Curaçaoan Jews in Coro and 500 francs from Curaçaoan Jews in Barranquilla.[7]

Most of these settlements had a very short existence, and their few Sephardic families did not constitute a community. A few, however, had a lasting life, and founded communal institutions for the practice of Jewish rituals and traditions. For example, in Panama City, then part of Colombia, Jews from Curaçao founded a Hebrew Benevolent Society in 1852. After the earthquake on St. Thomas in 1867, various Jews who had moved there from Curaçao now migrated to Panama. In 1876 the Benevolent Society was renamed Congregation Kol Shearith Israel.[8]

From Panama, a few of the Curaçaoan families that formed a satellite community spread into Central American cities such as Costa Rica and San Salvador, though they continued to maintain regular contact with the "mother" group in Curaçao. Frances P. Karner has noticed a marriage pattern by which Sephardim who moved abroad would return to Curaçao and eventually marry local Jewish women. Thus the departures during the mid-nineteenth century, which no doubt were caused by economic declines in Curaçao, often proved to be temporary, since changing fortunes on the island brought some of them back.

Barranquilla

By the middle of the nineteenth century Barranquilla was becoming a progressive city. Elisee Reclus, in 1855, noted the presence of a considerable number of foreign merchants—English, American, German, Dutch—which made Barranquilla the main exchange port for commerce with the interior, and the major market in Nueva Granada. The Dutch merchants were mostly Sephardim from Curaçao and other Caribbean Islands, among them H. J. Senior, A. Wolff, Isaias M. Solas, Israel Senior, and various members of the Alvarez Correa, Roiz Mendez, Cortizos, De Sola, and Curiel families. Many had already established successful businesses.

The founding of the Banco de Barranquilla in 1872 was a direct result of the city's economic development and the increased business of its customs, port, and railroads. The bank became Colombia's second-most-important financial institution after the Banco de Bogotá, and among its founders we find many Sephardic Jews of Curaçaoan origin, as well as a few Jews of German origin among others.[9]

The early Sephardim of Barranquilla attempted to preserve some of their traditions by meeting in each other's homes for prayers on the High Holy Days. By 1880 they were meeting more formally at the residence of Agustin Senior. However, by the beginning of the twentieth century the Jewish character of this "community" had been extinguished due to their total assimilation into the local population.

Perhaps the most outstanding personality among the Jews from Curaçao in Barranquilla was Ernesto Cortizos, the "father" of Colombian commercial aviation, who founded Scadta, later known as Avianca, the first commercial airline in South America. Many other Jews also held influential positions in the city's economic life.[10]

Costa Rica

There have always been very few Sephardim in Costa Rica, but the first Jews there were also from Curaçao. The situation changed rapidly, however. Thus a study indicates that in 1940 fully 700 of Costa Rica's 743 Jews were of Polish origin, and in 1978, more than 90 percent of its 1,586 Jews were of Polish origin, with the rest from other areas, including South America, and only a handful of Sephardic families. Nonetheless, an Ashkenazi informant on the early years of the twentieth century reported that Jewish religious life in Costa Rica was initiated by Sephardim: "We did not practice much religion. But we did celebrate Yom Kippur with the Maduro, the Sasso and the Robles [families]. We used to go to the home of Señor Maduro to pray. This we did for five or six years."[11]

The one or two dozen immigrant merchants who constituted the Curaçaoan satellite in Costa Rica were prominent in the economic structure and even attained political and civic offices. Moises Maduro, for instance, was appointed to public office before 1880, and years later Alfredo Sasso Robles became head of the Costa Rican Chamber of Commerce.[12]

Lima

We find a somewhat similar situation in the early community of Lima. Most of the Jews in Peru during the last half of the nineteenth century had come from Germany, while a few hailed from other West European countries and Russia. In 1870 they founded the Sociedad de Beneficencia Israelita.

Only three families belonged to the Curaçaoan satellite community, and all three arrived in Lima via the island of St. Thomas. Nevertheless, one of the most prominent members, and certainly a religious leader of the little group, was David Senior de Castro. A dentist by profession, De Castro arrived in Lima around 1871/72 in his late teens. In 1873 he became the treasurer of the society, and in 1887–89 its president. Moreover, given the lack of any religious functionary, Dr. Castro assumed the role of spiritual leader of the Sociedad de Beneficencia, performing wedding ceremonies and officiating as mohel at circumcisions. His religious leanings were evident from the fact that he arrived in Lima with a Torah scroll, which was later used at the religious services.[13]

Sephardim from Morocco in Belém

In addition to the Jews who migrated from Curaçao to the Latin American countries, other waves of Sephardim arrived there from overseas. They originated in two major regions: North Africa, especially Morocco, and the portions of the Ottoman Empire that today comprise Turkey, Greece, Syria, and Lebanon.

Individual Jews from Morocco first arrived in Latin America early in the nineteenth century, most probably as soon as they got word that the emerging nations there had adopted more liberal attitudes regarding non-Catholics.

At the beginning they came in small numbers, seeking to attain positions as merchants. Northeastern Brazil was the nearest point across the Atlantic, and the Moroccan Jews settled mainly in Belém, the capital of the state of Pará, where the Amazon meets the Atlantic Ocean. By 1824 there were enough Moroccan Sephardim in Belém to found a synagogue, which they named Porta do Ceu (Hebrew: Shaar Hashamayim, "Gate of Heaven").

Migration from Morocco continued at a slow pace until the 1870s. These adventurous merchants preferred northeastern Brazil, and a few went up the Amazon, establishing themselves in the various new towns and cities in the state of Amazonas. Gradually, some made their way to other cities, especially Recife, in the state of Pernambuco, and Rio de Janeiro, the capital.

Thus, in the early 1860s the naturalist Henry W. Bates reported seeing some Moroccan Jews during his exploration of the Amazon River.

> Near Ega we visited a village; several small but navigable streams or inlets here fall into the Ouaray; the land appeared to be of the highest fertility; we crossed a neck of land on foot, from one inlet to another. . . . One of the settlers was a Gibraltar Jew, established there many years, and thoroughly reconciled to the ways of life of the semi-civilized inhabitants. We found him barefoot, with trousers turned up to the knees, busily employed with a number of Indians—men, women and children—shelling and drying cacao, which grows with immense profusion in the neighborhood. . . . This was the only Jew I met with on the upper river. There are several settled at Santarem, Cameta, Para, where on account of their dealings being fairer than those of the Portuguese traders, they do a good trade, and live on friendly terms with the Brazilians.[14]

Many of these merchants succeeded economically. Some went back to their home cities in Morocco to marry and then returned to Brazil, but others intermarried and slowly lost their Jewish identity. In Belém, however, there was a larger concentration of Moroccan Jews. By 1869, it was reported, they still continued to gather for prayers in a private room, where they had three Torah scrolls. They also made collections for charitable institutions in Jerusalem. The Jewish merchants in towns up the Amazon would join the Belém group for the High Holy Days.[15]

Why the Moroccans Emigrated

During the last three decades of the nineteenth century, more considerable numbers of Jews from Morocco made their way to Brazil, Venezuela, and Argentina. Most of them hailed from Tetuán, though a few had lived in the coastal cities of Tangier, Larache, and Casablanca. This emigration was first stimulated by the Spanish-Moroccan war of 1859–60, when Spain set out to conquer Tetuán. The local Jews, who had suffered from pillage and massacres at the hands of their Muslim neighbors on the eve of the Spanish conquest, welcomed the Spaniards as saviors. The Spanish occupation, which lasted two years, was relatively good for the Jews. But with their departure on May 2, 1862, the Moroccan reaction led many of the city's Jews to emigrate.

The majority of the Jews who left Tetuán went to Algeria, especially to the city of Oran, but a growing number went to other areas in Spanish Morocco, including Tangier, Ceuta, and Melilla, while others settled in Gibraltar, Spain, and Portugal. Latin America, and especially Brazil at this early stage, attracted the most adventuresome.[16]

Jewish emigration was more pronounced from the coastal communities of Morocco than from those in the interior. In Meknès and Fez, contact with European culture and commerce was limited, while in Tangier and Tetuán there was constant intercourse with Europe. This induced many, especially the young, to try their fortune in commerce abroad.[17]

There were, moreover, differences between the two larger coastal cities, Tangier and Tetuán, that explain why most of the Moroccan immigrants to Latin America were from Tetuán. The Jews of Tangier, as Michael Laskier described,

> were not as economically impoverished as their counterparts in Tetuán. Even among the poorer segments of the Tangier community, one could engage in commercial activities of this strategic commercial port. . . . In Tetuán, on the other hand, there were hardly any important industries or commercial activities, and local Jews were in fact leaving town.[18]

Poverty, and lack of jobs and opportunities, proved to be the most compelling motivation for seeking amelioration abroad.

The Alliance Israélite Universelle

The creation of Alliance Israélite Universelle (AIU) schools in Tetuán (1862) and Tangier (1864) contributed enormously to the development of a new generation of Jews imbued with a spirit of progress.

The AIU schools played a central role in the modernization of the Jewish communities in the coastal cities, much more than in the interior, where the deeply rooted religious traditionalism of the Jews, and the opposition from rabbis and leaders, was much more intense. The AIU graduates spoke Spanish, French, and some English; they had been exposed to European mores, customs, and dress, and were motivated to reap the benefits of modern civilization.

The AIU schools also taught modern crafts and skills, hoping to change the occupational structure of the Jewish communities. However, for the period up to World War I no significant change took place in this area. Most young Moroccan Jews opted for either commerce or emigration as the best alternatives to escape poverty. Those who emigrated were "mainly from Tetuán, Larache and Elksar; some were from Tangier and fewer from Fez and Marrakesh. Many emigrants were in their teens."[19]

Even the graduates of the Alliance schools opted to emigrate due to the sparsity of economic opportunities in their hometowns. According to reports at the AIU, of the 417 graduates of the boys' school in Tetuán between 1862 and 1869, fully 182 emigrated. In other words, 43.6 percent of the school's graduates left the country. Of these, 104 opted for Algeria, 41 for Spain (including Ceuta, Melilla, and the Canary Islands), while 11 went to Brazil.[20] Those settling in Brazil stayed there several years, but many returned with fortunes to Tetuán or moved to other South American countries, due principally to the suffocating heat, yellow fever epidemics, insects, etc.[21] Figures for Tangier for the period 1875–1879 showed a trend of emigration to Algeria, Spain, Portugal and Brazil.[22]

Studies by Robert Ricard, Laskier, and Sara Leibovici indicate that in the 1880s and afterwards, the "emigration trends from the north, particularly from Tetuán, apparently gained additional momentum.... Whereas before 1880 more emigrants from Tetuán went to Algeria and Spain, the trend during the 1880's was more towards Latin America."[23] In his report on the AIU schools for 1884–85, David Cazés wrote:

> The school of Tetuán has only worked for export ... 95 percent of the students emigrate.... Today Algeria is not enough for this activity, and they go to Spanish America. There is a large number in Caracas, in Colón, in Panama, in Para-

maribo, in Buenos Aires; some have established themselves in the United States, they are in New York, Baltimore, Philadelphia, etc.[24]

The emigrants, as Spanish-speaking Jews, were naturally attracted by countries where their mother tongue, or a very similar one such as Portuguese, was spoken. Most of them were young, "between the ages of twelve and thirty," and were fleeing from the oppressive and sterile atmosphere of the *mellah*, "hoping to progress in new and free countries."[25]

Moroccan Settlements in Brazil

As a result of the rubber boom of the 1870s and afterward, Manaos, farther up the river from Belém, became an important commercial center. Fortunes were made, especially by British and American firms that exploited rubber, sugar, and cacao.

The prospects of rapid prosperity also attracted Jews to Manaos. While some were of Alsatian origin, most were Moroccan, often moving westward from Belém. Some went even farther up the Amazon into the Peruvian Amazonas region. In the 1880s, a substantial number of Jews settled in Iquitos, Peru, and in even smaller towns of the Peruvian forest region such as Yurimaguas, Caballococha, Santa Isabel, and Contamana.[26]

Many of the Sephardim represented Brazilian or European rubber companies. Others owned large stores in the cities and towns. Though their main motivations for living in the Amazon region, far from major cities, were obviously financial, they retained a modest Jewish identity. A correspondent for the *Jewish Chronicle* in London commented ironically in 1910 that the Jews of Iquitos ignored all the festivals except the Day of Atonement. Most did not observe Rosh Hashanah, "nor trouble to procure matzos for Pesach or any other requisites for religious observances."[27] However, they founded Jewish societies, and in Iquitos established a Jewish cemetery. Many of these Sephardic merchants became prominent citizens in their places of residence; some became mayors of their respective towns.[28]

A former teacher at the Alliance Israélite Universelle school in Morocco visited Iquitos in 1910, at the height of its prosperity. He reported that over 200 graduates of the school were living there, and many of them owned stores. "In Tangier one speaks about Iquitos as a fabulous city, with gold flowing through its streets."

Many of the Moroccan young men, he said, were full of visions of fortunes to be made.

> They do business in everything imaginable . . . English cloth, French novelties, German hardware, American machinery. They travel up the river in canoes or steamboats. . . . It's a hard life. At times they have to spend long months in their canoes, eat only rice and bananas, fight against the caimans, and wait for the Indians to come and buy their merchandise.

With respect to Jewish life, the teacher observed, "they only celebrate Yom Kippur, a day in which most boats are in port and the river is empty." He also noted that some returned to Morocco to marry, or established themselves in France, Spain, or England. "In Lisbon (Portugal) there is a sizable community of former immigrants from Peru and Brazil."[29]

The fall in rubber prices between 1910 and 1912 ruined many of the merchants and left the Amazon region impoverished. Most of its Jews left the area for Latin America's larger cities or even to return to the Old World.

The Moroccan migration continued, however, flowing now to Rio and São Paulo in Brazil, to Caracas in Venezuela, and especially to Argentina. In Caracas the Moroccans constituted the earliest segment of present-day Venezuelan Jewry. In the first few decades they met in private homes for their religious and social needs, but in 1926—now with the addition of Sephardim from the Ottoman Empire—they founded the Sociedad Benéfica Israelita, which in 1930 was renamed Asociación Israelita de Venezuela. In 1944 they built their synagogue in the El Conde section of Caracas.

Argentina

Moroccan Jews began to feel the lure of Argentina in the late 1870s, after the passage of liberal immigration laws in 1876, and additional legislation in the 1880s made the country even more appealing to Jewish immigrants. The impact of the liberal ideas of the eighties reduced the previously strong Catholic influence in Argentina's social and cultural institutions. After long-debated controversies between clericals and liberals, Congress passed a series of laws that stripped the church of many of its prerogatives. In 1884 the Ley de Educación Común made religious education no longer compulsory, relegating it to parental option, and limiting instruction to before or after class hours in all of the country's public schools. That same year the Civil Registration Law took away from the parishes the duty of registering births, marriages, and deaths. Finally, in 1888, civil marriage was made compulsory.[30]

On arriving in Buenos Aires, the Moroccan Jews found that there was already an existing Jewish society, the Congregación Israelita, founded in 1862 by immigrants from Central and Western Europe. Some of the Moroccans joined this congregation, even attaining positions on its board of directors. Most, however, settled in an area of Buenos Aires just south of the commercial district, where they organized their own societies. By 1891 the Congregación Israelita Latina had been founded, and by 1897 their burial society, Guemilut Hasadim, had acquired a lot for a cemetery just outside the city limits.[31]

From the 1890s until World War I the flow of Jews from Morocco to Argentina continued unabated. With the founding of the Jewish Colonization Association (JCA) and the launching of its agricultural colonies, another type of emigration of Moroccan Jews, more systematic but less numerous, was promoted by the AIU: that of teachers for the colonies' Jewish schools.

In April of 1895, four graduates of the École Normal of Paris left for Argentina.[32] In 1899, the Association des Anciens Élèves de l'Alliance à Tanger reported with elation that the subsidies for emigration to Latin America, usually limited to two people, had been considerably augmented. That year they were able to send twelve young candidates: five to Buenos Aires, two to Caracas, two to Belém, and one each to Maracaibo, Valparaiso, and Iquitos.

Similar efforts were made in Smyrna by an analogous association, which, at its own expense, sent young people who had been educated at the AIU school there and "who do not always find a remunerable job in their own town."[33] By the end of the century there were twenty schools in the JCA colonies, all directed by graduates of AIU schools in European Turkey, Smyrna, and Morocco. The advantage they had over teachers trained in other countries was their knowledge of Ladino and Spanish, which enabled them to teach the curriculum required by the Argentine education authorities.

The leaders of the AIU actually stimulated emigration from the poverty-stricken communities of Morocco. In their eyes the *oeuvre d'émigration* was justified by both its material and its educational value. Moroccan Jewry, with enormous pockets of misery and deficient education, benefitted from the prosperity that many emigrants attained in Latin America. The AIU, therefore, sought to impart to its students the skills they needed for success abroad.

A movement to encourage some alumni to emigrate to Senegal and Sudan, then under French domination, had little success. Evidently the cultural patterns of Latin America, modeled after those of Spain and Portugal, were more attractive than those of Black Africa.[34] Encouragement, moreover, was forthcoming from those already in Argentina.

Isaac Benchimol, who had been teaching for a number of years at the JCA colony of Mauricio, wrote in 1901 that Jewish emigration to South America was proving to be beneficial to the Jewish population of Tetuán. Letters describing economic success or visits to the city of birth after success had been attained had an impact on those who had not yet moved. They "did away with poverty, lifted morale . . . and developed individual initiative." Benchimol urged the AIU to introduce the teaching of Spanish at its schools in the interior of Morocco, where Jews spoke Arabic. This would provide students with an additional tool in case they contemplated migrating to Latin America, for "Latin America needs hands."[35]

In 1905, according to the calculations of Samuel D. Levy, reporting from Mauricio, there were 3,000 Sephardim in Argentina, 750 of them in Buenos Aires. Almost all were Moroccan, "85 percent . . . Tetuánese, and the rest from Gibraltar, from Tangier on the Moroccan coast, and Turks."[36]

It took most of the Moroccans Jews only a few years to create good economic situations for themselves in Argentina. Far from trying to restrict the immigration of more of their fellow countrymen, they made every effort to bring their families, relatives, and friends over.

Relatives usually stayed with those who had first arrived until they became acquainted with conditions in the new country. After that they would go to a city or town in the interior and establish a branch of the main house in Buenos Aires. An eyewitness reported at the turn of the century that "some Moroccan merchants [are] established in Buenos Aires and [have] up to five, six, and even eight branches of their business in the main centers of the Republic."[37]

A census conducted by Rabbi Samuel Halphon in 1909 confirms this. In the town of Villaguay, Entre Ríos province, there were only twelve Jews: a Russian family of six, five young men from Tetuán, and a widow who was also from Tetuán. The five Tetuanese men were managers of branch stores of firms owned by compatriots in Buenos Aires. The owners had become rich selling fabrics, linens, and clothing and were now wholesalers.

In the town of Gualeguaychu, in the same province, Halphon noted the presence of three Russian Jewish families, one French family, and five single Moroccan Jews. A decade earlier there had been some other Moroccan Jews, but they had left for Buenos Aires. Others came later and in turn left, to be replaced by more recent arrivals from Morocco: "It's a chain without end."[38]

Halphon's study also shows that Moroccans were the first Jewish settlers in many cities of the interior; some established themselves as early as the 1880s, though the majority arrived later.[39] Moroccan Jews began settling in the city of Santa Fé in the 1880s. Although they remained a small community (eleven families, totaling seventy-nine people, in 1909), they had acquired a cemetery by 1895.

Moroccan Jews also established themselves in rural towns along the railroad line west of Santa Fé, from La Sabana to Calchaqui. Halphon counted sixty-two families and ninety-six single persons for a total of 358 Moroccan Jews in these country towns. They ran general stores selling fabrics, haberdashery, shoes, and the like. Their knowledge of Spanish contributed to their commercial success, but, Halphon noted, while almost all were graduates of AIU schools, they lived in close contact with their Argentine countrymen and ended up abandoning many religious practices. For circumcisions and Passover needs, however, they resorted to the Jewish community of Santa Fé. They also buried their dead there.

In the final decades of the nineteenth century, Moroccan Jews settled in the towns of Villa María and Rio Cuarto, both in Córdoba province, and in Villa Mercedes and San Luis, both in San Luis province, as well as farther west in Mendoza.[40]

From the sources cited, as well as from documentation available in the archives of the Congregación Israelita Latina and Ets Ajaim in Rosário (also Moroccan), we infer that Moroccans moved into the interior of Argentina in larger proportions than did other Jewish immigrants.

In the interbellum period there was constant immigration of Jews from Tetuán and other areas of Morocco, though in more limited numbers than Eastern European Jews. An indication that the absolute numbers of Jews arriving from Morocco was dwindling is given by the 1936 Buenos Aires census. It showed just 420 persons born in Morocco, Spain, Tangier, Algeria, Gibraltar, Portugal, and Tunis who declared themselves to be Jewish. All the rest of the Moroccan community, numbering in the thousands, had been born in Argentina, some to Argentine parents. That the immigration of families with small children was almost nil is indicated by the fact that only five of the foreign-born Moroccan Jews were under the age of fifteen.[41]

For a few Moroccan Jews, emigration to Argentina was only temporary. They returned home after achieving economic stability, in some cases within ten years but sometimes as much as thirty. Many of the returnees had become Argentine citizens because an Argentine passport provided some protection in unstable Morocco. Thus, in 1927, seventy-nine of the ninety-five Argentines under the protection of the Argentine consul general in Rabat (i.e., 83 percent) were naturalized citizens who had been born in Morocco.[42] Indeed, even Jacob Bibas, the Argentine vice-consul in Spanish Morocco in 1935, had been born in Tangier and then lived in Rosário, province of Santa Fé, where he was active in local Jewish organizations.[43]

Jews from the Ottoman Empire

In addition to the Moroccan emigration, a second Sephardic migration developed from the Ottoman Empire toward the end of the nineteenth century. The financial debacle of the empire left a strong imprint on all elements of its population, Jews included. Many communities, lacking mineral wealth and industrial development, suffered grave impoverishment and were constantly threatened with overpopulation. Christians and Muslims were the first to leave, followed by the Jews. The emigrants from Beirut, Aleppo, Damascus, Istanbul, and Smyrna went to Egypt, Western Europe, and the United States, but also to several of the Latin American republics.[44]

Jews began to emigrate from the Ottoman Empire at the end of the nineteenth century. Egypt was the initial destination; from there a small number moved to Palestine, but most opted for the New World. Economic factors were the main impulse. The small communities in southeastern Turkey, as well as the large centers of Damascus and Aleppo in Syria, suffered from the diversion of international commerce to the newly opened Suez Canal and the subsequent demise of the caravan trade through their own regions.[45] Jews from Aleppo and Damascus in particular, who had previously represented English companies trading in cotton and woolen cloth, went to Manchester, starting in the nineteenth century, and remained there as merchants dealing in these commodities. The Syrian Jews in Manchester stayed in touch with the numerous new communities of compatriots mushrooming in America, especially in New York (Brooklyn) and Buenos Aires.[46]

During the first decades of the twentieth century, Jews left Ottoman territories in larger numbers. Two factors weighed heavily with them: letters from earlier emigrants enthusiastically describing life in the various Latin American countries, including their liberal laws and economic possibilities, and the 1908 revolution of the Young Turks. Aimed at securing constitutional government, the revolution paradoxically worked hardship on Jews and Christians by introducing compulsory military service.

Until that time, Jews and Christians had paid a special exemption tax to avoid conscription. Because serving in the army added to the difficulty of supporting a family and interfered with strict religious observance, escaping the draft became a force propelling Jews out of the empire.[47] Nevertheless, many Jews did serve during the Balkan wars and World War I. Though some served with distinction and many died, many more deserted after the collapse of the empire and sought to migrate.

The hardships wrought by the wars and the resulting political changes were also a major factor in emigration decisions. Some Jewish communities were more directly affected than others. The city of Adrianople, on the border of Turkey, Greece, and Bulgaria, suffered especially from the fighting. The resulting political instability there and the rule of the Greeks in many other cities of western Turkey—Smyrna in particular—led to the flight of thousands of Jews, many of whom migrated to Latin America, especially Argentina.[48]

Most Ottoman Jewish immigrants to Latin America settled in Buenos Aires. People originating in the same city tended to stay together, forming nuclei resembling their home communities. At the turn of the century, Ladino-speaking Jews from Smyrna, Constantinople, and other areas settled along the streets 25 de Mayo and Reconquista, not far from the port. By 1904 they were numerous enough to found their first charitable society, the Hermandad. That same year, a recently arrived Jew from Aleppo wrote to his family that he had found many acquaintances from his hometown. They took rooms in the Once district, still a center of Aleppine Jewish life. Damascene Jews arriving in Buenos Aires during the same period settled in the area of Boca and Barracas, a populous zone of predominantly Italian (especially Genoese) immigrants.

Old World ties thus proved important in determining patterns of settlement among Sephardic Jews, as they were for other immigrant groups.[49] Argentina, and in particular Buenos Aires, was always considered to be a major possibility when a Jew was choosing a destination. Ezra Garazi, who settled in New York in 1911, confirmed this when he reminisced, "I chose New York because it was reported that to peddle in Argentina one had to carry a heavier satchel than in New York."[50]

The first young men to arrive from Ottoman territories clearly intended to return home once they had earned enough money to live comfortably. The desire to reintegrate themselves into the closely knit family and community life of their early years weighed heavily on them. They were not *golondrinas*—southern European (mostly Italian) seasonal farm workers who came to Argentina each year to harvest the crops and then returned to their homes in Europe.[51] Turkish and Syrian Jews had other ways of making a living in mind—as businessmen.

For most, however, the process of capital accumulation took years because they started at the bottom, peddling in the streets of Buenos Aires or the interior towns. With heavy loads of cloth and other types of merchandise they made their rounds all day long. A few could not endure the effort, and their longing for family and friends impelled them to sail home.[52] But the majority stayed. Nissim Teubal, who left Aleppo in 1906 at the age of fifteen to join his brother Ezra in Buenos Aires, wrote in his memoirs:

> In the vicinity of Buenos Aires, I made a kind of covenant with myself. When I have earned my first 300 pounds, I said to myself, I shall return to Aleppo, and in Aleppo I will be considered a Croesus. . . . But when Buenos Aires came into sight, I increased the sum. Three hundred pounds was too little. I would wait until I had five hundred. The sum continued growing. I needed more and more. Mad with enthusiasm and ambition, I said to myself that I would not return to Aleppo other than with a real fortune.[53]

But Nissim and his brother never returned to Aleppo. In 1910 they brought their parents, brothers, and sisters to Buenos Aires. So it was with most of the Ottoman Jews. The revolt of the Young Turks, the Balkan wars, and finally World War I, with the disruption of transatlantic travel and the dismemberment of the Ottoman Empire, produced a radical change in the mentality of the Jewish emigrants. They now left for the Americas intending to make their permanent homes there. Those who went to Argentina had ample knowledge of conditions in the country. Many already had relatives and friends there; they were assured of jobs until they could start their own businesses.

Patterns of Organizational and Social Life

The Old World ties of Buenos Aires Sephardim still constituted a paramount factor in determining their patterns of settlement, and they continued to live in clusters based on cities or areas of origin. When they moved, they did so in chain migrations: Turkish Jews moved from Centro near the port to Villa Crespo; Damascene Jews moved in clusters from Boca-Barracas to Flores and Belgrano; Aleppine Jews settled in Ciudadela.[54]

By organizing separate mutual-aid societies, the Damascene, Aleppine, Turkish, and Moroccan Jews accentuated their separateness. The Turkish Jews organized a *kehillah*, or community, in March 1919, which centralized all their educational, religious, and welfare activities. Two years later, they expanded their charitable activities to provide the poor with the essentials for the Jewish holidays and medical services.

Typically, burial societies were independent of synagogues and schools, though the members and even officials of these institutions overlapped. The burial societies had a mutual-aid character, providing widows and orphans with a fixed stipend on the death of the head of family. In addition, friendship circles were created in many neighborhoods to provide for poor members in need.[55]

Although the distance between Ashkenazic and Sephardic immigrants in Buenos Aires is easily explained by their differing backgrounds, languages, traditions, and attitudes, the factors that caused the various Sephardic groups to remain apart from one another are more subtle. There were, for one thing, language differences. Traditions also differed. The two Syrian communities were estranged before coming to Argentina.[56]

Attachment to religion varied from one community to the other, Syrians being the most fervent believers, the Moroccans the most liberal. Further, each group settled in a different neighborhood, and most of their members worked nearby; their societies, quite understandably, were based in these neighborhoods, thus limiting the possibilities for socializing with members of other Sephardic groups. Finally, their strong emotional ties to their native communities prevented them from considering the benefits of stronger all-Sephardic societies.[57]

The Sephardic societies bear some resemblance to the landsmanshaften founded by Ashkenazim on the basis of common origin in the same town or area. However, the differences outweigh the similarities. The landsmanshaftn, which arose by the dozen in Buenos Aires during the World War I period and the 1920s, built a social atmosphere for immigrants from a specific area of origin in Poland, Galicia, Romania, or Bessarabia. But their main object was to facilitate the economic absorption of the immigrants. Members could borrow from the landsmanshaft, and because of its mutual-aid feature, their families had support in case of sickness, death, or unemployment. These funds, as well as others established in many Jewish neighborhoods, paved the way for the formation of hundreds of credit cooperatives, which began during the 1920s and survived for four decades. Whereas the Ashkenazic landsmanshaftn had a secular orientation, aiding members to establish themselves firmly, the Sephardic organizations were charitable in their approach.[58]

Other Latin American Countries

A similar pattern is evident in other major Latin American centers, such as Mexico City, Rio, and São Paulo. In these cities separate synagogues and schools were founded by the various immigrant Ottoman Jews. Mexican Jewry before World War I remained very small, but was made up of Jews from all parts of Europe and the Ottoman Empire. In 1912, under the initiative of a Greek Jew, Aaron Capon, a group of Jews of diverse origins founded Monte Sinai. By the end of World War I, however, this society came to be known as the general Sephardic synagogue, with a membership that included Balkan, Syrian, Turkish, and North African Jews. When the United States established immigration quotas in the 1920s, Jews who could not obtain visas opted to settle in Mexico or Cuba first with the goal of eventually moving north. Most remained in Mexico and Cuba, especially once they had succeeded economically. The Sephardim in Mexico were now numerous enough to have their own separate institutions. Thus the Aleppine group founded Sedaka Umarpe around 1931, and Ladino-speaking Jews from Turkey and Greece founded La Unión Sefaradí in 1924. Then Monte Sinai gradually became the congregation of the Jews from Damascus.

The Sephardim of Cuba founded Shebet Ajim in 1914. It remained their main community until the Castro revolution. After that about 90 percent of the Jews left, most to southern Florida, where they founded two "Cuban" congregations, one Sephardi and one Ashkenazi.

In smaller communities integration of all Jews was a necessity. Thus in Lima, when the first Sephardim from overseas arrived during the first two decades of the twentieth century, they quite naturally joined the Sociedad de Beneficencia Israelita, since it was already organized for religious services and owned a cemetery, Moreover, there was a common language, since the descendants of the original German immigrants spoke Spanish, while most Sephardim spoke Spanish or Ladino. In addition, Dr. David Senior de Castro, a Sephardi, was the "spiritual leader." By 1925 there were enough Sephardim in Lima to found the Sociedad de Beneficencia Israelita Sefardita, comprising Jews of varied Sephardic origins.[59]

Likewise, in Caracas, after some decades of growth, the Sephardic population was able to found the Asociación Israelita de Venezuela in 1930. The majority of its members were of Moroccan origin, but Jews from the Ottoman Empire joined as well.

Other medium-sized Jewish communities organized in similar ways. Both in Montevideo, Uruguay, and Santiago, Chile, Jews first organized by place of origin. Early in their development, separate communities of East European, Hungarian, German, and Sephardic Jews came into being. In both cities, the Sephardic community encompassed descendants of immigrants from all the Sephardic regions of the Old World.

In Chile, however, there was an interesting deviation from the general pattern. The first Sephardim did not go to Santiago, the capital and largest city, nor even to Valparaiso, its main port, but to Temuco, a developing town in the south of Chile. And almost all came from one city in Europe, Monastir (Bitoli), in Macedonia.

The exodus from Monastir began after the great fire of 1863 destroyed over 1,000 Jewish homes. Most of the city's Jews went to other parts of Yugoslavia, but some ventured to the United States or to Argentina, especially after railroad service between Monastir and Salonika was inaugurated in 1890, thus facilitating access to a port city.

The connection between Monastir and Temuco began in 1900, when Alberto Levy left Monastir and, after attempting to settle elsewhere in Europe, went to Argentina. From there he crossed the Andes to Santiago and found employment as a tailor in Temuco, a frontier town recently conquered from the Araucanian Indians. He wrote home of his success, and on the strength of his reports emigrating families from Monastir made Temuco their destination.

Thus, the newcomers had a strong common heritage in addition to close commercial and family links. In 1916 they formed their first organization, which they called Centro Macedónico. When news of the Balfour Declaration reached this remote community, their enthusiasm and Jewish pride were enhanced. In 1919 they officially changed their name to Centro Macedónico Israelita. In 1928 they became the Comunidad Israelita de Temuco, clearly asserting their Jewish identity.[60]

Starting in the 1920s and gradually in later decades, most of the Sephardim of Temuco moved to Santiago and Valparaiso, where they joined others who had migrated from Smyrna, Istanbul, and Salonika, as well as Monastir and other areas in the Sephardic world.

Later Newcomers

Jewish migrations to Latin America dwindled during the 1930s and afterward, for the world economic crisis and growing nationalist sentiments led to the closing of the doors of immigration throughout the Western Hemisphere. Nevertheless, small numbers of Jews managed to find a haven in Latin America during the Holocaust years. Few Sephardim arrived during this period or the ensuing decades, however, the only exception occurring in the aftermath of the Sinai Campaign of 1956 and the drastic political developments in Morocco, Algeria, and Tunisia around the same time.

At the time of Israel's War of Independence in 1948, there were about 80,000 Jews in Egypt, mostly in Cairo and Alexandria. Between May 1948 and January 1950, over 20,000 of them left, mainly going to Israel. Some, however, went to France, Italy, Switzerland, or Latin America.[61] The situation of Egyptian Jewry had totally deteriorated by November 1956. Once again, most made their way to Israel, but others opted for countries in the Diaspora. By 1960, there were only 8,000 to 10,000 Jews left in Egypt, and by 1967, only 2,500. Again, most moved to Israel, but a substantial number were helped by HIAS to resettle in the United States, Australia, Canada, and Latin America.

Between 1956 and 1963, however, 4,202 Egyptian Jews migrated to Latin America. The vast majority went to Brazil, mostly settling in Rio and São Paulo, but also in the secondary communities of Porto Alegre, Curitiba, Belo Horizonte, and Petropolis. A few went to Montevideo, Santiago (Chile), Caracas, and Buenos Aires. The chief rabbi of Alexandria, Aaron Angel, arrived in Buenos Aires in 1958, where he became the spiritual leader of the Balkan Sephardic community.[62]

Brazil also absorbed a relatively large number of Jewish families from North Africa during these years. This was due to the liberal immigration policy, favorable to admitting refugees, that was adopted by President Juscelino Kubitschek and continued by subsequent administrations. Thus for the period 1955–57, about 1,000 Jewish families from Morocco were allowed to enter in groups of fifty and to settle away from the large cities. In later years additional Moroccan Jews settled in Brazil.[63]

Sephardim and Ashkenazim: Subgroup Identities in Decline

We have already stressed that the cosmopolitan character of Jewish migration to Latin America facilitated the creation of separate institutions by the different groups along lines of place of provenance. This was more accentuated in the larger communities. But with the passing of more than half a century, the differences have become less significant, and an overall identification as Jews and with Judaism in the most inclusive sense has become more prevalent. This decline in subgroup identities can be seen throughout the continent, and in all aspects of Jewish life, including religious practices, Zionist activities, and Jewish education and culture.

The Sephardic immigrants, by and large, preserved stronger links with religious practices than the Ashkenazim. Quite naturally, there were differences among the various Sephardic communities of origin. The Syrian Jewish communities in Latin America had the strongest attachment to religious values. Their respective religious schools emphasized the teaching of Jewish observances and customs. In Buenos Aires, where the largest concentration of Syrians had settled, a strong rabbinic presence was established as early as 1912 with the arrival of Hacham Shaul Setton to lead the local Aleppine community. A recognized authority on Jewish law, Setton was respected in his home community of Aleppo and had the support of the chief rabbis of Palestine for his responsa.

The Ladino-speaking Jews from the Balkans, though Orthodox as well, were not as staunchly observant as the Syrians. Their knowledge of the Spanish language, and its great affinity with Portuguese, made their adaptation to Latin American mores much easier. The Moroccan Jews underwent the most rapid assimilation in Latin America.[64]

The second and third generations of Sephardic Jews were less observant. In addition, while Sephardic synagogues might retain traditional rituals, Sephardic Jews now often married Ashkenazim or even non-Jews. As a result, membership in a Sephardic or Ashkenazic synagogue did not necessarily indicate one's ethnic identity. Moreover with the proliferation of Conservative and Reform congregations, the Ashkenazi and Sephardi subgroup identities were diluted even more.

The Jewish press played an enormous role among Ashkenazic immigrants to Latin America, but had less influence among Sephardim. A number of Yiddish-language daily newspapers, as well as dozens of weeklies and monthlies, advocated every social, political, or cultural viewpoint, inundating the neighborhoods where East European Jews lived.

The local Yiddish press had more readers than there were members of Ashkenazic mutual-aid societies. Tens of thousands of immigrants throughout the continent used the Yiddish papers to search for job opportunities, social news, advice on how to survive in their new countries, guidance in understanding and adjusting to the wider community, information on local politics, economics, and social conditions, and news about Old World Jewish communities. The Yiddish press was a helpful tool in the search for "missing" husbands and fathers who had migrated to Latin America and had, for one reason or another, severed contact with their families in Europe.

Moreover, Yiddish newspapers launched crusades for or against specific issues. In Argentine there were diatribes concerning the local Yiddish theater and the involvement in it of Jewish white-slave dealers; the *kehillah* form of community organization versus an *alianza*, or federation; and such issues as whether to support or boycott Jewish colonization in Birobidzhan or in Palestine.

Before the Nazi era Sephardim did not participate in these controversies. Their concerns centered on earning a living and abiding as much as possible within traditional religious and cultural values, with little or no involvement in politics. In general terms, they were lukewarm to Zionism but very solicitous about helping their Jewish compatriots.

In the absence of specifically Sephardic newspapers, the Sephardim read the general press. Only in 1917 was a Sephardic newspaper, *Israel*, founded. It carried articles and notes about Sephardim, mainly about the Moroccan Jews of Buenos Aires. Correspondents in the interior of Argentina and neighboring countries contributed additional information.

The pro-Zionist leanings of *Israel* were atypical of Sephardim in Buenos Aires until 1930, when a new journal, *La Luz*, was initiated, raising the level of Sephardic journalism in Buenos Aires and throughout Latin America.[65] Finally, in 1984, the Federación Sefaradí Latinoamérica (Fesela), an umbrella organization of Latin American Sephardic institutions, founded in 1972, began publishing *Sefárdica*, a periodical that aims to promote research in Sephardic culture and make it available to the learned public.[66]

By 1991 the Latin American Yiddish press had lost its former luster. All Jewish communal publications are now either in Spanish or Portuguese, thus erasing a major element of subgroup cultural separateness.

It took much longer for the Sephardim in Latin America to warm up to Zionism than for their Ashkenazi neighbors. In several communities there was a short-lived sprouting of national feeling after the Balfour Declaration in 1917. It was evident among various Sephardic groups in Buenos Aires, but also in Temuco, as noted earlier, and in Santiago, Chile, and Montevideo, Uruguay, where only a small number of Sephardim lived at the time.[67] Though the local Zionist organizations, especially the Zionist Federation in Argentina, urged Sephardim to participate in the promotion of Zionist aims, their involvement in local or regional Zionist congresses or meetings was very low. The main obstacle in the early decades was one of language, since most Zionist activists spoke Yiddish.[68] In addition, many Sephardim were simply not interested, since they were convinced that Zionism was an endeavor promoted by East European Jews and geared solely to their needs. Others, especially the Syrian Jews, were opposed to political Zionism on religious grounds. Moreover, the factionalism created by the Zionist political parties was foreign to the Sephardim, who had difficulty understanding their existence in the Diaspora.[69]

The World Zionist Organization, nevertheless, sent a special delegate, Dr. Ariel Bensión, a Sephardi himself, to visit the Sephardic communities of Latin America in 1926. Bensión succeeded in establishing Sephardic Zionist committees, denominated Bené Kedem, in many of the larger communities and some of the secondary ones. These were independent of the regular Zionist organizations led by the Ashkenazim. The success, however, was only temporary.[70]

In Argentina, some fruits would be seen by 1929, when Sephardim made generous contributions to the special campaign launched as a result of the riots in Palestine. In the 1930s, with the rise of Nazism, and especially during the Holocaust and the subsequent creation of the State of Israel, more Sephardim adopted the Zionist cause. In many communities Sephardim had special activities geared to their own members, but as time passed, an amalgamation of efforts took place. During the last few decades many Sephardic leaders have attained positions of top leadership in the Zionist organizations of the various countries.[71]

In the field of Jewish education in the early decades, the different Jewish subgroups promoted their own schools in order to instruct their young in accordance with their particular traditions. Among Ashkenazi Jews there were schools that transmitted a definite political ideology, sometimes Zionist, at times totally anti-Zionist. The language of instruction was Yiddish. Sephardic schools emphasized Hebrew early on. Some Syrian schools even taught Arabic.

In general terms, the Sephardic schools have tended to be more oriented to religion, more inward looking, and more conservative.[72] In many instances, both Ashkenazi and Sephardi schools now have mixed enrollments, especially in communities too small to support more than one school. Moreover, since Yiddish has been replaced by Hebrew in the Ashkenazi schools, major subgroup identities have become much less protected. The protection of the wider group identity of Judaism is a sufficient challenge.

Finally, a major aspect of Jewish life in Latin America is the sports club. Huge institutions congregate tens of thousands of members in almost all sizable communities. In some, there are separate Sephardic clubs, but in this sphere too, as a general rule, the barriers between Ashkenazi and Sephardi have all but disappeared.

Neosefardismo!

In 1984, after many years of major negotiations, the Ashkenazi and Sephardi communities in Caracas agreed to combine efforts for the benefit of the whole Jewish populace, and in particular to strengthen Jewish education in the city. The words of one of the leaders at the signing ceremony apply not only Venezuela but to the whole Latin American continent:

> There is practically no Jewish family in Venezuela from either of the two kehillot that has not received a member of the other in its midst, attaining in this way the joining of all the branches in a progressively stronger trunk.[73]

Many changes have taken place. In the early decades of the century, Sephardic institutions discriminated not only against Ashkenazim, but also against Sephardim of different origins. Even in faraway Temuco, in southern Chile, the Centro Macedonico Israelita established higher "joining" fees for Ashkenazim, and only granted them "passive" membership, without the right to speak or vote at meeting.[74] Seven decades later, the vestiges of separateness find expression only in terms of nostalgia by the old-timers or in order to preserve a rich heritage on the verge of disappearance.

No Latin American Jew wants to return to the "old country," whether Russia, Poland, Syria, Turkey, or Morocco. Raised as citizens of their countries of birth, with strong links to the national culture, history, and destiny of these countries, the Jews of Latin America express themselves in Spanish and Portuguese, totally at home in their respective milieus. They speak about local authors and matters of regional concern, and, at the same time, contribute, as professionals or businessmen, to the economic and intellectual development of their countries.

In many respects, the Jews of Latin America, whether of Sephardic, Ashkenazic, or mixed descent, are *Latin American* Jews. Itic Croitoru Rotbaum has called them *Neosefardita* because their present origin is in the land of New Spain, or New Iberia, or *Neosefarad*. From this point of view, we might conclude that the strength of the Iberian culture and languages in Latin America has given the Sephardic tradition a somewhat more lasting strength in an area of the world where Sephardim represented 15 to 20 percent of the whole Jewish population.[75]

Notes

1. Isaac S. Emmanuel and Suzanne Emmanuel, *History of the Jews in the Netherlands Antilles* (Cincinnati, 1970), pp. 822-480.
2. Isidoro Aizenberg, "Efforts to Establish a Jewish Cemetery in Nineteenth Century Caracas," *American Jewish Historical Quarterly* 67, no. 3 (March 1978): 225 f.
3. Isidoro Aizenberg, *La Comunidad Judía de Coro, 1824-1900: Una Historia* (Caracas, 1983), pp. 33-92.
4. Ibid., pp. 99-105.
5. Frances P. Karner, *The Sephardics of Curaçao* (Assen, 1969), pp. 29 f.
6. Aizenberg, "Efforts to Establish a Jewish Cemetery," pp. 226-230.
7. Emmanuel and Emmanuel, *History of the Jews in the Netherlands Antilles*, pp. 167-168.
8. Karner, *Sephardics of Curaçao*, pp. 14, 30.
9. Eliseo Reclus, *Viaje a la Sierra Nevada de Santa Marta* (Bogota, 1947), p. 38, as quoted in Itic Croitoru Rotbaum, *De Sefarad al Neosefardismo* (Bogota, 1967), pp. 168 f.
10. Ibid., pp. 167-176.
11. Jacobo Schifter Sikora, Lowell Gudmundson, and Mario Solera Castro, *El Judío en Costa Rica* (San Jose, 1979), p. 251.
12. Lowell Gudmundson, "Costa Rican Jewry: An Economic and Political Outline," in *The Jewish Presence in Latin America*, ed. Judith Laikin Elkin and Gilbert W. Merckx (Boston, 1987), p. 220, n. 3.
13. Gunter Bohm, *Judíos en el Perú durante el Siglo XIX* (Santiago, 1985), pp. 86, 123 f., 142 f.; and Trahtemberg Siederer, *La Inmigración Judía al Perú, 1848-1948* (Lima, 1987), pp. 85, 114 f.
14. Henry W. Bates, *The Naturalist on the River Amazon* (1864), vol. 2, p. 175, as quoted in *Jewish Chronicle*, Feb. 26, 1864, p. 2.
15. *Jewish Chronicle*, Sept. 3, 1869, p. 11.
16. Sarah Leibovici, "Tétouan: une communauté écclatée," *Nouveaux Cahiers* 59 (Winter 1979-80): 13 f.; Isaac Benchimol, "La langue espagnole au Maroc," *Revue des Ecoles de l'Alliance Israélite* 2 (July-September 1901): 127.
17. Michael Laskier, *The Alliance Israélite Universelle and the Jewish Communities of Morocco, 1862-1962* (New York, 1983), p. 86.
18. Ibid., p. 64.
19. Ibid., p. 133.
20. Ibid., p. 134; see also Leibovici, "Tétouan," p. 16.
21. Robert Ricard, "Notes sur l'emigration des Israélites marocaines en Amérique espagnole et au Brésil," *Revue Africaine* 88, nos. 1-2 (1944): 84 f.
22. Laskier, *Alliance Israélite Universelle*, p. 135.
23. Ibid., pp. 135 f.

24. David Cazés, "Rapport sur les écoles de l'alliance de Tanger et de Tetuán," *Bulletin de l'Alliance Israélite Universelle*, 1884–85, p. 52.

25. *Association des anciens élèves de l'Alliance Israélite Universelle, Bulletin Annuel* (Tangier) 8 (1900): 13–17; Ricard, "Notes sur l'emigration des Israélites marocaines," p. 84. For Larache, see Eugene Aubin, *Le Maroc d'aujourd'hui*, 6th ed. (Paris, 1910), p. 91, where he asserts: "Parmi le juifs, quelques negociants et beaucoup d'artisans; un movement d'émigration vera l'Amérique du Sud commence à se dessiner dans la communauté qui est pauvre et peu organisée." For further details, see Victor A. Mirelman, "Sephardic Immigration to Argentina Prior to the Nazi Period," in Elkin and Merkx, *Jewish Presence in Latin America*, pp. 13–24.

26. Bohm, *Judíos en la Péru*, p. 101.

27. *Jewish Chronicle*, Oct. 21, 1910, p. 9.

28. Bohm, *Judíos en la Péru*, p. 101.

29. As quoted from *Bulletin de l'Alliance Israélite Universelle*, 1910, in *Archives Israélites*, 1910, pp. 253 ff.

30. Cf. José Luis Romero, *El desarrollo de las ideas en la sociedad argentina del siglo XIX* (Mexico City, 1965), pp. 9–46.

31. Victor A. Mirelman, *Jewish Buenos Aires, 1890–1930* (Detroit, 1990), pp. 14, 76–78.

32. *Bulletin de l'Alliance Israélite Universelle*, 1894, pp. 66 f.

33. As quoted in ibid., 1899, pp. 118 f.

34. Ibid., 1898, p. 102; 1899, pp. 118 f.; 1901, pp. 98 f.

35. Benchimol, "La langue espagnole au Maroc," p. 133.

36. Angel Pulido Fernández, *Españoles sin patria y la raza sefardí* (Madrid, 1905), pp. 643 f.

37. Benchimol, "La langue espagnole au Maroc," p. 128; M. L. Ortega, *Los Hebreos en Marruecos* (Madrid, 1919), pp. 301 f., quotes the same.

38. Samuel Halphon, "Enquête sur la population israélite en Argentine," JCA, *Rapport*, 1909, p. 285.

39. Ibid., pp. 303 f.

40. Ibid., pp. 251–310.

41. *Municipalidad de la ciudad de Buenos Aires, Cuarto Censo General* (Oct. 22, 1936), vol. 3 (Buenos Aires, 1939), pp. 310–323.

42. Ricard, "Notes sur l'émigration," p. 87.

43. Isaac Laredo, *Memorias de un viejo tangerino* (Madrid, 1935), p. 434.

44. Abraham Galante, *Histoire des Juifs de Rhodes, Chio, Cos, etc.* (Istanbul, 1935), p. 81; idem, *Histoire des Juifs d'Anatolie: Les Juifs d'Izmir (Smyrne)*, vol. 1 (Istanbul, 1937), pp. 161 f.; idem, *Histoire des Juifs d'Istanbul*, vol. 2 (Istanbul, 1942), p. 119; David de Sola Pool, "The Levantine Jews in the United States," *American Jewish Yearbook*, 1913–14, p. 209; Walter P. Zenner, "Syrian Jewish Identification in Israel" (Ph.D. diss., Columbia University, 1965), pp. 1–98, describes the economic, social, political, and religious situation of the Jews in Aleppo and Damascus during the later decades of the nineteenth century and the first of the twentieth; see also Philip K. Hitti, *The Syrians in America* (New York, 1924), pp. 48–52.

45. Hayyim J. Cohen, *The Jews of the Middle East, 1860–1972* (Jerusalem, 1973), pp. 76, 99 f.

46. Joseph A. D. Sutton, *Magic Carpet: Aleppo-in-Flatbush* (New York, 1979), p. 5

47. Pool, "Levantine Jews in the United States," p. 209; Zenner, "Syrian Jewish Identification," pp. 53 f.; Hitti, *Syrians in America*, p. 51. During World War I many Jews served in the Turkish army.

48. Cohen, *Jews of the Middle East*, pp. 76, 97.

49. Mirelman, "Sephardic Immigration," pp. 25–27.

50. Sutton, *Magic Carpet*, p. 13.
51. Robert Foerster, *The Italian Migration of Our Times* (Cambridge, Mass., 1924), pp. 261 f.
52. Nissim Teubal, *El inmigrante, de Alepo a Buenos Aires* (Buenos Aires, 1953), p. 83
53. Ibid., p. 75.
54. On the chain migration of Italians to Argentina, see S. I. Bailey, "The Adjustment of Italian Immigrants in Buenos Aires and New York, 1870–1914," *American Historical Review* 88, no. 2 (April 1983): 291.
55. Mirelman, "Sephardic Immigration," pp. 29 f.; Margalit Bejarano, "El cementerio y la unidad comunitaria en la historia de los Sefaradim de Buenos Aires," *Michael* 8 (1983): 24–31.
56. Zenner, "Syrian Jewish Immigration," p. 17; Cohen, *Jews of the Middle East*, passim.
57. In 1905 the Moroccans were the only group with a cemetery of their own. However, they would not admit other Jews. Their burial society decided that "all members who are not descendants of South European [i.e., Spanish and especially Gibraltan] or North African parents shall enjoy all rights ... except that of burial." Hesed Veemet, *Minutes*, 31 July 1905.
58. On Landsmanshaftn in Argentina, see L. Zitnitsky, "Landsmanshaften in Argentine," *Argentiner IWO Shriftn* 3 (1945): 155–161; Pinie Katz, *Yiddn in Argentina* (Buenos Aires, 1946), *Poilishe Yiddn in Dorem Amerika* (Buenos Aires, 1941); *Gilitziener Yiddn, Yoblbuch, 1925–1965* (Buenos Aires, 1966).
59. Trahtemberg Siederer, *La Inmigracion Judía al Perú*, pp. 111 f.
60. Moshe Nes-El (Arueste), *Historia de la Comunidad Israelita Sefaradí de Chile* (Santiago, 1984), pp. 43–54; Uri Oren, *A Town Called Monastir* (Tel Aviv, 1971), passim.
61. Michael Laskier, "Yahadut Mitzraim biTkufat Mishtaro shel Nasser (1956–1970)," *Mikedem Umiyam* (Haifa), 3 (1990): 216.
62. Ibid., pp. 226–231.
63. *American Jewish Yearbook* 59 (1958): 408 f.; 62 (1961): 218; and 64 (1963): 283.
64. Mirelman, *Jewish Buenos Aires*, p. 99. Cf. Shaul Setton Dabbah, *Dibber Shaul* (Jerusalem 1920).
65. Victor A. Mirelman, "Early Zionist Activities among Sephardim in Argentina," *American Jewish Archives* 34, no. 2 (November 1982): 190–205.
66. *Sefárdica* 1, no. 1 (March 1984).
67. Mirelman, "Early Zionist Activities," pp. 193 f.; Nes-El, *Historia de la Comunidad Israelita*, pp. 143–145; Haim Avni and Rosa Perla Raicher, eds., *Memorias del Uruguay: holocausto y lucha por fundación del Estado de Israel* (Jerusalem, 1986), pp. 38, 87.
68. Mirelman, "Early Zionist Activities," p. 199; Nes-El, *Historia de la Comunidad Israelita*, p. 145.
69. David Elnecave, "Los Sefaradim en el Mundo y en la Argentina." *Sefárdica* 1, no. 1 (March 1984): 105.
70. Nes-El, *Historia de la Comunidad Israelita*, pp. 147 f.; Mirelman, "Early Zionist Activities," pp. 199–201.
71. Avni and Raicher, *Memorias del Uruguay*, pp. 49 f.
72. Daniel C. Levy, "Jewish Education in Latin America," in Elkin and Merkx, *Jewish Presence in Latin America*, p. 182.
73. "Testimonios para la historia," *Escudo (Maguen)*, Caracas, 53 (October–December 1984): 13.
74. Nes-El, *Historia de la Comunidad Israelita*, p. 280.
75. Croitoru Rotbaum, *De Sefarad al Neosefardismo*, pp. 191–194.

Part III
Hidden Roots:
Sephardic Culture in North America

The Sephardim in North America in the Twentieth Century
Joseph M. Papo

Background

Sephardi communal life in North America came into being at the turn of the twentieth century as a result of mass emigration from the Ottoman Empire, which had been the center of the Sephardi world since the end of the fifteenth century. Sephardim first settled in the vast Ottoman domain, comprising much of the Balkans, North Africa, and the Middle East, as a result of the expulsion from Spain in 1492 and, four years later, from Portugal. Some of the more than 100,000 Jews exiled from the Iberian Peninsula found new homes in Holland, England, Italy, and other parts of Western Europe, but the great majority of them sought refuge under Ottoman protection. Sultan Bayazid II, seeing the Jewish refugees as a valuable asset, ordered his imperial officials to receive them kindly, and is said to have exclaimed, "Ye call Ferdinand a wise king! He who is impoverishing his own country by expelling the Jews, and we are enriching ours by admitting them."

Jews, of course, had been living in the Eastern Mediterranean area from early times. During the Byzantine period they had been restricted in their choice of places of residence and had been banned from full participation in the life of the country. Under the sultanate, however, they obtained freedom of residence, unrestricted trade, and religious autonomy. One of the exiles from Spain, Joseph Nasi, became a favorite of Sultan Salim, who gifted him with a group of Mediterranean islands and bestowed upon him the title of Duke of Naxos.

The native Jews, who had initially kept aloof from the newcomers, found themselves drawn into their orbit, and gradually Judeo-Spanish became the prevalent language and Iberian customs came to merge with the native ones. Under Ottoman rule, all non-Muslims were organized into national groups, or millets, and each millet was granted judicial autonomy, with its own court where conflicts and disputes were settled according to the laws of the respective minority group; moreover, the representative of each group to the Ottoman government was accorded the respect due an ambassador. The Jewish population enjoyed special respect and approval. Its chief rabbi, the hakham bashi, became an honored member of the Royal Council, able to represent and protect the interests of his people, as well as to exercise his authority over the life of the Jewish community. The last imperial investiture of a chief rabbi was conferred on Hai Nahoum Effendi in 1909.

It is relevant to future developments to note that the exiles did not congregate in a single area but settled, instead, in clusters of families hailing from the same province or township. Each settlement founded its own congregation and set up its own schools and courts, with each group faithfully preserving its own customs, characteristics, liturgy, and rituals. The various settlements soon began to prosper in many ways. The artisans among them had valuable knowledge and skills in the arts and crafts; the merchants, with their vast experience and extensive connections, contributed to the expansion of Turkish commerce and industry; and Sephardi physicians were highly regarded and enjoyed special respect, some serving as personal physicians to the court. Sephardi scientists, moreover, introduced the Turks to the use of gunpowder and the manufacture of firearms and cannon; they also installed Turkey's first printing press.[1]

Sephardi domestic life was organized around the observance of religious laws and precepts. Family roles were determined by tradition: the father was the head of the household and, as such, the voice of authority in all family affairs, but the mother was the ruler of her home. Customarily, young people married at an early age, with parents selecting the mates from among the children of their friends.

When the fortunes of the Ottoman Empire began to decline, Jewish prosperity began to wane as well. Thus, by the middle of the seventeenth century, only a small proportion of Ottoman Jews were still playing a significant role in commerce and high finance. Growing poverty, ignorance, and despair provided fertile ground for soothsayers and magicians promising cures for bodily ills and miraculous interventions. These conditions provided a ready audience for the teachings of Sabbatai Zvi, the self-proclaimed Son of God and bridegroom of the Torah. His conversion to Islam disillusioned and chastened the masses, and caused them to abandon their folly.

The centuries-long downward curve of the Ottoman Empire, with its deleterious effects on all of Turkish life, left its imprint on the cultural and spiritual life of the Jewish community.[2] Children attended the yeshiva to the age of thirteen, those of wealthy parents continuing their education to the age of sixteen.

By the middle of the nineteenth century, the Alliance Israélite Universelle had opened schools throughout the Ottoman Empire patterned after the French elementary school system. The Alliance was perceived by the Sephardim in a highly ambivalent way. On the one hand, so many parents wanted to enroll their children that classes were crowded beyond capacity. On the other hand, there was some quite strong opposition to the schools. The opponents argued that the schools, as centers of "proselytism," were alienating Sephardi children and youth from their ancient heritage. They also felt that the introduction of Gallicisms was despoiling the linguistic purity of Judeo-Spanish, and indeed that its status as the predominant language was being usurped by French.

In general, however, the schooling provided by the Alliance raised the educational level of the students and, thus, their economic potential. It helped thousands of young Sephardim to acquire not only the knowledge but the self-esteem, self-reliance, and dignity of demeanor required to enter professional or white-collar careers. In addition, the example of the educational system run by the Alliance inspired a number of Jewish communities to set up good, modern schools of their own for their children.[3]

The Young Turk Revolution of 1908 failed to live up to its promise of sweeping civic reform, but it did expand the civic rights of minorities, chief among them being the right and the duty to serve in the army. This carried with it the obligation of conforming to the Islamic laws observed in the army, which hitherto had been reserved for Muslims only. The imposition of military service led to the emigration of thousands of young Jews who did not wish to serve but could not come up with the high replacement tax which had to be paid during each of the all-too-frequent mobilizations. An additional impetus toward emigration came from the dislocations and economic hardships suffered by the Jewish communities during the 1911 Turkish-Italian war, the Turkish-Balkan wars of 1912–1914, the outbreak of World War I, and a series of natural disasters such as fires, earthquakes, and epidemics which had been plaguing the crumbling Ottoman Empire.[4]

Arrival and Adaptation

Some 3,413 Sephardi immigrants from the European and Asian parts of the Ottoman Empire arrived in the United States between 1885 and 1908. After 1908 Sephardi immigrants began to arrive in ever larger numbers, settling in the already overpopulated Lower East Side of New York, a factor which caused concern both to city officials and to the Commission of Immigration. In response to this concern, the Jewish Agricultural and Industrial Aid Society, operating on funds supplied by Baron de Hirsch, organized the Industrial Removal Office (IRO) for the purpose of relocating immigrants to less-congested parts of the country. With the assistance of the Federation of Oriental Jews of America, many Sephardim were settled in Seattle, Rochester, New Jersey, Indianapolis, Gary, Montgomery, and Atlanta, while Judeo-Spanish immigrants were encouraged to reemigrate to Central and South America. The majority of the immigrants, however, remained in New York City.[5]

A study by the American Civic League in 1912 showed that most of the immigrants were poor and had only a minimal formal education, but that their literacy level compared favorably with that of other ethnic groups. Thus, two-fifths of the Sephardim could read and write their own language, and another fifth could read but not write. Ninety percent of the literate group could read the Hebrew prayerbook. This sorry state of affairs for the descendants of the highly cultured Sephardim of the Golden Age must, of course, be viewed in the light of the poverty and ignorance of the masses among whom the majority of the Sephardim lived in the old country.[6]

It is a well-established fact that immigrants to a new country start out by drawing together into groups from the same cities and townships of origin, into landsmanshaften, such as were as formed by Ashkenazi immigrants. The Ashkenazim, however, had a unifying element which allowed them, in time, to transcend strictly local loyalties and expand into larger communal entities; they had a common language, Yiddish. The Sephardim from the Ottoman Empire, on the other hand, lacked a common language. Not only could they not communicate with the Ashkenazim but they were divided into Judeo-Spanish-, Arabic-, and Greek-speaking groups. They had to learn English in order to speak with each other. Furthermore, in the Ottoman Empire the Sephardic immigrants had lived in tightly knit, autonomous, and self-sufficient communal units, and it seemed only natural to them to continue this way of life in their new country.

Immigrants from the same city or locality formed societies in order to meet the immediate need of obtaining burial grounds for their dead. This done, societies expanded into serving other social and religious needs. They became the heartbeat of each Sephardi immigrant group and the center of its religious, cultural, and social activity. Mistrustful and fearful of all strangers, the Sephardi immigrants could feel secure only in their own enclaves and among their kinsmen. Some time passed before these small communities began to interact with each other and regain the consciousness of a shared Sephardi peoplehood.

The immigrant societies undoubtedly helped maintain the tradition, morale, sense of identity, and self-respect of their members. Yet they came to be a stumbling block to the formation of a centralized, effective Sephardi community. Thus, in considering the role of societies in the communal life of American Sephardim, a paraphrase of Rabbi Nissim Ovadia's dictum on the Alliance Israélite Universelle seems to sum it up best: The societies were so important to the initial survival and cohesion of the immigrant Sephardim that one cannot say anything bad about them, yet they proved so destructive to all efforts to unite and function on a broader, viable, communal Sephardi base, that one cannot say anything good about them.

The Arabic-speaking groups, which came mostly from Syria, stressed family unity and a thorough religious education for their children; the Greek Sephardim, mostly from Janina, maintained their individualism even within the framework of their own groups; while the Judeo-Spanish-speaking Sephardim, by far the largest of the three groups, were spurred on by a desire to regain their historic status and assert their equality with Ashkenazi Jewry.[7] The Ashkenazim, however, had a hard time accepting as Jews people who spoke no Yiddish, preferred spicy food to gefilte fish and knishes, pronounced Hebrew words in a totally different way, and chanted the familiar prayers in an Oriental rather than a Slavic or Germanic tonality—in short, whose customs were utterly alien to them.

An example in case is the tale of two Sephardi immigrants who went to Seattle, where a Greek friend put them to work in his fish store. When he introduced his new helpers to his Jewish customers, the latter refused to accept them as coreligionists and insisted that they were Turkish impostors, even after the young immigrants produced their prayerbooks and tefillin. They were not accepted until the local Reform rabbi intervened, not only legitimizing their claim to be Jewish but impressing upon his congregation that Sephardim were the heirs of the Golden Age.[8] Thus, Sephardi immigrants who in their native countries had enjoyed the security and status engendered from being rooted in a community for generations now found themselves in double jeopardy, as it were—strangers in the vast, complex world that was America, and strangers to their fellow Jews, the Ashkenazim.

The Ashkenazim, of course, held no patent on snobbishness. Sephardim regarded their own history and cultural heritage as by far the nobler and bemoaned the current conditions which placed them at a disadvantage. These mutually unfriendly feelings led the leaders of both groups to look for ways of bringing about a rapprochement. The Sephardi paper *La América* ran a series of articles in Yiddish on Turkish history and the Sephardic way of life in the Ottoman Empire. *La América* also urged its Sephardi readers to attend Jewish (read Ashkenazi) and Zionist meetings and picnics, since this would enable Jews from Russia, Galicia, and Romania to meet their brethren from the Middle East.

The Yiddish press, in turn, published a series of interpretative articles on the Sephardi newcomers and appealed to the general Jewish community to help them achieve a more satisfactory economic and cultural adjustment. Yet, as social interaction slowly began to increase, especially among the young, both groups began to evidence concern about their children marrying each other. Thus the May 1916 issue of the *American Jewish Chronicle* says rather plaintively: ". . . hardly does a daughter of the Orient marry a son of the West. She is given in marriage by her father, mother or guardian, who deem the Ashkenazi an unsuitable mate for a Sephardi woman, owing to differences of language, training and tradition."[9]

A study in 1969-70 by Hayyim Cohen of the Hebrew University shows that half of the third-generation Sephardi young men (especially among the Judeo-Spanish Sephardim) had married Ashkenazi women, while a survey by Marc Angel in 1972 shows that marriage between Ashkenazim and Sephardim has become quite common; "one might even say that it has become a rule rather than the exception."

The integration of Sephardim into the mainstream of American life was greatly speeded by America's entry into World War II. The erstwhile young immigrants were, by then, in their late forties and had assumed the responsibilities of raising and supporting families, and it was their children and grandchildren who responded to the draft. Full and partial responses by 272 Sephardi veterans show an average age of slightly over twenty on entering military service. Of the total, 243 were native-born, and 70 had enlisted. Their civilian occupations included salesmen (49), students (39), skilled workers (30), clerks (20), business owners (14), and manufacturers (6). Thirteen of the surveyed group had risen to officer rank, 74 had attained the grade of noncommissioned officer; among the awards received were presidential citations, Bronze Stars, good conduct medals, European, Asiatic, and Pacific Theatre medals, Victory Medals, Silver Stars, and the Croix de Guerre. The entire Sephardi community was mobilized to participate in the purchase of war bonds and to join the wartime work force. Sephardi political clubs, which had come into being before the war, intensified their activities. Thus, while not yet in a leadership position, the Sephardim still had the satisfaction of finding themselves an integral part of American economic and political life.[10]

Relations with the Established Sephardi Community

The Sephardi immigrants understood that the Ashkenazi reaction to them was based on ignorance, but they were bewildered and hurt when the old, established Sephardim did not accept them. The descendants of the twenty-three refugees who had landed in New Amsterdam from Brazil in 1654 knew well that the immigrants from the Ottoman Empire also had their ancestral roots in Spain, yet the affluent, educated, and well-respected American Sephardim found it difficult to receive the newcomers as members of their extended family. The manner in which they offered assistance made the immigrants feel that they were being relegated to the status of charity cases. The feelings of the newcomers were well expressed by Moïse Gadol, the publisher of *La América*:

> We must now tell them [the earlier Sephardim] in all fairness, that not only have we stopped believing in their earlier promises, but that their claiming credit [for helping us] prevents us from being able to obtain the actual help from other sources. We shall no more allow them to aggrandize themselves in public at the expense of our honest and sincere people. We shall not permit them to assail our dignity by claiming credit for assistance which, in fact, they had not provided.[11]

The extent to which the earlier Sephardim were willing to go to preserve their status as the quintessential Sephardim is especially manifest in their tendency to refer to the immigrants as Levantine Jews and even more in the request made in 1914 by Dr. David de Sola Pool, rabbi of the Spanish and Portuguese Synagogue of New York City, that HIAS rename its Committee on Sephardic Jewish Immigrants the Committee on Oriental Jewish Immigrants (a request to which HIAS acquiesced). While "Oriental" and "Levantine" are purely geographic terms and as such unobjectionable, the immigrants experienced this labeling as a form of social denigration, especially since "Levantine," in American usage, had come to stand for shiftiness and shyster tactics. One immigrant penned the following verse which summed up the collective immigrant resentment:

> We are but Jews
> and our name is Sephardim;
> never were we thought to be
> anything else but Sephardim
> from the day of our birth.

The term "Levantine" was quickly discarded, but "Oriental" remained in use for several years, since the established Sephardim could not see matters in the same light. Rabbi Marc Angel, himself the grandson of Sephardi immigrants, and current rabbi of Congregation Shearith Israel, aptly sums up the then prevailing situation:

> Some of the old line Sephardim felt uneasy because the new immigrants called themselves Sephardim. They were afraid the term would fall into disrepute and urged the new-comers to be called "Oriental." The immigrants, at first, accepted the new designation, but later came to resent it deeply as a slur against them. The impression had been created that the Sephardim were noble and rich while the Orientals were ignorant and poor. . . .The irony of it was that many of the immigrants were pure-blooded Spanish-speaking Sephardim who were being called "Orientals," while Shearith Israel members who were Ashkenazim and of mixed blood, were considered as the true Sephardim.[12]

While the leaders of both groups were grappling with the problem of identity, status, and recognition, the Congregation Shearith Israel sisterhood ignored abstract issues and welcomed the immigrants to its Neighborhood House on the Lower East Side, providing those who frequented it with a variety of services, including a synagogue (a departure from usual settlement-house procedure), religious education for the children, English day-classes, counseling on family and legal matters, a day nursery, a kindergarten, a dispensary, and a medical clinic. (Attendance at the Neighborhood House eventually dwindled as many Sephardic immigrants made sufficient economic progress to move to more desirable areas of residence, and the influx of newcomers fell off after 1924 because of restrictive new immigrations laws. After four decades of dedicated work, the sisterhood finally closed the settlement in 1950.)[13]

The immigrants and the old Sephardim continued having difficulties with each other until the early 1920s, when both groups began making concerted efforts to develop a better mutual understanding and relationship. It was in this spirit of rapprochement that the leaders of Congregation Shearith Israel gave their active support to the Sephardic Jewish Community of New York, which had come into being in 1924. Henry S. Hendricks, the parnass (president) of Shearith Israel, served as the Community's treasurer and took part in its financial management, while Dr. Pool served as chairman of its educational committee. In 1926, another prominent member of Shearith Israel, Mrs. H. L. Toledano, organized the Community Ladies Auxiliary, the "Sephardith," and served as its president for several years. In 1928 Shearith Israel as a whole affiliated with the Community, stating: "This action of the Congregation puts the Community in the historic line of service to the Sephardim of New York, which Congregation Shearith Israel has shouldered alone for nearly two and three-quarters centuries."[14]

In the 1950s the Shearith Israel joined the Central Sephardic Jewish Community of America, in the "hope that our association will draw closer together all the Sephardi elements of this city, so that we may act with greater strength in furthering our holy and common tradition." The Central Community, in turn, participated in the celebration of Shearith Israel's tercentenary in 1957, initiating the project of establishing a Jewish National Fund Tamar and David de Sola Pool Nachla in Israel.

Another effective interaction was established by the close working relationship in the pursuit of shared concerns which evolved between the women's division of the Central Community and the sisterhood of the congregation. Even this drawing together of the two Sephardi groups, however, failed to bring about a realization of Dr. Pool's vision of Shearith Israel's becoming the "Cathedral Synagogue" of the entire Sephardi community. The children and grandchildren of the twentieth-century Sephardi immigrants have established beautiful synagogues of their own throughout the country. A few well-to-do among them are affiliated with Shearith Israel, while others use it services only on special occasions. But the women's division and other groups hold meetings and social affairs in the Shearith Israel auditorium, and at such times Sephardi songs from various countries, the rhythm of Middle Eastern dancing, and the aroma of Sephardi cooking fill the synagogue's social hall, testifying to the many facets of the Sephardi heritage.[15]

Economic Adjustment

The economic fortunes of the Sephardi immigrants changed profoundly from one generation to the next. Enterprising Sephardim attending the New Orleans Centennial Exposition in 1885 and the Louisiana Purchase Centennial Exposition in St. Louis in 1904 found that they had indeed come to the land of opportunity. They managed, within a few years time, to become successful businessmen. Trade connections with the Orient enabled them to establish lucrative rug and antique businesses, while a few others built up a large amusement and recreation industry. The Schinasi brothers, having found an encouraging response to their hand-rolled Turkish cigarettes, proceeded to build a plant with cigarette rolling and packaging equipment designed to their specifications to handle rice and bamboo paper imported from Egypt and tobacco from Turkey.

The situation began to change after 1908, however, when increasing numbers of immigrants began to arrive, most of whom lacked both formal education and vocational skills and could speak neither English nor Yiddish. Many had to eke out a living by peddling, shining shoes, or selling postcards and flowers. Some found work as janitors or as candy and ice-cream vendors in movie houses or as checkroom attendants in hotels. Still others were hired by electrical and phonographic plants, garment factories, and tailoring shops—working long hours under unsanitary conditions for low pay. Taking in boarders was also a frequent means of supplementing one's income.[16]

It was estimated in 1916 that 10 percent of the immigrants were women, both married and single, and about half of them were employed, for the most part as unskilled workers. Married women mostly did piecework in their own crowded living quarters on material furnished by Sephardi subcontractors, earning a mere pittance. As for the women working outside the home, some of them were employed in small factories and shops run by their kinsmen, earning pitifully low wages and, in most cases, being required to pay for the use of the sewing machines on which they worked.

Sweatshop conditions, of course, were not invented by Sephardi entrepreneurs; they had long been part of the American immigrant scene. The Sephardi press and civic leaders strenuously advocated joining labor unions, but most Sephardi workers seemed to prefer security and low pay to the exertion and discomfort of union membership. In their view, being in a union meant having to associate with people whose language they did not speak, whose social mores seemed alien, and whom they did not trust. An editorial in *La Vara* in May 1923 mournfully depicted Sephardi workers as "sweating blood at their machines" rather than joining their comrades in the struggle for better working conditions.[17]

In the course of the 1920s the Sephardi needle-trade industry expanded from the exclusive manufacture of skirts and kimonos to include sportswear, women's coats and dresses, and children's clothing. With business improving and extending, working conditions began to change for the better. But the 1929 crash wiped out all the improvements along with the profits, and the fight for survival drove many of the manufacturers, both Ashkenazi and Sephardi, back to operating on a sweatshop level, fighting both unions and gangsterism. This state of affairs continued until the 1933 National Recovery Act permitted both the industry and the unions to recoup and start all over again.[18]

The gradual absorption of the Sephardim into general American economic life is reflected in two surveys which, although limited in scope, indicate the prevailing trend of their economic adjustment. In 1938 the largest society, the Sephardic Jewish Brotherhood of America, polled its membership, composed primarily of first-generation immigrants, and found the greatest number of respondents engaged in unskilled and semi-skilled labor in forty-three occupational categories, with 16 percent owning their own businesses and only a handful having reached professional status. A 1972 survey of second- and third-generation Sephardim by Rabbi Marc Angel, however, shows only a minuscule percentage of those polled falling into the category of unskilled labor, and they were in the age-range of forty and over. In the under-forty age-group, 53 percent were in business, 39 percent were professionals, 5 percent were artists, and 3 percent were skilled laborers.[19]

Looking back at the struggles and hardships the masses of Sephardi immigrants had to undergo (in common with most immigrants), and looking at the economic status of their children and grandchildren, one must acknowledge that they achieved what they set out to do when they left their homes to face the rigors of life in a new country—they ensured a better future for their offspring. Higher education is today considered an essential part of life by the descendants of the immigrants and of the refugees who arrived on these shores after World War II. They are to be found in all the professions. The fields of Romance languages and history are favored by those going into university teaching.

For the Sephardi immigrant, as for American Jewry as a whole, the decade of the 1940s constituted a watershed. Their wartime service and the general trend of the postwar period steered Sephardi youth toward greater integration into American life. Before World War II Sephardi manufacturers had survived by concentrating on high volumes at marginal profits. This effort stood them in good stead during the war, when the Office of Price Administration based its purchasing quota of raw materials on the applicant's previous volume of trade. This enabled many Sephardi manufacturers to fill a tremendous number of orders, bringing great wealth to several, with a few of them reaching the point of being listed on the stock market.

Several Sephardi manufacturers came to assume leadership in the garment industry. Three former presidents of the Central Sephardic Jewish Community of America served as presidents of the National Skirt and Sportswear Association, the Popular Dress Manufacturing Association, and the Federation of Apparel Manufacture Association, respectively.

The garment industry was one of the most important contributors to Sephardic economic development, but it was by no means the only one. A number of Sephardim went into the manufacture of yogurt, ice-cream cones, candy and halvah, and *lekum lehat*. Others entered the import-export industry, acquiring prestigious stores of their own; still others, more recently, engaged in electronics and banking.

Religion

While Sephardim and Ashkenazim are united in observing the basic tenets of Judaism and in abiding by the authority of the Babylonian Talmud, their divergent cultural backgrounds and historical experiences have left an imprint on their rituals, liturgy, and general attitude toward Jewish law. Sephardim have tended to stress the joyful and sustaining aspects of observing the commandments, and their strong sense of shared tradition and peoplehood enables them to tolerate patterns of observance that are less than absolute. Sephardi music reflects Iberian and Arabic elements; in consequence, the musical range of Sephardi chants is limited, and thus the congregation is able to join with the cantor in the recital and chanting of the prayers. As for the *piyutim* (hymns), it has been said that the Ashkenazi ones are "mediators between the Nation and its God," while those of the Sephardim are "mediators between the Soul and its Creator." Sephardi *piyutim* are derived from the poets of the Golden Age, such as Solomon Ibn Gabirol, Judah Halevi, Abravanel, Abraham Ibn Ezra, and many others.

Thoughtful Sephardim have been concerned about preserving Sephardi religious rituals and traditions since the early years of mass immigration, which produced a proliferation of small, societal synagogues. While the birth of each new synagogue served as an occasion for neighborhood celebrations marked by so much religious fervor that their Ashkenazi neighbors took to referring to the Sephardim as "Jews of Jerusalem," the synagogues proved too small to accommodate everyone who wanted to worship on the High Holidays, so that services on these occasions had to be held in movie houses, lofts, and halls, losing out on both proper conduct and decorum.

In 1913, a commission set up by concerned leaders of the Federation of Oriental Jews, the Spanish and Portuguese Synagogue, and the Kehillah of New York attempted to bring a measure of unity into the spiritual life of the Sephardim. The idea of setting up a chief rabbinate, with Rabbi Abraham Galante of Turkey as incumbent, was proposed but failed to gain a consensus among the commission's members. Deliberations continued until the outbreak of World War I made it impossible for Rabbi Galante to leave Turkey.[20]

Matters stood still until 1941, when Rabbi Nissim J. Ovadia arrived in this country as a refugee from France. The force of his magnetic personality and the strength of his leadership drew all the societies of the three Sephardi groups into his ambit, and they agreed to unite into the Central Sephardic Jewish Community of America, electing him as their chief rabbi—a position he filled for a tragically short time until his death the following year. He was succeeded as chief rabbi by Dr. Isaac Alcalay, a refugee from Yugoslavia, who served in this capacity until his retirement in 1968. As one of his responsibilities,

Rabbi Alcalay served as a consultant to the Bet Din which the immigrants had established in 1920. Upon his retirement this Bet Din ceased its activity, leaving as the only Sephardi Bet Din extant today the one maintained by the Syrian Sephardi community.[21]

As demographic changes brought on by economic improvement served to loosen societal ties, congregations began to form on an inclusive neighborhood basis, recognizing a common Sephardi heritage which transcends regional roots. Newly arriving immigrants from North Africa, Iran, Iraq, and Cuba, however, still sought the security and comfort of forming their own congregations.

Thoughtful Sephardim had recognized early on that what Sephardi synagogues needed, in addition to the spiritual leadership exerted by a chief rabbi, was to obtain trained Sephardi rabbis, able to preserve and pass on Sephardi religious rituals and traditions as well as to exercise the kind of communal leadership needed in the environment into which they all had been transplanted. In 1956, the Central Sephardic Jewish Community, aware of the dire shortage of trained Sephardi rabbis, asked Yeshiva University to initiate a program of Sephardi studies, with the focus on rabbinical training. Matters did not begin to move, however, until 1964, when the chief rabbi of Great Britain, Dr. Solomon Gaon, joined the Yeshiva faculty; under his aegis the Sephardic Studies Program (now the Jacob Safra Institute of Sephardic Studies) came into being.[22]

A survey by the American Sephardi Federation in 1975 showed that half of the forty-six Sephardi congregations were headed by Sephardi rabbis, one-third by Ashkenazim, and the rest were without a rabbi. The 1989–90 Diary of the Spanish and Portuguese Congregation indicates that out of sixty-nine congregations, over two-thirds are headed by Sephardi rabbis, 19 percent by Ashkenazim, and an equal number have no rabbis, showing that the number of Sephardi congregations is growing and that they are increasingly being served by Sephardi rabbis.

Education

Much like the question of religious observance and synagogue life, Jewish education for the young—a matter of course in the Ottoman

Empire—was a problem for the Sephardi immigrants. Societal fragmentation was the main roadblock. Because the societies were made up of relatively small, tightly knit groups, and were reluctant to join forces with each other, they were unable to provide their members with many needed services, and especially with adequate religious schools for their children.

When *La América* urged its readers to send their children to Ashkenazi neighborhood Talmud Torahs, some of the societies were stirred into opening schools of their own where their children would learn "our Hebrew language, our religion and the glorious history of our ancient great nation." By 1912 there were two schools on the Lower East Side and one in Harlem, the latter receiving an accolade from the *Jewish Daily Forward* for its achievements.

Unfortunately, the schools were plagued by lack of funds, and this made it difficult for them to accommodate new pupils and maintain a level of excellence. Only the Syrian community mustered the required resources to maintain steadily growing schools. In the late 1920s the Sephardi Jewish Community of New York tried to consolidate the various downtown societal schools into one well-functioning institution, but the effort was unsuccessful.[23]

The next major communal push to safeguard the Sephardi heritage through improved Jewish education came from the Central Sephardic Jewish Community of America, which not only subventioned some of the existing schools but was able to consolidate several in Brooklyn and the Bronx. This accomplishment was hailed by knowledgeable leaders as "the turning point in the evolution of the Community from a hope and a wish into a fact and reality."

Nonetheless, the number of children attending these schools was very small. A survey conducted by the Central Sephardic Community in 1946 in the Metropolitan New York area showed that only 643 children were attending Sephardi schools. The next two decades produced some progress, albeit limited. A 1963 survey showed that the number of religious schools had increased from five to eight and the number of students had almost doubled, with an enrollment of 1,083 students, 950 of whom were attending schools sponsored by the Brooklyn Syrian Sephardi community. The survey also indicated that an indeterminate number of Sephardi families were sending their children to Ashkenazi-sponsored schools and yeshivot.

In 1976, a study conducted by Rabbi Abraham Hecht, chairman of the Education Committee of the American Sephardi Federation, found that very little progress has been made in the endeavor to increase the number of students and provide them with an adequate religious education. The only positive development registered in the study was the fact that a number of Ashkenazi schools had successfully introduced Sephardi history and culture into their curricula.[24] To date, all Sephardi religious schools are maintained by Sephardi congregations, with the exception of a few all-day schools and a growing number of schools sponsored by the Syrian Sephardi communities, which have maintained religious education as an integral part of their communal life.

Culture

While integration into the prevailing culture was a necessary part of the immigrants' economic progress and social adjustment, Sephardi intellectuals early on became concerned that this might bring in its train a sense of unrootedness and alienation. In 1930 a "lest we forget our glorious heritage" campaign was launched, and the sponsorship of Columbia University was elicited for the creation of a Sephardic Studies Group, directed by Professor Mair J. Benardete and Henry J. Besso. The Group published Besso's *The Dramatic Literature of the Spanish and Portuguese Jews in Amsterdam, Holland in the 17th Century* and Benardete's *Study of the Hispanic Culture and Heritage of the Sephardic Jews*, published in 1951. This done, however, the Group dissolved for lack of further interest and support.

The Central Sephardic Jewish Community of America, in turn, successfully sponsored a scholarship program in 1959, aimed at encouraging Sephardi students to complete their general academic education as well as their religious studies. It also launched an essay contest on Sephardi life in the United States, but this effort evoked only scant interest. The Community subsequently encouraged Yeshiva University to establish the Jacob E. Safra Institute of Sephardic Studies. Yeshiva also opened a Sephardic Reference Room containing manuscripts, books, periodicals, and artifacts and holds lectures and exhibits on Sephardi culture.[25]

The 1960s saw a burgeoning of cultural activity. Reproached by historian David N. Barocas for the shameful neglect of living Sephardi scholars, a group of Sephardi intellectuals bestirred themselves to organize the Foundation for the Advancement of Sephardic Studies and Culture, headed by Professor Mair Benardete and, subsequently, by Louis N. Levy. The Foundation published "tracts" containing a wealth of data on the background of Sephardi immigrants gathered over the years, which were shared with scholars throughout the country. Upon Barocas's death, the objectives of the Foundation were integrated into the program of the Sephardic House established by Rabbi Marc Angel and Louis N. Levy, an Institute for Researching and Promoting Sephardic History and Culture. Directed by Rabbi Angel, the Sephardic House offers classes and programs of Sephardi interest, is preparing educational materials on Sephardi history and culture to be used in Jewish schools, and publishes books by Sephardi authors. In 1992 it sponsored its second annual contest for college youths. It also issues a newsletter that goes out to its members and to Sephardi congregations throughout the country.

In 1967, Professor Isaac Jack Lévy at the University of South Carolina, with the sponsorship of Yeshiva University, organized the American Society for Sephardic Studies (ASOSS). Its publication, the *Sephardic Scholar*, provided a forum for young scholars, and their articles, in turn, provided valuable material for present-day researchers. Yet the funds for this publication ran out after four issues, and the financial and moral support needed to revive it have failed to materialize. At present, according to its current president, David J. Altabé, the ASOSS continues a merely nominal existence, in the hope, however, that a new wave of interest and support might bring it back to life.

The Institute for Sephardic studies, organized by Professor José Faur in 1972, had the especially promising focus of developing a cadre of young leaders with a mandate to actively participate in communal life and work on making cultural programs part and parcel of Sephardi communal and family events. The Institute also introduced credit-earning Sephardi studies programs in a number of universities and awarded scholarships for doctoral degrees in religion, history, and Sephardi studies. Unfortunately, this truly effective, progressive program came to an end when Institute's leaders were unable to resolve some basic disagreements about future goals and objectives.

Yeshiva University is, at present, the nation's only academy to offer a Sephardic major leading to a B.A. or B.S. decree, but several universities offer courses on Sephardi Judaism, its history, culture, and folklore, and a number of Sephardi, Ashkenazi, and non-Jewish academics are engaged in research in this field.[26]

Zionism

Throughout their long sojourn in the Ottoman Empire, Sephardim had been constrained to express their Zionist aspirations only in prayers and on Passover, since political Zionism was considered an irredentist movement in Turkey. It took a few years for the immigrants to absorb the fact that in America people were free to express their ideas and to join together to promote their beliefs, and that it was okay to be an active Zionist.

In 1913 the Oriental Jewish Maccabee Society was formed in order to "develop the physical well being of its membership, to propagate the Hebrew language, to defend the national honor of the Jew whenever attacked and to work closely with the Federation of American Zionists." The immigrants, however, were not as yet ready for sustained organizational work and the group folded after a few months.

A similar fate overtook the Zionist Sephardic Society, founded in July 1914 by Moïse Gadol. Even though its first open meeting was attended by more than 400 people, among them many Ashkenazim, and notwithstanding its participation in Jewish National Fund drives, affiliation with the Federation of American Zionists, and participation in Prayers for Peace meetings called by President Woodrow Wilson, the Society was unable to maintain its cohesion, and by the end of 1915 it had ceased to exist.

Undeterred by these failures the Agudath Zionist Maccabee came into being in 1916. Under the leadership of Simon Nessim, it enriched and expanded the traditional Maccabee program to include courses in Jewish history and culture. It also took an active part in raising funds for the Jewish National Fund and the Jewish Colonial Trust.

Several young Sephardi women joined the society, a sufficiently unusual occurrence in those days to attract considerable attention, prompting a delighted Nissim Behar, a revered Sephardi luminary, to assert gallantly that" a society without young women is like a spring without roses." Its publication, *La Renanciencia* ("Renaissance") began in March 1917 as a bimonthly, continued through 1918, and then appeared irregularly until 1922.[27]

The issuance of the Balfour Declaration on November 2, 1917, evoked a resurgence of enthusiasm among the Sephardi community. Judeo-Spanish-, Greek-, and Arabic-speaking groups held mass meetings expressing support for a Jewish National Home in Palestine and participated in fund-raising activities on behalf of Zionist projects. There were, however, some who feared giving overt support to the establishment of a Jewish homeland lest it lead to reprisals against the Jews of Turkey. Sephardi socialists were also opposed, disagreeing with the Zionist credo on ideological grounds, but they were a very small minority. The main contributing factor in the demise of the Agudath Maccabee Society in the late 1920s was the dispersal of its members into outlying neighborhoods, though Simon Nessim held that an important role was also played by the fatalism which many Sephardim had absorbed during their sojourn in the Ottoman Empire, a feeling that individual activity and initiative are irrelevant and futile.

Ideological conflicts, psychological conditioning, and demographic changes notwithstanding, Sephardim did not lose the desire to express their Zionist aspirations as Sephardim. In 1937 a number of former Agudath Zionist Maccabee members obtained a partial subvention from the Zionist Organization of America (ZOA) and launched the *Sephardic Bulletin*, devoting space to Zionism and world Jewish affairs, and responding to those who were averse to taking a strong Zionist stand by citing the splendid wartime record of the young Sephardim in the Jewish Battalion who had fought for the liberation of Palestine.

The anti-Zionist voice gradually grew weaker, and in 1942 *La Vara* was able to declare editorially that Zionism had ceased to be a subject of debate among the Sephardim, everyone having recognized its vital importance. In 1943 a group of young Syrian Sephardim formed the

Syrian Division of the ZOA, but subsequently they joined the Mizrachi. Thirty years later a group of Syrian women organized a chapter of the Mizrachi Women's Organization of America.[28]

Sephardim, as a collective entity, have, of course, always strongly supported the concept of a Jewish national homeland. The history of Sephardi settlements in Palestine, going back to the eleventh century, and of the many nineteenth-century Sephardi forerunners of latter-day Zionism, was recounted in 1947 in a joint supportive statement to the United Nations Ad Hoc Committee on the Palestinian Question by the Central Sephardic Jewish Community of America, the American Branch of the Sephardi World Federation, and the Union of Sephardic Congregations. At its reorganization conclave in 1972, the American Sephardic Federation affiliated with the American Zionist Federation.

The Press

The desire to unite the fragmented Sephardi immigrant groups into a pursuit of common objectives led Moïse Gadol, while visiting from Bulgaria in 1910, to decide to stay in New York in order to publish a Judeo-Spanish newspaper. *La América*, and the publications that followed, became the life-blood of the immigrant community, providing its members with much-needed information, serving as a means of intercommunication, extending leadership, and formulating communal goals.

Judeo-Spanish, or Ladino, has its base in the pre-classical, pre-Columbian fifteenth-century Castilian Spanish that was the spoken language of the Jews in Spain until the Edict of Expulsion in 1492, since Hebrew was reserved for scholarly treatises, philosophy, and poetry. Having no formally codified structure, Judeo-Spanish remained flexible and adaptable to the postexilic needs of the Sephardim and integrated many of the grammatical rules of their respective host-countries. It is written in cursive Rashi characters.

Having sunk all of his capital of $880 into this venture, Moïse Gadol published the first issue of *La América* in November 1910. Its stated objectives were to play a most sacred, the most holy role in helping our brethren to unite into a community, and to serve as medium of all important events, as well as an organ representing their rights and, finally, to raise its humble but strong voice to put an end to the injustice and antagonism existing between the Ashkenazim and the Sephardim.

Publishing English, Yiddish, and Judeo-Spanish glossaries (with the English transliterated into Rashi characters), *La América* strove to acquaint the immigrants with the immigration laws, urged them to obtain citizenship papers, and offered help on such practical matters as the amount of tax levied on pushcart peddlers, the location of neighborhood hospitals, pharmacies, and public baths, and the cost of riding subways, streetcars, and elevated trains, where "there are no divided sections, the poor and the millionaires sit together."

The articles also dealt with mandatory school attendance for all children under sixteen, free access to libraries, museums, and parks, and even the low cost of electricity, "cheaper than anywhere in the world." Subsequent Sephardi publications followed *La América*'s example of providing English vocabulary columns, publishing biographical sketches of American historical figures, and urging readers to avail themselves of the help HIAS was offering immigrants in securing first papers.

The post–World War I economic depression, the near cessation of Sephardi immigration, and last but not least, the competition posed by other Sephardi papers, chiefly *La Vara*, combined to endanger not only the expansion but the very existence of *La América*. Gadol fought hard to keep his paper alive but had to admit defeat by July of 1925.[29]

An overview of the publications which followed, one after the other, in rapid succession testifies to the ease with which the interest of the Sephardi immigrants could be aroused as well as to the difficulty in maintaining it for very long. The most short-lived of the papers was *La Aguila* ("The Eagle"), launched by Alfred Mizrahi in February 1912 on the assumption that his drive to sell one thousand $5 shares would provide the necessary funds to publish a daily newspaper. His assumption, however, proved wrong, and the first of issue of *La Aguila* was also its last.

El Progresso, which appeared in October 1915 and changed its name to *La Bos del Pueblo* in its December issue, was started by the

Nessim-Torres Press "as a weekly journal of pleasure and enlightenment, devoted to the intellects of the Sephardic Jews in America." Its Salonika-born chief editor, Maurice Nessim, had been an active member of the Salonika Socialist Federation, and after America's entry into World War I, his editorials began to alarm the government censors, who interpreted them as communist propaganda, a state of affairs which induced Nessim to leave the country in 1919.

Undeterred by his earlier failure, Alfred Mizrahi decided to take over the paper and renamed it *La Epoca de New York*, adding English sections of general interest in order to attract not only Ashkenazi but non-Jewish readers. But this venture proved to be ill-starred as well, closing down in February 1920.

El Kirbatch Americano ("The American Whip"), a humorous weekly with a satirical bite, edited by Albert Levy, appeared in 1917 and closed down that same year. So did Albert Covo's *El Emigrante*, designed to improve the immigrants' social and moral conditions.[30]

The first postwar attempt to start a new publication came in September of 1921, when Simon S. Nessim began putting out the weekly *La Luz*, dedicated to bringing about better mutual understanding among the various Sephardi groups and to raising their educational and cultural level. For lack of sufficient communal support *La Luz* folded in 1922.

At the very time that one Sephardi publication was failing, another was starting what was to be an uninterrupted run of twenty-six years. *La Vara* ("The Staff") made its appearance in September 1922, with a masthead depicting an angel beating a hypocrite with a staff. The motto above this, printed in both Judeo-Spanish and Hebrew, proclaimed: "And the staff you shall take in your hand and shall not leave a hypocrite among you."

In 1923 *La Vara* passed into the hands of the Nessim-Torres Press, and a few years later Albert Torres became its sole owner and editor. Throughout its life *La Vara* was a strong supporter of every effort to form a central community organization. In the early 1930s, it dropped its humor pages to focus on world affairs and on the promotion of good communal leadership, also adding an English-language section. Due to Albert Torres's ill-health and ensuing financial problems, the very last

Judeo-Spanish paper to be printed in Hebrew characters, not only in America but in the entire world, came to an end in February 1948.

Two more publications form a part of the annals of the Sephardi press in North America. *El Luzero* ("The Beacon"), a monthly illustrated review, first saw the light of day in 1927 and was forced to close a year later because of insufficient interest. And *Progress*, an English-language monthly which began publishing in Seattle in September 1934 and was distributed free of charge to all of the city's Sephardi households, expired with its thirteenth issue.[31]

The *Sephardic Home News*, primarily an organ of the Sephardic Home for the Aged, appears ten times a year. An eight-page publication dealing mostly with events concerning the Home, it has a wide circulation throughout the country and, in most issues, carries articles of a cultural nature and news of general Jewish interest.

The *Sephardic View International*, published by Ruth Abade, is an organ of the International Sephardic Exchange, a nonprofit organization, which appears irregularly with news and views from Sephardi communities all over the world.

Community Organization

Communal organizations owe their inception to the realization that basic needs can be met most constructively by mutual cooperation and assistance. Sephardi immigrants, coming into a totally new and alien environment, naturally gravitated to people from their home regions, deriving comfort from shared language and customs. Once established, the mutual-aid societies became the centers of communal and social life, with all the strengths and weaknesses that such small, closed-in social units tend to possess.

The situation might have continued unchanged throughout the adjustment process were it not for the inner strength derived from the feeling of being part of *Klal Yisrael*, the totality of the Jewish people, that the Sephardim had developed during the era of dispersion. Thus, having achieved an initial economic adjustment, Sephardi civic leaders began to examine the total Sephardi cultural inheritance, reaffirming Sephardi values, rituals, and traditions and transmitting them to the young.

The best way to do this, they found, was by uniting their many disparate synagogues and obtaining the services of trained rabbis, by providing good schools with qualified teachers, and by establishing coordinated welfare agencies. The inability of the individual societies to provide programs of this kind to their members and to unaffiliated Sephardim served as a prod to civic leaders and the press, and they repeatedly urged the societies to join forces in order to build a comprehensive, strong communal organization.

In the event, it was an appeal for help for the victims of the devastating 1910 fire in Constantinople (Istanbul) which brought about the first joint action by the societies. The subsequent influx of thousands of immigrants from Turkey, the Balkans, and the Near East gave further impetus to the twelve Judeo-Spanish-, Arabic-, and Greek-speaking societies then in existence to form an agency that would represent the total community, without, however, impinging on individual societal rights.

In April 1912, the concerted leadership of Moïse Gadol, Joseph Gedalecia, and Albert Amateau resulted in the formation of the Federation of Oriental Jews of America (the word "Oriental" having been strongly suggested by the leadership of the Spanish and Portuguese Synagogue), with an advisory board that included prominent Ashkenazi personalities and members of Shearith Israel as well as some prominent Sephardim. Joseph Gedalecia was elected president of the Federation, which cited among its objectives

> to Americanize the Spanish, Greek and Arabic speaking Jews from the Orient whose influx, of late, has increased considerably . . . to engender and promote a feeling of unity and love among the members thereof and to extend voluntarily a helping hand in time of need to one another and to other Jews from the Orient and also to have a common place where the members shall gather from time to time to discuss charitable, social and educational matters.[32]

Following the initial enthusiastic affirmation of cooperation and proud Sephardi self-reliance came the realization that if the Federation was to achieve this goal, the individual societies had to commit themselves to active participation and ongoing financial support. The knowledge that concerted action was in the best interest of the whole Sephardi community prevented societal leaders from arguing against it, but their reluctance to abandon their deeply rooted modi operandi pushed them into a stance of passive resistance, as it were. They manifested their resistance by dilly-dallying on submitting their financial contributions and by a merely sporadic attendance at meetings.[33]

Yet some of the Federation's efforts did meet with success. It brought to the attention of the general Jewish community the suffering of the Jews during the Balkan Wars, resulting in the formation of a community-wide Committee for the Relief of Jewish Sufferers by Wars and Massacre. Volunteers came forth to provide the newly arrived immigrants with advice and referrals to various hospitals and Jewish charitable and recreational institutions. The Federation also provided the leaders of the societies, who previously had been isolated from each other, with opportunities to meet and get acquainted, with the additional benefit of learning how to conduct orderly meetings according to parliamentary rules.[34]

The Federation's leaders wanted to increase its effectiveness by opening an office with a paid secretary, installing a chief rabbi, and most of all, acquiring a building which would house a centralized synagogue and a Talmud Torah. But these goals proved unattainable even with the financial aid offered by the Kehillah of New York. When the United States entered World War I in April 1917, the Federation suspended its activities in order not to appear to be operating illegally, since most of the not yet naturalized Jews from Turkey were, technically, subjects of an enemy nation. After the war, due to lack of manpower and funds, and most importantly because of the indifference of its member societies, the Federation was unable to regain whatever momentum it had been able to develop. It went out of existence in 1918.[35]

The next successful move toward communal unity and cohesion came, surprisingly enough, from within the societies themselves, instigated by the Salnician Brotherhood. Thirteen Judeo-Spanish-speaking societies responded to the call, and in January 1920, the Sephardic Community of New York was founded, with Joseph A. de Benyunes as president. Its objectives included the centralization of religious services and Jewish education, settling of domestic problems, fund-raising for war victims, and last but not least, becoming an authorized and effective representative of the Sephardi community in all dealings with other Jewish institutions and with the government, thus enabling Sephardim to enjoy the same recognition and privileges as their Ashkenazi brethren.

The Community was given office space in the Spanish and Portuguese Sisterhood Neighborhood House. Its part-time executive secretary dealt with problems pertaining to immigration, obtained work permits, and assisted in filing for citizenship papers; he also worked with the State Board of Charities and the United Hebrew Charities, and settled domestic quarrels—all highly valued services at no cost to the recipients.

Impressed with the work done by the Community, the Spanish and Portuguese Synagogue considered joining on an equal basis with the societies but withheld a final commitment until it could be sure that the leaders of the societies truly wanted the Community to exist and were ready to work with it and for it. This skepticism, alas, proved to be well grounded, and even the rousing encouragement of Chief Rabbi Nahum Effendi of Egypt, visiting in New York, failed to counteract the lack of interest displayed by the societies. The lack of financial and moral support made it impossible to maintain the services of the part-time executive secretary, and this, in turn, brought about the demise of the Community in the spring of 1922.[36]

Social and political entities, like nature, abhor a vacuum; thus, no sooner had the Sephardic Community of New York ceased to exist than signs of a new surge of interest and sentiment toward achieving communal integration and cohesion began to appear in the Sephardi press. By the early 1920s the struggle for economic survival had become largely a thing of the past for most Sephardi immigrants. The thrust now came from the desire to foster the health and development of Sephardim as a group, as bearers of a distinct and proud Jewish tradition and history of their own who were ready to take their rightful place in the life of their new country.

In June of 1924, seven societies, with a combined membership of 1,600 and annual dues of $2 per member, affiliated into the Sephardic Jewish Community of New York, with the following objectives:

> To promote the general welfare of the Sephardic Jewish community of New York and other cities in the United States and to perpetuate the ideals and traditions of the Sephardic people; to cooperate with existing Sephardic organiza-

tions; to promote the organization of societies to take charge of specific lines of communal activity and to help every individual member of the Community to avail himself of such advantages and facilities as are already available.

Membership, open to all Jews, was divided into five categories: societies, groups, philanthropic organizations, patrons, and individuals at large.[37] Edward Valensi was the first elected president; Robert Franco served as executive secretary and upon his death was succeeded by Victor Tarry.

Over the next few years the Community raised the level of social and educational services, coordinated fund-raising activities, achieved a degree of communal unity, and acted as the official representative of America Sephardim for overseas Sephardi communities. Most importantly, it was able to realize a long-cherished dream by purchasing a building in Harlem. Housing an enlarged synagogue and a Talmud Torah, and able to accommodate a great many youth and adult activities, the Community's new home was a true center of Sephardi cultural and communal life.

Despite this most promising beginning, the Community's continued growth required an expanding financial base and active communal participation, and this support was not forthcoming to the needed extent. Moreover, the Great Depression was having its effect on the Sephardi community. By the fall of 1931, the Community found its membership greatly depleted due to demographic changes and its financial support falling due to the ravages of the depression.

When the Federation of Jewish Philanthropies refused its request for an allocation, the Community was forced to close its center, which had been the core and mainstay of its educational, religious, and recreational activities and their social services. The Talmud Torah was moved to rented quarters, and staff-time and salaries were cut in half. Yet expenses continued to exceed income, forcing the board to discontinue all of its activities. The Community's death knell was sounded in November 1932 when its constituent societies voted to disaffiliate.[38]

The demise of the Sephardic Jewish Community of New York did not lay to rest the conflicts which were pulling asunder the body politic of the Sephardi immigrant community: the conflicts between those who wanted to maintain the status quo, i.e., the preservation of the accustomed, society-oriented life, and those who strove to transcend the divisions of the past and give rise to a united, strong Sephardi community. Throughout the 1930s both factions lived up to their respective natures, the status quo preservers by digging in their heels and resisting all efforts by communal leaders to rouse them out of their passive resistance, and the activists by living up to the admonishment "if at first you don't succeed, try, try again"!

Several efforts made during the 1930s proved unsuccessful, however. The tide turned in April 1941, when Dr. Nissim J. Ovadia, the chief rabbi of Paris, arrived in New York. Ovadia, who had escaped from France with the help of both Jews and Gentiles, threw the weight of his charismatic personality on the side of those who sought change and progress. It was he who issued the next clarion call for a centralized Sephardi communal structure for the sake of keeping faith with the Sephardi heritage.

The news of Rabbi Ovadia's arrival traversed the Sephardi community with the speed and impact of an electric current, eliciting interest and anticipation even in the Greek- and Arabic-speaking groups, which since the dissolution of the Federation of Oriental Jews had held aloof from involvement in Sephardi communal life. Fifteen hundred people came to a meeting called to greet and honor him. Speaker after speaker stressed the need for a united, active Sephardic community and for a strong, inspired leader to help Sephardim to achieve this goal.

Dr. Ovadia proved, indeed, to be an inspired and inspiring leader. He offered his fellow Sephardim a historical perspective of their communal struggles and gave them credit for having begun the attempt to achieve communal unity while still wrestling with basic survival problems. Their early attempts, he said, had been doomed to failure not only by language barriers and cultural diversity but also by their total lack of experience in forming and maintaining a centralized pluralistic community structure. Now, however, Sephardim had achieved a degree of communal maturity that would enable them to forge ahead and form a strong, united, vital community, following the traditional concept which throughout the ages had enabled Jews to survive as a people, and which still had the force to evoke the adherence of modern youth. He viewed Sephardi unity

> not as an act of separatism but as an attempt to recruit forces which are now divided and dispersed in order to press them into service of the Jewish cause. . . . For the time being we, Sephardim and Ashkenazim, must remain separately strong so that we might become strong together. We need each other and the world needs us all. . . . It was for this purpose that I accepted with deep humility the invitation of the dispersed Sephardi community of the United States to cooperate with Dr. Pool and other spiritual leaders in the United States in forming an organization to serve our own group, Jewry as a whole and, last but not least, the world.

Assurance was given to each and all groups that the Central Community was in no way aiming at reducing their independence, and that its goal would be to achieve coordination of all the various activities so as to avoid waste and duplication and allow communal resources to be used to the best advantage of all Sephardim. As a result of these efforts, the societies decided to affiliate and to permit a Central Community to take on the supervision of their synagogues and Talmud Torah, as well as to effect any reorganization deemed necessary. The societies also agreed that the amount of the communal membership fee would be determined by the numerical strength of each society, and lastly, they pledged to inform their members that in joining a Central Community dedicated to enhancing the welfare of the Sephardim, they, as members, would be making "a definite contribution to Judaism."

The Central Sephardic Jewish Community of America came into being in 1941, with Dr. Ovadia elected its chief rabbi, Henri J. Periah its president, and an assembly of delegates and board of directors composed of societal delegates and communal lay leaders. The affiliation of all the societies was celebrated on May 4, 1942. Near the end of the month Dr. Ovadia had his first premonition of heart trouble; in August he was felled by a fatal heart attack.[39]

Dr. Ovadia's death stunned the Sephardi community and was experienced as a crushing blow by its leaders. They felt orphaned, rudderless, and overwhelmed, yet were mindful of their obligation to their fallen leader and gave voice to it in their eulogy:

> He was a conqueror of hearts, an intellectual giant, a dreamer. . . . If his spirit were audible here tonight, he would say to us: "In the name of God do not forsake what I have begun! If you have love in heart for my memory, continue this

work!" Let us, therefore, go forward until we attain the good for which he labored and gave his life.

The appeal not to betray the leader they were mourning rallied the assembly of delegates and board of directors to formulate the objectives of the Central Community along the lines drawn up by Dr. Ovadia.[40]

To establish community-wide communication, the Central Community, in 1943, began publishing an organ of its own, the *Sephardi*, a periodical intended to serve the central organization and also to be

> a connecting link between the various communities in the United States and Latin America, so that the united Sephardic Jewry could work alongside the World Jewish organizations ... to help our brethren in devastated grope and in Africa. ... this is an obligation which historic circumstances have placed upon us.

With the exception of an occasional article in Judeo-Spanish by Rabbi Isaac Alcalay, who had been appointed chief rabbi, the *Sephardi* was published in English. It appeared three times a year for the next ten years and, sporadically until 1959, reaching 4,000 individuals, organizations, and out-of-town communities.[41]

By 1944 it became evident to some members of the board of directors that fund-raising, no matter how successful, was not an end in itself and communal needs would not be met by mere resolutions and statements of goals, but that a competent staff-person was needed to transform lofty aims into actual deeds. With the employment of a trained and experienced community organizer as executive director, the Central Community, in the course of the following five years, proceeded to realize many of its objectives.

Among other things, the *Sephardi*, which had appeared only once in 1943, was relaunched, a Sephardi Veterans Post was established, and a Centralized Location Service was set up to assist survivors of the Holocaust to locate their relatives in this country and to help American Sephardim find their relations abroad. Special funds raised for overseas needs were distributed by the Joint Distribution Committee, and packages of food and clothing were sent overseas. Small neighborhood congregations were assisted to join together to achieve better standards of Jewish education and religious services. Studies of the needs of Sephardi aged resulted in the eventual establishment of the Sephardic Home for the Aged, and studies of the needs of Sephardi youth led to the employment of a full-time youth director. In addition, the Women's Division became active in the war effort, working closely with the American Red Cross, the National Council of Jewish Women, and other organizations.

At the very moment, however, when the Central Community seemed to be on the way to realizing the dream cherished by enlightened Sephardi immigrants, that of developing an authentic Sephardi cultural life, divisiveness and apathy, the old enemies of Sephardi communal unity, made themselves felt again. In the course of 1946–47 it became evident that a change of mood was setting in, manifested by the fact that the usual complaints that the Community was not doing enough were being replaced by allegations that it was doing rather too much and was, thus, overshadowing the societies.

The Community did its best to allay the concerns of the societal leaders, stressing the fact that it was a communal organization composed of diverse but equal parts working toward common goals. But these efforts notwithstanding, the attitude of the societal leaders was reminiscent of Heinrich Heine's famous dictum: "I was baptized but not converted."

The resistance to being "converted," to being bona fide partners in a centralized communal structure, was manifested by poor attendance at board meetings and diminishing campaign contributions, and seemed to gather strength with each and every demonstrated success in activities and service performed by the Central Community. This situation led to the resignation of the executive director, followed by that of his replacement some two years later, leaving Dr. Alcalay to shoulder a great deal of administrative work in addition to the responsibility of spiritual leadership.[42]

Over the next few years, the Central Community attempted a number of structural changes that met some of the societal demands while allowing it to proceed with its main goals. In 1955 the Community went a step further, putting the societies in control of the organization. It soon became evident, however, that a structural reorganization was unable to effect any changes in the basic problems besetting the Community, let alone solve them. The Community still lacked the money to fund needed services, and the level of participation by the societal representatives remained woefully low.

The retirement of Dr. Alcalay in 1968 left the Central Community in a state of suspended animation, as it were, with nothing left but its name—a name kept alive by the work of its Women's Division. As for the societies which constituted the legal base upon which every one of the organized community structures had been based, they themselves began to lapse into inactivity during the 1960s, their sole function now being to provide burial services. The Syrian Sephardim were the only exception; their communal life continues to develop and progress.[43]

In 1972 this author, in person and by questionnaire, contacted the Central Community's former leaders and those still serving, albeit nominally, to sound them out on their views of the Community's past effectiveness and its chances for an eventual comeback. All of the respondents agreed that the Central Community had, indeed, provided services which the societies had been unable to provide on their own. These included the standardization and formalization of Jewish education and religious services; the financial and moral support of religious schools and congregations; coordination of fund-raising drives; helping Sephardi World War II refugees adapt to the American scene; sponsorship of citywide youth activities and provision of scholarships; being instrumental in the establishment of the Sephardic Home for the Aged and the Sephardic Center of the Bronx; providing a forum for the discussion of common problems; giving societal leaders the opportunity to meet and work out more cooperative modi operandi; and last but not least, serving as spokesman for all Sephardim.

On the other hand, some felt that the mutual-aid societies and congregations met the basic needs of their members to a degree which precluded any need to belong to and identify with an overall communal structure, citing the Home for the Aged as an example of a flourishing communal enterprise which, according to many respondents, had, indeed syphoned off both leadership and funds from the Central Community. The growing number of Ashkenazi-Sephardi marriages were also perceived to be contributing to the disintegration of the Community, as well as a growing rift between wealthy Sephardim called upon to provide money and intellectuals bent upon preserving the purity of their ideas.

Nonetheless, a clear-cut majority of the respondents came out in favor of a revitalized Community with the following updated objectives: to infuse the young generation with a greater knowledge and commitment to Sephardi history, tradition, and values; to persuade them to become active members of the Sephardi fold; to participate actively in efforts to meet the needs of the Sephardi and general Jewish communities in America and abroad; to obtain better services for Sephardim in Israel and serve as a spokesman for all Sephardim. But all agreed that only a leader of the stature of Dr. Nissim Ovadia would be able to achieve so sweeping a revitalization, and some expressed hopes that such a leader might yet emerge: ". . . the chances are minimal but—who knows? After all man has reached the moon!"

At present, however, despite valiant efforts by the Women's Division to prod it out of its total inactivity, the Community has remained moribund. In January of 1990, Mrs. Emily Levy, who had served as president of the Central Community for the preceding eight years, announced that the parent organization had turned its remaining assets over to the Women's Division, which would become the representational body for the entire Central Community.[44]

The American Sephardi Federation

While struggling to create a unified, viable Sephardi community on American soil, Sephardi leaders had retained their ties to Sephardim across the world and had felt the urge to join with historically conscious Sephardim in other countries and resume an active, creative role in the life of *Klal Yisrael*. This led to the establishment of the Sephardi World Federation in 1925 and to the opening of an American branch in 1951, using the Central Sephardic Jewish Community as a core from which to communicate with communities and groups throughout the land. The decline of the Central Community affected the branch's ability to sustain the interest and allegiance it had managed to build up, and the death of its chairman, Simon Nessim, further scaled down its activities.

This situation became a serious concern to the Sephardi World Federation, which went to work on bringing the American branch back to life. Some fifty Sephardi leaders from across the land, as well as outstanding members of the World Zionist Organization and the Jewish Agency, assembled in Chicago in October 1972 and worked out plans to revitalize the organization under the name of the American Sephardi Federation. Its first convention, in February 1973, was attended by 250 delegates who reaffirmed their determination to strengthen and foster Sephardi religious and cultural life in America, as well as to serve Sephardi communities in Israel and the world.

Under the leadership of its first president, Daniel J. Elazar, the American Sephardi Federation was especially successful in stimulating enthusiasm among the youth. National conclaves of young adults were organized. Congregations and communities were inspired to develop cultural interests and activities. Teenagers were enabled to spend a summer in Israel and came back with a strengthened feeling and insight into their Sephardi identity. And with increased self-esteem came also a greater participation in all phases of general Jewish life in their respective communities.

In spite of these successes, however, the initial impetus began to weaken within the next few years. Attendance at board meetings began to decline, diminishing financial support led to the resignation of the executive director and to the discontinuance of the productive youth programs, and Sephardi public interest seemed to vanish. For all these reasons the work of the American Sephardi Federation slowed down considerably.

Still, all the sparks had not been extinguished, and in 1985, the newly elected president, Leon Levy, decided to bring the Federation back to life. Gifted with vision and leadership, using his own funds and enlisting further financial support from individuals and organizations, he succeeded in reactivating the Federation. To ensure continued interest, he instituted, in addition to general membership dues, a President's Circle of Advisers, with each member pledging to contribute a minimum of $1,000 to support the Federation's ongoing activities and committing themselves to play an active role in guiding its future activities.

During Levy's presidency the American Sephardi Federation has held three national conventions, the largest, in Seattle in 1989, attracting 600 delegates. In 1987, the Federation's Young Leadership Division began publishing the *Sephardic Connection*. The year 1988 saw the employment of a full-time social worker with many years of experience in the field of community organization. More recently, a full-time youth director and a public relations director were added to the staff. The Federation's current organ, *Sephardi Highlights*, keeps members apprised of its activities.

The American Sephardi Federation hopes to promote the maintenance of a Sephardi cultural identity and at the same time to forge a new direction for the future of American Jewish life as a whole. Its seven-pronged program includes an increased advocacy for Jews in distressed lands, coordinating its activities with those of the World Organization of Jews of Arab Countries, the International Coalition for Rescue of the Jews of Yemen, and other such groups. The Federation has also established a new Sephardic Resource Center which provides books and audiovisual materials to "teach teachers" about Sephardi culture; and it plans a major demographic study to facilitate planning and to bring Sephardi concerns to the attention of world Jewry.

Federation efforts to develop young Sephardi leaders include ongoing seminars, workshops, and shabatons throughout the country and planning for Project Sepharad 1992, commemorating the expulsion of the Jews of Spain and the warm welcome they received in the Ottoman Empire. This last consideration led a large number of Sephardim to form the American Association of Jewish Friends of Turkey, a group seeking to ensure a proper stress on the beneficent role the Ottoman Empire had at the time of Jewish need.

In late 1989, world Jewish leaders announced the formation of the International Jewish Committee for Sepharad 1992. Yitzhak Navon, former president of Israel and current minister of education and culture, was its founder and chairman, and it was spearheaded by the World Sephardi Federation and its president, Nessim D. Gaon. Headquartered in New York City, the Committee was directed by the executive vice-president of the American Sephardi Federation, Hal M. Lewis.

We have seen initial successes followed by deterioration, and we have seen dedicated civic and religious leaders refuse to admit defeat, choosing instead to start all over again. In the end, their dream of achieving a strong, united, viable Sephardi community was defeated by a combination of forces—external ones, such as demographic shifts and upward economic mobility, and internal ones, such as the resistance of the entrenched leaders of the societies and other groups to yield any of their autonomy, as well as the unwillingness of those who had achieved affluence to join or to contribute funds to a united central community.

The current interaction between Sephardim in America and in Israel is mutually beneficial. Limited as this rebirth may be, it represents a tribute to the determination and dedication of the early immigrants, who, their failures notwithstanding, were able to preserve enough Sephardi cohesion, self-respect, and drive to allow their grandchildren to embark on a quest of their own. It is a quest to unearth the neglected wellsprings of Sephardi creativity and to ensure that these treasures find their rightful place in the cultural heritage of Jewry as a whole.

The continued existence of the American Sephardi Federation as a communal umbrella organization which offers its services to an estimated 150,000 to 200,000 American Sephardim holds the best hope for the preservation of a Sephardi communal identity in the United States. All its efforts need and deserve substantial support from the total Jewish community. This support will be well justified because Jewish life in America today must gather and cherish all its cultural sources in order to ensure its continued well-being and growth.

Nissim Behar

I cannot bring myself to close this bird's-eye view of twentieth-century Sephardi immigrant life in North America without paying at least a brief tribute to an outstanding Sephardi personality who dedicated his life to the service of his people, without ever seeking the limelight and without hesitating to share his all-too-meager means with those whose needs he deemed to be greater than his own.

Born in Jerusalem in 1848 into a distinguished rabbinical family, Nissim Behar received his talmudic instruction from his father and his maternal grandfather, a famous kabbalist. A recipient of an

Alliance Israélite Universelle scholarship to the Ecole Orientale in Paris, Behar graduated in 1869 and was appointed to open up Alliance schools in Aleppo, Syria, and Samacoff (Samakov), Bulgaria. In 1875, he was entrusted with the directorship of the most prestigious of the Alliance schools, that in Constantinople (Istanbul).

Seven years later, Nissim Behar returned to Jerusalem to open a school there which would incorporate his pedagogic vision. In what was at the time a revolutionary departure from the norm, he combined an academic curriculum with a vocational workshop to better meet the needs of the city's children, and also taught Hebrew by what came to be called the *Ivrit b'Ivrit* method. This decision provided a badly needed job for Eliezer Ben Yehuda, who was then toiling on the first modern Hebrew dictionary.

On opening day, the school had one student. It took enormous persistence and courage and all of Behar's powers of persuasion and personal magnetism to overcome the antagonism and resistance of Jerusalem's Sephardi and Ashkenazi religious leaders and induce them to allow children to attend the school, whose reputation soon began to attract non-Jewish children. By 1897, when Behar was sent to Europe to mobilize interest and support for the Alliance schools, the Jerusalem school counted 400 students; at the time of his death thirty-four years later, its student body numbered more than 1,500.

In his three years of traveling through Europe, Behar engaged the interest of leading non-Jewish as well as Jewish personalities and was received in audience by King Victor Emmanuel II of Italy and by Pope Pius X. In 1901 Behar was sent to America to revitalize the Alliance chapters there and organize new ones. He conscientiously executed his assignment but soon found his attention claimed by a multitude of problems.

Becoming an American citizen turned Behar, ipso facto, into an American activist. In 1903, galvanized into action by the Kishinev massacre, he persuaded influential Christian ministers to condemn, ex cathedra, pogroms against a religious minority. In addition, he launched a nationwide campaign urging the U.S. government to abrogate its 1832 Commerce and Friendship Treaty with Russia because of the latter's refusal to grant visas to American citizens of Russian Jewish descent. This so-called Passport Question, which alarmed and upset many Jewish establishment leaders, culminated in President Taft's abrogation of the treaty in 1912.

Troubled by the plight of immigrants, Behar founded the National Liberal Immigration League and recruited Charles W. Eliot, the president of Harvard, and Woodrow Wilson, president of Princeton, among the board members. In 1906, perceiving that Jewish rights could best be protected and Jewish causes most effectively championed if American Jewry's diverse organizations coordinated their efforts, he founded the Federation of Jewish Organizations—an unprecedented event which evoked displeasure and opposition on the part of many Jewish power-brokers. As journalist Abraham Goldberg recalled,

> The enemies of the new organization kept on saying: "Who is Behar? Who invested him with authority?" They pointed to the fact that he was a Sephardic Jew and not a member of the majority. Nevertheless, his maligners plagiarized his ideas and put them to their own use. . . . But it was he and he alone who was the progenitor of the various Jewish political movements in this country.

Space does not permit me to touch on a great number of other achievements of this remarkable man, who, unfortunately, has been overlooked by the scholars and chroniclers of Jewish life. I can only hope that future historians will correct this injustice and grant Nissim Behar his rightful place in the history and esteem of the Jewish people.[45]

Notes

1. Moïse Franco, *Essai sur l'histoire des Israélites de l'Europe Ottoman* (Paris, 1847).

2. Michael Molho, *Usos y Costumbres de Los Sefardíes de Salónica* (Madrid: Instituto Arias Montano, 1950).

3. Ibid.; Franco, *Essai sur l'histoire des Israélites*; Jacques Bigard, "Alliance Israélite Universelle," *American Jewish Year Book*, 1900–1901, pp. 75 ff.

4. Michael Molho, *Le Judaisme Grec en général et la Communaté Juive en particulier entre les deux guerres mondiales* (Barcelona, 1956), p. 73. Eliot Grennel Mears, *Modern Turkey* (New York, 1924), p. 96; Cecil Roth "On Sephardi Jewry," *Kol Sepharad*, November–December 1966, pp. 62 ff.

5. B. D. Bogen, *Jewish Philanthropies* (New York, 1917), pp. 26 ff.; Albert Amateau to Papo, January 1973, March 18, 1976.

6. "New York Is a City Set Apart Where Live Jews Who Know No Yiddish," *New York Tribune*, Sept. 22, 1912, pt. II, pp. 4, 7.

7. *La América*, Nov. 11–25, Dec. 9, 1910; April 11, May 12, June 20, July 7, 1911; Jan. 12, March 8, May 12, 1912; Feb. 21, 1913; Oct. 10, 1919; *La Bos del Pueblo*, March 16, June 29, 1917; Oct. 10,

1919; Joseph A. D. Sutton, *Magic Carpet in Flatbush: The Story of a Unique Ethnic Jewish Community* (New York, 1979); interview with Mazal (Mrs. Nissim) Ovadia, Summer 1946.

8. Joan Dash, "Sephardim in Seattle," *National Jewish Monthly*, May 1963, pp. 12, 13, 49, 50.

9. *La América*, April 28, May 12, May 19, June 2, July 7, Aug. 4, Dec. 29, 1911; Dec. 13, 1912; Jan. 31, June 27, 1913; June 4, 1915; Jan. 21, Feb. 25, 1916; July 22, 1917; May 31, 1918; Park and H. A. Miller, *Old World Traits Translated* (New York, 1921), p. 200; Bernard Drachman, *The Unfailing Light: Memoirs of an American Rabbi* (New York, 1948), p. 357; Celia Silbert, "Characteristics of the Daughters of the Orient," *American Jewish Chronicle* (New York), May 16, Aug. 25, 1916; *La Bos del Pueblo*, July 21, July 28, Sept. 8, 1916; Jan. 5, Jan. 12, Feb. 9, Feb. 16, March 25, June 8, 22, 1917; *Haivri* (New York), vol. 7, June 22, 1917.

10. Hayyim Cohen, *Dispersion and Unity* (Jerusalem: World Zionist Organization, 1971–72), pp. 151–160; Marc Angel, "The Sephardim in the United States: An Exploratory Study," *American Jewish Year Book*, 1973, pp. 116 ff.

11. *La América*, May 16, Oct. 5, 1913; Jan. 30, 1914.

12. Minutes of Shearith Israel Sisterhood board of directors (hereafter cited as SIS), Jan. 24, 1914: minutes of HIAS board of directors (hereafter cited as HIAS), Feb. 10, 15, 1914; Angel, "Sephardim in the United States," p. 101.

13. Shearith Israel Sisterhood Annual Reports, 1911–1921; SIS, Jan. 25, 1925.

14. *Bulletin of Shearith Israel League*, May 1927, quoted in *Community Activities*; Shearith Israel to Central Community, April 9, 1928; *Community Activities Bulletin*, April 28, 1928.

15. Central Community to Shearith Israel, Oct. 28, 1955; Shearith Israel to Central Community, Nov. 3, 1955; *Sephardi*, March 13, 1959; minutes of Women's Division board of directors (hereafter cited as WD), April 28, 1969: *Shearith Israel Bulletin*, April 28, 1928.

15. Central Community to Shearith Israel, Oct. 28, 1955; Shearith Israel to Central Community, Nov. 3, 1955; *Sephardi*, March 13, 1959; WD, April 28, 1969; *Shearith Israel Bulletin*, May–June, 1972.

16. *La América*, Nov. 11, Nov. 25, Dec. 10, 1910.

17. Leon Saunders, "Sephardic Oriental Bureau," *HIAS Annual Report*, 1911; David M. Perahia to Papo, Jan. 1, 1978; Simon Nessim, *La Bos del Pueblo*, Aug. 11, Aug. 18, Sept. 27, Oct. 6, Nov. 12, 1916, *La America* Sept. 15, Sept. 27, 1916; Cecilia Silbert, "Economic Conditions of the Oriental Jewess in New York," *American Jewish Chronicle*, October 1916, pp. 666 ff.

18. *La Vara*, Feb. 9–23, March 9–30, Apr. 20, May 4, June 8, 1923; *La América* July 23, 1919, Sept. 8, Sept. 15, 1922; Mar. 23, 1923; June 6, Sept. 19 1924; *Sephardic Brotherhood Review*, April 1923, 1928.

19. Sephardic Brotherhood Occupational Census, March 1938; Victor D. Sann, "A Study of the Adjustment of Sephardi Jews in the New York Metropolitan Area," *Jewish Journal of Sociology* 9 (June 1967): 25 ff.; Angel, "Sephardim in the United States," pp. 116 ff.

20. *Jewish Encyclopedia*, 4:198: M. J. Benardete, *Hispanic Culture and Character of the Sephardic Jews* (New York, 1952), pp. 117 ff.; Marc D. Angel, "Sephardim in America," *Present Tense*, Summer 1976, pp. 12 ff.; *La America*, Jan. 10, Jan. 17, Oct. 1, Dec. 26, 1913; Mar. 6, June 12, Sept. 11, Oct. 9, Nov. 3, 1914; Louis M. Hacker, *The Communal Life of Sephardic Jews of New York City*, May 1926.

21. Joseph M. Papo, "The Sephardic Community of America," *Reconstructionist*, October 29, 1946, pp. 12 ff.

22. Minutes of Central Community board of directors (hereafter cited as CC), Sept 29, 1942; Nov. 30, 1961; Jan. 28, March 22, 1962; Lou C. Gerstein to Yeshiva University, Feb. 1959 (written at the request of the Central Community). Herbert C. Dobrinsky, Victor Tarry, Marc D. Angel, and M. Mitchell Serels to Papo, 1965–1978.

23. *La América*, Dec. 10, 1910; May 26, 1911; Jan 5, Feb. 9, Feb. 23, Aug. 9, Sept. 6, Oct. 11, Oct. 18, Nov. 29, 1912; Albert Amateau to Papo, Dec. 31, 1974; *Sisterhood Annual Reports*, 1913, 1914; *La Vara*, Sept. 8, 1922, Feb. 16, 1923; Oct. 18, 1926; July 18, 1928.

24. Moïse Bensignor, "On the Religious Front of Our Community," *Sephardi*, March 1944 (not circulated); Joseph M. Papo, "Report on Jewish Education," *Sephardi*, September 1946; Jewish Education Committee of New York, *Report*, Nov. 4, 1949; Central Community Survey, 1946; L. S. Alvo, "Survey of Religious and Educational Activities of the Synagogues and Centers Affiliated with the Community," Fall 1962, *Sephardi World*, May 1976; Sutton, *Magic Carpet*, pp. 92 ff.

25. *La Vara*, Sept. 17, 1937; Simon Nessim to Central Community, April 1962; *Kol Sepharad*, March 1963.

26. *Sephardic Scholar*, 2nd series, 1972–73, pp. 5 ff; Yeshiva University reports, pamphlets, and literature; extended correspondence with Louis N. Levy and David N. Barocas; *Shearith Israel Bulletin*, February 1979; *Sephardic Home Bulletin*, Jan. 14, 1980 and others.

27. *La América*, Nov. 11, 1910; March 13, 1913; Feb. 6, July 3, Aug. 7, Oct. 9, 1914; April 9, June 25, Aug, 20, 1915; March 10, Sept. 27, Oct. 20, 1916; May 18, 1917; Feb. 8, Mar. 17, Nov. 15, 1918; May 4, 1920; *La Bos del Pueblo*, Nov. 3, Dec, 29, 1916; Feb. 9, May 11, 1917; April 15, 1918; Simon Nessim in *La Renanciencia*, October 1919; *La Luz*, Nov. 20, 1922.

28. *Sephardic Bulletin*, September 1937, November 1938; *La Vara*, September 1942.

29. *La América*, Nov. 11, 1910; April 21, 1911; Oct. 11, Dec. 13, 1912; March 7, Nov. 14, 1913; *New York Tribune*, Sept. 22, 1912; *El Progresso*, Nov. 5, 1915; *La Bos del Pueblo*, Aug. 13, 20, 1917; July 3, 1925.

30. *La América*, Nov. 7, 1919; *La Bos del Pueblo*, Nov. 28, 1919; Albert J. Amateau to Papo, June 30, 1978.

31. *La Vara*, Sept. 1, 1922; Oct. 26, Nov. 9, Dec. 28, 1923; interview with Albert J. Torres, Aug. 9, 1937; Joel H. Halio, "Some Aspects of the Sephardi Press in America" (unpublished monograph, 1972); Marc D. Angel, "*Progress*," *Seattle Sephardic Monthly*, 1934–35; *American Sephardi* 5 (Autumn 1971): 90 ff.

32. *La América*, Mar. 22, April 5, 1912; Nov. 15-19, Dec. 22, 1912; May 2, 1913, June 16, 1916; *La Bos del Pueblo*, April 26, 1918.

33. Albert J. Amateau to *La Luz*, Jan 22, Feb. 5, 1922; *Sephardic Brotherhood Review*, November 1936; Joseph Gedalecia, *La Vara*, Aug. 26, 1937; interview of Albert J. Amateau, Aug. 13, 1937.

34. Joseph Gedalecia to Felix Warburg, Dec. 22, 1912, May 2, 1913.

35. *La América*, Jan. 25, July 12, 1918; *La Bos del Pueblo*, Apr. 5, May 3, 17, 1918; Albert J. Amateau to Papo, Mar. 18, 1976.

36. *La América*, Jan. 9, 21, 30, Feb. 6, Mar. 19, Apr. 2, Oct. 8, Nov. 19, 1920.

37. *La Luz*, Jan. 1, 1922; *La America*, Sept. 22, Dec. 22, 1922; Feb. 16, Mar. 2, June 1, 1923; *La Vara*, Nov. 1922; Jan. 12, June 8, Aug. 3, Oct. 5, Nov. 16, 1923.

38. CC, Nov. 20, 1926; Jan. 19, Feb. 19, Mar. 9, 1927; Dec. 11, 1931; Jan. 25, 1932; *Community Activities Bulletin*, March 23, 1928; *Commuunity Sephardic Bulletin*, April 1929; interview of Victor Tarry, June 1972.

39. *La Vara*, Apr. 25, May 16, 1941; businessmen's committee minutes, May 26, June 6, July 4, 1941; *Independent Jewish Press*, Aug. 1, Sept. 26, 1941

40. Henry J. Perahia, Simon S. Nessim, Moise Bensigor in *La Vara*, Sept. 6, 1942; John Hezekiah Levy, CC, Sept 10, 1942.

41. Simon Nessim to Central Community, Aug. 31, 1944; Simon Nessin to Papo, Sept. 12, 1944; community personnel committee minutes, Sept. 29, 1944; CC, Oct. 1, 1944; Mar. 12, April 12, May 1, Oct. 30, 1945; Nov. 25, 1946; April 15, 1947; Isaac Asseo to *La Vara*, Dec. 6, 1946, Mar. 14, 1947;

Papo to Central Community, Mar. 28, 1947; ADCC minutes, May 1947; John J. Karpeles to Central Community board of directors, Oct. 19, 1948.

42. CC, April 14, 18, June 6, 1955; May 21, June 18, 1956; Ten Volunteers minutes, April 16, 1955; Central Community to Sephardi leaders, May 17, 1960; Simon Nessim to Sephardi Community, April 21, 1961; CC, June 12, 1961; Central Community Report, 1961–63; Victor Tarry to Papo, Dec. 20, 1965; Joseph Kattan to Papo, Oct. 3, 1972.

43. Emilie Levy to Papo, Jan. 30, 1990.

44. *Report of the Sephardic Delegation to the American Zionist Convention, Chicago,* October 1972; *News and Views* (American Zionist Federation); *Jewish Telegraphic Agency,* Feb. 27, 1973; *B'nai B'rith Messenger,* Mar. 7, 1973; *Jewish Floridian,* Mar. 2, 1973; *Sephardic Home News,* April 1973; *Young Sephardi News Bulletin,* June–July 1979; *Sephardic World,* March 1976, p. 2, April 1979; Victor Tarry to Papo, Oct. 29, Nov. 17, 1981; June 14, 19, 1982; Jan. 11, 1985; American Sephardic Federation minutes, Jan. 6, 1985; *Sephardic Highlights,* 1989, January and February 1990; Joseph M. Papo, *Sephardim in Twentieth Century America in Search of Unity* (San Jose, Calif., 1987) pp. 250 ff.; *Jewish Journal,* Dec. 28, 1989, Jan. 3, 1990.

45. E. R. Lipsett, "Nissim Behar, the Man, His Battles and His Responsibilities," *American Hebrew,* March 29, 1918, pp. 564 ff; Z. Szajkowsky "The Alliance Universelle in the United States," *American Jewish Historical Society Quarterly* 39 (June 1950): 389–443; Abraham Goldberg, "Nissim Behar," in *Pioneers and Builders: Biographical Studies and Essays,* p. 192; Nissim Behar's correspondence with the Alliance (1901–1920); Papo, *Sephardim in Twentieth Century America.*

Language of the Sephardim in Anglo-America
Denah Lida

Introduction

At the end of the fifteenth century, when the Jews were expelled from the Iberian Peninsula, Castilian was still in the formative process that would eventually crystallize in its modern configuration. It was that language, with its irregularities of pronunciation and spelling, some of its archaic grammatical forms and structures, which was transported into the Diaspora. Subsequent changes occurred in the Spanish of the Sephardim, depending in part on their geographic proximity to Spain, as in North Africa and Holland or the Ottoman Empire, but the fundamental traits remained static, and innovations generally came from the languages to which each community was exposed.

When the first twenty-three Jewish arrivals to the so-called New World reached New Amsterdam in 1654, the Spanish or Portuguese they spoke was not unlike that spoken in the Iberian Peninsula. Their ancestors had taken refuge in the Netherlands at the time of the expulsion and subsequently. The frequent contact with Spain in particular, to which many traveled under Hispanic and Portuguese names, although some assumed their Jewish names and maintained a kind of dual identity, helped to keep them abreast of linguistic changes and to maintain a highly literary form of expression. The playwright Miguel (de) Barrios, also known as Daniel Levi and as a combination of both names, serves as a good example. Travelers pursued commercial enterprises and often served in diplomatic missions. A very important factor is that they had access to peninsular publications. That these Jews, first in Antwerp, then in Amsterdam, read Spanish literature in the original is attested to by the fact that some of them cultivated the same genres and had their works published locally. These were read not only in the Diaspora but in Spain as well.

The first Jewish immigrants to North America, as is well known, settled, after a harrowing voyage and considerable difficult negotiations with Peter Stuyvesant, in what is now New York City and, shortly thereafter, in the thriving commercial community of Newport in Rhode Island. They had been Dutch settlers in Brazil when Portugal overtook their colony. In a frustrated attempt to return to Holland, they finally landed in another Dutch colony. These people, educated and hard-working, were backed by rich merchants in the motherland. They assimilated quickly, amassed fortunes, sponsored many philanthropic activities, gained the respect of their neighbors and, gradually, the rights of citizenship even before some of their European and Ottoman coreligionists. While most clung to their Judaism, it was naturally harder to preserve their Iberian heritage at such a great distance from its source, amid a vastly different emerging culture. As a consequence, the first streams of early settlers in the seventeenth century, while they retained their given and family names and their self-image as Sephardim, soon lost most other identifying traits, especially their language, with a very few exceptions which we can determine from their wills and tombstones. It is not of them that we shall speak in the pages which follow, but of the language brought by the larger influx of immigrants who came in the late nineteenth and early twentieth centuries, especially before and after World Wars I and II.

Linguistic Background

Linguistic evolution is a very slow process, as we can realize if we consider that the Romans first introduced Latin into the Peninsula in the second century B.C.E. Once conquered, the local populations, except perhaps for the Basques as far as language is concerned, were heavily influenced by the invaders, who came with advanced organizational abilities as well as a hierarchical social structure, codified laws, engineering skills for constructing roads, aqueducts, etc., and a language which became that of the church when the Romans were christianized. We should also take into account the fact that the new Romanic language emerged from the everyday Latin the soldiers spoke rather than from the more cultured written language. Thus the

Language of the Sephardim

early forms of speech of the peoples under Roman dominion were known as Vulgar Latin, that is, the common and colloquial language used by the populace.

Naturally, there was also some evidence of the languages which had been spoken previously in the Peninsula, such as Iberian, Celtic, and Basque. The development continued into the early centuries of the Christian era under the domination, between the fifth and eighth centuries, of the Goths, Visigoths, and Barbarians who came from the north. The presence of these hordes left relatively few traces on the language, except for a small vocabulary and some names.

It was during this period that Vulgar Latin, acquiring its own particular regional forms in the Peninsula, became known as *romance* (pron. in three syllables: *ro-man-ce*). In spite of its geographic isolation from the rest of Romanla, the Latin derivative tongue was preserved, but because of that isolation and lack of exposure to more modern Latin, it remained rather archaic and also developed peculiarities of its own in the following centuries, especially during the long Moorish invasion and the period of Reconquest.

By the eleventh century a primitive form of Spanish emerged which was a mixture of pre-Roman words, popular Latin, Gallicisms introduced by French pilgrims on their way to Santiago and the tomb of Saint James, and *romance*. This early tongue was also called *ladino*, from the Latin *latinus*. Thus, *favlar en ladino* came to signify "to speak clearly, in a straightforward manner," i.e. intelligibly. Among Jews *ambezar la Torah en lashon y en ladino* was "to learn the Pentateuch in Hebrew and in *romance*."[1] A speaker of medieval romance, such as a translator or interpreter, who expressed himself clearly and directly, could be known as a *ladinador* or a *ladinante*. The transitive verb *ladinar* meant "to render into medieval 'Spanish' from another language" such as Arabic. The Bible and prayers were also translated, most often by Jews, into Latin and pre-expulsion romance.[2]

During the twelfth and thirteenth centuries the regional dialectic variants took shape: Castilian in the central plains, Gallego-Portuguese on the Atlantic coast, Asturian-Leonese in the northwest, Navarro-Aragonese in the northeast, Catalan (and its variant Valencian) on the Mediterranean coast, and Andalusian in the south. The spread of Castilian loosely followed the Reconquest of the Peninsula by the Christians against the Moors throughout the Middle Ages to the fall of the last Moorish kingdom, Granada, in 1492.

The archaic "Spanish" was characterized by many irregularities as well as phonetic instability and hesitation. While Latin continued to be used for what was considered "serious" writing in prose, poetry, viewed as a more frivolous genre and meant for entertainment, could be and was rendered in the vernacular, spoken form of the language. Except for translations of Arabic narrative prose and some politico-moral catechisms and clerico-didactic prose, it was not until the second half of the thirteenth century that *romance* prose emerged, during the reign of the scholar-king Alfonso the Wise. Its development continued throughout the fourteenth century, as it was cultivated by learned noblemen who pursued a life of letters, such as Don Juan Manuel.

Before the Jews were expelled, the transition from this medieval "Spanish" to the pre-classical form had already taken place, so that structure was fairly solidified. But classical Spanish, which reached its peak in the sixteenth and early seventeenth centuries, would elude most of the Jews, except those near enough to have frequent contact with the living language, either through clandestine visits to Spain or through visitors from Spain. It was primarily the Sephardim of the Netherlands and North Africa who reaped the benefits of these contacts. For example, Jews from those areas adopted the use of *usted*, the polite form of 'you', derived from *vuestra merced*, in lieu of the third-person *él, ell a*, commonly used by other Sephardim: 'How are you?' asked of an elderly lady, is rendered *Cómo está ella*? Those in the Mediterranean countries and the Ottoman Empire were more isolated and, therefore, more conservative. We shall have occasion to follow these two very diverse general groups into the New World, where their histories—linguistic and social—are very different from each other.

Although we must recognize that living languages are always in subtle flux, it is sufficiently accurate for our purposes to say that during the seventeenth century the transformation took place in the oral tradition, sounds became pretty well fixed regionally, and written prose reached new heights of eloquence. What remained to be standardized was the spelling, but that would not occur until the Royal

Academy of the Language was created in 1713. One of its first major undertakings was the publication of the *Diccionariodo Autoridades*, 1726–1739. This was followed by *Ortografía* ("Spelling"), 1741 which reflects the changes in pronunciation, and *Gramática* ("Grammar"), 1771. The Academy then proceeded to publish certain major works in accordance with the new standards. Some minor vacillation—*s* for *x* before a consonant, for example—continued into the nineteenth century, but later editions of the Dictionary and the Grammar continued to establish norms which are followed today in almost all parts of the Spanish-speaking world.

The Medieval Language

The differences in the pronunciation of typically romance words between Sephardim and speakers of modern Spanish can best be understood by an examination of the spelling of some medieval texts, always recognizing that these do not necessarily provide unquestionable evidence. Unfortunately, few original medieval Spanish manuscripts are known to exist, so that what manuscripts we do have are those of scribes of a period later than the original, where individual errors and norms can be found. If, however, we limit ourselves to frequently used words which show the same traits in many manuscripts, we can be fairly certain of their validity. We will quote several passages from works which appeared between the eleventh and late fifteenth centuries.

1. Dixo el cid, el que en buen hora nasco:
   Graçias, don abbat, e so vuestro pagado.

   Dues fijas dexo niñas, e prendetlas en los braços;
   ....
   dellas e de mi mugier, fagades todo recabdo.[3]
2. Aun otro miraclo vos querría contar
   Que fizo la Gloriosa, non es de olbidar.
   Fuent perenal es ella de qui mana la mar,
   Que en sazon ninguna non çessa de manar.[4]

The narrator of a work introduces a couplet with the moral of the tale in some variant of "Et porque don Iohan tovo este por buen enxiemplo, fozolo escriuir en este libro et fizo estos viessos que dizen assi," after which the couplet follows, as, for example:

3. Por quexa non vos fagan ferir,
   ca siempre vençe quien sabe sofrir.[5]
4. Como dize el sabio, cosa dura e fuerte
   es dexar la costumbre, el fado e la suerte.
   Con grand ira e saña, Saúl que fue rey,
   el primero que los judios ovieron en su ley . . .
   Desque calló el coxo, dixo el tuerto . . .[6]
5. Asi vos fyncastes del   Para muncho turar[7]
   E fazer lo que el   cobdiçiaua librar.

   Vida al fumo trae   El fuego que se amata.

   Enel rrey mete mientes, Toma enxemplo del:
   Mas lazra por las gentes, Que las gentes por el.[8]
6. Dauid, santo e loable,
   sabio e caualleroso,
   quanto noble e glorioso
   fue, non cale que se flable . . .[9]
7. Entonçes perdi la honor, quando dixe mal é oy peor.
   Fallado avedes la gritadera.
   Nin vo, non vengo; was qual sesso tuve, tal cabeça tengo.[10]
8. Nesciuelo, loquito, angelico, perlica, simplezico. . . .
   Mala landre te mate.[11]

Ladino Characteristics

A. Phonetics

In these passages we see that the written *x* in words which in modern Spanish take a *j* (*dixo, dexo, coxo, enxiemplo, quexa*) represents a sound still heard in Judeo-Spanish, the equivalent of our *sh* in English. It is the same *x* which was found in Cervantes' epic *Don Quixote* until the Academy established in the eighteenth century that *x* would have its Latin value and that the sound which had evolved from that *sh* would be represented by *j* in writing. Incidentally, given the original pronunciation of the title of the novel, we can understand why so many European languages preserved the sound (Italian: Chicciotto, French: Quichotte, etc.), while English preserved the spelling (Don Quixote) and changed the sound.

The medieval silent fricative sound *sh* has been preserved by the Sephardic communities until the present time. In Anglo-America, wherever there are speakers of Judeo-Spanish, this and other archaic forms can still be heard. It is one of the most distinguishing characteristics together with the voiced africate *g (dj)* as in 'general,' where modern Spanish has a written *ja, jo, ju* or *ge, gi*. From this we may hypothesize that in the archpriest of Hita's stanza 309 (see above) the word for 'Jews' was probably pronounced with its acute accent, as Sephardim still say it and the voiced *g (dj) judiós*. Equally idiosyncratic is the Judeo-Spanish voiced fricative of French *je* or the *s* of English 'measure', which also appears as a written *j* in Castilian before *a, o,* and *u* or as a *g* before *e* or *i* (i.e., *hija, ija; ajo, ajo; mujer, mujer; diriqir, dirijir*). Another sound which readily identifies the Judeo-Spanish speaker is the voiced fricative *z*, as in English 'dazer, days, these, lazy', which no longer exists in Castilian in an intervocalic position, although in some regions we may hear an *s* followed by certain consonants pronounced as a voiced consonant. Judging from old written texts, we see that *romance* distinguished between a single *s* and a double *ss* or *ç*. Words such as *passar, braços* 'arms', *naçe* 'is born', *çessar* maintain the silent *s* sound and give us *pasar, brasos, nase, sesar*. On the other hand, words written with a single *s* or *r*, which are now pronounced the same as the silent *s*, in Judeo-Spanish are voiced, so that we have *dezir* 'to say', *azer* 'to do', *caza* 'house' and *ermozo* 'beautiful'.

Related to the consonantal variations, we are not surprised to come upon cases of metathesis similar to those encountered today in rural areas and among the less literate in Spain and Hispanic America. The group *rd* easily becomes *dr* (*acodarse, acodrarse* 'to remember', *borde, bodre,* 'border', *gordo, godro* 'fat', *tarde, tadre* 'late, afternoon', *verde, vedre* 'green'). *Prove*, as was said in old Spanish and is still heard today, continues to be the form used in Ladino for 'poor'. The group -*rede* becomes -*dere*, as in *alrededor, alderedor* 'around'; and *cuidado* is rendered *cudiado* 'care'.

While the above represent the most striking holdovers from medieval *romance* that distinguish Ladino from modern Castilian, there are other differences which are exemplary of the pure state of some stressed vowels which in Spanish subsequently either evolved into or from diphthongs. The most frequently used radical changing verbs, such as *pensar, pienso* 'to think, I think', *querer, quiero* 'to want, I want', or *dormir, duermo* 'to sleep, I sleep', are generally rendered as *penso, quero, durmo*, although we find that *tener* 'to have' is conjugated as in modern Spanish *tengo, tienes, tiene* 'I have, you have s/he has'. An undiphthongized *o* is maintained in *scola* for *escuela* 'school', *sola* for *suela* 'sole'. In contrast, we occasionally encounter a reversal of this phenomenon among people, aware of diphthongization, who apply it by analogy to infinitives, giving *quierer*; other verb forms, such as *puedemos* for *podemos* 'we can', *sietiré* for *sentiré* 'I will regret'; *siervo* for *sirvo* 'I serve'; and nouns such as *biervo* for *verbo* 'verb or word', *bandiera* for *bandera* 'flag', *lutio* for *luto* 'mourning', or the adverb *adientro* for *adentro* 'inside'. Diphthongs formed with the semi-vowel *w* (i.e., *au, eu, iu*) tend to maintain their archaic form (*av, ev, iv*): *cavsa, causa* 'cause' and by analogy *cavso, caso* 'case'; *Evropa, Europa, devda, deuda* 'debt'; *civdad, ciudad* 'city'. We should keep in mind that engraved *u* appeared as *v*, and that the confusion was transmitted in printing, along with the further complication that the bilabial *b* and the labiodental *v* were, in fact, pronounced in the same way, depending on their position in the word. We do not need the support of the graphic form to explain the oral survival of the labiodental *v*, since so many other archaisms remain, and the phenomenon appears in scattered regions of the Hispanic world as well.

Finally, as far as the phonics are concerned, it should be noted that Ladino belongs to the large family of Spanish speakers whose pronunciation of words written in Castilian with a double *ll* is equivalent to that of the fricative palatal *y* or *hi* followed by *e* (*ayer* 'yesterday', *yerva, hierba* 'grass', *yelo, hielo* 'ice') and thus we see *yamar, llamar* 'to call', *eva, ella* 'she', *cavayo, caballo* 'horse', etc. Since there is no rule without its exceptions, we can find a limited number of instances where the lateral palatal is preserved, as in *talya, talla* 'figure, form,' and a few in which the *ll* is replaced by a single lateral sound, as in *caleja, calleja* 'street' or *luvia, lluvia* 'rain'.

In light of the general adherence to old *romance* and to variants that are not uncommon in the rest of the Hispanic world, it is striking that many, if not most, Sephardic dialects have lost the very characteristic distinction between the simple vibrant *r* and the multiple *rr*. In the areas which were geographically closest to Spain or where frequent travel to the Peninsula was involved for commercial and other reasons, the trilled or multiple vibrant *rr* is preserved and there is no confusion between *pero* 'but' and *perro* 'dog' or between *caro* 'dear, expensive' and *carro* 'car, cart', as happens in the speech of other areas.

B. Syntax

As we continue to describe the language which was to make its way to the New World, a few observations on syntax and morphology are in order. Basically, the grammatical structure of the sentence, which was already established by the end of the fifteenth century, is maintained with a few variants common to many parts of the Hispanic world. Some medieval carryovers remain, such as the order of pronouns found in combination. Modern Castilian has resolved to place an impersonal reflexive pronoun before a personal pronoun when both are used: *Se me olvidó, te olvidó* 'I forgot, you forgot', whereas Judeo-Spanish still says *Me se olvidó, te se olvidó*, although the modern order occurs in the third person (*Se le olvidó*) and in the plurals. In the instances where we have a direct and an indirect object pronoun ('Give it to her' *Dáelo*), the Castilian order of indirect before direct prevails, as it did in old *romance*: 'I gave it to him' *Se lo di*.

Another case where a medieval form persists, as it does in many places and, especially among children, by analogy with similar constructions is the combination of the preposition *con* 'with' and the singular prepositional pronouns. Correct modern usage is *conmigo, contigo, consigo* 'with me, with you, with her, him, you (polite)! Judeo-Spanish, in accordance with all the other prepositional pronouns, says *con mí, con ti, con él, con eya* (cf. Latin *mecum, tecum* ...).

Adjectives and adverbs present no peculiarities, although Judeo-Spanish does not often avail itself of the fine nuance in meaning achieved by placing an adjective before a noun rather than after, as is more usual. Verbs and tenses function fundamentally as they do in contemporary Spanish. The subjunctive has maintained its place in the language with minor distinctions, such as the general use of the imperfect subjunctive form in *-ra* rather than that in *-se: avlara,* *comiera, escriviera*. At times this imperfect subjunctive is avoided in favor of the imperfect indicative: instead of the conditional statement 'If it weren't so late, I would wait for them', Castilian *Si no fuera tan tarde, les esperaría*, Ladino gives *Si no era tan tadre, los esperaría*.

In lieu of the future of probability ('It is probably 3 p.m.' *Serán las tress de la tarde*) we often find *Deven de ser las tres de la tadre*. The Judeo dialects conserve, as might be expected, a number of grammatical constructions common to regional and folk speech retained in some cases from the medieval language. Such is the case of the double gerundive: 'As, while I was walking, As I went walking along, I met my cousin' *Estando caminando, encontrí a mi prima*; 'As she traveled around, along, she met many people' *Indo viajando, conosió a muncha djente*. Intensive action is expressed as in popular Castilian: *avla que avla, gritan que gritan* 'he talked and talked, they shouted and shouted'.

Other verbal phenomena include the occasional transformation of a reflexive verb into a transitive one: *Se nos pasó el dolor > Mos pasó la dolor*; the use of the auxiliary *tener* in the present perfect: *Le he dicho que no venga > Le tengo dicho que no venga*, while preserving *haber, aver* in other tenses, sometimes interchangeably with *tener*; and the preservation of the old Spanish impersonal *aver* where Castilian now employs *hacer: Hace dos días que se fue > Ay dos días que se fue*.

Prepositions and conjunctions are generally used as in Castilian, although there is confusion in the distinction between *por* and *para*, as often happens to this day among native Spanish speakers. Also, Ladino-speaking people limit themselves to the two basic forms for 'and' and 'or', which are the conjunctions *y* and *o*, even as the average speaker does, eschewing *e* and *u* where the phonics calls for them.

C. Morphology

On the subject of morphology there is somewhat more divergence than in syntax, albeit Ladino remains in its fundamental character a part of the greater Spanish-speaking world. Encounters between Spaniards or Hispanic Americans and Sephardim immediately produce a sense of recognition and affinity. After all, many of the differences, as we have noted, can be attributed to the conservation of archaic forms, a phenomenon common in other parts of the Hispanic world as well.

Such is the case, for example, of words ending in -*or*, which are masculine in Castilian (*el calor, el color, el sabor*, etc.) and feminine in most instances in Ladino (*la calor, la color, la savor*, etc.), although some exceptions are *el vapor* 'boat' and *el amor*. Other old feminines are *la mar*, very widespread in Castilian rural, rustic, and poetic speech, and *la fin*. Furthermore, those nouns beginning with an unstressed *a* are also feminine in Ladino, while some may be masculine in Castilian (*el azúcar, la asúcar* 'sugar', *el alfiler, la alfinete* 'pin'). This use of the feminine article also occurs with feminine words beginning with a stressed *a*, which in Castilian take the masculine article in the singular to avoid the double *a* (*la agua*).

Plurals are formed in the same way as in Castilian, with a few exceptions. One is the use of the Hebrew plural ending in -*m* or -*im* either in Hebrew words or in words related to religion and the Sephardic tradition. Therefore, we find *sefardim, haverim* 'partners', *hahamim* 'rabbis'. Another Hebrew ending which finds its way into an occasional Hispanic noun formed from an adjective is -*oth*, as in the old word for 'lazy', *haragán*, which gives 'laziness' *haraganuth*.[12]

One area in which we recognize the impoverishment of the language is in the reduced number of diminutive suffixes, in which Spanish is so rich. The most prevalent ending is the old -*ico*, -*ica*, and in some Mediterranean and Mid-Eastern dialects it is the only one. Even in these, though, there remains a trace of -*ito*, -*ita* in double diminutives such as *chiquitico* 'tiny' and *poquitico* 'very small amount'. In other dialects -*ito*, -*ita* is more common, either because of the proximity to Spain or because it has been picked up from contemporary Spanish. With proper names we also encounter -*ucha* for women and -*achi* for men, as terms of endearment. While augmentative endings are not frequent (the preferred form is the use of the Turkish adjective for 'large' in some areas: *kodjá*, with the noun), the endings -*in*, -*ona*, and -*anca* do exist.

Collective suffixes are -*ado*, -*ada*, as in *vezindado* 'neighborhood', *calderada* 'potful'; -*dero*, -*dera*, as in *gritadero* 'great shouting', *voradera* 'crying spell'; -*oria*, *dientoria* 'crowd' and -*ería*, *ropería* 'bundle of clothes'. Many suffixes denoting place of origin are similar or identical to the Castilian, with the frequent -*ano*, -*ana* also applied to some forms which Castilian renders in different ways. One of the most prevalent suffixes in this category, reserved primarily for Sephardic people of the Mid-East, is *-lí, -lía* (*izmirlí, izlmirlía, saloniclí, stambolí, chunacalí, monastirlí, castorialí, adjemlí* 'Persian', etc.). Other occasional endings are *-és, -esa* (*francé, inglés*); *-ezo, -eza* (*milanezo, maltezo*); and *-ino, -ina* (*maroguino, turguino*).

Most of the days of the week bear strong resemblance to Castilian or are identical. Such is the case with 'Monday', 'Tuesday', 'Wednesday', and 'Friday' (*lunes, martes, miércoles,* and *viernes*). 'Thursday' is only a phonetic variant of *jueves* (*djugueves*); and 'Saturday' *sábado* is rendered as in the Hebrew from which it comes (*shabat* or *shabá*). The only really divergent day is 'Sunday' (*domingo* in Castilian, from Latin *dominus*), which comes from the Arabic *alhad* or *alhá*. Cardinal numbers retain the Spanish forms closely, except for some pronunciations, but the ordinals present variants: after 'third' the remaining numerals up to 'tenth' end in *-eno* (*cuar teno, cinqueno,* etc.). After that it would be *j* (*la*) *de onze, dodje,* etc. This last is also an alternative form for numbers 'second' through 'tenth'.

While one could detail many traits of the pronunciation, usage, and unique forms of pronouns, we will limit ourselves here to a few outstanding features. Immigrants who arrived before World War II brought with them the use of the third person as a polite form of address. This is probably still the case among the few older people who remain in North America as well as in Europe and the Mid-East. Respect toward parents and between spouses was, until a generation or so ago, expressed by the use of *vos*, as was once the case in Castilian. At the present time most speakers, except the very old, have reduced all second-person pronouns to the familiar *tú* and its plural *vozotros*.

Ladino preserves only two forms of demonstrative pronouns and adjectives, as in English: one for 'this, these' *este, esta, estos, estas,* and one for 'that, those' *aquel, aqueya, agueyos, aqueyas.* Castilian distinguishes between that which is near the person to whom one speaks and that which is far from both speaker and addressee: the former being *ese, esa, esos, esas* and the latter *aquel, aqella, aquellos, aquellas.* The interrogative pronouns are similar to Castilian, if we allow for slight variations in pronunciation not uncommon in the Hispanic world. However, Ladino treats *cuál,* 'which one' as a masculine form, using *cuálo* for the feminine (plurals: *cuáles, cuálos, cuálas*) and *cuála* for the neuter. *Cuál, cuáles* are the only forms in Castilian, and there is no neuter, for that is rendered by *qué*. Also unlike Castilian, which has a differentiating indefinite pronoun for persons (*alguien* 'someone', *nadie* 'no one'), Ladino uses *alguno, -a, ninguno, -a* for persons as well as for inanimate objects, and also to indicate 'one' or 'none' of a group of persons or objects, as in Castilian.

With regard to verb forms, as for other parts of speech, the basic rules that pertain are the same as in Castilian, with some variations. Once again, we will not go into differences in pronunciation. Perhaps the most prominent trait is the application to first-conjugation verbs (*avlar* 'to speak') of the preterite endings common to the second (*comer* 'to eat') and third (*bivir* 'to live') conjugations, ending in stressed *avlí* for *hablé* 'I spoke', etc. This does not occur in the preterite of irregular verbs, which follow tradition (*dishe, dije* 'I said', *pude, pude* 'I could'). However, some archaic forms, common also to rural areas of Spain, are conserved. Thus we have *trushe* 'I brought' for *traje*, and *vide* 'I saw' for modern *vi*. The imperfect of the verb 'to see' *ver*, which in Old Spanish was *veer*, has lost its initial *e* and is rendered *via*, as also occurs in medieval *romance*.[13] It is an instance in which the dialects and rural speech, normally so conservative, drop an old form still preserved in modern Spanish. This phenomenon also applies to the verb *leer* 'to read', but it, at least, still maintains both *e*'s. The Judeo-Spanish dialects rarely use this verb, preferring *meldar*, of Hebrew extraction. It should also be mentioned that like *veer* the verb 'to be' *ser* was originally *seer*, but its conjugations are irregular in both imperfect and preterite, and Ladino conforms to the Castilian.

Another feature of the various Judeo-Spanish dialects which they share with regions of the Hispanic world is the prefix *a* before many verbs: *rascar* 'to scratch' becomes *arascar*, *limpiar* > *alimpiar* 'to clean', *bajar* > *abashar* 'to descend', Other examples are *alevantar(se)* 'to raise, pick up, get up', *arazgar* 'to tear', *aremendar* 'to mend', *asentar(se)* 'to seat, be seated', *araviarse* 'to get angry'. One curious instance is that of *amatar* 'to extinguish' as opposed to *matar* 'to kill' (see above, example 5).

D. Vocabulary

In order to give some sense of the linguistic patchwork that has woven itself into the basic Spanish language over five centuries and which survives to this day, we include a sampling of words from the languages which have left a lasting mark on Judeo-Spanish. Any of these words may appear in any of the dialects from North Africa to Istanbul, especially the Hebrew, most of which are basic to the life of Jews. Of course, one can expect more Arabic in North Africa and little or no Turkish there, while the Mid-East communities use more Turkish. Words which exist in Castilian are not included. We have chosen as an example to list words all of which appear in the dialect originally from Izmir and now spread throughout North America. Other words, Serbo-Croatian in Monastir, more Greek in Salonica, for instance, pepper those dialects. Concentrating a bit on the configuration in one area will illustrate the mosaic well.

HEBREW

aftahá - hope, confidence
balabay - male head of household
beemá, behemá - animal
berahá - blessing
birith - ceremony of circumcision
cahal - synagogue
cavod - respect
gaviento - proud
haber - news
haftoná - spanking

hamor - donkey, stupid
haver - partner
hohmá - wisdom
kehilá - synagogue
lashón - language, chatter
mijpahá - family
muel - circumciser
seclet - worry, trouble
sedacá - alms, charity
sehorá - pain, disillusionment
tanith - fast
tifilá - prayer

FRENCH

adreso - address
amator - amateur, lover of
antica - antique
azardo - chance (cf. It.)
arivada - arrival
arivar - to arrive
berber - barber
bijuc - jewel
botoniera - buttonhole, boutonniére

casqueto - cap
cordela - ribbon
cuvierta - blanket
dandjerozo - dangerous
dantela - lace
data - date
dezabiyé - woman's loose garment
engagé - arm in arm
englutir - to swallow

envelop - envelope
espondjar - to sponge
factoría - factory
furnitura - furniture
gravata - necktie
mashina - machine
mashinistro - machinist
matmazel - young lady, mademoiselle
mostarda - mustard
pantuflas - slippers
parada - parade
pelerina - cape, cloak
polís - policeman

postier - postman
propozar - to suggest, propose
pruna - prune
pudra - face powder
refusar - to refuse
regretar - to regret
reushir - to succeed
sharpa - scarf
sezón - season
vacansas - vacation
validja - suitcase, valise
visaví - closet with full-length mirror

ITALIAN
achetar - accept
adío - goodbye
avocato - lawyer
capache - capable
carosa - carriage, coach
carosero - coachman
djaqueta - jacket
Djermania - Germany
djermano - German
empidegado - employee

forqueta - hairpin
grizo - gray
lavoro - work
peto - lapel
pirón - fork
posta - mail
putana - prostitute (cf. Fr.)
salata - salad (cf. Gr.)
sigareto - cigarette
valuta - value

GREEK
bamia - okra
bizel (also *pizel, pinzel*) - pea
bira - beer (cf. It.)
bleta - pleat
chanta - handbag, purse
chapura - carp (ichth.)
fildján - cup (cf. Turk.)
foresiá - suit
fustán - dress

gravata - necktie (cf. Fr., It.)
horó - dance
indiano - turkey
maimona - monkey
nicocherá - housewife
patrioti - patriot
perdé - curtain
prasa - leeks
quinezo - Chinese

GREEK (cont.)
reclama - advertisement (cf. Fr.)
sardela - sardine
scara - spit (cooking)
soy - lineage, family
spirto - match

TURKISH
aharvar - to strike, spank
ahchí - cook
amán - interjection
apansiz - suddenly
arabá - cart, wagon, wheelbarrow
aversís - ugly
bacal - grocer
bahchován - farmer
batal - idle
beguenear - to accept
bezer - tired
bicliador - meddlesome
bicliar - to meddle
bilbil, bilbul, bulbul - nightingale
bilibiz - pea, garbanzo
boy - size
boyá - paint
boyadjí - painter
buchuc - twin
buz - ice
buzaná - freezing, icy
calabalic - crowd, to-do
capac - pan lid
carar - amount
carpuz - watermelon
casap - butcher
chadir - umbrella
chalum - airs (to put on airs)
chamashir - undershirt
charshí - market
chiní - plate
chizmez - boot
churap - stocking
clapá - lapel
colay - easy
condjá - rose
condjero - rosebush
cuchunduria - beets
cushac - belt
cutí - box
daúl - tambourine
dest - trouble
djam - window pane
dolap - closet
dumán - smoke, vapor
enbenear - to mount
farashaná - dust pan
findján - cup
furcha - brush
haír - profit, benefit
hal - problem, trouble
hiram - blanket
hodjá - master
kióstec - chain
kirikic - peanut
libric - Turkish coffee pot
meraclí - neat, fastidious
musafir - guest
mushamá - oilcloth, linoleum
mushterí - client, customer

TURKISH (cont)
nishán - scar, sign
pachá - leg
pailón - large pot
patladearse - to burst
peltec - tongue-tied
saraf - moneylender
sekiliar(se), secliar(se) - to worry
shacá - joke
shadriván - fountain
shamatá - noise
sharsheo - dizziness

shushulera - diarrhea
tahtás - flat slippers
tavá - tray
taván - ceiling
tashtiriar - to mix, stir
tendjeré - tin
tifsín - oven pan, tray
trushí - pickles; *en* - pickled
utí - iron (for pressing)
yelec - vest

ENGLISH
adrés - address
bel - bell
djanitor - janitor
envelop - envelope
farma - farm

farmero - farmer
fridjider - refrigerator
vedjiteble - vegetable
yok - egg yolk

ARABIC
alhad - Sunday

alminara - candle holder

SLAVIC
rizá - handkerchief

Conclusion

We have attempted to provide an abbreviated analysis of those features which, in one degree or another, characterized the speech of the Sephardic people when they immigrated to America in the late nineteenth and early twentieth centuries. To a large extent, the newcomers seem to have gravitated to many of the same places as those who arrived in colonial times. While the latter no longer preserved the language of their heritage, except where it may have been assimilated into the Sephardic ritual, they seem to have blazed a trail for the later arrivals, by making their way south and west for commercial reasons in the seventeenth century, as participants in the War of Independence and in the Civil War, or in search of fortune during the Gold

Rush. Many forged on northward into Canada seeking commercial opportunities and a better life, first in the East, later in the West. It should be noted, however, that early settlements and congregations tended to develop along the coasts, where seaports favored entrepreneurial activities. Those centers received the first Jewish immigrants from Germany, Austria, and other parts of Europe. Even though the newcomers were not Sephardim, they initially joined the Sephardic congregations. These Ashkenazim eventually outnumbered the Jews of Iberian origin and founded their own congregations.

The earliest communities were formed in Newport, Rhode Island, in what is now New York City, and in Philadelphia. The former, which still maintains the oldest Sephardic synagogue in North America, was gradually depleted by migrations to Massachusetts, notably the Boston area, and other parts after the 1812 war with England ended the prosperity of the community. Before the Revolutonary War the colonies already had three other congregations in Richmond, Savannah, and Charleston. In the early nineteenth century Judah Touro had left Newport and established himself in New Orleans, where he amassed a large fortune and was an important participant in Andrew Jackson's defense of that city in 1814–15.

By the mid-nineteenth century we also find affluent communities of merchants, manufacturers, and developers in Montreal. Although congregations remained small, since there were never very large numbers of Sephardim, they continued to organize in Canada and the United States in Atlanta, Louisville, Los Angeles, Seattle, and other cities. In some cases brotherhoods and sisterhoods were established according to the city of origin, but even when immigrants from one area dominated, there tended to be a mixture of Sephardim from various communities abroad. There are, indeed, a few cases in which a whole group was settled in one locale, and their lingüistic and cultural features were best preserved.

In reviewing the language of the Spanish Jews across North America, two factors stand out which underlie their entire history from the time of the expulsion five hundred years ago. First and foremost is the amazing capacity to preserve their linguistic heritage and, second, the gradual and unobtrusive absorption of features of the local and contemporary cultures in which they lived. Pronunciation was never much influenced by exposure to a new language; it was mainly vocabulary that infiltrated. The same pattern is found to be true in Anglo-America. All the Spanish, Hebrew, Turkish, Greek, Serbo-Croatian, etc., which the immigrants brought with them, remained. To that were added some new words, which those who live in heavily Hispanic neighborhoods will recognize as having filtered into the speech of the local Hispanic population as well, such as *grosería* 'grocery store'.

While there are still speakers of the various Judeo-Spanish dialects, it must be noted, with sadness, that Ladino is rapidly disappearing as a living language. Extraordinary efforts are being made to record it, and there is a revival of the folklore, in particular the music, of which there are now many recordings. But the strength of English for second- and third-generation Americans has been great to overcome. The language is disappearing likewise in other parts of the world for different reasons, such as the ease of adapting to modern Spanish in the Hispanic countries and the ease of adapting to the Sephardic pronunciation of Hebrew in Israel. That is why it is essential to recognize and record, not only the significance of this well-preserved heritage to scholars of Spain and Portugal, but the great wealth of history, lore, music, and language which seeped into the cultures of all the scattered areas which the Sephardic passage has touched.

Notes

1. In modern Spanish *ladino* refers to any foreign language (*hablar en ladino*), and in Latin American countries it denotes Indians who speak Spanish.

2. The adjective *ladino, ladina* was used in the fifteenth century to describe works written in a cultured, artistic language close to educated Latin. Toward the end of the sixteenth century, when Castilian was fairly stabilized, the adjective had acquired the quality of a personal characteristic, moving from "artful" to "artificial," from "cultured" and "Latinate" to "clever" and "crafty," until it took its present acceptation of "astute, foxy, sly."

3. *Cantar de Mío Cid* (12th cent.), paleographic edition of Ramón Menéndez Pidal (Madrid, 1946), pp. 916–917. "The Cid said, 'Thank you, Sir Abbot, and I am your debtor'" (v. 248). "I leave two small daughters, and take them into your arms" (v. 255). "Take every care of them and of my wife" (v. 257).

4. Poem by Gonzalo de Berceo (13th cent.), ed. C. Carroll Marden, *Revista de Filología Española* 9 (Madrid, 1928). "I would like to relate another miracle—which the glorious Virgin performed, that shouldn't be forgotten. / She is the eternal foundation from which the sea emerges, which at no time ever ceases to flow" (p. 45).

5. Don Juan Manuel, *Libro de los Enxemplos del Conde Lucanor et de Patronio* (13th cent.), ed. J. M. Blecua (Madrid, 1969). "And because Don Juan considered this a good lesson, he had it written in this book and composed the verses which say..." (p. 176). "Don't be upset because of complaints, for the one who is patient always conquers" (p. 112).

6. Juan Ruiz, archpriest of Hita, *Libro de Buen Amor* (14th cent.), ed. Raymond S. Willis (Princeton University Press, 1972). "As the wise man says, it is a hard and difficult thing to get free of custom, fate, and fortune" (pp. 52–53). "From great wrath and anger, Saul, who was king, the first that the Jews had under their laws [religion]" (pp. 91–92). "When the lame man stopped speaking, the one-eyed one said..." (pp. 128–129). Other examples of *judíos* with acute accent appear in strophes 1063 (p. 293), 1193 (p. 327), 1657 (p. 447).

7. Other examples of *muncho* for *mucho* appear in lines 1262, 1270, 1320, and 1385. This alternates with numerous cases of *mucho*.

8. Santob de Carrión (Shem Tob ibn Ardutiel b. Isaac), *Proverbios Morales* (14th cent.), ed. Ignacio González Llubera (Cambridge University Press, 1947). "In the same way you were left by him, to last a long time / And to do what he longed to carry out" (p. 64). "The fire which is extinguished brings life to the smoke" (p. 101). "Pay attention to the king, take an example from him: / He toils more for the people, than the people for him" (p. 104).

9. Fernán Pérez de Guzmán, *Coplas de Vicios Virtudes*, in *Generaciones y Semblanzas* (14th cent.), ed. R. B. Tate (London, 1965). "David was saintly and praiseworthy, wise and chivalrous, as well as noble and glorious, one must not speak of it..." (p. 76).

10. Iñigo López de Mendoza, marquis of Santillana, *Proverbios* (15th cent.), in *Páginas Escogidas*, ed. Fernando Gutiérrez (Barcelona, 1939). "I lost my honor when I spoke ill and heard worse" (p. 266). "You've discovered where the noise is coming from. / (Now you've uncovered the truth.)" (p. 266). "I'm neither coming nor going; but the brains I had give me the head I have" (p. 268).

11. Fernando de Rojas, *Comedia de Calisto* (1499, 1502), ed. R. Foulché-Delbosc (Barcelona and Madrid, 1902). "Little fool madcap, angel, little gem, simpleton... / May a terrible tumor kill you" (p. 23).

12. Note that *h* is now silent in Castilian. It is used in our text to represent sound in Ladino.

13. Analogic forms are as common in Judeo-Spanish as they are in the larger Hispanic community in the speech of rural dwellers, of people with little formal education, and of course, of children. Thus it is that on the pattern of some irregular forms in the first-person singular of the present tense (e.g., *traigo* 'I bring'), we find *creigo* 'I believed', *veigo* 'I see', *fuygo* 'I flee', *destruygo* 'I destroy', *riygo* 'I laugh', *friygo* 'I fry', and the corresponding present subjunctives which are formed like the present indicative. In the case of *ir* 'to go' the irregularity is limited to the present subjunctive *vaiga*, while the present indicative is *vo*, as in medieval *romance*, for *voy* in Castilian (cf. also *so* for *soy*). A similar case is that of *aiga* for *haya*, the present subjunctive of *aver, haber* 'to have', very common among Spanish speakers.

Selected Bibliography

Barocas, David N. *Ladino, Judezmo and the Spanish-Jewish Dialect*. New York, 1976.
Benoliel, J. "Dialecto judeo-hispano-marroquí o hakitía." *Boletín de la Real Academia Española* 13 (1926).
Bunis, David N. "Problems in Judezmo Linguistics." *Working Papers in Sephardic and Oriental Jewish Studies*, vol. 1. New York, 1945.

———. *The Historical Development of Judezmo Orthography: A Brief Sketch.* New York: Yivo Institute for Jewish Research, 1974.

Crews, Cynthia. *Recherches sur le Judeo-Espagnol dans les pays balkaniques.* Paris, 1935.

Lapesa, Rafael M. *Historica de la Lengua Española.* Madrid.

Levy, Denah. *El Sefardi Esmirniano de Nueva York.* Mexico City, 1952.

———. "Pronunciación del sefardi esmirniano de Nueva York." *Nueva Revista de Filologia Hispanica* 6 (1952).

Luria, Max. *A Study of the Monastir Dialect of Judeo-Spanish Based on Oral Material Collected in Monastir, Yugoslavia.* New York, 1930.

Nehama, Joseph, with Jesús Cantera. *Dictionnaire du Judeo-Espagnol.* Madrid, 1977.

Pascual Recuero, Pascual. *Diccionario Basico Ladino-Español.* Barcelona, 1977.

Sephiha, Haim Vidal. *Le Ladino (Judeo-Espagnol Calque).* Paris, 1973.

The Sacred and Secular Musical Traditions of the Sephardic Jews in the United States

Israel J. Katz

For almost a century and a quarter (1654–1776), Jewish religious and cultural life during the colonial period was dominated entirely by the Sephardim. The liturgical practices followed were those established in the early part of the seventeenth century by Portuguese conversos in the emancipated congregations of Amsterdam,[1] and which also served as the model for synagogues in London (Sahar Asamaim, also known as Bevis Marks),[2] Bayonne (Nefusoth Yehudah), Bordeaux (Sha'are Rachamim), and Hamburg (Beth Israel).[3]

The year 1654 marked the arrival in Nieuw Amsterdam of twenty-three Jews who had fled from Recife (Pernambuco), Brazil, when the Portuguese conquered this vital port—held since 1630 by the Dutch, under whom it had become a refuge for Portuguese Marranos. More than a decade earlier, in 1642, the Haham Isaac Aboab de Fonseca (1605–1693), leader of the Amsterdam Sephardic community, and Hazzan Moses Raphael de Aguilar (d. 1679) had sojourned in Recife for the purpose of ministering to "the spiritual needs of the large community of Marranos who had recently declared their Jewish identity."[4]

The twenty-three men, women, and children who survived the perilous sea journey were undoubtedly among those instructed by the learned rabbi and hazzan in matters of Judaism and the liturgy. In the year following their arrival in Nieuw Amsterdam, they formed their own congregation, naming it Shearith Israel, and it was here that the Amsterdam liturgy was transplanted on North American soil.[5] In succeeding generations, other Sephardic communities were established on the East Coast, all of which have continued to practice the Amsterdam rite up to the present time.[6]

Documentation is sparse concerning the music and manner in which the varied Sephardic synagogue services were conducted during the colonial period, even though we have learned from historical sources that the liturgy was almost entirely dominated by music, either intoned, chanted, or sung to strophic and non-strophic melodies. The role and responsibilities of the hazzan are explicitly documented in the minutes of the trustees of each congregation, wherein the changing attitudes toward music during the Sabbath and holiday services, as well as toward social events—particularly weddings—in the synagogue, are also reflected. While it is difficult to reconstruct the earliest worship services of the New York congregation and of the other Sephardic congregations that evolved in colonial times, we must assume that their traditional melodies were totally of Old World origin.[7]

The earliest musical compendium containing the so-called "traditional melodies" was that of a sister congregation, Bevis Marks in London, which was published in 1857.[8] Of the seventy melodies printed therein, sixty-nine of which are harmonized, D. A. de Sola (1796–1860),[9] hazzan and preacher at Bevis Marks, had the temerity to date two of them "prior to the settlement of the Jews in Spain" and forty-seven as "melodies composed in Spain, and subsequently introduced by the Israelites into the various countries in which they took refuge from the persecution in the Iberian Peninsula."[10] Jacob Hadida, who was entrusted with the task of revising the melodies in 1948, made reference to de Sola's classification of "the so-called traditional tunes," stating that the "only truly traditional melodies . . . are those interpreted from Tangameem [*te'amim* ("tropes")] for the Parashah, Haftorah, Megilot, and the Tehilim."[11]

Apart from the traditional songs which they sang during synagogue worship services for the Sabbath, High Holidays, and festivals, the Sephardim maintained a rich repertoire of paraliturgical melodies for use in the home on Sabbaths, holidays, and feasts—Sukkot, Simhat Torah, Hannukah, Tu b'Shvat, Purim, Passover, Lag b'Omer, Shavuot, and including the elegies (*kinnot*) chanted on Tisha b'Av and during the week preceding it. Strophic hymns sung in Hebrew, Portuguese, and, in recent times, Judeo-Spanish also played an important role in both the synagogue and home.[12] In addition, there were numerous paraliturgical songs that accompanied the circumcision and wedding ceremonies, as well as special dirges (*endechas*) connected with death and burial rites.

An example of the musical links between Amsterdam's K.K. Talmud Torah, London's Bevis Marks, and Shearith Israel can be found in the *zemer* for the High Holidays, *Et sha'are ratzon* (see Ex. 1).[13] However, here, taking the London example (1a) as the earliest published melody, we can compare it with the tune that was known in Amsterdam (1b). Examples 1c and 1d are presently sung on the High Holidays at Shearith Israel. Comparisons such as this will yield greater insights into the transmission of tunes among the three dominant communities (London, Amsterdam, and New York).[14]

Example 1: *Et sha'are ratzon*
a. Bevis Marks (D. A. de Sola, *The Ancient Melodies*, no. 30).
b. Talmud Torah (transcribed by M. R. Kanter, *Traditional Melodies* p. 569).[15]
c. Shearith Israel (D. and T. de Sola Pool, *An Old Faith*, p. 150).[16]
d. Shearith Israel (A. L. Cardozo, *Sephardic Songs of Praise*, p. 68).[17]

continued on next page

(N.B. The cadential portion of the first melody phrase is seen immediately in the Shearith Israel examples. In phrase 2, the initial portion of the London tune, and its ascent to a', sets it apart from the others. At the beginning of phrase 3, the text "Ana [O God]" is rendered with a melisma, whose axis appears to be the tone g; yet oddly enough the Shearith Israel version [1c] concurs with London's cadential tone, while the other [1d] concurs with the Amsterdam. And in the last phrase, 1c differs in the opening portion, while the three [1a, 1b, and 1c–d] differ remarkably in their final cadences.)

Among other examples exhibiting differences between the musical liturgies of Shearith Israel and Bevis Marks are *Haskivenu*, *Adon Olam*, and *Az yashir Moshe* (from the Sabbath liturgy); *Ki eshmera shabbat*, a variant (a *zemer* for Shabbat); *Adonai bekol shofar*, a variant (sung during the High Holidays); *Schachar Abakeschka* (sung on weekdays before the morning service); and *Beruchim atem*, a variant (sung at circumcision ceremonies).

* * *

The earliest phonograph recordings of Judeo-Spanish songs made in the United States were produced by Kaliphone Records, Mayesh Phonograph Record Co., Me Re Records, Metropolitan Recording Co. and Polyphon. The latter dates back to the early 1920s. Kaliphone, Mayesh, Me Re, and Metropolitan were popular labels among the Sephardim in the early 1940s. The recorded repertoire featured lyric, wedding, and Zionist songs, *romances* ("ballads"), etc., and even Hebrew songs by such popular vocalists as Victoria Hazan and Jack Mayesh. Many of these recordings were advertised, together with their contents, in the popular Judeo-Spanish newspaper *La Vara*.

However, the first scientific attempt in the United States to make field recordings of Judeo-Spanish songs occurred at Columbia University in 1930. Under the advice of Professor Franz Boas of the anthropology department, Zarita Nahón, a graduate student from Tangier, undertook a study of the Moroccan Sephardic dialect (*haketía*). Upon returning from a six-month field trip to Morocco, she enlisted the aid of her sister, Simy (Suzanne) Nahón de Toledano, to sing a goodly number of the ballads and songs she had collected. The recordings were made under the supervision of Professor Boas.[18]

Later that year Professor Federico de Onís of the Spanish department invited Simy to record some of the ballads at the Casa de las Españas. Subsequently de Onís himself recorded informants from the Sephardic communities of Salonika (Mentesh Amiras, Elvira Ben David, Ishak Sustiel, Maria Vivas) and Rhodes (Clara Turiel) for the purpose of archiving specimens of Judeo-Spanish from the Eastern Mediterranean.[19] Also in the early 1930s, Emma Adatto Schlesinger recorded ballads, songs, and folktales among Turkish and Rhodian informants residing in the Sephardic community of Seattle, Washington.[20]

It was not until the 1950s that academic interest in Judeo-Spanish folklore and music was renewed. Informants from Rhodes residing in Atlanta, Georgia, supplied the sung texts for two important studies that contain the earliest musical transcriptions of Judeo-Spanish songs made directly from field recordings. In the first, published in 1951, Daniel D. Stanley transcribed five ballad melodies and two lyrical songs directly from gramophone recordings.[21] In the second study, actually a master's thesis, Isaac Jack Lévy enlisted the aid of Garret Laning, Harry Kruger, and Robert M. Arnett respectively, to provide musical transcriptions for three of his collected song texts.[22]

A third study, published in 1960, lacked the musical component but merits mention because it was the first of a collaborative effort aimed at studying systematically the ballad corpus (*Romancero*) of Judeo-Spanish informants from the Balkan region who had recently immigrated to the United States (Los Angeles, Seattle, San Francisco, and New York).[23] Professors Samuel G. Armistead and Joseph H. Silverman, who initiated this study in August of 1957, soon realized the importance of an interdisciplinary link with musicology, whereupon Israel J. Katz joined their endeavor in 1959.[24]

The trio had completed three decades of collaborative research by the time of Professor Silverman's death on March 23, 1989. The first of their multi-volume series, bearing the title *Judeo-Spanish Ballads from Oral Tradition* (Berkeley and Los Angeles, 1986), was published before he died, and his wisdom and untiring dedication will continue to inform subsequent volumes.[25]

Numerous musical transcriptions provided by other researchers have been published since 1971. They too were made directly from field tapes and comprise material collected in San Antonio, Texas

(1971),[26] Los Angeles (1972–1973 and 1984),[27] Seattle (1973),[28] and New York (1979).[29]

We know very little about the traditional secular songs that the Sephardim of the Western European communities—primarily Amsterdam and London—brought to the United States. However, since the turn of this century, immigrants from the diverse Sephardic communities of the Eastern Mediterranean region have carried with them a rich storehouse of song. Its relics comprise such genres as *romances* ("ballads"), *muwashshahat, zejeles, coplas* ("couplets"), and *endechas* ("dirges"), which date from pre-expulsion times on the Iberian Peninsula.

We are fortunate that many traditional song texts have been preserved in manuscript and printed sources from fifteenth- and sixteenth-century Spain and Portugal, yet very few of them contain musical notation. A goodly number of their opening verses were cited as tune indicators in Judeo-Spanish songsters, chapbooks, and broadsides (utilizing Rashi characters), as well as in Hebrew songsters and hymnals that enjoyed wide circulation among the Mediterranean Sephardic communities from the sixteenth century on.

In spite of these invaluable textual links, we lack evidence upon which to reconstruct earlier musical practices. Nonetheless, there are other stylistic links that bear relevance to the Iberian tradition, namely formal structure, modes, traditional cadences, and regional melodic traits that were known to exist prior to the sixteenth century.

In two previous studies, recently republished as one, I examined the musical aspects of the Judeo-Spanish *Romancero*, wherein I distinguished two basic styles which separate the sung repertoires of the Eastern Mediterranean from those of the North African Sephardic communities, and postulated a third which emanated from Greece.[30] Inasmuch as the Eastern style was the more dominant among the Sephardic immigrants who came to America during the first half of this century, it is truly sad to report that this tradition will not survive beyond the second generation that was nurtured by them.

The greater part of all the material gathered to date in the United States, and most recently from Canada,[31] which still awaits both textual and musical transcriptions, will enable present and future scholars to study the entire repertoire brought to these shores. Moreover, it will eventually be linked to the vast material recorded throughout Latin America, North Africa, the Eastern Mediterranean, and Israel.

* * *

Of the eleven representative textual examples provided by my colleague, Professor Samuel G. Armistead, seven were sung (see his essay in this volume). All were recorded from informants who immigrated from the Eastern Mediterranean region. While Armistead's comments relate specifically to the linguistic, literary/thematic, and folkloric aspects of their contents, it should prove interesting to examine the sung examples from the standpoint of their actual performance, and to provide published tunes of Eastern Mediterranean provenance for those which were recited. While room does not permit a complete transcription of each, I have notated either the initial or subsequent strophe of each example, indicating, in the latter case, the specific one. As mentioned above, the Eastern Mediterranean examples conform to stylistic principles which differentiate them from those practiced among the Sephardic communities of North Africa (mainly Morocco and Algeria). Hereon I shall follow the order of my colleague's presentation (enclosed in parentheses).

Example 2 (= Armistead 1.1): *Gaiferos jugador*

continued on next page

Musical Traditions of the Sephardic Jews

The highly melismatic rendition of the ballad *Gaiferos jugador* ("Gaiferos the Gambler") clearly exhibits a style that was foreign to the Iberian Peninsula. Here, in the span of eight melody phrases, the informant, from Salonika, has completed four textual hemistichs, the second of which is repeated:

⌐———1———⌐
Por los palacious de Carlo
—2—⌐—3—⌐—4—
y non pasan sinon ǧugare
————5————⌐
y non pasan si non ǧugare
—6—⌐—7—⌐
y non gugare plata ni oro,
⌐———8———⌐
sino vias y sivdades.

Notice the similarity between the second and sixth and between the initial and fifth melody phrases. The range comprises an octave. The dotted bar lines indicate the singer's accentuation of the sung text. I have avoided a discussion of mode, due to the nature of the informant's erratic intonation. To my knowledge this is the only published musical example for this ballad.

Example 3 (= Armistead 1.2): *El pozo airón*

The version edited by Armistead was recited. Tunes for *El pozo airón* ("The Bottomless Well") from the Eastern tradition have been collected by Manrique de Lara (in Sofia) (see Ex. 3), Michael Molho (Salonika), and Isaac Levy (Jerusalem and Turkey).[32] Molho's tune is a close variant of Manrique de Lara's. Both comprise a quatrain strophe ABCD, with C carrying the refrain burden " ¡Y guay que dolor!," and D, the repeated second textual hemistich. They are also based on a Major hexachord, ending on the third degree. Levy's Jerusalem tune encompasses a Major pentachord (b to f-sharp), and that from Izmir, an octave (e-flat to e-flat; based on *finalis* f). The former bears the strophic structure $A^{w+x}A^{w+y}A^{w+z}BC$, wherein melody phrases B and C each carry the fourth textual hemistich. In the latter tune, the relationship between the melody phrases and textual hemistichs can be depicted as $\begin{array}{c} ABABCDCD. \\ ababcdcd \end{array}$

Example 4 (= Armistead 2.1): *La moxca y la mora* (from Rhodes)

The cumulative song *La moxca y la mora* ("The Fly and the Moorish Girl") can also be found among Alberto Hemsi's tunes from the tradition of Rhodes.[33] Here we give the initial and final cumulative strophes. It is sung in a simple duple meter (2/2), whereas the Hemsi variant is notated in a compound duple meter (6/8). Both are based on a Major pentachord.

Example 5 (= Armistead 2.2): *Un cavretico*

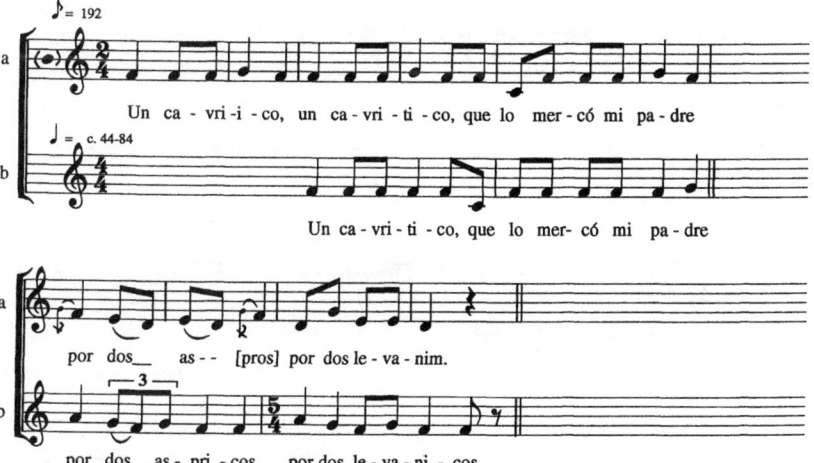

It is unfortunate that Armistead's informant recited this well-known allegorical Passover song, *Un cavretico* ("A Little Goat"), for which Léon Algazi cited three melodic versions (1958: nos. 25–27), the latter of which is reproduced here (see Ex. 5a), and for which both Isaac Levy and Abraham A. Schwadron collected many other examples.[34] Among the numerous tunes from the Eastern Mediterranean region that accompany this text, it should prove instructive to compare a rendition from Salonika (Algazi, no. 27), recorded by Constantin Braïloïu and Léon Algazi in Paris, with that from Monastir, recorded by Abraham Schwadron in Brooklyn, New York, in 1976 (see Ex. 5b).[35]

Though both tunes share the same *ambitus*, a Major 6th, and basically the same meter, the former comprises a Dorian hexachord (based on the *finalis* d̲), while the latter, a Major hexachord (based on f̲).

Example 6 (= Armistead 3.1): *Cantiga de parida* (from Salonika)

continued on next page

Our *cantiga de parida* ("Birth Song") comprises yet another melodic version which can be added to those collected by Edith Gerson-Kiwi, Isaac Levy, and Susana Weich-Shahak.[36] Here I have transcribed only the second textual stanza.

Example 6 conforms to the basic musical characteristics discussed by Susana Weich-Shahak, who studied this genre. It is in duple (2/4 meter), and its melodic movement is mainly diatonic (with occasional intervals of a minor 3rd). However, its range, comprising a minor hexachord (d-e-f-g-a-b-flat), is an exception to her inclusion of wide ranges (exceeding a 7th and above) in her breakdown of characteristics. The tune's structure, ABCB'DE, mirrors the textual stanza, while the refrain strophe, *Ya es . . .*, is rendered as *FGHI*. Notice the singer's use of ornamentation as well as the recurring motive "x" in melody phrases A, B, and G.

The version collected by Weich-Shahak carries the same refrain as our Example 6; those of Lévy (Izmir and Turkey), only its initial verse "Ya es ya es buen *simán* esta alegría [var. `criatura' (Izmir)]." Yet Gerson-Kiwi's example includes an entirely different refrain text comprising three verses: "Fino fin' e florido / todo bien complido / che viva el parido." Only Lévy's example (from Jerusalem) was sung without a refrain. All were rendered in duple meter (2/4); however, marked differences among them can be seen in their text-tune relationships, *ambitus*, and mode.

1. Gerson-Kiwi (Salonika): $\frac{ABAB'CDE}{abcdefg}$, Major 7th, Minor mode ending on the third degree. It should be mentioned that melody phrase E carries bears basically the cadential figuration as phrase B'.

2. Lévy (Jerusalem): $\begin{smallmatrix}\text{ABC}DAB,\\ \text{a b c d e f}'\end{smallmatrix}$ minor 7th, Major mode ending on the third degree, or it may be analyzed as the E mode ending with a Phrygian cadence.

3. Lévy (Izmir): $\begin{smallmatrix}\text{ABAB}CBCD,\\ \text{a b c d}efef'\end{smallmatrix}$ minor 7th, same modal analysis as previous example.

4. Lévy (Turkey): two strophes, $\begin{smallmatrix}\text{ABABAB}'CD\ /\ \text{EFGHIJ}KL,\\ \text{a b c d e f }gh\qquad \text{i j k l m n}gh\end{smallmatrix}$ diminished 12th, bi-modal characteristics (Major/minor), falling into same analytical category as the two previous examples.

5. Weich-Shahak (Salonica). $\begin{smallmatrix}\text{ABABCD}EFGH\\ \text{a b c d e f}ghij\end{smallmatrix}$ Major 9th. The analysis rendered in her article (p. 101) favors the E mode, also bearing the Phrygian cadence, and which she places in the *maqam Huzam*.

Thus, compared with textual counterparts from the Eastern Mediterranean region, our example can be documented as authentic, even though its modality is basically minor (*finalis* d). Note also that only its melodic phrase B is repeated.

Example 7 (= Armistead 3.2): *Canto de boda* (from Salonika)

continued on next page

Musical Traditions of the Sephardic Jews

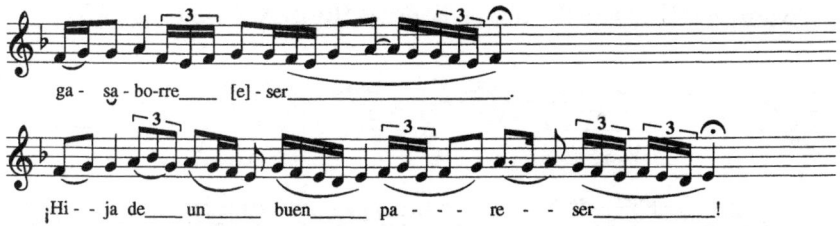

ga - sa - bo-rre___ [e] - ser___

¡Hi - - ja de___ un___ buen___ pa - - re - - ser___!

The wedding song *Hija mía, si te vas* ("My daughter, if you are departing") (Ex. 7) hardly conforms to the highly spirited and tuneful songs that are known in Sephardic communities throughout the Mediterranean region.[37] The text, which Armistead alludes to as fragmentary, and whose second verse appears to belong to another nuptial song, bears an uneven number of verses in each stanza. No other tunes have been discovered for this text.

The initial melody phrase appears to hover around the tonal axis a' before descending to the cadential tone f, which accounts for four of the phrasal cadential tones, while the remaining three end on e. Upon reaching the cadential tone of the third melody phrase, the informant raised her actual pitch level a semitone higher—which is not reflected in the notation. Such fluctuations have been encountered in renditions of this type—particularly among aged singers—when either concentration on the text or faltering memory tends to provoke erratic intonation.

Here the style, lacking a basic rhythmic pulse, corresponds to that exhibited in the ballad rendition of *Gaiferos jugador* (see Ex. 2). Yet, unlike the latter example, here our informant absorbed the first eight hemistichs in seven melody phrases:

⌜―――1―――⌝
Hija mia, se te vas

⌜―――2―――⌝
mira bien y apara mientes.

⌜―――3―――⌝
Por los caminos que tu vas,

⌜―――4―――⌝
no hay primos ni parientes.

⌜―――5―――⌝
Las estrañas son tu ǧente;

⌜―――6―――⌝
no to hagas aborreser.

⌜―――7―――⌝
¡Hija de un buen pareser!

Example 8 (= Armistead 3.3): *Endecha* (from Rhodes)

Endechas ("dirges") have become, in the course of centuries, a kind of regionally-bound communal repertoire, which enabled the bereaved to share their burden of grief.[38] Following an ancient custom, it was natural that the mourner's personal thoughts were borne out in spontaneous song. *Y me viego con poca fuera* is a unique text among Judeo-Spanish *endechas*, for which our transcription records for posterity an example of this practice. The genre also carries special significance as a body of song with which to commemorate the destruction of the Second Temple (in the year 70 C.E.) on and during the week preceding Tisha b'Av.

The tune comprises a quatrain strophe (ABCD). Encompassing a range that surpasses an octave (Major 9th), the informant rendered it in the Major mode (*finalis* f). Its final cadence on c conveys a feeling of circularity. Notice the ornamental cadences in the initial and third melody phrases.

Example 9 (= Armistead 4.1): Lyric song (from Rhodes)

The Sephardic tradition abounds with lyric songs. The two texts contributed by Professor Armistead are rare specimens, and here, for the first time, are registered the melodies to which they were sung. The first, *Morena de rufios caveyos* (Ex. 9), bears a transcription of the second textual stanza. The tune is unmistakably Mixolydian (here base on *finalis* c), disregarding the intentional lowered third degree that the informant rendered in nearly every strophe. Here we have yet another example of a disjointed text-tune relationship. The text comprises a distich and a refrain, "Por [var.' pur'] la madrugada." The tune, a quatrain strophe (ABCD), accommodates the text in the following manner:

⌜———A———⌝⌜—B—⌝
Cavayero, me engrañates

⌜————⌝⌜———C———⌝
pur la gura que me gurates.

⌜———D———⌝
¡Pur la madrugada!

The melodic repetitions, designated "x," are a most peculiar feature of this tune. The latter repetition constitutes melody phrase C, while the former functions as the cadential portion of A, continuing as the opening portion of B.

Example 10 (= Armistead 4.2): Lyric song (from Rhodes)

A second lyric song, *Echa agua en la tu puerta* (Ex. 10), for which only the first textual stanza was collected, was sung as a simple quatrain strophe in the minor mode (*finalis* d). Notice the Turkish interjection, ¡Amán! ("alas, mercy"), which bridges melody phrases 3 and 4.

Example 11 (= Armistead 5.1): Prayer for rain (from Rhodes)

Although bearing intermittent and intricate metric changes, this otherwise simple, yet animated, tune appears to revolve around the tonal axis f̱, spanning a minor penatchord (ḏ-e̱-f̱-g-a̱), and ends with a strictly metrical incantation. The rendition is totally syllabic.

* * *

This survey has touched upon the sacred and secular musical traditions of the Sephardim, whose history in the United States has been exemplary. In particular, the secular musical examples that have been notated here, together with those that have been and continue to be contributed by musicologists throughout the Western Hemisphere, bear testimony to an Old World tradition transplanted on American soil. It was the tenacious nature of the Sephardim, particularly those from North Africa and the Eastern Mediterranean, to retain in their oral tradition textual vestiges from their centuries-long existence on Iberian soil. Much work lies ahead in linking, where possible, their post-exilic Old World tunes to the Iberian Peninsula, as well as reconstructing their musical practices.[39]

Notes

1. The earliest congregation, founded in 1597, was Bet Ya'akov, named after its founder, Jacob Tyrado. Neveh Shalom (1608) and Bet Yisrael (1618) followed, and ultimately merged as a unified congregation, named Kahal Kodesh Talmud Torah (1639). The latter inaugurated its present building on Rapenburgerstraat, the so-called "Great Synagogue," on August 2, 1675.

Regarding the musical life and musical liturgy of the Amsterdam Jewish community, see Israel Adler, *La Pratique musicale*, and Maxine Ribstein Kanter, "Traditional Melodies," wherein she discusses the "High Holiday Hymn Melodies of the Portuguese Synagogue of Amsterdam," pp. 303–373. David Pinna contributed four pages of musical transcriptions for the Pentateuch and Prophets modes as rendered according to the tradition of the Portuguese Jews of Amsterdam in D. E. Janowski, *Biblia Hebraica*, Introduction, fol. d4.

2. Sahar Asamaim, modeled upon the "Great Synagogue" in Amsterdam and erected on the street named Bevis Marks, was inaugurated in 1701.

Specimens of its liturgical music can be found in (1) E. Aguilar and D. A. de Sola, *The Ancient Melodies*; see the more recent edition by Elias Jessurun, *Sephardi Melodies: Being the Traditional Liturgical Chants of the Spanish and Portuguese Jews' Congregation, London* (London: Bevis Marks and Oxford University Press, 5691/1931), as well as the recording *Music of the Spanish and Portuguese Synagogue*, supervised by John Levy (New York: Folkways Records and Service Corp. Record Album no. FR8961, 1960); (2) Franz Reizenstein transcribed 103 liturgical items from recordings made by Hazzan Eliezer Abinun and Hazzan Joseph Papo (of the London and Paris synagogues, respectively) in Obadiah Camhy, ed., *Liturgie séphardie* (London: World Sephardic Federation, 1959); and (3) M. R. Kanter "High Holy Day Hymn Melodies," pp. 12–44;

3. H. P. Salomon, "Hispanic Liturgy Among Western Sephardim," provides background information concerning liturgical practices of the Sephardic communites founded in Western Europe and the Americas during the seventeenth century. See also A. L. Cardoso's short essay "The Music of the Sephardim," which deals mainly with liturgical music. Among the published sources of liturgical music from these and other Western European Sephardic communities, we cite the following:

A. *France*: (1) Paris (Temple Israëlite): Emile Elihu Jonas, comp. and ed., *Shirot Yisraël: Recueil des chants hébraïques anciens et moderne exécutés au Temple du Rite Portugais de Paris* (Paris: A. Durlacher, 1854); (2) Emile Jonas, comp., *Shire Yisrael; Chants hébraïques exécutés dans les temples consistoriaux et au temple du rit portugais de Paris*; (3) Paris (Bérith Halom): Lein Algazi, *Chants séphardis*; see also O. Camhy, ibid.; (4) Comtat Venaissin (comprising the four communities: Avignon, Carpentras, Cavaillon, and l'Isle-sur-Sorgues): Jules Salomon and Mordochée Crémieu, comps., *Zmirot Yisraël: Chants hébraïques, suivant le rite des Communautés Israëlites de l'ancien Comtat Venaissin* (Marseilles: Delanchie, 1885); and (5) Southern France (synagogues of Bayonne and Bordeaux): M. J. Benharoche-Baralia, comp., *Chants traditionnels hébraïques en usage dans la communaute séphardie de Bayonne* (Biarritz: Zadoc Kahn, 1961).

B. *Germany* (Hamburg): Fourteen traditional Sephardic melodies are included in the *Sammlung von gottesdienstlichen Gesängen nach der Ordnung des Hamburger Tempel-Gebetbuches* (Hamburg, 1852), compiled by Gerson Rosenstein (1790–1851) of the Reform Temple.

C. *Italy*: (1) Livorno (= Leghorn) (Comunitá Israelitica): Federico Consolo, comp. and ed., *Libro dei canti d'Israele. Antichi canti liturgici del rito degli Ebrei Spagnoli* (Florence: Bratti, 1892); and (2) Rome (Tempio Maggiore on the Lungotevere Cenci): Elio Piattelli, comp., *Canti liturgici ebraici di rito italiano* (Rome: Edizione de Santis, 1967).

Sources for liturgical and paraliturgical music of Sephardic communities in North Africa and the Eastern Mediterranean region can be found in:

A. *North Africa*: (1) Abraham Zvi Idelsohn, *Gesänge der marokkanischen Juden* (Berlin and Vienna: Benjamin Harz Verlag, 1929)(= vol. 5 of the *Hebräisch-orientalischer Melodienschatz*); (2) Robert Lachmann, *Jewish Cantillation and Song in the Isle of Djerba* (Jerusalem: Archives of Oriental Music, Hebrew University, 1940); and (3) Arcadio de Larrea Palacin, *Canciones rituales hispano-judias* (Madrid: Instituto de Estudios Africanos, 1954).

B. *Eastern Mediterranean*: (1) Romania: Bucharest: M[auricu] Cohen-Linaru, *Tehillot Yisrael* (for Sabbath, Rosh Hashanah, and Yom Kippur), 2 vols. (Paris: A. Durlacher, 1910); (2) Abraham Zvi Idelsohn, comp., *Gesänge der orientalischen Sefardim* (Jerusalem, Berlin, and Vienna: Benjamin Harz Verlag, 1923) (= vol. 4 of the *Hebräisch-orientalischer Melodienschatz*); and (3) Isaac Levy, comp., *Antología de liturgia judéo-española*.

4. M. R. Kanter, "Traditional Melodies," p. 319.

5. For a more detailed account of the founding congregation, see David de Sola Pool and Tamar de Sola Pool, *An Old Faith in the New World*, especially pp. 3–36. Relations between Shearith Israel and London's Sahar Asamaim are discussed by S. Gaon, "Some Accounts," pp. 1–13.

Portions of the musical liturgy of Shearith Israel have been preserved in: (1) Leon M. Kramer and Oskar Guttmann, comps. and eds., *Kol Shearith Yisrael: Synagogue Melodies of Congregation Shearith Israel* (New York: Transcontinental Music, 1942) [containing melodies for the Shabbat service only]; and (2) A. L. Cardozo, *Sephardic Songs of Praise*.

6. The following sister congregations were established during the colonial period: Mikveh Israel (Savannah, Georgia, 1735), Beth Elohim (Charleston, South Carolina, 1749), Yeshu'at Israel (Newport, Rhode Island, ca. 1750), Mikveh Israel (Philadelphia, 1771), and Beth Shalome (Richmond, Virginia, 1789). In 1768, a group of Sephardim from New York's Shearith Israel established

a congregation in Montreal, Canada, retaining the same name. For information concerning the subsequent development of American Sephardic communities, see the excellent and concise overview by M. D. Angel, "The Sephardim of the United States," pp. 77–137. Regarding ritual practices among both Western and Eastern Sephardim residing in the United States, see H. C. Dobrinsky's most useful *A Treasury of Sephardic Laws and Customs*.

J. Reider, "Jewish Music in Pennsylvania," presents interesting material concerning Mikveh Israel of Philadelphia. See also D. A. Jessurun Cardozo, "Sephardi Music in America since 1654."

7. This assumption is based on the fact that during the early Colonial period the majority of hazzan-ministers in the early American congregations were sought from sister Sephardic congregations overseas, particularly Amsterdam and London. For a chronological survey of the religious leaders of Shearith Israel, beginning officially with Saul Pardo (d. 1702/1703) from Amsterdam, see D. and T. de Sola Pool, *An Old Faith*, pp. 158–210.

8. E. Aguilar and D. A. de Sola, *The Traditional Melodies*.

9. Cf. Abraham de Sola, *Biography of David Aaron de Sola, Late Senior Minister of the Portuguese Jewish Community of London* (Philadelphia: Wm. H. Jones & Sons, 1864). Abraham, the sixth child of D. A. de Sola and Rebecca (Rica) Meldola, had distinguished himself as minister, hazzan, lecturer, and biblical scholar of Shearith Israel from 1846 until his death. For an interesting account of his professional life, see Evelyn Miller, "The 'Learned Hazan' of Montreal: Reverend Abraham de Sola, LL.D.: 1825–1882," *American Sephardi* 7–8 (1975–76): 225–243.

10. D. A. de Sola, "The Ancient Melodies," p. 16.

11. From his prefatory remarks to the index of tunes in S. Gaon, ed., *Book of Prayer*, p. 243.

12. An excellent anthology, *Sephardic Songs of Praise*, compiled by Rabbi A. L. Cardozo, contains many hymns. For a compilation of the more popular Hebrew texts, see Nosson Scherman, *Zemiroth: Sabbath Songs*, to which Macy Nulman contributed information on the Sephardic songs (pp. 287–305). For examples of Judeo-Greek hymns, see Rachel Dalven and Israel J. Katz, "Three Traditional Judeo-Greek Hymns," pp. 191–208. The latter were recorded at the Sephardic Home for the Aged in Brooklyn.

13. For an interesting commentary on this *piyyut*, attributed to Yehuda Semuel Abbas (ca. 1163), see H. P. Salomon, "A Magnificent Sephardic Song," pp. 7–21. D. A. de Sola, "The Ancient Melodies" (p. 16), placed its tune in the category of "melodies composed in Spain."

14. Here, Jacob Hadida's remarks, alluding to the melodic changes which he discovered in his revision, begun in 1948, of the tunes associated with daily and occasional services at Sahar Asamaim, are most appropriate:

> An earnest endeavor has been made to eliminate as many errors as possible that have crept into the tunes during the past century—errors in notes in time—and today we are as near as we shall ever get to the rendering of de Sola's régime. That these errors have crept in is a direct result of a delightful feature of our services—the Congregational singing. This must naturally lead to an everlasting conflict between choir and Congregation. But if the melodies are to be preserved from further distortion, the efforts of the choir must prevail over the efforts of the less musical members. The melodies are the heritage of the Congregation, in the care of the choirmaster; to be guarded and cherished fiercely. Perhaps the worst case of distortion of a melody is to be found in our Rosh Hodesh Hallel. The version as it appears on page 24 of the de Sola–Aguilar book is truly delightful; and it must have suffered some very rough treatment to have developed into what we sing today.
>
> (Solomon Gaon, ed., *Book of Prayer*, p. 243).

15. In the early 1970s, the entire liturgy of its Sephardic community was recorded by Hazzan Solomon Nunes Nabarro (b. 1920). Nabarro's rendition was transcribed by M. R. Kanter. For

additional information concerning these recordings, see Kanter, "Traditional Melodies," pp. 356–358.

16. Our example was taken from chapter 4 of D. and T. de Sola Pool, *An Old Faith in the New World* (pp. 145–151), which contains thirteen musical transcriptions from the Shearith Israel liturgy. Both Siegfried Landau and Margo Mendes Oppenheimer were acknowledged by the authors (p. ix) for these transcriptions.

17. Rabbi Cardozo distinguished himself as hazzan at Shearith Israel from 1945 to 1985.

18. According to Zarita Nahón, in S. G. Armistead and J. H. Silverman, *Romances judeo-españoles de Tánger* (p. 9), George Herzog, then of Columbia University's anthropology department, made the musical transcriptions. Unfortunately, to date they have not been located. However, the Moroccan examples recorded by Professor de Onís were studied by S. G. Armistead and J. H. Silverman, ibid., and with I. J. Katz in "Judeo-Spanish Folk Poetry from Morocco," pp. 59–75.

19. Earlier, during the 1922–23 academic year, Mair José Benardete collected ballads in New York among Eastern Mediterranean Sephardic immigrants for his master's thesis, entitled "Los romances judeo-españoles en Nueva York" (Columbia University, 1923). This was subsequently edited by S. G. Armistead and J. H. Silverman and published under the title *Judeo-Spanish Ballads from New York*. A redacted version of Benardete's comments can be found in the latter edition, pp. vii–viii.

20. See E. A. Schlesinger, "A Study of the Linguistic Characteristics."

21. R. R. MacCurdy and D. D. Stanley,. "Judaeo-Spanish Ballads from Atlanta," pp. 221–238. A critical analysis of Stanley's transcriptions can be found in I. J. Katz, *Judeo-Spanish Traditional Ballads* 1:96–102.

22. I. J. Lévy, "Sephardic Ballads and Songs." Lévy recorded additional items in private residences in Atlanta and Los Angeles, and at the Sephardic Old Age Home in Brooklyn. See I. J. Katz, *Judeo-Spanish Traditional Ballads*, 1:99, n. 1 and 114, n. 1. The bulk of Lévy's musical examples were taken from Isaac Levy's *Chants judéo-espagnols* and Vicente T. Mendoza, *El romance español y el corrido mexicano: estudio comparativo* (Mexico City: Ediciones de la Universidad National Autonoma, 1939).

23. S. G. Armistead and J. H. Silverman, "Hispanic Balladry" pp. 229–244. See also their survey, "Judeo-Spanish Ballad Collecting in the United States," pp. 156–163.

24. For a discussion of their interdisciplinary collaboration, see I. J. Katz, "The Musical Legacy" pp. 72–85.

25. The first volume contains, in its introduction (pp. 5–33), a history of their collaboration.

26. Transcriptions of five Judeo-Spanish songs were made by Isaac Salinas and Rosa Samuelson in W. Samuelson, "Romances and Songs of the Sephardim," pp. 527–551.

27. J. H. Mauleón contributed thirty musical transcriptions to R. Benmayor's study, *Romances judeo-españoles de Oriente*, and C. Merrill-Mirsky, "Judeo-Spanish Song from the Island of Rhodes," included ten.

28. Mauleón, ibid.

29. R. Greenstein, *La Serena*. The collection, containing eight musical transcriptions, was made at the Sephardic Home for the Aged in Brooklyn, New York.

30. I. J. Katz, "The Musical Legacy," pp. 45–58.

31. See J. R. Cohen, "Judeo-Spanish Song in the Sephardic Communities of Montreal and Toronto: Survival, Function and Change" (Ph. D. diss., University of Montreal, 1988).

32. Manrique de Lara's unpublished example is cited in S. G. Armistead, *Romancero judeo-español en el Archivo Menéndez Pidal*, no. X13.1; M. Molho, *Usos y costumbres*, p. 330; and I. Levy,

Antología 4:nos. 210–211, pp. 325 and 328, respectively. In all three sources its incipit is given as "Ya se van [var. = fueron] los siete hermanos."

33. A. Hemsi, *Coplas séfardies*, Op. 8, no. 5 "Estávase la mora en su bel estar . . ."

34. L. Algazi, *Chants séphardis*, nos. 25–27; I. Levy, *Antologia* 4:nos. 292 (Izmir), 293, 295–296 (Sarajevo), 299 (Istanbul), and 10:no. 130 (Salonika). See A. Schwadron, "Un Cavritico: The Sephardic Tradition," *Journal of Jewish Music and Liturgy* 5 (1982–83): 24–39. See also his definitive study of the multiple tunes he collected in "Chad Gadya: A Passover Song." He also produced a recording, *Chad Gadya [One Kid]*, based on diverse examples from his collection, Folkways Records Album no. FR 8920 (New York, 1982), side 1, bands 3b (from Salonika), 6 (from Istanbul), 7d–e (from Rhodes), and side 2, band 4d (from Tangier).

35. The Braïloïu and Algazi example can be found on a recording issued as a series, World Collection of Recorded Folk Music, by the Archives International de Musique Populaire, UNESCO (Paris, 1951), 9A1 62, side 2, no. 3, and that notated by A. Schwadron in "Un cavritico en la tradición sefardi" (ex. 13).

36. E. Gerson-Kiwi, "The Legacy of Jewish Music," p. 164 (from Salonika); I. Levy, *Antología*, 4:nos. 239–241 (pp. 374–377) (from Jerusalem, Izmir, and Turkey, respectively); and S. Weich-Shahak, "Childbirth Songs," ex. 3 (p. 3)(from Salonika).

The customs surrounding birth and circumcision in the Sephardic community of Salonika are described by Molho, *Usos y costumbres* , pp. 49–90.

37. For important background material, M. Alvar, *Cantos de boda*, pp. 3–39; Molho, *Usos y costumbres*, pp. 15–47.

38. See M. Alvar, *Endechas judeo-españolas*, pp. 9–70; Molho, *Usos y costumbres*, pp. 17–201.

39. Taking the tunes of the extant Sephardic *Romancero* as their point of departure, Judith Etzion and Susana Weich-Shahak have provided a good start in their recent contribution, "The Spanish and the Sephardic Romances." I. J. Katz discusses the popular practice of "Contrafacta and the Judeo-Spanish Romancero."

Bibliography

Adler, Israel. *La Pratique musicale savante dans quelques communautés juives en Europe aux XVIIe et XVIIIe siècles*. 2 vols. Paris: Mouton & Co., 1966.

(Part IV was revised and enlarged in *Musical Life and Traditions of the Portuguese Jewish Community of Amsterdam in the XVIIIth Century* [Jerusalem: Magnes Press, 1974].)

Aguilar, Emanuel, and D[avid] A. de. Sola. *The Ancient Melodies of the Liturgy of the Spanish and Portuguese Jews*. London: Wessel & Co., 1857.

Algazi, Léon. *Chants séphardis*. London: Féderation Séphardite Mundial, 1958.

Alvar, Manuel. *Endeehas judeo-españoles*. Edición refundida y aumentada. Con notacion de melodías tradicionales de Maria Teresa Rubiato. Madrid: Instituto Arias Montano, C.S.I.C., 1969.

———. *Cantos de boda judeo-españoles*. Con notación de melodias tradicionales por Maria Teresa Rubiato. Madrid: Instituto Arias Montano, C. S. I. C., 1971.

Angel, Marc D. "The Sephardim of the United States: An Exploratory Study." *American Jewish Yearbook* 74 (1973): 77–138.

Armistead, Samuel. *Romaneero judeo-español en el Archivo Menéndez Pidal (Catálogo-Índice de romances y canciones)*. 3 vols. Madrid: Cátedra-Seminario Menéndez Pidal, 1978.

——, and Joseph H. Silverman. "Hispanic Balladry among the Sephardic Jews of the West Coast." *Western Folklore* 19/4 (1960): 229–244.

——, eds. *Romances judeo-españoles de Tánger recogidos por Zarita Nahón*. Con la colaboración de Oro Anahory Librowicz. Transcripción musicales de Israel J. Katz. Madrid: Cátedra-Seminario Menéndez Pidal, 1977.

——. "Judeo-Spanish Ballad Collecting in the United States." *La Corónica* 8, no. 2 (1980): 156–163.

——, eds. *Judeo-Spanish Ballads from New York: Collected by Mair José Benardete*. Berkeley and Los Angeles: University of California Press, 1981.

——, and Israel J. Katz. "Judeo-Spanish Folk Poetry from Morocco (The Boas-Nahón Collection)." *Yearbook of the International Folk Music Council*, 11 (1979): 59–75.

——. *Judeo-Spanish Ballads from Oral Tradition. I. Epic Ballads*. Berkeley-Los Angeles: University of California Press, 1986.

Benmayor, Rina. *Romances judeo-españoles de Oriente. Nueva recolección*. Transcripciones musicales de Judith H. Mauleón. Madrid: Cátedra-Seminario Menéndez Pidal/Editorial Gredos, 1979.

Cardozo, Abraham Lopes. "The Music of the Sephardim." *The World of the Sephardim*, pp. 37–71. New York: Herzl Institute, 1960.

——. *Sephardic Songs of Praise: According to the Spanish-Portuguese Tradition as Sung in the Synagogue and the Home*. Cedarhurst, N.Y.: Tara Publications, 1987.

Cardozo, D. A. Jessurun. "Sephardi Music in America since 1654." *Jewish Music Notes* (January 1955): 3–4.

Cohen, Judith R. "Judeo-Spanish Song in the Sephardic Communities of Montréal and Toronto: Survival, Function and Change." Ph.D. diss. Montreal: Université de Montréal, 1988.

Dalven, Rachel, and Israel J. Katz. "Three Traditional Judeo-Greek Hymns and Their Tunes." In Rae Dalven, *The Jews of Ioannina*, pp. 191–208. Philadelphia: Cadmus Press, 1990.

de Sola, Abraham. *Biography of David Aaron de Sola, Late Senior Minister of the Portuguese Jewish Community of London*. Philadelphia: Wm. H. Jones & Sons, 1864.

de Sola, D[avid] A. "The Ancient Melodies . . . An Historical Essay on the Poets, Poetry and Melodies of the Sephardic Liturgy." In E. Aguilar and D. A. de Sola, *The Ancient Melodies of the Liturgy of the Spanish and Portuguese Jews*, pp. 1–17. London: Wessel & Co., 1857.

Dobrinsky, Herbert C. *A Treasury of Sephardic Laws and Customs: The Ritual Practices of Syrian, Moroccan, Judeo-Spanish and Spanish and Portuguese Jews of North America*. Hoboken, N.J., and New York: Ktav Publishing House and Yeshiva University, 1986.

Etzion, Judith, and Susana Wiech-Shahak. "The Spanish and the Sephardic *Romances*: Musical Links." *Ethnomusicology*, 32/2 (1988): 1[173]–37[210].

Gaon, Solomon, ed., *Book of Prayer of the Spanish and Portuguese Jews' Congregation, London*. Vol. 1. Oxford: Oxford University Press, 1958.

——. "Some Aspects of the Relations between Sha'ar Hashamayim of London and Shearith Israel of New York." In *Migrations and Settlement, Proceedings of the Anglo-American Jewish Historical Conference*, pp. 1–13. London: Jewish Historical Society of England, 1971.

Gerson-Kiwi, Edith. "The Legacy of Jewish Music through the Ages." *In the Dispersion*, 3 (Jerusalem: World Zionist Organization, 1963–1964): 149-172.

Greenstein, Robin. *La Serena: A Collection of Ladino Song*. (Washington, D.C.): American Jewish Congress, CETA Program, 1979, published as a mimeographed pamphlet.

Hemsi, Alberto. *Coplas sefardies*. 5 fascs. Alexandria: Editions Orientale de Musique, 1932–1938.

Jablonski, David Ernest. *Biblia Hebraica* contains Pentateuch and Prophets only. 2 vols. in 1. Berlin: J. H. Knebel, 1699.

Kanter, Maxine Ribstein. "Traditional Melodies of the Rhymed Metrical Hymns in the Sephardic High Holiday Liturgy: A Comparative Study." Ph. D. diss. Evanston: Northwestern University, 1978.

———. "High Holy Day Hymn Melodies in the Spanish and Portuguese Synagogue of London." *Journal of Synagogue Music*, 10, no. 2 (December 1980): 12–44.

Katz, Israel. *Judeo-Spanish Traditional Ballads from Jerusalem: An Ethnomusicological Study* 2 vols. New York: Institute of Mediaeval Music, 1972–75.

———. "The Musical Legacy of the Judeo-Spanish *Romancero*." In *Hispania Judaica: Studies on the History, Language, and Literature of the Jews in the Hispanic World*, edited by Josep M. Solà-Solé, Samuel G. Armistead, and Joseph H. Silverman, vol. 2, pp. 45–58. Barcelona: Puvill, 1982.

———. "Jewish-American Music: Sephardic." In *The New Grove Dictionary of American Music*, edited by H. Wiley Hitchcock and Stanley Sadie, vol. 2, pp. 569–573. London: Macmillan, 1986.

———. "Contrafacta and the Judeo-Spanish *Romancero*: A Musicolgocial View." In *Hispanic Studies in Honor of Joseph H. Silverman*, edited by Joseph V. Ricapito, pp. 169–187. Newark, Del.: Juan de la Cuesta, 1988.

———. "Pre-Expulsion Tune Survivals among Judeo-Spanish Ballads? A Possible Late Fifteenth-Century French Antecedent." In *Hispanic Medieval Studies in Honor of Samuel G. Armistead*, edited by E. Michael Gerli and Harvey L. Sharrer (Madison: Hispanic Seminary of Medieval Studies, 1992), pp. 171–192.

Levy, Isaac, ed. and coll. *Chants judéo-espagnols*. Introduction by O. Camhy. Vol. 1. London: World Sephardi Federation, 1959; vols. 2–4. Jerusalem: Author, 1970–73.

———. *Antología de liturgia judeo-española*. 10 vols. Jerusalem: Ministerio de Educación y Cultura, 1964–1980.

Lévy, Isaac Jack. "Sephardic Ballads and Songs in the United States: New Variants and Additions." M.A. thesis. Iowa City: University of Iowa, 1959.

MacCurdy, Raymond R., and Daniel D. Stanley. "Judaeo-Spanish Ballads from Atlanta, Georgia." *Southern Folklore Quarterly* 15 (December, 1951): 221–238.

Merrill-Mirsky, Carol. "Judeo-Spanish Song from the Island of Rhodes: A Musical Tradition in Los Angeles." M.A. thesis. Los Angeles: University of California, 1984.

Miller, Evelyn. "The `Learned Hazen' of Montreal: Reverend Abraham de Sola, LL.D.: 1825–1882." *American Sephardi* 7–8 (1975–1976): 225–243.

Molho, Michael. *Usos y costumbres de los sefardíes de Salónica*. Madrid-Barcelona: Instituto Arias Montano, C.S.I.C., 1950.

Pool, David de Sola, and Tamar de Sola Pool. *An Old Faith in the New World*. New York: Columbia University Press, 1955.

Reider, Joseph. "Jewish Music in Pennsylvania in the Eighteenth Century." *Church Music and Musical Life in Pennsylvania in the Eighteenth Century*, edited by the National Society of the Colonial Dames of America, vol. 3, part II, 331–333, 350. Philadelphia: Printed for the Society, 1947.

Salomon, Herman P. "Hispanic Liturgy among Western Sephardim." *American Sephardi*, 2, 1–2 (1968): 49–59.

———. "A Magnificent Sephardic Song *Et sha'arei ratzon*: Literal Translation and Commentary." *American Sephardi*, 7–8 (1975): 7–21.

Samuelson, William. "Romances and Songs of the Sephardim." In *The Sephardi Heritage: Essays on the History and Cultural Contribution of the Jews of Spain and Portugal*, edited by Richard D. Barnett, pp. 527–551. London: Vallentine, Mitchell, 1971.

Scherman, Nosson, comp. and ed., *Zemiroth: Sabbath Songs with Additional Sephardic Zemiroth.* Brooklyn, N.Y.: Mesorah, 1979.

Schlesinger, Emma Addato. "A Study of the Linguistic Characteristics of the Seattle Sefardi Folklore." M.A. thesis. Seattle: University of Washington, 1935.

Schwadron, Abraham A., ed. and coll. *Chad Gadya [One Kid]: Aramaic, "One Kid"; circa 15th–16th Century, Central Eastern Europe. Aramaic / German / Yiddish / Greek / Ladino / Judeo-Provencial / Italian / Arabic / Persian / Kurdistan / Yemen.* New York: Folkways Records FR 8920, 1982.

———. "*Chad Gadya*: A Passover Song." *Selected Reports in Ethnomusicology* 4 (Los Angeles, 1983): 125–155.

———. "Un cavritico de la tradición sefardi." *Escudo*, no. 54 (Segunda época)(January–March, 1985): 19–34. Translated by Jacob Carciente.

Weich-Shahak, Susana. "Childbirth Songs among Sephardic Jews of Balkan Origin" *Orbis Musicae* 8 (1982–1983): 87–103.

Judeo-Spanish Traditional Poetry in the United States

Samuel G. Armistead

To the memory of Joseph H. Silverman, peerless colleague and beloved friend.

The first Jews to arrive in what would later be the United States were Sephardim.[1] Refugees from the Dutch settlement at Recife in Brazil, recently reconquered by the Portuguese, arrived at Nieuw Amsterdam in 1654. The congregation of Shearith Israel came into existence in 1655, when the Dutch West India Company—counter to the demands of Governor Peter Stuyvesant—granted permission for the immigrants to remain. Yeshuath Israel, the congregation in Newport, Rhode Island, was founded in 1658. The destiny of these two earliest Jewish settlements is inseparable from that of Amsterdam and London, and by extension of Dutch Brazil, Surinam, and the West Indies.

Though some early settlers probably came directly from Portugal or even Spain, a great majority of the pioneers were undoubtedly Portuguese crypto-Jews or their descendants—unwilling converts to Catholicism who, on arrival in Amsterdam, the "Dutch Jerusalem," starting in the final years of the sixteenth century, gladly returned to their ancestral faith.

These Portuguese conversos, many of whom were originally of Spanish origin, posessed an essentially Renaissance Iberian culture. In Holland, they enthusiastically cultivated many of the literary genres characteristic of the Spanish Golden Age.[2] At home and, to a degree, even in their formal writing, they came to use modalities of Spanish and Portuguese in which the two Iberian languages exerted strong reciprocal influences.[3]

If the earliest immigrants to the future New York spoke Spanish and Portuguese—as they most certainly did—then they would surely have remembered, among other oral literary forms, certain ballads, riddles, and folktales, and would have enlivened their daily speech with pungent Iberian proverbs, but we have no extant textual evidence to support such a reasonable supposition.⁴ Indirectly, however, we can perhaps form some idea of the sort of traditional literature the early American Sephardim may have known from the contents of a Portuguese miscellany put together in Holland in the late seventeenth century: *Relações, cantigas, adeuinhações, e outras corizidades, Trasladadas de papeis Velhos e juntados neste caderno en Amsterdam, 1683* ("Narratives, songs, riddles, and other curiosities, copied from old papers and assembled in this notebook, in Amsterdam, 1683"). The nostalgic character of this booklet's title, *Trasladadas de papeis Velhos*, unequivocally foreshadows the eventual disappearance of Hispanic oral literature among the Dutch Sephardim. Though their Hispano-Portuguese language would linger on vestigially even down to the early twentieth century, it was already taking on an aura of antiquarian nostalgia in the last years of the 1600s.⁵

The distinctive conditions encountered in Nieuw Amsterdam–New York were even less propitious for the survival of Sephardic Hispano-Portuguese or of its oral literature. Though certain ritualized announcements in the synagogue continued to be made in Spanish or in Portuguese, and a specialized religious vocabulary was to survive even in modern times, the old languages seem to have died out in colonial America by the end of the eighteenth century at the very latest.⁶ In 1783, no less a figure than the distinguished hazzan Gershom Mendes Seixas, who ministered to the New York community and, during the Revolution, served at Mikveh Israel in Philadelphia, could nonetheless allow that he was "unacquainted with the Spanish and Portuguese languages which have ever been used since the first establishment of the synagogue."⁷ Barring the discovery of new documents—always a distinct possibility—we cannot know what oral literature may have circulated among the early Sephardic settlers in colonial America, nor exactly when it ceased to exist.

In the first decades of the present century, a new and culturally quite different wave of Sephardic immigration began to arrive in the United States. With their expulsion from Spain in 1492, Jews who had been unwilling to convert, even nominally, to Christianity had settled in various Eastern Mediterranean cities under Ottoman rule, as well as in North Africa. In contrast to the Renaissance culture of the conversos who took refuge in Holland and other parts of Western Europe in the sixteenth century, the exiles of 1492 took with them a more conservative, essentially medieval Hispanic culture and language. Unlike the Western Sephardim, who gradually lost their Hispanic languages, the Eastern Mediterranean and North African Jews kept alive and cherished their Judeo-Spanish dialects and oral literature down to the present day.

During the early years of the twentieth century, a variety of interrelated developments—the disintegration of the Ottoman Empire, the Young Turk Revolution (1908), resurgent Balkan nationalism, and the Balkan Wars (1912–1913)—combined to pose a grave threat to the integrity of the Eastern Sephardic communities. Many Sephardim felt it was time to leave. By 1926, some 25,000 Sephardic Jews are estimated to have emigrated to the United States.[8] These Eastern Spanish Jews brought with them to America an extraordinarily rich repertoire of traditional oral literature, in which elements dating back to pre-expulsion Spain were complexly interwoven with other features acquired in the Balkans and the Middle East.[9]

In 1957, in collaboration with my deceased friend Professor Joseph H. Silverman, I began a research project aimed at collecting, studying, and editing Sephardic oral literature. In 1959, we were joined by our friend, the distinguished ethnomusicologist, Professor Israel J. Katz. Since that time, we have done fieldwork, individually and collaboratively, in the United States, Spain, Morocco, and Israel, and have interviewed a total of 241 informants in all: 164 from the Eastern Mediterranean communities and 77 from North Africa.[10]

Though our principal efforts have been aimed at bringing together a massive collection of narrative ballads (*romances*), we have, whenever possible, collected other forms as well, and our collection has come to include examples of all the major genres of Sephardic folk literature. On the following pages, at the kind invitation of Professor Martin A. Cohen, I have edited, with brief critical remarks and the bibliography essential for further reading, a representative sample of some of these folk-literary materials.

Our fieldwork in the United States has for the most part been limited to Eastern informants—a total of 85 in all—so the present selection will include only Eastern Sephardic materials.[11] Though other divisions can be defended, I have classified our texts into the following generic categories: (1) ballads, (2) cumulative songs, (3) songs of passage, (4) lyric songs, (5) prayers and charms.[12]

1. Ballads

Judeo-Spanish ballads (*romansas* = Spanish *romances*) are narrative poems, typically with sixteen-syllable verses, made up of two eight-syllable hemistichs, with assonant rhyme in every second hemistich. Originating from fragments of long medieval epic poems, the ballads became established as a separate genre in the early fourteenth century, and the form was subsequently used to narrate numerous events in Spanish history, to recreate a variety of medieval narratives, to adapt stories borrowed from the balladic traditions of other European peoples (notably from France), and also as a vehicle for poems known only in the Hispanic tradition. From its medieval origins, the genre has survived down to the present day in the living oral tradition of all Hispanic peoples.[13]

Of all the genres of Sephardic oral literature, the ballads have the closest links to early Spanish counterparts, and, hence, Hispanists have lavished attention on them, unfortunately to the unwarranted neglect of other genres.[14] Because of its conservative character, Judeo-Spanish balladry offers invaluable evidence for the comparative study of the Pan-Hispanic *Romancero* and, indeed, of the Pan-European ballad as well.[15]

From our collection of some 1,485 ballad texts, here are two previously unedited versions collected from Eastern Sephardic informants in the United States:

1.1	*Gaiferos jugador*	Gaiferos the Gambler
	Por los palasios de Carlo	In the halls of Charlemagne's palace,
	y non pasan sinon ǧugare.	they do nothing but gamble.
2	Y non ǧugan plata ni oro,	They don't gamble for silver and gold,
	sino vías y sivdades.	but for cities and towns.
	Ganó Carlo a Gaifero	Charlemagne won from Gaiferos
	sus vías y sus sivdades.	his cities and his towns.
4	Ganó Gaifero a Carlo	Gaiferos won from Charlemagne
	y a la su spoza reale.	his royal wife.

	Más s'acontentava piedrere,	Better to have lost her,
	piedrere que no ganare.	to lose her and not to win her.
6	—¡Y sovrino, el mi sovrino,	"Nephew, my nephew,
	y el mi sovrino caronale!	blood nephew of mine!
	Yo vos creí chequetico	I raised you from childhood;
	y el Dio te hizo barragane.	God made you a valiant young man.
8	Y El te dio barvica roxa	He gave you a red beard
	y en tu puerpo fuersa grande.	and great strength in your body.
	Yo te di a Lindabera	I gave you Lindabella
	y por mujer y por iguale.	for your wife and equal.
10	Vos fuetex hombre covado	You were cowardly;
	y que vola dexatex yevare.	you let her be carried off.
	Espozada la tengo en Fransia	I have betrothed her in France
	y por sien rublas y por maze.	for a hundred rubles and more.
12	Vos que sox hombre garrero	But you are a warrior
	y vola puedíax ganare.—	and you could still win her."
	Y la topó a Lindaibeya	He encountered Lindabella
	y mañanicas de Sanğiguare.¹⁶	on the morning of St. John.

1.2	*El pozo airón*	*The Bottomless Well*
	Ya se van los siete hermanos,	Now the seven brothers depart,
	ya se van para Aragó.	now they depart for Aragón.
2	Las calores eran fuertes;	The heat was intense;
	agua non se les topó.	they could find no water.
	Por en medio del camino,	Along the way,
	toparon un poğo airó.	they found a deep well.
4	Echaron pares y nones;	They drew lots;
	a el chico le cayó.	it fell to the youngest.
	Ya lo atan a la cuedra;	Now they tie him to the rope;
	lo echan al poğo airó.	they lower him into the well.
6	Por en medio de el poğo,	Halfway down that well,
	la cuedra se le rompió.	the rope broke.
	La agua se le hizo sangre;	The water became blood for them;
	las piedras culevros son.	the stones became serpents.
8	—Si vos pregunta el mi padre,	"If my father asks you,
	le dizéx: "¡Al poğo airó!"¹⁷	tell him: `He was left in the well!'"

Gaiferos jugador exemplifies the medieval origins of so many ballads in the Sephardic repertoire. Nowhere else in European balladry, except among the Eastern Sephardim (and in the similarly archaic traditions of Portugal, Galicia, León, and Catalonia), can there still be heard a narrative song ultimately derived from the tradition of the *Waltharius* epic and its various medieval Germanic congeners.[18] By contrast with the medievalism of *Gaiferos*, *El pozo airón* is a direct and close translation of a modern Greek ballad. It is one of a small but significant number of *romanzas* which, except for their language and formulaic style, have nothing to do with the ballad genre's medieval Hispanic origins, but derive from Eastern Mediterranean prototypes.[19] This particular ballad, because of its tragic implications, is used as a dirge to be sung on the ninth of Av.

2. Cumulative Songs

Sephardic cumulative songs have never been studied as a genre. In addition to the two poems edited here, there are a number of others. *The Twelve Numbers* (*¿Quién supiese y entendiese?*) corresponds to the universally popular *'Eḥād mî yôdēa?*[20] *The Hours of the Day* (*La cantiga de las horas*), an exclusively Eastern children's song, associates the hours with a variety of everyday activities.[21] *Vivardueña*, known both in the East and in Morocco, follows the procedures involved in planting, harvesting, and making bread.[22] *Our bride says* (*Dice la nuestra novia*), current in the East and in North Africa, involves a metaphorical description of the bride's beauty.[23] Each of these songs has abundant counterparts in other branches of the Hispanic tradition, as well as in those of other European speech communities. A systematic study of the genre would be most welcome. Here are two examples from our collection:

2.1	*La moxca y la mora*	*The Moorish Girl*
1	S'estávase la mora en su bel estar.	The Moorish girl was sitting in her sweet repose.
	Venía la moxca por hazerle mal.	The fly came along to do her harm.
	La moxca a la mora, mesquina la mora, qu'en sus campos moros . . .	The fly harmed the girl, poor Moorish girl, in her Moorish fields . . .
12.	S'estávase'l šoḥet en su bel estar.	The butcher was sitting in his sweet repose.

Venía el malaḥ a-mave	The Angel of Death came along
por hazerle mal.	to do him harm.
El malaḥ a-mave al šoḥet,	The Angel of Death harmed the butcher,
el šoḥet al buey,	the butcher the ox,
el buey al agua,	the ox the water,
el agua al fuego,	the water the fire,
el fuego al palo,	the fire the stick,
el palo al perro,	the stick the dog,
el perro al gato,	the dog the cat,
el gato al ratón,	the cat the mouse,
el ratón a la rana,	the mouse the frog,
la rana a l'abezba,	the frog the wasp,
l'abezba a la moxca,	the wasp the fly,
la moxca a la mora,	the fly the girl,
mesquina la mora,	poor Moorish girl,
en sus campos moros.[24]	in her Moorish fields.

2.2 *El cavretico* — *The Little Goat*

1 Un cavretico, — A little goat
   que me lo mercó mi padre, — my father bought for me,
   por dos aspros, — for two small coins,
   por dos levanim. — for two little coins.

2 Vino el gato — The cat came along
   y modrió el cavretico, — and bit the little goat
   que me lo mercó mi padre, — my father bought for me,
   por dos aspros, — for two small coins,
   por dos levanim . . . — for two little coins . . .

9 Vino el malaḥ — The Angel came along
   y acuzó al šoḥet, — and accused the butcher,
   porque degoyó a la vaca, — because he killed the cow,
   porque bevió a la agua, — that drank the water,
   porque amató al ḥuego, — that put out the fire,
   porque quemó al palo, — that burned the stick,
   porque aḥarvó al perro, — that beat the dog,
   porque modrió al gato, — that bit the cat,
   porque modrió al cavretico, — that bit the little goat
   que me lo mercó mi padre, — my father bought for me,
   por dos aspros, — for two small coins,
   por dos levanim.[25] — for two little coins.

Ultimately, *The Moorish Girl* and *The Little Goat* embody the same Pan-European song-type. *The Moorish Girl* represents the song's Pan-Hispanic "secular" form, while *The Goat* is a Judeo-Spanish adaptation of the beloved haggadic Ḥad gadyā', itself a late and rather imperfect Aramaic translation of one of the song's Central European modalities. The Eastern Sephardic tradition knows yet a third form: *The Good Old Man* (*El buen viejo*), which is a close translation of the poem's Greek variant.[26] The three songs, all variations on the same text-type, eloquently illustrate the variegated cultural traditions—Hispanic, Hebraic, and Balkan—which have contributed to the Sephardic repertoire.

3. Songs of Passage

Songs of passage, pertaining to the major transitions of life, have not been investigated as such, though Manuel Alvar's editions and studies of Moroccan Sephardic wedding songs and dirges are model contributions, and Paloma Díaz-Mas's authoritative catalogues and studies of both Eastern and North African dirges can be considered essentially definitive surveys.[27] In regard to such liminal songs, there are notable differences between the two Sephardic traditions. While we are fortunate to have Alvar's richly documented Moroccan evidence, much less is known about Eastern wedding songs.[28] Thanks to Díaz-Mas, dirges from both areas are well known, but the songs in question seem to have a rather different character in the two subtraditions. Little is known of birth songs from Morocco, and in the East also the evidence is scarce.[29] Here are three texts from our collection, concerning, respectively, birth, marriage, and death:

3.1 *Cantiga de parida*   Birth Song
1   Y cuando la cumadre dize: When the midwife says:
     —¡Dale, dale!—,   "Keep on, keep on!"
     responde la parida: the woman in labor answers:
     —¡A Dio escapáme!—   "May God help me!"
     Dize la criatura: The child says:
     —¡A salvo quitáme!—   "May I be delivered!"
     Responde la su ǧente: All the people answer:

	— ¡Amén, amén, amén!—	"Amen, amen, amen!"
	Ya es, ya es buen simán	Indeed this child
	esta criatura.	is a good omen.
	¡Bendicho'l que mos ayegó	Blessed be He who brought us
	a esta ventura!	to this good fortune!
2	Ya viene el parido	Now the new father arrives
	con los convidados.	with all his guests.
	Qu'yeva' la mano	In one hand he carries
	resta de pexcado;	a serving of fish
	por la otra mano	and in the other
	siento y un ducado.	a hundred and one ducats.
	Ya es, ya es buen simán	Indeed this joy
	esta alegría.	is a good omen.
	¡Bendicho'l que mos ayegó	Blessed be He who brought us
	a ver este día!	to see this day!
3	Ya viene el parido	Now the new father arrives
	a los pies de la cama.	at the foot of the bed.
	Le dize la parida:	The young mother tells him:
	—Hoy no comí nada.	"I've eaten nothing today."
	—Presto que le tra'	"Quickly have them bring her
	gayina enxundiada.³⁰	a fattened chicken."

3.2 *Cantiga de novia* — *Wedding Song*

1 Hija mía, si te vas, — My daughter, if you are departing,

mira bien y apara mientes. — look out and pay attention.
Por los caminos que tú vas, — On the roads you will travel,
no hay primos ni parientes. — there are no cousins or relatives.
Las estrañas son tu ğente; — Unknown women will be your family;

no te hagas aborreser. — be sure you're not disliked.
¡Hija de un buen pareser! — Beautiful girl!

2 —Cuando m'iva para'l baño, — "As I was going to the baths,
todos me quedan mirando: — everyone looked at me:
"¿Quién es eya la que pasa?" — `Who is that who's passing by?'
"La mujer del mercader".— — `It's the merchant's wife.'"
¡Hija de un buen pareser!³¹ — Beautiful girl!

3.3 *Endecha* — *Dirge*

	—Y me veigo con poca fuersa,	"And I have little strength left,
2	echado'n cama ḥazino.	lying sick in my bed.
	Y a fin di la media nochi	And after midnight,
4	y la puerta me batió.	someone knocks at my door.
	¿Y quén es est' hombre boracho,	And who is this drunkard
6	que la puerta me batió?	who's knocking at my door?"
	—Yo no so hombre boracho	"I am no drunkard,
8	y ne por bever vin'aquí.	nor did I come here for drink.
	Y so mandado de los sielus,	I am a messenger from Heaven
10	qu'el alma me dex a mí.	come to ask for your soul.
	Avremíx vos la puerta;	Open the door for me,
12	yo vola tumaré.—	so I can take your soul."
	Ya l'avrió la media puerta,	Then he opened half the door,
14	di cara y no di curasón.	pretending and unwillingly.
	—Y avrimíx la otra media	"Open the other half for me
16	y ávremela de corasón.—	and open it willingly."
	Ya le avrió l'otra media;	Then he opened the other half
18	el cuerpo ya lo'stiró.	and he lay down to die.
	Las ojadas se siravan;	His eyes were closing
20	despartisión de l'empañó.	and death turned him pale.
	Ya le lavan pies y manos	Now they wash his hands and feet
22	con agua de turunǧá.	with orange-scented water.
	Ya le quitan las comidas;	Now they take away his food;
24	el garón no puede'nglotar.	his throat cannot swallow.
	—¡Y qué dichas y qué endechas,	"And what songs of mourning
26	endechas para mí me haráx!	you will compose for me!
	Y sin hora y sin tiempo,	Now there's no time left:
28	il alma ya vola vo dar.—	I will give up my soul."
	Y con xofletico en boca	And with hardly a breath left,
30	y él ya se encorajó,	then he took courage,
	porque la hora le vino;	for his hour had come,
32	a punto él se la dió.	and he delivered up his soul.
	—¡Y qué picado y qué manzía,	"And what sorrows and lamentations
34	que yorarán por mí!	they will weep for me!
	Y más y más los mis parientis,	And even more my family,
36	que los ojos no s'enxugarán!³²	whose eyes will not be dry!"

Our *Cantiga de parida* offers a graphic evocation of the harrowing, though ultimately joyous, circumstances surrounding the birth of a

Sephardic child.³³ The somewhat startling detail that the child itself should speak out before birth, calling for its own delivery, reflects a widely known folklore motif.³⁴ Our *Wedding Song*, which embodies urgent advice to the departing bride, is fragmentary.³⁵ The fact that the girl is now "the merchant's wife" stresses, of course, the economically advantageous character of her marriage. This second strophe, not found in any other version I have seen, doubtless originally belonged to some other nuptial song. The *Endecha* sung for us by Mrs. Perla Galante is, to my knowledge, unique. There is nothing exactly like it among the Eastern and Moroccan texts exhaustively catalogued by Paloma Díaz-Mas. I would guess that this song was improvised for our benefit, using authentic motifs and formulas to evoke a no-longer-practiced traditional custom with which Mrs. Galante was, all the same, still intimately familiar. The crucial motif of Death personified, who comes knocking at the victim's door to carry him off, has medieval origins and is still well known in modern Sephardic dirge poetry.³⁶

4. Lyric Songs

The Moroccan Sephardic tradition of lyric poetry has been exhaustively documented and studied by Manuel Alvar. Much less is known about the Eastern tradition. All the same, as in the case of various other genres, we can distinguish songs of very different types and origins. The two texts published here exemplify the repertoire's cultural and chronological diversity.

4.1

1	Morena de rufios caveyos,	Dark girl with blond hair,
	se queréx ganar denero.	if you want to earn money.
	¡Por la madrugada!	At dawn!
2	Cavayero, me engañates,	Knight, you deceived me,
	pur la ǧura que me ǧurates.	by the oath you swore to me.
	¡Por la madrugada!	At dawn!
3	Y se te ǧuro por el sielo	And if I swear to you by Heaven
	y de no tocarte el dedo.	not even to touch your finger.
	¡Por la madrugada!	At dawn!
4	Y morena de rufios entrinsados,	Dark girl with blond tresses,
	se queréx ganar ducados.	if you want to earn ducats.

	¡Y por la madrugada!	At dawn!
5	Y cavayero, me engañatis,	Knight, you deceived me,
	por la ǧura que me ǧurates.	by the oath you swore to me.
	¡Por la madrugada!	At dawn!
6	Y se te ǧuro por la luna	And if I swear to you by the moon
	y de no tocarte en la uña.	not even to touch your fingernail.
	¡Y por la madrugada!³⁷	At dawn!

4.2

Echa agua en la tu puerta — Throw water on your doorstep
y pasaré y mi cairé. — and, passing by, I'll slip and fall.
Tuparé una chica cavza; ¡amán! — I'll find a small excuse
entraré y te havlaré.³⁸ — to go in and speak with you.

Our first text, *Morena de rufios caveyos*, clearly attests, prosodically, thematically, and stylistically, to its medieval Peninsular origins.³⁹ These verses, with their synonymous rhyme words (*caveyos/entrinsados; denero/ducados; sielo/luna; dedo/uña*), relate to the multi-secular Hispanic tradition of parallelistic couplets, typical of Galician-Portuguese songs and not unknown in the medieval Castilian repertoire, which have also survived in Moroccan Sephardic wedding songs and in marginal areas of Portugal down to the present day.⁴⁰ The twin rhyme words *ducados* and *dineros* appear in a Castilian *villancico* included in the sixteenth-century gothic-type broadside, *Cantares de diversas sonadas*:

0	Mis ojuelos madre	My eyes, mother,
	valen vna ciudade	are worth a city.
1	Mis ojuelos madre	My eyes, mother,
	tanto son de claros	are so bright,
	cada vez que los alço	each time I raise them
	merescen ducados	they obtain ducats;
	ducados mi madre	ducats, mother.
	valen vna ciudade.	They're worth a city.
2	Mis ojuelos madre	My eyes, mother,
	tanto son de veros	are so brilliant,
	cada vez que los alço	each time I raise them
	merescen dineros	they obtain coins;
	dineros mi madre	coins, mother.
	valen vna ciudade.⁴¹	They're worth a city.

The topic of the dark girl (*morena*)—even if here her hair is blond—also ties this song to an ancient and polysemic lyric tradition.⁴² At the same time, our song's enigmatic, elliptical, intuitive style is typical of the early *villancicos*: What is really going on here? On one hand, there is the suggestive allusion to "earning money" and, on the other, a courtly promise not even to touch the girl—the same girl who, at the same time, reproaches the knight for having "deceived" her. Here too the allusion to dawn is highly ambivalent according to the poetic code of the traditional lyric.[43] The exact details of this amorous minidrama remain a mystery, as the poem invites us to imagine and to elaborate upon its unlimited possibilities. Clearly these Judeo-Spanish verses became part of the Sephardic tradition at an early date.

Echa agua en la tu puerta offers a very different perspective on Judeo-Spanish lyric poetry. Octosyllabic quatrains, with assonant rhyme in the even verses, were extremely popular in the recent tradition, and hundreds of texts are known, though they have never been systematically studied. Our song represents a word-for-word translation of a Modern Greek distich, thus exemplifying once again the significant—though, from a scholarly point of view, gravely neglected—impact of Eastern Mediterranean folk literature on the Judeo-Spanish repertoire. In translation, the Sephardic song's Neohellenic parent text reads: "Throw water on your doorstep,/ so that passing by I may slip,/ so, for your mother, I may find an excuse/ to go in and talk with you."[44] The correspondence could hardly be more exact.

5. Prayers and Charms

Sephardic popular prayers and medicinal charms have hardly been studied at all. Here are two texts—a prayer for rain and a charm against the evil eye—from among the materials we have collected over the years.

5.1	*Agua, O Dio*	
	¡Agua, O Dio!	
2	Que la tierra la demanda.	*Prayer for Rain*
	Chicos, chicos y piqueños	Water, O God!
4	pan queremos;	The earth requires it.
	agua no tenemos.	Children and little ones

6   ¡Abre los sielos,
     arrega los campos!
8   ¡Arregador, arregador,
     echa trigo al montón!⁴⁵

5.2 *Contra el ainará*
     Con el nombre del Dio,
2   Abraam, Itshak, Yakov,
     Aarón, David, Šelomó:
4   Yo meto la mano
     y el Dio mete la melezina.
6   Como la señora de Miriám,
     a-neviá,
8   que sanava y melezinava

     y todo el mal eya quitava
10 y a la fondina de la mar
     lo echava,
12 ansí yo quito el mal
     de fulana,
14 hija de sistrana.
     Todo el que la miró,
16 con mala ojada,
     con mala ariada:
18 Si es hombre,
     que no pierda el nombre;
20 si es mujer,
     que no piedra el saver;
22 si es ave muda,
     a-Kadúš Baruḥú
24 esté en su ayuda.
     Caminando por un camino,
26 encuentrí a un viejezico:
     Fierro vestía,
28 fierro calsava.
     — ¿Onde vas?
30 —Ande fulana,
     hija de sistrana,
32 a quitarle todo el ainará.
     Todo el que la miró,

we need bread;
we have no water.
Open the heavens,
irrigate the fields!
Waterer of the land,
pile up mounds of wheat!

Against the Evil-eye
In the name of God,
Abraham, Isaac, Jacob,
Aaron, David, Solomon:
I put in my hand
and God puts in the medicine.
Like Miriam
the prophetess,
who performed cures and gave
   medicine
and took away all the sickness
and threw it
into the depths of the sea,
so I take away the sickness
of so-and-so,
daughter of such-and-such.
Every person who looked upon her
with an evil look
or with bad demeanor:
If it be a man,
may she not lose her name;
if it be a woman,
may she not lose her knowledge;
if it be a mute bird,
may the Holy One, Blessed-be-He,
give help to her.
As I was walking along a path,
I met a little old man:
He was dressed in iron,
with iron shoes.
"Where are you going?"
"To the house of so-and-so,
daughter of such-and-such,

34	con mala ojada,	to take from her all the evil eye.
	con mala ariada,	Every person who looked at her
36	y a la fondina de la mar	with an evil look
	yo lo echava.	and with bad demeanor:
38	Y el Dio la melezinava.[46]	I threw him
		into the depths of the sea.
		And God cured her."

The little rain prayer must have been widely known in the Sephardic East.[47] Such prayers, with classical antecedents, are also well known in Greek tradition,[48] but there can be little doubt as to the origin of our Sephardic text. In his *Vocabulario de refranes y frases proverbiales*, compiled in 1627, Gonzalo Correas includes an essentially identical incipit: "¡Agua, Dios, agua, ke la tierra lo demanda! Klamor a Dios en tiempo seko" ("Water, O God, water, for the earth requires it! Outcry to God in time of drought").[49] The Judeo-Spanish prayer is, then, without doubt of ancient Hispanic provenience.

The charm against the evil eye, despite its distinctively Jewish invocations of God, the Patriarchs, and Miriam the prophetess,[50] is closely related to ancient Pan-European folk-charms and folk-beliefs. The idea of a supernatural or divine apotropaic figure traveling or being met along a road as part of his curative mission is prominent in many folk-charms. Spanish texts continue to represent a meeting with the curing agent while on a journey.

San Pedro e San Pablo	St. Peter and St. Paul
viñan de Roma;	were coming from Rome;
encontraron con Nuestro Señor	they met our Lord
e díxoles:	and he said to them:
— ¿Dónde vés, Pedro?	"Peter, where are you coming from?"
—Veño de Roma.	"I'm coming from Rome."
—¿Qué hai de novo alá?	"What's new over there?"
—Moito Mal de Osipela	"Many people suffer
e de Sipilón . . .[51]	from erysipelas . . .

St. Peter then describes the cure or turns back to put it into effect. The verses concerning who may have looked with an evil eye (vv. 15–21) are used differently in Salonika to refer to hiccups.[52] Such enumerations of possible offending individuals (or creatures) are also well known in Hispanic charms: ". . . se-é de mala muller, vaite pra mala muller,/ se-é de sapo, vaite pro sapo,/ se-é de culebra, vaite pra culebra . . ." ("if it's from an evil woman, turn back upon her; if it's from a toad, go back to the toad; if it's from a serpent, go back to the serpent").[53] That the little old man should be dressed and shod in iron is highly significant. Metal, and particularly iron, has been seen as magical and proof against all sorts of evil influences since time immemorial. The figure of the old man as helper is also widely known.[54] Again, the allusion to the depths of the sea suggests the practice of sympathetic magic, in which some object brought into contact with the sufferer is thrown into the sea or buried in the earth, thus taking the sickness with it and effecting the cure.[55]

* * *

The Sephardic tradition has often been regarded as a precious relic, a fossilized, archaic survival from medieval times. On the foregoing pages, I have attempted to show that it is indeed notably important for what it has preserved and for what it can teach us about ancient Spanish traditions. At the same time, the Sephardic heritage also represents much more. It records the vital, dynamic creativity of the Sephardim, who have shaped their distinctive tradition in relation to all the diverse peoples—Hispanic and Balkan—with whom they have interacted during their long and eventful history.

Notes

1. See David de Sola Pool and Tamar de Sola Pool, *An Old Faith in the New World* (New York: Columbia University Press, 1955), pp. 3–12 et al. Actually, Jacob bar Simson, who arrived a few months before the refugees from Recife, may well have been Ashkenazic (pp. 12–13, 16, 24, 26, 467). I take into account here the important work of a number of scholars concerning early Jewish settlements in America: Isaac S. and Suzanne E. Emmanuel, Lee M. Friedman, Hyman Grinstein, Morris Gutstein, Seymour B. Liebman, Jacob R. Marcus, Cecil Roth, and Peter Wiernik. For reasons of space, I will dispense with full citations. I wish to thank my friends and colleagues, Rabbi Pinchas Giller and Professors Israel J. Katz and John M. Zemke for their learned advice on bibliographical and Hebraic problems. Steve Kidner's excellent technological help in preparing master tapes is greatly appreciated.

2. See, e.g., Henry V. Besso, *Dramatic Literature of the Sephardic Jews of Amsterdam in the XVIIth and XVIIIth Centuries* (New York: Hispanic Institute, 1947); Kenneth R. Scholberg, *La poesía reli-*

giosa de Miguel de Barrios (Columbus: Ohio State University Press, 1962); also E. M. Wilson, "Miguel de Barrios and Spanish Religious Poetry," *Bulletin of Hispanic Studies* 4 (1963): 176–180.

3. See, e.g., William Davids, "Bijdrage tot de studie van het Spaansch en Portugeesch in Nederland," *Nederlandsche Philologencongress* (Leiden: A. W. Sijthoff, 1910), pp. 141–154: Max L. Wagner, *Os Judeus Hispano-Portugueses e a sua Língua no Oriente, na Holanda e na Alemanha* (Coimbra: Universidade, 1924). The same was certainly the case also in other European Marrano communities: Kenneth Adams, "Castellano, judeoespañol y portugués," *Sefarad* 26–27 (1966–67). On diasporic Judeo-Portuguese, see especially Paul Wexler, "Marrano Ibero-Romance," *Zeitschrift für Romanische Philologie* 98 (1982): 59–108; "Lingüística Judeo-Lusitánica," *Judeo-Romance Languages*, ed. Isaac Benabu and Joseph Sermoneta (Jerusalem: Hebrew University, 1985), pp. 189–208. Note also Cecil Roth, "The Role of Spanish in the Marrano Diaspora," *Hispanic Studies . . . I. González Llubera*, ed. Frank Pierce (Oxford: Dolphin, 1959), pp. 299–308.

4. In 1910, the 86-year-old Amsterdam patriarch, David Montezinos, still remembered a few notable proverbs. Among them: "Sahiu de Egypte e entrou en Mizrajiem" (lit. "He left Egypt and went into Egypt [Heb. *Miçraîm*]"; i.e., He went from the frying pan into the fire). See Davids, "Bijdrage," pp. 152–153; Wagner, *Os Judeus*, p. 11.

5. See our articles: "El Romancero entre los sefardíes de Holanda," *Études . . . Jules Horrent* (Liège: Gedit, 1980), pp. 535–541; "Three Hispano-Jewish *romances* from Amsterdam," *Studies . . . John E. Keller* (Newark, Del.: Juan de la Cuesta, 1980), pp. 243–254.

6. On the disappearance of Spanish and Portuguese, see Pool and Pool, *An Old Faith*, pp. 87–89, 460, 489. Inscriptions on tombstones persisted until 1796, but David de Sola Pool concludes that "the use of Portuguese or Spanish had given way completely to English by the middle of the eighteenth century, except in some homes of Sephardim" ("The Use of Portuguese and Spanish in the Historic Shearith Israel Congregation in New York," *Studies . . . M. J. Benardete*, ed. Izaak A. Langnas and Barton Sholod [New York: Las Américas, 1965], pp. 359–362). For more on the disappearance of Spanish and Portuguese and the acculturation of the early Sephardim in New York, see Hyman B. Grinstein, *The Rise of the Jewish Community of New York, 1654–1860* (Philadelphia: Jewish Publication Society, 1945), pp. 206–207, 166–167.

7. Pool and Pool, *An Old Faith*, p. 87; on Mendes Seixas and his distinguished service: pp. 167–168, 170–174. Note, all the same, that Mendes Seixas is using his ignorance of Spanish and Portuguese as a possible excuse for not returning to his duties at the New York synagogue, thus implying perhaps that the languages were still used, at least in ritual. In any event, "these languages were abandoned by the congregation after the Revolution" (p. 87).

8. Compare the figures cited by Louis M. Hacker, "The Communal Life of the Sephardic Jews in New York City," *Journal of Jewish Communal Service* 3 (1926–27): 32–40 (p. 34); Joseph M. Papo, *Sephardim in Twentieth-Century America: In Search of Unity* (San Jose and Berkeley: Pelé Yoetz Books and Judah L. Magnes Museum, 1987), p. 22. On modern Sephardic communities in New York and elsewhere in the United States, see Papo, "The Sephardic Jewish Community of New York," *Studies in Sephardic Culture: The David N. Barocas Memorial Volume*, ed. Marc D. Angel (New York: Sepher Hermon, 1980), pp. 65–94; Abraham D. Lavender, "The Sephardic Revival in the United States," *Journal of Ethnic Studies* 3, no. 3 (1975–1976): 21–31; and Marc D. Angel's beautiful and deeply moving book, *La America: The Sephardic Experience in the United States* (Philadelphia: Jewish Publication Society, 1982). Note also Angel's crucial article: "The Sephardim of the United States: An Exploratory Study," *American Jewish Yearbook* 74 (1973): 77–138. For an indication of the cultural richness and linguistic diversity of Eastern Sephardic immigration to New York City in the early years of this century, see Max A. Luria, "Judeo-Spanish Dialects in New York City,"

Todd Memorial Volumes, II: Philological Studies, ed. John D. Fitz-Gerald and Pauline Taylor (New York: Columbia University Press, 1930), pp. 7–16.

9. See our *En torno al romancero sefardí: Hispanismo y balcanismo de la tradición judeo-española* (Madrid: Castalia, 1982), pp. 149–239; and for additional folk-literary genres, "Sephardic Folkliterature and Eastern Mediterranean Oral Tradition," *Musica Judaica* 6, no. 1 (1983–84): 38–54. Ethnomusicological analysis corroborates such findings: Israel J. Katz, *Judeo-Spanish Ballads from Jerusalem: An Ethnomusicological Study*, 2 vols. (Brooklyn, N.Y.: Institute of Mediaeval Music, 1972–75); "The Musical Legacy of the Judeo-Spanish Romancero," *Hispania Judaica*, ed. Joseph M. Sola-Solé et al., 3 vols. (Barcelona: Puvill, 1980–84), 2:45–58.

10. Concerning our collection, see our book, *Judeo-Spanish Ballads from Oral Tradition*, vol. 1, *Epic Ballads* (Berkeley and Los Angeles: University of California Press, 1986), pp. 4–21. For collecting and research on Sephardic folk literature, particularly ballads, in a worldwide perspective, see our *Judeo-Spanish Ballads from New York Collected by Maír José Benardete* (Berkeley and Los Angeles: University of California Press, 1981), pp. 4–11.

11. Oro A. Librowicz has brought together a particularly rich collection of Moroccan Judeo-Spanish ballads in Canada. See her *Cancionero séphardi du Québec* (Montreal: Collège du Vieux Montréal, 1988).

12. For an authoritative survey of all genres of Judeo-Spanish literature, both written and oral, see Iacob M. Hassán, "Visión panorámica de la literatura sefardí," *Hispania Judaica* (Barcelona: Puvill, 1982), 2:25–44. In the present article, I omit paraliturgical songs, which, although many have become traditional, ultimately go back to written sources: they stand, in a sense, at the frontier between written and oral literature. For reasons of space, riddles, proverbs, and folktales have also been omitted here. I have limited the article to poetic genres in the strictest sense.

13. For the ballads, see, as a starting point, our "The Judeo-Spanish Ballad Tradition," *Oral Tradition* 2, nos. 2–3 (1987): 633–644.

14. See Reginetta Haboucha, "The Folklore and Traditional Literature of the Judeo-Spanish Speakers," in *The Sepharadi and Oriental Jewish Heritage*, ed. Issachar Ben-Ami (Jerusalem: Hebrew University, 1982), pp. 571–588.

15. See my "Judeo-Spanish and Pan-European Balladry," *Jahrbuch für Volksliedforschung* 24 (1979): 127–138.

16. Version from Salonika (Greece), sung by Esther Varsano Hassid, 67 years, collected by S.G.A. and J.H.S., The Bronx, August 22, 1959.

17. Version from Salonika, recited by Sarah Nehama, 84 years, collected by S.G.A. and J.H.S., Brooklyn, August 20, 1959.

18. See, for now, our *The Judeo-Spanish Ballad Chapbooks of Yacob Abraham Yoná* (Berkeley and Los Angeles: University of California Press, 1971), pp. 87–99; and my *Romancero judeo-español en el Archivo Menéndez Pidal (Catálogo-Indice de romances y canciones)*, 3 vols. (Madrid: C.S.M.P., 1978), no. B15. Note that in the Eastern Judeo-Spanish versions, the motif of the wife as wager (here vv. 3–5) is an extraneous intrusion.

19. See our *En torno*, pp. 154–157; for other *romances* derived from Modern Greek, see pp. 151–178.

20. The Sephardic versions have not been studied. Among many others that could be listed, see Léon Algazi, *Chants séphardis* (London: Fédération Séphardite Mondiale, 1958), no. 28; Isaac Levy, *Antología de liturgia judeo-española*, 10 vols. (Jerusalem: Ministerio de Educación y Cultura, 1964–80), 3:330–350 (nos. 285–290). It is particularly interesting that this song should also form part of the traditions of certain Marrano and Hispanic crypto-Jewish communities. See Henry León, "Les juifs espagnols de Saint-Esprit: Chansons et prières," *Bulletin Hispanique* 9 (1907):

279–280; Jaume Riera i Sanz, "Oracions en catalá dels conversos jueus: Notes bibliográfiques i textos," *Anuario de Filología* (1975): 345–367; Angela Selke, *Los chuetas y la Inquisición* (Madrid: Taurus, 1972), pp. 284–285. For a detailed study of the song's origin and Pan-European analogs, see Aurelio M. Espinosa, "Origen oriental y desarrollo histórico del cuento de las doce palabras retorneadas," *Revista de Filología Española* 17 (1930): 390–413. For international parallels, see also Stith Thompson, *Motif-Index of Folklore*, 6 vols. (Bloomington: Indiana University Press, 1955–58), Z22. *Ehod mi yodea*.

21. See my *Catálogo-Indice*, no. Y1.
22. See our *En torno*, pp. 110–117.
23. See my *Catálogo-Indice*, nos. Y5–Y6.
24. Version from Rhodes (Greece), sung by Mrs. Leah Huniu, 67 years, collected by S.G.A. and J.H.S., Los Angeles, July 31, 1958. The following forms require comment: *šoḥet* (12*aef*) "butcher (qualified to slaughter animals according to ritual requirements)" (Heb. *šōḥēt*); *malaḥ a-mave* (12*ce*) "angel of death" (Heb. *malā'kh ha-māweth*). For the transcription of Hebrew used in the present article, see our *Chapbooks*, pp. 18–20.
25. Version from Çanakkale (Turkey), recited by Mr. Isaac Zacuto, ca. 60 years, collected by S.G.A., Los Angeles, Spring 1958. The word *aspro* (1*c*) is from Greek *'áspron* "money, coin: a farthing" (from *'áspros* "white"); *levanim* (1*d*) is simply the Hebrew equivalent: *lābān, lĕbānîm* "white; silver coin(s)". For *malaḥ* (9*a*) and *šoḥet* (9*b*), see the previous note.
26. See our study of the three songs and their Pan-European analogs: "A Judeo-Spanish Cumulative Song and Its Greek Counterpart," *Revue des Etudes Juives* 137 (1978): 375–381 (or *En torno*, pp. 183–188); also Abraham A. Schwadron, "Chad Gadya: A Passover Song," *Selected Reports in Ethnomusicology* 4 (1983): 125–155.
27. See Manuel Alvar, *Cantos de boda judeo-españoles* (Madrid: C.S.I.C., 1971); *Endechas judeoespañolas*, 2nd ed. (Madrid: C.S.I.C., 1969); Paloma Díaz-Mas, "Poesía luctuosa judeo-española" (Licenciatura thesis, Universidad Complutense, Madrid, 1977); idem, "Temas y tópicos en la poesía luctuosa sefardi" (Ph.D. diss., Universidad Complutense, Madrid, 1981).
28. See now Susana Weich-Shahak, "The Wedding Songs of the Bulgarian-Sephardi Jews: A Preliminary Study," *Orbis Musicae* 7 (1979–80): 81–107. On Moroccan wedding songs, see now also Oro A. Librowicz and Judith R. Cohen, "Modalidades expresivas en los cantos de boda judeo-españoles," *Revista de Dialectología y Tradiciones Populares* 41 (1986): 189–209; Judith R. Cohen, "*Ya Salió de la Mar*: Judeo-Spanish Wedding Songs among Moroccan Jews in Canada," in *Women and Music in Cross-Cultural Perspective*, ed. Ellen Koskoff (Westport, Conn.: Greenwood Press, 1987): pp. 55–67. Note also Sarah Leibovici, "Nuestras bodas sefarditas: Algunos ritos y costumbres," *Revista de Dialectología y Tradiciones Populares* 41 (1986): 163–187.
29. See, however, S. Weich-Shahak, "Childbirth Songs Among Sephardic Jews of Balkan Origin," *Orbis Musicae* 8 (1982–83): 87–103.
30. Version from Salonika, sung by Esther Varsano Hassid, 65 years, collected by S.G.A. and J.H.S., Van Nuys, Calif., August 22, 1957. The following words need comment: *simán* (1*i*, 2*g*) "sign, omen" (Heb. *şîmān*); *resta* (2*d*) here perhaps "serving"; usually "string (of fish, figs, coins)": other versions allude to a "resta de ducados" (= Sp. *ristra*); *enxundiada* (3*f*) "fattened" (Sp. *enjundia* "fat, grease [of an animal]"). The sentiment expressed in vv. 1*kl* and 2*ij* echoes the benediction *šeheḥĕyānû* ("who has granted us life ... and permitted us to reach this season").
31. Version from Salonika, sung by Esther Varsano Hassid, 65 years, collected by S.G.A. and J.H.S., Van Nuys, Calif., August 22, 1957. The *baño* (2*a*) clearly refers to the second ritual bath (*bĕthûlîm*) discussed by Michael Molho, *Usos y costumbres de los sefardies de Salónica* (Madrid and Barcelona: C.S.I.C., 1950), p. 35.

32. Version from Rhodes, sung by Perla Galante, ca. 75 years, collected by S.G.A. and J.H.S., Los Angeles, January 8, 1958. The following forms need comment: ḥazino (2) "sick" (O. Sp. hazino "sad, poor, afflicted"; from Ar. ḥazīn "sad"); agua de turungá (22) "orange water" (?) (turungá = toronjal "tree producing the toronja fruit"; the meaning of Sp. toronja varies regionally: "grapefruit; citron; types of orange"; it is not certain exactly what meaning toronğa has in E. J.-Sp.; if the word, seemingly limited to poetic contexts and not in current use, has been influenced by T. turunc, which seems probable, then it may well denote the bitter Seville orange; garón (24) "throat" (Heb. gārôn); englotar (24) "swallow" (cf. E. J.-Sp., O. Sp. englutir); xofletico (29) "light breath" (cf. Sp. soplar).

33. For other texts, see Edith Gerson-Kiwi, "The Legacy of Jewish Music Through the Ages," In the Dispersion 3 (1963–64): 149–172 (p. 164); Levy, Antología, 4: 374–378 (nos. 239–240); Max A. Luria, The Monastir Dialect of Judeo-Spanish (New York: Instituto de las Españas, 1930), p. 94; Baruh Uziel, "Ha-fôlklôr šel ha-yĕhûdîm ha-sĕfārādîm," Rĕšumôth 5 (1927): 324–337; 6 (1930): 359–397: 375–376 (or the inaccurate transcription in Arcadio de Larrea Palacín, "El cancionero de Baruh Uziel," Vox Romanica 18 [1959]: 324–365 [p. 341]).

34. See our Chapbooks, pp. 188–189 and n. 4.

35. For other texts, see Molho, Usos y costumbres, p. 44; Uziel, "Ha-fôlklôr," p. 383 (or Larrea Palacín, "El cancionero," pp. 345–346); Leo Wiener, "Songs of the Spanish Jews in the Balkan Peninsula," Modern Philology 1 (1903–1904): 205–216, 259–274 (no. 1).

36. See our En torno, pp. 89–95. Vv. 13–14, 21–22, 25–26, and 33 embody formulas that are well known elsewhere in Judeo-Spanish traditional poetry.

37. Version from Rhodes, sung by Rebecca Peha, 71 years, collected by S.G.A. and J.H.S., Los Angeles, July 23, 1958.

38. Version from Rhodes, sung by Victoria Hazan Kassner, ca. 55 years, collected by S.G.A. and J.H.S., Los Angeles, October 27, 1957. The word amán (= T. aman "have mercy!") is a popular poetic exclamation used in the traditional songs of all Balkan peoples. See our En torno, pp. 214–227.

39. Published variants are rare: see my Catálogo-Indice, no. AA11; Michael Molho, Literatura sefardita de Oriente (Madrid and Barcelona: C.S.I.C., 1960), pp. 97–98; Uziel, "Ha-fôlklôr," p. 382 (= Larrea, "Cancionero," pp. 344–345).

40. See the exhaustive studies of Eugenio Asensio, Poética y realidad en el cancionero peninsular de la Edad Media, 2d ed. (Madrid: Gredos, 1970), pp. 69–229; M. Alvar, Cantos de boda, pp. 65–94; Maria Aliete Farinho das Dores Galhoz, "Une note de plus pour l'étude du petit corpus de chansons parallelistiques de Marmelete," Litterature Orale Traditionnelle Populaire (Paris: Fondation Calouste Gulbenkian, 1987), pp. 39–58.

41. Margit Frenk, ed., Cancionero de galanes y otros rarísimos cancionerillos góticos (Valencia: Castalia, 1952), pp. 62–63; as the editor observes (p. xli), veros doubtless corresponds to Old French vair "variable, changeable, of different colors; shining, brilliant, grey-blue, clear (of the eyes)." For more on this song, see M. Frenk, Corpus de la antigua lírica popular hispánica (Siglos XV a XVII) (Madrid: Castalia, 1987), no. 128.

42. See our Judeo-Spanish Ballads from Bosnia (Philadelphia: University of Pennsylvania Press, 1971), pp. 99–100; John G. Cummins, The Spanish Traditional Lyric (Oxford: Pergamon, 1977), pp. 99–101; Paula Olinger, Images of Transformation in the Traditional Hispanic Lyric (Newark, Del.: Juan de la Cuesta, 1985), pp. 18–22 et al.; Frenk, Corpus, pp. 62–69.

43. See S. G. Armistead and James T. Monroe, "Albas, Mammas, and Code-Switching in the Kharjas," La Corónica 11, no. 2 (1982–83): 174–182.

44. For variants of the Greek and Sephardic verses, see our study in En torno, pp. 179–182. For other close translations of lyric songs from Greek, see Moshe Attias, Cancionero judeo-español

(Jerusalem: Centro de Estudios sobre el Judaismo de Salónica, 1972), no. 75, and our "Sephardic Folkliterature," pp. 43–44. For numerous examples of Eastern Sephardic lyric poetry, some of it of relatively recent origin, see Attias, *Cancionero*, and Isaac Levy, *Chants judéo-espagnols*, 4 vols. (London and Jerusalem: Fédération Séphardite Mondiale–Edition de l'auteur, 1959–73).

45. Text from Rhodes, sung by Rebecca Amato Levy, 46 years, collected by S.G.A and J.H.S., Los Angeles, February 16, 1958. Mrs. Levy is now the author of an invaluable book on her native Judeo-Spanish tradition: *I Remember Rhodes* (New York: Sepher-Hermon, 1987). On the Rhodian community, see also Marc D. Angel's splendid book, *The Jews of Rhodes* (New York: Sepher-Hermon, 1978).

46. Text from Rhodes, recited by Rebecca A. Levy, 46 years, collected by S.G.A and J.H.S., Los Angeles, February 16, 1958. The following forms need comment: *a-neviá* (7) "the prophetess" (Heb. *ha-nĕbî'āh*); *a-Kadúš Baruḥú* (22) -Heb. *ha-Qādôš Bārûkh-hû*; *ainará* (32) "evil eye" (Heb. *ʽēyn hā-rāʽ*).

47. For a variant from Salonika, see Joseph Nehama, *Dictionnaire du judéo-espangnol*, ed. Jesús Cantera (Madrid: C.S.I.C., 1977), p. 14*b*.

48. See John C. Lawson, *Modern Greek Folklore and Ancient Greek Religion* (New Hyde Park, N.Y.: University Books, 1964), pp. 23–25, 49–50.

49. Gonzalo Correas, *Vocabulario de refranes y frases proverbiales* (1627), ed. Louis Combet (Bordeaux: Université de Bordeaux, 1967), p. 65*b*. For other Hispanic rain prayers, see Enrique Casas Gaspar, *Ritos agrarios: Folklore campesino español* (Madrid: Escelicer, 1950), pp. 40–47. Note also the rain song published in *Revista de Dialectología y Tradiciones Populares* 1 (1944–45): 368–369. Its obviously modern character bespeaks continuity of belief in the efficacy of such prayers.

50. Note the entire issue of *Yeda-'Am* 9, no. 1 (Autumn 1963), devoted to "The Patriarchs and Matriarchs in Jewish Folk-Life." For analogous texts, see Abraham Galante, *Histoire des juifs de Rhodes, Chio, Cos, etc.* (Istanbul: Fratelli Haim, 1935), p. 119; Matilda Koen-Sarano, "El aynara en el reflan djudeo-espanyol," *Aki Yerushalayim* 10, no. 4 (1989): 42–45.

51. Víctor Lis Quibén, *La medicina popular en Galicia* (Pontevedra: Torres, 1949), p. 144, also pp. 26, 68–69, 122, 128, 139–140, 145–149, 161, 163, 201. For other instances, also involving the question "Where are you going?", see Augusto César Pires de Lima and Bertino Daciano, "Tradições de Azurara," *Douro-Litoral* 4, nos. 1–2 (1950): 117; Joaquim and Fernando Pires de Lima, *Tradições populares de Entre-Douro-e-Minho* (Barcelos: Editora do Minho, 1938), pp. 163, 168; Joan Amades, *Folklore de Catalunya* (Barcelona: Selecta, 1951), nos. 3458, 3474, 3482; Claude Roy, *Trésor de la poésie populaire française* (Paris: Seghers, 1954), p. 352.

52. See Molho, *Usos y costumbres*, p. 290.

53. Quibén, *La medicina popular*, p. 77; also pp. 134, 141, 144, 275, 281, 285, 286.

54. For iron, see our *Epic Ballads*, pp. 53–55, nn. 30–34; for the old man, Thompson, *Motif-Index*: N825.2, *Old man helper*.

55. See Wayland D. Hand, "The Magical Transfer of Disease," in *Magical Medicine* (Berkeley and Los Angeles: University of California Press, 1980), pp. 17–42. For further instances, see Molho, *Usos y costumbres*, pp. 278–280; Amades, *Folklore de Catalunya*, nos. 3494–3495; Luis L. Cortés, *Antología de la poesía popular rumana* (Salamanca: University of Salamanca, 1955), pp. 136–137, 144–145.

Tradition and History: Sephardic Contributions to American Literature

Diane Matza

Sensitivity to cultural diversity in our national literature has propelled us to reexamine our literary histories and critical canon, a necessary undertaking even for a narrow specialization such as American Jewish belles lettres. Among the general reading public, Jewish or not, names like Malamud, Roth, Gold, Bellow, Charyn, Ozick, Paley, and numerous others of primarily Eastern European background are well known. Much less familiar are writers of Sephardic background, though two exceptions readily come to mind, Emma Lazarus and Robert Nathan. Other Sephardic belletrists generally have reputations only among scholars and critics.[1] For example, historians know Mordecai Manuel Noah as a playwright as well as a politician, journalist, and proponent of Jewish causes; educators may know Annie Nathan Meyer, a founder of Barnard College, also as a playwright, short fiction writer, and memoirist; critics specializing in contemporary American Jewish literature will be familiar with Stanley Sultan's novel *Rabbi* and Stephen Levy's poetry, and so on. Several histories and critical works on American Jewish literature, however, have excluded figures like Meyer and Sultan; and nowhere have Sephardic writers been examined as a group.

While surely there have been and are American writers of Sephardic background, the question of whether the Sephardic Jewish writer exists as a class with special concerns and approaches different from the German or Eastern European Jewish writer is a complex one. The paucity of evidence may explain why this issue has not so far been addressed. Sephardic writers are relatively few in number, and their works are scattered across several periods in American literature and diverse literary forms. Some of them are or were professional writers and rather prolific, but others were amateurs, and a few produced only one work—and that not distributed widely. The works of some Sephardic authors have a strong Jewish content, those of others have no Jewish characters or identifiably Jewish themes, leading one to ask whether the category of "Jewish writer" should include all Jews who write or only those who write on matters of Jewish concern. Further, the national backgrounds of the writers we will discuss are considerably varied. Mordecai Manuel Noah, Penina Moïse, Emma Lazarus, Elizabeth Cardozo, Annie Nathan Meyer, Robert Nathan, and Nancy Cardozo were all American-born descendants of the earliest Sephardic settlers in the United States, and their connections to Judaism ranged from the devout to the unconcerned.[2] The Sephardic Jewry of the eastern Mediterranean, which has a much shorter history in the United States, is represented by Leon Sciaky, who was born in Salonika; Stephen Levy and David Raphael, whose families originated in the Levant; and Stanley Sultan, whose family came here from Syria.

The question for us here is whether the members of such a diverse group display a common sensibility derived from their Sephardism and whether the Sephardic heritage infuses their literary work. To determine this requires examining their personal histories as American Sephardim, when possible, as well as their writings. I believe that subtle commonalities exist among several of the writers I have mentioned, most notably in a cosmopolitan outlook bequeathed them by either of two strains of Sephardic cultural background. Among the descendants of the early Sephardic settlers this expresses itself as a tendency to espouse traditional democratic and sometimes religious values, and among the Levantine Sephardim as a preoccupation with memorializing and revitalizing Sephardic history. In both groups, furthermore, heritage has influenced the writers' relationships to America, which in turn affected their chosen subjects.

Among those writers whose ancestry goes back to the early Sephardic settlers—Mordecai Manuel Noah, Penina Moïse, Emma Lazarus, Annie Nathan Meyer, and Robert Nathan—we find that they all displayed a Jewish consciousness in their personal lives and expressed it in their writing.[3] Yet we find nothing parochial in this group: they possessed an impressively broad range of interests and were fully engaged in the wider American culture, even if, like Penina Moïse and Emma Lazarus to a degree, they led sheltered and domestic-centered lives.

Whether they regarded Judaism piously or cursorily, these writers did not shun the Gentile community and were not shunned by it in turn. Discord was not the general tone of their relations with Christians, although most of them were familiar enough with anti-Semitism, either through direct experience or through their knowledge of history and contemporary events. Despite some personal tensions between their American nationality and Jewish group identity, their literary efforts—even when critical of American institutions—as a rule display tremendous faith in America's democratic promise, and they consistently affirm the qualities of the America they value: the individual's importance at the center of life, dissent, liberty, and identification with the suffering of others. Their families' long history without persecution in America, and the subsequent security most of them felt as American Jews, encouraged them to espouse these values, to urge equal opportunity for others as well, and to take up Jewish or other causes in their writing. In the case of most of the writers I plan to discuss, mixing a chronological and thematic framework, both their personal lives and their writings illuminate their relationships to tradition, to history, and to their adopted home.

Penina Moïse

Ill-health and poverty kept Penina Moïse (1797–1880) physically close to home throughout most of her life, but the domestic sphere did not limit her outlook or narrow the subjects of her poetry. She was a respected figure in the cultural, religious, and educational affairs of the Jewish community, holding salons for the intellectually inclined, keeping abreast of current literary trends, writing hymns for the synagogue, and establishing a school with her sister. Biographical data suggest that Gentiles also esteemed her and that she had quite friendly relations with them, although she firmly rejected intermarriage for herself and frowned on it among her coreligionists.[4]

Throughout her life Moïse contributed poems and essays to numerous periodicals, and her cosmopolitan outlook is certainly revealed in her wide subject and style range. She is best known for her religious poetry, especially the hymns still included in several prayerbooks. The conventional style that marks most of her poetry, making some of it seem unimaginative, is appropriate to hymns, which must have traditional appeal. Accessibility, ability to provide comfort, and simplicity of images mark these works, which reveal a sincere, unquestioning, and almost absolutist faith. Some of the hymns discuss salvation and death, but life is the true subject of most, a life completed and vitalized by religious faith. The God of these works is generous and forgiving, a source of truth and goodness.

Moïse downplays her own imaginative powers in the hymns; instead, she relies on standard ways of showing God's power and so reveals her own humility before God. For example, the idea expressed in "The lmmutability of God" is a simple one: huge changes take place over time; these changes are beyond human conception, but God's presence is constant and thus comforting.[5]

Further, the rhyme schemes are not innovative, as in,

> Oh! bless the meek
> who daily seek
> Thy praise to speak;
> Whose efforts blend,
> Faith to extend
> In thee, man's never-changing Friend!
> [p. 5]

No effort to reveal passion, intensity, or sensuality marks such lines; neither are the images fresh and striking—"wings of light," "rain-drops large and bright," "tears of recent storm" (p. 14). To describe creation Moïse will use the phrase "vivid colors" rather than duplicate the colors for the reader. Again, Moïse's purpose, not innovation but illustration of the force and constancy behind religious tradition, is satisfied by such poetic language.

Moïse asserts her own acceptance of God's law, despite her personal hardships, with rather upbeat resignation, actively espousing traditional verities about the afterlife and other Jewish teachings. Often, she aims to cheer:

> To ev'ry evil that annoys,
> to every trial fearful,

> Thou bringest some light counterpoise.
> [p. 11]

And in a similar vein,

> Meek faith converts the couch of pain
> Into a bed of roses;
> For there we moral vigor gain,
> To bear what G-d disposes.
> [pp. 13–14]

Or consider Moïse's poem about personal loss, "Immortality of the Soul." She begins with grief: "A mournful lament for the dead! Woe unto me!" However, this is the most complaint she allows herself, and by the fifth stanza she avows, "Excessive grief is unbelief." The words she has God speak in this poem are ones she accepts:

> Death, my messenger of peace,
> Frees the soul my grace will save....
> Then tremble not at empty names
> Ye who mercy's word believes.
> [p. 34]

A poem about her brother's death continues this optimism, ending with the charge that mourners should

> celebrate with one united voice
> Thy first birthday among immortal souls.
> [pp. 294–295]

Moïse is not interested in the philosophical complexity of how faith lightens pain; this is left for others with a more analytic bent and a more questioning relationship to God.

Nothing in Moïse's religious poetry prepares us for her humorous justification of card-playing and writing as mental sport in "The Muses' Vindication of Cards," or for the wit displayed in "Love and Law," in which a lawyer, smitten with a woman who spurns his love, imagines her trial and the verdict convicting her. Personal poems about her family, nature poems such as "The Apple," "The Comet Again," and "The Gift of the Snowdrop," and historical poems about the United States further exhibit the range of her poetic style and interests. Most interesting, Moïse's political and historical poetry reveals that she felt no tension about being a Jew in America; in fact, her secure American identity contributed to her ability to express personal outrage in poems about the Maryland Jew Bill, which imposed religious restrictions on public officials, and the persecution of Jews in Damascus, and to speak out vehemently about non-Jewish issues such as the Irish famine and the plight of Civil War widows.

Moïse was both a religious traditionalist and a person sure of her secular democratic values. Both of these attitudes were possible because her heritage was generally respected by those around her, though, of course, she did see some crumbling of the Jewish world as her coreligionists intermarried and even converted. Still, her community was well established, she experienced no personal anti-Semitism, and she received considerable praise for her efforts on behalf of the Jewish community. Her life, reflected with little distortion in her writings, represents a common adjustment of mid-nineteenth-century Sephardic Americans to the new land: traditionalism and assimilation appear to coexist, each with a circumscribed sphere of influence.

Mordecai Manuel Noah

Mordecai Manuel Noah (1785–1851) provides both a contrast and a parallel to Moïse. His penchant for full involvement in the life of the United States and the Jewish community was similar to Moïse's. However, not hampered by gender, isolation, or ill-health, and blessed with an exuberant, egotistical, and energetic nature, Noah had a more dramatic and public career than Moïse. He was a playwright, a journalist, a publicist for the Jewish community, a diplomat, and a politician.

Despite the repeated praise for the American experiment in democracy in Noah's speeches and writings, a defensive insecurity about his American identity comes through in his highly patriotic plays. He was also overtly concerned about anti-Semitic remarks directed at him in the press, and he addressed these in his own newspaper columns. Further, he believed that anti-Semitism was responsible for his recall as envoy to the Barbary States, although the historian

Jonathan Sarna suggests that this problem was more perceived than real, and that Noah's sloppy financial arrangements led to his recall.[6] No doubt, he experienced some tension between his religious and national identities, a point I will raise again later.

As a dramatic issue, anti-Semitism appears in none of Noah's plays, but Sol Liptzin suggests that Noah's avoidance of the ubiquitous evil Jewish character so popular on the stage in his day evinces his concern with anti-Semitism in the American theatre.[7] Whether theatregoers noticed this oblique technique is, of course, unknown; however, it seems safe to say that Noah's Jewishness propelled him to write repeatedly about democracy's promise of tolerance, justice, and equality.

Noah is probably known better for his failed Ararat plan, the attempt to colonize Jews in upstate New York, and for his journalism than for his plays, which even he called amateurish. Nonetheless, many critics have regarded these efforts as worthy contributions to a budding native theatre, and it is certainly worth examining how his private values and infatuation for the American Dream gain full expression in the dramas.

Noah's historical plays focus on the nature of virtue and honor, loyalty and liberty. They are conventional in style: three of the four extant plays use the familiar device of the woman disguised as a man, and all of them depend on predictable intrigue and some contrived circumstances. Still, they are paced well and are quite entertaining.

She Would be a Soldier; or, The Plains of Chippewa, which takes place during the War of 1812, offers an excellent example of Noah's political intentions. It begins with a paean to the American Dream spoken by a Frenchman, Jasper, who is "imbued with the spirit" he had felt as one of La Fayette's soldiers during the Revolution.[8] After the war he became a true pioneer, taming the wilds, settling down, and raising a daughter, Christine. This opening establishes both Jasper's and the play's values, and though Jasper errs in promising Christine to Jerry, a man she cannot love (mostly because he studiously keeps out of the fighting when his militia unit confronts some British troops), and so sets in motion Christine's escape, his values are the ones affirmed in the end. Christine loves Lenox, a soldier, and, disguised as a soldier herself, follows him to the battlefront to save herself from bumbling and cowardly Jerry. Despite her bravery, her emotions are stereotyped, as when she quickly concludes that Lenox does not love her when she sees him conversing with another woman. To other soldiers, Christine seems a suspicious character because she lurks around her lover's tent, and when she refuses to reveal her identity or motives she receives a death sentence. By the end of the play, all threats to a happy resolution disappear, Lenox and Christine are reunited, and the British are defeated.

Although the play depends on humor and expected plot turnings, Noah conveys a serious message through his repeated mocking of the cowardly Jerry and his scorn for the British General's paternalism toward the Indian Chief and for Captain Pendragon's self-inflation as a "man of fashion." The humbler and rawer Americans receive full praise, and from their lips come the idealistic closing words, "enemies in war—in peace, friends."

The Fall of Athens offers another example of Noah's political intentions, though it is a much more ambitious theatrical venture than *She Would Be a Soldier*. Characterized by an elaborate setting, several subplots, and much intrigue, it admirably avoids predictability by involving the Greek heroes in plans for liberation that are neither simplistic nor easily fulfilled. Further, the heroes and heroine face personal and political struggles and so are not one-dimensional. As in his other work, however, Noah's decidedly American values emerge clearly: he praises individual and collective action for freedom, stresses the right of choice, and urges full equality for all classes of people.

For Noah the playwright there was, apparently, no conflict in a Jew's using the stage as a platform to espouse the democratic ideal. Nonetheless, one wonders about his motivations. Did he fear that if America could not live up to its promises the Jews would suffer? If so, did he feel a special responsibility as a Jew to remind American audiences of their country's principles? In his fine book, *Jacksonian Jew: The Two Worlds of Mordecai Manuel Noah*, Jonathan Sarna suggests that Noah's Ararat plan revealed the fragile underpinnings of his espoused beliefs in American opportunity for equality.

> Neither his patriotic allusions nor his sweeping assertions could conceal the Ararat-American tensions inherent in his plan. If, as he claimed in his address, "in this free and happy country distinctions in religion are unknown," how

could a separate Jewish colony be countenanced? How could a "government of the Jews" be organized if the constitution and laws of the U.S. were to be binding? How could Jews in Ararat be loyal to America if the asylum was "temporary and provisional"?[9]

Likewise, if Noah felt these tensions, as Sarna convincingly asserts, he very well might have seen the theatre as a forum for safeguarding Jewish interests. For Noah, the century-long history of Sephardic Jewry in America was apparently not enough to assuage his concern that the Jews were living in a country not their own and governed by a people other than themselves. Perhaps Noah believed that through a public and dramatic medium he could influence his audiences to believe and practice the ideals of the democratic tradition.

Emma Lazarus

Emma Lazarus (1849–1887), the best-known of the Sephardic writers, has received comparatively substantial critical attention, and much has been written about her development of a strong Jewish consciousness. Thus, what follows is not new textual or historical analysis but a consideration of Lazarus's similarities to other writers in this study.

Raised in a consciously Jewish but minimally observant home, Lazarus looked not to her own history but to classical Greece, the German poets, and transcendentalism for poetic inspiration. She showed her allegiance to tradition by "rarely stray[ing] off beaten methods of versifying " or "tried-and-true subjects."[10] Like other writers in this Sephardic group, Lazarus had numerous Gentile friends and became part of the general intellectual community through her personal and/or written relationships with Ralph Waldo Emerson, E. C. Stedman, Turgenev, Robert Browning, and William Morris. She did not seek out other Jewish writers, nor did she use Jewish subjects extensively in her work until she awakened to her own minority status during the great migration of Eastern European Jews to New York after 1880.

Lazarus's poem "In the Jewish Synagogue at Newport," written in 1867, is instructive of her attitude about Judaism prior to the last decade of her life. As Dan Vogel explains in his *Emma Lazarus*, it reveals "the impersonality, the dispassionate objectivity of her review of the highlights of history." Lazarus sees the Jews "only as a `relic of the days of old'" (p. 73). In this poem, nothing vital exists in the contemporary Jew but memory.

A shift in Lazarus's relationship to Judaism and to other Jews began in 1880, when mounting brutality drove thousands of Russian Jews to emigrate, arousing her awareness of persecution and of the meaning of continuity in Jewish identity. Vogel helps us understand Lazarus's perspective: "The fountainhead of modern culture was poisoned in her mind, and even classical culture appeared to be relatively empty, if not suspect" (p. 141). Further, in an essay titled "The Jewish Problem," Lazarus revealed a new consciousness that even America could not fulfill the Jews' need for safety, decency, and opportunity: "in America every Jew knows that the host society never equates the Jewish community with the best Jews; rather security for the Jew is dependent on the conduct of 'the meanest rascal who belongs to the tribe' " (p. 142).

To the end of her life Lazarus's subject remained the Jews and Judaism.[11] Of the three writers discussed thus far, she was by far the least religious and the most assimilated. Yet neither characteristic hindered her identification with other Jews in time of crisis. Lazarus's experience must, then, raise the question, What binds the Jewish people together, and to what extent are they assimilable?

Clearly, in Lazarus's case anti-Semitism compelled her to examine an identity she had neglected. However, her natural sympathy with the persecuted was not the only factor in her conversion. Rabbi Gustav Gottheil influenced her not only to visit the immigrants on Ward's Island but to expand her deficient education in Judaism and Jewish history. Like Joseph Victor, the protagonist of Robert Nathan's *A Star in the Wind*, a work written eighty years after her death, Emma Lazarus discovered that Jewishness remained a vital tradition and could be a compelling force in her own life, manifested in part by a commitment to Zionism, a commitment Mordecai Manuel Noah might have made had he lived during the same period.

Annie Nathan Meyer

A strong contrast to Emma Lazarus is her cousin, Annie Nathan Meyer (1867–1951), who minimized the existence of anti-Semitism in the United States and remained firmly opposed to Zionism during all of her long life. A prolific fiction writer, dramatist, and essayist, Meyer was proud of her Sephardic heritage, her familial connection to Rabbi Gershom Seixas, and her family's long history in America, all of which helped her to move very successfully between the Jewish and Gentile worlds. These attributes, I believe, also contributed to Meyer's traditionalism; yet she repeatedly claimed for herself a position in the literary and social avant garde. In fact, her own appraisal ignores a palpable tension between the radicalism and traditionalism of her thought.

As a Jew, Meyer maintained an affiliation with Shearith Israel, the oldest Sephardic synagogue in the United States, but she wrote very little about her religious education or the extent of her own observance. She once referred to herself in print as an agnostic, and after her marriage to Dr. Alfred Meyer—for whom science rather than spirituality was the significant force in the universe—she rarely attended religious services or fulfilled religious rituals at home. During the Great Migration period, Meyer's attitudes toward newcomers were similar to those of the establishment German Jews who feared an anti-Semitic reaction to the influx of Eastern European and Ottoman Jews. She urged the new immigrants to be as unobtrusive as possible, and in fact this founder of Barnard College, so often sought out for her advice about higher education, occasionally discouraged Eastern European Jewish women from applying to Barnard. Also praising Israel Zangwill's play *The Melting Pot* in her article "The Ghetto in Literature," she nevertheless warned that such works might incite "racial" hatred by emphasizing the exoticism of the Jews. Jewish writers, she asserted, should write about the Jewish bourgeoisie, just as Gentile prose artists had for decades written of their own middle-class.[12] Meyer herself never undertook such a project; in fact, absent from her creative work is any reference to Jewish characters, themes, or issues.[13]

Meyer's attitudes about anti-Semitism reflect her privileged position in a line of Sephardic Jews with a long and comfortable history in America, and a certain ambivalence about prejudice as well. In her autobiography, *It's Been Fun*, she briefly notes but minimizes one childhood experience with anti-Semitism in the Midwest, and she claims in the book's closing pages that anti-Semitism exists only for those who look for it.[14]

For a Jewish woman writing in the 1980s, so close in time to the decimation of Jewish communities in Europe and the Levant, and not long after a nasty period of anti-Semitism in the United States, this might suggest ulterior motives. Meyer seems also to have been obtuse about being the object of anti-Semitism, having ignored the possibility that her Jewishness was the reason that Barnard's administration granted her a less than prominent position even though she was a founder of the college. On the other hand, she was aware quite early of the ugliness in Hitler's racial policies and urged Barnard officials not to invite German scholars with fascist leanings to the campus.[15]

Meyer's varying views of Jewishness match the separation between tradition and the avant-garde in other areas of her life. She seems to be straddling a fence dividing two worlds. While acknowledging that tradition was necessary for group survival as well as to maintain her own position of privilege, she also saw it as exercising as a stranglehold on groups that were without privilege in American society. Her play *Black Souls*, written in 1932, expresses her outrage about the indignities black people still suffered in the United States, and her special concern with their lack of educational opportunity.

Black Souls was controversial in both its subject, a love affair between a young black man and a young white woman, and its style, for its black characters do not speak in dialect. Meyer was one of the few white writers of her time to depict educated black characters speaking as whites did; and to assure herself that she was right to do so she had James Weldon Johnson read her play for stylistic authenticity. He gave it his blessing. As we will see in what follows, the play reveals a great deal about Meyer's conflicted attitudes toward the world she lived in.

In addition to displaying Meyer's sincerity and passion about equality, *Black Souls* is generally a well-written play, often compelling, tightly organized, with sympathetic and interesting characters. The setting is a black-run institution of higher learning for blacks in the South. Among the ingredients are the headmaster's enthusiasm about working for his race, his wife's secret history as a forced paramour to Senator Verne, and a romantic attachment between Verne's daughter and a young black poet. While the play is thoroughly enjoyable as a drama and as a historical document, Meyer's manipulating hand is highly visible, as when the senator's daughter, Luella, pursues her lover though he has repeatedly warned her of the South's hostility to their romance. Eventually the young lover relents and takes Luella to his secret room in the woods, thus setting in motion a series of events that lead to his death. The play's resolution, showing a repentant Verne, may satisfy Meyer's need for optimism, but is hardly believable. Violence in the form of a lynching reveals Meyer's understanding of southern realities, but her conversion of the evil and hypocritical Verne displays her need not merely for happy endings but for trust in the American system and in the ultimate success of democratic values.

In most of Meyer's earlier fiction and drama, primarily in the area of women's issues, tradition prevented her from being as radical as she considered herself. Nonetheless, she frequently wrote eloquently about the unsatisfactory position of women in contemporary American life and in the institution of marriage; and her work displays seriousness, commitment, wit, and sensitivity to the complexity of human relationships.

Her first novel, *Helen Brent, M.D.*, is radical in its deploring of high society's materialist values and double standard of sexual morality; its condemnation of society's silence on venereal disease, and of men who deny their wives' achievements; and its suggestion that many women ignore women's collective best interests. In this novel Annie Nathan Meyer sacrifices novelistic subtlety to create a platform for her own views, but she has still given us a detailed and memorable picture of a particular social world. For example, in explaining how difficult it is to combine marriage and career, Helen Brent says, "Women are often more against us than men because they live life in a narrow sphere," and adds that she has "never found a man willing to take irregular meals and give up vacations."[16]

Despite these attitudes, Meyer's novel sticks to the traditionalism of happy endings and heroines as models of all the correct views. What is troublesome about Helen Brent as a model, however, is that Meyer too firmly emphasizes her separateness from all other women; thus, Helen may be a model of correct views, but she is not a model to be emulated by other women. Even her best student falls into the trap of willingness to give up all for a man.

Helen Brent is a young and attractive doctor who has refused to relinquish her career for marriage to the highly traditionalist lawyer she loves. Firm in her conviction not to become merely a domestic machine when she marries, Brent is also committed to fighting battles for other women, often with little success. For example, outraged that her prize student's sister is to wed a profligate man known to carry venereal disease, she confronts the mother. Her effort to have the marriage called off or even to warn the bride fails, and later she must witness the young bride's death. But it is not only in this that Helen Brent is unsuccessful. She is also unable to convince her student's mother that this daughter deserves love as much as the more social and less intellectual child. As she rails privately and publicly about the crimes she alone seems to see, other women describe her as sour, never examining their own opinions.

Perhaps the greatest disappointment for the contemporary reader is the novel's closing hint that Helen and her lawyer will eventually marry. Harold has been so blind, intransigent, and stupid that his incipient change of heart is not quite credible, no more so than Verne's conversion in *Black Souls*. We feel that the novel's denouement into traditionalist roles was preordained. Nor is there anything radical in the central premise of *Helen Brent, M.D.*—that it takes a highly unusual woman, of which there are very few, to question traditional values effectively.

A later play by Meyer, *The Dominant Sex*, written in 1911, advances the same message. Here, Meyer uses humor and irony to highlight the main character's folly. Mrs. Cora Mason confuses women's equality with an unthinking espousal of any cause related to women and a total rejection of domestic responsibilities toward her husband and child. Prey to fashionable thoughts about woman's emancipation, Mrs. Mason becomes a neglectful wife and mother and a shallow thinker, for which Meyer soundly chastises her. There are amusing portraits here of the secretary who spends her whole salary on modish but inappropriate and uncomfortable clothing, a gossiping wealthy matron who pretends interest in political issues but listens most closely to the latest sex scandal, a hard-nosed and somewhat masculine female journalist. Clearly these are all stereotypes, and Meyer relies on them to advance her own views: women should be sensible, immune to fashion, feminine, and involved in women's issues but only if participation means attending to traditional roles. After reading *Helen Brent, M.D.* we might expect Meyer to show how Mrs. Mason learns to integrate both sides of her life; yet the play closes with Cora's assertion that if women have filled their lives with causes it is because "Man forsook women." Traditionalism wins all.

The conflict between traditional and radical impulses appears again in Meyer's antisuffrage views, which may seem surprising for such a strong champion of women's higher education. The notion of female moral superiority proclaimed by some women's suffrage factions was anathema to Meyer. And on a more practical side, she believed that many women were too unastute politically and intellectually to add an experienced voice to the electorate. Even those utterly sympathetic to these concerns might wonder how Meyer reconciled them with her view that many men were hardly more astute, and why Meyer clung to her antisuffragism until her death in 1951.[17]

The contradictions in Meyer's work are perhaps not so surprising if we remember that her intellectual coming of age occurred during a period the historian Henry F. May has called "the end of Victorian calm and the beginning of cultural revolution."[18] Radical thought in the social, political, intellectual, and economic realms of American life was increasingly common among the educated and the working class. For a time, the custodians of America's genteel tradition were moderately successful in restraining these impulses, but tension and contradiction characterized many of the period's great debates. In Meyer's case, the Sephardic Jewish heritage and her social position worked to make her a traditionalist, while her own intelligence and vision propelled her toward change.

Robert Gunthal Nathan

The most contemporary of American writers of old Sephardic stock was Robert Gunthal Nathan (1894–1985), an extraordinarily prolific writer whose work spans some sixty years. He was active in the same period as the immigrant and second-generation Eastern European Jewish writers who influenced American literature so dramatically. But Nathan was different from them, a genteel, urbane scion of an old Sephardic family for whom dual Jewish and American identity was never a source of discomfort and even rage, as it was for his East European coreligionists, the newer Americans.

Sol Liptzin, in *The Jew in American Literature*, asserts that

> Nathan . . . and Louis Untermeyer, a descendant of pre–Civil War Israelites, expressed in their prose and verse a far more positive approach to the Jewish past, a far deeper understanding of the Jewish present and a far greater faith in the Jewish future than did the no less talented but only semi-integrated children of the Eastern immigrants.[19]

Nathan did not see the Jew, as the Eastern Europeans did, as the quintessentially modern alienated victim; instead, in his poems and novels, he emphasized the Jew's singular position as reviled and suffering but still chosen and surviving. From this foundation springs his concern with a larger humanity and belief in the regeneration of the spirit.

Many of Nathan's novels contain Jewish minor characters, such as Gus the taxi driver in *Portrait of Jennie* and Rosenberg the violinist in *One More String*, who comment ironically on the agonies that are part of the general human condition. The novels *Jonah* and *Road of Ages* refer more specifically to the Jewish exile, but they make clear that the possibilities for humans to reveal their spirituality and morality rest in a Judeo-Christian tradition, not just a Jewish one.

Nathan wrote all of these works prior to 1940. It is in *A Star in the Wind* (1962) and in some of his poetry, especially *A Winter Tide* (1940), that we find full exploration of his personal relationship to Jewishness. For Nathan, Jewish history is sacred and compelling, and Jewish survival depends on memory of this history. Hitler's measures against the Jews in the 1930s, the war, and its aftermath aroused in

Nathan a specifically Jewish consciousness and stirred his natural proclivity to evoke Jewish memory.

As Clarence Sandelin notes in his excellent book-length study of him, Nathan was aware of the Jews' essential conflict in maintaining a tradition that sets them apart from others and makes them the object of scorn, hate, and brutality. Though Nathan often suggested that a secular view of Judaism, not dependent on Orthodox observance, would check tensions with other groups, he understood that religious tradition has a compelling power, and he never advocated abrogation of the covenant. Nor did the inextricable connection he saw between Christianity and Judaism lead him to ignore their distinctiveness.

Two early poems paint a highly positive picture of the Jewish world. "He Attends the Funeral of a Jew" exhibits Judaism's power to sustain a people physically, emotionally, and historically. Serenity and peace characterize the poem. The Jewish heritage surrounds and welcomes its adherents. In "The Poet Contemplates the Exile," Nathan invokes biblical Judaism, mourning the dead glory of Jerusalem and the loss of its spirituality. Here he hints at the dangers posed by the modern world, with its temptations to stray from righteousness.[20]

A Winter Tide, especially the section titled "The Root and the Flower," sets a new tone in Nathan's poetry. It establishes the Jew as exile and victim, but also as survivor.[21] In these poems Nathan is a witness. Distance and objectivity may characterize the authorial voice in some of the poems, but in most the poet's tone is urgent. He describes a 1930s world of terrible danger and the human folly of egotism, stupidity, and moral vacuousness. Despite all this, Nathan remains optimistic, believing that human hopes, the desire for peace, and nature's cyclical renewal make the future one of possibility, not despair.

Regarded from a post–World War II perspective, Nathan's philosophy is simplistic. Consider the argument in "This Faith, This Violence":

> For if those of us of one blood and mind were ever to destroy
> Finally and irreparably, once and for all, forever,
> Those others whose differing blood or ideas lash us to fury,
> How bare would earth seem, how lonely her hills and watercourses.
> [pp. 37–39]

The apparent naivete is rooted in Nathan's focus on the simplest, most ordinary, most common of human actions and the accompanying, perhaps extraordinary, belief that if we were to attend to these with seriousness of purpose, without vanity, with awareness of other human lives, then the world would be at peace. Coming from an American Jew sustained by the long and secure history his people had experienced in the United States, such views may conflate gratitude and optimism.

Most interesting to the contemporary reader is the tension that exists among Nathan's Jewish-content poems. For example, "On the Jewish Exile" affirms with genuine certainty his belief in the Jews' continued survival. Yet in another poem his outrage and fear are palpable: "what madness has the world?" he cries in "Letter to Europe," a poem strewn with prophetic images of fire, flame, embers, ashes, fever, stubble, and waste (pp. 32–33).

Similarly, "Moses on Nebo" reveals Nathan's questioning of God. Moses, still the faithful disciple who praises God for leading the Jews out of Egypt, says he is waiting for a new sign that God has not forsaken his people. He hears "tocsins of alarm" throughout Europe, but so far God is still silent. The poem ends with Moses waiting, and we feel sure that Nathan is waiting too, not necessarily for a sign from God but for intervention on behalf of the Jews by human beings all over the world (pp. 19–21). But Nathan is not one to wait idly, and as he waits he will exhort, warn, chastise, and pray.

Many of these poems implicitly call for the Jews' defense. "The Root and the Flower" explains the strong link between Judaism and Christianity; if one cannot exist without the other, then a threat to either is a threat to both. Though many Christians recognize Christianity's debt to Jewish thought and to biblical Israel, not all would rush to defend the contemporary Jew. But Nathan demands such a defense, and he repeats his plea in the collection's last poem, "Epistle."

> Christian, be up before the end of day,
> Before the last, the fading hour dies;
> Sleep not until the light has fled away,
> and night's black trumpet cries.
>
> [pp. 22–25]

Much of the world failed Nathan's Jews during World War II. His next discussion of the Jewish dilemma in a full-length work appeared in 1962 in *A Star in the Wind,* his only novel to focus on an individual Jewish consciousness and the role of tradition in that consciousness. Although the novel is frequently sentimental and occasionally annoyingly mysterious in probing the protagonist's uncertainty about where and to what he belongs, it is also an affecting work about a man who rejects an American Jewishness that he associates with smothering families, strong patriarchal rule, and desires for greatness. After a long sojourn in Palestine, Joseph Victor finally commits himself to a spiritual and historical, though not necessarily religious, Jewishness. He learns that Jewish exile, Jewish suffering, and Jewish deaths have meaning because they have molded survivors who understand how to build again, who have the "hunger for life" he did not have before his Palestinian odyssey.

As is true of many of Nathan's novels, *A Star in the Wind* is essentially a love story, and it is in Joseph's relationships with two women, the secure, young, untested, and thoroughly New England and Gentile Priscilla, and the tortured and sad Jewish Anna, that he learns how the power of Jewish memory and tradition hold him, however reluctant he was to realize this in the novel's early pages.

Comparing the language describing Joseph's two affairs reveals that innocence, dreams, and sweetness characterize the relationship with Priscilla. They meet in the spring when evidence of Rome's lush rebirth is everywhere: "water falling, fountains playing, flowers and bushes sending out their fragrance on the air."[22] When the two spend a weekend together away from the city, "they felt far away from everything and everybody, together, by themselves, alone—wonderfully secure, hidden from the world, comforted and safe" (p. 75).

Yet we know from the beginning that this idyllic relationship cannot last. Priscilla claims that Joseph's Jewishness makes him more of a person, but she also admits to herself that his darkness and strangeness are disturbing and will never yield to her. More telling of the gulf between them are Joe's dreams of death and entrapment. To his query whether she has ever felt the same, her reply is a curt "Certainly not."

By contrast, on a ship bound for Palestine, Joe encounters Anna, a survivor of a death camp. He immediately recognizes her pain though he doesn't understand it at first, and he is impressed by "the proud and frightened way she held her child close to her" (p. 120). Here, the passengers sleep in an "airless hole lit by a few unshaded bulbs" (p. 113), and when Joseph and Anna first make love in Tel Aviv, it is not in a quiet sun-lit pensione but in a dark and just-emptied bomb shelter.

If the affair with Priscilla has taught Joseph about the nature of love, it has also pressed him to confront his yearning for meaning—as yet unconnected to his heritage. The language describing his responses to Anna, a "soft brave strong sad beautiful woman" (p. 184), evokes Joseph's entrance into a more mature, serious, responsible, and suitable relationship. Even without Nathan's editorial comment that Anna is part of Joseph's "homeward dream," we know Joseph belongs with Anna because he learns to identify deeply with her immediate personal past and with the historical tradition that surrounds them and binds them to other Jews.

A Star in the Wind suggests that America as ideal will not make Joseph whole. Though typical of many second-generation American Jews, Joseph does not feel his American identity very deeply, and remarks early in the novel that he has no country. Later, Anna touches again on America's lack of a hold on Joseph as she tries to imagine living in Cleveland, not Tel Aviv; and when the novel ends Joseph has found new direction—as he says, "I am committed," though we don't know whether this commitment is to living in Israel and to a new Jewish identity, whatever form it may take, or to helping Israel from a distance.

In any case, the novel implies that even centuries of life in America have not provided Jews with the kinds of traditions and bonds they need and want, that something more than absence of persecution and promises of opportunity are necessary. It is interesting that this possibility is expressed by a man descended from the first Jews in America, the very people whose history in the United States attests to the Jews' having successfully made the country theirs. But perhaps this is not surprising in the wake of the Holocaust.

Post–World War II: Levantine Sephardic Writers

A major change in the literary productions of Sephardic writers occurred after World War II, when for the first time in the United States we have works that illuminate a specifically Sephardic Jewish life. These works memorialize a minority culture, reveal its vitality as a subject for literature, and explore how collective and individual memory restores the past and makes it understandable. These contemporary Sephardic writers trace their lineage to the Ottoman world, and their connection to Sephardic cultural and religious traditions is much closer than that of the writers of old American stock examined so far.

Leon Sciaky

Leon Sciaky's *Farewell to Salonika*, written in 1946 and his only book, was the first literary work in English by a Levantine Jewish immigrant to be published in America. It is the autobiography of an educator, peace activist, and explorer, a man deeply moved and affected by his physical surroundings—both the Ottoman world in which he grew up and the upstate New York that became his adopted home.[23]

A sentimental and nostalgic book, *Farewell to Salonika* provides a lovingly crafted picture of a world destroyed by greed, corruption, force, and murder. Through a compassionate, intelligent, and sensitive consciousness, it describes the Levantine world from which many Sephardic immigrants came and examines the importance of place to Sciaky, his strong attachment to the smells, sights, and sounds of the city and countryside, and his yearning for these after having emigrated.

The Levantine world shaped Sciaky's intellectual development and later the content and texture of his memories. Sciaky was strikingly similar in some ways to the American-born Sephardic writers. Just as they were generally secure in their sense of being American and belonging on American soil, praising the country's best values, Sciaky, too, was cosmopolitan in outlook, passionately attached to his homeland, and promoted the democratic values for which many in the Levant were striving.

Like other post–World War II Sephardic writers, Sciaky differs from most of the writers previously discussed in his direct preoccupation with history. Both Sephardic cultural tradition and his family's secular outlook had shaped him, and while one sharpened his predilection to preserve cultural traditions, the other committed him to reform and to liberal social and political thought. In the aftermath of emigration and the massacre of the Jews, Sciaky's desire for preservation and for change both intensified, creating *Farewell to Salonika*'s dual focus: the author's private memories and the violence of history.

Sciaky's concern is with violence done to land, people, ideals, and the individual consciousness, and with the inevitable destruction of religious and cultural traditions. He suggests that the secular Jew can pay homage to the past through memory, but that memory preserves only for the individual who remembers. In a similar vein, *Farewell to Salonika* records tradition but cannot transmit it. Neither can culture, in Sciaky's view, be transplanted.

What saves his autobiography from being a sad memorial to a dead world is Sciaky's continued optimism about the idealistic secular values of peace and harmony that he learned in the Levant. He ends his book with an exhortation to the United States to fulfill these ideals, but unfortunately he wrote no sequel to evaluate his half a century of life in this country.

David Fintz Altabé

David Altabé is a professor of Spanish, a translator of Judeo-Spanish and Spanish writings, a poet who writes in English, Judeo-Spanish, Spanish, and French, and the current president of the American Society of Sephardic Studies. His poetry is notable for its simplicity of language, its strong conviction about the universality of human pain and joy, and its directness of emotion. The poems in his collection, *Chapter and Verse*, cover a wide range of subjects; love and marriage, fatherhood, the nature of art, mourning, religious heritage, are among the most prominent.

In the section "Poems of the Nations and Races" emerges a distinctly American Sephardic Jewish sensibility, a combination of identification with others' suffering and a clear-eyed sense of history's disruptions, injustices, and promises. "March 17, 1975" addresses the poet's horror of the current Irish bloodshed. The color green in stanza 1 symbolizes harmony and hope, while red dominates the last stanzas as the poet's donning a red shirt reveals his firm commitment to speak of private and communal agony. The poem's last line, intentionally colloquial and, hence, jarring, suggests that even the poet's facility with language fails before the ubiquity of contempory terrorism. In another poem, "Hey There, Whitey," the perspective of a writer who is himself a member of a minority group within another minority group, allows Altabé to express sympathy with African-American aspirations and anger while urging the understanding that race is not the only determinant of want and discrimination.[24]

"Homage to our Turkish Brethren," a new poem written to commemorate the sultan's welcome of the Jews after the expulsion, helps to explain why some Sephardic Jews are so fierce in their loyalty to Turkey, even glossing over that country's present-day repressive policies:

> The benevolence granted by your forefathers did not end in 1492,
> For five hundred years we have lived side by side, Turk and Jew;
> We have shared your destiny, we have eaten your food;
> Our Spanish is enriched by your words, our music by your tunes.

Stephen Levy

Stephen Levy (b. 1947) is an American poet whose work has been consciously influenced by his Sephardic heritage. Levy is a preservationist, like Sciaky, but at the same time demonstrates the life still to be found in Sephardic culture. For example, he founded the Judezmo Society and its magazine, *Adelantre!*, whose purpose was to promote not only the study but the use of Judeo-Spanish.[25]

Preservation may also be a key motive of the poignant poem "With My Father," which addresses the pain of loss a young boy feels when he sees for the first time the now "boarded up storefront, a synagogue with the word Sephardic on the door," where his father attended services with his immigrant grandfather.

Another poem about memory, rather than being merely elegiac in tone, is also redemptive and determined to build on memory. The poem begins, "For hundreds and hundreds of years my fathers and brothers in three countries along the Mediterranean soon made their way to their synagogues . . . to pray in a language strange to me—I am ignorant." The pain of loss is apparent, but in the poem's closing line, "Lord, listen, listen to me: I am humming home," there is a new element suggesting a religious and cultural continuity, a reclaiming of the past to the present.

In contrast, a lovely short poem called "English" expresses the difficulties the American Sephardi experiences in trying to bridge past and present. The immigrant generation and the intellectually aspiring second and third generations are unable to understand each other's needs.

> quit school go out
> and work and all day my father in the coffeehouse or with the holy books
> . . . but even when
> I was very young
> I wrote I wrote
> I loved to write
> compositions poems
> I'm still writing I don't
> stop I'll get
> all of it published yet
> I'll get them all.[26]

David Raphael

David Raphael, a physician by profession, has written two novels and is working on a third. All set in medieval Spain, they reenact the converso and expulsion period of Jewish history. *The Alhambra Decree* depicts the violence during this period of Jewish history and the Jews' concomitant tenacity in clinging to tradition. Another of Raphael's purposes is to emphasize the universality of Jewish exile, to show parallels between the Spanish expulsion and other Jewish persecutions, and to suggest that a heroism based on faith continues to be possible. In this Raphael is optimistic that Jewish religious culture can be transplanted by those who keep its tenets firmly and are willing to fight and even die for them.

Don Isaac Abravanel, the hero of *The Alhambra Decree*, speaks for Raphael, suggesting the core idea behind his interest in the historical novel. Addressing the Segovia Jewish community after the expulsion edict has been announced, Abravanel says,

> The right to reside in this kingdom is nothing compared to our Jewish inheritance.... What greater loss is there than to surrender one's very being? What is the price, the inner price, for cutting oneself off from one's people? What is the price for exchanging the truths of Torah for a life of falsehood and hypocrisy?[27]

Abravanel comes to the congregation shortly after delivering his eloquent final speech to King Ferdinand and Queen Isabella, a speech that Raphael intends to be a challenge to all oppressive regimes: "We destroy *you*?" he asks the sovereigns,

> It is indeed the very opposite. Did you not admit in this edict to having confined all Jews to restricted quarters and to having limited our legal and social privileges, not to mention forcing us to wear shameful badges? Did you not tax us oppressively? Did you not terrorize us day and night with your diabolical Inquisition? ... The unrighteous decree you proclaim today will be your downfall. And this year, which you imagine to be the year of Spain's greatest glory, will become the year of Spain's greatest shame.... In your heart of hearts, you distrust the power of knowledge, and you respect only power. With us Jews it is different. We Jews cherish knowledge immensely. In our homes and in our prayerhouses learning is a lifelong pursuit. Learning is our lifelong passion; it is at the core of our being; it is the reason, according to our sages, for which we were created. [p. 153]

Memory, learning, tradition—these are the keys to a civilization's survival. Raphael's primary task in this novel is to teach history, to restore memory of centuries-old traditions, and to convey the Jews' heroism and the Spanish rulers' treachery. Thus, the novel provides a panoramic view of Jewish life in fifteenth-century Spain, including extensive biographical information on the political figure and philosopher Don Isaac Abravanel, Don Abraham Senior the tax collector, King Ferdinand and his possible Jewish origins; exhaustive detail about the preparations for expulsion and the brutal persecutions Jews faced after they left Spain; and a picture of Jewish life that explains Spanish proverbs, Hebrew prayers, religious customs, feasts, and terminology. Further, Raphael provides several long disquisitions on the philosophical distinctions between Judaism and Christianity.

Historical references and authentic detail receive most of Raphael's attention in this work. Recreating experience is much less important to him than a careful retelling of events. The work, then, is more in the style of documentary than fiction, resulting occasionally in a rather artificial integration of background information into the story.

In one scene, for example, Rabbi Maimi is walking to the tax collector's house to discuss new taxes. To introduce a page-long discussion of the Marranos, Raphael tells that us Maimi is worried not about money but "about the Converso problem."

At another point, to explain that Jews live in a highly restrictive and often threatening environment, where the political and social authority they answer to is not their own, Raphael sets Senior, the tax collector, the task of finding some decree he can fight. What follows are four pages of Don Abraham Senior summarizing numerous documents, a device that provides useful historical information but tells us little about Senior's personal struggle to be a good leader, a matter of much concern to him, we are told later.

Elsewhere, Abravanel leads Senior to explain King Ferdinand's relationship with the Jews by saying, "Tell me, Don Abraham, I have heard the strangest things about King Ferdinand's origins." Again, a long aside follows, this time about Ferdinand's possible Jewish heritage.

Most of the information presented in this manner is not superfluous to our understanding of the expulsion period. Nonetheless, novelistically, the distinction between fiction and nonfiction is too obvious, and the emphasis on telling rather than showing denies us access to the characters' interior consciousness and motivation, thus making them—and the issues that define them—much less complex than they should be.

Still, the novel often succeeds in engaging the reader's emotions. The story itself is so dramatic and the characters so passionate that Raphael's audience will surely hold its breath, sigh with relief, or express outrage at every turn of the plot. Raphael is particularly effective in showing the fanatical De la Pena arouse the Christian populace against the Jews on Rosh Hashanah. Here we recognize the priest's emotional frenzy and irrationality, feel the inherent drama of competing allegiances as the Hermandad's security chief weighs and casts aside his responsibility to the Jews, and applaud the sensitive and intelligent fighter Don Isaac Abravanel, who forcefully and rationally defends the Jews' religious position. Appearing throughout the text, such incidents define Jewish history as violence, oppression, sacrifice, and pain, but also triumph, endurance, faith, action, and survival.

Stanley Sultan

The last novel I will discuss here, *Rabbi* by Stanley Sultan (b. 1928), is the most interesting recent work by an American Jewish writer. Heartbreaking in its evocation of the physical, psychic, and moral losses engendered by the immigrant experience and the Holocaust, the novel makes us confront the loss of meaning in twentieth-century life—its leaving human beings without anchor, its acceptance of sham and deceit, and of the inability to distinguish between good and evil, the insensitivity to the life-sustaining promise a new land might offer, divorce from homeland language and values, dependence on material prosperity for sustenance, and entrapment in dissatisfying intellectual reasoning.[28]

The novel begins during Passover, 1948, in the prosperous Syrian Jewish community of Sea Beach in Brooklyn. The Djubal family is at the center of the tale, and the immigrant Rabbi Jacob Djubal—intelligent, devoted to the Law, unwavering in his judgments of human character, sensitive to and understanding of the unspoken—is the most admirable character in the novel, his narrow judgments of women and Ashkenazim coming across almost as quirky endearments. Through the eyes of the rabbi's grandson Jason, a confused but often sensitive adolescent who alternately eschews and accepts personal responsibility, we see much of the novel's intrigue.

The central moral question of the story is raised when Rosalie, a Holocaust survivor and cousin of Reuben Djubal's Ashkenazi wife, introduces the Djubals to the horrors that struck down the vast majority of Europe's Jews during the war, including the Sephardim of the Balkan lands, but did not, of course, touch their brethren in Syria. The Holocaust itself and the current shenanigans of Rosalie's vengeful, powerful, and morally ambiguous former betrayer and present lover force moral dilemmas upon the Djubals as well as upon the reader.

Upon hearing Rosalie's story, young Jason asks himself what connection Jews should feel to one another. He answers the question by deciding he must adopt a life dominated by Jewishness. As Jewish observance and Jewish identity are inextricably linked, he becomes increasingly devout.

Later he struggles with this resolution. Witnessing hypocrisy among those whose ritualistic piety lacks the spirit of the Law, and realizing that his community no longer fully understands and accepts biblical Judaism, he wonders what values to trust when confronted with evil. Slowly Jason discovers that while his grandfather's absolutism does not work for him, a relativistic morality is dangerous, as it may make evil unrecognizable and judgments of behavior impossible.

Sultan's most interesting strategy in exploring the relationship between meaning, morality, and action is to focus on language. The characters speak three languages, Arabic, Hebrew, and English, with varying degrees of facility; the Sea Beach Jews listen to gossip and pass on rumor; there are unsympathetic figures whose manipulation of language reveals the self-interest at the heart of all their communications; the rabbi's search for truth is a struggle against rumors, hints, and the ambiguity of language; and Jason strives mightily to explain himself in word, thought, and deed.

The languages of the home and of prayer once provided individual and community meaning, but such linguistic rootedness is no longer possible in a land of a myriad cultural transplantings. The dominance of English demonstrates how difficult it is to maintain cultural continuity in the new environment. For some members of the Sea Beach community, the new language, surroundings, and values bring such distance from the past as to lead to a kind of moral obtuseness and vacuity. The only ones who escape this are Rabbi Djubal, in his devotion to religious teachings and to memory, and Jason, whose painfully learned moral lessons and self-awareness are the rabbi's secular counterpart.

Yet Sultan does not equate the two characters. Jason's identification with English speech and with the English rather than the Hebrew form of his name displays his distance from historical and religious memory. It is the role of Rabbi Djubal's moral and personal example throughout the novel to tacitly insist that to achieve a coherent identity, Jason must eventually integrate his intellectual yearnings with his racial past.

Sultan's novel reminds us that the United States, beneath its monolithic mass-media surface, is land of small groups rich in ritual, language, ethics, and history, surviving in willed or forced isolation from mainstream American culture and sometimes sending us an interpreter who enriches us by speaking in the rhythms of another community and sharing with us details of another world. The novel's larger themes capture the quintessential American experience of self-examination, but contrary to the dominant theme of earlier works by American Jews in which self-exploration requires severing ties with the past, here the past demands understanding, engagement, reconciliation.

Summary

This study has aimed to familiarize a general audience with Sephardic writers and to outline the similarities in their concern with tradition and history.

The older group of Sephardic writers traced their ancestry to Jews who had settled in America when the country's population was largely homogenous and the Jews' small numbers generated little severe discrimination. These early settlers established a financially stable community, one that was religious but usually not strictly observant, and whose members associated often and freely with Gentiles in business and social affairs.

The Sephardic writers who were descendants of these settlers maintained or developed a Jewish consciousness while also being well-assimilated in mainstream American culture. A dual identity that generated little conflict made them active proponents of America's democratic values and the American system in their lives and literary works. However, we have seen occasions in which this faith in a sustaining American civilization was strained. In these cases the authors' traditionalist sentiments were bolstered, not abandoned, though of course by means that were varied and individualistic.

Mordecai Manuel Noah, for example, feeling tensions between his Jewish and American identities, and uncertain about America as a genuinely safe haven for the Jews, devised a plan for a self-governing Jewish enclave. Years later, when historical events made them face questions of Jewish identity and solidarity in times of crisis, Emma Lazarus and Robert Nathan were no less optimistic than ever about their own assimilated position in the United States, but their writings displayed a highly personal attachment to Jewish tradition that had not been evident before.

American writers of Levantine Sephardic background have also been concerned with tradition, but their focus has consistently been on a distinctly Sephardic religious, cultural, and historical tradition. Profoundly affected by the massacres of World War II and the disruptions caused by the Jewish migrations in the late nineteenth and early twentieth centuries and after the war, the Levantine Sephardim have also emphasized in their work the violence and disruptions of Jewish history and their effect on Jewish survival.

Their focus on their own culture is no doubt especially pronounced because the very large Eastern European Jewish population in the United States has dominated definitions of Jewishness, and Sephardic Jewish history and culture have received little attention. It is interesting to note that in comparison to the Sephardim, the writers of Eastern European Jewish background who so greatly influenced American literature between 1930 and 1970 did not explore the European past or write directly about the Holocaust. The concern with morality in Malamud, for example, emerges from his reaction to the Holocaust but is more universalist than Jewish in content. More recently, however, non-Sephardic Jewish writers like Thomas Friedmann and Jerome Badanes have begun to display the same concern with historical memory and its relation to Jewish survival that animates Stanley Sultan and Stephen Levy.

Notes

1. I am defining "Sephardic" in the broadest sense to include Jews of non-Ashkenazi origin, i.e., descendants of colonial Sephardim, Levantine Jews from Greece and Turkey, and Middle Eastern Jews.

2. Vera Caspary, in her autobiography, *The Secrets of Grown-ups* (New York: McGraw-Hill, 1979), pp. 7–8, says that her Sephardic origin is a matter of speculation, and so I have excluded her from this study.

3. There is little to indicate a distinctly Jewish consciousness in the writings of either Elizabeth Cardozo, the nineteenth-century poet, or Nancy Cardozo, the twentieth-century poet and biographer of Maude Gonne, and so I have not considered them here.

4. Charleston Section, Council of Jewish Women, *Secular and Religious Works of Penina Moïse with a Brief Sketch of Her Life* (Charleston, 1911).

5. Ibid., p. 3. All subsequent page references to this work appear in the text.

6. Jonathan D. Sarna, *Jacksonian Jew: The Two Worlds of Mordecai Manuel Noah* (New York: Holmes & Meier, 1981), p. 122.

7. Sol Liptzin, *The Jew in American Literature* (New York: Bloch, 1966), p. 25.

8. Mordecai Manuel Noah, *She Would Be a Soldier; or, The Plains of Chippewa*, in *Representative Plays by American Dramatists. 1765–1819*, ed. Montrose J. Moses (New York: Benjamin Blom, 1918, reissued 1964), p. 640.

9. Sarna, *Jacksonian Jew*, p. 70.

10. Dan Vogel, *Emma Lazarus* (Boston: Twayne, 1980), p. 109. Subsequent references to this thorough and insightful study appear in the text.

11. Marc D. Angel, "The Jewish Poems of Emma Lazarus," *American Sephardi* 2 (1968): 60–63.

12. Annie Nathan Meyer, "The Ghetto in Literature," *Bookman* 10 (February 1900): 532–534.

13. Myrna Gallant Goldenberg, "Annie Nathan Meyer: Barnard Godmother and Gotham Gadfly" (Ph.D. diss., University of Maryland, 1987), p. 251. I found the reference to *Barriers* here; I have not yet been able to locate it.

14. Meyer, *It's Been Fun* (New York: Henry Schuman, 1951), p. 109.

15. Lynne D. Gordon, "Annie Nathan Meyer and Barnard College: Mission and Identity in Women's Higher Education, 1889–1950," *History of Education Quarterly* 26 (Winter 1986): 518.

16. Annie Nathan Meyer, *Helen Brent, M.D.: A Social Study* (London: Cassell, 1892). p. 108.

17. See *It's Been Fun*, p. 207. Also see Gordon, "Annie Nathan Mayer and Barnard Collge," p. 512, fn. 17.

18. Henry F. May, *The End of American Innocence* (Chicago: Quadrangle Books, 1959), p. ix.

19. Liptzin, *Jew in American Literature*, pp. 151–152.

20. Robert Nathan, *Youth Grows Old* (New York: Robert M. McBride, 1922), pp. 8 and 9.

21. Robert Nathan, *A Winter Tide* (New York: Alfred H. Knopf, 1940), pp. 22–25. Subsequent page references to this work appear in the text.

22. Robert Nathan, *A Star in the Wind* (London: W. H. Allen, 1962), p. 28. Subsequent page references to this work appear in the text.

23. Leon Sciaky, *Farewell to Salonika* (New York: Current Books, 1946).

24. David Fintz Altabé, *Chapter and Verse* (New York: Fintzenberg, 1978).

25. Stephen Levy, "Some Sephardic Poems" *Adelantre!* (1975). In addition to poems this section contains translations of Ladino proverbs and a poem about the Nazi destruction of the Monastirli Jews: "Snowflakes Falling from the Black Sky," based on Uri Oren's book, *A Town Cailed Monastir*.

26. Stephen Levy, "English," in *Voices within the Ark: Modern Jewish Poetry*, ed. A. Rudolph and H. Schwartz (New York, 1980), p. 522.

27. David Raphael, *The Alhambra Decree* (North Hollywood, Calif.: Carmi House Press, 1988), p. 165.

28. Stanley Sultan, *Rabbi* (West Whately, Mass.: American Novelists Cooperative Publications, 1977).

The Secret Jews of the Southwest
Frances Hernández

The Holy Office spread its inquisitional activities into the New World along with the Catholic faith. King Ferdinand of Spain decreed its establishment soon after the first colonists were settled, appointing Juan Quevedo, the bishop, as inquisitor general, with discretionary powers, in 1516. Charles V, the Holy Roman emperor, heard stories of the harassment of the natives in New Spain, decided that the Holy Office had been committing excesses in its zeal, and decreed, on October 15, 1538, that only European colonists would be subject to the examinations of the Inquisition. But Philip II, stringently pious, increased its powers in Spanish territory only three years later, designating the new provinces of Lima, Mexico, and Cartagena as strong centers.

One curious, though typical case of the friars' dealings with the indigenous people is described by Rabbi Floyd S. Fierman from documents of the Holy Office in the National Archives of Mexico City.[1] The trial of an Indian, Martin of Coyoncán, on November 18, 1539, is recorded. Through an interpreter who speaks his own language, Suchmitl, the offender is asked to affirm that he is a Christian; he avers that he was baptized some ten years earlier. Then he is questioned about his sexual relations with four sisters, which he understands is against both Catholic law and his tribal custom. After he explains that the first two sisters had died before he became a Christian and married the third one in the church, he then confesses that he has lain with the fourth sister. His punishment is to be publicly beaten and shaved in his village—and admonished against any further relationship with either his wife or her sister on threat of burning at the stake.

In another case history, possibly the first New Christian in Mexico was Hernando Alonso, a blacksmith who arrived from Cuba with Pánfilo de Narváez in 1520, after previous service with Hernán Cortés. Alonso's name turns up as a witness or defendant in various actions from 1529 to March 9, 1558. On one occasion he was called to give evidence against Cortés, who was being charged with failure to make a fair distribution of the spoils of war among his men. Later Alonso was accused of selling beef and pork from his own ranch located about sixty miles north of Mexico City at prices cheaper than those of his competitors. Finally, it is reported that he has been imprisoned because he had twice baptized a child, the second time according to the law of Moses.

Naturally, these decades of oppression by the Holy Office, involving spies and informers in all sectors of the Spanish-dominated society, caused increasing unease among conversos and anyone else who might be—for any reason—fingered for suspicious practices. In 1570 Philip II grew concerned about stories he was hearing from his clergy in New Spain of witchcraft, Lutheranism, recalcitrant Indians, and, most painful, heretics—especially those New Christians who were suspected of backsliding into Jewish observances. Although he had authorized priests to take whatever action they deemed necessary to combat these evils, a charge many of them accepted enthusiastically, he decided to establish strengthened headquarters for the Inquisition in Mexico City and in Lima that same year.

The first full *auto-da-fé* was celebrated in Mexico four years later—the same year Hernán Cortés died. This event increased the reign of terror that reached its climax on April 11, 1649, when thirteen Spaniards, all accused of judaizing, were burned at the stake at the *auto-general* in the city. In 1821 this activity was formally ended, although one more victim died in the flames five years later, the good fathers being unwilling to let their years of patient investigation on the case go for naught. The Holy Office was not legally closed down until 1834, by which time more than a hundred persons had been barbarously executed, with thousands more tortured, mutilated, deprived of property, and intimidated.

One of the most famous cases of the Inquisition in the New World was completed during that frenetic initial sixteenth century: that of the Carvajal family of Nuevo León.[2] Luis de Carvajal y de la Cueva had first sought his fortune in New Spain as a merchant and then cattle rancher in Pánuco in 1567. He earned such a reputation as an Indian fighter and skillful colonizer that he won an appointment from the crown as governor of a vast territory in northern New Spain, to be called the New Kingdom of Nuevo León. He also received the unusual dispensation to bring a boatload of relatives and employees with him without any documents attesting to their Catholic orthodoxy. In New Spain his nephew, whom he had designated as his successor, became a fervent judaizer and something of a mystic in the classic Spanish tradition. Because of Luis the Younger's open devotion to his ancestral faith, he was tortured and burned alive in the great *auto* of 1596.

An appreciable number of New Christians settled in remote areas of New Spain. Those who could not survive on the rugged frontier burrowed into anonymity. North into the desolate mountain fastnesses of what is now New Mexico was a forbidding destination. Several expeditions started up from Mexico in the 1580s and 1590s, looking for silver mines like those that had been discovered in Zacatecas half a century earlier, but their organizers found it difficult to recruit colonists. Too many stories had filtered down about the marauding Comanches and Utes, the high mountain blizzards, the distances between water sources.[3]

Fray Marcos de Niza made the rugged journey north in 1539, looking for the fabled cities of Cíbola; he found nothing like the splendid centers he saw in his mind's eye, only a far glimpse of Hawikuh, now known as Zuñi Pueblo. His guide, the gigantic black slave Estevanico, brought him into Apache territory, but was himself killed by the Indians before the two explorers could return. Estevanico remains a figure in the songs and folk drama of New Mexican villages.

In 1598, when Juan de Oñate took the first colonists north to make a permanent settlement, his band of 135 soldiers, farmers, and their families were reluctant travelers. But some of them were under investigation by the Inquisition, making removal to even so unpromising a destination advisable. Indication is strong that several of those on the muster roll of January 8 were conversos who had been recruited because they were already on the lists of the Holy Office. Juan, Miguel, and Antonio Rodríguez and Francisco Hernández had, in fact, already been burned in effigy two years before. Their families and friends could only have wished to follow them into the wilderness to find freedom, however limited and tenuous, to preserve the traditions of their ancestors. Many did in the subsequent decades.

Most of the judaizers came after the Oñate expedition, seeking refuge in New Mexico in the seventeenth century. The first arrivals struggled up the Río Grande to the Española Valley, where they took over a pueblo called Okeh, near present-day San Juan Pueblo, renaming it San Juan de los Caballeros. Some moved into another Indian town, Yuquegunque, on the other side of the river, near where the Chama joins it. This was the first Spanish capital: San Gabriel.

In spite of the rigorous conditions, there were distinct advantages for the secret Jews. Primarily, there were very few priests around. As late as 1827, there were only seventeen clergymen in the entire territory.[4] No one was around to inquire about strange-sounding prayers, comment on overfrequent bathing in a land where there was usually a water shortage, or observe a suspicious repugnance for pork in communities where any kind of meat was rare. The few missionaries who came confined themselves to their estates and concentrated on the Pueblo Indians, who turned out to be particularly recalcitrant about forced labor on the white men's lands. The Franciscans committed numerous atrocities in their attempts to repress the indigenous religion, destroying kivas, burning the sacred kachinas, and beating or killing religious leaders. The gross oppression led to the Pueblo Revolt of 1680, when the tribes attacked Santa Fé, which had been the capital and the location of most church activity for seventy years.

Not only were there few priests, but there were also few Europeans of any kind. Before the rebellion, the Spanish population never exceeded 3,000 in a vast area. The government of New Spain tried repeatedly to collect settlers into defensible towns, but they resisted all such efforts, remaining in widely distributed family groupings. They found that they were safer from raids by the plains Indians, who preferred more profitable attacks on larger communities with bigger stores of grain and other commodities. The colonists could pursue illegal trade without interference from the viceroy's officers; they shared labor and defense in communal arrangements led by headmen to whom they were related, known as *tatas*, rather than the *patrones* who treated their neighbors as bound servants. They could also work out understandings with nearby pueblos when the Indians were not threatened by the ministrations of priests.

Secret Jews of the Southwest

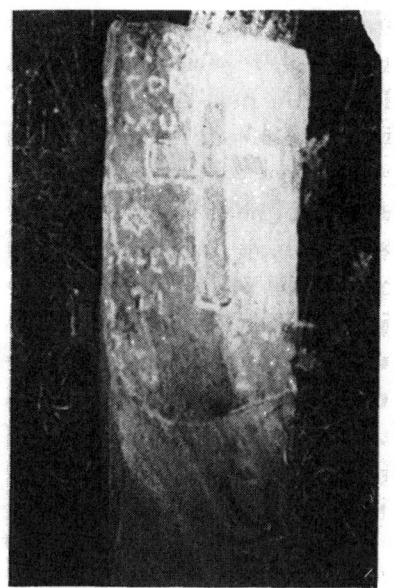 

Tombstones from Catholic cemeteries in the American Southwest with Jewish symbols (Courtesy Frances Hernández)

The early colonists who had come with Oñate had received *encomiendas* from the government in Mexico—land grants complete with rights to force the natives to work on them. Two generations later, the scattered, isolated communities had taken on a social leveling; by the eighteenth century there were no more hereditary aristocrats nor paupers. With fewer than 2,500 Spaniards and some 24,000 Pueblo Indians on the Río Grande, Chama, El Rito, and Nutrias rivers, there was inevitable mixing of the gene pools. Local folk applied the name *coyotes* to those among them who were part-Spanish, or Spanish and some other European blood, such as that of the French trappers who occasionally followed the muskrat and beaver down from Canada. The nomadic Indians from the eastern plains were *gentiles*, and the rare crosses of Indian and black parents—all those who claimed to be descendants of Estevanico—were known as *zambos*.

After the Pueblo Revolt, when Spaniards from the larger towns fled back to El Paso del Norte, Diego de Vargas returned from exile with fewer than forty families who were willing to try the risks of colonization again. In 1693–94, de Vargas was able to recruit sixty-seven more families from central Mexico, followed the next year by another twenty-seven. To the already established residents, these newcomers were known as *españoles mexicanos*, since most were Mexican-born and part-Indian. Another group formed in northern New Mexico by the eighteenth century was the *genízaros*, Pueblo Indians who had been separated from their tribes by capture by plains Indians or by forced military service for the Spaniards. These displaced persons received communal land grants in exchange for acting as a reserve military force to be called up if needed. Their town grants comprised one square league with water rights, all held in common. Some of these exist today, such as Tortugas in the south and Abiquíu on the Chama River; the Indian inhabitants must speak Spanish, since they have no common tongue, and their tribal customs are a pastiche of borrowed or remembered practices. While all these population movements were taking place, the secret Jews persevered unmolested in their isolated groups, completely out of touch with coreligionists anywhere in the world, but applying what they could recall of the law of Moses from generation to generation.

The Secret Jews of New Mexico

Four hundred years after the New Christian judaizers began to arrive in the upper Río Grande Valley and its tributaries, there may be some 1,500 families within the wider Hispanic population who have legitimate claim to be their decendants. Their cognizance of this heritage ranges from the rare few who have a full understanding of their history and what it means, to those who have vague family references and realize that there are customs, taboos, and attitudes among their relatives that are unusual or unexplained, to those who have no comprehension of Judaism and their possible connection to it at all.

But there are clues. To the alert observer, unusual customs and attitudes among members of the native Hispanic population reveal much about their ancestors. In some families candles are lit on Friday nights, sometimes in the bottom of deep jars; approved marriage partners are limited to a few known and often related groups; active sports are discouraged on Saturdays; regular bathing is insisted upon, even in cold weather; and a pride in reading and general educational attainments is fostered.

One avenue for investigation is through the records of the Inquisition with their detailed lists of suspicious behavior that may indicate the New Christians' involvement in judaizing. The tribunal in Mexico City was alerted by any observed reluctance to eat pork or shellfish; the rumor of a secret room, especially interior or underground, that might be used for proscribed prayers; an evident concern for the burial of deceased relatives in shrouds of new linen without using coffins; the discovered possession of copies of the Bible, especially the Old Testament; or a noticed avoidance of lighting fires for cooking on Saturday, even in the chill mountains of New Mexico. Sometimes conversos displayed an exaggerated piety among their Christian neighbors; others evaded contact with the church whenever possible, submitting to confession only when required.

Initially, the fear of the Inquisition was fundamental. The first colonists arriving in the sixteenth century carried with them stories of relatives and acquaintances who had fallen victim to the Holy Office in Spain or Portugal. The institution, which had been formed as recently as 1480, did not function under the authority and control of the pope, but received its administrators by direct appointment of the monarchs. Almost a hundred years after its appearance in Spain, the Inquisition was established in Lima and Mexico City by King Philip II to "free the land, which has become contaminated with Jews and heretics."

The threat of the Inquisition did not disappear until 1821, and it rarely penetrated into the upper reaches of the Río Grande Valley. There were, however, some highly visible prosecutions well into the seventeenth century. For example, the friars pursued Bernardo López de Mendizábel, the Spanish governor of New Mexico from 1659 to 1661, and his wife with charges of judaizing. López died before the case was brought before the judges, who ultimately decided that there had been no real evidence against the couple after all and announced a postmortem exoneration. Though infrequent, such events could not have been encouraging to the secret Jews.

Even though the Inquisition was always a distant threat to those above the Paso del Norte, there were real enough dangers nearby. If a family were exposed as judaizers, they could lose title to their land, no matter how long they had occupied it, since Spanish land grants could be held only by bona fide Christians. If settlers who used land that they did not own came under suspicion, they could be denied their water rights—a sentence of extinction in the arid Southwest. Even years after these rights were stabilized by secular government, inhabitants who were denounced by their neighbors faced formal banning from the local pulpit and ostracism that could make social interaction uncomfortable and earning a living unlikely. In the necessarily communal villages of the Rocky Mountains, where survival depended on a barter economic system, exclusion by one's neighbors had to result in departure and loss of property.

To this day, revelation of their background is strongly resisted by those who still live in ancestral villages or in enclaves within what have become urban areas. Most of the information about them that has emerged comes from individual members who have left their communities, moving out for education, jobs, marriage. Clemente Carmona, for example, who comes from the largest remaining Sephardic enclave in New Mexico, located in the Atrisco Grant south of Albuquerque, reports the anger of his relatives when he described to an interviewer some of their traditional observances. Dennis Durn encountered strong resistance from family members when he publicly converted to Judaism after his genealogical research through fourteen generations in New Mexico disclosed an unbroken line of New Christian judaziers. Daniel Yocum, a south valley engineering student, recalls how irate his grandmother became when her husband carved a menorah and displayed it in a window where it could be seen by passersby, even though she was rigorous herself in her clandestine religious observance. For persons who have guarded their secret through so many generations, this final probing of their private practices is still perceived as dangerous. Many of them are also members of Catholic parishes, an association that they value and regard as protective. Local ostracism and the disdain of their neighbors continue to be feared, even in this era of multiculturalism and ethnic pride.

In spite of the centuries of hiding, some awareness of the presence of the crypto-Jews has always existed among the Hispanic populace. William Day, director of city services for senior citizens in El Paso, recalls a schoolyard situation when he was growing up in southeastern New Mexico in the 1920s. Raised on an isolated ranch in Sierra County, he was sent by his parents to live with relatives in order to attend school in the village of San Antonio on the Río Grande some twenty miles south of Socorro. The only school there then, as in all the rural counties of the state before the Second World War, was parochial. There the new boy noticed that the Hispanic children seemed to divide themselves into two groups, one much smaller than the other. Occasionally, teasing and fights broke out between them, at which point the nuns would rush into the larger crowd, dispersing them with cries of, "Now, you leave those little hebreos alone!" Day did not realize until many years later what the term meant and believes that none of the children did at the time.[5]

Suspect Names

One of the first clues that the Dominican and Franciscan officers of the Inquisition pursued was the names, both surname and given, of suspected conversos. When Jews submitted to conversion in Spain, they often adopted the names of their religious sponsors: López, Gómez, Domínguez, Rodríguez, Sánchez, Ramírez, García, Hurtado, Varela (also spelled Barela locally), all common in the Southwest. José Estrudo lists, in an essay titled "Nombres Apellidos Sefarditas," the most frequently used Jewish names during and after the Inquisition: Marcos, Vidal, Mercado, León, Andrade, Arias, Benavides, Castro, Henríquez (or Enríquez), Ferro, Hernández, (or Hernández), Franco, Medina, Méndez, Mendoza, Pérez, Rodríguez, and Salazar.[6]

Alfonso Toro, in *La familia Carvajal*, records the names of families persecuted by the Inquisition in Mexico during the sixteenth century: Almeida, Alvarez, Andrada, Carmona, Carvajal (or Carbajal or Carabajal), de la Cueva, de León, Delgado, de Nava, Duarte, Enríquez, Espejo, Espinoza (or Espinosa), Ferro, Hernández, Herrera,

López, Martínez, Morales, Muñoz, Núñez, Pérez, Rivera, Rodríguez, Salado, Sánchez, Saucedo (or Saucedos or Salcido). All of these names, except Ferro and de Nava, appear in the early records of New Mexico settlements. Among the original settlers of San Gabriel, the village that became Oñate's capital, are the following names that were recognized as usually Jewish: Cáceres, Carrasco, Castro, Durán, Espinosa, Fernández, García, Gómez, Griego, Hernández, Herrera, Ledesma, León, López, Morales, Pérez, Ramírez, Rivera, Robledo, Rodríguez, Romero, Sánchez, and Varela.

The most common names today in northern New Mexico (Taos, San Juan, Río Arriba, Bernalillo, San Miguel, and Mora counties), many of which have previously been cited as of Sephardic connection, include Abeyta, Alarid, Alire, Aragón, Archuleta, Armijo, Atencio, Baca, Barreiro (one of the few clearly Portuguese names) Benavides, Bustos, Candelaria, Casías (Casillas), Cerda, Chaves (and Chávez), Cisneros, Cordova, Corrales, Enríquez, Espinosa, Gallegos, Gamboa, García, Girón (also spelled Jirón), Gómez, González, Griego, Gurulé, Gutiérrez, Hernández, Herrera, Jacques (also Jáquez), Jaramillo, León, Lobato (Lovato), López, Lucero, Maez (Maes), Maestas, Manzanares, Marques, Martín (which became Martínez in the eighteenth century and now belongs to 20 percent of the population), Medina, Miranda, Montoya, Muñiz, Olivares, Ortega, Ortiz, Pacheco, Pérez, Pino, Quintana, Rivas, Rodríguez, Romero, Saes (apparently lost in the current generation), Salazar, Sánchez, Sandoval, Santiestevan, Serna, Serrano, Silva, Sotelo, Suazo (Jewish in Portugal), Tafoya, Telles, Tenorio, Torres, Trujillo, Ulibarrí (almost the only Basque surname in the region), Valdez, Velarde, Velásquez, Vigil, and Zamora.

Of these names and some that appear in other parts of the state, there are interesting backgrounds. Loggie Carrasco of Albuquerque claims that her family name has a Hebrew root, meaning "oak tree," and that the surnames Pino, Jaramillo, Ramírez, and Durán are similarly derived.[7] Some names indicate national origin: Griego means "Greek"; Frésquez means "Flemish"; Gallegos refers to the Spanish province of Galicia. Two surnames are evolutions from the French: Archebeque comes from L'Archeveque, and Gurulé from Grollet.[8] The name Rael is believed to have been originally Israel (spelled Ysrael in preceding centuries), and Cobos was once Jacobo. Benavides (often spelled Benavíez in analogous form to the other *ez*-ending names) probably began as Ben David. Lucila Benavíez, a native of Tierra Amarilla near the Colorado border, told me of a surprising incident involving her family name. After her parents both died before she was five, she was raised in a Catholic orphanage in California, knowing little of her family background. As a middle-aged woman in 1989, she walked into a small crafts shop in Los Angeles, where she paid for her purchase with a check. The shopkeeper looked at her name and commented, "Oh, you are a Sephardic Jew." She had no idea what that meant, but has since researched her family tree five generations back to find the names Sánchez, Velasques, Chávez, Manzanares, Delgado, Martínez, and López among the Benavídezes.

One family that is certain of Jewish connection are the Cocas of Taos and Las Vegas; their name is Portuguese in origin, as are most of the surnames that are spelled with the *es*, instead of the *ez*, ending, which in both cases means "son of." The actual surname Sefardita did not turn up in New Mexico to our knowledge, but it is in the family of Cecilia Concha of El Paso. Her great-aunt, who was also the aunt of the famous Mexican painter Diego Rivera, was Emilia Rivera y Sefardita. She had emigrated in the nineteenth century from Galicia in Spain to Guanajuato, Mexico. Another local surname of particular interest is that of the Amézquitas of Doña Ana County. Having emigrated from central Mexico four generations ago, they are aware that their name is of Arabic derivation from a phrase that means "to the mosque." Perhaps their ancestors were among the *mozarabes*, or forced converts, in the Muslim population of Spain.

In regard to the given names of certain families, favored ones for girls are Sara, Ester, Judit, Raquel, Rebeca, Susana, Josefina, Betsabé, and Rosa. In fact, my first cognizance of the remnants of Sephardic culture in New Mexico involved a girl's first name. Some thirty years ago a little girl in Santa Fé named Ester García told me excitedly that her parents were planning a party for her name day. It is the custom of Hispanics in northern New Mexico to celebrate the official days of the saints for whom their children are named, whether or not they were born on those days. Since there is no Saint Esther on the Catholic calendar, I was puzzled. After asking her the date, I consulted the Hebrew calendar for the month of Adar and discovered that her date was Purim that year—the Feast of Esther. I knew that her parents were educated persons who must have known what they were about. But what was going on here? In the years since then, I have learned that *el día de Ester* has been observed in many mountain villages as long as anyone can remember.

The names for men that recur in some areas are often from the Old Testament: Arón, Abrán, Adán, Benjamin, David, Daniel, Efrán, Emanuel or Manuel, Eliu, Eliseo, Esequías, Ezequael, Gedeón, Isac, Isidro, Jacobo, José, Jeramías, Jons, Josías, Josué, Moisés, Natán, Noé, Rubén, Salomón, Sansón, Zacarias or Zecarias. Names for boys were sometimes chosen by the *rezador*, or prayer leader, of the community, a sort of circuit-riding rabbi among the isolated settlements who consulted his prayer book or Bible for suitable selections. The custom of naming children after dead relatives can be observed, as newborns carried forward the given name from a departed great-uncle or grandmother.

It is instructive occasionally to note the name choices listed for family members in obituaries. Thus, when Raquel Orona died on May 29, 1991, in Mesquite at the age of ninety-four, it was reported that she had been preceded in death by her husband, Manuel; her brothers, Eliseo and Marcos; and two sisters, Ester and Rosa. Her nine sons include Moisés, Benjamin, Salomón, Elías, Daniel, Eliseo, David, and Issac. The family is, incidentally, Protestant: members of the Church of God of Prophecy.

Similarly, when Abraham Daniel Gonzales died in Pueblo, Colorado, on October, 1990, also at ninety-four years, his sons included Leví, Daniel, and Benjamin. He did not belong to a church, but was buried with a graveside service at the Old Fort Garland Cemetery, under the direction of the Romero Funeral Home. Another old-timer from the village of La Madera in Río Arriba County was Manuel Rafael Griego, who died in the fall of 1991 at the age of ninety-eight. His wife and his sister shared the same first name: Siria Trujillo and Siria Gallegos. He was buried in the "nondenominational" cemetery at La Madera by Lujan's Funeral Home.

The absence of affiliation with the Roman Catholic Church in three small communities that are almost entirely Catholic, as well as the presence of so many Old Testament names in the family trees, suggests an adherence, at some level, to their ancient Judaic heritage. One family that Dr. Stanley Hordes studied in the village of Questa, west of Taos, has been prominent in the civic affairs of the region for several generations: the Raels of the homestead at El Valle del Oso on the upper Río Colorado. From father to son, the names Moisés, Salomon, and Jacobo have alternated through the years. Although there are several other indications of a Jewish connection, the family resists the identification.

The Sacred Sabbath

Of all the suggestions of a Jewish presence in the native population, the persistent observance of the Sabbath is most often mentioned. I have heard many reports of lamps lit at Friday sunset, left burning all night with a long linen wick, and the explanation that the light was an offering for the repose of the souls of dead relatives. Sometimes the wick was placed in a bowl of pure olive oil, which might continue to glow for a week. Women lighted candles for the Friday-evening meal, presumably in honor of the Catholic saints, but they did not say which ones. Daniel Yocum of the Atrisco enclave remembers the Friday-night candles in his home, around which the Old Testament stories were retold. Ana Rael Delay, a forty-five-year-old Santa Fe woman, recalls her grandmother's Friday candles;[9] so does Carlos Vélez-Ibáñez, an anthropologist at the University of Arizona. Berta Trillo, using an assumed name, reports that all draperies at the windows of her home in Las Cruces have always been drawn before the lighting of the Sabbath candles, a custom that her grandmother told her had been in the family for five hundred years.[10] There were Sabbath candles and Hebrew prayers in the home of Dr. Efrén Martínez, a dentist in Denver, whose mother continued the practices of Judaism, even though she was married to a Catholic.

Women of these families did their shopping and food preparation early on Fridays, rushing home as soon as possible to arrange the festive meal of the week. Some fathers or grandfathers returned home from their week of labor bearing loaves of freshly baked bread, often formed by rolls of dough braided together before going into the oven in some unidentified kitchen. Several residents of Old Town in Albuquerque remember a certain Italian priest named Father Libertini who was posted in this old Spanish-speaking neighborhood during the first quarter of our century; known as a Jew-baiter in this community with many converso families, he was fond of dropping in on certain households on Friday evenings to ascertain if more candles than usual were aflame or had just been doused.

On Saturdays the judaizers devoted themselves to diligent bathing and trimming of their finger and toe nails, with gentle attention to the elders for whom these tasks of personal care were difficult. The bed linens were changed, and everyone acquired clean underwear, over which they donned their best attire. Dennis Durán remembers his family getting all cleaned up and staying home, except to make short visits to relatives in the neighborhood, especially if anyone had been reported sick during the week. While the fathers of other children usually worked on Saturdays and lounged around the local cafés on Sundays after mass, his father worked on Sunday. The approved occupations on Saturday were prayer, study, and quiet games. In Daniel Yocum's family, the youngsters were chastised if they became

Tombstones from Catholic cemeteries in the American Southwest with Jewish symbols (Courtesy Frances Hernández)

too active or noisy. The Yocums attended mass, but on Saturdays, when that option was available in their parish; at church they were warned by their mother to concentrate on God and not to digress with prayers to the saints.

In the Carrasco family of Atrisco, the prayers were the standard Catholic petitions, but without any reference to the Trinity. Loggie Carrasco remembers that when the Virgin Mary was mentioned, her grandmother reminded her to think of the other Mary—Miriam, the sister of Moses. Michael Atlas-Acuna says that his great-great-grandmother taught her descendants not to pray to Jesus, usually delivering her instructions while lighting the Friday night candles. Study of religious materials, after they became more available in the nineteenth century, was an important duty on the Sabbath. Josephine García of Albuquerque claims that she had heard the stories of the Old Testament read aloud to her so often that she was able to recite many of them verbatim before she entered school. On the other hand, she never saw a copy of the New Testament until she was in high school. Ramón Salas, who is employed as a materials analyst at Digital Equipment Company in Albuquerque, recalls that it was his task to write out the family prayers, which usually ended with the words, *Que Diós y la ley de Moisés nos protegen!* ("May God and the law of Moses protect us!").[11]

One of the most intriguing stories of Sabbath observance I have heard involves an old Hispanic Catholic family of Albuquerque. The account was given to me by Laura Stacy, a Las Cruces girl who was attending a temple in that city, where the Cosdens were a new couple recently arrived from the East. They told her about a strange experience they had as newcomers to the community. One Friday evening they were invited to dinner at the home of friends who are members of a family that has been prominent in the area for generations. They all sat down to a lovely candle-lit table, but before she joined them, the hostess turned to the wall of the dining room on which hung a picture of Jesus of the style that is standard in Roman Catholic homes. She twisted the cord from which the portrait was suspended until the image faced the wall. The she sat down at her end of the table without comment on her action. The Cosdens were embarrassed, assuring her that she need not have made that gesture to acknowledge the fact that they were Jews on their Sabbath. The lady of the house expressed surprise, declared that she had not realized that they were Jewish, and explained that her action was merely a custom that had always been observed in her family on Friday evenings.[12]

The Holidays

As with the persistent observance of the Sabbath, various judaizing customs also coincide with some of the traditional holy days of the Hebrew calendar. As in the case of little Ester Garcia of Santa Fé, the *día de Ester* in March has been a regular festival in many northern New Mexico communities and in such now-urban enclaves as Atrisco. Clemente Carmona remembers that it was primarily a women's festival, during which mothers explained domestic tasks to their girl children. They fried *empanadas*, small pastries filled with beef, pumpkin, or whatever dried, spiced vegetables were left from the winter hoard. Sometimes the triangular pies were referred to as *hamantashin* ("Haman's hat"). These pies were consumed with much drinking and singing by neighbors dressed up in their new spring clothes. Women lit candles to Saint Esther and other favorite personas, always including the *Gran Santo*—Moses. The oldest person present for the occasion—man or woman—was asked to say the blessing over the wine.[13] On February 12, 1964, a new archbishop arrived in Santa Fé: James Peter Davis, an Anglo unfamiliar with local ways and indisposed to be tolerant of them. He soon announced ex cathedra that Esther was not a Catholic saint and should no longer be so venerated.

In April, when the Spanish villages were busy with their passionate celebration of Easter, some families were repeating their own ancient customs related to the season. Dennis Durán recalls that his people baked unleavened bread for several spring days, which the children looked forward to because of its surprising crispness. Other special foods marked that week or two: *sopa*, a bread pudding with cinnamon and raisins; *capirotada*, layers of bread, dried fruit, cheese, and syrup baked together as a festive dessert; and the *lentajas*, or lentils, cooked with venison. The Saturday before Easter, the men prepared a large salad, featuring the earliest vegetables in the spring garden—and that was all that the families ate until sundown. On Good Friday, *tortas de huevo* were the only food served: thick slices of potato dipped in egg batter and fried in hot chile sauce. To celebrate the holy Sunday, all groups, both Catholic and suspect Catholic, baked or roasted whole kids, *cabritos*, in underground ember pits. But certain families drained blood from the slaughtered animals and used it to mark unobtrusive signs on their doors. Inside those houses some ferocious spring cleaning had been going on in preparation for this event, too.

At the end of May, about the time that the Americans had introduced their Memorial Day in the nineteenth century, Ana Rodríguez and Silvia Carmona-Durán remember that their aunt used to read to them the story of Ruth from the Bible. I know of no other vestigial observance of Shavuot in the month of Sivan. But in June all the villages up and down the Chama, Pecos, Río Grande, and even the smaller streams celebrated San Juan's Day by taking their first summer plunge into the icy mountain rivers. Some particular families bathed together in the fast-running *acequias*, or irrigation ditches, which served as a communal mikveh.

The most solemn observances of the year were the High Holy Days of the early fall. Rosh Hashanah, was known as *el Día Grande*. Young people realized that it was an important day for their elders, with their grandfathers praying in the cellars, but they did not often comprehend that it marked a "new year," different from the one they had learned on the common calendar. Soon afterward came an even more awe-striking day, when the Carmonas and their neighbors from Atrisco would vanish into the fields along the irrigation ditches from dawn until sunset. Although they appeared from a distance to be picking spinach, they spent the hours reciting prayers and singing mournful songs.[14] At Abiquíu, Truchas, and other villages in Río Arriba and Taos Counties, some families had the custom of walking from house to house on a certain fall day, forgiving any offenses that they might have suffered from their neighbors and asking absolution for any unkindness or oversight they might have committed during the year. Some women were reported to have tucked peas or wheat grains into their shoes so that the discomfort during the day would remind them of any forgotten transgressions.

A few citizens from the ranches near Bernal and Tecolotito in San Miguel County recall powerfully moving chants sung in someone's barn on the night before the sacred Day of Atonement, when they heard the claim that all personal vows that they might have made during the preceding year were now declared annulled before the majesty of the Lord: a *Kol Nidre* of the mountains. In a quite different kind of observance, along the lower Chama River of Río Arriba County, two communities, the Indian Pueblo of San Juan and the Hispanic village of Chamisa, have for many generations shared a new moon festival in the early fall. Old records indicate that at these annual joint gatherings, the Tewaed speakers and the Spanish-speaking neighbors renew ancient agreements involving some fairly elaborate codes of compensation payments in the event of injury to person or property, as well as the promise to honor the right of asylum for any fugitives. Some investigators have concluded that aspects of these covenants for peaceful negotiation appear to be based on Mosaic law. It is also significant that interpretations of the agreement, as well as administration of its provisions, were often left to members of the Penitentes, the secret religious brotherhood that frequently provided the leadership in isolated settlements.

One of the most memorable stories that has come to me about Yom Kippur was related by our great-aunt, Loyola Hernández, who spent her life as a nun in the convent of Loretto in Santa Fé. Sister Loyola described a close friend of hers in the 1920s, another elderly nun, who always went into seclusion one certain day in early October. When her sisters asked if she were fasting for a special intention, she explained that her own aunt, who had also been a member of the convent, had instructed her as a child to spend this annual day in prayer, asking for forgiveness of her sins against others. She believed that the observance had been imposed by some long-forgotten personal vow or dedication to a lost patron saint; neither of them had ever heard of Yom Kippur. Later in October the children of some families looked forward to the *día de los jacales*, when they helped their parents construct branch-roofed huts in their yards, where they ate jolly meals in the golden autumn weather and sang songs of thanksgiving for a fruitful harvest. Clemente Carmona remembers his grandmother's stories of the temporary shelters they built at reaping time, where they ate festive meals of the bountiful valley crops before night frosts set in. He did not realize until middle age that the occasion was the Feast of Tabernacles. Bishop Davis, however, soon comprehended what was going on in the little booths and banned Sukkot as well.

The last of the year's major holidays was Hanukah, which seemed to come in conjunction with the Christmas festivities in which almost everyone was involved to some extent. Since the only school system in New Mexico, outside of the three or four larger towns, was Catholic until the middle of the century, all children took part in the Christmas pageants and parties. Most people set out *farolitos*, small paper bags half filled with sand into which candles were lodged. On Christmas Eve they also set ablaze *luminarias*, small bonfires in front of their homes, intended to light the Christ child's way to shelter. Ramón Salas and Daniel Yocum remember that the women of their families lit one candle in a sack the first night, two sacks on the second night, and so on, increasing the number for eight days, usually ending with nine flames at once around Christmas Eve.[15] Others remember a week in midwinter that they called the *fiesta de Los Reyes*, during which eight or nine candles burned on the family altar. One memory connected with that holiday, which is shared by several informants, is that of playing with a special toy for that period: a *trompita*, or four-sided top, which resembles the traditional dreidel of European Hanukah games.[16]

One more custom is recalled, which occurred regularly in the homes of the secret Jews at the beginning of each month. As in the case of most ritualistic events, especially in the home, the women had charge of the ceremony. They placed two glasses on the household altar, one containing several stalks of grass, and the other, coins. Although the symbolism is apparently a wish for fertile crops and fiscal prosperity, the women refused to divulge to the men in the family what they were doing. Their secret incantations were often chanted in Ladino, the ancient Judeo-Spanish dialect—now remembered only in phrases and some pronunciation differences in New Mexico.

Foods

Most unusual foods among the secret Jews in New Mexico, Arizona, and southern Colorado were connected to their observance of the Sabbath or other holy days. But there were enough regular habits—especially those of which the Inquisition in Mexico City took particular notice—to set them apart in matters of diet. Even in these remote outposts of the New World, they tended to adhere to the age-old proscriptions. They could not eat bacon or other pork, which was not a temptation since pigs were not introduced into the region until the late eighteenth century. They had to eschew reptiles or fish without scales—not a problem in a land so far from the sea. They were forbidden animals that chew the cud but lack cloven hoofs, as well as bisulcate beasts that do not ruminate. But that allowed them to consume the common domestic animals: sheep, goats, and cattle, in addition to the rabbits, deer, elk, and antelope that were basic supplements. When they ate chickens, turkeys, or wild fowl, they were careful not to choke or suffocate the creatures, decapitating them cleanly with sharp knives and draining out the blood. They remembered that they were not to eat the fat or blood of their victims. Ray Padilla heard of heated arguments between his great-uncles about the condition of a knife to be used in slaughter—whether it was adequately sharp and unblemished to conform to the humane laws of Leviticus.

Another more esoteric law regarding the preparation of meat involved the *landrecilla*, or small round tumor in the glandular tissue of the leg of a ritually clean animal. This *nervus ischiadicus* must be removed from any creature to be eaten, except from poultry. Since this deveining was a difficult task to accomplish without demolishing the haunch, many cooks simply did not serve the hindquarters, merely feeding the sections to the dogs or making a present of them to their less circumspect neighbors.[17]

Another infraction of Catholic custom was the eating of meat on Friday, as happened in many households. This aberration, however, was looked upon tolerantly because flesh was hard to come by at any time—and the New Mexican Catholics had enjoyed a dispensation from this injunction for many years. Table manners included the habit of women to serve their menfolk first, without seating themselves to eat until the others had finished their meals. Traditionally the mother of the family served the eldest son first, after which his father helped himself to the dishes. For the women, a period known as the *dieta* extended for forty days of rest and seclusion following childbirth. During this period, they were fed by relatives or *comadres*, the godmothers of their children, with strengthening food: *chaqueue*, or "blue-corn gruel" in the Tewa tongue, boiled lamb, chicken or rabbit stews with chile, the flesh of a male black goat, and as much goat's milk as could be garnered.

Some dishes were especially appropriate for holidays: sweet, gooey *fichuelas*, smeared with honey, appeared around Christmas time; *pastel* or *pastelico*, a popular meat pie, could be expected for weddings and fiestas; and *pan de León* or *de España* was a round, sweet loaf baked in the outdoor ovens (*hornos*) when distant relatives came to visit. Special treats were the candies: *leche quemada*, or "burned milk," was a caramel syrup served over bread pudding or *atole*, finely ground corn gruel. Certain other fudge-like confections were wrapped in little decorated squares of paper, which were carefully smoothed, pressed, and preserved between occasions for their use. Some of these three-inch fragments were printed with dim pictures of a crowned, patriarchally bearded head—*maguen Davids*.

Everyday menus always included some form of bread. In northern Mexico and upward into the Río Grande Valley, the usual grain was wheat rather than corn; the flour tortillas, flat, round, and as unleavened as matzos, were fried on grills or hot stones. *Pan de semita*, or "Semitic bread," was, on the other hand, baked in sun ovens. Yeast-raised loaves were usually purchased from a baker for special events, such as Friday evenings in some households, when the farmers would come in early from the fields bearing the fresh, fragrant loaf from some nearby kitchen.

Many families preserved old recipes and styles of cooking from their ancestors in Spain, adjusting the ingredients to what was available in the distant West. Some have always used much garlic and onion, fried in vegetable rather than animal fat, which probably gave their dishes a distinctive—and suspect—flavor. Eggs were served with tomatoes and/or onions; lamb chops, *avas frescas con carne*, were broiled with stewed fava beans; and the *costilla de ternera* was veal cutlets with minced garlic. Hunks of lamb or venison were braised on skewers; *media de calabaza* was stuffed summer squash; and cookies or *biscochos* were flavored with anise, sesame seed, and piñon nuts—all in method very similar to the Sephardic dishes still served in Rhodes, Istanbul, Damascus, and Jerusalem. Josephine García remembers her mother's unconventional tamales, assembled only with chicken and bits of beef—never with the more common chunks of pork. These filling "Mexican sandwiches" were roiled up in a scrupulously clean kitchen, where dishes containing milk were kept strictly separate from those involving meat, though Señora García never offered any clear explanation for why this odd rule was imposed.

Songs and Narratives

In the northern communities some linguistic hints in pronunciation and word form, occasional alternative lyrics to popular *romances* and to the *alabados*, or hymns of praise, and unusual themes in a few traditional tales suggest a Ladino influence.

The archaic speech has a distinctive accent noted by contemporary Spanish speakers, as in *bendishimos* instead of *bendecimos*, *mos* and *muestro* in place of *nos* and *nuestro*, and such forms as *vide* and *guiso/guisa*, which are retained by Ladino speakers around the world. When asked if the term *marrano* had ever been applied to them, some older persons assured an investigator that it was an insult applied to all Spaniards by Italians. In addition, they commented that the Spaniards called the Italians *moros blancos*, or "white Moors."[18] Among the popular songs, John Morgan has heard alternative lyrics involving "the little Sefardita" to the well-known ballad, "Las Golondrinas."

Extensive collections of songs and folklore have been assembled by Dean John Robb of the department of music and Professor Ruben Cobos of the department of modern and classical languages at the University of New Mexico, both compiled during the 1940s and 1950s. Today this material is being thoroughly analyzed and collated by Dr. Rowena Rivera of Albuquerque. Among the old narratives, one or two have as protagonist a rabbi who overcomes his tormentors, and there is one in which the hero searches for the true religion and finally "returns." Rivera comments, "I have come across some songs that derive almost directly from Jewish prayers. The question is how did they get to New Mexico?"[19]

Religious songs, graces, and laments reveal other details. Two prayers, usually offered after a meal, are reminiscent of the Jewish grace after meals. One has the refrain:

Siempre mejor,	May we always improve, never
nunca peor,	grow worse, never to lose our
nunca mos perdimos	table from our
la mesa del muestro Criador.	Creator.

Another is:

El Padre Grande	Great father, who cares
que mande el chico,	for even the smallest,
asegun tenemos de menester	according to your law,
para muestra casa	we guide our house
y para muestros hijos.	and our children.

Occasionally the Hebrew blessing *Hodu L'Adonai qui tov qui le'olam chasdo* was quietly added.

At funerals, the mourning wails, or *llantos*, accompanied the corpse without embalming or coffin (at least into the 1920s) to its rapid burial. Certain *alabados*, or hymns, were appropriate for these solemn occasions, which sound much like the grieving dirges, or *endechas*, of the Sephardim. The *cantor*, or song leader of the community, started the stanzas, often singing several lines before the rest of the group joined in responses. Most of the *alabados*, which were sung for vigils, wakes, Lenten and Holy Week observances, are suggestive of a Sephardic milieu.

The Book

No Hebrew writing has survived from the early period except for some fragmentary inscriptions on pottery shards and on a large stone that could have been a door lintel, found in San Miguel County. The Jews of New Spain suffered from a lack of Hebrew texts. One scriptural scroll has been found: the "Little Torah," with some sixteenth-century Spanish comments inscribed inside its ark, now residing at Temple Albert. It was discovered in a tin box, buried somewhere near Los Lunas, a community south of Albuquerque on the Río Grande that was colonized by New Christians. The circumstances of its discovery and delivery are a secret guarded by the congregation. It is known to have been dated by the department of anthropology at the University of New Mexico as pertaining to the late seventeenth or early eighteenth century.

Obtaining Bibles was difficult in a Catholic country, where priests assured the faithful that the misinterpretation of Scripture was a dangerous sin to be scrupulously avoided. In fact, Andrés Palacio, the author of the Edict of Expulsion of the Jews in 1492, had urgently warned against trying to understand the subtleties of the word of God without ordained guidance. Colonists in New Spain arrived with admonitions ringing in their ears about refugees who had settled in northern European countries and been infected with Protestantism, even to the point of demanding translations of the sacred texts into their own tongues. Since those days, Spaniards in the New World have continued to associate the presence of a Bible in the home, especially a copy in Spanish, with Protestantism.

The secret Jews had to resort to radical strategies to obtain texts. The earliest and most common was to give a son to the church; not only was this sacrifice a protective cover, but with a priest in the family, a Bible in the house was justified. If he turned out to be scholar, he could even acquire Hebrew volumes for them without anyone looking askance. One of the last of the young men so dedicated was Clemente Carmona of Atrisco, now a man in his sixties. Although he learned from his grandfather that he was a Jew while he was still in his teens, Carmona was sent, as firstborn son, to begin training for the priesthood at the Aquinas Newman Center on the University of New Mexico campus. After that initial study, he entered the Dominican seminary in northern California. While he was a student there, he was seriously injured in an automobile accident. During the leisure of his convalescence, he rethought his religious commitment, concluding that he must abandon the Catholic masquerade and emerge openly as a Jew. This decision deeply upset his family, who had earnestly adhered to their Judaic faith over many generations in secret, because it would estrange them from the Hispanic Catholic community in which they had always lived.

The first major opportunity for the crypto-Jews of New Mexico to acquire Bibles that they could all read occurred in the middle of the nineteenth century, when the first Protestants filtered into this remote section of Mexican territory. Hardy Scottish Presbyterian missionaries rode up into the hidden valleys, six-shooters on their hips and saddlebags full of cheap Bibles printed in Spanish. Many a lonely sheepherder and isolated ranch wife taught themselves to read with the aid of these rare books. Some villagers murmured about those who so readily reached out for the forbidden volumes, commenting that they were probably Jews anyway. And many of them were indeed judaizers.

Rites of Passage

The customs of birth, marriage, and death are probably the most tenacious in any culture. Among the secret Jews some attitudes about parturition, the choice of mates, and appropriate burial still survive. For some women, confinement meant staying apart from their husbands for three months after childbirth. A few appear to have been observing the Levitical law that requires forty days of separation after the delivery of a boy and eighty after a girl. The practice of circumcision for newborn boys was spotty, depending on how isolated a Jewish enclave was from the surrounding community. Revelation of the condition was immediate when village children swam in rivers or the *acequias*—and soon reported to the local priest, if there was one. Nevertheless, a few old itinerant mohels operated up and down the territory, covering great distances between remote ranches and settlements. Clemente Carmona remembers one such wizened elder who always appeared from somewhere within a week after the birth of a boy in Atrisco, demanding plenty of boiling water for the sterilization of his instruments. The father and grandfather of Nora García Herrera were both circumcised by the same old man in their community; when the elder died, her father carved a star of David on his gravestone. In the 1870s, when the Presbyterians began to open their hospitals, where all male babies were routinely circumcised, most of the practitioners disappeared.

The customs of death began when a moribund person was gently removed from her bed and laid on the ground, so that the spirit actually left the body while it was in contact with the earth, resting on two large boards with candles at both ends. The body was turned on its side, facing a wall. At the moment of expiration, the attendants shouted the *llanto*, or death call, which echoed through the neighborhood. Some families throughout the region preferred quick burials for their dead—before sundown of the day of demise, if not obstructed by a coroner or other official. Their neighbors were often shocked by the deprivation of a night-long *velorio*, or wake. The preparation of the corpse was ritualistic, usually done by women relatives or sometimes by the men of the Penitente Brotherhood, who carefully bathed the body, trimming hair and nails. After the 1920s the work of the Penitentes, who were repeatedly in trouble with the bishop, was taken over in many places by the Unión Protectiva, which also helped orphans, providing dowries for destitute girls.

I have heard stories from two or three generations back about the stitching of shrouds, described by some as long tunics, cut from new linen if the family could afford it. More recently the dead have been buried in their own clothing, with hems and pockets cut out of the garments. The body was lowered into the grave wrapped in a blanket but casketless—a custom to which the Inquisition always took particular exception. María Sánchez remembers that all her relatives threw handsful of dirt into the grave, murmuring, "*Eretz Ysrael!*" On one such occasion she asked her grandmother, "Are we Jewish?" To which the older woman replied, "*Somos Israelitas.*"

After the *endechas* were chanted, the mourners returned to the family home for a ritual meal of eggs and cheese, during which a curious custom was sometimes followed. A fertilized egg in its shell was set aside to present to the first stranger who might call at the house, with the idea that he would carry away the sting of death and at the same time a potential new life. Then the immediate family observed a week of mourning in seclusion, with all mirrors in the building covered or turned to the wall. No music sounded until after the funeral. A year later the dead loved one would be remembered with lighted candles.

Burial usually took place in the local Catholic cemetery, generally the only ground available for that purpose. But areas of the *campo santo* were set aside for individual groups of relatives. In some of these sections the headstones all face east and are blank except for the names and dates of the deceased. In some locales, the northern village of La Madera, for example, there is a tiny, hidden "nondenominational" graveyard, and in the exclusive burial grounds of the Penitente Brotherhood at such places as Santa Rosa and Tecolotito, gravestones can be uncovered in the underbrush that have stars of David and menorahs carved on them. Beto Ponce knows where a private graveyard lies off the highway to Romeroville; in a photograph of a tombstone there, marked with two stars of David, he has covered the family name with masking tape. In many cemeteries, markers can be found with both Jewish and Christian symbols, or occasionally the Masonic symbol as well. Emilio and Trudi Coca of Santa Fé have produced an extensive photographic study of these revealing stones, comparing them to pictures of stones with similar designs in authentic Jewish cemeteries in other parts of the country. In the old Penitente cemetery at Santa Rosa, for example, where the latest stone uncovered is dated 1911, they found etched beneath the standard crosses clear outlines of stars of David, menorahs, six-petaled flowers, hands with fingers spread to form six groupings—all Judaic symbols recognizable to the initiated. Michael Atlas Acuna of Pueblo, Colorado, has found Hispanic Catholic cemeteries in that area where stones are decorated with stars of David, eternal lights, and six-point lilies. He also reports that in a 170-year-old rural church near Trinidad, one can see stars of David with "Adonai" inscribed in the centers, menorahs, and the Ten Commandments in Hebrew all worked into the stained-glass windows.[20]

Endogamous marriage has probably been the most critical of the measures taken to maintain this culture in the hinterlands. Researchers are mapping the patterns of intermarriage, finding frequent connections through many generations of the Espinosas, Villanuevas, Castros, Atencios, Carrascos, Gómezes, Luceros, and Lópezes. Although Dennis Durán was not apprised of his Jewish heritage while he was growing up, his mother made clear to him that he must select his wife from a list of specific families. In certain closed communities, such as the village northeast of the town of Roy, or the settlement southwest of Gallup, or the Atrisco enclave, the men are regarded as very clannish by their neighbors, who learn that they strongly—even violently—oppose any match contemplated by one of their women with a man outside of the clan. Symeon Carmona, who was told by his grandfather that the family were Jews, can identify some thirty-five families in and around the Atrisco community, some as far south as Tomé, with whom they could contract marriage. Members of this group make themselves known to each other with cryptic phrases or hand signals; the children's future alliances are often arranged by relatives.

This endogamous tradition can be traced in the Carmona family as exemplars of the tendency. To avoid inbreeding in the small gene pool, men of the line have occasionally traveled far south to Zacatecas in Mexico, where cousins settled during the seventeenth-century Mexican Exodus, to find wives. The parents of Clemente and Symeon are José Santano-Matrovio Carmona and Victoriana Consuelo Pérez. José's parents were Juan de Diós Carmona and Eponsea Ramírez; Juan de Diós's mother was Susana Espinosa, one of the Zacatecas brides, and his father, Clemente Carmona. Susana's parents were Rafael Espinosa and Leandra Arcuna; Rafael's parents were José Espinosa and Julia Arcuna, all from the Zacatecas enclave.[21]

The church frowned upon marriage between two single, unrelated persons who both happened to serve as godparents for the same child. Even today a man and woman linked in the responsibility of *compadrazgo*, or co-parenthood, can cause a scandal in New Mexico by marrying each other against the ingrained taboo. Such marriages were countenanced, however, in family groups where the pool of appropriate partners was limited. The church did occasionally allow dispensation for nuptials within the first and second degrees of cousinhood, especially if pregnancy was involved, but the injunction against matches between step-parent and step-child or between step-siblings was inviolate. Nevertheless, such connections did occur within the Sephardic group, and there were even a few rare cases of polygamy, usually a man who had taken to wife two sisters, one of whom might be tubercular or deformed. Such unorthodox alliances were often arranged to keep property intact—as was common in

Christian marriages, too—as well as to maintain blood lines, sometimes with the public justification of heredity. The secret Jews always regarded themselves as *hidalgos*, Spanish aristocrats of pure blood line.

Other marriage customs included the expectation that the oldest son of the family would remain unmarried until the youngest son was adult. This restraint was imposed upon him because it was his duty to distribute the family estate upon the death or incapacity of the parents; it was felt that he would be more fair in dealing with his siblings if he did not yet have a family of his own to consider. On the other hand, the youngest boy or girl, known as the *socoyote*, had the charge of staying home to care for aging parents, often remaining unmarried until they died, or for life. When a child left home permanently for marriage or employment, he accepted his father's formal blessing with a kiss for the paternal hand. María Sánchez reports that in her family, following a nuptial mass, a private ceremony was held at home under a canopy.

Economic conditions of the family could postpone marriage, especially for the men. Even though the economy of the northern New Mexico–southern Colorado region was essentially based on *camblache*, or barter trade, with little money passing through any hands before the nineteenth century, it was possible to acquire some substance in property and goods. Those who were not prosperous by village standards postponed marriage. Steve Almond, a reporter for the *El Paso Times*, found an old electrician in a nondescript shop guarded by a Great Dane in downtown El Paso; he identified himself as a Jew who had left his northern New Mexico village when he was thirteen. He remembered that the elders of his clan had told stories about their ancestors all the way back to the first colonists of New Spain; that they wore prayer shawls for morning worship; that they ignored the Christian festivals and scrupulously followed Mosaic law. He stated that he had followed the way of his male relatives; if they could not find a Jewish bride, they did not marry.[22]

Young persons of the current generation who are seeking their roots have discovered unknown relatives in distant locations, as a result of the constant effort to find suitable spouses. Dennis Durán, who has painstakingly reclaimed the family tree for fourteen generations in the Santa Fé area, has discovered that he is related to several families that he never heard of—and that some of them are still practicing Jews. George Martínez, who now lives in Montbello, Colorado, has sought out nine generations, finding relatives all over northern New Mexico and southern Colorado. Ramón Salas, on the same quest, discovered that he is related to Daniel Yocum. Salas has been able to document seventeen generations in the state, without finding any indication of official conversion to or from Judaism. In the process, he met an unknown third-cousin, María Sánchez, with connections at Romeroville, near Las Vegas, and at San Elizario, a far south village on the Río Grande below El Paso. He asked her if she was aware of their shared Jewish roots. She responded that if he had been using his good Jewish head, he would have become aware of his heritage long before.

One of the most charming stories I know is about a case of semi-exogamy, in which a New Mexico Sephardi married a New York Ashkenazic woman in the 1950s. Trudi Rattner came out to Santa Fé soon after the Second World War. There she met a handsome young native man, employed in nearby Española. When he asked her for a date, she replied primly that she was Jewish and did not go out with men of other faiths. Emilio Coca, however, informed her that one of her attractions for him was her background, since he was Jewish himself. Trudi, looking at a dark, dimpled Hispano, decided that the local fellows would go to any length to date an exotic New Yorker. But Emilio was finally able to convince her, with photographs of his grandmother wearing a star of David at her throat and with the recitation of Hebrew prayers, albeit in an odd accent, that he was indeed a Jew.

The Cocas of Taos and Las Vegas are descended from Miguel Coca de Vega, first recorded at the sixteenth-century fortified colony at Las Golondrinas near La Ciénaga, some twenty miles south of Santa Fé. His sons moved northward, probably when the capital was assigned priests. Emilio's branch settled in the Taos Valley; five Coca families are now listed in Las Vegas. One group, of which Miguel Coca y Lucero has now identified himself, reached and settled Guadalupita, north of Tecolote, one of the few settlements in the state that is still too isolated to receive television signals. His distant cousin Emilio and Trudi Coca have now been married thirty-two years.

Christian Connections

The secret Jews of New Mexico overwhelmingly present themselves to the world as Catholics. The façade required of them as conversos remains largely intact today. Ben Shapiro, working on a research grant funded by the New Mexico Endowment for the Humanities, spent two years interviewing Hispanics in Albuquerque, Santa Fé, and the small towns up and down the Río Grande Valley; all his respondents identified themselves as Catholics, even though they retain vestiges of judaizing rituals in their traditions and folklore.[23] The parents of Bertha Cobos Muskey, who now lives in Colorado Springs, Colorado, grew up in the lower-valley village of San Elizario, where they were Catholics, in spite of the fact that her father did not attend mass, but, instead, went to "meetings" with other men of the community on Saturday mornings, and that Mrs. Cobos, in her old age, has become more and more obsessed with the possibility of pork entering the house or meat and milk dishes being served at the same meal. There are a few, however, who have always avoided contact with the church, while, on the other hand, others have made connections with certain Christian organizations.

Four Gentile groups have had some influence among the Sephardim from the late sixteenth century through the nineteenth: the Jesuits, the Penitentes, the Protestants (Presbyterians and Seventh-Day Adventists), and the Masons. Each of these religious and social institutions seems to have offered some protection, initially, against the militant officers of the Inquisition, and at last, against isolation and ostracism resulting from nonparticipation in parochial activities.

The Society of Jesus offered sympathetic instruction and intellectual rigor in the Southwest, as well as in other parts of Latin America. Gabino Rendón, like many other northern New Mexican boys, had his first opportunity to begin learning English in the Jesuit school that opened in Las Vegas, New Mexico, in 1877. In those classrooms children were allowed to read the Bible in Spanish and English, an experience totally forbidden by other priests.

Another Catholic connection was the Hermanos Penitentes, which some believe is a perverted remnant of the Third Order of St. Francis.[24] The fraternity had chapters, or *moradas*, in many isolated villages, even as far south as San Elizario, and conducted religious and social activities in communities that often did not see a priest from one year to the next. The groups did not proselytize, but simply brought in teenaged sons or nephews from one generation after another. The members undertook communal responsibility for each other, tending the sick, assisting the disabled, and helping to support widows. One Penitente family would address the members of another as *mano* from *hermano*, or "brother." The leader of the *morada*, or *hermano mayor*, usually came from the most prestigious family of the community. Far into the twentieth century, it has been difficult to be elected to any political post in the northern counties without membership in or at least support by the Penitentes.

The history of the Brotherhood is currently being studied by several researchers. It is not certain when the first *moradas* were established, but Bernardo Abeyta is credited with building the ancient church in the village of Chimayo, known as El Santuario, which may have been one of the first buildings of the Penitentes. This famous shrine, with a hole in its floor from which magic earth is scraped out to achieve miraculous cures, is very similar to one in Guatemala. And, in fact, the village was settled by the Ortegas, a clan of weavers that moved up from the Central American country in the late eighteenth century. Other old meeting houses are in the San Juan basin farther north; the chapter at Los Martinez moved to Cañada Bonita in 1920, apparently to avoid interference from the local church.

The services conducted in the chapter buildings—small, thick-walled, windowless adobe fortresses—were relentlessly secret, a situation that has always worried the church. Several New Mexican archbishops, especially Fathers Lamy and Salpointe, both of whom were French, did their best to eradicate the order. Its most renowned celebration was the annual re-enactment of the Crucifixion on Good Friday, or *Tinieblas*, with one of the members elected each spring to bear the cross at the head of a long, solemn procession of self-flagellants, accompanied by groans, rattling chains, and the rhythmic beat of *matracas* made of dried gourds. Prayer leaders, or *rezadores*, were protected by the silence of their neighbors if any stranger came asking questions. In Chama, for instance, the *rezador* appeared to lead devotions at weddings and births, where he often had the honor of naming the child with a selection from his prayer book. Whether or not some *moradas* actually provided worshipers for judaizing enclaves is still debated. Dr. Rowena Rivera has found no direct evidence in their records, although many of their chants sound like prayers from old Sephardic communities in other parts of the world and their cemeteries contain gravestones with Jewish symbols.

The next Christian connections came much later in the history of the territory: the nineteenth century, when the first intrepid Protestant missionaries entered what was now part of the United States. Mexico had won its independence from Spain in 1821, but lost almost half of its land when General Kearny of the American army announced in 1846 at Las Vegas that he was annexing New Mexico, a claim that became official two years later with the Treaty of Guadalupe Hidalgo. Scotch and English Presbyterians rode in by the middle of the century, distributing tracts and selling Spanish Bibles for about forty cents. The Reverend Mr. Alexander Darley, called "the apostle of the Southwest," covered the sparsely populated territory of the San Luis Valley in southern Colorado and northern New Mexico. Among his first customers were the Penitente families, who were especially interested in the Old Testament. Many of them subsequently became Presbyterians.[25]

One of the first Hispano ministers was Antonio José Rodríguez, who was invited by the Ute tribe in 1895 to found a school at Ignacio, Colorado. With the Indian leader, Julian Buck, as one of the first converts, Rodriguez's school continued into the 1920s, offering the Ute children their first exposure to education in English and Spanish. Prominent native preachers included John Whitlock y Lucero, the great-grandfather for whom my husband is named; Tomás Atencio; and Gabino Rendon. They founded mission schools and churches all over the northern reaches, creating a small but active Presbyterian community that has provided many educational and political leaders in the state over the past century. Rendón converted the entire villages of Trementina and Peñasco; Atencio helped found the English-speaking Allison-James School in Santa Fé and the Menaul School in Albuquerque; Whitlock's son-in-law, Benigno Hernández, both a Penitente and a Presbyterian, became the first congressman when New Mexico achieved statehood in 1912. One of Whitlock's grandsons became a regent of the University of New Mexico; another is a judge and former U.S. ambassador.

Becoming a Protestant was indeed a difficult decision in the area, requiring strong moral fiber to combat the threatening hostility of the community. Villagers recalled that one of the most suspect forms of behavior mentioned in the lengthy Edict of Faith published by the Inquisition in Valencia in 1519 was reading—anything, but especially the Bible. The purpose of the edict, read from all New Spain pulpits, was to enlist the populace in the search for judaizers. Those who indulged in the dubious habit of reading usually displayed a curiosity about the forbidden translations; and that frequently led right to the ardent little chapels of the Presbyterians. Almost everyone who could read was captivated by the books that the missionaries made available; those who could not often saw them as an opportunity to become literate. Relatives sometimes disowned these adventurous dissenters from the wisdom of Mother Church; others whispered that they were probably Jews anyway.

The Reyes family moved into northern New Mexico from Mexico, escaping from the Revolution of 1910 and bringing along a prosperous trade in liquor, as well as a Jewish identity. They married into the local Madero and Gallegos families, who had already become Presbyterians in Gabino Rendón's congregation at Las Vegas. Dr. Tomás Atencio, son of the minister, is now a cultural historian at the University of New Mexico; he says that his family takes their Jewish roots for granted. Dr. Gabino Rendón, another minister's son, teaches sociology at Highlands University; he is also interested in pursuing the hints and connections of a perceived Jewish past within the small Protestant community of northern New Mexico. Another, more recent Protestant group that has attracted converts in the region is the Seventh-Day Adventists; they observe the Sabbath on Saturday and conform to the Levitical dietary laws.

A second non-Catholic connection that seems to have been a latter-day analogue to the Penitentes for some communities has been the Masonic lodges, the first chapter of which in New Mexico was organized about 1878 at Fort Union, near Las Vegas. The Catholic Church was almost as inimical to the Masons as to the Brotherhood, and for the same reason: they incorporated religious motifs into their ceremonies, which, because of their policy of strict secrecy, the church could not control. The Masons suffered the same threats as had the Presbyterians when they were bringing the Reformation to New Mexico three hundred years after it took place in Europe. Most of the Masonic founders were English-speaking Protestants, who encouraged education in their recruits and bestowed a status on them that was recognized in the wider community. Gravestones in the cemeteries at Monticello, Anton Chico, Bernal, San Marcial, and Tecolote feature Masonic symbols, sometimes along with disguised Jewish signs. On a few markers in the separate graveyards around Puerta de Luna, the Masonic symbols bear Hebrew inscriptions within them.

The Future of the Crypto-Jews

Dr. Stanley M. Hordes, the leading researcher in this field in New Mexico, believes that the Hispanic-Jewish culture is rapidly dying out, succumbing to the influences of radio, television, and public education available in every corner of the territory. Although some villages and enclaves cling stalwartly to their customs, most of their children are leaving for higher education, jobs, and an inevitable melding into the larger community

Nevertheless, certain families cling to their background. They keep in close touch with each other, and settle in cohesive family groups in small towns, like the Mirabals and the Olivareses southwest of Gallup. Their habits include a refusal to hang pictures on their walls, an avoidance of kneeling during prayer and of kindling fire on Saturdays, and insistence that their children stay in school, in spite of the general preference among Hispanics for going to work as soon as possible. For a long time to come, some women will object to cutting out garments on Fridays, explaining that things will surely happen to prevent the completion of the project; oppose their sons' purchase of automobiles, even when they can afford a down payment, with the argument that they might be killed on the mountain roads; and refrain from sweeping dirt out their front doors, carefully pushing it out the back way or lifting it through a window instead. Although they defend this last practice as avoiding bad luck, the usual explanation for any odd habit, Dr. Jack E. Tomlins points out that the same precaution is taken by women in open Sephardic communities in Greece and Turkey in order to avoid dishonoring the mezuzahs attached to their doorposts.[26]

Specifically religious observances have managed to persist, probably because there have always been few priests in the northern villages to correct these aberrations. Even today many churches open for mass by a traveling cleric no more than once a month—or even once a year for a general baptism of children. Before the annexation by the United States in 1846, most of the native-born priests married and produced offspring. The famous Padre Martínez of Taos did much for his people in the late nineteenth century, promoting their education by opening schools and founding a newspaper that is still printed, *El Crepúsculo* ("Evening"). Archbishop Lamy excommunicated him, but he defiantly continued to minister to his flock. The fact that a considerable percentage of the citizens of Taos and Río Arriba Counties are now surnamed Martínez is credited to him, since he gave his name to all the foundlings and homeless children whom he took into his orphanage.

In a crypto-Jewish village, the clandestine religious activities centered around the *rezadores* who served as "rabbis." They supervised the laborious hand-copying of psalms and prayers in Ladino, which were handed down from father to son, and appointed the *levantadores*, who lifted the sacred texts during secret meetings in different houses, sometimes in underground prayer rooms or, apparently, in the *moradas* of the Penitentes. Though Ladino is now largely forgotten, there was always a *rezador* available somewhere who remembered the prayers, for which the men stood with their heads covered.[27] Ramón Salas has recorded one of the favorite prayers, translated from the Ladino as follows:

Holy Savior of the world,

I, Ramón, call on you this holy day.
They have eyes; may they not see me.
They have hands; may they not use them against me.
They have feet; may they not reach me,
By the angels of Number 43.

The most important line in this incantation is the last one, referring to the chapter in Isaiah in which God promises to rescue His people and bring them home to the Promised Land.[28] And then there is the unknown carver from among the many crypto-Jewish families around the plaza who decorated the Church of San Felipe de Neri in the center of Old Town in Albuquerque with a star of David above its altar.

Some treasured artifacts remain: silver amulets chiseled with one or two Hebrew characters, said to be protectors against disease; Daniel Yocum's photograph from the 1920s of his grandparents' wedding pose, with the young groom wearing a tallit over his shoulders; a Christ doll, handed down in a family that called it a representation of the Messiah still to come, claiming that the real Mary was the sister of Moses—*El Gran Santo*. More than twenty years ago, an elderly lady of the numerous Chaves clan in Santa Fe—herself a Chaves on both sides and married to a Chaves as well—showed me a leather phylactery of the sort manufactured in western Europe in the nineteenth century. She had found it among her dead grandfather's possessions; when I asked her what she thought it was, she guessed a charm against the evil eye. In spite of all this evidence, when Stanley Hordes interviews persons in Atrisco, he is told that they do not want to hear that they are Jews, since they have enough trouble just coping with being Hispanic.

In many families the tradition of judaizing seems to have been shepherded through the women. It has often been through mothers and grandmothers that adolescents learned of their background. Berta Trillo discovered, when she was in her thirties, a stenographer's pad left by her grandmother, in which were recorded strange prayers consisting of Hebrew phrases written in the Roman alphabet, plus a few Hebrew letters, and the confession: "*Judía. Tu eres judía. Somos judíos.*" This revelation explained to Berta the hidden worship, dietary peculiarities, and distrust of Catholicism that were typical of her childhood. Teresa Fajardo, a Las Cruces woman now in her forties, who is related to the Cocas of Taos and Las Vegas, had a similar experience of finding a notebook in which her grandmother had written the word *Judía*. Carlos Vélez-Ibáñez, an professor in his fifties, learned of his heritage about thirty years ago at the funeral of his only sister. On that occasion, his mother leaned close to him and whispered, "I'm going to tell you a secret that has always been passed on through the women of our family. But now I must tell you. *Somos judíos*. We are Jews."[29] As he looked back on his childhood, the only indication of this news that he could recall was the family's strict aversion to pork.

As guardians of the secret, the women were also severe about disclosure. Daniel Yocum remembers that his grandmother made her husband hide his carved menorah in the garage. There is also a strong suggestion that in some families a choice was made about which members would be told of the heritage and which ones would be allowed to merge, unaware, into the mainstream. Inevitably, some members also made the choice for themselves. This situation had led to families in which one branch of the line continues its judaizing practice, while another does not. An example of this is reported by Ed Martínez of Albuquerque, who comes from a tightly knit clan in a village south of Las Vegas. His parents and siblings lived on one side of a small river; his father's sister and her family were ensconced on the other side. Martínez knew that his aunt lighted candles on Friday nights, in spite of their cost in this impoverished community. When he was thirteen, his grandfather told him that his cousins across the river were Jews, but that they were close kin and that their practices must never be exposed.

Elsewhere, in areas where the crypto-Jewish families felt more secure against the censure of their Catholic neighbors, the grandfathers undertook the training of children as they reached the age of puberty. They explained that Moses is the great saint, that God is the only focus of prayers, and that they must perform such niceties as carefully washing their hands before eating, after which ablutions they were each to fold a napkin and place it on his shoulder. Grandmothers taught the Friday-night rituals, sometimes commenting that the men did not remember the prayers accurately, while the women could be counted on. Fathers taught their sons the values of respect, honesty, and family responsibility, often mentioning that a youth must not consider marriage until he is able to give his own future son a secure start in life. Mothers bestowed the most powerful blessings on their children, constituting the sign of family approval. They taught their daughters the scrupulous management of the home, with fervent housecleaning each spring around Easter, and attentive care of their own bodies, with regular bathing and special modesty during menstrual periods, sometimes requiring a separation from the family for a few days. Girls also learned their community duties to care for the sick, help the poor, and work through women's organizations, such as the Union Protectiva, to provide dowries for orphan or indigent brides. Many of these family-centered concepts will continue to be instilled and cherished.

Since the publicizing of this research, many persons have contacted investigators with questions and confidences. Cecilia Concha of El Paso, whose brother is a local priest, asks for information and tells me that her family is sure of its Jewish or Moorish descent. Ana Nuñes of Houston understands more about her roots since she talked with an elderly man of the Old Town section of Albuquerque, who explained that his method of testing the sharpness of a knife to be used for slaughtering was to try scraping the ink off newspaper print. Rachel Soles of El Paso reports that her study of ancestors has netted Diego de Montoya, some Godoys (a Basque name), and a Gonzalez who worked on the cathedral in Santa Fé—all of whom are related to Felix Torres in Socorro, as well as to some clandestine Jews in the villages of Tomé and Tortugas. Melissa Amado, a twenty-six-year-old graduate student at the University of Arizona, learned of her heritage by seeking out among her progenitors the descendants of the first Amado family in America, which left Valencia around 1700, apparently to evade the later activities of the Inquisition. During her search, she located a distant relative who told her that he is a Jew and that Judaism was the faith of the Amados. Michael Atlas-Acuna began to look into his background after reading in a newspaper about Stanley Hordes's research. He had heard that several of the Acunas had been with New Mexico's first colonists, among those who had hastily left Mexico, where they had been marked for death by the Holy Office. Although he is married to a Jewish woman himself and can remember his own great-grandmother lighting Friday-night candles and warning him not to pray to Jesus, Atlas-Acuna was unaware of his own background until he happened upon the article.

Others have met with the realization in unusual ways. Ruth Flores Reed, now retired as an administrative assistant from the Mexican-American Studies and Research Center at the University of Arizona, regularly wore at her throat a curious silver amulet that had been passed down to her through the women of her family. One day Dr. Abraham Chanin, who serves as director of the Southwest Jewish Archives, explained to her that the tiny marks on the little plate were the Ten Commandments in Hebrew. She then remembered that when she was growing up in Mexico, her family ate no pork, read the Old Testament, believed in one deity—the God of Israel, and told stories about a prominent forebear, Ruíz de Apodaca, who had been her great-grandfather's first cousin, Mexico's last viceroy from Spain, and a secret Jew.[30] Somehow she had not made the connection from these details.

Ana Rael Delay of Santa Fé, who has been teaching school in Colorado since 1982, also read about the discoveries and was moved to recall unusual habits in her own family, which has traced its arrival in New Mexico to 1610. She can remember the days of *matanza*, or butchering, at her grandparents' rural homestead, when her grandfather repeatedly sharpened the *jífero*, or slaughtering knife, before cutting the throats of calves and goats, allowed the carcasses to drain their blood for a long time, and removed the sciatic nerve from the hindquarters, while repeating prayers through the whole process. Her grandmother went into a frenzy of activity around Easter time, baking a special yeastless bread that she called *gallecitas*, washing all the dishes in the cupboards, and lining all the shelves with fresh paper. Delay also recalls the stern warnings from her parents that she must never tell anyone about the family's habits.[31] Since then she has learned that the family surname, Rael, is believed to have derived from Israel, and that she is connected to the Cocas of Taos, who know they are Jews.

Dr. Ray Padilla, the forty-seven-year-old director of the Hispanic Research Center at Arizona State University, emphasizes that he is a Catholic but, nevertheless, is fascinated by research into his Sephardic ancestry in Jalisco, three hundred miles north of Mexico City. He first became aware of the possibility when he read an essay by Dr. Raúl Padilla López, the rector of the University of Guadalajara, in which the educator describes his descent from judaizers in the Jalisco community. Subsequently, Ray Padilla and his brother made a journey to their parents' native village, where they noticed that the church had no crucifixes inside or out. They also saw that the men dressed with dignity, as their own father did habitually, always appearing in long-sleeved shirts and never leaving their homes without hats on their heads. The Padillas sought out neighbors who remembered their grandfather and his brothers, mentioning heated arguments among them on *día de matanza* over whether the butchering knife was sharp enough and completely free of nicks and whether the animal carcass had drained thoroughly before being taken down to divide.

The question remains now about what the future will hold. How are these Hispanos reacting to the unexpected knowledge—or revelation—of their Jewish connection? The range of responses is wide. Some villagers in isolated areas are still fearful, uneasy, and resentful that their secret is out. They are faced with the choice of denying the claims and continuing in their old unobtrusive ways, of joining the mainstream, or of deciding to practice Judaism openly, perhaps with some connection to an established Jewish community, even though the present-day cosmopolitan Ashkenazim seem more foreign to them than do the Spanish-speaking Catholics who have always surrounded them. Any of these routes requires courage for both the predictable and the unknown. A national debate goes on about how these long-separated, uneducated, often uncircumcised Jews should be accepted. Rabbi Marc D. Angel, leader of Shearith Israel, the historic Spanish and Portuguese Synagogue in New York City, and president of the Rabbinical Council of America, insists that they must prove matrilineal descent and/or go through valid halakhic conversion. In spite of a compassionate attitude toward these people who have endured so much in New Spain, Angel claims that "to eliminate these standards is to undermine the distinctiveness of the Jewish people."[32] Some local rabbis have assisted those seeking help into the assimilation process: in Albuquerque, Lynn Gottlieb, a Reform rabbi, has served as a discreet contact for the hidden Jews, and Isaac Chelnick of a Conservative congregation, B'nai Israel, is assisting several in their formal adoption of Judaism.

Among persons outside the villages and enclaves who have recently learned of their background, there is also the range of responses, from staying with the Catholicism in which they were raised, to full conversion and participation. Marina Vaca, a fifty-two-year-old teacher's aide in Albuquerque, traces her descent from Leví Melendres, a trading-post proprietor who helped to establish Doña Ana County. Although she is not a practicing Jew, she plans to honor her ancestors by praying at the Wailing Wall in Jerusalem and walking the streets of the prophets in Israel.[33] Paul Márez, a twenty-four-year-old graduate student, belongs to a split family; some attend mass, while he goes to the temple with others. Dr. Efrén Martínez, the Denver dentist who is a native of Longmont, has recently seen his son through his bar mitzvah. Berta Trillo, who was called a Jew by her fellow Catholics in younger days, now sees her grandchildren being brought up as Jews and guarding the five-century-old rituals of her ancestors.[34] Ramón Salas has converted to Judaism after his family search, as has Dennis Durán, among his relatives. Durán, a contracts administrator at the Los Alamos laboratory, discovered that he is descended on both maternal and paternal sides from Gómez Robledo, who came to northern New Mexico with Oñate in 1598. This early settler is famous in colonial history as one of the few judaizers whom the Inquisition chased all the way from Mexico City into the upper Río Grande Valley; his was also an extremely rare case of acquittal, probably due to his strong armed guard. More than two hundred pages of the trial records of the Holy Office are devoted to this proceeding.

There are a few remarkable persons who have managed to maintain their Judaism more or less openly. One such is Loggie Carrasco, a woman in her eighties from Atrisco, who speaks Ladino fluently. She has charted her family tree back to the Iberian Peninsula, which her ancestors left, from Seville and Madrid, in the early 1600s. She holds a proprietary right in the Spanish land grant bestowed on Don Fernando Durán y Chaves in 1692, now known as the Atrisco Grant. In the landmark Heirship Case of early in this century, her parents were awarded the claim interest No. 833174. She was brought up in a leading family of the Atrisco enclave, being told as a teenager by her mother that Catholicism was superstitious nonsense. She remembers an oft-told story about an ancestor named Manuel Carrasco who was tried by the Inquisition in Mexico City in 1648 for the unlikely crime of being apprehended, while traveling, with a matzo cake hidden beneath his hat. Although he tried to convince the Catholic authorities that unleavened bread was a popular remedy for headache, he was tried for Judaism and ended up with his sugar plantations confiscated and himself "disappeared." For many years, Loggie Carrasco has been a member of the congregation at Temple Albert, where she assists other crypto-Jews to embrace formal Judaism, and where she and her brother have long served as teachers in the Sunday school.

With the new openness and appreciation, the possibility of renewal may be at hand. I recently overheard this brief conversation after a lecture on the subject of the conversos. One man in the audience said quietly to another: *"Cuáles de nosotros son los judíos?"* (Which of us are the Jews?) The answer was, *"Los agudos"* (The smart ones).

Notes

1. Floyd S. Fierman, *Roots and Boots: From Crypto-Jew in New Spain to Community Leader in the American Southwest* (Hoboken: Ktav, 1987); Kathleen Teltsch, "Scholars and Descendants Uncover Hidden Legacy of Jews in the Southwest," *New York Times*, November 11, 1990, p. 16A.

2. Alfonso Toro, *La familia Carvajal: Estudio histórico sobre los judíos y la Inquisición de la Nueva España en el siglo XVI, basado en documentos originales y en su mayor parte inédutism qye seconservant en el Archivo General de la Nación de la Ciudad de Mexico* (Mexico City: Editorial Patria, 1944).

3. Frances Leon Swadesh, *Los Primeros Pobladores: Hispanic Americans of the Ute Frontier* (Notre Dame: University of Notre Dame Press, 1974); Richard C. Greenleaf, *The Mexican Inquisition of the Sixteenth Century* (Albuquerque: University of New Mexico Press, 1969).

4. Swadesh, *Los Primeros Pobladores*, p. 74.

5. Described in conversation at the Unitarian church of El Paso on May 19, 1991.

6. Harry S. May, *Francisco Franco: The Jewish Connection* (Washington, D.C.: University Press of America, 1978), p. 97.

7. David Nidel, "Modern Descendants of Conversos in New Mexico: 500 Years of Faith" (unpublished essay), p. 34.

8. Teltsch, "Scholars and Descendants."

9. Patricia Gininger Snyder, "America's Secret Jews: Hispanic Marranos Emerge from Centuries of Hiding," *Jewish Monthly*, October 1991, pp. 26–38; Steve Almond, "Secret Faith: Did Jews Fleeing the Inquisition Hide Their Heritage in New Mexico?" *El Paso Times*, March 5, 1990, p. 1F.

10. Almond, "Secret Faith."

11. Snyder, "America's Secret Jews"; Henry J. Tobias, *A History of the Jews in New Mexico* (Albuquerque: University of New Mexico Press, 1978).

12. Conversations with Laura Stacy on several occasions between July 1982 and September 1984. This custom has been confirmed by Nieves Bushell, a native of Barcelona who is now a professor in New Zealand; she reports that a painting of the Last Supper was turned to the wall in her home during certain family celebrations.

13. Nidel, "Modern Descendants of Conversos"; Swadesh, *Los Primeros Pobladores*.

14. Almond, "Secret Faith."

15. "Converso Descendants: The Long Road Back," *Hadassah Magazine*, January 1992, pp. 18–20; "Torn Between Two Faiths," *San Jose Mercury News*, May 11, 1991, p. 1B.

16. Elaine DeRosa, "Uncovering a Hidden Past: Descendants of Crypto-Jews Seek Answers," *Greater Phoenix Jewish News*, March 8, 1991, p. 11.

17. Fierman, *Roots and Boots*, pp. 12–13, mentions this action of removing the leg gland as a focus of prosecutions by the Inquisition. The Leibman index of trials lists eight cases based on this charge, including those of Mariana de Mirabel in 1602 and of Marta de San José in 1654.

18. Dr. Edgar Ruff has confirmed the usage, as reported in William Byron's *Cervantes*, p. 88. Guzmán de Alfarache says that the common Spanish epithet of *moros blancos* was particularly applied to the Genose.

19. "Hispanics Rediscover Jewish Identity," *New Mexico Magazine*, June 1991, p. 27.

20. In telephone conversations on November 12 and 14, 1990

21. Nidel, "Modern Descendants of Conversos," p. 26.

22. Almond, "Secret Faith," p. 27.

23. Shapiro, report on National Public Radio, April 28, 1988.

24. Gabino Rendón, *Hand on My Shoulder* (New York: Board of National Missions, Presbyterian Church in U.S.A., 1963), p. 65.

25. Swadesh, *Los Primeros Pobladores*, p. 77.

26. Reported in conversations in 1976–78.

27. Nidel, "Modern Descendants of Conversos," p. 26.

28. "Converso Descendants," p. 19.

29. "Torn Between Two Faiths," p. 1.

30. Snyder, "America's Secret Jew," p. 23.

31. "Converso Descendants," p. 19.

32. Marc D. Angel, "Crypto-Jews Should Meet Halachic Standards," *New York Jewish Week*, May 24, 1991, p. 25.

33. Almond, "Secret Faith," p. 1.

34. Virginia Culver, "Hispanics Discover Surprising Heritage," *Denver Post*, May 12, 1991, p. 6.

CONTRIBUTORS

SAMUEL G. ARMISTEAD is Professor of Spanish and Comparative Literature at the University of California, Davis. He specializes in the literature of medieval Spain and modern Hispanic literature (especially traditional poetry of the Sephardim). The author or editor of more than twenty book-length publications on the oral literature of Hispanic peoples, he has, for the past thirty-five years, collaborated with the late Joseph H. Silverman and Israel J. Katz on extensive field work in Sephardic communities in America, Spain, North Africa, and Israel.

MARTIN A. COHEN is Professor of Jewish History at the Hebrew Union College–Jewish Institute of Religion, New York. He has also taught at Antioch College, Temple University, and Hunter College of the City University of New York. He is a past president of the American Society of Sephardic Studies and Chairman of the Board of the Jewish Historical Society of New York. He served as the editor of three major sections on Sephardica for the *Encyclopaedia Judaica* and contributed numerous articles on the subject. Among his books in the field are *The Martyr*, on the Mexican Inquisition; the translation from the Portuguese of Samuel Usque's *Consolation for the Tribulations of Israel;* and the forthcoming *The Canonization of a Myth*, on the Portuguese Inquisition.

FRANCES HERNÁNDEZ is a member of the faculty at the University of Texas at El Paso. She has also taught at the Universidad de Puerto Rico and at universities in Chile and Malaysia. Among her best-known works are *The Catalan Chronicle of Francisco de Moncada* and *The Turks with the Catalan Company, 1305–1312*. She is presently translating Alfonso Toro's history of the Inquisition in the Americas, *The Carvajal Family*.

ISRAEL J. KATZ is presently a Research Associate with the University of California, Davis. He has taught at McGill and Columbia Universities as well as the City University of New York. His specialization is in the music of the Mediterranean region with a particular emphasis on the musical traditions of the Sephardic Jews. A former Guggenheim Fellow, Professor Katz is the author of numerous works dealing with the folk music and poetry of Spain and Portugal. Among his best-known works are *Judeo-Spanish Traditional Ballads from Jerusalem: An Ethnomusicological Study* (1972–1975) and (with the late Joseph H. Silverman and Samuel G. Armistead) the multi-volume edition of *Judeo-Spanish Ballads from Oral Tradition* (1986).

EMMA FIDANQUE LEVY was born in Panama and raised in the tradition of Congregation Kol Shearith Israel, the synagogue founded by her great-grandparents. She is a trustee of New York's Central Synagogue and heads the Oral History Project of the National Council of Jewish Women's New York section.

DENAH LIDA is Professor of Spanish and Comparative Literature at Brandeis University, Waltham, Massachusetts. She has also taught at Harvard University, Middlebury College, Sweet Briar College, the University of Pittsburgh, and the University of Southern California. The author of nearly two dozen scholarly works, Professor Lida is completing a book entitled *A Century of Judeo-Spanish Scholarship: An Overview*.

DIANE MATZA teaches writing and twentieth-century American literature at Utica College. She has written about cultural transmission among American Sephardim and conducted oral histories with Judeo-Spanish- and Greek-speaking immigrants. She is currently writing a literary biography of Annie Nathan Meyer.

ALLAN METZ is Reference Librarian at Drury College, Springfield, Missouri. He is the author of nearly two dozen scholarly articles on Latin America and Latin American Jewry. He has just published a full-length study, *Leopoldo Lugones y los judíos: as contradiccioneas del nacionalismo argentino* (Buenos Aires, 1992).

VICTOR A. MIRELMAN is the rabbi of West Suburban Temple Har Zion, River Forest, Illinois. He holds the Ph.D. in Jewish history from Columbia University. Rabbi Mirelman has published extensively in journals such as *Jewish Social Studies*, *Conservative Judaism*, and *American Jewish History*. His book *Jewish Buenos Aires, 1890–1930: In Search of an Identity* was published in 1990.

JOSEPH M. PAPO was born in Upper Galilee, Israel, and is descended from a long line of Sephardic rabbis. He was educated in Egypt and the United States, where he emigrated in 1925. He was one of the founders of Masada, the National Zionist Youth Organization. Mr. Papo has devoted his professional life to Jewish communal service and has served as the executive director of the Central Sephardic Jewish Community in America. He has published a number of works on Sephardic culture and history, including *Sephardim in Twentieth Century America: In Search of Unity* (1987).

MALCOLM H. STERN is widely acknowledged to be the dean of American Jewish genealogists. The fifth member of his family to be ordained at the Hebrew Union College, Rabbi Stern is a member of the faculty at the Hebrew Union College–Jewish Institute of Religion, New York, and the genealogist of the American Jewish Archives. He is best known for two important genealogical works, *Americans of Jewish Descent* (1960) and *First American Jewish Families; 600 Genealogies, 1654–1977* (1978).

ROCHELLE WEINSTEIN is Professor and Deputy Chair in the Department of Music and Art at the Borough of Manhattan Community College/City University of New York. She is also Research Associate at the Institute for the History of German Jewry, University of Hamburg. Professor Weinstein is completing a book entitled *The Stones of Amsterdam: Sepulchra Monuments of the Jews of the Netherlands in the 17th and 18th Centuries*.

Index

Abade, Ruth, 290
Abd al-Majid I (Ottoman sultan), 57
Abd-ar-Rahman III (Cordovan caliph), 15
Abd-er-Rahman II (Cordovan emir), 16
Abd-er-Rahman III (Cordovan caliph), 17
Abeniacar, Abigail, 105, 106
Abeniacar, Isaac, 89, 90, 105
Abeniacar, Jacob, 89
Abeniacar, Mordechay, 89, 90
Abeniacar family, 89
Abenjacar, Mordohai, 106
Abeyta (surname), 420
Abeyta, Bernardo, 442
Abiquiu, N.Mex., 416, 427
Abner of Burgos, 36
Aboab, Abraham de Isaac Semach, 106
Aboab, Daniel Semach, 81, 85, 129, 130
Aboab, Immanuel, 56, 76
Aboab, Isaac Semach, 104
Aboab, Ribca Semach, 85, 104
Aboab de Fonseca, Isaac
    in Amsterdam, 93, 107, 109, 111
    as Bible commentator, 107-108, 109, 118
    as Hebrew poet, 218-219
    portraits of, 109, 118, 120
    in Recife, 77, 109, 141, 218, 331
    and Mordechay Senior, 109
Aboab family (Curaçao), 184
Abraham (biblical patriarch), 90, 98, 108, 110, 112, 117
Abraham bar Jahacob, 118
Abraham Ibn Daud, 20
Abraham Ibn Ezra, 280
Abrahams, Abraham I., 160, 161
Abrahams, Florence, 152
Abrahams, Robert D., 152
Abran (given name), 422
Abravanel, Isaac, 59, 182, 280, 405
    Raphael's fictionized portrait of, 403
Abravanel, Judah, 61
Absiel, Francois, 95
Aby Yetomim (Amsterdam charitable society), 130
Acapulco, Mexico, 223

Acculturation and assimilation
    of American Sephardic writers, 381, 399, 407
    and Judeo-Spanish press, 288
    in Latin America, 216, 224, 237, 240, 259
    of Lazarus, 388
    in Minorca, 10
    of Moroccan Jews, 259
    in Muslim Spain, 21
    of Noah, 384, 386-387, 407
    of Nathan, 398
    in Ottoman Empire, 61, 67
    of Sciaky, 399
    and Sephardic identity, 205, 283, 406
    in Spain and Portugal, 28
    in U.S., 273, 278, 283, 288, 399, 406, 407, 408
Acosta (Jamaican official), 149
Actors, 172
Acuña, Hernando de, 41
Acuna, Michael Atlas, 437
Adan (given name), 422
Adarbi, Isaac, 58
Adonai bekol shofar (hymn), 335
Adon Olam (hymn), 335
Adrianople, Turkey, 252
Aelantre! (periodical), 401
Afonso I (Afonso Henriques) (Portuguese king), 32
Afonso II (Portuguese king), 32
Afonso III (Portuguese king), 30
Afonso IV (Portuguese king), 35
Agricultural colonies, in Argentina, 235, 247, 248
Agriculture
    in Muslim Spain, 17
    in Christian Iberia, 27
    in New World, 217, 219, 226
    in Roman/Visigothic Iberia, 10, 13
    in Western Sephardic Diaspora, 73
    See also Viticulture
Agrippa and Berenice (New Testament figures), 114
Agua, O Dio (prayer), 369, 371

Agudath Maccabee Society, 286
Agudath Zionist Maccabee, 285
La Aguila (newspaper), 288
Aguilar, Moses Raphael de, 77, 93, 141, 218, 331
Ahasuerus (biblical king), 101
Ahmed III (Ottoman sultan), 57
Al-Andalus, 14, 23
    during Reconquista, 23, 24
    Golden Age of, 15, 16
Alaric II (Visigothic king), 13
Alarid (surname), 420
Albert Einstein Day School (Panama), 197
Albert Einstein Institute (Panama City), 202
Albigensians, 50
Albo, Joseph, 38
Albuquerque, Afonso de, 70
Albuquerque, N.Mex., 418, 423-424, 425, 441, 444, 447, 452
Alcalay, Isaac, 280, 281, 297, 298, 299
Aleppo, Syria, 251, 253, 258
    Alliance schools in, 304
Alexander, Abraham, 166
Alexandria, Egypt, 257
Al-Fadil (Saladin's vizier), 21
Alfaquim (court physician), 28
Alfasi, Isaac, 19
Alfonso V (Aragonese king), 38
Alfonso X (Alfonso the Wise) (Castilian king), 28, 33, 312
Alfonso XI (Castilian king), 33, 36
Algazi, Leon, 342
Algeria, 250
    Jewish immigration to, 243
    Moroccan Jews in, 244
    musical tradition of, 338
    Spanish exiles in, 55
Al-Ghazali, 61
The Alhambra Decree (Raphael), 402-405
Alire (surname), 420
Aljamas, 17
Aljubarrota, Battle of, 36
Alkmaar, Netherlands, 90
Allen, Ruth, 204
Alliance Israélite Universelle, 67, 239
    Ovadia's view of, 271
    school system of, 304
    in Argentina, 247, 248
    in Morocco, 243-249 *passim*
    in Ottoman Empire, 269, 304
    U.S. chapters of, 304
Allison-James School (Santa Fe), 444
Almagro, Diego de, 220
Almeida (surname), 419
Almeida, Jorge de, 211
Almoli, Solomon ben Jacob, 62
Almond, Steve, 439
Almosnino, Moses, 61, 65
Alonso, Hernando, 411-412
Altabé, David F., 284, 400-401
Altman, Paul, 146
Altona, Germany, 182
Alvar, Manuel, 364, 367
Alvarez (surname), 419
Alvares Correa, Jahacob, 94
Alvarez Correa family (Barranquilla), 239
Amado, Melissa, 449
Amado family (Valencia & New Mexico), 449
Amador de los Rios, José, 5
Amalgamated Synagogue (Jamaica), 150
Amateau, Albert, 291
La América (newspaper), 272, 274, 282, 287, 288
America, discovery of, 2, 209-210
American Association of Jewish Friends of Turkey, 302
American Bicentennial (1776), 169
American Civic League, 270
American Jewish Chronicle, 273
American Jewish Congress, 146
American Jewish Historical Society, 161
American Red Cross, 298
American Revolution
    Charleston during, 166
    Curaçao during, 188
    Newport during, 158, 161
    New York during, 158-159
    Philadelphia during, 166, 168
    Savannah during, 164
    St. Eustatius during, 153, 188
American Sephardi Federation, 281, 287, 301, 302, 303
    Education Committee, 283
    Young Leadership Division, 302

American Society of Sephardic Studies, 284, 400
American Zionist Federation, 287
Amézquita (surname), 421
Amiens, Treaty of, 187
Amiras, Mentesh, 336
Amsterdam, 238
    Brazilian Jewish emigres in, 141
    and Coro, 238
    and Curaçao, 147
    Fidanque family in, 182-183, 185
    Jewish community of, 127, 128, 130, 188, 283, 309, 331
    as Jewish cultural/spiritual center, 76, 146, 217, 357
    messianic currents in, 63
    as mother city of other Sephardi communities, 77, 93, 156, 156, 157
    New Christians in, 53, 76, 357
    poverty among Sephardim of, 73
    publishers' guild of, 93, 111
    Sephardi secular music in, 337
    synagogues of, 105, 127
Amsterdam Jewish Museum, 127
Amsterdam Municipal Archives, 85, 104, 143
Amusement and recreation industry, 277
Andalusian (Spanish dialect), 311
Andrada (surname), 419
Andrade, Benjamin da Costa, 146
Andrade, Gaspar de, 133
Angel, Aaron, 258
Angel, Marc D., 273, 275, 278, 284, 451
Anshei Sfarad, as synagogue name, 174
Antioquia, Colombia, 221
Antique business, 277
Anti-Semitism
    in Barbados, 144
    in Curaçao, 138
    in Damascus, 384
    and guild membership, 93
    and immigration, 389
    and Lazarus, 388
    and Meyer, 389, 390
    and Noah, 384, 385
    in Ottoman Empire, 57
    in pre-Expulsion Spain, 404
    in Reconquista Iberia, 29
    in Savannah, 163
    in Surinam, 143
    in U.S., 381, 388, 389, 390
    in Venezuela, 237
Anton Chico, N.Mex., 445
Antwerp, Jewish community of, 309
Apocalypticism. *See* Messianism and apocalypticism
Apodaca, Ruíz de, 450
Apostasy, 180
"The Apple" (Moise), 383
Appraisers, 187
Aquinas, Thomas, 61
Aquinas Newman Center, 434
Arabic
    and Alliance schools, 248
    Jewish knowledge of, 18, 21, 56
    Spanish translations from, 312
    in Syrian Sephardic schools, 261
Arabic-speaking Jews, 248, 271
    in U.S., 291, 295, 406
Aragon, 2, 23, 30, 32, 35, 36, 37, 38, 40, 41, 51
    Fidanc family in, 180
    intermarriage with New Christians in, 43
    mass conversions in, 52
Aragon (surname), 420
Ararat plan, 385, 386-387
Araujo, Juan (Julio) de, 147
Arba'ah Turim (Jacob ben Asher), 64
Archebeque (surname), 420
Archivo da Torre do Tombo (Lisbon), 220
Archuleta (surname), 420
Arcuna, Julia, 438
Arcuna, Leandra, 438
Argentina
    agricultural colonies in, 235, 247, 248
    Catholic influence in, 247
    in colonial era, 216, 222-223
    Jewish immigration to, 246
    Moroccan Jews in, 242, 245-250
    passim, 254
    Ottoman Jews in, 252-253
    Russian Jews in, 235, 249
    Spanish and Portuguese Jews in, 222, 248
    Zionism in, 260, 261
Arians, 12
Arias (surname), 419

Aristotle/Aristotelianism, 20, 22, 26, 61
Arizona, University of, 449
  Mexican-American Studies and Research Center, 450
Arizona State University
  Hispanic Research Center, 451
Armijo (surname), 420
Armistead, Samuel G., 336, 338, 340, 341, 342, 344, 345, 347, 348
Arnett, Robert M., 336
Arón (given name), 422
Arredondo family (The Hague), 105
Artisans and craftsmen, 73, 273
  in Muslim Spain, 17
Artists, 154
The Artist's Studio (Vermeer), 102
Asceticism, 27
Ashkenaz, Ashkenazim (Hebrew terms), 3
Ashkenazim
  in Argentina, 254, 259
  in Costa Rica, 240
  in Curaçao, 148
  and Federation of Oriental Jews of America, 291
  intermarriage with, 259, 262, 273, 405
  in Jamaica, 150
  and Judeo-Spanish press, 289
  naming practices of, 173
  in New Amsterdam, 157
  in Ottoman Empire, 56
  religious attitudes of, 163, 258, 279-280
  schools of, 261, 282, 283
  in Seattle, 272
  in Sephardi synagogues, 159, 160, 162, 168-169, 281
  in Surinam, 226
  in Venezuela, 262
  and Zionism, 260
Asociación Israelita de Venezuela, 246, 256
Assa, Abraham, 65
Assimilation. *See* Acculturation and assimilation
Association des Anciens Élèves de l'Alliance à Tanger, 247
Astrologers, 28
Astronomers, 27, 210
Asturian-Leonese (Spanish dialect), 311

Asturias, 23
Atencio (surname), 420
Atencio, Tomas, 443, 444
Athias, Joseph, 93, 111
Atlanta, 67
  Ottoman Jews in, 270
  Sephardic Jews in, 336
Atlas-Acuna, Michael, 425, 449, 450
Atrisco Grant (New Mexico land grant), 418, 423, 425, 427, 434, 435, 438, 447, 453
Autos-da-fé, 48
  episcopal, 227
  in Mexico (New Spain), 211, 223, 227, 412, 412
  in Peru, 215, 220, 221, 222, 225
  in Portugal, 218, 219
  in Spain, 46
Aveele, Johan van den, 106, 108, 110, 118, 127
Averroes, 16, 26
Avianca (airline), 240
Aviation industry, 240
Avicebrol, 21
Avicebron, 21
Avila, Abraham, 165
Azriel of Gerona, 27, 28
Az yashir Moshe (hymn), 335

Babylonian Exile, 3
Baca (surname), 420
Badanes, Jerome, 408
Baeck, Leo, 205
Baerle, Casper van, 103
Baeza brothers, 145
Baghdad, 18
  gaonate of, 26
Bahia, Brazil, 217, 219
Bahya Ibn Pakuda, 20, 65
Balboa, Vasco Núñez de, 211
Balearic Islands, 36, 38, 46
Balfour Declaration, 257, 260, 286
Balkan Wars, 251, 253, 270, 292, 359
Ballads (*romances*), 65, 335, 336, 337, 340, 357, 359, 360-362
Baltimore, Moroccan Jews in, 245
Banco de Barranquilla, 239-240
Banco de Bogota, 240

Banking and insurance, 56, 57, 73, 201, 239-240, 240
Barbados, 85, 143-146
   and Amsterdam Jewry, 77, 93
   Brazilian Jews in, 77, 219
Barbados Museum, 145
Barcelona, 23, 24, 26
   Disputation of, 35
Barela (surname), 419
Barnard College, 379, 389, 390
Barocas, David N., 284
Barranquilla, Colombia, 238, 239, 240
Barreiro (surname), 420
Barreto de Menezes, Francisco, 141
Barrios, Daniel Levy de, 130
Barrios, Miguel de, 309
Barsely, Joseph, 94
Barsimson, Jacob, 156, 157
Baruch, Jacob, 129
Baruch family (Hamburg), 85
Basque (language), 311
Bates, Henry W., 242
Bayazid II (Ottoman sultan), 56, 57, 267
Bayonne, New Christians in, 72
Beck, Nicolaas van, 134
Behar, Nissim, 286, 303-305
Beirut, Lebanon, 251
Bejarano, Hayim, 67
Belém, Brazil, 241-242, 245, 247
Bellow, Saul, 379
Belmonte, Isaac Nunes, 103, 127
Belmonte, Manuel Baron, 103, 127, 130, 131
Belo Horizonte, Brazil, 257
Benardete, Mair J., 283, 284
Benavides (surname), 419, 420-421
Benavidez (surname), 421
Benavíez (surname), 420-421
Benavíez, Lucila, 421
Benchimol, Isaac, 248
Ben David, Elvira, 336
Benedict XIII (antipope), 35, 38
Bene Kedem (Zionist organization), 261
Ben Israel, Manasseh, 76, 103
   portraits of, 118
Benjamin (given name), 422
Bension, Ariel, 261
Bentinck, William, 110, 111

Benveniste, Hayyim, 65
Ben Yehuda, Eliezer, 304
Benyunes, Joseph A. de, 292
Berab, Jacob, 62
Bernagie, Bastiaan, 134, 137
Bernal (seaman with Columbus), 210
Bernal, N.Mex., 428, 445
Bernalillo, N.Mex., 420
Beruchim atem (song), 335
Besso, Henry J., 283
Bet-Din Hagadol (Great Court), 62
Beth Ahabah (Richmond synagogue), 171
Beth El Emeth (Philadelphia synagogue), 169
Beth Elohim (Charleston synagogue), 165, 167, 186
Beth Haim van Ouderkirk van de Amstel, 183
Beth Israel (Hamburg congregation), 182, 331
Beth Shalome (Richmond synagogue), 171
Beth Yangakob (Jamaica synagogue), 151
Bet Israel (Amsterdam synagogue), 107
Bet Jacob (Amsterdam synagogue), 107
Betsabé (given name), 421
Bet Yosef (Caro), 64
Bevis Marks (London synagogue), 182
   and Bridgetown synagogue, 145
   and Charleston synagogue, 165
   and Georgia colony, 162
   liturgy of, 331, 332, 333, 335
   names of, 331
   rabbis of, 111
Bibas, Jacob, 250
Bible
   and Catholicism, 417, 434, 442, 444
   commentaries on, 61, 62, 66, 107-108, 182
   Ferrara edition of, 76
   illustrated editions of, 93, 94, 95, 97, 112, 124-125
   literary themes drawn from, 102, 126
   names drawn from, 91, 160, 422
   New Christian use of, 53, 423, 425, 427, 434, 435, 447, 450
   quoted, 185
   as source of tombstone illustrations/inscriptions, 81, 90, 95, 97, 98, 99, 108, 110, 111, 147, 237
   translations of, 65, 76, 93, 101
   See also names of biblical books

Biblia Sacra, 124
Birth customs
   birth songs, 364, 366
   in Southwestern U.S., 435
Black Code, 171
Blacks, 215, 390, 401, 413, 415. *See also* Slavery; Slave trade
Black Souls (Meyer), 390-391, 392
B'nai B'rith, 148
B'nai Israel (Albuquerque synagogue), 452
B'nai Jeshurun (New York synagogue), 159
Boas, Franz, 335
Bocarro, Gaspar, 180
Bolivar, Simon, 236
Bordeaux, New Christians in, 72, 75
La Bos del Pueblo (newspaper), 288
Bosnia, Judeo-Spanish dialect of, 65
B'racha V'shalom Ugemiluth Chassadim (St. Thomas synagogue), 154, 190
Brailoiu, Constantin, 342
Brandão, Ambrósio Fernandes, 217
Brandon, Bartolomeus, 111
Brandon, David Henry, 199, 200
Brandon, Inez, 199
Brandon, Judith Maduro, 199
Brazil
   Alsatian Jews in, 245
   assimilation in, 220 rubber industry
   Egyptian Jews in, 257
   expulsion of Jews from, 141, 142, 143, 146, 147, 156, 219, 226
   immigration policy of, 258
   Inquisition in, 219-220
   Jewish community of, 183, 357
   Moroccan Jews in, 241-246 *passim*, 258
   North African Jews in, 258
   Senior family in, 89, 108, 109, 129
   sugar industry, 89, 217, 218
   under Dutch rule, 77, 77, 81, 141, 218, 219
   under Portuguese rule, 77, 81, 141, 211, 213, 216-219, 218, 226, 310
Brazil Company (Portuguese), 128
Brazil wood, 217
Bredero, Gerbrand, 102
Breviarium Alaricianum (law code), 13
Briceño, Diego Peñalosa, 211

Bridgetown, Barbados, 144, 165
Brokers, factors, and commercial agents, 85, 130, 132, 185, 186, 187, 189, 197, 201
Bronx, N.Y., Sephardi schools in, 282
Brooklyn, N.Y.
   Monastir Jews in, 342
   Ottoman Jews in, 251
   Sea Beach community, 405, 406
   Sephardi schools in, 282
   Syrian Jews in, 282, 405, 406
Brooklyn Heights, Battle of, 158
Brown, Saul, 157
Browning, Robert, 387
Buck, Julian, 443
Buenos Aires
   Ashkenazim in, 247
   census figures for, 248, 250
   Inquisition in, 222
   Egyptian Jews in, 257
   Moroccan Jews in, 247, 249, 250
   Ottoman Jews in, 251, 252, 253
   Portuguese conversos in, 213, 222
   Syrian Jews in, 251, 258
   Zionism in, 260
Bulgaria, Alliance schools in, 304
Bulgarian Jews, in U.S., 287
Burke, Edmund, 153
Business and commercial activities
   in Amsterdam, 97, 130, 156
   in Argentina, 222, 249, 251-253
   in Barbados, 85, 144, 144, 219
   in Brazil, 85, 89, 129, 147, 217, 218, 241-246 *passim*, 249
   in Christian Spain and Portugal, 25, 27
   in Colombia, 236, 238, 239-240
   in colonial North America, 159, 160, 161, 163-164, 165, 169
   in Costa Rica, 240
   in Curaçao, 85, 98, 122, 124, 130, 132, 219, 235, 236, 238
   in Denmark, 105
   in England, 251
   and evolution of Judeo-Spanish, 309
   of Fidanque family, 190, 193, 197, 202
   in Haiti, 155
   in Jamaica, 151
   in Latin America, 214, 227

Index   463

in Mexico, 211, 412
in Muslim Iberia, 17
in Netherlands, 128, 129, 130, 156
in Ottoman Empire, 56, 56-57, 66, 267-268
in Panama, 193, 200, 201, 202
in Peru, 214, 225, 245, 246
of Portuguese conversos, 214
of Senior Henriques family, 122
in St. Thomas, 190, 191, 193
in Surinam, 141, 143, 226
in U.S., 197, 251, 273, 277-279, 287-290, 335
in Venezuela, 236-237, 238
in Visigothic Iberia, 9-10, 10, 13
in Western Sephardic Diaspora, 73
in West Indies, 141, 225
See also names of business and commercial activities
Bustos (surname), 420
Butchers, 157

Caballococha, Peru, 245
Cabral, Pedro Álvares, 216
Cácaeres, Diego García de, 220
Cacao, 237
Cáceres (surname), 420
Cairo, Egypt, 257
Calchaqui, Argentina, 249
Caliphate, Almohad, 15
Calle, Alfonso de la, 210
Calvinism, 47
Cameta, Brazil, 242
Campanall, Mordecai, 159
Campeche, Mexico, 223
Canada
　Sephardi music in, 337
　See also Montreal
Canada Bonita, N.Mex., 442
Canary Islands, 244
Candelaria (surname), 420
Candioti, Teodoro, 225
Cantares de diversas sonadas (song), 368
La cantiga de las horas (song), 362
Cantiga de novia (song), 365, 367
Cantiga de parida (song), 342-344, 364-365, 366
Canto de boda (song), 344-345
Cape Verde Islands, 211
Cap-Haïtien, Haiti, 155

Capon, Aaron, 255
Capsali, Moses, 62
Capuchins, 133, 137
Caracas, Venezuela
　and Curaçao Jewry, 190, 236, 238
　Egyptian Jews in, 257
　Moroccan Jews in, 244, 247
　Sephardi-Ashkenazi cooperation in, 262
　synagogues of, 246, 256
Cardoso family (Amsterdam and Curaçao), 85
Cardosos, Batseba Aboab, 85
Cardoze, David, Jr., 154, 195
Cardoze family, (Panama)
Cardozo, David Nunes, 164
Cardozo, Elizabeth, 380
Cardozo, Isaac (Fernando), 76
Cardozo, Nancy, 380
Cardozo family (Curaçao), 184
Carilho, Sarah, 121
Carilho Marchena, Ester, 97
Carilho Marchena, Rachel, 97
Carilho Marchena, Sarah, 97
Carmona (surname), 419
Carmona, Clemente, 418, 427, 429, 434, 435, 438
Carmona, Eponsea Ramírez, 438
Carmona, José Santano-Matrovio, 438
Carmona, Juan de Diós, 438
Carmona, Susana Espinosa, 438
Carmona, Symeon, 438
Carmona, Victoriana Consuelo Pérez, 438
Carmona-Duran, Silvia, 427
Carmona family, (New Mexico) 427
Caro, Joseph, 60, 62, 64, 65
Carrasco (surname), 420
Carrasco, Loggie, 420, 425, 452-453
Carrasco, Manuel, 453
Carrasco family (New Mexico), 425
Carrera, José Miguel, 220
Cartagena
　and Curaçao Jewry, 133, 190, 238
　Inquisition tribunal in, 90, 133-136 *passim*, 221
Cartographers, 27, 210
Carvajal, Catalina, 211
Carvajal, Guiomar, 211
Carvajal, Isabel, 211
Carvajal, Leonor, 211

Carvajal (Carbajal, Carabajal) de la Cueva, (surname), 419
Carvajal family, 211
Carvajal y de la Cueva, Luis de, the elder, 211, 412
Carvajal y de la Cueva, Luis de, the younger ("El Mozo"), 211, 413
Carvalho, Emanuel Nunes, 168
Carvalho e Mello, Sebastian Joseph de, 54
Casablanca, 242-243
Casa de Contratación, 210
Casías (surname), 420
Casillas (surname), 420
Cassuto, Alfonso, 182
Casta, Ana de, 225
Castila del Oro, Panama, 211
Castile, 2, 30, 32, 33, 34, 35, 37, 38, 40, 41, 51, 52
Castilian (Spanish dialect), 309, 311-312
Castro (surname), 419, 420
Castro, Isaac de, 218
Catalan (language), 311
Catalonia, 23, 38
    Jews of, 210
Catani family (Ottoman Empire), 57
Cathari, 50, 51
Cats, Jacob, 103
Cavallo y La Cerna, Martin de Gomez de, 134
El (or Un) cavretico (song), 341-342, 362-363
Cayenne, Surinam, 143
Cazes, David, 244
Celtic (language), 311
Cemeteries
    in Barbados, 144, 144, 145
    in Brazil, 219
    in Caracas, 238
    in Charleston, 165, 166
    in Coro, 237, 238
    in Curaçao, 85, 86, 90, 95, 97, 127, 137, 147, 149, 185
    in Czernowitz, 92
    in Gluckstadt, 91
    in Haiti, 155
    in Hamburg/Altona
        Konigstrasse, 91, 182
        Ohlsdorf, 91
    in Iquitos, 245
    in Jamaica, 149, 150, 150, 151
    in La Madera, N.Mex., 422
    in Lima, 255
    in Nevis, 152
    in Netherlands
        Groet, 90
        Muiderberg, 91
        Ouderkerk, 81, 86, 90, 92, 95, 96, 97, 117, 127, 183
        Scheveningsweg, 91, 111
    in New Amsterdam, 157, 186
    in New Orleans, 172
    in Newport, 159, 160, 161
    in Panama, 193
    in Philadelphia, 167
    in Prague, 92
    in Pueblo, Colo., 422
    in Rhode Island, 159
    in Río Hacha, 238
    in Richmond, 171
    in Santa Fe, Argentina, 249
    in Savannah, 163, 164
    in Southwestern U.S., 437, 445
    in St. Croix, 154
    in St. Eustatius, 152, 153
    in St. Thomas, 154
    in Surinam, 143
Centinela contra judíos de sangre (Torrejoncillo), 45
Central Sephardic Community of America, 297
    essay contest on Sephardic life in U.S., 283
    and synagogues, 296
Central Sephardic Jewish Community of America, 279
    Centralized Location Service, 297
    demise of, 299-300
    educational activities of, 282, 283, 296, 297
    and mutual-aid societies, 298
    and Ovadia, 280
    services provided by, 297, 299
    and Shearith Israel, 276
    Women's Division of, 298, 299, 300
    during World War II, 299
    and Yeshiva University, 281, 283
    and Zionism, 287
Central Sephardic Jewish Community of New York, 297-298
Central Synagogue (Nassau County, N.Y.), 200

Centro Macedónico (Temuco), 256
Centro Macedónico Israelita (Temuco), 257, 262
Cerda (surname), 420
Ceuta, Spanish Morocco, 243, 244
Chama, N.Mex., 443
Chamisa, N.Mex., 428
Chanin, Abraham, 450
Chapter and Verse (Altabé), 400-401
Charcas Province, Peru, 213
Charlemagne (Frankish king), 14
Charles I (Spanish king), 71
Charles II (English king), 149
Charles Martel (Frankish king), 14
Charleston
    in colonial period, 78, 163, 165-167
    first Jewish settler in, 165
    synagogues of, 78, 165, 166, 186, 326
Charlestown, Nevis, 151
Charles V (Holy Roman emperor), 71, 210, 411
Charles XI (Swedish king), 110
Charlotte Amalie, St. Thomas, 190, 191
Charyn, Jerome, 379
Chaves (surname), 420
Chaves family (New Mexico), 447
Chávez (surname), 420, 421
Chazars, 17
Chelnick, Isaac, 452
Chicago, 67
Chief rabbinates, Sephardi
    of Egypt, 293
    of Great Britain, 281
    of Ottoman Empire, 67, 268
    in U.S., 280, 281, 295, 297
Chile
    in colonial era, 216
    conversos in, 220-221
    Sephardic Jews in, 256, 257
Chillon, Abraham, 93
Chilon, Johan Lopes, 93
Chimayo, N.Mex., 442
Chindaswinth (Visigothic king), 11
Chintila (Visigothic king), 11
Chmielnicki massacres, 63
Christianity
    Nathan's view of, 394-396 *passim*
    Raphael's view of, 404
    See also names of churches and denominations
Christianstad, St. Croix, 154
Christmas, 429, 431
Chumaceiro, Aron Mendes, 148
Chumaceiro, Joseph H., 167
Church of God of Prophecy, 422
Cibola, cities of, 413
Cigarette industry, 277
Cincinnati, 67
Circumcision
    in American colonies, 158, 160
    and Jewish identity, 91
    liturgical melodies for, 332, 335
    in colonial Mexico, 224
    of New Christians and crypto-Jews, 160, 224, 435
    records of, 104
Cisneros (surname), 420
Citizenship, U.S., 288, 293
Civil War, U.S., 167
Clement VII (pope), 59
Clothing and dry goods, 190, 249
Cobos (surname), 420
Cobos, Ruben, 432
Coca (surname), 421
Coca, Emilio, 437, 440, 441
Coca, Trudi Rattner, 437, 440, 441
Coca de Vega, Miguel, 440
Coca family (New Mexico), 440, 448, 450
Coca y Lucero, Miguel, 440
Cock, Hieronymous, 122
Cocoa, 73, 129
Code Noir (Black Code), 146, 155, 171
Cohen, Abraham, 143
Cohen, Hartwig, 166
Cohen, Hayyim, 273
Cohen, Jacob Raphael, 168
Cohen, Martin A., 359
Cohen, Moses, 165, 166
Cohen, Samuel, 146
Colbert, Jean Baptiste, 146
Colombia, 194, 236
    in colonial era, 216, 221
Colon, Panama, 193
    Moroccan Jews in, 244
Columbia University

Sephardic Studies Group, 283
studies of Judeo-Spanish songs at, 335, 336
Columbus, Christopher, 142, 149, 170, 210, 226
"The Comet Again" (Moïse), 383
Commentary on the Earlier Prophets
(Abravanel), 182
Commercial agents. *See* Brokers, factors,
and commercial agents
Committee for the Relief of Jewish Sufferers
by Wars and Massacre, 292
Communal organizations, 290-300 *passim See
also names of organizations*
Communal solidarity and kinship feelings
and commercial activities, 57, 73, 89,
121, 133, 185, 186, 190, 193, 249, 251
and marriage patterns, 186, 239, 437-438
among Moroccan Jews, 248, 249
among Ottoman Jews, 252, 253
and residential/organizational patterns,
247, 251, 252, 253, 254, 256, 271, 326
with *K'lal Yisrael* and world Sephardi
Jewry, 300
Communal structure
in Curaçao, 147, 184-185
in Dutch Brazil, 219
in Hamburg, 182
in Holland, 147, 219
New Orleans, 172
Compadrazgo (co-parenthood), 438
Complicidad Grande, 72, 221, 225
Comunidad Israelita de Temuco, 257
Concepción de Chile, 220
Concha, Cecilia, 421, 449
Congregación Israelita (Buenos Aires), 247
Congregación Israelita Latina (Buenos Aires),
247, 250
Conquistadors, 211
Conservative Judaism, 259
and crypto-Jews, 452
Consolation for the Tribulations of Israel
(Usque), 75, 76
Constantinople (Istanbul)
aid to fire victims in, 291
Alliance school in, 304
emigration from, 251, 252, 257
foods of, 432
Jewish publishing in, 65-66

Judeo-Spanish dialect of, 65
New Christians in, 66, 89
Contamana, Peru, 245
Contra el ainaré (charm against evil eye), 370, 371
Conversion, to Catholicism
of New Christians, 44, 216
of North African Jews, 68
recidivism from, 11, 68
among Southwestern crypto-Jews, 440
in Spain and Portugal, 11, 29, 36, 37, 38,
39, 43, 44, 52, 68, 210
in Visigothic Iberia, 11, 13-14
Conversion, to Islam, 58, 269
Conversion, to Judaism
of New Christians, 160
in Ottoman Empire, 58
of Southwestern crypto-Jews, 451-453
passim
in Spain and Portugal, 24, 29
in Visigothic Iberia, 10
Conversion, to Protestantism, 68, 118, 163,
443-444
Conversionists, 35, 36, 38, 39, 42
Conversos. *See* New Christians
Córdoba Province, Argentina, 250
conversos in, 222
Cordova (surname), 420
Cordova, Jacob de, 108, 111
Cordova, Joshua Hezekiah de, 78
Cordova, Moses de Isaac, 111
Cordova e Brazil, Jacob Haim ben Moses
Raphael de, 106-107
Cordovero, Moses, 63
Coro, Venezuela, 138, 236-239 -1passim-0
Corrales (surname), 420
Corsica, 14
Cortés, Hernán, 223, 411, 412
Cortizos, Ernesto, 240
Cortizos family (Barranquilla), 239
Cosden family (Albuquerque, N.Mex.), 425
Costa Rica, 239, 240
Courtiers, Jewish, 28
Covo, Albert, 289
Craft guilds, 93
Creatione Mundi (Manasseh Ben Israel), 103
El Crepusculo (newspaper), 446
Cromwell, Oliver, 71, 72, 144, 149

Crypto-Jews, in Latin America, 213, 215, 217, 223, 451
Crypto-Jews, in Southwestern U.S.
  aristocratic self-image of, 439
  bathing and grooming customs of, 424
  and Bible, 425, 433-434, 450
  birth and parturition practices of, 431, 435
  and Catholicism, 418, 422, 425, 428, 430, 433, 437, 439, 441-442, 451
  circumcision practices of, 435
  custom of not sweeping dirt out door, 446
  death and funerary practices of, 433, 436, 437, 448
  dietary practices of, 423, 427, 430-432, 436, 441, 448, 449, 450
  and Freemasonry, 445
  future prospects of, 445, 451-453
  genealogical studies of, 439, 440, 449, 452
  Hebrew among, 433, 433, 440, 445, 447, 450
  holiday celebrations of, 427-429, 450
  Judeo-Spanish among, 429, 432, 433, 446, 452
  and mainstream Judaism, 451-452
  marital practices of, 417, 437-439, 447
  naming practices of, 419, 419-423, 422
  and Protestantism, 422, 433-444-, 435
  ritual slaughter among, 451
  Sabbath practices of, 423, 425, 445, 448, 450
  and "Saint" Esther, 426
  secretiveness of, 418
  songs and narratives of, 432-433
  subterfuge of having sons enter priesthood, 434
  turning of picture of Jesus to wall by, 425, 445
  women's role among, 418, 423, 425, 428, 429, 441, 445-446, 448, 449
Cuba, 142, 149, 238
  Jews from, in U.S., 281
  Sephardim in, 255
Culi, Jacob, 66
Cumana, Venezuela, 236
Curaçao
  during American Revolution, 188
  and Amsterdam Jewry, 77, 148, 235, 238
  archival sources on, 85
  B'nai B'rith chapter in, 148
  Brazilian Jews in, 77, 219
  business activities in, 132, 133, 147, 186, 187, 189
  and Caribbean "diaspora," 152, 153, 154, 193, 236, 236, 238, 239, 240, 241, 246
  cemetery of, 85, 86, 97
  in colonial period, 130, 146-148, 187, 326
  and Dutch West India Company, 137-138
  economic decline of, 236, 239
  emigration to U.S. from, 168
  factionalism and communal conflicts in, 148, 189, 193, 239
  Fidanque family in, 183, 189
  Jewish community of, 77, 130, 146-147, 183, 184, 190, 235-236, 238
  Jewish Historical Museum, 97
  Koeymans assiento, 130
  National Guard, 187
  and North American Jewries, 146, 186
  rabbis and religious functionaries of, 94, 166
  self-governing institutions of, 147, 184, 185
  Senior family in, 85, 104, 112, 121, 122, 129, 137, 138
  synagogues of, 97, 184-185, 189
  during War of 1812, 189
Curiel, Moses, 93, 127, 128
Curiel family, 239
Curitiba, Brazil, 257
Customs and superstitions
  avoidance of sweeping dirt through front door, 446
  bathing and grooming, 424
  evil eye charms, 369, 370-372, 447
  of Greek and Turkish Jews, 446
  naming of children, 173
  of Southwestern crypto-Jews, 445-446
  turning picture of Jesus to wall, 425-426, 445
  See also Birth customs; Marriage customs; Death and mourning
Cuzari (Ha-Levi), 20

Da Costa, Gabriel (Uriel), 53
Da Costa, Isaac, 147, 165, 166, 184
Da Costa, Jeronimo Nunes, 93, 127, 128
Da Gama, Vasco, 70

D'Aguilar (De Aguilar), Moses Raphael, 77, 93, 141, 218, 331
Damascus, 251
    foods of, 432
Damascus incident, 384
Daniel (given name), 422
Daniels, Edward S., 145
Darley, Alexander, 443
Da Silva, Jacob, 105
Da Silva Rosa, J. S., 109
David (given name), 422
David, David, 169
David (biblical king), 98, 99, 119
Dávila, Pedrarias, 211
Davis, James Peter, 427, 429
Day, William, 419
D'Costa, Alfred, 151
Death and mourning
    among Southwestern crypto-Jews, 433, 435, 436, 437, 448
    See also Endechas
De Castro, Celina, 203
De Castro, David Senior, 241, 256
De Castro family (Curaçao), 184
De Castro family (Panama), 195
De la Motta, Emanuel, 164
De la Motta, Jacob, 164, 167
De Lara, Manrique, 340
Delay, Ana Rael, 423, 450
De Leon (surname), 419
DeLeon family (Curaçao), 184
Delff, Willem, 118
Delgado (surname), 419, 421
De Liz family (The Hague), 105
Del Medigo, Joseph, 118
Delvalle, Benjamin Shalom, 193, 195
Delvalle, Rebecca Fidanque, 193-194, 197
Demography
    AIU Jerusalem school enrollment (1897, 1931), 304
    al-Andalus Jewry, 17
    American Sephardi Federation convention attendance (1973), 301
    Aragon Jewry (13th cent., 1492), 2, 35
    Barbados Jewry (17th cent.), 144
    Brazilian *engenhos* owned by New Christians (1550, 1600), 217
    Brazilian Jewry (1645, 1654), 141, 141
    Brazilian Jews emigrating (1659), 183
    Castilian Jewry (1492), 2
    Catholic clergymen in New Mexico (1827), 414
    Charleston Jewry (1849), 165, 166
    Christian percentage of Iberian population (before 8th cent.), 6
    Coro Jewry, 236
    Costa Rican Jewry (1940, 1978), 240
    Cuban Jews emigrating (after Castro revolution), 255
    Curaçao Jewry (1745), 146, 148
    Dutch Jews in Curaçao, 184
    Egyptian Jews emigrating after 1948, 257
    Egyptian Jews in Latin America (1956-63), 257
    females among Sephardi immigrants to U.S. (1916), 277
    Haiti Jewry (1765), 155
    Iberians in New World (mid-16th cent.), 69
    Jamaica Jewry, 149, 150
    literacy of Sephardic immigrants to U.S. (1912), 267
    Martinique Jewry (1680), 146
    massacre victims in Spain (1391), 2
    Moroccan AIU graduates emigrating, 244
    Moroccan-born Argentine nationals in Rabat (1927), 250
    Moroccan Jews along La Sabana-Calchaqui railroad, Argentina (1909), 249
    Moroccan Jews in Argentina (1905), 248
    Moroccan Jews in Brazil (1955-57), 258
    Moroccan Jews in Buenos Aires (1936), 250
    Moroccan Jews in Santa Fé, Argentina (1880s), 249
    Navarre Jewry (1492), 2
    Nevis Jewry (1678), 152, 152
    New Amsterdam Jewry (1664), 157
    New Christians indicted for judaizing, 46
    New Mexico population (18th cent.), 415
    Newport Jewry (1760, 1774), 161
    New York City Sephardi schools enrollment (1946, 1963), 282
    occupations of Sephardim in U.S. (1938, 1972), 278

occupations of Sephardi World War II veterans, 273
Paramaribo Jewry (1694), 143
Peruvian conversos (1646), 215
Philadelphia Jewry (1778), 168
Portuguese in Buenos Aires (1620), 222
Portuguese Jewry (1492), 2
rabbis of U.S. Sephardi congregations (1975, 1989-90), 281
Salonika Jews killed in Holocaust, 67
Sephardi circulation (1943-59), 297
Sephardic Jewish Community of New York (1924), 293
Sephardic Jews in Ottoman Empire (after 1492), 267
Sephardic/Ottoman immigrants in New York (1924), 67
Sephardic percentage of world Jewry (1990s), 5
Sephardim in Argentina (1905), 248
Sephardim in Buenos Aires (1905), 248
Sephardi/Ottoman immigrants in U.S. (1885-1908), 267
Spanish and Portuguese Jewish exiles (1492, 1496), 2, 267
Spanish colonists in New Mexico (1598), 413, 416
Spanish Jewry (Reconquista period), 24
St. Eustatia Jewry (1722), 152
St. Thomas Jewry (1837), 154
Villaguay (Argentina) Jewry (1909), 249
De Nava (surname), 419
Dentists, 241
Denver, Colo., 423
De Onís, Federico, 336
De Silva, Jehoshua, 111
De Sola, Abraham, 170
De Sola, David Aaron, 332
De Sola family (Barranquilla), 239
De Sola Mendes, Frederick, 78
Deza, Diego de, 210
De Zeeuwsche Naghtegael (Cats), 103
Dhimmis, 17
Día de Ester, 422, 427
Día de los jacales (Sukkot), 428
Día Grande (Rosh Hashanah), 427
Dialoghi d'amore (Ebreo), 61

Dialogos das Grandezas do Brasil (Brandao), 217
Dias, Luis, 144
Diaspora, Sephardic, 4
Díaz de Cáceres, Antonio, 211
Díaz del Vivar, Rodrigo (El Cid), 23
Díaz-Mas, Paloma, 364, 367
Diccionariodo Autoridades, 313
Dice la nuestra novia (song), 362
Dietary laws (kashrut)
  and Inquisition, 135, 222, 417
  among Mexican conversos, 224
  Sephardi laxity vs. Ashkenazi rigidity, 163, 174
  among Seventh-Day Adventists, 444
  shochetim and bodekim, 158, 166
  among Southwestern crypto-Jews, 430, 432, 441, 448, 449, 450, 451
Dieussart, François, 105
Dignity, in Sephardi worship, 158, 174
Dimont, Max I., 191
Diniz the Farmer (Portuguese king), 32
Diplomats and consuls, 309
  of Argentina, 250
  of Belgium,
  of Muslim governments, 17, 57, 89
  of Spain and Portugal, 28, 127-128, 130-131
  of U.S., 384
Dirges. See *Endechas*
Dirksen, Manuel, 129
Dole, Victor de, 137
The Dominant Sex (Meyer), 392
Domínguez (surname), 419
Dominicans, 434
  burning of Maimonides' writings by, 26
  conversionist activities of, 38
  and Disputation of Barcelona, 35
  and Inquisition, 50, 419
Doña Ana County, N.Mex., 421, 452
Don Quixote (Cervantes), 314
El Dorado, legend of, 142
Dotar (Holy Company for Dowry of Orphans and Young Girls), 85, 106, 109, 124, 130
Doweries, 449
The Dramatic literature of the Spanish and Portuguese Jews in Amsterdam (Besso), 283
Duarte (surname), 419
Duarte, Diego, 103

Duarte, Francesca, 103
Duarte, Gaspar, 103
Duarte, Jacob, 103
Duarte-Rodriguez-Fidanque, David, 180
Du Fay, Jan Noach, 138
Du Pont, Henry S., 145
Duque, I., 182
Durán (surname), 420
Durán, Dennis, 424, 426, 437, 439, 452
Durán y Chaves, Fernando, 452-453
Durn, Dennis, 418
Dusart, François, 105
Dutch Guiana. *See* Surinam
Dutch Reform Congregation Emanu-el (Curaçao synagogue), 148
Dutch Reformed Church, 156
Dutch Republic, 71, 237
    cultural life of Jews of, 358
    New Christians in, 55, 72, 75, 91
    Sephardim in, 69
    States General, 85, 93, 133, 137, 188
Dutch West India Company, 357
    Amsterdam Chamber of, 129, 133
    attack on Bahia by, 217
    and Curaçao, 97, 137, 147, 183, 188
    Jewish stockholders of, 72, 156
    and Moses Senior Henriques, 129
    and New Amsterdam, 72, 137, 156, 357
    and slave assiento, 132, 133
Duties of the Heart (Ibn Pakuda), 65
Duyster, Willem, 118
Dyeing, 217

Easter, 426, 450
Ebbelaer, Johannes, 95
Ebreo, Leone, 61
Ecclesiastes, Book of, 61
Echa agua en la tu puerta (song), 348-349, 369
École Normal (Paris), 247
École Orientale (Paris), 304
Edicts of Faith, 45
Edicts of Grace, 45, 50
Edward the Black Prince, 33
Efran (given name), 422
Ega, Brazil, 242
Egica (Visigothic king), 10, 14
Egypt, 55, 257

'Ehad mî yôdéa? (song), 362
Ein Yaakov (Ibn Habib), 64
Elazar, Daniel J., 301
Eleazar (biblical personage), 100
Eliot, Charles W., 305
Eliseo (given name), 422
Eliu (given name), 422
Elizabeth I (English queen), 72
Elksar, Morocco, 244
El pozo airón (ballad), 340, 362
El Santuario Church (Chimayo, N.Mex.), 442
Elvira, Council of, 10
Emancipation Proclamation, 191
Emanuel (given name), 422
Emerson, Ralph Waldo, 387
El Emigrante (newspaper), 289
Emma Lazarus (Vogel), 388
Emmanuel, Isaac S., 96, 121, 126, 148-149, 186
Emmanuel, Suzanne, 186, 187
Emunah Ramah (Ibn Daud), 20
Encomiendas, 415
Endechas (dirges), 332, 337, 346, 364, 365-366, 367
    and Southwestern *alabados*, 433, 436
England, 70, 71, 74
    and Iberian Jewish exiles, 267
    Jews in, 142
    and New Christians, 72
    New Christians in, 75
English (language), 402, 406
    as common language for Ottoman Jews in U.S., 271
    instruction in by Judeo-Spanish press, 288
Enrique (count of Trastamara), 33
Enrique II (Castilian king), 33-34
Enrique III (Castilian king), 36
Enrique IV (Castilian king), 40
Enriquez, Juana, 43
Enriquez (surname), 419, 420
Entre Ríos Province, Argentina, 249
La Epoca de New York (newspaper), 289
Erwig (Visigothic king), 10, 14
Esequias (given name), 422
Eskrich, Pierre, 124
Espanyol. *See* Judeo-Spanish
Espejo (surname), 419
Espejo diel de vidas (Laguna), 77
Espinosa (surname), 420

Espinosa, José, 438
Espinosa, Julia Arcuna, 438
Espinosa, Leandra Arcuna, 438
Espinosa, Rafael, 438
Espinosa, Susana, 438
Espinoza (surname), 419
Ester (given name), 421
Estevanico (Southwestern explorer), 413, 415
Esther (biblical queen), 101
   Book of, 102
   Feast of, 422
   Saint, 426
Estrudo, José, 419
Ethics of the Fathers, 66
Ets Ajaim (Rosario synagogue), 250
Et sha'are ratzon (hymn), 333-335
Ets Haim Library (Amsterdam), 109
Eudes (duke of Aquitaince), 14
Euric (Visigothic king), 12
Expulsion, Edict of, 1, 43, 287, 309, 434
   500th anniversary celebration, 302
Ezequael (given name), 422

Factors. *See* Brokers, factors, and commercial agents
Factory workers, 277
Faith, Edicts of, 45
Faithful Mirror of Lives (Laguna), 77
Fajardo, Teresa, 448
Falaquera, Shem Tob ibn, 22
The Fall of Athens (Noah), 386
La familia Carvajal (Toro), 419
Family unity, 271
Farda (charity fund) 224
Far Eastern trade, 73
Farewell to Salonika (Sciaky), 399-400
Faro, Rebecca Henriques, 130
Fatalism, of Ottoman Sephardim, 286
Faur, Jose, 284
Federación Sefaradí Latinoamérica (Fesela), 260
Federation of American Zionists, 285
Federation of Apparel Manufacture Association, 279
Federation of Jewish Organizations, 305
Federation of Jewish Philanthropies, 294
Federation of Oriental Jews, 280, 295
Federation of Oriental Jews of America, 270, 291
   and new immigrants, 292
   philanthropic work by, 292
Feldheym, Norman, 196, 202
Fernandes, Diego Dias, 217
Fernandez (surname), 420
Fernandez de Oviedo, Gonzalo, 211
Fernando I (Aragonese king), 38
Fernando (Ferdinand) II (Aragonese king)
   Bayazid's view of, 56, 267
   colonial policies of, 210, 411
   and Columbus, 2
   and Edict of Expulsion, 1
   and Isabella of Castile, 1, 40
   Jewish ancestry of, 43, 403, 404
   Raphael's fictional portrait of, 403
Fernando III (Castilian king), 23, 28, 30
Ferrara, 70
   "Marrano Press" at, 76
   New Christians in, 72
Ferrer, Vincent, 38
Ferro (surname), 419
Fez, Morocco, 63, 243, 244
Fidanc, Azmel, 180
Fidanque, Abraham Haim, 187, 188, 189
Fidanque, Bathsheba Jesurun Henriquez, 187
Fidanque, Benjamin (1635-1704), 182
Fidanque, Benjamin (1893-1981), 201
Fidanque, Benjamin Delvalle (1863-1937), 194, 197, 198-199
Fidanque, Benjamin Delvalle (b. 1912), 201
Fidanque, Benjamin Earle, 202
Fidanque, Bertha Toledano, 201-202
Fidanque, Cecil, 202
Fidanque, Celina de Castro, 203
Fidanque, David of Isaac, 183
Fidanque, Elaine Maduro, 202, 203
Fidanque, Elias Alvin ("Bill"), 179, 180, 195, 196, 202, 203
Fidanque, Emma (Emita) (b. 1912), 201
Fidanque, Emma Levy Maduro (1850-1935), 180, 193, 202
Fidanque, Frederick Reuben, 204
Fidanque, Gladys Toledano, 202
Fidanque, Hannah, 187
Fidanque, Henry Brandon, 201
Fidanque, Ines, 201
Fidanque, Inez Brandon, 199, 200, 201

Fidanque, Jack (b. 1914), 201
Fidanque, Jack (Jacob) (1891-1948), 203
Fidanque, Jacob (1801-1885)
Fidanque, Jacob (1858-1942), 197, 198
Fidanque, Jacob (Jahacob) (d. ca. 1739), 182, 185
Fidanque, Jacob de Abraham (d. 1702), 182
Fidanque, Jacqueline, 202
Fidanque, J., & Co., 193
Fidanque, Joseph (1844-1933), 180, 190, 191, 193, 197, 201, 201, 202
Fidanque, Joseph (1890-1970), 197
Fidanque, Joseph, Jr. (b. 1940), 201, 204
Fidanque, Josseph, 183, 185, 203, 205
Fidanque, Lucille Wallenstein, 201
Fidanque, Lynda, 203
Fidanque, M., and Brothers, 193
Fidanque, Mordechay (1760-1826), 187, 188, 189
Fidanque, Morris (1888-1966), 190, 193, 197, 198, 199, 200, 201, 201, 202, 204
Fidanque, Nelson, 201
Fidanque, Rachel Devalle (1837-1896), 193
Fidanque, Rae (Rachel) (1907-1946), 204
Fidanque, Rebecca (1868-1947), 193-194, 197
Fidanque, Rebecca Henriquez Fereyra (ca. 1777-1845), 189
Fidanque, Rebecca Mendes-Monsanto (1810-1863), 190, 191
Fidanque, Rebecca Sasso, 198
Fidanque, Ruth Allen, 204
Fidanque, Sara (daughter of Yacob and Bathsheba), 187
Fidanque, Sara Jesurun Henriquez (d. 1768), 185
Fidanque, Stanley (b. 1918), 201
Fidanque, Stanley (son of Benjamin Delvalle and Rebecca), 197
Fidanque, Sybil Maduro, 201
Fidanque, Vito (Joshua Vivian), 191, 204
Fidanque, Ya'acob (Rif), 182
Fidanque, Yacob (1717-1791), 185-187
Fidanque, Zelia, 201, 202
Fidanque de Castro, Morris, 155
Fidanque family
    in Amsterdam, 182-183
    business activities of, 193, 197, 201, 203, 204
    and controversy over Hazzan Piza, 190
    in Curaçao, 183, 190
    in Hamburg, 179, 180, 182
    and Inquisition, 179, 180
    members of in Altona cemetery, 182
    name of, 179, 180
    in New York City, 197, 198, 203, 204
    in Panama, 194, 195, 197, 200, 200, 201
    and Reform Judaism, 196, 198, 205
    relics of, 191
    in Saragossa, 179
    in St. Thomas, 155, 190, 191
Fierman, Floyd S., 411
Fiesta de Los Reyes (Hanukah), 429
Figueroa, Gomez de, 134
Financial advisers, 187
Florence, 70
Florida, 164
    Cuban Jews in, 255
Folklore. *See* Oral tradition, Sephardi
Fonseca, Abraham da, 106
Fonseca, Abraham van Aaron da, 94
Fonseca, Daniel de, 57
Fonseca, David da, 105
Fonseca, Moses Lopez da, 158
Fonseca, Rodrigo Henrique de, 220
Fons Vitae (Ibn Gabirol), 21
Food and confections industry, 279
Food customs, 423, 427
Fortalitium Fidei (Spina), 48
Fort Union, N.Mex., 445
Foundation for the Advancement of Sephardic Studies and Culture, 284
Four Captives, Legend of, 19, 20
France, Jews and New Christians in, 70, 71,72, 142, 146
Franciscans, 50, 137
    in New World, 414, 419
Franco (surname), 419
Franco, Robert, 294
Franks, David, 167
Frederick Henry (Dutch stadholder), 103
Freemasonry
    Savannah lodge, 164
    and Southwestern crypto-Jews, 437, 441, 445
    symbols of, on gravestones, 437
French and Indian War, 160, 169
Frésquez (surname), 420
Friedmann, Thomas, 408

Index

Fundam, Abraham, 85, 121
Fundam, Abraham de Jacob, 129
Fundam, Ester de Jacob, 106
Fundam, Jacob, 85
Fundam, Rachel Senior, 85, 104
Fundam, Ribca Senior, 85
Funerals. *See* Death and mourning
Fur traders, 169

Gabirol, Solomon ibn, 19, 20
Gadol, Moïse, 274, 285, 287, 288, 291
Gaiferos jugador (ballad), 338-339, 345, 360-362
Galante, Abraham, 280
Galante, Perla, 367
Galle, Philip, 114
Gallego-Portuguese, 311
Gallegos (surname), 420
Gallegos family (New Mexico), 444
Gallup, N.Mex., 438, 445
Gama, Gaspar da, 216
Gamboa (surname), 420
Gans, Moses, 109
Gans, Moses Heiman, 109
Gaon, Nessim D., 302
Gaon, Solomon, 182, 281
Garazi, Ezra, 252
García (surname), 419, 420
García, Ester, 427
García, Josephine, 425, 432
García Herrera, Nora, 435
García IV (Navarrese king), 30
Gardis family (Bordeaux), 155
Garment industry, 277, 278
Gary, Ind., Ottoman Jews in, 270
Gedalecia, Joseph, 291
Gedaliah ben Tam Ibn Yahia, 61
Gedeón (given name), 422
Genoa, 70, 71
George II (English king), 150
Georgia, Jews in, 162
German Jews
  in Peru, 241
  in Richmond, 171
Gerson-Kiwi, Edith, 343
"The Ghetto in Literature" (Meyer), 389
Gibraltan Jews, Brazil, 242
Gibraltar, 243, 248, 250

origin of name of, 14
"The Gift of the Snowdrop" (Moïse), 383
Giron (surname), 420
Glorious Revolution, 71, 76
Gluckstadt, Denmark, 91, 105, 129
Goa, India, 70
Godoy (surname), 449
Gold, Herbert, 379
Goldberg, Abraham, 305
Gomez (surname), 419, 420
Gomez de Oliva, Leon, 222
Gonzales, Abraham Daniel, 422
Gonzales, Benjamin, 422
Gonzales, Daniel, 422
Gonzales, Levi, 422
Good Friday, 426, 442
The Good Old Man (song), 364
Goths, 311
Gottheil, Gustav, 388
Gottlieb, Lynn, 452
Gould, Alice B., 210
Government officials, 74
  in Christian Spain and Portugal, 28, 47, 130, 210, 403
  in Muslim Spain, 17, 18
  in New World, 153, 155, 164
  in Ottoman Empire, 57, 89
  in U.S., 155, 384
  See also Diplomats and consuls
Gramatica, 313
Grammarians, 19, 25
Granada
  Christian conquest of, 22, 312
  Jewish community of, 18
  under Muslims, 15
La Gran Colombia, 194, 236
El Gran Santo (Moses), 447
Gratz, Rebecca, 167
Great Conspiracy, 72, 221, 225
Great Depression, 278, 294
Greater Colombia, 194, 236
Great Sanhedrin (Napoleonic), 75
Greece, 241
Greek Jews
  oral tradition of, 364, 371
  superstitions and customs of, 446
Greek-speaking Jews, in U.S., 271, 291, 295

Griego (surname), 420
Griego, Manuel Rafael, 422
Griego, Siria Gallegos, 422
Griego, Siria Trujillo, 422
Guadalajara, Mexico, 224
　　Univerity of, 451
Guadalupe Hidalgo, Treaty of, 443
Guadalupita, N.Mex., 440
Gualeguaychu, Argentina, 249
Guanajuato, Mexico, 421
Gudiel, Francisco de, 222
Guemilut Hasadim (Buenos Aires burial society), 247
Guide of the Perplexed (Maimonides), 20, 21-22, 26
Gundemar (Visigothic king), 11
Gunpowder, 57, 268
Gunst, P. van, 118
Gurule (surname), 420
Gutieres, Leonore, 105
Gutiérrez (surname), 420
Gutteres, Ludovico Luis, 144

Ḥad gadyā (song), 364
Hadida, Jacob, 332
The Hague, 91
Hai Nahoum Effendi, 268
Haiti, 142, 155
Halakhah. *See* Jewish law
Ha-Levi, Jehuda (Judah), 19, 20, 28, 280
Halevy, Uri Phoebus, 93, 111
Halphon, Samuel, 249
Haman (biblical figure), 101, 102
Hamburg
　　cemetery of, 91-92, 182
　　Duarte-Rodriguez-Fidanque family in, 179, 180, 182
　　Jews and New Christians in, 85, 129, 130, 331
Hamilton, Alexander, 151
Hamon, Joseph, 57
Hamon, Moses, 57
Hanton (captain of *William & Sarah*), 162
Hanukah
　　liturgical melodies for, 332
　　among Southwestern crypto-Jews, 429
Harby, Isaac, 166
Harlem (New York City), Sephardim in, 282, 294

Harpendinck, John, 157
Harrison, Peter, 160
Haskivenu (hymn), 335
Hay—Bunau-Varilla Treaty, 194
Hays, Moses Michael, 161
Hayyuj, Judah ben David, 19
Hazan, Victoria, 335
Hazzanim (Cantors). *See* Rabbis and religious functionaries
"He Attends the Funeral of a Jew" (Nathan), 395
Hebrew, 406
　　in Jewish education, 261, 304
　　as language of prayers, 186, 270
　　among Ottoman Jews, 270
　　in Reconquista Spain, 25
　　Sephardic pronunciation of, 172, 173, 272
　　songs in, 335
　　among Southwestern crypto-Jews, 433, 437, 440, 445, 447, 450
　　in tombstone inscriptions, 237
　　and Zionist activities, 285
Hebrew Benevolent Society (Panama City), 239
Hebrew Immigrant Aid Society (HIAS), 257
　　Committee on Oriental Jewish Immigrants, 274
　　Committee on Sephardic Jewish Immigrants, 274
　　and Ottoman immigrants, 288
Hebrew Union College—Jewish Institute of Religion, 148, 154, 196
Hebrew University, 273
Hecht, Abraham, 283
Heemskerch, Martin van, 122
Heine, Heinrich, 298
Helen Brent, M.D. (Meyer), 391-393
Hemsi, Alberto, 341
Hendrick, Jan, 111
Hendricks, Henry S., 275
Henri II (French king), 72
Henri IV (French king), 89
Henriques, Abigail Isidro, 85, 129
Henriques, Afonso, 89
Henriques, David Lopes, 81, 129, 129, 130
Henriques, Ester Senior, 81, 105, 130
Henriques, Jacob de Jeuda Senior, 103, 106, 128
Henriques, Jacob Lopes, 130

Henriques, Judah de Jacob Senior, 81, 121
Henriques, Moses de Jacob Senior, 128
Henriques, Moses Lopes, 130
Henriques, Philippe, 85, 90, 112, 122, 129, 132
Henriques, Raquel Lopes, 130
Henriques, Ribca Lopes, 81, 129
Henriques, Sara de Moses Gabay, 130
Henriques, Selomo de Jacob Lopes, 130
Henriques de Castro, David, 96
Henriques Pimentel family, 89
Henriquez (surname), 419
Henry VII (English king), 72
Henry VIII (English king), 72, 76
Heremenegild (Visigothic king), 12
Hermandad (Buenos Aires charitable society), 252
Hermandad (Inquisition enforcement arm), 405
Hermanos Penitentes.
    See Penitente Brotherhood
Hernandez (surname), 419, 420
Hernandez, Benigno, 444
Hernandez, Francisco, 413
Hernandez, Loyola, 428
Herrera (surname), 419, 420
Herrera, Gabriel de, 211
"Hey There, Whitey" (Altabé), 401
HIAS. *See* Hebrew Immigrant Aid Society
Hidalgo y Castilla, Miguel, 47
Hides and leather, 57, 237
High Holidays, 241, 280
    liturgical melodies for, 332
    among Southwestern crypto-Jews, 427
    See also Rosh Hashanah; Yom Kippur
Highlands University, 444
Hija mía, si te vas (song), 345
Himmelblau, George, 204
Himmelblau, Rae (Rachel) Fidanque, 204
Hirsch, Baron de, 270
Hispaniola, 142, 155
Historia social, politíca y religiosa de los judíos de España y Portugal (Amador de los Rios), 5
History of the Goths (Isidore of Seville), 9
History of the Jews of Spain and Portugal (Lindo), 5
History of the Jews of the Netherlands Antilles (Emmanuel and Emmanuel), 186

The History of the Marranos (Roth), 5, 183
Hitler, Adolf, 390
Holland. *See* Dutch Republic Holocaust
    and European Sephardim, 67, 257, 297
    and Latin American Sephardim, 261
    and Malamud, 408
    and Meyer, 390
    and Nathan 397-398,
    and Sultan, 405
    and Zionism, 261
Holy Week, 433
"Homage to Our Turkish Brethren" (Altabé), 401
Honen Dalim (St. Eustatia synagogue), 152, 153
Honendel Synagogue (The Hague), 105
Honor, as Spanish behavioral concept, 53-54
Hooft, Pieter, 102, 103
Hooghe, Romeyn de, 94, 110, 127
Hordes, Stanley, 423, 445, 447, 449
Host desecration charges, 29, 72
Hovot ha-Levavot (Ibn Pakuda), 20
Huancavélica, Peru, 214
Huesca, 24
Huguenots, 71, 71, 75
Hurtado (surname), 419
Huygens, Constantijn, the elder, 103
Huygens, Constantijn, the younger, 103

Iberia
    bifurcated Jewish identity in, 40
    geography of, 9
    Hebrew designation of, 3, 4
    linguistic history of, 310-311
    Muslim name of, 14
    population of, 3
    See also Spain; Portugal
Ibn Adret, Solomon, 26
Ibn Daud, Abraham, 20
Ibn Ezra, Abraham, 280
Ibn Ezra, Moses, 19
Ibn Gabirol, Solomon, 19, 20, 21, 280
Ibn Habib, Jacob, 64
Ibn Habib, Levi, 62
Ibn Janah, Jonah, 19
Ibn Labrat, Dunash, 19
Ibn Nagrela, Samuel (Ismail), 18, 19
Ibn Pakuda, Bahya, 20, 65

Ibn Shaprut, Hasdai (Hisdai), 17, 18, 19
Ibn Shoshan, Meir, 28
Ibn Yahia, Gedaliah ben Tam, 61
Ibn Yaish, Solomon, 57
Icharri y Daois, Miguel, 135
Ignacio, Colo., 443
Immigration
    of Eastern European Jews, 387-388, 389
    from Germany, 167, 171, 174
    from Morocco, 241-252 *passim*
    from Turkey and Levant, 67, 251-254, 267, 270, 359, 380
    and Lazarus, 387-388
    to Argentina, 246-252
    to Brazil, 241-246
    to U.S., 159, 168, 267, 270-273, 387-388, 389
Immigration Commission, U.S., 270
Immigration laws, U.S., 255
"Immortality of the Soul" (Moise), 383
"The Immutability of God" (Moise), 382
Import-export enterprises, 129, 159, 160, 193, 197, 237, 277, 279
Independence National Historic Park (Philadelphia), 169
India, 70
Indianapolis, Ottoman Jews in, 270
Indians, 164, 165
    and Inquistion, 411
    See also names of tribes
Indian trade, 164
Industrial Removal Office, 270
Inquisition
    abolition of, 46, 54, 235, 238, 412
    American compared to Spanish, 212, 228
    archives and records of, 41-42, 220, 411, 416-417, 452
    in Argentina, 213, 214, 222
    in Balearic Islands, 46
    in Brazil, 217
    in Chile, 221-222
    Christian opposition to, 45
    Christians tried by, 212, 225
    in Colombia, 90, 133, 212, 213, 214, 221, 227, 411
    conversionary efforts by, 135
    and Dominicans, 50
    economic and financial aspects of, 215, 222, 223
    Edicts of Grace and Faith, 50, 444
    and emigration to New World, 210
    establishment of, 40
    evidentiary and judicial procedures of, 45, 46, 50, 136, 411
    and Freemasons, Protestants, and liberals, 47, 49, 52
    and Indians, 411
    as instrument of social control, 47, 48
    and *La Ovandina*, 220
    and *limpieza de sangre* myth. See *Limpieza de sangre*
    in Mexico, 211, 214, 215, 223, 224, 227, 227, 411, 412, 417, 419, 430, 450, 452
    in New Mexico, 417, 418
    nonreligious aspects of, 48, 49, 51
    offenses prosecuted or investigated by, 45, 46, 50, 90, 135, 142, 212, 213, 215, 222, 224, 411, 412, 417, 430, 444, 453
    overviews of, 41, 42, 216
    Papal, 50, 51
    penalties inflicted by, 46, 50-51, 215, 222, 223, 412. *See also* Autos-da-fé
    periodicity of activities of, 51-52
    in Peru, 211-212, 214, 215, 220, 222, 225, 227, 411, 412, 417
    racism and totalitarianism of, 54
    and secular authorities, 51
    and Southwestern crypto-Jews, 441
    in Spain and Portugal, 45, 50, 51, 160, 162, 180, 417
    use of informers, torture, and terror by, 46, 48, 50, 412
    victims of, 46, 213, 419, 449
    Hernando Alonso, 411, 412
    Diego Peñalosa Briceño, 211
    Teodoro Candioti, 225
    Manuel Carrasco, 453
    Carvajal family, 412
    Catalina Carvajal y Díaz de Cáceres, 211
    Francisca Nunez Carvajal, 211
    Isabel Carvajal y Herrera, 211
    Leonor Carvajal y Almeida, 211
    Luis de Carvajal "El Mozo," 211
    Luis de Carvajal y de la

Cueva, 211
Ana de Castra, 225
Isaac de Castro, 218
Francisco de Gudiel, 222
Rodrigo Henrique de Fonseca, 220
Luis de León, 49-50
Juan de Loyola y Haro, 225
Francisco Maldonado de Silva, 220, 222, 225
Martin of Coyoncán, 411
Juan Rodríguez Mesa, 221
Samuel Nuñez, 162
Manuel Bautista Pérez, 225
Luis de Riverso, 221
Gómez Robledo, 452
Jacob Senior (Philippe Henriques), 134-135, 136, 137
Simón Vaez Sevilla, 215
Antonio José da Silva, 219
Institute for Researching and Promoting Sephardic History and Culture, 284
Institute for Sephardic Studies, 284-285
Intermarriage, 180
    between New and Old Christians, 39, 43, 46
    of conversos and crypto-Jews in Latin America, 216
    among Southwestern crypto-Jews, 437
    with Ashkenazim, 204, 259, 262, 273, 299, 405, 440
    with non-Jews, 10, 68, 78, 144, 151, 171, 172, 204, 220, 242, 381
International Coalition for Rescue of the Jews of Yemen, 302
International Jewish Committee for Sepharad 1992, 302
International Sephardic Exchange, 290
International trade, 56. *See also* Import-export enterprises
"In the Jewish Synagogue at Newport" (Lazarus), 387
Iode, Gerard de, 112
Iquitos, Peru, 245, 246, 247
Iranian Jews, in U.S., 281
Iraqi Jews, in U.S., 281
"I Remember Panama" (Inez B. Fidanque), 201

Isaac (biblical patriarch), 90, 99, 108, 117
Isaac bar Sheshet Perfet (Ribash), 27-28
Isaac of Fez, 19
Isaacs, Isaiah, 171
Isaacs, Rufus Daniel, 197-198
Isaac the Blind, 27
Isabella, Haiti, 155
Isabella (Isabel) I (Castilian queen), 1, 40, 210
    Raphael's fictional portrait of, 403
Isac (given name), 422
Isidore of Seville, 9
Isidro (given name), 422
Isidro, Abigail, 85
Isidro, Isaac Baruch, 129
Isidro, Isaac Rodigues, 129
Isidro, Manuel, 129
Isidro family (Hamburg), 85
Israel, State of, 261
    and American Sephardim, 301, 303
    Sephardi community of, 67-68
    and Sephardi identity, 301
    Sephardi oral literature in, 359
Israel (Buenos Aires newspaper), 260
Isserles, Moses, 65
Istanbul. *See* Constantinople
Italia, Salomo, 118
Italo-Turkish War, 270
Italy, 70, 71
    Jews and New Christians in, 44, 55, 69, 74, 76
It's Been Fun (Meyer), 390
Ivrit b'Ivrit (teaching methodology), 304
Izmir, Turkey
    Judeo-Spanish dialect of, 322
    musical tradition of, 340, 343, 344
    printing in, 66

Jabez press (Salonika), 66
Jackson, Andrew, 326
Jacksonian Jew: The Two Worlds of Mordecai Manuel Noah (Sarna), 386
Jacob (biblical patriarch), 99, 112
Jacob ben Asher, 64
Jacob Ibn Habib, 64
Jacobo (given name), 420, 422, 423
Jacobs, Manis, 172
Jacques (surname), 420

Jalisco, Mexico, 451
Jamaica, 142, 186, 193, 199
  and Amsterdam Jewry, 77
  Curaçao Jews in, 190
  Eastern Mediterranean Jews in, 151
  and St. Thomas, 154
  synagogues of, 149-150
Jamestown, Va., 151
Janina, Greece, 271
Janitors, 277
Jáquez (surname), 420
Jaramillo (surname), 420
Jaume I (Aragonese king), 30, 32, 35
Jeramias (given name), 422
Jerusalem
  Alliance school in, 304
  foods of, 432
  musical tradition of, 340
  Sephardim in, 303
Jesuits, 146, 441, 442
Jesurun family (Curaçao), 184
"Jew," as synonym for "merchant" and "Portuguese," 222
Jewelry industry, 57
The Jew in American Literature (Liptzin), 394
Jewish Agency, 301
Jewish Agricultural and Industrial Aid Society, 270
Jewish Battalion, 286
Jewish Chronicle, 245
Jewish Colonial Trust, 285
Jewish Colonization Association, 247, 248
Jewish Daily Forward, 282
Jewish education
  and Alliance Israélite Universelle, 67
  and communal organizations, 291
  in Latin America, 258-259, 261, 262
  and *Me'am Lo'ez*, 66
  and mutual-aid societies, 282
  in Ottoman Empire, 64, 269, 270, 281-282
  and Sephardic Community of New York, 292
  Sephardic themes in Ashkenazic curricula, 283
  Sephardi studies programs, 283, 284
  among Syrian Jews, 258, 261, 271
  under Maccabee aegis, 285

  in U.S., 281-283, 285, 292
Jewish identity, 74
  of Lazarus, 388, 408
  of Meyer, 389
  of Nathan, 394-395, 397-398, 408
  of New Christians in Brazil, 331
  of Noah, 407
  and religious observance, 406
  of Sephardic writers, 380
Jewish law (Halakhah), 18-19, 64-65. *See also* Talmud and rabbinic literature
Jewish National Fund, 285
"The Jewish Problem" (Lazarus), 388
Jewish Theological Seminary, 169
Jirón (surname), 420
João I (Portuguese king), 32
Joden Savanne, Surinam, 143
Johan Maurits (John Maurice) (governor of Brazil), 81, 218
Johnson, James Weldon, 390
Joint Distribution Committee, 297
Jonah (Nathan), 394
Jonah Ibn Janah, 19
Jons (given name), 422
José (given name), 422
Josefina (given name), 421
Josías (given name), 422
Josué (given name), 422
Juana (Aragonese queen), 43
Juana I (Navarrese queen), 34-35
Juan I (Castilian king), 34
Juan II (Aragonese king), 38
Juan II (Castilian king), 39
Judah, Isaac H., 171
Judaizing
  in Argentina, 222
  as charge in political cases, 47
  in Chile, 220-221
  extent of, 227
  fictional treatments of, 42
  and Inquisition, 45, 48, 227
  in Latin America, 235
  and martyrdom, 44
  among New Christians, 41, 42, 227, 235
  in Nuevo Leon, 416
  in Peru, 142, 225
  in Portugal, 162

in Southwestern U.S., 412, 413, 414, 417, 418
and traditional Judaism, 44
Judeo-Spanish, 248
    adaptational benefits of in Latin America, 248, 258-259
    and Alliance schools, 269
    Arabic influences on, 322
    and Castilian Spanish, 65, 287, 309, 311-312
    current status of, 326-327, 401
    among East Mediterranean and North African Jews, 359
    folklore of, 327
    Gallicisms in, 269
    grammar of, 65
    Greek influences on, 322
    Hebrew influences on, 65, 319, 322
    literature in, 65-66
    morphology of, 318-321
    music of, 327
    names of, 65, 311
    among Ottoman Jews, 267, 271
    phonetics of, 314-317
    printing and publishing in, 66
    pronunciation of, 272, 313-314, 432
    regional dialects of, 65, 322-325
    religious usage of, 65-66, 165, 166, 173, 325, 332, 358, 446-447. *See also* Liturgy and synagogue ritual
    Serbo-Croatian influences on, 322
    among Southwestern crypto-Jews, 429, 446, 452
    syntax of, 65, 317-318
    translations from Hebrew into, 65
    Turkish influences on, 322
    as unifying agent, 65, 66, 256, 358
    vocabulary of, 321-325
    written form of, 287
Judezmo. *See* Judeo-Spanish
Judezmo Society, 401
Judit (given name), 421
Kabak, A. A., 42
Kabbalah, 62-63
Kadoorie family (Ottoman Empire), 57
Kahal Kadosh Neve Tsedek (Jamaica synagogue), 149
Kaliphone Records, 335
Karaites, 56, 60

Karner, Frances P., 239
Kashrut. *See* Dietary laws
Kaspi, Joseph ben Abba Mari ibn, 22
Katz, Israel J., 336, 359
Kayserling's Academy (Hanover), 197, 198
Kearny, Stephen W., 443
Kenesset ha-Gedolah (Benveniste), 65
Kesef Mishneh (Caro), 62
Keter Malkhut (Ibn Gabirol), 20, 21
Keur van Grafsteenen (Henriques de Castro), 96
Keys, Abraham Israel, 168
Ki eshmera shabbat (hymn), 335
Kingston ("King's Town"), Jamaica, 150, 165
Kishinev massacre, 304
El Kirbatch Americano (newspaper), 289
Kol Nidre (prayer), 428
Kol Shearith Israel (Panama City synagogue), 194, 195
    adoption of Reform liturgy by, 196
    Anniversary Volume, 201
    clergy and officers of, 196, 200, 201, 203
    names of, 197, 239
    sisterhood of, 200, 202
Kol Shearith Israel Benevolent and Burial Society (Panama City), 193, 195
Koningen Esther (ship), 185
Koran, 16
    Jewish familiarity with, 18
Kranenburg, Fidanque J., 183
Kruger, Harry, 336
Kubitschek, Juscelino, 258
Kursheedt, Gershom, 172
Kursheedt, Israel Baer, 171, 172
Kuzin, Isaac Hisquiahu de Cordova, 111

Labor unions, 277-278
La Cienaga, N.Mex., 440
Ladino. *See* Judeo-Spanish
Lag b'Omer, 332
La Guaira, Venezuela, 237, 238
Laguna, Daniel Israel Lopez, 77
Lamy, John B., 442, 446
Landsmanshaften, 254, 255, 271
Laning, Garret, 336
Larache, Morocco, 242, 244
La Sabana, Argentina, 249
Las Cruces, N.Mex., 423, 448

"Las Golondrinas" (ballad), 432
Las Golondrinas, N.Mex., 440
Laskier, Michael, 243, 244
Las Vegas, N.Mex., 421, 440, 441, 443, 444, 448, 448
Latin, in Iberian Peninsula, 310-311, 312
Latin America. See names of countries
Lawyers, 164
Lay prayer leaders, 157, 164, 170, 171-172, 215. See also Rezadores
Lazarus, Emma, 379, 380, 381, 387-388, 389
Lea, Henry Charles, 212
Leather and hides, 237
Lebanon, 241
Ledesma (surname), 420
Leeser, Isaac, 168-169, 172, 173, 174
Leghorn, New Christians in, 72
Leibovici, Sara, 244
Lent, 433
León, Luis de, 49
León (kingdom), 23, 30
León (surname), 419, 420
Leonor (Castilian queen), 36
Leovigild (Visigothic king), 12
Lepanto, Battle of, 57
Leusden, Johannes, 93
"Levantine," as pejorative term, 274, 275
Levantine Jews, in U.S., 408. See also Syrian Jew
Levi, Daniel, 309
Levi Ibn Habib, 62
Levy, Albert (publisher of *El Kirbatch Americano*), 289
Levy, Alberto (Monastir Jew in Temuco), 256
Levy, Asser, 157, 165
Levy, David, 167
Levy, Emily, 300
Levy, Isaac (colonial Philadelphian), 167
Levy, Isaac (musicologist), 340, 342, 343, 344
Lévy, Isaac Jack, 284, 336
Levy, Leon, 301, 302
Levy, Louis N., 284
Levy, Nathan, 167
Levy, Samuel D., 248
Levy, Stephen, 379, 380, 401-402, 408
Lewis, Hal M., 302
Libertini, Fr. (Italian priest in

Albuquerque), 424
El libro del judío (Ossado), 224
Lievens, Jan, 118
La Ligne, Battle of, 72
Lima, 241
    Complicidad Grande, 221
    Inquisition tribunal in, 222
    Sephardim and conversos in, 223, 255, 256
Limpieza de sangre, 40-54 passim, 223
Lindes, Sarah, 105
Lindo (London Sephardic merchant), 163
Lindo, Elias Hayyim, 5
Linguists and translators, 18, 19, 28, 164, 165
Liptzin, Sol, 385, 394
Literacy level
    of Ottoman Jewish immigrants to U.S., 270
The Little Goat (song), 363, 364
Liturgy and synagogue ritual
    in Amsterdam, 76, 331, 333
    of Bevis Marks, 331-333
    in colonial synagogues, 157, 160, 162, 165, 166, 167, 169, 170, 171, 172, 331-332
    dignity of, 158, 174
    grace after meals, 433
    musical aspects of, 272, 280, 331-332, 333
    of Penitente Brotherhood, 443
    rain prayer, 218
    Sephardic, 157, 166
    translations of, 158, 166
Liuva II (Visigothic king), 11
Llantos (mourning wails), 433, 436
Lobato (surname), 420
Lobatto, Abraham Cohen, 93
Lobatto, Isaac (Rehuel), 93
Lobatto, Ruleff, 93
London, 85, 165, 337
Lopes, Eliau, 94
Lopes, Ester, 81
Lopes, Sarah, 81
Lopes de Liz family, 103
López (surname), 419, 420, 421
Lopez, Aaron, 160
Lopez, David, 166
Lopez, Duarte, 160
Lopez, João, 160
Lopez, José, 160
Lopez, Michael, 160

Lopez, Moses, 161
Lopez, Rodrigo, 72
Lopez, Sally, 167
Lopez de Fonseca, Moses, 158
López de Mendizábel, Bernardo, 417
Lopez family (Newport), 161
Lopez Padilla, Raul, 451
Loretto, convent of (Santa Fe, N.Mex.), 428
Los Angeles, Sephardi Community of, 67, 337
Los Martinez, N.Mex., 442
Louisiana, 171
Louisiana Purchase Centennial Exposition, 277
Louis XI (French king), 72
Louis XIV (French king), 146
Lovato (surname), 420
"Love and Law" (Moise), 383
Lower East Side (New York City), 270
    Ottoman Jewish immigrants on, 275
    Sephardi schools on, 282
Loyola y Haro, Juan de, 225
Lucena, Abraham de, 156
Lucero (surname), 420
Lujan's Funeral Home (La Madera, N.Mex.), 422
Luminarias (festive bonfires), 429
Luminary (Maimonides), 21
Los Lunas, N.Mex., 434
Luria, Isaac, 63
Luther, Martin, 59
Lutheranism, 47, 59
La Luz (Buenos Aires newspaper), 260
La Luz (New York newspaper), 289
El Luzero (periodical), 290
Lyon, Abraham de, 163
Lyon, Isaac de, 164
Lyon (Leoni), Myer, 150

Macedonia, 256
    Judeo-Spanish dialect of, 65
Machabeu, Judah, 106
Machado family (The Hague), 103
Madariaga, Salvador, 210
Madeira, 217
La Madera, N.Mex., 422, 437
Madero family (New Mexico), 444
Madinat az-Zahra, Cordova, 15
Madrid, Spain, 452
Maduro, Joshua ("Jossy") L., 148, 185
Maduro, Judith, 199
Maduro, Moises, 240
Maduro, Samuel Levy, 193, 195
Maduro family (Costa Rica), 240
Maduro family (Panama), 194
Maestas (surname), 420
Maez (Maes) (surname), 420
Magen Abraham (Mauricia synagogue), 108, 141, 218
Maguen Davids (Southwestern confection), 431
Maimonides, Moses, 19, 20, 21, 22, 26, 62
Maimunists and anti-Maimunists, 26-27
Majorca, 42, 210
Malacca, 70
Malamud, Bernard, 379, 408
Maldonado de Silva, Francisco, 220, 225
Manaos, Brazil, 245
Mancera, marquis de, 215
Manchester, England, 251
Manuel (given name), 422
Manuel, Juan, 312
Manuel I (Portuguese king), 216
Manufacturing, 273, 277, 278, 279
Manzanares (surname), 420, 421
Mappah (Isserles), 64-65
Maracaibo, Venezuela, 247
Marache, Solomon, 168
"March 17, 1975" (Altabe), 401
Marchena, Abraham de, 121
Marchena, Isaac de, 97
Marchena family (Curaçao), 184
Marchena y Carilho, Ester de, 112, 124
Marco (physician to Columbus expedition), 210
Marcos (surname), 419
Márez, Paul, 452
Marie de Médicis (French queen), 92
Marks, A. J. "Roley", 172
Marot, Daniel, 105
Marques (surname), 420
Marrakesh, Morocco, 244
"Marrano," as pejorative term, 42, 209, 217, 432
Marriage patterns and customs
    arranged, 268
    first-cousin marriages, 173
    Meyer on, 391
    in Ottoman Empire, 268
    returning home for wife, 242, 246

among Southwestern crypto-Jews Jews,
　417, 437-440
uncle-niece marriages, 173
　See also Wedding songs
Marti, Raymund, 35
Marti (Castilian king), 38
Martín (surname), 420
Martínez (New Mexico priest), 446
Martínez (surname), 420, 421
Martínez, Ed, 448
Martínez, Efrén, 423, 452
Martínez, Ferran, 36
Martínez, George, 440
Martínez de Oviedo, Gonzalo, 36
Martinique, 146, 154
　New Christians in, 75
Martyrdom, 44, 53
Maryland Jew Bill, 384
Maslin, Simeon, 148
Massachusetts, 159
Mauricia, Brazil, 141, 219
Mauricio, Argentina, 248
Mayesh, Jack, 335
Mayesh Phonograph Record Co., 335
Mazarin, Jules, 71
Me'am Lo'ez (Culi et al.), 65-66
Medina (surname), 419, 420
Medina, Samuel di (Rashdam), 61
Meir Ibn Shoshan, 28
Meknès, Morocco, 243
Meldola de Sola, Aaron David, 170
Melendres, Leví, 452
Melilla, Spanish Morocco, 243, 244
The Melting Pot (Zangwill), 389
Memorboek (Gans), 109
Menahem ibn Saruk, 19
Menaul School (Santa Fe), 444
Mendes, David Franco, 138
Mendes, Henry Pereira, 78
Mendes, Isaac Pereira, 165, 171
Mendes, Jacob, 165
Mendes, Joseph Jesurun, 144
Mendes de Castro, Manoel, 218
Mendes family (Bordeaux), 155
Mendez (surname), 419
Mendoza, Argentina, 250
Mendoza (surname), 419

Menendez y Pelayo, Marcelino, 28
Mercado (surname), 419
Mercado, Abraham de, 144
Mercado, David, 144
"Merchant," as synonym for "Jew" and
　"Portuguese", 222
Merchants and shopkeepers, 56, 73, 159, 169,
　185, 185, 211, 242, 245, 246, 249, 279, 290,
　412
Me Re Records, 335
Mesa, Juan Rodriguez, 221
Mesiah, Abraham, 93
Mesquita, Joseph Bueno de, 157
Mesquite, N.Mex., 422
Messianism and apocalypticism, 59-60, 63
Metropolitan Recording Co., 335
Mexico, 238, 255
　in colonial era, 210, 216, 223
　Inquisition in, 211, 227, 411, 453
　National Archives, 411
　New Christians in, 42, 73, 142, 211, 215,
　　223, 223, 224
　Ottoman Jews in, 255
　War of Independence of, 47
Meyer, Alfred, 389
Meyer, Annie Nathan, 379, 380, 389-393
Mezuzah, 446
Mickve Israel (Savannah synagogue), 163, 164,
　165
Mikveh Israel (Jamaica synagogue), 150, 169
Mikveh Israel (Philadelphia synagogue), 168,
　358
Mikve Israel (Curaçao synagogue)
　and Amsterdam Jewry, 105, 147, 188, 189
　buildings of, 97, 148
　and Caracas Jewry, 238
　clergy and officers of, 185, 187, 189, 193
　conflicts in, 188, 189, 191
　donations to, 105, 122, 185
　founding of, 147, 184
　hascamoth of, 147, 184, 187, 188, 195
　and North American Jewry, 146, 158
　Torah scrolls of, 185
Milan, Gabriel, 153
Milan, New Christians in, 72
Military service
　in Bolivar's army, 236

in Chile, 222
in Christian Iberia, 27
in Dutch Brazil, 218
in Hessian and British armies, 159
in Jamaica, 151
in Jewish Battalion, 286
in Muslim Spain, 17, 18
in New Amsterdam, 157
in Ottoman Empire, 251, 269
as privateers, 73
in Roman/Visigothic Iberia, 10
in Surinam, 143
in U.S., 273
in Western Sephardic Diaspora, 74
in World War I, 286
Millás Vallicrosa, José María, 210
Mining, 211
    of bauxite, 151
    of gold, 73
    of mercury, 214
    of silver, 73, 214, 222
Minis family (Savannah), 164
Minorca, 10
Miranda (surname), 420
Miriam (biblical prophetess), 371, 425
Mishnah, 21
Mishneh Torah (Maimonides), 19, 21, 26, 62
Mizrachi Women's Organization of America, 287
Mizrahi, Alfred, 288, 289
Mizrahi, Elijah, 62
Modena, 70
Mohelim (circumcisers), 160, 161
Moïse, Penina, 380, 381, 381-384
Moisés (given name), 422, 423
Molho, Michael, 340
Molkho, Solomon, 59, 60
Monastir (Bitoli), Macedonia
    emigration from, 256, 257
    Judeo-Spanish dialect of, 322
    musical tradition of, 342
Monsanto, J. (Jacob Fidanque), 192
Montalto, Elijah, 92
Monterrey, 211
Monte Sinai (Mexico City synagogue), 255
Montevideo, Uruguay, 256, 257
    Zionism in, 260

Montferrat, 70
Montgomery, Ala.
    Ottoman Jews in, 270
Monticello, N.Mex., 445
Montoya (surname), 420
Montoya, Diego de, 449
Montreal, P.Q., 169-170, 326
The Moorish Girl (song), 362-363, 364
Mora, N.Mex., 420
Morais, Sabato, 169
Morales (surname), 420
Mordecai (biblical personage), 101, 102
Moreh Nevukhim (Maimonides), 20, 21-22, 26
Morena de rufios caveyos (song), 347, 367-369
Morgan, John, 432
Moribal family (N.Mex.), 445
Morocco
    emigration from, 241-248 *passim*, 258
    Judeo-Spanish dialect of, 335
    kabbalistic activities in, 62
    music of, 335, 338, 364
    oral literature of, 359, 367
    Spanish exiles in, 55, 56
Morris, William, 387
Morteira, Saul Levi, 76, 106, 111
Moses (biblical prophet), 98, 110
    as Gran Santo, 427, 447, 448
Moses ben Enoch, 19
Moses ben Maimon. *See* Maimonides, Moses
Moses ben Shem Tob, 27
Moses Ibn Ezra, 19
"Moses on Nebo" (Nathan), 396
Motthe, Jacques de la, 156
La moxca y la mora (song), 340-341, 362-363
Moya, marquis of, 210
Mozarabes, 421
Muhammad III (Ottoman sultan), 57
Muiderberg literary circle, 103
Munitions industry, 57
Muñiz (surname), 420
Muñoz (surname), 420
Murad III (Ottoman sultan), 57
"The Muses' Vindication of Cards" (Moise), 383
Music, Sephardi
    in Greece, 337
    Iberian and Arabic elements of, 280

in North Africa, 335, 337, 338, 364
in pre-Expulsion Spain and Portugal, 337
recordings of, 335
in synagogue liturgy, 332
in the U.S., 331-356
in Turkey and Levant, 337, 338
See also Birth songs; *Endechas*;
Wedding songs
Musicians, 74
Muskey, Bertha Cobos, 441
Mutual-aid societies, 247, 254
in Argentina, 247, 252
in Buenos Aires, 254
and communal organization, 292, 295
demise of, 299
and Jewish education, 282
in Latin America, 239, 239, 245
and new immigrants, 291
of Ottoman Jews, 254, 255, 290
regional basis of, 258
services provided by, 299
and synagogues, 280
in U.S., 271, 290, 326
in Venezuela, 246
See also names of societies
Myers, Myer, 161
Mysticism, 26-27, 59, 60, 63-63
Mytilene, dukedom of, 57

Naghtegael, Aernout, 118
Nahon, Zarita, 335
Nahon de Toledano, Simy (Suzanne), 335, 336
Nahum Effendi (Egyptian chief rabbi), 293
Name day, celebration of, 421
Names, Sephardi
of biblical (Hebrew) origin, 74, 91, 160, 420, 422
of converts to Catholicism, 419
of firstborn children, 173
given names, 421-422
indicating national origin, 420, 421, 449
of Southwestern crypto-Jews, 420-421
as subject of Inquisition scrutiny, 419
surnames, 419-420, 421
in Turkish Republic, 67
Nantes, Edict of, 71, 75
Naples and Sicily, 70

Napoleon I (French emperor), 75
Narboni, Moses ben Joshua, 22
Narváez, Panfilo de, 411
Nasi, Gracia Mendes, 64
Nasi, Joseph, 57, 267
Nassy (Nassi), David Cohen, 143, 226
Nassy, Joseph Cohen, 143
Nassy, Samuel, 143
Natan (given name), 422
Nathan, Moses N., 173
Nathan, Robert G., 379, 380, 388, 394-398
National Council of Jewish Women, 298
National Liberal Immigration League, 305
National Museum of American Jewish History, 169
National Recovery Act (1933), 278
National Skirt and Sportswear Association, 279
Navarre, 2, 6, 23, 30, 32, 35, 37, 52
Navarro-Aragonese (Spanish dialect), 311
Navas de Tolosa, Battle of, 23
Navon, Yitzhak, 302
Naxos, dukedom of, 57
Needle-trade industry, 278
Nefusoth Yehudah (Bayonne congregation), 331
Nefutzoth Yehudah (New Orleans synagogue), 173
Neoplatonism, 20, 26, 27
Neosefardismo, 262
Nessim, Maurice, 289
Nessim, Simon S., 285, 286, 289, 300
Nessim-Torres Press, 289
Netherlands. *See* Dutch Republic
Neveh Shalom (Jamaica synagogue), 150
Neve Shalom (Amsterdam synagogue), 107
Neve Shalom (Paramaribo synagogue), 143, 148
Neve Tsedek (Jamaica synagogue), 149
Nevis, 151-152
New Amsterdam
cemetery of, 157, 186
and Dutch West India Company, 72, 156, 357
English conquest of, 157
Jewish community of, 77, 219, 274, 309, 310
Jewish worship in, 156, 186, 331, 357
Stuyvesant's opposition to Jews in, 72, 156, 357

Index

"New Christian," connotations of term, 39
New Christians
   allegations against, 39-40. *See also* Limpieza de sangre
   and Catholicism, 53, 75
   as demonized enemy, 47
   in Italy, 44, 55
   Jewish practices and identity among, 41, 42, 44, 53, 74-75, 76, 417
   in Latin America, 73, 218, 226-227, 228. *See also names of countries*
   in Muslim countries, 55. *See also* Ottoman Empire
   in Netherlands, 55
   reponsa pertaining to, 61
   in Spain and Portugal, 44. *See also* Portugal; Spain
   in Western Europe, 70-72
New England, first Jewish community in, 159
New Granada, 227
New Kingdoms of Leon, 211
New Mexico
   Inquisition in, 417, 417-418
   New Christians in, 413
   Spanish colonization of, 211, 413-416 *passim*, 449-450, 452
   U.S. annexation of, 443, 446
   See also names of towns and counties
New Mexico, University of, 432, 434, 444
   anthropology department, 434
   Aquinas Newman Center, 434
   and "Little Torah," 434
New Mexico Endowment for the Humanities, 441
New Netherlands, 72. *See also* New Amsterdam
New Orleans, 171-173, 326
New Orleans Centennial Exposition, 277
Newport, R.I.
   commercial activities in, 159-160, 186
   and Curaçao Jewry, 186
   during American Revolution, 158, 161
   Jewish community of, 159-160, 310
   and New York Jewry, 78
   See also Yeshuath Israel
New Spain. *See* Mexico
Newspapers and periodicals, Sephardi
   and Americanization, 288
   and communal cohesion, 293
   in English, 290, 297
   Hebrew characters abandoned by, 290
   in Latin America, 260
   in U.S., 286, 287-290
   See also names of newspapers and periodicals
New York City
   ballads recorded in, 337
   commercial activities in, 203, 204
   Fidanque family in, 191, 197, 198
   Moroccan Jews in, 245
   newspapers in, 287-289
   Ottoman Jews in, 251, 252, 270
   proposed Sephardi chief rabbinate of, 280
   schools in, 282
   Sephardi culture in, 287-289, 358
   Sephardim in, N.Y.; 67, 280, 326.
   See also Bronx; Brooklyn; Harlem
   synagogues of. *See* Shearith Israel
   under Dutch rule. *See* New Amsterdam
   under English rule, 157, 357
New York Kehillah, 280, 292
New York State Board of Charities, 293
Nicholas V (pope), 40
Nicomachean Ethics (Aristotle), 61
Nidhe Israel (Barbados synagogue), 144, 145, 146
Nieto, David, 77
Nieuw Amsterdam. *See* New Amsterdam
Niza, Marcos de, 413
Noah, Mordecai Manuel, 379, 380, 384-387, 407
Noble, Luis, 222
Noé (given name), 422
"Nombres Apellidos Sefarditas" (Estrudo), 419
Non-Jews, social relations with, 9-10, 28, 89, 103, 160, 174, 381, 387, 397, 415, 451.
   See also Intermarriage
Noronha, Fernando de, 216
North Africa, 241, 358
North African Jews, in U.S., 281
Nueva Granada, 194, 239
Nuevo León, 413
Nuñes, Ana, 449
Nunes de Fonseca, Joseph, 143
Ñúñez (surname), 420
Nunez, Daniel, 163, 164

Nunez, Moses, 163, 164
Nunez, Samuel, 162
Núñez de Carvajal, Francisca, 211
Núñez de Fonseca, Joseph, 226

Obadiah, Book of, 3
Obituaries, of Southwestern crypto-Jews, 422
Occident and American Jewish Advocate (periodical), 169, 172
Occupations, 237, 238. *See also names of occupations*
Office of Price Administration, 279
Oglethorpe, James, 163, 164
Okeh pueblo (New Mexico), 414
Old Fort Garland Cemetery (Pueblo, Colo.), 422
Old Guard-New Guard (historical construct), 12, 13, 30-41, 48-54 *passim*, 68-75 *passim*
Olinda, Brazil, 218
Olivares (surname), 420
Olivares family (New Mexico), 445
Omepezoa, Pedro de, 222
Oñate, Juan de, 413, 415, 452
One More String (Nathan), 394
"On the Jewish Exile" (Nathan), 396
Oral tradition, Sephardi, 358
    alabados (hymns), 433
    ballads. See Ballads
    cumulative songs, 362-364
    Dirges. See *Endechas*
    folklore and folktales, 357, 432
    Hispanic roots of, 369, 371, 372
    lyric songs, 367-369
    of North African and East Mediterranean Jews, 359
    prayers and charms, 369-372, 433
    proverbs, 357
    songs of passage, 364-367
    of Southwestern crypto-Jews, 432-433
Oran, Algeria, 243
Oranjestad, St. Eustatia, 152
Ordination, 58, 62
Orgonos, Rodrigo de, 220
"Oriental," as pejorative term, 274, 275
Oriental Jewish Maccabee Society, 285
Ormuz, 70
Orobio de Castro, Isaac (Baltasar), 76-77
Orona, Benjamin, 422

Orona, Daniel, 422
Orona, David, 422
Orona, Elías, 422
Orona, Eliseo, 422
Orona, Ester, 422
Orona, Isaac, 422
Orona, Manuel, 422
Orona, Marcos, 422
Orona, Moisés, 422
Orona, Raquel, 422
Orona, Rosa, 422
Orona, Salomon, 422
Ortega (surname), 420
Ortega family (Chimayo, N.Mex.), 442
Orthodox Judaism
    in Charleston, 167
    and crypto-Jews, 451
    in Curaçao, 148
    in Richmond, 171
Ortiz (surname), 420
Ortografía, 313
Ossado, Ricardo, 223-224
Ottoman Empire, 241
    Altabé's view of, 401
    chief rabbinate of, 268
    communal autonomy in, 57, 58, 60
    conflicts and problems in, 60-61
    decline of, 57, 63, 66, 269, 270, 359
    emigration from, 67, 170, 241, 246, 247, 250-253, 269, 270, 359
    fatalism and inwardness of Jews of, 286
    Jewish life in, 60-61, 267, 268-269, 270
    loyalty to, 401
    millet system, 58, 268
    musical tradition of, 336, 340
    native Jews of, 56
    New Christians in, 55, 56, 267, 302, 358, 401
    Rose Law (1839), 57
    secularization of, 67
    Sephardic contributions to, 56-57, 268
    and World War I, 280
    Young Turks Revolt, 67, 269
    and Zionism, 285, 286
Ottoman Jews, in U.S., 399
    adaptational needs of, 288
    economic achievement of, 278

as "enemy" aliens during World War I, 292
and established Sephardic community, 274, 275
lack of common language among, 271
studies of, 284
Ovadia, Nissim J., 271, 280, 295-297, 300
La Ovandina (pamphlet on New Christian ancestry), 220
Ozick, Cynthia, 379

Pacheco (surname), 420
Pacheco, Moses, 159
Padilla, Ray, 430, 451
Paiewonsky, Ralph, 154
Painters, 74
Palacio, Andres, 434
Palestine
    during World War I, 286
    in medieval period, 287
    Sephardim in, 287, 303
Paley, Grace, 379
Pallars, 23
Panama
    Fidanque family in, 193, 202
    history of, 194
    Jews from St. Thomas in, 154
Panama Canal, 193, 194
Panama City, Panama, 239
Panama Railroad, 194
Pan de España (Southwestern food), 431
Pan de León (Southwestern food), 431
Pan de semita (Southwestern food), 431
Pantel, Pieter, 95
Papal States, 70
Papiamento (language), 190
Para, Brazil, 242
Parafrasis Comentado Sobre el pentateucho (Aboab), 108, 109-110
Paraguay, 245
Paramaribo, Surinam, 143
Paraphs, 108, 109
Pardo, Josiau (Josia), 94, 147
Pardo, Saul, 157
El Paso, Tex., 419, 421, 439
El Paso del Norte, N.Mex., 416
El Paso Times, 439

Passover (Pesach), 245, 249
    in colonial Mexico, 453
    liturgical music for, 332, 342
    among Southwestern crypto-Jews, 426-428, 450
    and Zionism, 285
Paul, St., 114
Paul of Burgos, 29
Peddlers, 277
Peddling, 252, 253
Pedro I (Castilian king), 33
Pedro III (Aragonese king), 35
Pedro the Justicer (Portuguese king), 32
Peixotto, Selomoh Cohen, 166
Pelayo (Visigothic nobleman), 22
Penasco, N.Mex., 444
Penha, Daniel de la, 130
Penitente Brotherhood, 428, 441, 442, 446
    and burial rites, 436, 437
    and judaizing, 443
Pereira family (The Hague), 103, 105
Pere the Great (Aragonese king), 32
Pere the Punctilious (Aragonese king), 32
Pérez, Manuel Bautista, 225
Pérez (surname), 419, 420
Periah, Henri J., 296
Pernambuco, Brazil, 141, 217
Peru
    Inquisition in, 225, 227
    Moroccan Jews in, 245
    New Christians in, 42, 73, 77, 142, 213-215, 225
Peter, St., 371
Petersen, Solomon, 156
Petit Val, David du, 126
Petropolis, Brazil, 257
Philadelphia
    in colonial era, 166, 167-169
    Moroccan Jews in, 245
    synagogues of, 78, 167-169 *passim*, 186, 326
Philanthropy
    by Curaçao Jewish community, 238, 239
    in colonial Mexico, 224
    for Eretz Israel, 182, 182, 195, 195, 224
    farda, 224
    sedaca, 219
    for synagogues, 105, 122, 158, 160, 185, 186

for victims of Constantinople fire, 291
for yeshibot, 64
Philip II (Spanish king), 71, 213, 412, 417
Philip III (Spanish king), 214, 226
Philip IV (Spanish king), 214
Philippines, 70
Philosophers, 20, 21, 26
and mysticism, 27
Phylacteries, 447
Physicians and surgeons, 402
in Amsterdam, 144
in Christian Spain and Portugal, 28
in Muslim Spain, 17, 19, 21
in New World colonies, 144, 163, 220, 222, 225
in Ottoman Empire, 57, 57, 61, 268
to royalty, 28, 57, 72, 74, 92
Pieters, Solomon, 156
Pimentel, Alvaro, 89
Pimentel, Garcia, 89, 90, 105
Pimentel, Manuel, 89, 90
Pimentel, Prudentia, 105
Pimentel, Violante, 105
Pimiento, Juan Dias, 134
Pinelo, Antonio de León, 222
Pino (surname), 420
Pinto, David de, 127
Pinto, Isaac, 158
Pinto Delgado, Juan, 126
Pinto Delgado, Mosseh, 126
Pires, Diogo, 59
Pissaro, Camille, 154
Pius X (pope), 304
Piyyutim (hymns), 280
Piza, David, 170
Piza, Joshua, 189, 190, 195
Plaza de los Bomberos (Panama City), 200
Poema de la Reyna Ester (Pinto Delgado), 126
"The Poet Contemplates the Exile" (Nathan), 395
Pogroms, Russian, 37
Polish Jews, in Costa Rica, 240
Political activism
in Costa Rica, 240
in Jamaica, 151
in Latin America, 245
in Venezuela, 237

Polygamy, 438
Polyphon Records, 335
Pombal, marquis of, 54
Ponce, Beto, 437
Pool, David de Sola
and Fidanque family, 182
and Ottoman immigrants, 274-276 *passim*
Popular Dress Manufacturing Association, 279
Porat Yosef (Taitazak), 61
Porta do Ceu Congregation (Belém), 242
Portales, Diego, 220
Portland, Oreg., 67
Porto Alegre, Brazil, 257
Porto Bello, Panama, 213-214
Portrait of Jennie (Nathan), 394
Port Royal, Jamaica, 147, 149, 150
Portugal, 30, 32, 70
and Brazil, 211, 213. *See also* Brazil
colonial empire of, 69, 70
conversion to Christianity in, 2, 52
Inquisition in, 42, 160, 162, 417
Jews in 2, 35, 37, 52, 55
modernization in, 41
Moroccan Jews in, 243
musical tradition of, 337
New Christians in, 44, 52, 55, 91, 220
union of with Spain, 212, 222
Portuguese (language), 193, 245, 311, 357-358.
See also Judeo-Spanish
"Portuguese," as synonym for "Jew," 186, 215, 222
Portuguese-Israelitisch Begraafplaats Wergroep, 96
El Porvenir Society (Curaçao), 148
Potosí, Bolivia, 214, 223
El pozo airon (ballad), 362, 340
Prayers for Peace, 285
Presbyterians, 435, 441, 443
Printing and publishing, 66, 66, 111, 287-290
in Amsterdam, 76
of Bibles, 65, 76, 101
in Ferrara, 76
in Judeo-Spanish, 67, 76
in Ottoman Empire, 66, 268
secularization of, 67
Privateers, 73
Progress (periodical), 290

El Progresso (newspaper), 288
Project Sepharad 1992, 302
"Prosopopeia" (Teixeira), 217
Protestantism, 434
    and Southwestern crypto-Jews, 422, 435, 441, 443-444
    See also names of Protestant churches and denominations
Proverbs, 357
Providence, R.I., 161
Provisioners, 128
Pueblo, Colo., 422, 437
Pueblo Indians, 414, 415, 416
Pueblo Revolt, 414, 416
Puerta de Luna, N.Mex., 445
Puerto Bello, Colombia, 238
Puerto Cabello, Venezuela, 236
Puerto Rico, 142, 149, 238
Pugio Fidei (Marti), 35
Pulido y Fernandez, Angel, 3
Purim, 332. *See also* Dia de Ester, 422
Puritanism, 159

Questa, N.Mex., 423
Quevedo, Juan, 411
¿Quien supiese y entendiese? (song), 362
Quintana (surname), 420

Rabat, Morocco, 250
Rabbi (Sultan), 379
Rabbinical Council of America, 451
Rabbis and religious functionaries
    Ashkenazim as, 158, 281
    education and duties of, 58, 281, 332
    laymen as, 157, 164, 165
    ordination of, 58
    titles of, 58, 165, 174
    in U.S., 281
    See also names of rabbis and religious functionaires
Rachel (biblical matriarch), 99
Rael (surname), 420, 450
Rael family (El Valle del Oso, N.Mex.), 423
Raleigh, Walter, 142
Ramírez (surname), 419, 420
Ramírez, Eponsea, 438
Ranchers, 412

Raphael, David, 380, 402-405
Raquel (given name), 421
Rashi script, 287
Rattner, Trudi (Mrs. Emilio Coca), 440
Real estate businesses, 187
Reason and Faith (Cordova), 78
Rebeca (given name), 421
Rebecca (biblical matriarch), 100, 114
Reccared (Visigothic king), 10, 11
Receswinth (Visigothic king), 10, 12, 13
Recife
    Jewish community of, 85, 141, 156, 219
    Moroccan Jews in, 242
    New Christians in, 81, 108
    Portuguese conquest of, 81, 331, 357
    rabbis of, 108, 109, 331
    and rain-prayer responsum, 218
    under Dutch rule, 81
Reclus, Elisee, 239
Reconstructionist Judaism, 148
Recording industry, 335
Reed, Ruth Flores, 450
Reformed Society of Israelites (Charleston), 166
Reform Judaism, 205, 259
    in Charleston, 166-167
    in Curaçao, 148
    Leeser's opposition to, 169
    in New Orleans, 173
    in Panama, 196
    in Savannah, 165
    and Southwestern crypto-Jews, 452
    in St. Thomas, 154
Regimiento de la Vida (Almosnino), 65
Relações, cantigas, adeuinhações, e outra corizidades, 358
Religious observance
    attentuation of, 235, 249, 259, 401, 402
    of Balkan Jews, 258-259
    in Curaçao, 184, 185, 188, 189
    documented by Inquisition, 179
    of Fidanques in Hamburg, 179, 182
    and Jewish identity, 406
    in Lazarus household, 387
    of Meyer, 389
    of Moroccan Jews, 245, 249, 259
    Nathan's view of, 395
    of New Christians, 91, 215, 217, 224

of Ottoman Jews, 254
Sephardi vs. Ashkenazi patterns of, 258, 279-280
of Southwestern crypto-Jews, 440
of Syrian Jews, 258
See also Liturgy and synagogue ritual
Rembrandt van Rijn, 118
La Renanciencia (periodical), 286
Rendon, Gabino, 441, 443, 444
Responsa literature, 61, 218
Reubeni, David, 59
Reyes family (New Mexico), 444
Rezadores (prayer leaders), 422, 443, 446
Rhode Island, first Jews in, 159
Rhodes
    foods of, 432
    musical tradition of, 336, 341, 346, 347
Ribagorza, 23, 30
Ribeiro, Diogo Nunez, 162
Ricard, Robert, 244
Richelieu, Armand Jean Duplessis de, 126
Richmond, Va., 170-171, 326
Rif (Ribi Ya'acob Fidanque), 182
Río Arriba County, N.Mex., 422, 427, 428, 446
Río Cuarto, Argentina, 250
Río de Janeiro
    Egyptian Jews in, 257
    Moroccan Jews in, 242, 246
    New Christians in, 219
    Ottoman Jews in, 255
Río de la Plata, New Christians in, 77
Río Hacha, Colombia, 238
Rios y Quizada, Diego de los, 134
Ritual murder accusations, 29
Rivas (surname), 420
Rivera (surname), 420
Rivera, Diego, 421
Rivera, Jacob, 160
Rivera, Rowena, 432, 433, 443
Rivera family (Newport), 161
Rivera y Sefardita, Emilia, 421
Riverso, Luis de, 221
Road of Ages (Nathan), 394
Robledo (surname), 420
Robledo, Gomez, 452
Robles, Alfredo Sasso, 240
Robles family (Costa Rica), 240

Rochester, N.Y., Ottoman Jews in, 67, 270
Rodelph Shalom (Philadelphia synagogue), 168
Rodney, George Brydges, 153, 154
Rodríguez (surname), 419, 420
Rodríguez, Ana, 427
Rodríguez, Antonio (colleague of Juan de Oñate), 413
Rodríguez, Antonio Jose (Presbyterian minister), 443
Rodríguez, Juan, 413
Rodríguez, Miguel, 413
Rodríguez de Matos, Francisco, 211
Roemer, Anna, 103
Roemer, Maria, 103
Roiz Mendez family (Barranquilla), 239
Roman Catholic Church
    and Arians, 12
    and Freemasonry, 445
    judaizing among clergy of, 222
    legislation of regarding Jews, 9-10, 11
    marriage rules of, 438
    New Christian officials of, 47
    and Penitente Brotherhood, 445
    and Southwestern crypto-Jews, 423, 424, 426, 429, 433, 441
    among Western Sephardim, 68
    See also Inquisition
Romancero. *See* Ballads
Romances. *See* Ballads
Romania, Judeo-Spanish dialect of Romaniotes, 56
Romansas. *See* Ballads
Rome, Iberian Jews in, 71
Romero (surname), 420
Romero Funeral Home (Pueblo, Colo.), 422
Romeroville, N.Mex., 437, 440
"The Root and the Flower" (Nathan), 396
Rosa (given name), 421
Rosario, Argentina, 250
Rosh Hashanah (New Year), 245, 427
Rosh Hodesh (New Moon), 429
Rotbaum, Itic Croitoru, 262
Roth, Cecil, 5, 183
Roth, Philip, 379
Rotterdam, 130
Roville, Guilleaume, 124
Roville, Phillipe, 124

Roy, N.Mex., 438
Royal Academy of the Language (Spain), 313, 314
Royal African Company (Portugal), 85, 132
Rubber, 245
Ruben (given name), 422
Rubens, Peter Paul, 103
Rug business, 277
Ruisdael, Jacob van, 92
Ruiz, Juan, 317
Russia, 74, 235, 304
Russian Jews
  in Argentina, 249
  in Peru, 241
Russian-Swedish War, 63
Ruth, Book of, 427
Ruyter, Michiel de, 131

Sabbath
  among crypto-Jews, 423-426
  in Dutch Brazil, 218
  and Inquisition, 222, 416
  liturgical melodies for, 332
  observances of, 173, 430
  among Seventh-Day Adventists, 444
  among Southwestern crypto-Jews, 430, 445, 448, 450
Sabbatha, Campoe, 149
Sabbatian movement, 63, 65
Sadeler, Jan, 112, 114
Saes (surname), 420
Safed
  kabbalism in, 60, 62-63
  printing in, 66
Sahar Asamaim (London synagogue), 331. *See also* Bevis Marks
St. Catherine (ship), 156
St. Charles (ship), 156
St. Croix, 153, 153-154, 186
La Sainte Bible, 126
St. Esprit, Battle of, 72
St. Eustatius, 152-153, 188, 190
St. Jago de la Vega, Jamaica, 149
St. Jean de Luz, France, 72
St. Joseph, Lucas de, 134
St. Louis Exposition, 277
St. Martin (St. Maarten), 153
St. Pierre, Martinique, 146
St. Thomas
  clergy of, 166, 173
  commercial activities in, 190, 191, 193
  Curaçao Jews in, 190, 239, 241
  Fidanque family in, 190, 193
  Jewish community of, 153, 189, 191
  synagogues of, 154, 191
Saladin (Egyptian sultan), 21
Salado (surname), 420
Salas, Ramón, 425, 429, 440, 446, 452
Salazar (surname), 419, 420
Salcido (surname), 420
Salesmen, 273
Salim (Ottoman sultan), 267
Salnician Brotherhood, 292
Salomón (given name), 422, 423
Salomon, Bernard, 126
Salonika
  emigration from, 257
  during Holocaust, 67
  Jewish community of, 58, 218
  Judeo-Spanish dialect of, 65, 322
  kabbalism in, 62-63
  musical tradition of, 336, 339, 340, 342, 343, 344
  oral tradition of, 371
  printing in, 66
  Sciaky's description of, 399
Salonikan Jews
  in Curaçao, 148
  in U.S., 289, 380
Salonika Socialist Federation, 289
Salpointe (Catholic archbishop), 442
Saluzzo, 70
Samacoff (Samakov), Bulgaria, 304
Samuel (Ismail) Ibn Nagrela, 18, 19
San Antonio, Texas, 419
  Sephardim in, 336
Sánchez (surname), 419, 420, 421
Sánchez, Gabriel, 210
Sánchez, Maria, 436, 439, 440
Sanchez de Segovia, Rodrigo, 210
Sancho II (Portuguese king), 30
Sancho III ("el Mayor") (Navarrese king), 30, 34
Sancho the Fat (Asturian king), 17
Sandelin, Clarence, 395

Sandoval (surname), 420
San Elizario, N.Mex., 440, 441, 442
San Felipe de Neri Church (Albuquerque), 447
San Gabriel, N.Mex., 414, 420
Sanhedrin, 62
San Juan Pueblo, N.Mex., 414, 420, 428
San Luis, Argentina, 250
San Marcial, N.Mex., 445
San Miguel County, N.Mex., 420, 428, 433
San Salvador, 239
Sansón (given name), 422
Santa Fe, Argentina, 249
Santa Fe, N.Mex., 414, 421, 423, 427, 437, 440, 441, 447, 450
Santa Isabel, Peru, 245
Santa Marta, Colombia, 238
Santángel, Luis de, 210
Santarem, Brazil, 242
Santa Rosa, N.Mex., 437
Santiago, Chile
   New Christians in, 220, 221
   Ottoman Jews in, 256, 257
   Zionism in, 260
Santiago, Spain, 311
Santiestevan (surname), 420
Santo Domingo, 142, 190
São Paulo, Brazil
   Egyptian Jews in, 257
   Moroccan Jews in, 246
   New Christians in, 219, 222
   Ottoman Jews in, 255
São Tomé, 217
São Vicente, Brazil, 219
Sara (given name), 421
Saragossa (Zaragoza), Spain, 23, 24, 179
Sardinia, 14
Sarfati, Aaron, 93
Sarna, Jonathan, 385, 386, 387
Sasportas, Jacob, 118
Sasso, Moses David, 154-155
Sasso, Rebecca, 198
Sasso family (Costa Rica), 240
Sassoon family (Ottoman Empire), 57
Saucedo (Saucedos) (surname), 420
Savannah, 78, 162-165, 186, 326
Savoy, 70
Scadta (airline), 240

Schachar Abakeschka (hymn), 335
Schinasi brothers, 277
Schlesinger, Emma Adatto, 336
Scholars and sages
   in Christian Iberia, 27-28
   in Muslim Spain, 17, 18-19
   in Ottoman Empire, 57, 61-62, 64
Scholasticism, Christian, 27, 28
Schurman, Anna Maria, 103
Schwadron, Abraham A., 342
Sciaky, Leon, 380, 399-400
Scientists, 27, 73, 74
Sculpture gardens, 111
Seattle
   American Sephardi Federation convention in, 302
   Ottoman Jewish immigrants in, 270, 272
   Sephardic community of, 290, 336, 337
Sedaca (charity fund), 219
Sedaka Umarpe (Mexican synagogue), 255
Seder (or *Sefer*) *Ha-Kabbalah* (Ibn Daud), 120
Sefardica (periodical), 260
Sefardita (surname), 421
Sefer Elim (Del Medigo), 118
Sefer ha-Halakhot (Alfasi), 19
Sefer Ikkarim (Albo), 38
Segovia, Spain, 403
Seixas, Gershom Mendes, 158, 168, 171, 172, 358, 389
Seixas, Isaac B., 171
Seixas, Moses, 161
Seixas family (Newport), 161
Selim I (Ottoman sultan), 57
Selim II (Ottoman sultan), 57
Semach David (Barbados synagogue), 144
Senegal, 248
Senior, Abraham (son of Benjamin S.), 90, 117
Senior, Abraham (son of David S.), 122
Senior, Abraham (son of Isaac Haim S.), 121
Senior, Abraham (son of Mordechay de Judah S.), 81, 403, 404
Senior, Agustin, 240
Senior, Batseba Aboab Cardoso, 85
Senior, Benjamin, 81, 103, 104, 105, 117, 128
Senior, David (Afonso Henriques), 89
Senior, David (son of Benjamin S.), 104
Senior, David (son of Mordechay de Judah S.),

81, 85, 97
    commercial activities of, 122, 138
    in Curaçao, 85, 98, 106, 130, 138
    tombstone of, 106, 121, 138
    will of, 120, 122
Senior, Ester, 105, 124, 128
Senior, H. J., 239
Senior, Isaac (son of Mordechay de Judah S.), 81, 85, 117, 122
Senior, Isaac Raphael (son of Benjamin S.), 90, 117
Senior, Ishac Haim, 97, 106, 109, 121
Senior, Israel, 239
Senior, Jacob, 85, 90, 98, 103, 106, 108, 109, 121, 130, 132, 133, 134, 136, 137
Senior, Jacob (son of David S.), 122
Senior, Jacob de Jeuda (son of Judah S.), 129, 130
Senior, Jeuda de Benjamin, 104
Senior, Judah (grandfather of Mosseh S.), 89
Senior, Judah (son of Mordechay de Judah S.), 81, 105, 121
Senior, Judah (Philippe), 105
Senior, Judah de Jacob, 81, 109, 128, 129
Senior, Juda van Benjamin, 104
Senior, Manuel, 89
Senior, Mordechay (son of Selomoh S.), 124
Senior, Mordechay de Isaac, 97
Senior, Mordechay de Jacob, 104
Senior, Mordechay (Mordechai) de Judah, 89, 106, 121
    in Amsterdam, 108-109, 130
    in Brazil, 81, 108
    paraph of, 108
    will of, 85
Senior, Mordechay Haim, 104, 122
Senior, Mosseh de Mordechay, 94, 109, 128
    Amsterdam house of, 97, 128
    and Benjamin Senior, 85
    business monogram of, 98, 101
    library and art collection of, 103-104
    New Christian ancestry of, 91
    tombstone of, 81, 82, 83, 85, 90, 97-102, 108, 117
    will of, 103, 105, 106
Senior, Rachel, 81, 106, 120-121, 128
Senior, Ribca, 81

Senior, Sarah, 121, 122
Senior, Selomoh, 81, 85, 97, 104, 121, 124
Senior Henriques, Judah, 128, 129
Senior Henriques, Moses, 101
Senior Henriques family, 90, 103, 104, 105
Senior Teixeir family, 90
Sentencia-Estatuto, 39-40, 47
Sepharad (biblical place-name), 3
Sepharadi, Sepharadim (Hebrew terms), 3, 4
Sephardi (periodical), 297
Sephardi, Sephardim (Hebrew terms), 3, 4
Sephardic Bulletin, 286
Sephardic Center (Bronx, N.Y.), 299
Sephardic Community of New York, 292, 293
Sephardic Connection (periodical), 302
Sephardic Home for the Aged, 290, 298, 299
Sephardic Home News, 290
Sephardic House, 284
Sephardic Jewish Brotherhood of America, 278
Sephardic Jewish Community of New York, 275, 276, 293-294
Sephardic Jewry
    bifurcated identity of, 41
    Christian allegations against, 39-40
    considerations relevant to study of, 1-6 *passim*
    cultural heritage of, 60, 65-66, 281, 282, 283-285, 303, 359. See also Judeo-Spanish
    customs of. See Customs and superstititions
    designations applied to, 39
    Eastern Diaspora of, 8. See also Ottoman Empire
    Golden Age of, 19-21, 25, 76
    historical development of, 8
    and Jewish law, 64, 66
    and Kabbalah, 62-63. See also Messianism and apocalypticism; Mysticism
    minhag of. See Liturgy and synagogue ritual, Sephardi
    misconceptions regarding, 6-7
    modernization of, 41
    Muslim influences on, 14, 18, 25, 56-58. See also Ottoman Empire
    naming practices of. See Names, Sephardi
    "occidentation" of, 8

oral literature of. *See* Ballads; *Endechas*;
  Oral tradition, Sephardi
ordination among, 58, 62
present state and future prospects of, 78
and Roman Catholicism, 27, 68
self-governance among, 17, 18, 25, 29, 57, 58
self-image and traits of, 14, 61, 174, 272
Silver Age of, 25
in Spain and Portugal, 9, 24-30, 55. *See also* Spain; Portugal
and Spanish Expulsion, 58-59
in State of Israel, 67-68, 303
and the Holocaust, 67
under Muslim rule, 8, 14-22
under Romans and Visigoths, 8, 9-14
unifying factors of, 62, 64, 65, 66, 271, 281
in U.S., 67, 78, 174, 326, 357-358
Western Diaspora of, 68. *See also* Amsterdam
See also New Christians
Sephardic Resource Center, 302
Sephardic Scholar (periodical), 284
Sephardic View International (periodical), 290
Sephardi Highlights (periodical), 302
Sephardi Jewish Community of New York
  and Jewish education, 282
Sephardi studies, university courses in, 284, 285
"Sephardith" (Sephardic Jewish Community of New York ladies' auxiliary), 276
Sephardi Veterans Post, 297
Sephardi World Federation, 300
  American Branch, 287, 301
Serbia, Judeo-Spanish dialect of, 65
Sermons, 111, 174
Serna (surname), 420
Serrano (surname), 420
Setton, Shaul, 258
Seventh-Day Adventists, 441, 444
Severus (bishop of Minorca), 10
Sevilla, Simon Vaez, 215
Seville, 36, 37, 452
  composicion of, 210
Sexual morality, 391
Shaangare Yosher (Jamaica synagogue), 150
Sha'are Rachamim (Bordeaux synagogue), 331
Shaare Tsedek (Curaçao synagogue), 148

Shaarey Tefila (New York synagogue), 78, 198
Shaar Hashamayim (Belem synagogue), 242
Shaar Hashamayim (Jamaica synagogue), 150
Shabbetai, Chayyim, 218
Shanarai-Chasset (New Orleans synagogue), 172, 173
Shapiro, Ben, 441
Shavuot (Pentecost)
  liturgical melodies for, 332
  among Southwestern crypto-Jews, 427
Shearith Israel (Montreal synagogue), 169, 170
Shearith Israel (New York synagogue), 281
  and Amsterdam Jewry, 331
  and Annie N. Meyer, 389
  Ashkenazic members of, 167
  Benjamin D. Fidanque social room, 199
  clergy and officers of, 78, 157, 158, 182, 198, 203, 204, 274, 451
  and Curaçao Jewry, 158, 186
  and Federation of Oriental Jews of America, 280, 291
  and Fidanque family, 182, 198
  founding of, 77, 157, 186, 331, 357
  liturgy and minhag of, 157, 158, 159, 331, 332, 333, 335
  Mill Street building of, 157
  names of, 77, 158
  Neighborhood House, 275, 293
  and other North American congregations, 78, 158, 160-162, 167, 170
  and Ottoman Jewish immigrants, 274, 275, 276
  and proposed chief rabbinate, 280
  and Sephardic Community of New York, 293
  sisterhood of, 275, 276
Sheba, Queen of, 99
Shebet Ajim (Cuban synagogue), 255
Sheftall, Levi, 165
Sheftall, Mordecai, 164, 165
Sheftall family (Savannah), 164
Shelomo Molkho (Kabak), 42
Shem Tov ibn Shem Tov, 22
Shepherd, Rezin, 173
She Would Be a Soldier (Noah), 385-386
Shilstone, Eustace M., 145
Shipbuilding, 73

Index

Shippers and shipowners, 85, 89, 101, 124, 185, 185, 188
Shulhan Arukh (Caro), 64-65, 66
Sicily, 14
Sierra County, N.Mex., 419
Signora, Benjamin, 94
Silva (surname), 420
Silva, Antonio José da, 219
Silva, Jehosua de, 111
Silva, Simao Vaz, 105
Silverman, Joseph H., 336, 359
Silversmiths, 161
Simhat Torah, 332
Simson, Nathan, 157, 158
Sinai Campaign, 257
Singers, 335
Sir Moses Montefiore Congregation (Richmond synagogue), 171
Sisebut (Visigothic king), 10
Sisenand (Visigothic king), 10
Sixtus IV (pope), 1
Slavery
    in Curaçao, 185, 187
    in Iberia, 11, 13
    in Mexico, 215
    in Surinam, 143, 226
Slave trade, 143
    in Brazil, 213, 218
    in Colombia, 222
    and Curaçao, 132, 133, 147, 183
    and Newport, 160
Smith, John, 151
Smyrna, Turkey, 247, 251, 252, 257
    Judeo-Spanish dialect of, 65
Soap and oil processing, 105
Sobarbe, 23, 30
Social clubs, 160
Socialism, 286, 289
Sociedad Benefica Israelita (Caracas synagogue), 246
Sociedad de Beneficencia Israelita (Lima synagogue), 241, 255
Sociedad de Beneficencia Israelita Sefardita (Lima synagogue), 256
Socorro, N.Mex., 419, 449
Sofia, Bulgaria, 340
Solas, Isaias M., 239
Soles, Rachel, 449
Solis, Jacob da Silva, 171-172
Solomon, Herman P., 180, 182
Solomon (biblical king), 99
Solomon ha-Levi of Burgos, 29
Solomon Ibn Adret, 26
Solomon Ibn Gabirol, 19, 20, 21, 280
Solomon Ibn Yaish, 57
Sotelo (surname), 420
South Carolina, University of, 284
South Sea Company, 132
Southwest Jewish Archives, 450
Souza, Sr. (member of Shanarai-Chasset), 172
Spain
    anti-Jewish pressures in, 16, 29, 35-36, 37, 42, 44, 402, 403, 417. *See also* Conversionists
    colonies of. See *names of colonies*
    cultural heritage of, 359. *See also* Judeo-Spanish; Sephardic Jewry, cultural heritage of
    expulsion from, 1, 2, 25, 39, 55, 68, 69, 210, 287, 302, 358, 402, 434
    Golden Age of, 16, 280, 357
    Inquisition in, 42-51 *passim*, 180, 417
    Jewish life in, 17-22, 24-29, 39, 41, 210, 211
    Jewish music in, 337
    medieval period, 402
    modernizing processes in, 41
    Moroccan Jews in, 243, 244
    Muslim (Moorish) period, 14-22, 311
    as name for non-Portuguese Iberia, 1-2
    New Christians in, 44, 210, 211
    and Portugal, 212, 222
    Reconquista period, 22-30, 28, 311-312
    Roman period, 9, 310-311
    Visigothic period, 9-14, 311
    See also names of kingdoms and towns
Spanish (language), 245, 248, 249, 311, 357
    medieval, 313-314
    in synagogue use, 166, 186, 358
    See also Judeo-Spanish
Spanish-American War, 149
Spanish and Portuguese Synagogue (London). *See* Bevis Marks
Spanish and Portuguese Synagogue (New York). *See* Shearith Israel (New York synagogue)

Spanish-Moroccan War (1859-60), 243
Spanish Morocco, 243
Spanish Town, Jamaica, 149, 150
Speightstown, Barbados, 144
Spices, 129
Spina, Alfonso de, 48, 71
Sports clubs, 261-262
Stacy, Laura, 425
Stanley, Daniel D., 336
A Star in the Wind (Nathan), 388, 394, 397-398
Stedman, E. C., 387
Stephen, St., 10
Stern, Malcolm H., 151, 152
Stiles, Ezra, 161
Stopendael, Daniel, 131
Stradanus, Johan, 114
Stratford, Conn., 161
Stuyvesant, Peter, 72, 156, 157, 183, 310, 357
Suasso, Antonio (Isaac) Baron Lopes I, 105
Suasso family (The Hague), 103
Suazo (surname), 420
Sudan, 15, 248
Sugar
    Brazilian, 89, 129, 217, 218, 219
    importation of, 73, 89, 219
    plantations, 151, 217, 226
    refining and processing of, 105, 217, 218
    West Indian, 73, 151, 219, 226
Suicide, 144
Sukkot (Tabernacles)
    liturgical melodies for, 332
    among Southwestern crypto-Jews, 428-429
Suleiman I (Ottoman sultan), 57
Sultan, Stanley, 379, 380, 405-407, 408
Sura, academy of, 18
Surinam, 142-143, 216, 226, 357
Susana (given name), 421
Sustiel, Ishak, 336
Sweden, 74
Swintila (Visigothic king), 11
Synagogues
    communal and societal basis of, 280, 281, 291
    in Latin America, 143, 218
    neighborhood basis of, 281
    in North America, 156, 326
    of Ottoman Jews, 255
    in West Indies, 146, 151, 153, 155
    See also Rabbis and religious functionaries; *names of synagogues*
Syria, 66, 241
Syrian Jews
    in Argentina, 251, 252, 254, 258, 260
    communal institutions of, 281, 283, 299
    in U.S., 251, 282, 380, 405
    Zionism among, 260, 286-287

Tafoya (surname), 420
Taft, William Howard, 305
Taifas, 15
Tailors, 256
Taitazak, Joseph, 60, 61
Tallit (prayer shawl), 447
Talmud and rabbinic literature
    Christian allegations against, 38
    and Dominicans, 35
    and Jewish self-government, 17, 25
    in Muslim Spain, 18-19
    religious authority of, 279
    study of, 18-19, 77
    tombstone inscriptions drawn from, 98
Talmud Torah (Amsterdam synagogue)
    and Aboab, 107, 218
    founding of, 76, 107
    liturgy of, 333
    and Recife Jewry, 218
Tangier, Morocco, 242, 243, 244, 246, 247, 248, 250
Taos County, N.Mex., 420, 421, 427, 440, 446, 448, 450
Tarik (Muslim general), 14
Tarry, Victor, 294
Tartas, David de Castro, 93, 111, 127
Tavora, Christovao de, 143
Teachers and professors, 279, 400
    of Romance languages, 279
Tecolote, N.Mex., 440, 445
Tecolotito, N.Mex., 428, 437
Tedeschi, Portuguese for "Germans", 158
Teixeira, Bento, 217
Teixeira Pinto, Bento, 217
Telles (surname), 420
Temple Albert (Albuquerque), 434, 434, 453
Temple Sinai (New Orleans), 173

Index

Temuco, Chile, 256, 257, 262
   Zionism in, 260
Tenorio (surname), 420
Tesselschade, Maria, 103
Tetuán, Morocco, 242, 243, 244, 248, 248
Teubal, Ezra, 253
Teubal, Nissim, 253
Textile industry, 57
Theatrum Biblicum, 111
Theatrum Sacrarum, 117, 118
Theodosian Code, 10, 12-13
Thesaurus Sacrarum, 112
Thirty Years War, 215
"This Faith, This Violence" (Nathan), 395-396
Tierra Amarilla, N.Mex., 421
Tinoco, Miguel, 215
Tisha B'av (Ninth of Ab), 1
   music for, 332, 346
Tiverton, R.I., 160
Tobacco, 73, 129
Tobago, 142
Tobias, Joseph, 165
Toldedano, Mrs. H. L., 276
Toledano, Bertha, 201, 202
Toledo, 11, 24
Tombstone inscriptions and monuments
   in Coro, 237
   in Curaçao, 94, 104, 106, 110, 147, 185, 187, 237
   of Dutch Christians, 92, 94, 95
   of Dutch Sephardim, 91-92
   of Josseph Fidanque, 185
   Masonic symbols on, 445
   meaning and significance of, 131-132, 138
   narrative and allegorical reliefs on, 92
   in Nevis, 152
   of Daniel and Ester de la Penha, 130
   of Penitente Brotherhood, 443
   of Senior family, 85, 95-97
   of Abraham and Isaac Raphael Senior, 117
   of David Senior, 86, 121
   of Ester Senior, 86, 124, 126, 127
   of Ishac Haim Senior, 86, 118, 120
   of Jacob Senior, 112
   of Mosseh de Mordechay Senior, 81, 90, 110, 111, 112, 118, 126, 196
   of Rachel Senior, 86, 120-121

   in Southwestern U.S., 415, 424, 435, 437, 445
   in St. Thomas, 154
   See also names of persons memorialized
Tome, N.Mex., 438, 449
Tomlins, Jack E., 446
Torah Or (Amsterdam yeshiva), 109
Torah scroll, found in Southwestern U.S., 433-434
Toribio Medina, José, 212
Toro, Alfonso, 419
Torrejoncillo, Francisco de, 45, 48
Torres (surname), 420
Torres, Albert, 289
Torres, Felix, 449
Torres, Luis de, 210
Tortosa, Disputation of, 38
Tortugas, N.Mex., 416, 449
Tournes, Jean de, 126
Touro, Abraham, 161
Touro, Isaac, 160, 161
Touro, Judah, 161, 167, 172, 173, 326
Touro Synagogue (Newport synagogue). *See* Yeshuath Israel
Touro Synagogue (New Orleans), 173
Translators. *See* Linguists and translators
Translators of Toledo, 28
Trastamara, Fernando de, 38
Trastamara family, 33, 34
Trementina, N.Mex., 444
Trillo, Berta, 423, 447, 452
Trinidad (West Indies), 142
Trinidad, Colo., 437
"Triumpho del govierno popular" (Barrios), 130
Trompita (dreidel), 429
Truchas, N.Mex., 427
Trujillo (surname), 420
Truman, Harry S., 154
Tu b'Shvat, 332
Tucumán, Argentina, 222
Tunis, 250
Turgenev, Ivan, 387
Turiel, Clara, 336
Turkey. -1See-o Ottoman Empire
The Twelve Numbers (song), 362

Ulibarrí (surname), 420

Union of Sephardic Congregations, 287
Union Prayer Book, 196
Union Protectiva, 436, 449
Union Sefaradi (Mexico), 255
United Company of Spermaceti Candlers, 160
United Hebrew Charities, 293
United Nations, Ad Hoc Committee on the Palestinian Question, 287
United Netherlands. *See* Dutch Republic
United States
    Ottoman immigrants in, 267-305 *passim*
    Russian treaty (1832), 304-305
    Sephardic writers in, 379-408
    See also Immigration
Untermeyer, Louis, 394
Urgel, 23
Usque, Samuel, 75, 76
Ute Indians, 443

Vaca, Marina, 452
Valdez (surname), 420
Valdivia, Pedro de, 220
Valencian (Spanish dialect), 311
Valenica, David, 237
Valenica, Spain, 24, 34, 449
Valensi, Edward, 294
Valentine, Simon, 165
Valparaiso, Chile, 247, 256, 257
Vandals, 14
Van den Broeck, Crispin, 114
La Vara (newspaper), 278, 286, 288, 289 335
Varela (surname), 419, 420
Vargas, Diego de, 416
Vase, Pierre du, 124
Vass, Emmanuel, 154
Velarde (surname), 420
Velasques (surname), 421
Velásquez (surname), 420
Velez-Ibanez, Carlos, 423, 448
Venereal disease, 391
Venezuela
    Curaçao Jews in, 236-237
    Jews in political life of, 237
    Moroccan Jews in, 242, 246, 256
    Ottoman Jews in, 256
Venice, 70, 89
    New Christians in, 72, 91

Veracruz, Mexico, 223, 224
Verhulst, Rombout, 105
Vermeer, Jan, 102
Victor Emmanuel II (Italian king), 304
Vidal (surname), 419
Vigil (surname), 420
Villaguay, Argentina, 249
Villa María, Argentina, 250
Villa Mercedes, Argentina, 250
Virginia State Chamber of Commerce, 151
Virgin Islands, U.S. purchase of, 154
Visigoths, 9-14 *passim*, 34, 311
Visscher, Claes Jansz, 111-114
Visscher, Roemer, 103
Vital, Hayyim, 63
Viticulture
    in Georgia, 163-164
    in Iberia, 10, 13, 27
    in Ottoman Empire, 57
Vitoria, Francisco de, 222
Vivardueña (song), 362
Vivas, Maria, 336
Vocaulario de refranes y frases proverbiales (Gonzalo Correas), 371
Vogel, Dan, 388
Vondel, Joost van, 102, 114
Vorsterman, Lucas, 103
Vos, Martin de, 112, 114, 117

Waldensians, 50
Wallenstein, Lucille, 201
Waltharius (epic poem), 362
War of 1812, 189
War of Independence, Israeli, 257
Washington, George, 158, 171
Weddings. *See* Marriage patterns and customs
Wedding songs, 332, 364, 367
Weich-Shahak, Susana, 343, 344
Well-poisoning allegations, 29
Whale-oil candles, 160
Whaling, 160
White-collar workers, 273
Whitlock y Lucero, John, 443, 444
Wholesalers, 249
Wierix, Anthony, 112
Wijbrandts, Gillis, 93
Willemstadt, Curaçao, 148, 184

Index

William & Sarah (ship), 162
William II (Dutch stadholder), 103
William III (Dutch stadholder, English king), 81, 90, 94, 103, 105, 110, 111, 128
William of Orange, 193
Williams, Roger, 159
Willoughby of Parham, Lord, 143, 226
Wills and testaments
    of Josseph Fidanque, 185
    of Sarah Lopes, 85
    of Jeuda Senior Henriques, 128
    of David Senior, 120, 122, 124, 129, 133
    of Mosseh Senior, 85, 103, 106, 122, 129
    of Mordechay Senior, 85, 105
Wilson, Woodrow, 285, 305
Wine-making, 57. See also Viticulture
A Winter Tide (Nathan), 394, 395
"With My Father" (Levy), 401
Witteric (Visigothic king), 11
Wolff, A., 239
Wolff, Egon and Frieda, 108
Women
    and Annie N. Meyer, 391
    and *Dia de Ester*, 427
    among Ottoman immigrants to U.S., 277
    as transmitters of traditions, 418, 423, 425, 428, 429, 441, 445-446, 447, 448, 449
    as Zionist activists, 286, 287
World Organization of Jews of Arab Countries, 302
World Sephardi Federation, 302
World War I
    and Federation of Oriental Jews of America, 292
    and *La Bos del Pueblo*, 289
    and Ottoman Jews, 251, 253, 270, 280
World War II
    and integration of American Sephardim, 273
    and Sephardic businessmen, 279
World Zionist Organization, 261, 301
Wouk, Herman, 154
Writers and poets, 309, 309
    in Christian Spain, 25, 28
    in Jamaica, 77-78
    Jewish identity of, 388, 398, 399
    in Latin America, 217, 219, 222, 223-224

    in Muslim Spain, 18, 19
    in Netherlands, 102-103, 126
    in Ottoman Empire, 64-65
    Sephardic identity of, 380, 399, 400
    in U.S., 379, 381, 384, 398
    See also names of writers and poets
Yad ha-Hazakah (Maimonides), 21
Yale University, 161
Yeshiva University
    and American Society for Sephardic Studies, 284
    Jacob E. Safra Institute of Sephardic Studies, 281, 283
    Sephardic Reference Room, 283-284
    Sephardi studies at, 281, 285
Yeshuath Israel (Newport synagogue), 160, 186, 326, 357
Yeshuot Mashiho (Amsterdam charitable society), 108, 109
Yiddish, 271, 272
    and Sephardi immigrants, 288
Yiddish press
    articles on Sephardim in, 272
    in Latin America, 259, 260
Yigdal (hymn), 150
Yllan, Joao de, 147, 183
Y me viego con poca fuera (dirge), 346
Yocum, Daniel, 418, 423, 424, 429, 440, 447, 448
Yom Kippur (Day of Atonement)
    in Amsterdam, 75
    Jamaica Assembly adjourned for, 151
    in Latin America, 240, 245, 246
    among Southwestern crypto-Jews, 428
Young Men's Hebrew Association (YMHA) Panama branch, 196
Young Turkish Committee of Union and Progress, 67
Young Turks Revolt, 67, 251, 253, 269, 359
Ysrael (given name), 420
Yugoslavia, Sephardic Jews of, 280. *See also* Monastir
Yuquegunque, Nuevo León, 414
Yurimaguas, Peru, 245

Zacarias (given name), 422
Zacatecas, Mexico, 438
Zacut, Abraham, 210

Zamora (surname), 420
Zangwill, Israel, 389
Zaragoza (Saragossa), Spain, 23, 24, 179
Zecarias (given name), 422
"Zekher Asiti le-Nifle'ot El" (Aboab), 219
Zevi, Shabbatai, 63, 64, 66, 108-109, 269
Zionism
    in Latin America, 260-261
    music of, 335
    in Ottoman Empire, 285
    Sephardi views of, 257, 260, 285-287
    in U.S., 285-287, 389
Zionist Organization of America, 286
    Syrian Division, 287
Zionist Sephardic Society, 285
Ziryab the singer (Muslim poet), 16
Zohar, 27, 63
Zuni Pueblo, N.Mex., 413
Zur Israel (Recife synagogue), 108, 141, 218